An Introduction to Business Decision Making:

Text and Cases

Methuen: Canadian Business Administration

Canadian Business Law
E. Amirault, M. Archer

Principles of Public Finance
D. A. L. Auld, F. C. Miller

Public Administration in Canada:
Selected Readings, 3rd Edition
W. D. K. Kernaghan

Acquisitions and Mergers in Canada, 2nd Edition
D. B. Morin, W. Chippindale

Business and Government in Canada, 2nd Edition
K. Rea, J. McLeod

Business Interests and the Reform
of Canadian Competition Policy, 1971-1975
W. T. Stanbury

An Introduction
To Business
Decision Making:
Text and Cases

Michael R. Pearce, D.B.A.
Assistant Professor of Business Administration
School of Business Administration
The University of Western Ontario

David G. Burgoyne, M.B.A.
Associate Professor of Business Administration
School of Business Administration
The University of Western Ontario

John A. Humphrey, D.B.A.
Associate Professor of Business Administration
School of Business Administration
The University of Western Ontario

Methuen
Toronto • New York • London • Sydney

Canadian Cataloguing in Publication Data

Pearce, Michael R., 1946-
    An introduction to business decision making

ISBN 0-458-92750-3

1. Business - Case studies. 2. Industrial
management - Canada - Case studies. 3. Decision-
making - Case studies. I. Burgoyne, David, 1933-
II. Humphrey, John, 1937-   III. Title.

HF5351.P42   658.4'00971   C77-001355-4

Printed and bound in Canada

4 5   81 80

CONTENTS

Section VIII   An Introduction to General Management   411

Case Contributors

R. Archibald

P. M. Bishop

D. G. Burgoyne

T. F. Cawsey

S. N. Chakravorti

M. V. Conlin

J. A. Craig

R. B. Dow

J. A. Erskine

B. Floyd

G. R. Forsyth

D. Francis

M. G. Hagerman

J. A. Humphrey

F. W. P. Jones

R. M. Knight

M. R. Leenders

R. A. Lefebvre

D. S. R. Leighton

J. C. Lemmon

R. C. Malanchuk

R. E. M. Nourse

R. D. Oliver

R. W. Orser

D. A. Peach

M. R. Pearce

J. K. Pliniussen

O. Richardson

H. Uren

M. G. Webb

J. R. Weber

J. J. Wettlaufer

S. R. Wilkinson

Harvard University

Kings College, Halifax

Government of Canada

Harper and Row Publishers

The cases presented in this book were prepared to provide a basis for discussion and were not designed as illustrations of either correct or incorrect handling of administrative problems. In some instances, names of people and places and data have been disguised.

TO OUR WIVES:

Janet
Gerd
Lib

PREFACE

This book is designed for students embarking on their first case study course in management. Such a course (Business 020) has been offered at the Western Business School for over forty years. This experience clearly indicates that a certain amount of textual materials combined with a selection of real management problems ("cases") provide the blend both students and faculty find most effective and exciting.

This is predominantly a casebook. It represents the culmination of a great deal of effort by many people. Most of their names are listed in the table of contents, but we would like to add a few comments of appreciation here.

First, this book is in the tradition established by its predecessors, *Canadian Business Administration,* published in 1957, and *Business Administration in Canada,* originally published in 1961. The pedagogical foundation laid by Professors W. A. Thompson, L. W. Sipherd, D. H. Thain, J. J. Wettlaufer, S. A. Martin and M. R. Leenders is much in evidence and greatly appreciated.

Second, real management problems could not be presented as case studies without the full cooperation and participation of numerous executives. Their willingness to contribute information, time and financial assistance has enabled us to offer a variety of contemporary problems to the student. We think this is essential to an informed understanding of how business operates today.

Third, many hours have been spent by our Business 020 faculty in the past few years to make this collection of material pedagogically effective. These faculty members have researched, written, tried, criticized and rewritten materials in this book. Any attempt to acknowledge specific contributions to the textual materials would not fully recognize the team effort involved. Further, since Business 020 faculty are graduates of Western, their treatment of materials has been significantly influenced by their ongoing involvement with all the faculty of this School. Those involved in the process include Gary Boydell, Marilyn Campbell, Michael Conlin, John Craven, Robin Dow, Michael Hagerman, Rudi Kuhlman, Ron Lefebvre, Chuck Lemmon, Bob Malanchuk, John Pliniussen, Rob Orser, Dale Oliver, Olga Richardson, Steve Wilkinson and Mark Webb. All three of us have had the pleasure of working closely with these faculty members in the capacity of Chairman of the Business 020 Group. That has been a most rewarding experience for each of us.

Fourth, several other individuals have contributed meaningfully to this effort. Professor George Forsyth has continued to provide us with general management material of high quality, as has Professor M. R. Leenders in the production/operations area. Professor David Shaw, former Chairman of the Research and Publications Program for the School, has provided encouragement and support for this project over the past several years. Professor Jim Hatch, Acting Chairman of Research and Publications, added his enthusiasm to the project. Professors Al Mikalachki, David Peach, and Walter Thompson helped us with the textual material. Ruth Wright, Linda Collins, Norene Culp, Betty Freeborn, Jean Fish, and Jean Rennie, Fay Henderson, Marianne Malo and Phyllis Jackson have efficiently and willingly handled a heavy and hectic schedule in the preparation of the manuscript. Col. Fraser Rowland and Professor Walter Thompson have continued to provide a sterling example of concern for teaching an introductory course of high quality. Their leadership by example has inspired all of us. Finally, Dean J. J. Wettlaufer and Associate Dean C. B. Johnston have offered us every encouragement to complete this project.

We are indebted especially to the Associates' Plan for Excellence which has provided funds to support much of our casewriting activities. The Associates are a group of corporations and individuals which provide financial and other support to the School.

Finally, we are grateful for permission to reprint the "outside" cases. As noted in the table of contents, cases are included which are not Western cases. We have found them to be good exercises in problem solving which complement our internally developed materials.

We appreciate the meaningful contributions of all these people, but willingly take responsibility for any errors in this book.

We sincerely hope that this collection of text and cases will engage your attention, challenge your abilities and improve your understanding of and skill in management decision making.

Michael R. Pearce
David G. Burgoyne
John A. Humphrey

London, Ontario, 1977

SECTION I

An Introduction to the Case Method

WHAT IS A CASE?

A case as it applies to this book is a situation that a decision maker faces at some time. Although names, places and data have sometimes been disguised, almost all of the cases are real situations faced by real people. The objective of each case is to leave you at a decision point with the kinds of information (and the lack of information) available to the decision maker when he or she attempts to resolve a problem and/or grasp an opportunity.

In each case, the real decision maker was expected to analyze the situation, determine the problems and opportunities involved, generate and evaluate alternative courses and implement a plan of action. The expectation is that you will go through this same process, except that you will not have the opportunity to actually implement action and see results.

A number of frustrations commonly face decision makers: a shortage of information on which to base decisions, a shortage of time in which to make those decisions, and seldom any opportunity to test the consequences of choosing one course of action versus alternative ones. You will have to cope with these same limitations when dealing with the cases.

WHAT IS THE CASE DISCUSSION METHOD?

The case discussion method differs from the traditional lecture method in many ways. A major one is that it is highly participative. Students interact with other students and with the instructor. The instructor's role is to guide the discussion—to probe, question and add some inputs rather than to give the "answers." Students, not surprisingly, are interested in what "really" happened or what the instructor would do given that situation. Rarely will this be forthcoming. The learning issue is what you would do and why. Developing your decision-making skills and knowledge is the objective of the process.

In real situations when a group of managers address issues such as these in the cases, there are nearly always different views on interpretation of the data and on what could and should be done. Accordingly, you should expect that there will be different views expressed by your classmates in a case discussion. The essence of the case method is the process of stating points of view, defending positions, and actively listening so as to understand and constructively criticize the positions of others. Rarely will you leave the classroom, after discussing a case, unchanged in your position or perspective.

In spite of the common interest of students in resolving the case issues and in spite of the guidance of the instructor, class discussions may seem repetitious and unorganized at times. This is unavoidable, particularly in the early stages of a course. This will become much less of a problem as the class as a group develops its decision-making ability. The class will be able to handle a case more efficiently and effectively as students gain practice in the case method.

THE ROLE OF THE STUDENT

The very nature of the case discussion method demands that students be present, be prepared and actively participate in discussions by both talking and listening.

To prepare for class, students should go through the following process.

1. Read the case for general understanding.
2. Reread the case from the viewpoint of the decision maker, underlining key information and jotting down data and ideas that are important.
3. At this point, you should be in a position to "push" the data to see the relationships and thereby understand what is going on, how the situation developed, what problems and opportunities exist, what *could* be done to resolve the problems and grasp the opportunities, what the advantages and disadvantages are of what *could* be done, and thereby decide what you think *should* be done, who should do it, how it should be done, when it should be done, etc.
4. Ideally, you will have the opportunity to discuss informally your preparation of the case with some of your classmates prior to the class. This should be a sharing situation in which you discover ideas you may have overlooked or did not weight heavily. Your colleagues will also benefit from your inputs. Meeting at a designated time and place is ideal, but if this is not possible, a bull session in the lounge, coffee shop or someone's room with three or four others can be most useful.
5. Your instructor may or may not assign questions to be considered in preparing the case. When questions are assigned, they should only be considered as a means of assisting you in getting into the case and not the limits of your case preparation.
6. Watch out, the process can be deceiving! Some students have thought they were on top of the situation without really doing too much work. They read over cases rather casually once or twice, jot down a few ideas, go to class and listen to the discussion. As points come up they feel, "I touched on that" or "I would have reached the same conclusion if I had pushed the data a little further." When exam time arrives and they are asked to do a case on their own, they find they are in serious difficulty. Such students spend the exam period trying to learn how to deal with a case, rather than dealing with the issues in the case for that exam. This situation is not surprising since, in fact, this is the first case these students have really tried to do. They are in somewhat the same position as someone entered in a track event at an official track meet whose training consisted of watching others practise for a number of months.
7. The need to be a skillful communicator arises repeatedly in management. The case method presents an ideal opportunity to practise talking and listening skills. For some, talking in a group situation is difficult. The only way to overcome this problem is to jump in and begin. Do not wait until you have a major presentation to make where you will hold the floor for a lengthy period. Adding a key piece of information or questioning something can be done in a few sentences and may be the best way for you to begin active involvement. Your instructor and your classmates will be supportive of your efforts—they will learn from you whether you are "on target" or not. For others, listening is a poorly developed skill. Some individuals, in fact, do not listen; they simply wait for their turn to talk. The case method depends on the willing interaction of the students. Without that essential ingredient, the cases become interesting stories rather than opportunities to develop the ability to make management decisions.

A PROCEDURE FOR CASE ANALYSIS

1. **Read Case Twice** (at least)

   A. Quickly, to see what it is about
   B. Carefully, making marginal notes

2. **Statement of Decisions To Be Made** (first attempt)

Briefly, what decisions must you tackle?
Which decisions must be made first?

3. **Situation Analysis**

What questions do you need to answer to enable you to make reasoned decisions?
What information do you have to address those questions? Should you ''push'' some numbers? Why? How?
Do not rehash the case! If you write something down, ask yourself: What does it mean? How does it help me make a decision? So what?
What information are you lacking? Do you have to make some assumptions? If so, label them as assumptions.

4. **Problem Identification** (second attempt)

In more detail than #2 above, what are the problems you discovered in your analysis of the situation?
Which problems are most important?
What opportunities have you uncovered? Which look most attractive?

5. **Alternative Courses of Action**

For each problem or opportunity:
A. What alternative actions could reasonably be tried?
B. What are the advantages and disadvantages of each alternative course of action? (Refer to your analysis of the situation and your expectations as to ''what would happen if we did it'' for each alternative.)

6. **Decision Statement**

Based on #5 above, what specifically do you recommend be done about each problem and opportunity?
Who should do it?
How?
When?
How will you know if your recommendation was a good one? (How will you measure results?) What would you suggest if your plan does not work?
If you had to make some assumptions and guesses, how critical were they to your decision? (In other words, if your assumptions were proved incorrect, would you change your recommendations?)

SECTION II
An Introduction to Financial Statements

The purpose of this chapter is to introduce and explain financial statements. Financial statements give a picture of a company's operating results and its financial condition. This chapter will discuss:

1. The balance sheet
2. The income statement
3. The relationship between the income statement and the balance sheet

All incorporated companies are obliged by law to provide annual financial statements to their shareholders. This information is usually presented in a firm's annual report. In addition to financial statements, these reports often contain a message from the president describing the corporation's past and planned activities including new product developments, plant expansion, and assessment of changes in market conditions.

The balance sheet and the income statement provide the basic information which a businessman, investor, lender, or shareholder needs to gauge the financial well-being of a company. Learning and understanding financial statements is not difficult. Elementary calculations in addition, subtraction, multiplication and division are the only basic requirements.

This chapter will concentrate on the definition of the two financial statements. The "Introduction to Financial Management" chapter will focus on analyzing these statements and the statement of changes in financial position. Proper use of financial tools aids financial decision making. However, before analytical concepts can be used for decision making, there must be understanding of the basic financial vocabulary and the relationships that exist between different statements and terms.

PART 1: THE BALANCE SHEET

The balance sheet presents the financial position of an enterprise as of a particular day, such as December 31, 1976. It is like a photograph of a firm's financial condition at a particular point in time.

The purpose of a balance sheet is to show what a company owns and what it owes. The assets—what a company owns—are listed on the left side of the statement. The liabilities—what a company owes—are listed on the right side. The net worth (known as shareholders' equity for incorporated companies)—the difference between what a company owns and what it owes—is also listed on the right side. Both sides are always in balance.

Assets represent all the physical goods and things of value *owned by* the company. Assets include finished and unfinished inventory, land, building, equipment, cash and money owed to the company from credit sales or money lent to others.

Liabilities consist of all debts or claims *owed by* the company, such as loans from the bank, unpaid accounts due to suppliers.

Shareholders' equity (net worth) represents the interest, stake, or claim the owners have in the company. It is the owners' original investment plus the accumulation of all profits that have been retained in the firm since the company's inception.

Individuals can formulate personal balance sheets. What does it mean when Howard Hughes's net worth was estimated at several billion dollars? This amount is what is left when his liabilities (debts) are subtracted from his assets, physical holdings, cash, and any money owed to him.

Before studying a business balance sheet, try to formulate your own personal balance sheet. As an example, a balance sheet has been prepared for one of the course instructors. A disguise is used by calling him D. B. Stevens.

D. B. STEVENS
Balance Sheet
as of June 26, 1976

ASSETS			LIABILITIES	
Current assets			Current liabilities	
Cash		$ 500	Notes payable—Bank	$2 000
Bonds at cost			Notes payable—	
(market value, $1 200)		1 000	General Motors	1 000
Stocks at cost			Notes payable—Father	1 500
(market value, $700)		1 000	Total current liabilities	$4 500
Prepaid car insurance		300		
Life insurance (cash			Long-term liabilities	
surrender value)		200	Notes payable (5 yr. @7%)	1 000
Total current assets		$3 000	TOTAL LIABILITIES	$5 500
Fixed assets			NET WORTH (EQUITY)	
Automobile	$5 200		Capital	$1 500
Less: acc. dep.[1]	2 000			
		$3 200		
Stereo system	$ 700			
Less: acc. dep.[1]	300			
		400		
Television	$ 500			
Less: acc. dep.[1]	200			
		300		
Apartment				
furniture	$ 400			
Less: acc. dep.[1]	300			
		100		
Total fixed assets		4 000		
TOTAL ASSETS		$7 000	TOTAL LIABILITIES AND NET WORTH	$7 000

[1]Accumulated depreciation

Another more complicated statement is presented for XYZ Manufacturing Co. as of December 31, 1976. Each of the XYZ accounts will be discussed in turn.

XYZ MANUFACTURING CO. LTD.
Balance Sheet
as of December 31, 1976

ASSETS

Current assets		
Cash		$ 14 000
Marketable securities at cost		
(market value $106 000)		102 000
Accounts receivable	$252 000	
Less: allowance for doubtful accounts	12 000	
Net accounts receivable		240 000
Raw materials inventory	120 000	
Work in process inventory	74 000	
Finished inventory	130 000	
Total inventories		324 000
Prepayments		14 000
Total current assets		$ 694 000
Investment in subsidiary		40 000
		—
Fixed assets		
Land		$ 54 000
Building	$456 000	
Less: accumulated depreciation	168 500	
		287 500
Machinery	$114 000	
Less: accumulated depreciation	43 200	
		70 800
Office equipment	$ 12 000	
Less: accumulated depreciation	4 300	
		7 700
Total fixed assets		420 000
Intangibles: goodwill		10 000
TOTAL ASSETS		$1 164 000

LIABILITIES

Current liabilities

Accounts payable	$ 120 000
Notes payable (due June 1977)	102 000
Accrued expenses payable	39 600
Taxes payable	18 400
Total current liabilities	$ 280 000

Long-term liabilities

First mortgage bonds (10% interest, due 1985)	424 000
TOTAL LIABILITIES	$ 704 000

SHAREHOLDERS' EQUITY

Capital stock

Preferred shares, 5% cumulative, $100 par value each; authorized, issued and outstanding 600 shares	$ 60 000	
Common shares, $5 par value each; authorized, issued and outstanding 30 000 shares	150 000	
Capital surplus	104 000	
Retained earnings	146 000	
Total shareholders' equity		460 000
TOTAL LIABILITIES AND SHAREHOLDERS' EQUITY		$1 164 000

ASSETS

The size of the company is measured often in terms of its assets. Two major categories of assets are current assets and fixed assets.

CURRENT ASSETS

Current assets include cash and items which in the normal course of business will be converted into cash within an operating cycle, usually a year from the date of the balance sheet. Each current asset item should be listed in order of liquidity (ease of conversion to cash). Current assets generally consist of cash, marketable securities, receivables, inventories and prepayments.

Cash

Cash is the money that is on hand and the money on deposit in the bank.

Cash	$ 14 000

Marketable Securities

This asset represents investment of the company's funds in some other organization for the purpose of earning interest. Because these funds may be needed on short notice, it is usually considered wise to make investments that are readily convertible to cash and subject to minimum price fluctuations (such as certificates of deposit and commercial paper). The general practice is to show marketable securities at cost with the market value listed parenthetically.

Marketable Securities at Cost
(market value, $106 000) $ 102 000

Accounts Receivable

Accounts receivable are funds owed to the company by customers who have purchased on credit and usually have 30, 60 or 90 days in which to pay. The total amount due from customers as shown in the balance sheet is $252 000. However, some customers fail to pay their bills. Therefore, a provision for doubtful accounts is estimated (based on previous experience) so that the net accounts receivable amount will represent the actual amount that is expected to be collected. The balance of $240 000 is thus shown as the net accounts receivable on the balance sheet.

Accounts Receivable $ 252 000
Less: Allowance for Doubtful Accounts   12 000
Net Accounts Receivable $ 240 000

Inventory

Retailers' and wholesalers' inventories consist of the goods they have for sale to their customers. The functions these companies perform are to store, promote, sell and distribute goods. The goods themselves are not changed in any major way from the time they are received to the time they are sold. The inventory is valued at its original cost or its present market value, whichever is lower.

A manufacturing company's inventory will consist of raw materials; work in process (subassemblies and partially completed products); and finished products manufactured but not yet sold. Finished and semi-finished products are given a higher cost than the raw materials: the cost of labour content, the cost of energy consumed in production and other manufacturing costs are to be added to the raw material cost.

Raw Materials Inventory $ 120 000
Work in Process Inventory   74 000
Finished Inventory   130 000
Total Inventories $ 324 000

Prepayments

At times it is necessary or convenient to pay for items in advance. When the items are short-term, such as property or equipment rental and fire insurance, they are called prepaid expenses.

Although the payment is made at one time, the contract (in the case of rent) or the anticipated benefit or reward (in the case of insurance) is expected to last over a span of time. As the "value" is not fully received when the payment is made, the "unused" portion, or the benefit to come, is considered an asset of the company. For example, if two years of insurance are still unused on a five-year policy which originally cost $100, then $40 will be shown on the balance sheet as prepaid expense.

Prepayments	$ 14 000

To summarize, current assets include cash, marketable securities, accounts receivable, inventories and prepayments.

Total Current Assets	$ 694 000

Investment in Subsidiary

XYZ Manufacturing Co. Ltd. owns a small wholesale business that aids in the distribution of its manufactured products. Investments in subsidiary in this case represent a controlling interest, more than 50 per cent, of the common stock. The common stock is not a tangible asset, and, therefore, not included with fixed assets. XYZ Manufacturing Co. Ltd. has no intention of selling its investment. As a consequence, the investment is listed in this separate category after current assets.

Investment in Subsidiary	$ 40 000

FIXED ASSETS

Fixed assets are physical items which will last more than one year. They include those items not intended for resale which will be used in the operation of the company such as land, buildings, machinery, equipment, furniture, automobiles and trucks. Fixed assets, with the exception of land, are shown at their original cost, less accumulated depreciation. This presentation may be conservative: the original cost may well be lower than either present market value or replacement cost. For example, land which appears on the books as $54 000 may actually be worth $100 000. Fixed assets should be stated in order of "permanence," with land generally considered the most permanent.

Depreciation

Fixed assets, with the exception of land, become useless over the years, through wear or obsolescence. In order to allow for this loss of use, the asset is "written-down" or depreciated. These reductions are based on the expected useful life of the asset and estimated salvage value. The allowances for depreciation are usually accumulated separately so that the asset's original cost figure on the balance sheet is preserved. The accumulated depreciation amount then reflects that part of the original cost of the asset which has been depreciated and charged to the company as an expense. Thus, the net balance after accumulated depreciation (net book value) is not intended to reflect current or market value of an asset as of the balance sheet date.

There are a number of ways to calculate depreciation. The simplest one is a straight line method whereby the cost of the fixed asset is allocated evenly over its useful life. For example, suppose a machine is bought for $100 000 and it has an estimated life of 10 years, and zero salvage value. Its cost will be allocated at the rate of $10 000 each year. The accumulated depreciation would be $10 000 at the end of the first year; $20 000 at the end of the second year; $30 000 at the end of the third year, etc. By the end of the tenth year, the net book value of the machine would be zero. Other methods are also used; one, double declining balance, is a model for the calculation of depreciation for tax purposes.

The accumulated depreciation for each fixed asset is best shown separately, although sometimes only one total is shown for all the fixed assets.

Building	$456 000	
Less: Accumulated Depreciation	168 500	
		$ 287 500
Machinery	$114 000	
Less: Accumulated Depreciation	43 200	
		$ 70 800
Office Equipment	$ 12 000	
Less: Accumulated Depreciation	4 300	$ 7 700

Fixed assets, in summary, are the investments in property, plant and equipment. As explained, they generally are expressed in terms of their cost diminished by the depreciation accumulated as of the date of the financial statement.

Total Fixed Assets	$ 420 000

Intangibles

Most of a company's assets can be seen and touched. There are, however, some items of value that are not so tangible yet are customarily recorded as assets. For example, patents and franchise rights are intangible assets. Another intangible, "goodwill," is encountered only when companies change hands. When a company is purchased, establishing a price for it is difficult. Often a purchaser will pay more for a company than it seems "worth" on the balance sheet because he believes the loyalty of existing customers, or the company's reputation, etc., are worth a premium over the tangible assets. The purchaser's balance sheet for the company after it is purchased will include an account called goodwill that reflects the premium paid. Over time, goodwill is generally amortized, which means it is written down just like the depreciation on a tangible fixed asset. One might expect to find listed under intangibles the value of trained, competent personnel, but the "human resources" of a company are not typically valued and reported on the balance sheet, primarily because there is no agreement on how to arrive at an appropriate value. Organization costs by accounting rules may be recorded as an intangible asset.

Intangibles	$ 10 000

All assets are added together:

TOTAL ASSETS	$1 164 000

LIABILITIES

Liabilities refer to all the debts a company owes. They are categorized into current liabilities and long-term liabilities

CURRENT LIABILITIES

Current liabilities reflect the amount of money the company owes and must pay within the coming year. Some of these debts include unpaid wages, bank and bond interest, legal fees, pension payments and taxes. In addition, it is usual to include in current liabilities the portion of long-term debts due within the year.

Accounts Payable

Funds owed by the company for goods and services provided on credit by its suppliers are accounts payable. The company usually has 30, 60 or 90 days in which to pay. Sometimes, the suppliers offer a cash discount of, say, 2 per cent, as an inducement to pay promptly.

Accounts Payable $ 120 000

Notes Payable

Companies often need additional cash to operate. Thus, money is borrowed from banks or other lenders. In return, the borrower gives the lender a written promissory note, stating that borrowed funds will be returned within a year (plus any other agreed-upon arrangements such as interest, etc.). These are called notes payable. Also, suppliers sometimes request formal recognition of amounts owed them.

Notes Payable (due June 1976) $ 102 000

Accrued Expenses Payable

In addition to its debt to suppliers and lenders, a company may owe for various goods not yet delivered in full or for services not yet fully performed. Examples are salaries and wages prior to payday, interest, fees to lawyers, architects, etc., for partially completed undertakings. Accrued expenses are expenses that have been incurred, but because of an incomplete transaction, they have not been recorded.

Accrued Expenses Payable $ 39 600

Taxes Payable

Like a citizen, a business is required to pay taxes. Tax payments are made throughout the year. The residual is the outstanding balance after tax is determined in the income statement.

Taxes Payable $ 18 400

To review, total current liabilities is the sum of all the debts that the company will have to pay within one year from the balance sheet date.

Total Current Liabilities $ 280 000

LONG-TERM LIABILITIES

Current liabilities were defined as debts due within one year. Long-term liabilities are debts due after one year from the date of the balance sheet. The principal portions of mortgages, bonds and some loans are examples. The interest on these items may be payable quarterly, semi-annually or annually. This year's or any previous year's interest, if not yet paid, would therefore be shown as an accrued expense payable or a current liability. Interest is charged against only those periods which have already passed. The interest that will be payable for the future may be known, but it is not considered a debt until it has been incurred (but not paid) and does not appear as a liability on the balance sheet. In the sample balance sheet, one long-term liability is the 10 per cent first mortgage bonds due in

1985. The money was received by the company as a loan from the bondholders, who in turn were given a certificate called a bond as evidence of the loan. The bond is really a formal promissory note issued by the company, which agreed to repay the debt at maturity in 1985 and agreed also to pay interest at the rate of 10 per cent per year. The term "first mortgage" is a safe-guard initiated by the lenders. This means that if the company is unable to pay off the bonds in cash when they are due, the bondholders have a claim or lien before other creditors on the mortgaged assets. The mortgaged assets may be sold and the proceeds used to satisfy the debt.

First Mortgage Bonds	
(10% interest, due 1985)	$ 424 000

Finally, all liabilities, current and long-term are added and listed under the heading of total liabilities.

TOTAL LIABILITIES	$ 704 000

SHAREHOLDERS' EQUITY

The total equity interest that all stockholders have in a corporation is called shareholders' equity or net worth. It is what is left after subtracting total liabilities from total assets. Equity is separated, for legal and accounting reasons, into three categories: capital stock, capital surplus and retained earnings.

Capital Stock

The capital stock account reflects the owners' equity in the company. This account is treated differently depending on the company's form of ownership. (Forms of ownership will be discussed in more detail in the next chapter.) In a sole proprietorship, this will appear as a single account, for example:

Scott Meddick, capital	$ 50 000

In a partnership, the accounts will show the respective amounts of the partners' shares of the ownership equity, for example:

Scott Meddick, capital	$ 50 000
Bill West, capital	30 000
Total capital	$ 80 000

In a public or private company the shares of ownership are called capital stock. Anyone can purchase shares in a public firm whereas the sale of a private company's shares is restricted. Shares are represented by stock certificates issued by the company to its shareholders.

The number of shares of capital stock which a company is authorized to issue and the par value, if any, of these shares is specified in the articles of incorporation. The company usually requests authorization of a larger number of shares than it will issue immediately. Thus, if more capital is needed in future years the company will not have to change the charter of its company by increasing the number of authorized shares. Outstanding shares represent the shares that are in the hands of shareholders. The term "par value" is the dollar value given to each share of stock on authorization. "No par value shares" have no such predeclared value.

A company often issues more than one kind of stock in order to appeal to as many investors as possible.

Preferred Shares

Preferred shares have preference over common shares. Normally, dividends are not declared on common shares until preferred shareholders have received their full dividend. If the company should be liquidated, preferred shareholders have first claim on remaining assets, after creditors (those to whom the company owes money as shown in the liabilities section) have been repaid. Dividends to preferred shareholders are normally limited to a stated percentage of share value and are not related to the level of profit. In the XYZ Manufacturing Co. example, the preferred stock is designated 5 per cent cumulative, $100 par value each; this means that each share is entitled to $5 in dividends a year when declared by the Board of Directors. The word "cumulative" means that if in any year the dividend is not paid, it accumulates in favour of the preferred shareholders and must be paid to them before any dividends are distributed to common stock shareholders. In general, preferred shareholders do not have voting rights in the company, unless dividends are in arrears, i.e., have not been paid. There are many different kinds of preferred shares; the terms are specified on the balance sheet.

> Preferred shares, 5% Cumulative $100 Par Value
> Each: Authorized, Issued and Outstanding
> 600 Shares $ 60 000

Common Shares

Common shareholders control the company because the shareholders vote for a board of directors and vote on other management issues at shareholder meetings. While preferred shares are usually fixed as to par value and dividend, common shares may not have a par value, nor is any dividend guaranteed to the holder. Therefore, in prosperous times when company earnings are high, dividends may also be high, and when earnings drop, so may dividends on common shares.

> Common Shares, $5 Par Value Each:
> Authorized, Issued and Outstanding 30 000
> Shares $ 150 000

Capital Surplus

When a company sells shares, the buyers' investment is recorded under capital stock. However, shares may be sold for different prices at different times. To simplify the recording procedure, all shares sold are recorded first at the price of the first shares sold (original issue). When shares are sold at higher prices than the original issue, the difference is considered capital surplus. For example, if 10 000 common shares were sold at $5 each when the company was incorporated, this would have been recorded under capital stock as $50 000. If, at a later date 20 000 additional common shares were issued and sold at $10.20 per share, then $20\ 000 \times \$5 = \$100\ 000$ would be added to capital stock. The *additional* capital [$20\ 000 \times (\$10.20 - \$5) = 20\ 000 \times \$5.20 = \$104\ 000$] would be recorded under capital surplus. (Underwriter's fees would normally be deducted, but for simplicity, this detail is omitted here.)

> Capital Surplus $ 104 000

Retained Earnings

The third component of equity is retained earnings. These represent the accumulated total of after-tax profits and losses from operations over the life of the company that have been retained in the enterprise, i.e., not paid out in dividends. Profits add to the total and losses subtract from it. If a company has had more losses than profits, the amount in retained earnings will be negative (usually shown in brackets) and labelled ''Net Deficit.'' Any dividends paid are also subtracted from the running total. XYZ Manufacturing Co., since it started, has retained a net total of $146 000 from its operations.

Retained Earnings $ 146 000

Shareholders' equity accounts are then totalled.

TOTAL SHAREHOLDERS' EQUITY $ 460 000

All liabilities and shareholders' equity items are added together. This amount balances with the total assets.

TOTAL LIABILITIES AND SHAREHOLDERS'
EQUITY $1 164 000

THE AUDITOR'S REPORT

The financial statements of a company are relied upon by management, shareholders, creditors and potential investors. Statutory regulations require an independent auditor for public corporations and for some private companies. Auditors report to the shareholders, not to the management, stating whether, in their opinion, the statements present fairly the financial position of the firm, in a consistent manner with the previous year's report.

FOOTNOTES

Financial reports are condensed and formalized. Footnotes are used where explanation may be necessary, and to give additional relevant information, such as stock options, details of long-term debt and the details of unconsolidated subsidiaries. It is essential to read footnotes in addition to the numbers in the balance sheet.

Before proceeding to the income statement, here is a summary of the important points to remember about the balance sheet.

FACTS TO REMEMBER ABOUT THE BALANCE SHEET

1. The balance sheet shows the financial picture as of a certain point in time.
2. The company name and date must also appear in the title.
3. Assets are on the left, liabilities and shareholders' equity are on the right. (Sometimes they are listed one after another on a page—this is acceptable but not desirable.)
4. Current assets are first, followed by fixed assets.
5. Current assets are listed in order of liquidity, from most liquid to least liquid.
6. Fixed assets are listed in order of permanence, from the most permanent to the least.
7. Current liabilities are first, followed by long-term liabilities.
8. There is no necessary order to the listing of liabilities under current and long-term headings.
9. Shareholders' equity is capital stock +
                                  capital surplus +
                                  retained earnings
10. Assets = Liabilities + Equity. A balance sheet always balances.

PART 2: THE INCOME STATEMENT

The income statement, also referred to as a profit and loss statement or statement of earnings, shows how much money the corporation made or lost during a particular period. While the balance sheet shows the financial position of a company at a given date, the income statement often is of greater interest to investors because it shows the record of its operating activities for an operating cycle, normally a year.

An income statement matches the revenue generated (usually from selling goods) against all the expenses incurred during the same period to generate these revenues. The difference is a net profit or loss for the period. The phrase "for the period" in the previous sentence is important. For example, if the period ended December 31, and a sale was made on December 30, it would be recorded as a revenue for the period even if the customer did not pay for the product until January. Similarly, expenses incurred but not yet paid, such as an employee's wage, are recorded for the appropriate period. Thus, the income statement does not relate to the actual movement of cash in a company, only to the generation of revenues and the incurring of expenses.

Examine the components and format of the income statement for the XYZ Manufacturing Co. Ltd. below.

Net Sales

Net sales represent revenue earned by the company from its customers for goods sold or services rendered. When a company sells services rather than goods (e.g., a railroad, theatre, or dry cleaners), its net sales are usually called "operating revenues." The net sales item covers the amount received after taking into consideration returned goods and discounts for quick payment. Remember, net sales refer to sales made during the period, not cash collected.

Sales		$1 370 000
Less: Sales returns and		
allowances	$ 30 000	
Sales discounts	20 000	50 000
Net Sales		$1 320 000

XYZ MANUFACTURING CO. LTD.

Statement of Earnings
for the year ending December 31, 1976

Sales			$1 370 000
Less: Sales returns and allowances	$30 000		
Sales discounts	20 000		50 000
Net sales			$1 320 000
Cost of goods sold:			
Finished goods inventory, December 31, 1975			$ 115 000
Raw materials inventory, December 31, 1975		$125 000	
Purchases		667 000	
Less: Raw materials inventory, December 31, 1976		120 000	
Raw materials used		$672 000	
Direct labour		120 000	
Factory overhead		211 000	
Work in process inventory, December 31, 1975		70 000	
Less: Work in process inventory, December 31, 1976		74 000	
Cost of goods manufactured			999 000
Cost of goods available for sale			$1 114 000
Less: Finished goods inventory, December 31, 1976			130 000
Cost of goods sold			984 000
Gross profit			$ 336 000
Operating expenses:			
General and administrative expenses			$ 66 000
Selling expenses			102 000
Depreciation expense			36 000
Total operating expense			204 000
Operating profit			$ 132 000
Plus: Other income			6 000
Less: Other expenses, interest			42 400
Net profit before tax			$ 95 600
Estimated income tax expense			38 240
Net earnings			$ 57 360

Cost of Goods Sold

A major expense associated with making sales is the cost to the company of the product itself, either to make it or buy it. To a non-manufacturing distributor, this cost is simply the price paid to the supplier plus freight, duty and any other acquisition expenses. A non-manufacturing company calculates its "cost of goods sold" during a given period by adding the cost of goods available for sale at the beginning of the period to the cost of goods purchased during the period, and then subtracting the cost of goods unsold at the end of this period. Thus:

Non-Manufacturing Company

Cost of beginning inventory (on first day of period)
Plus cost of purchases (during period)
Plus freight-in
Minus cost of ending inventory (at end of period)
Equals cost of goods sold.

To a manufacturing company, the cost of goods sold includes not only the cost of the raw materials but also the costs related to making those goods. Thus:

Manufacturing Company

Cost of beginning inventory, finished goods
Plus cost of goods manufactured
Equals cost of goods available for sale
Minus cost of ending inventory, finished goods
Equals cost of goods sold

Note that an additional calculation is done for cost of goods manufactured. First the cost of raw materials used must be determined:

Cost of beginning inventory, raw materials
Plus purchases, raw materials
Less cost of ending inventory, raw materials
Equals raw materials used.

The next step is to add

Direct labour
Plus factory overhead
Plus cost of beginning inventory, work in process
Minus cost of ending inventory, work in process
Equals cost of goods manufactured.

"Manufacturing overhead" includes all the costs of production except raw material and direct labour such as, indirect labour, power, heat, light and depreciation of equipment and machinery used in the production of the goods manufactured. Depreciation of other items such as office furniture is not included in "Manufacturing overhead" but is considered an operating expense.

Cost of Goods Sold $ 984 000

Gross Profit

Gross profit or margin is determined by subtracting the "cost of goods sold" from "net sales." It represents the markup or margin the enterprise charges or earns on its product costs.

Gross Profit $ 336 000

Operating Expenses

Operating expenses are generally categorized as "general" and "administrative" and "selling" expenses. The categories are usually separated, but this is not always necessary. Executive salaries, office payroll, office expenses, rent, electricity and the like are the usual items included as general and administrative expenses. Selling expenses include salesmen's salaries and commissions, advertising, promotion and travel.

Operating Expenses
    General and Administrative $ 66 000
    Selling Expenses   102 000

Depreciation Expense

As mentioned earlier, depreciation is the allocation of the cost of an asset over its useful life. The income statement, for a period of time, records all the costs associated with obtaining revenues. Such expenditures as production equipment or trucks to deliver goods, if charged against the revenues generated during the first year of expenditure, though the asset had a few more years of use, would understate profits in the first year and overstate profits in subsequent years. To overcome this, the purchase cost of the asset is spread over several income statement periods. (Please refer to page 10 for methods of depreciation determination.) First, the amount of depreciation allocated to the income statement period is called *depreciation expense* and is shown on the income statement under operating expenses (or as already mentioned, under "manufacturing overhead"). Second, a running total of all depreciation expenses to date for each asset is listed on the balance sheet in an account called "accumulated depreciation."

    Depreciation Expense $ 36 000

Operating Profit

"Operating profit" represents the net gain from the enterprise's normal operating activities. It is calculated by subtracting "operating expenses" from "gross profit."

    Operating Profit $ 132 000

Other Income and Other Expenses

The company may have revenues that are not directly related to its primary business (such as interest earned on investments, sale of land or equipment). To include them under net sales would distort this item and make comparison of performance over several years unrealistic. Other expenses often include interest the company must pay on money it has borrowed. The XYZ's first mortgage bonds, carried on the balance sheet as a long-term liability, bear 10 per cent interest on $424 000. Thus, the interest expense on the income statement is equal to $42 400 per year. "Other income" and "Other expenses" are usually reported after operating profit has been calculated.

    Other Income $ 6 000
    Other Expenses, Interest   42 400

Net Profit Before Tax

"Net profit before tax" represents the company's determination of its income before estimation of its tax liability.

    Net Profit Before Tax $ 95 600

Estimated Income Tax Expense

Corporations earning profits must pay income tax. The tax rate is calculated on the net profit. The net profit before taxes is $95 600. If the tax rate was 40 per cent, the estimated income tax would be $38 240.

Estimated Income Tax Expense	$ 38 240

Net Earnings

After all revenues (the plus factors) have been added and all expenses (the minus factors) subtracted, the residual is "net earnings." If expenses exceed revenues, the residual is a "net loss."

Net Earnings	$ 57 360

A SUMMARY OF FACTS TO REMEMBER ABOUT THE INCOME STATEMENT

1. The income statement covers a period of time. (The balance sheet shows the financial position of the enterprise at one point in time.)
2. Sales (revenues) made *during* a period are recorded. This does not necessarily mean that cash was collected.
3. Expenses incurred during the period to make these sales are recorded. This does not necessarily mean that cash was paid out.
4. The formal structure of an income statement is: sales first, then expenses, then net earnings (or loss).
5. Above all, remember an income statement matches expenses to revenues, for a specified period of time.

PART 3: THE RELATIONSHIP OF THE INCOME STATEMENT AND THE BALANCE SHEET

Retained Earnings

The balance sheet portrays the financial condition of a firm at a single point in time. Retained earnings represent the account that is the nexus for the balance sheet and the income statement. The retained earnings are the earnings remaining after dividends on preferred and common stock have been paid; that is, the earnings retained in the company. When an enterprise starts in business it has no retained earnings but as soon as it has any profits or losses, the retained earnings account is affected. (If losses are greater than earnings, the account is listed as "net deficit.") For example:

Net Earnings for the Year 1976		$ 57 360
Less: 1976 Dividends Paid		
on Preferred Shares	$ 3 000	
on Common Shares	15 000	
		18 000
1976 Net Increase in		
Retained Earnings		$ 39 360

The statement of retained earnings for XYZ Manufacturing Co. Ltd. is presented below.

XYZ MANUFACTURING CO. LTD.
Statement of Retained Earnings
for the year ended December 31, 1976

Retained earnings: December 31, 1975		$106 640
Net earnings for the year, 1976		57 360
		$164 000
Less: 1976 dividends paid on:		
Preferred Shares	$ 3 000	
Common Shares	15 000	
		18 000
Retained earnings: December 31, 1976		$146 000

Transactions[1]

Some transactions will have an impact solely on the balance sheet accounts. For example:

1. On September 1, the ABC Co. is established by buying $5000 worth of capital stock in the corporation and putting the money in a bank account.

ASSETS:		LIABILITIES:	
Cash	$ 5 000		
		SHAREHOLDERS' EQUITY	
		Capital Stock	$ 5 000
	$ 5 000		$ 5 000

2. The company buys and pays cash for office equipment which costs $1000.

ASSETS:		LIABILITIES:	
Cash	$ 4 000		
Equipment	1 000	SHAREHOLDERS' EQUITY	
		Capital stock	$ 5 000
	$ 5 000		$ 5 000

3. The company buys an automobile for $3000. It pays $2000 cash and takes out a bank loan for $1000.

ASSETS:		LIABILITIES:	
Cash	$ 2 000	Notes payable—bank	$ 1 000
Automobile	3 000	SHAREHOLDERS' EQUITY	
Equipment	1 000	Capital stock	5 000
	$ 6 000		$ 6 000

4. $7000 of capital stock is sold to new investors.

ASSETS:		LIABILITIES:	
Cash	$ 9 000	Notes payable—bank	$ 1 000
Automobile	3 000	SHAREHOLDERS' EQUITY	
Equipment	1 000	Capital Stock	12 000
	$13 000		$13 000

---

[1] In many accounting texts, transaction analysis is taught by the use of debits and credits. Debits and credits will not be used in this text.

Other transactions have impacts on both the balance sheet and income statement.

Revenues for sales of products or services are sold for cash or credit. If cash is received then the cash item on the balance sheet will increase appropriately. If the product is sold on credit then the accounts receivable item on the balance sheet will increase. Expenses, such as wages, rent, advertising, which are incurred may be paid immediately or later. If paid by cash now, the cash account must be decreased by the appropriate amount. If the company incurs the expense but does not pay in cash immediately, the expense is shown as a payable in the liabilities section.

Sometimes, the relationship between the balance sheet and the income statement is difficult. Not all the possible solutions which might occur will be listed here. Here are a few situations:

1. Changes in inventory: close inspection of cost of goods sold section of an income statement can demonstrate how inventory can increase (via purchases) and decrease (via sales). The ending inventory figure on the income statement is the same as the inventory figure on the balance sheet as of the last day of the period covered by the income statement.
2. Prepaid expenses: if at the beginning of an income statement period, there is a prepaid expense (insurance) that is incurred during the income statement period, the value of the asset on the balance sheet will decrease by the appropriate amount at the end of the period rather than reducing the cash amount.
3. Paying for debts, buying and selling assets. With some exceptions these transactions do not appear on the income statement, yet most beginning students seem to think they should. Paying a bank loan with cash changes both the bank loan payable (a liability) and the cash (an asset) accounts.
4. Retained earnings and the cash accounts. Some beginning students persist in thinking that profits equal cash increases, and that retained earnings are cash. The first idea is not necessarily wrong—if all transactions were on a cash basis. The second idea, that retained earnings are a ''second bank account,'' is never true. It represents a claim on the balance sheet, a claim that arises by the amount of profits retained in the company. The actual money it represents could be in cash, but just as likely may be invested in new inventory, desks in the office, and so on. The cash shown in the cash account in the current assets section is the total cash in the company as of that point in time!

Problems in Balance Sheet Construction

Problem 1
Stan Hardy Retail Florist

Capital, S. Hardy	$9300
Accumulated depreciation, store fixtures	4000
Accounts payable	4100
Goodwill	2000
Store fixtures, cost	7500
Inventory	2500
Bank loan (90-day note)	2200
Cash	3700
Accrued expenses payable	300
Accounts receivable	4200

Assignment

Different accounts are listed above, in random order, for the florist business of Stan Hardy. The accounts are as of January 31, 1977.

1. Determine whether the account is a current asset, fixed asset, intangible asset, current liability, long-term liability or net worth account.
2. Prepare a balance sheet as of January 31, 1977 for the business.

Problem 2
Robinson Hardware Store Ltd.

Land	$ 7 800
Prepaid expenses	5 100
Accrued expenses payable	4 200
Notes payable, due in 90 days	15 000
Long term debt	20 500
Accumulated depreciation, building and equipment	22 900
Marketable securities	1 700
Accounts payable	29 500
Accounts receivable	24 000
Capital stock[1]	20 500
Organization expenses	1 000
Buildings and equipment, cost	47 600
Retained earnings	52 600
Taxes payable	2 100
Cash	7 300
Inventory	72 800

Assignment

Different accounts as of January 31, 1977 are listed above in random order for Robinson Hardware Store Ltd.

1. Determine whether each account is a current asset, fixed asset, intangible asset, current liability, long-term liability or an equity item.
2. Prepare a formal balance sheet as of January 31, 1977, for Robinson Hardware Store Ltd.

[1] Authorized 2500 shares, $10 par value.

Problem 3
Best Furniture Manufacturer Ltd.

Accumulated depreciation, buildings	$ 27 200
Patents	3 600
Building, cost	77 300
Accumulated depreciation, equipment	62 600
Bank loan, short-term	69 700
Common stock[1]	26 600
Equipment, cost	104 800
Inventory	136 000
Accrued expenses payable	7 400
Long-term debt, due within one year	4 000
Cash	?
Investment[2]	36 200
Prepaid expenses	4 100
Taxes payable	8 800
Marketable securities	5 600
Land	10 500
Mortgage, due in 1993	45 700
Goodwill	7 300
Organization expenses	1 500
Accounts receivable	134 700
Preferred stock[3]	23 700
Retained earnings	158 400
Accounts payable	81 300
Debentures, due 1986	20 000

Assignment

The above accounts are taken from the records of Best Furniture Manufacturer Ltd. as of December 31, 1976. Prepare a balance sheet for the company and determine the cash position.

[1] Authorized and issued 10 000 shares of no par value stock.
[2] Represents a 50 percent ownership in a major hardwood lumber supplier.
[3] Authorized 10 000, $10 par value shares.

Problems on Income Statements

Problem 1
Jones Department Store Ltd.
(in 000's of dollars)

Net sales	$3700
Cost of goods sold	2900
Other income	20
Selling expenses	480
Gross margin (profit)	800
Net operating profit	210
Administrative expenses	110
Other expenses	30

Assignment

Different income statement items for the Jones Department Store Ltd. are listed above in random order. All refer to the year ending December 31, 1976, and are in thousands of dollars. The tax rate is 45 per cent.

1. Prepare a formal income statement for the period ending December 31, 1976, for the Jones Department Store Ltd.

Problem 2
J. T. Ross Retail Sales Co. Ltd.
(in 000's of dollars)

Gross profit	$217
Selling expenses	64
Ending inventory	190
General and administrative expenses	57
Net sales	850
Net profit before tax	96
Beginning inventory	157

Assignment

Different income statement items of J. T. Ross Sales Co. Ltd. are listed above in random order for the three-month period ending April 30, 1976.

1. Prepare a formal income statement for the period ending April 30, 1976, for J. T. Ross Retail Sales Co. Ltd. Assume the income tax rate is 50 per cent.

Note: To complete this exercise the following items will have to be calculated:
   (a) Cost of goods sold
   (b) Purchases
   (c) Net profit after tax

Problem 3
Adanac Textile Mills Ltd.
(in 000's of dollars)

Direct labour	$ 251
Goods in process, December 31, 1976	128
Sales discounts	9
Manufacturing overhead	193
Goods in process, December 31, 1975	130
Raw materials, December 31, 1976	163
Administrative expenses	98
Finished goods, December 31, 1975	74
Selling expense	49
General expense	85
Sales returns and allowances	11
Raw materials, December 31, 1975	166
Finished goods, December 31, 1976	73
Other expense, interest	28
Sales	1 830
Indirect labour	33
Other expense, royalty	6
Material purchases	986
Other income	25

Assignment

Income statement items are listed above in random order. All are period accounts for the year ending December 31, 1976, except where noted. Assuming a tax rate of 40 per cent prepare a formal income statement for Adanac Textile Mills Ltd. for the year ending December 31, 1976.

Problem 4
Canlan Pulp and Paper Ltd
(in 000's of dollars)

Selling expenses	$ 126
Sales returns and allowances	11
Finished goods, December 31, 1975	151
Other revenue	71
Depreciation, manufacturing equipment	212
Indirect labour	330
Depreciation, office equipment	24
Direct labour	495
Sales discounts	15
Administrative expenses	235
Other manufacturing overhead	81
Net sales	3839
Goods in process, December 31, 1975	73
Gross profit	630
Estimated income tax expense	17
Raw materials, December 31, 1976	540
Raw materials used	2095
Cost of goods manufactured	3212
General expenses	157
Net earnings	29
Other expenses, interest	113
Raw materials, December 31, 1975	529
Net operating income	88

Assignment

Income statement items for Canlan Pulp and Paper Ltd. are listed above in random order. All are period accounts for the year ending December 31, 1976, except where noted. Prepare a formal income statement for Canlan Pulp and Paper Ltd. To complete the assignment sales, material purchases, ending goods in process and finished goods inventories, and cost of goods sold will have to be calculated.

Problems on the Relationship
of the Income Statement
and Balance Sheet

Problem 1
Cut Rate Stores Incorporated
(in 000's of dollars)

Inventory, June 30, 1976	$ 316
Accounts payable	120
Gross profit	357
Store fixtures, net	60
Selling expenses	142
Income tax expense	5
Retained earnings, June 30, 1975	220
Cash	20
General and admin. expenses	180
Accrued expenses payable	40
Long-term notes payable	13
Accounts receivable	135
Notes payable	105
Inventory, June 30, 1975	285
Capital stock	15
Sales	1416
Depreciation expense	15
Income tax payable	3

Assignment

Different balance sheet and income statement accounts are listed above in random order. The balance sheet accounts are as of June 30, 1976, except where noted. The income statement amounts are for the year July 1, 1975, to June 30, 1976, in thousands of dollars.

1. Determine whether each account is a balance sheet or income statement item.
2. Prepare a formal income statement for Cut Rate Stores Incorporated for the year ending June 30, 1976.
3. Prepare a statement of retained earnings for the year ended June 30, 1976.
4. Prepare a formal balance sheet as of June 30, 1976, for Cut Rate Stores Incorporated.

Problem 2
Garnier Wholesalers Incorporated
(in 000's of dollars)

Retained earnings, December 31, 1975	$ 190
Cash	17
Retained earnings, December 31, 1976	216
Net sales	1663
Accounts receivable	159
Gross profit	394
Capital stock	45
Net profit before taxes	35
Income tax expense	9
Purchases	1347
Long-term bank loan	10
Prepaid expenses	11
Depreciation expense	20
Accumulated depreciation, December 31, 1975	140
Inventory, December 31, 1975	316
Accrued expenses payable	13
Selling expenses	168
Equipment, cost	200
Notes payable—bank	200
Inventory, December 31, 1976	394
Income taxes payable	4
Cost of goods sold	1269
Accounts payable	133
General and administrative expenses	171

Assignment

Different balance sheet and income statement accounts are listed above in random order in thousands of dollars. The balance sheet accounts are as of December 31, 1976, except where noted. The income statement amounts are for the year ending December 31, 1976.

1. Determine whether each account is a balance sheet or income statement item.
2. Prepare a formal income statement for the year ending December 31, 1976, for Garnier Wholesalers Incorporated.
3. Prepare a statement of retained earnings for the year ended as at December 31, 1976.
4. Prepare a formal balance sheet as of December 31, 1976, for Garnier Wholesalers Incorporated.

Problem 3
NRS Co.

PART A

On August 30, 1976, Nick West, Rob Taber and Steve Rand, university students, decided to combine their summer earnings and invest the money in a small record and poster store. Their total combined investment was $1500 in cash with each member contributing $500. Draw up a balance sheet showing the financial position of NRS Co. as of August 30, 1976.

PART B

On August 31, 1976, the following events occurred:

1. Nick and Steve found a basement retail outlet vacant near the university campus. Remodelling would be required. The rent for the store was $75 per month, with the first month and the last month of the lease payable on signing the lease contract. Nick and Steve signed a 12-month lease.
2. A contractor estimated the costs of the remodelling improvements would be $600. A contract to complete the work was signed by Nick.
3. Nick purchased three counters, a cash register, two chairs and a desk from a second-hand shop for $300 in cash.
4. Steve contacted a record supplier and bought $900 worth of records. He paid $200 in cash and agreed to pay the remaining $700 in 30 days.
5. Rob travelled to Toronto and purchased for cash $200 worth of posters.
6. Nick and Steve negotiated a bank loan of $1000 at 8 per cent interest per annum. The bank was to be repaid in two installments as follows:
   August 30, 1977 $500 + interest
   August 30, 1978 $500 + interest

Assignment
Prepare a balance sheet as of August 31, 1976, for NRS Co.

PART C

During the next six months Nick, Rob and Steve felt that the business had been doing well. The following events occurred:

1. In early September the contractor completed the remodelling and was paid $600.
2. Sales of $2500 in records had been made. The records sold had cost NRS $1500. In addition $250 in posters had been sold which originally cost $100. Of the record sales, $2000 had been received in cash and $500 had been billed to student organizations, but not paid for. All poster sales were cash sales.
3. The $700 owing to the record supplier for the August 31 purchase had been paid.
4. An additional $1700 worth of records had been purchased and $1400 had been paid in cash and $300 was still owed as of February 28, 1977.
5. An insurance policy covering the inventory for two years, starting September 1, 1976, had been purchased for $200 cash.
6. Interest on the bank loan was calculated to be $40 but had not been paid.
7. Light and power had amounted to $100 and had been paid in cash.
8. The three owners had each withdrawn $100 in cash.
9. Rental payments were made regularly on the first day of the month.

Assignment

1. Prepare an income statement for the 6-month period that the company had been in operation. How much profit was made?
2. Draw up the balance sheet as of February 28, 1977.

SECTION III
An Introduction to Financial Management

The purpose of this chapter is to introduce the basic techniques used by financial managers and analysts to assess and project the financial performance and position of a business. An understanding of the basic financial statements from the previous chapter is essential to an understanding of this chapter. Several financial analysis tools will be discussed and their application to the financial management cases will be summarized. Financial analysis and management is not just number pushing; judgment must be exercised as to what numbers to look at and how to interpret them. Often, a "qualitative factor," something not expressed in numbers, is more important to the solution of a problem than all the numbers involved.

PART 1:   FINANCIAL GOALS

There are four basic financial goals: profitability, growth, liquidity and stability. To survive, every business must meet each of these goals to some extent, although a business must determine for itself the relative emphasis to place on each of the four goals.

Profitability refers to the generation of revenues in excess of the expenses associated with obtaining it. This is the "bottom-line" test of how successful a firm's operators have been as shown at the bottom of the income statements.

Growth refers to increasing in size or acquiring more of something. A businessman may assess his financial performance by calculating, for example, how much sales or assets have increased this year over last year. While there are many widely held concerns about growth in general (for example, the zero population growth movement), businessmen and investors remain very interested in financial growth.

Liquidity refers to a business's ability to meet short-term obligations. For example, a manager may wish to invest as much of his firm's cash in inventory and equipment as possible but, if he overdoes it and cannot pay his employees or creditors on time, he can be forced into bankruptcy. A good financial manager maintains a balance between profit, growth and liquidity.

Stability refers to a business's overall financial structure. For example, a businessman may wish to invest as little of his own money as possible in his firm and finance his operation mainly with debt. If the debt-equity mix is too far out of balance, the firm may topple should some of the debtors want their money back at an "inconvenient" time. Many of the spectacular financial disasters reported in the newspapers resulted from neglect of the stability goal of sound financial management.

There are no clear-cut guidelines on how much or how little financial performance is adequate or on how to trade off performance on one financial goal in favour of another. For example, 10 per cent sales growth may be terrible for a firm in one industry but excellent for a firm in another. Similarly, a high level of liquidity may be preferable to growth for a firm at one time and detrimental for the same firm at another.

Financial analysis and projections are used to assess achievement of financial goals. The financial statements of the LMN Retail Co. Ltd. will be used to illustrate the development of the Statement of Changes in Financial Position and the financial ratios. Exhibit 1 presents the income statements of LMN Retail Co. Ltd. for 1975, 1976 and 1977; Exhibit 2, the balance sheets as of January 31, 1975, 1976 and 1977.

In addition to discussing the Statement of Changes in Financial Position and financial ratio analysis, this chapter will illustrate an elementary process for developing projected financial statements. It will also examine the forms of business organization, credit evaluation and sources of short-term and intermediate term financing for small and medium sized businesses.

Exhibit 1
LMN Retail Co. Ltd.
Income Statement
For the Years Ending January 31
(in 000's of dollars)

	1975		1976		1977	
Sales		$875		$849		$1 086
Cost of goods sold:						
Beginning inventory	$152		$153		$ 168	
Purchases	678		662		874	
Cost of goods available for sale	$830		$815		$1 042	
Less: Ending inventory	153		168		200	
Cost of goods sold		677		647		842
Gross profit		$198		$202		$ 244
Operating expenses:						
General and administrative	$ 67		$ 76		$ 90	
Selling	76		84		113	
Depreciation	15		15		14	
Total operating expenses		158		175		217
Net operating profit		$ 40		$ 27		$ 27
Other expenses—interest		3		2		2
Net profit before tax		$ 37		$ 25		$ 25
Estimated income tax		16		10		10
Net earnings		$ 21		$ 15		$ 15

Exhibit 2
LMN Retail Co. Ltd.
Balance Sheet
as of January 31
(in 000's of dollars)

	1975	1976	1977
Assets			
Current assets			
Cash	$ 2	$ 12	$ 6
Net accounts receivable	80	72	80
Inventory	153	168	200
Total current assets	$235	$252	$286
Fixed assets, net	49	34	32
TOTAL ASSETS	$284	$286	$318
Liabilities			
Current liabilities			
Accounts payable	$ 68	$ 64	$ 71
Notes payable—bank	18	18	30
Taxes payable	16	10	12
Accrued expenses	5	12	8
Total current liabilities	$107	$104	$121
Long-term liabilities	30	20	20
TOTAL LIABILITIES	$137	$124	$141
EQUITY			
Capital stock	$ 15	$ 15	$ 15
Retained earnings	132	147	162
Total equity	147	162	177
TOTAL LIABILITIES AND EQUITY	$284	$286	$318

PART 2: THE STATEMENT OF CHANGES IN FINANCIAL POSITION[1]

The statement of changes in financial position shows changes between two balance sheets. Up to this point, only one balance sheet has been used. Over a period of time a company will have several balance sheets or "statements of financial position." There are a number of ways to analyze a set of balance sheets; one is by the statement of changes in financial position. Examine the 1975 and 1976 balance sheets of LMN Retail Co. Ltd. The changes in balance sheet accounts are as follows:

	(in 000's of dollars)
Cash, an increase of	$ 10
Net accounts receivable, a decrease of	8
Inventory, an increase of	15
Fixed assets, a decrease of	15
Accounts payable, a decrease of	4
Notes payable—bank, no change	
Taxes payable, a decrease of	6
Accrued expenses, an increase of	7
Long-term liabilities, a decrease of	10
Capital stock, no change	
Retained earnings, an increase of	15

This procedure shows what has happened in each account, but does not give much insight into the way these changes relate to one another to result in a change in total assets of $2000 (or a change in total liabilities and equity of $2000).

Some of these changes represent money coming into the company. For example, the reduction of accounts receivable represents an incremental cash collection of $8000. In other words, the reduction through collection of accounts receivable is a source of cash to the LMN Retail Co. Ltd. Similarly, the reduction of fixed assets, either through sale or depreciation, has an incremental impact on cash (i.e., it is a source of cash).

An increase in a creditor's claim represents the postponement of a cash payment; therefore it is also a source of cash. For example, the $7000 increase of accrued expenses is a source of cash. The last source of cash is retained earnings, which represents the increase in the cash position created by the postponement of dividends. Total sources of cash for the year ending January 31, 1976, for the LMN Retail Co. Ltd. are:

Sources	*(in 000's of dollars)*
Net accounts receivable collected	$ 8
Fixed assets, net	15
Accrued expenses	7
Earnings retained in business	15
Total sources	$45

Inspection of the income statements, Exhibit 1, reveals that in the 1976 fiscal year, LMN Retail Co. Ltd. charged $15 000 of depreciation expenses. If LMN Retail Co. Ltd. were on a cash basis (i.e., all sales were for cash and all expenses paid as incurred), the impact of the operations in the fiscal year would have been to increase cash $30 000—the net earnings plus depreciation. The cash was used when the fixed asset was purchased. Depreciation is a non-cash allocation of the original expenditure.

Some of the changes represent cash outflows or uses of money. The investment in in-

---

[1] Only the Statement of Changes in Financial Position on a cash basis will be presented.

ventory increased by $15 000. This represents a reduction in the cash position of LMN Retail Co. Ltd. to purchase the additional items. Similarly, a reduction in a creditor's claim represents a cash outflow or use of cash. For example, the decrease of accounts payable by $4000, taxes payable by $6000 and long-term liabilities by $10 000 are uses of cash. In summary, for the fiscal year ending January 31, 1976, the uses of cash by LMN Retail Co. Ltd. were:

Uses	*(in 000's of dollars)*
Inventory	$15
Accounts payable	4
Taxes payable	6
Long-term liabilities	10
Total uses	$35

For the 1976 fiscal year, the sources of cash for the LMN Retail Co. Ltd. were $10 000 greater than the uses of cash. In other words, the firm had a net cash inflow of $10 000 as represented by the increase in the cash account. Exhibit 3 presents the statement of changes in financial position of LMN Retail Co. Ltd. for the year ending January 31, 1976.

Exhibit 3
LMN Retail Co. Ltd.
Statement of Changes in Financial Position
for the Year Ending January 31, 1976
(in 000's of dollars)

Sources of cash:		
Net accounts receivable	$ 8	
Fixed assets, net	15	
Accrued expenses	7	
Retained earnings	15	
Total sources		$45
Uses of cash:		
Inventory	$ 15	
Accounts payable	4	
Taxes payable	6	
Long-term liabilities	10	
Total uses		35
Net cash increase		$10
Cash, January 31, 1975		2
Cash, January 31, 1976		$12

In summary, sources of cash are decreases in assets, increases in liabilities and increases in equity. Conversely, uses of cash are increases in assets, decreases in liabilities and decreases in equity. For the sake of clarification it might be useful to take the viewpoint of an owner of a small enterprise at his cash register. The collection of a sale immediately increases his cash. If the customer wishes to pay his bill by credit card rather than cash, the impact on the retailer is the foregone cash collection and the increase in his accounts receivable. If he subsequently sells the accounts receivable to a bank, his cash position will increase and his accounts receivable will decrease. In contrast, if a supplier on delivery of goods demands immediate payment, the owner must reach into his cash register to make payment. However, if the supplier states he does not wish payment immediately, the impact is the postponement of a payment and the preservation of or incremental impact on cash. Subsequently, when the account payable is paid, there will be a use of cash.

As an analytical tool, statements of changes in financial position can be prepared for any period the analyst desires, providing balance sheets are available. Exhibit 4 presents the statement of changes in financial position for the LMN Retail Co. Ltd. for a two-year period ending January 31, 1977.

Exhibit 4
LMN Retail Co. Ltd.
Statement of Changes in Financial Position
for Two Years
Ending January 31, 1977

Sources of cash:	
Fixed assets	$17 000
Accounts payable	3 000
Notes payable—bank	12 000
Accrued expenses	3 000
Retained earnings	30 000
Total sources	$65 000
Uses of cash:	
Inventory	$47 000
Taxes payable	4 000
Long-term liabilities	10 000
Total uses	$61 000
Net cash increase	$ 4 000
Cash, January 31, 1975	2 000
Cash, January 31, 1977	$ 6 000

In analyzing the statements, *first* identify the major changes (Exhibit 4), which are as follows:

Sources	
Retained earnings (profits)	$30 000
Fixed assets decrease	17 000
Bank loan increase	12 000
Uses	
Inventory increase	$47 000
Payment of long-term debt	10 000

The analyst cannot tell whether the profits were used to increase inventory or whether the bank loan was used to pay off the long-term debt. Instead, a general flow of cash can be observed. Also, without more information, the decrease in fixed assets can be a result either of depreciation or the sale of fixed assets. On this point, the income statement records that the total depreciation expense for 1976 and 1977 was $29 000 ($15 000 + $14 000). If the only change in fixed assets had been an increase in accumulated depreciation on the balance sheet, the decrease in fixed assets would have been $29 000, not $17 000. It appears LMN bought $12 000 worth of fixed assets. In other words, reported changes in financial position would be more accurate if a $29 000 source (increase in accumulated depreciation) and a $12 000 use (increase in cost of fixed assets) were shown.

The second step in analysis is to interpret the desirability of these major changes. Essentially, LMN management has used cash generated from operations (profits and depreciation) to (a) invest in inventory, (b) buy more fixed assets and (c) pay off some of the long-term debt. Because cash from operations was not sufficient for this purpose, LMN management has, in effect, substituted short-term debt (bank loan) for long-term debt (the $10 000 paid off). Were all of these moves appropriate? It depends. For example, it appears that LMN's sales are now beginning to grow (see Exhibit 1). It is possible that the inventory increase was in anticipation of growth; or it is possible that it made the growth feasible by making a larger variety or quantity of goods available for sale. The relative amount of inventory will be examined in the next section of this chapter to see whether LMN management increased it too much. Because the terms of the long-term debt are not known, it is impossible to comment on the appropriateness of retiring some of the debt. Ordinarily, more information would be available to make better judgments about the desirability of changes. The LMN example is only an illustration of the analytical approach.

The statement of changes in financial position is a valuable tool, but clearly it is limited in its uses. For example, the analyst is not able to determine in the LMN example whether the increase in inventory was excessive or not relative to the increase in sales for LMN. Ratio analysis is required to complement the statement of changes in financial position.

PART 3: FINANCIAL RATIO ANALYSIS

As changes occur in the size of a company's various accounts, it is difficult to analyze what is happening by casual inspection of several income statements and balance sheets. If only one or two accounts changed and the rest stayed the same, it would be a relatively straightforward task to identify and interpret such developments. However, everything usually appears to fluctuate. Further, the bigger the numbers, the more difficult it is to tell how much they have changed.

An approach developed to assist in identifying and interpreting changes in financial performance and condition is called ratio analysis. A ratio is simply a fraction: it has two parts, a numerator (the top) and a denominator (the bottom). Using the LMN example, there are endless possible ratios that could be calculated by taking various numbers on the income statements and balance sheets and making up fractions. Most of the calculations would be meaningless. However, financial analysts have agreed upon a common set of fifteen to twenty ratios that are useful in assessing financial performance and financial position. Exhibit 5 presents several ratios for the LMN Retail Co. Ltd. The following are some observations of Exhibit 5:

1. The ratios are grouped into four categories; the headings refer to the four financial goals. In other words, the ratios help analyze the company's progress towards each of these financial objectives.
2. The ratios do not look like fractions! Each fraction has been simplified as much as possible.

3. Some ratios are percentages; others are in days; others are in the form of proportions, etc. The differences are the result of the various numbers used in the fractions.
4. Each ratio has been calculated for three years in order to compare ratios over time and to identify changes in them. A single ratio does not provide much insight as to the direction in which a firm is heading.

Exhibit 5
LMN Retail Co. Ltd.
Ratio Analysis
for the Years Ending January 31

	1975	1976	1977
	%	%	%
Profitability:			
(i) Vertical analysis[1]			
Sales	100.0	100.0	100.0
Cost of goods sold	77.4	76.2	77.5
Gross profit	22.6	23.8	22.5
Operating expenses: General and administrative	7.7	9.0	8.3
Selling	8.7	9.9	10.4
Depreciation	1.7	1.8	1.3
Subtotal	18.1	20.6	20.0
Net operating income	4.6	3.2	2.5
Other expenses	0.3	0.2	0.2
Net profit before tax	4.2	3.0	2.3
Estimated income tax	1.8	1.2	0.9
Net earnings	2.4	1.8	1.4
(ii) Return on investment[2]	14.3%	9.7%	8.8%

Growth:[3]	1975-1976	1976-1977	
Sales	(3.0%)	27.9%	
Profits, after tax	(28.6%)	—	
Assets	0.7%	11.2%	
Equity	10.2%	9.3%	

Liquidity:	1975	1976	1977
Current ratio	2.2/1	2.4/1	2.4/1
Acid test	0.8/1	0.8/1	0.7/1
Working capital	$128 000	$148 000	$165 000
Age of receivables[4]	32.9 days	30.5 days	26.5 days
Inventory in days cost of goods sold[4]	81.4 days	93.5 days	85.5 days
Age of payables[4]	36.1 days	34.8 days	29.2 days

Stability:			
Net worth to total assets	51.8%	56.6%	55.7%
Long-term debt interest coverage	13.3 times	13.5 times	13.5 times

[1] Detail may not add to totals because of rounding.
[2] Return on investment is based on average equity except for 1975, which is on year-end equity.
[3] Brackets indicate negative amounts.
[4] A 360-day year was used.

Interpretation of Ratios

Interpretation of ratios will be discussed before outlining how to calculate each ratio. As an example, the net profit/sales ratio is comprised of two numbers from the income statement, net profit after tax and net sales. The objective is to gain an indication of the change in profit relative to the change in sales. From LMN's income statements, Exhibit 1, net profit after tax declined from $21 000 to $15 000 and then remained at $15 000. Also, because sales declined from 1975 to 1976, some decrease in profits could be expected. Did profits decline more or less than sales? That is a hard question to answer without preparing the net profit/sales ratio. If both profits and sales had declined together to the same extent, the relationship between them would have remained the same; that is, the ratio of net profit to sales would be constant. From the ratios in Exhibit 5, the analyst can see that the relationship has changed: formerly profits were 2.4 per cent of sales; now they are 1.8 per cent of sales. In short, profits declined more than sales. From 1976 to 1977 sales increased but the ratio of net profit to sales deteriorated. Was this decline in the profitability ratio good or bad? If LMN's objective is to make as much profit as possible, this decline was bad, but this conclusion might be premature. First, because other firms in LMN's industry might have fared even worse, LMN might be doing very well in that respect. It would be useful to look at a set of industry ratios to check this possibility. Second, maybe LMN was trading off profitability for some other financial goal intentionally, in which case the decline in profitability may be an expected consequence. To address this possibility, other ratios are inspected and the goals of management investigated.

Ratios are indicators of change. They simplify relationships between numbers but net profit/sales has shown us that LMN's profitability on one dimension has declined. The ratio does not tell us whether that was good or bad or even why the decline occurred. Clearly, a ratio can change if the numerator changes, the denominator changes or both change. In order to understand the trend of net profit/sales from 2.4 per cent to 1.8 per cent to 1.4 per cent, the cause of that change must be found. Why did profits change? Why did sales change? In short, a close look at the components of the ratio is required.

Ratios are similar to traffic lights: red, yellow and green. Changes in the ratios (such as the net profits/sales example) signal whether the analyst should "stop" (take a close look at something), "be prepared to stop" (a problem may be developing), or "go" (so far, so good). In short, ratios are *indicators* of problems (or success) that can be monitored relatively easily.

Calculation of Ratios

It is suggested that in the following examples the student insert the data from the financial statements (Exhibits 1 and 2) of LMN Retail Co. Ltd. to verify the calculations in Exhibit 5.

Profitability

Vertical analysis is the restatement of the income statement in percentages, using sales for the year as the base, i.e., 100 per cent. The term vertical arises from the fact that percentages are calculated on a vertical axis, in contrast to growth ratios, such as sales growth, which make a horizontal comparison. The purpose of the analysis is to eliminate the impact of absolute dollar sales on expense amounts. For example:

$$\text{Cost of goods sold to sales} = \frac{\$ \text{ Cost of goods sold}}{\$ \text{ Net sales}} \times 100 = \underline{?} \ \%$$

This ratio indicates the amount spent to provide the products sold; its complement is as follows:

$$\text{Gross profit to sales} = \frac{\$ \text{ Gross profit}}{\$ \text{ Net sales}} \times 100 = \underline{?}\ \%$$

This ratio measures the percentage of each sales dollar left to pay operating expenses and contribute to profits after paying for cost of goods sold. An increasing gross profit to sales ratio trend may be the result of a reduction in cost of goods sold (better cost control in a manufacturing firm, more astute buying in a retailing firm, etc.) or the result of an increase in selling prices or both. The opposite is true of a declining trend in gross profit to sales. Because cost of goods sold is usually the major expense associated with obtaining sales revenue, financial managers pay close attention to changes in this ratio. For manufacturing concerns, percentages should be calculated for each component of the cost of goods sold.

The next area for study is the level of operating expenses:

$$\text{Operating expenses to sales} = \frac{\$ \text{ Operating expenses}}{\$ \text{ Net sales}} \times 100 = \underline{?}\ \%$$

or the residual after deducting operating expenses from gross profit

$$\text{Net operating income} = \frac{\$ \text{ Net operating income}}{\$ \text{ Net sales}} \times 100 = \underline{?}\ \%$$

The net operating income ratio indicates what percentage of each sales dollar is left after meeting operating expenses. For LMN Retail Co. Ltd., despite no change in the net operating profit in dollars from 1976 to 1977, the net operating profit percentage is down. Reviewing the operating expense ratios and cost of goods ratio, the factor creating the downward trend is the cost of goods sold. Despite the decrease in operating expense ratios between 1976 and 1977, the analyst may wish to investigate the substantial increase in selling expense ratios for the same period. A possible explanation may be that LMN management, after suffering a decline in sales in 1976, decided to expand sales volume through price cuts and increased promotion expenses. Other explanations are feasible. The analyst uses the ratios to decipher management's intent and measure their capabilities.

$$\begin{aligned}\text{Return on investment} &= \frac{\$ \text{ Net profit, usually after tax, before dividends}}{\$ \text{ Average year's equity}} \times 100 = \underline{?}\ \% \\ \text{(R.O.I.)}\end{aligned}$$

$$\text{Average year's equity} = \frac{\text{Year's beginning equity} + \text{Year's ending equity}}{2}$$

Because there are several ways to calculate R.O.I., care should be exercised in using this ratio. There are other methods of calculating these components that are equally good. The important thing is to be consistent and to label what method was used. If the average year's equity cannot be calculated, year end equity is used as the denominator as was done in 1975 for LMN.

R.O.I. is a way of measuring how much money was made from operations relative to the shareholders' investment. (A company's equity section includes the original investment of the shareholders plus the profits retained in the company.) For the LMN shareholders, R.O.I. has been declining from 14.3 per cent in 1975 to 8.8 per cent in 1977.

To assess R.O.I., look both at the trend (it is downward for LMN) and at alternative investment returns shareholders might make. For example, if a shareholder is comparing LMN to government bonds, he would have to assess the relative returns (it has been higher, on average, in LMN) with the relative risks (risk is much lower with government bonds). If the R.O.I. is the same or less for LMN stock versus government bonds over time, prudent shareholders will invest their money in the lower risk bonds.

Growth Ratios

Growth ratios are easy to calculate and can be done for any financial item. Usually, four growth rates are calculated before any more intensive growth analysis is made. Growth can be calculated over *any* period of time, one week or one decade. The Exhibit 5 ratios for LMN are for one-year periods. Growth is expressed as a percentage change from one point in time to another using the first point in time as a base.

$$\text{Sales growth} = \frac{\text{Year 2 sales} - \text{Year 1 sales}}{\text{Year 1 sales}} \times 100 = \underline{?}\ \%$$

$$\text{Profit growth} = \frac{\text{Year 2 profits} - \text{Year 1 profits}}{\text{Year 1 profits}} \times 100 = \underline{?}\ \%$$

Profit growth may be calculated before or after tax. In either case the approach used should be acknowledged.

$$\text{Asset growth} = \frac{\text{Year 2 total assets} - \text{Year 1 total assets}}{\text{Year 1 total assets}} \times 100 = \underline{?}\ \%$$

$$\text{Equity growth} = \frac{\text{Year 2 equity} - \text{Year 1 equity}}{\text{Year 1 equity}} \times 100 = \underline{?}\ \%$$

Liquidity Ratios

There are a number of ways to assess liquidity for a company. Liquidity is the capability of a company to meet its short-term obligations. Ratio analysis is used to indicate whether liquidity problems appear to exist and whether more complex analysis is warranted.

$$\text{Current ratio} = \frac{\text{Total current assets}}{\text{Total current liabilities}} = ?/1$$

The current ratio is a measure of a company's short-term liquidity. It reflects the relative balance between short-term assets and short-term debts. In the LMN example the 1975 current ratio is 2.2/1 (also expressed 2.2:1), which can be interpreted as $2.20 in current assets for every $1.00 in current liabilities. The rationale for using this ratio is that a company must meet its short-term obligations with short-term assets. So long as the company has more current assets than current liabilities, there is a margin of safety in case it becomes necessary to pay off some or all of the current liabilities. Every industry has found a different level of current ratio to be appropriate. There are no firm guidelines as to the "right" current ratio for a company.

The current ratio can be too high as well as too low. If too much money is kept in cash or inventory, for example, that money may not be being put to work as effectively as it could be.

$$\text{Acid test ratio} = \frac{\text{Cash} + \text{marketable securities} + \text{accounts receivable}}{\text{Current liabilities}} = ?/1$$

The acid test ratio (A.T.R.) is a tougher test of liquidity than the current ratio. Usually, the main difference between the two calculations is the amount of money invested in inventory. Because inventory is often the least liquid current asset (the most difficult to convert into cash in a hurry), its inclusion in a liquidity ratio may overstate a company's immediate liquidity. For example, a distillery with an inventory of one-year-old whiskey cannot readily convert its inventory into cash when the whiskey requires five years of aging before it can be sold. There is no firm standard of an appropriate A.T.R.

$$\text{Working capital} = \text{Current assets} - \text{Current liabilities} = \$ \ ?$$

The working capital expressed in dollars (not as a percentage) is another way to assess liquidity. The rationale is that after the enterprise has enough current assets available to cover its current liabilities, the money left over—working capital—is available to "work with." Again there are no standards, but most managers appear to think "more is better."

There are three common "interval" ratios: the age of receivables, inventory in day's cost of goods sold and the age of payables. The intent in each case is to relate the position of the asset with the undertaking of an operating activity. Accounts receivable are generated by credit sales. The control of the receivables in terms of collection is how many days' sales have been foregone by the enterprise in granting and supervising credit. Finished goods inventory (the only inventory of LMN Retail Co. Ltd.) is available for sale. Normally, management plans its inventory to meet sales expectations. The analyst does not have the management's expectation. Consequently, the most recent cost of goods sold is substituted for the sales estimate. Because inventories are valued at the lower of cost or market, cost of sales is used for the calculation, not sales as measured in selling prices (i.e., net sales). Accounts payable usually are generated from credit purchases. Consequently, the willingness or capability of the company to meet its supplier obligations is measured in terms of the day's purchases outstanding. In summary, interval ratios use the following matched pair components:

Numerator	*Denominator*
receivables	sales
inventory	cost of goods sold
payables	purchases

$$\text{Age of accounts receivable} = \frac{\$ \text{ Accounts receivable}}{\$ \text{ Average daily sales}} = ? \text{ days}$$

$$\$ \text{ Average daily sales} = \frac{\text{Total period sales}}{\text{Number of days in period}} = \$?/\text{day}$$

The average daily sales term in the denominator of the interval ratio is simply the total for the period, divided by the number of days in the period. For example, average daily sales for LMN Retail Co. Ltd. in 1975 would be calculated as follows:

$$\frac{\$875\ 000}{360} = \$2431/\text{day}$$

Of course, there are more than 360 days in a year, though most businesses do not have 360 operating days in a year. Therefore, the use of 360 in the denominator may appear questionable. It is used, however, because it is simpler to think of a year with twelve months of thirty days each. A different denominator—such as 365 days or 260 days (52 weeks × 5 days)—can be used instead, as long as the base chosen is noted and consistently used for all calculations.

Age of accounts receivable, expressed in days, shows the average number of day's sales that remain uncollected. In other words, on January 31, 1975 LMN had 32.9 average day's worth of sales for which money had not been received. In 1976 and 1977 sales and receivables changed for LMN. Management was able to reduce the amount of money invested in receivables, relative to sales level, from about thirty-three days to thirty-one days to twenty-seven days. An inspection of the balance sheet (Exhibit 2) may not have yielded the extent of this improvement in the receivables position.

Another way to think of the age of receivables is in terms of the length of time a company must wait, on average, after making a sale before collecting its money. If the LMN Retail Co. Ltd. had credit terms of "due in ten days," an age of receivables of thirty days indicates poor credit management. The opposite would be true if its terms were "due in sixty days." The longer the age of receivables, the more money it takes to operate the firm because the company's customers have use of the company's money between the time goods are delivered and the time they are paid for. On the other hand, credit terms and procedures that are too stringent may drive customers away.

Sometimes the "average" nature of the age of receivables ratio is misleading because some accounts may be very short-term and others long overdue. One approach to analyzing this problem is the preparation of an "aging schedule," which groups various accounts receivable according to the number of days they have been outstanding. For example, an aging schedule may look like this:

Age	% of Accounts Receivable
0-30 days	60%
31-60 days	30
over 60 days	10

$$\text{Inventory in day's cost of goods sold} = \frac{\$ \text{ Ending inventory}}{\$ \text{ Average daily cost of goods sold}} = \text{? days}$$

$$\$ \text{ Average daily cost of goods sold} = \frac{\text{Period cost of goods sold}}{\text{Number of days in period}} = \$ \text{?/day}$$

The inventory interval measure, expressed in days, indicates how fast merchandise moves through the business—from the date received to the date sold. For example, even though LMN substantially increased its investment in inventory between 1976 and 1977, the flow of inventory to sales improved.

A trend toward longer interval measures may indicate that the company is carrying excessive inventory for its sales level or that its inventory is becoming obsolete. Higher inventory levels represent larger amounts of money a company has tied up. Reducing inventory will not only release money which may be used more productively elsewhere, but usually it will also cut down on storage costs, obsolescence, etc. However, firms can lose business by not having inventory (known as "stock-outs") when the customer requests goods. Most companies try to balance the costs of running out of inventory and the costs of keeping large stock levels.

Another ratio for examining inventory is "inventory turnover." This ratio measures the number of times inventory turned over, that is, was sold. Inventory turnover is calculated by dividing cost of goods sold by the ending inventory:

$$\text{Inventory turnover} = \frac{\$ \text{ Cost of goods sold}}{\text{Ending inventory}} = \text{? times}$$

The results for LMN Retail Co. Ltd. by year are: 4.4 times in 1975, 3.9 times in 1976 and 4.2 times in 1977.

$$\text{Age of accounts payable} = \frac{\$ \text{ Accounts payable}}{\$ \text{ Average daily purchases}} = \underline{?} \text{ days}$$

$$\$ \text{ Average daily purchases} = \frac{\text{Total period purchases}}{\text{Number of days in period}} = \$ \underline{?}/\text{day}$$

Age of payables, expressed in days, shows how long the company takes to pay for what it buys on credit. Compared with industry figures and the terms of credit offered by the company's suppliers, this ratio indicates whether the company is depending too much on its trade credit. If the age of payables is excessive, creditors may demand repayment immediately, causing cash problems for the company, or may stop supplying the company until it pays for its previous purchases. Even though stretching the age of payables generates funds for a firm, a bad credit reputation can be developed which may cost the company dearly in the long term.

Good management of payables can save a company money. Many suppliers offer terms such as "1/10, net 30," which means a 1 per cent discount if the invoice is paid within ten days, and the total bill must be paid within thirty days. The savings possible by paying 1 per cent less within ten days work out to an annual interest rate of about 18 per cent. Because bank loan rates are usually less than 18 per cent, borrowing to take advantage of such discounts can increase profits.

If the age of payables is very low in comparison with industry practice, it may indicate the company is foregoing a potential source of cash.

Stability Ratios

$$\text{Net worth to total assets} = \frac{\$ \text{ Total net worth (i.e. Equity)}}{\$ \text{ Total assets}} \times 100 = \underline{?} \%$$

$$\text{Debt to total assets} = \frac{\$ \text{ Total liabilities}}{\$ \text{ Total assets}} \times 100 = \underline{?} \%$$

Net worth to total assets (%) + Debt to total assets (%) = 100%

The net worth to total assets ratio, expressed as a percentage, indicates the amount of assets which were financed by the owners. In general, the higher the ratio, the more interested prospective lenders will be in advancing funds. If the ratio is too low, there is danger of encouraging irresponsibility by the owners and of having inadequate protection for the company's creditors. There are no general rules for evaluating the size of this ratio: look for trends and seek comparative industry data to assess the appropriateness of the ratio. An unfavourable trend may forebode difficulty in raising additional money should it be required.

The debt to total assets ratio is another way of expressing the same thing. Because total liabilities plus equity equal total assets, the net worth and debt ratios equal 100 per cent. For example, in 1975 LMN's net worth to total assets ratios was 51.8 per cent; therefore, its debt ratio was 48.2 per cent.

$$\text{Long-term debt interest coverage} = \frac{\text{Period net profit before interest on long-term debt and taxes}}{\text{Period interest on long-term debt}} = \underline{?} \text{ times}$$

The long-term debt interest coverage calculation indicates how many times the company's profit could pay the interest on the debt it owes before tax profit is used, because income taxes are calculated after deducting interest expenses. Thus, the ability to pay interest expenses is not affected by income taxes. If a company cannot cover the interest payments from its profit, it will have to delve into its cash and other assets. Failure to meet debt obligations can cause bankruptcy. An unfavourable trend or comparison with the industry average may also give the company a poor credit rating, impairing its ability to obtain additional debt. This ratio can be altered to include any fixed charges or obligations the company may incur to make this ratio more inclusive and indicative of potential problems in meeting long-term obligations.

Other Ratios

There are many other ratios that are useful in certain circumstances. Here are three ratios investors often use to assess investment performance:

$$\text{Stock yield} = \frac{\text{Annual dividend per share}}{\text{Current market price per share}} \times 100$$

$$\text{Price earnings ratio} = \frac{\text{Current market price per common share}}{\text{Earnings per common share}}$$

$$\text{Earnings per common share} = \frac{\text{Net profit after tax less preferred dividends}}{\text{Number of issued common shares}}$$

PART 4: PROJECTED FINANCIAL STATEMENTS

Every financial statement reviewed so far reflects past performance or position but, in order to plan future operations, anticipation of future performance or position is required. Statements prepared in anticipation of the future are called projected or pro forma statements. There are three basic reasons for preparing projected statements:

1. To forecast financial performance or position (e.g., what will profit likely be next year?);
2. To examine the interrelationship of financial policies with changes in marketing and production policies (e.g., if sales double, how much more money will be required in inventory investment?); and
3. To forecast cash needs, debt needs, capacity to expand operations, etc. (e.g., how big will the bank loan have to be six months from now?).

The financial statements can be projected if enough information is available to prepare meaningful estimates of future performance and position. However, a projected statement is only as good as the estimates, assumptions and judgements that went into its preparation. Three basic types of information can be used to prepare projected statements:

1. Managers' estimates (e.g., a sales forecast);
2. Past financial relationships (e.g., financial ratios of previous years); and
3. Assumptions and guesses as to what might occur.

It is important to explain the source of every number on a projected statement, usually with footnotes which outline the basis of the calculations. For example, a footnote for an inventory estimate may be as follows:

> Inventory calculated on the basis of thirty-five days average daily cost of goods sold. The age of inventory during the previous five years ranged between thirty and forty days.

There are two basic types of projected statements. One is a projection based on the assumption management will continue to follow past financial policies. The objective of this approach is to show what would happen if this were so. Proponents of change in financial policy often use this technique to show impending disaster unless changes are made. The other type of projection is based on a suggested set of changes. The objective of this approach is to show the impact on likely future performance and position if these changes were followed. Often these two approaches are mixed in practice.

Need for a Balancing Figure

For both the projected balance sheet and the projected income statement, a balancing figure is needed. Seldom can each account on each statement be projected in such a way as to make the statement ''work out.'' For example, it is common when projecting a balance sheet to leave either ''cash'' or ''bank loan payable'' to the end and then insert a number that makes the balance sheet balance. For the income statement, the account often used to offset other estimates is purchases in the cost of goods sold section. No two projected statements are likely to be identical: individuals tend to use different assumptions about the future and, consequently, to have different balancing figures.

Projected Income Statement

Always begin a set of projected statements with the income statement, then the balance sheet and, finally, if desired, the statement of changes in financial position. Inventory, receivables and payables are based on the income statement. Also it is pointless to estimate the change in retained earnings on the balance sheet before attempting to project net profit on the income statement.

The following procedure should be used:

1. Estimating a new sales volume is the first and most important step. Use managers' estimates and/or past growth trends as guidelines.
2. Use the relationships among income statements accounts on past statements to estimate cost of goods sold, gross profit and operating expenses. Modify these for new information or for a developing trend.
3. The last period's ending inventory is the opening inventory in the projected costs of goods sold section. Usually, it is best to estimate ending inventory using the inventory interval measure. Then, using the fact that purchases equal cost of goods sold plus ending inventory minus beginning inventory, calculate purchases as a balancing figure.
4. The extent of detail in the operating expenses section depends on the quality of the information available and the objectives in preparing the projected income statement.
5. Sometimes it is appropriate to do more than one projected income statement. For example, if sales volume estimates vary significantly, statements based on a high, reasonable or low projected sales volume may prove useful.

Projected Balance Sheet

Preparing a projected balance sheet is usually more difficult than preparing a projected income statement. The main reason for this is that there is no one key account, similar to sales on the income statement, that helps determine many others on the balance sheet. Generally, each balance sheet account must be calculated separately. Here are a few guidelines:

1. Begin by deciding what the balancing account will be (usually cash or bank loan payable).

2. Fill in all the accounts that probably will remain the same (e.g. land will be the same if none will be bought or sold).
3. Fill in the accounts already calculated. For example, retained earnings will change in accordance with the estimated profit (from the projected income statement) and in accordance with any plans for dividend payments.
4. Estimate the other accounts. Usually, a good way to begin is by using averages or trends of previous years' ratios and then adjusting these as needed. For example, suppose the estimated next year's sales were $36 000 and, based on previous patterns, the age of accounts receivable was expected to be thirty days. All but one component of the formula used to calculate age of accounts receivable, the $ accounts receivable total, is known. Solve the formula to get an estimate of this missing number.

$$\text{Age of accounts receivable} = \frac{\text{Accounts Receivable}}{\dfrac{\text{Sales}}{360}}$$

Therefore,

$$30 \text{ days} = \frac{?}{\dfrac{\$36\ 000}{360}}$$

Therefore, estimated accounts receivable is $3 000 (30 × $100). Use this same approach for ending inventory and accounts payable.
5. After filling in all but the balancing figure, calculate it.

Interpretation of the balancing figure is sometimes tricky when the resulting figure is negative. For example, suppose cash was the balancing figure and the amount was ($30 000). This negative amount means the company will need an infusion of $30 000 from somewhere, just to have zero in the cash account. Usually a company requires some positive cash, so the "loan" required in this example may be $35 000 to $40 000. Suppose in another set of figures the bank loan payable was used as the balancing account and the amount turned out to be ($30 000). This is equivalent to saying the bank owes the company $30 000, which is similar to a bank deposit. In this example, the bank loan would be reduced to zero and cash increased by $30 000.

No projected statement is "right"—the analyst can, and often should, continue to try new possibilities to see "what would happen if. . . ."

Projected Statement of Changes in Financial Position

This statement is rarely prepared, but not because it is difficult. After preparing a projected income statement and balance sheet, most analysts do not find much cause to do a projected statement of changes in financial position statement. It is easy to construct one after one or more projected balance sheets have been completed. Follow the same procedures that are outlined for historical statements of changes in financial position.

PART 5: FORMS OF OWNERSHIP

There are three major legal forms of ownership: the sole proprietorship, the partnership and the limited company. It is important to note which form of ownership is involved because the different characteristics of each form will have implications for the operation of the firm. The following section explains the various forms of ownership, their advantages and disadvantages.

Sole Proprietorship

A sole proprietorship is a business owned and usually operated by a single individual. Its major characteristic is that the owner and the business are one and the same. In other words, the revenues, expenses, assets and liabilities of the sole proprietorship are also the revenues, expenses, assets and liabilities of the owner. A sole proprietorship is also referred to as the proprietorship, single proprietorship, individual proprietorship and individual enterprise.

A sole proprietorship is the oldest and most common form of ownership. Some examples include small retail stores, doctors' and lawyers' practices and restaurants.

Advantages

A sole proprietorship is the easiest form of business to organize. The only legal requirements for starting such a business are a municipal licence to operate a business and a registration licence to ensure that two firms do not use the same name. The organization costs for these licences are minimal.

A sole proprietorship can be dissolved as easily as it can be started. A sole proprietorship can terminate on the death of the owner, when a creditor files for bankruptcy or when the owner ceases doing business.

A sole proprietorship offers the owner freedom and flexibility of making decisions. Major policies can be changed according to the owner's wishes because the firm does not operate under a rigid charter. Because there are no others to consult, the owner has absolute control over the use of the company's resources.

Disadvantages

As mentioned earlier, the financial condition of the firm is the same as the financial condition of the owner. Because of this situation, the owner is legally liable for all debts of the company. If the assets of the firm cannot cover all the liabilities, the sole proprietor must pay these debts from his own pocket. Some proprietors try to protect themselves by having assets such as their house and automobiles put in their spouse's name.

A sole proprietorship often has difficulty in obtaining capital because lenders are leery of giving money to only one person who is pledged to repay. As a result, the sole proprietor often has to rely on friends, relatives and government agencies for funds or loan guarantees.

A proprietorship has a limited life, being terminated on the death, bankruptcy, insanity, imprisonment, retirement or whim of the owner.

A proprietorship may experience difficulties in attracting new employees because there are few opportunities for advancement, minimal fringe benefits and little employment security.

Partnerships

A partnership is an unincorporated enterprise owned by two or more individuals. A partnership agreement, oral or written, expresses the rights and obligations of each partner. For example, one partner may have the financial resources to start the business while the other partner may possess the management skills to operate the firm. There are three types of partnerships: general partnerships, limited partnerships and joint ventures. The most common form is the general partnership, often used by lawyers, doctors, dentists and chartered accountants.

Advantages

Partnerships, like sole proprietorships, are easy to start up. Registration details vary by province, but usually entail obtaining a licence and registering the company name. Partners' interests can be protected by formulation of an ''Agreement of Partnership.'' This agreement specifies all the details of the partnership.

Complementary management skills are a major advantage of partnerships. Consequently partnerships are a stronger entity and can attract new employees more easily than proprietorships.

The stronger entity also makes it easier for partnerships to raise additional capital. Lenders are often more willing to advance money to partnerships than to proprietorships because all of the partners are subject to unlimited financial liability.

Disadvantages

The major disadvantage of partnerships is that partners, like sole proprietors, are legally liable for all debts of the firm. In partnerships, the unlimited liability is both joint and personal. This means that the partners together are responsible for all the firm's liabilities. If one of the partners cannot meet his share of the debts, the other partner(s) must pay all debts.

Partners are also legally responsible for actions of other partners. Many partnerships include in their agreements stipulations as to what decisions—financial or otherwise—can be made without the consent of all partners. Even with this agreement, however, partners are still liable for actions under the firm's name. In these cases, a suit can be brought against a partner's actions that were not in accord with the agreement.

Partnerships are not as easy to dissolve as sole proprietorships. Partnerships terminate on the death of any one partner or when one of the partners breaks the partnership agreement or gives his notice to leave. It is often difficult for firms to find new partners to buy an interest. As a result, partners often take out term insurance on the lives of other partners to purchase the interest of a deceased partner and sale prices are pre-set.

Limited Companies

Limited companies, unlike proprietorships or partnerships, are created by law and are separate from the people who own and manage them. Limited companies are also referred to as corporations. In limited companies, ownership is represented by shares of stock. The owners, at an annual meeting, elect a board of directors which has the responsibility of appointing company officers and setting the enterprise's objectives.

Advantages

Limited companies are the least risky from an owner's point of view. Shareholders of corporations can only lose the amount of money they have invested in company stock. If an incorporated business goes bankrupt, owners do not have to meet the liabilities with their own personal holdings unless they, as individuals, have guaranteed the debts of the corporation.

Corporations can raise larger amounts of capital than proprietorships or partnerships through the addition of new investors or through better borrowing power.

Limited companies do not end with the death of owners. A limited company can terminate only by bankruptcy, expiry of its charter or by a majority vote of its shareholders. With this continued life and the greater growth possibilities, limited companies can attract more diversified managerial talent.

Disadvantages

It is more expensive and complicated to establish corporations than proprietorships or partnerships. A charter, which requires the services of a lawyer, must be obtained through provincial governments or the federal government. In addition to legal costs, a firm is charged incorporation fees for its charter by the authorizing government.

Limited companies are subject to federal and provincial income taxes. Dividends to shareholders are also taxed on an individual basis. Thus, limited companies are taxed twice: on the profits they earn and on the dividends which come out of the profits. In proprietorships and partnerships earnings are only taxed once—as the personal income of the individuals involved.

With diverse ownerships, corporations do not enjoy the secrecy that proprietorships and partnerships have. A company must send each shareholder an annual report detailing the financial condition of the firm.

PART 6: CREDIT

When customers can purchase goods or services without paying cash immediately, they are buying "on credit." Credit is a major factor in today's business environment for both the seller and the buyer. Consumers use credit cards; firms purchase from suppliers on credit; banks lend short-term money to help companies or individuals. Attractive credit terms can increase sales—by keeping present customers and attracting new ones.

Credit is riskier and more expensive than cash operations. The decision to offer credit means the credit-granting company must also be ready to accept the risk that some customers will not pay their debts. Credit management attempts to differentiate good risk customers from poor risk ones. Credit managers look at four characteristics to differentiate these firms. These are called the "four C's of Credit": business conditions, character, capacity to repay and collateral. The principles of credit analysis apply to bank loans, applications for charge accounts and numerous other instances where credit is involved.

Business Conditions

Current or pending legislation (which could drastically affect the operations of a firm), economic conditions (such as seasonal and cyclical sales patterns, growth and profit potential, etc.), social trends (such as changes in market and in customer buying behaviour) and technological changes (such as innovations) are important indicators of a firm's likely potential success within an industry. Credit officers and bankers look at a firm in the context of its industry to determine, "What does the firm have to do in order to operate successfully? Is this possible for this firm?"

Character

An important consideration is the character of the borrower. Past credit records are good indications of a firm's (or individual's) chances and inclinations of paying liabilities. The experience and financial expertise of the management are critical in sizing up the "character" of a corporation.

Capacity to Repay

Projected statements provide useful information about possible future financial performance and position. Such statements illustrate both need for money and possible time for repayment. The assumptions used in arriving at these statements should be scrutinized carefully in order to determine if (and when) the money will be repaid. Often, lenders will place restrictions on the borrower to ensure a higher likelihood of repayment.

Collateral

Lenders often seek protection in the event of a default (the credit loan is not repaid in full or in the time specified). This protection is usually in the form of collateral, which refers to assets pledged against the loan. For example, a company may offer its accounts receivable as collateral for a short-term loan or an individual may offer her car as collateral for a vacation loan. The amount of collateral sought and the willingness to accept certain assets as collateral varies according to lender and the loan situation.

The above are guides to intelligent credit analysis. Every credit situation requires judgement, not just mathematical computation.

PART 7: SOURCES AND TYPES OF FINANCING

There are several sources of financing. The costs, availability and conditions must be analyzed for each source in order to obtain the right "fit" for the firm. Financing sources can be categorized into three maturities: short-term, medium-term and long-term. The cost of financing varies directly with the investor's perception of the risk of financing.

Short-Term Financing

Enterprises can obtain short-term financing from trade creditors, chartered banks, finance companies, factor companies and the short-term money market. Short-term financing is usually for a period of less than one year.

Trade credit refers to purchasing goods or services from suppliers on credit. It appears on the balance sheet as accounts payable. The buyer is allowed a period of time, usually thirty or sixty days, in which to pay for the goods or services that have been received. To encourage prompt payments of credit sales, sellers often offer a discount from the invoiced amount if payment is made within ten days of billing. If the purchaser cannot pay the account within the given period, the creditor will often charge an interest penalty.

The Canadian chartered banks are another important source of short-term financing. Demand loans with a "line of credit" are the most common type of credit given by banks. A line of credit means the bank can arrange for an individual or a company to borrow up to an agreed sum over a certain period time. This helps companies with seasonal products who may experience cash shortages in the off-season. The borrower is charged a rate of interest for demand notes and a fractional percentage for a line of credit. However, a bank can demand repayment of these loans at any time.

Finance companies, such as HFC and AVCO, also lend money but usually charge higher rates of interest than chartered banks because of higher risks and higher costs of money.

Another method of short-term financing is "factoring." Instead of pledging accounts receivable for a bank loan, a borrowing company will sell the accounts receivable to a "factoring" company. Thus, except for paying the factoring company a fee, the firm does not have to concern itself with collecting the accounts or the risk of a bad debt. Customers' payments go to the factoring company rather than the seller.

Medium-Term Financing

Medium-term financing is for a period of over one year but not greater than ten years. Firms often require medium-term financing for growth, either for additional working capital or for new assets such as plant expansion, equipment or machinery. Medium-term financing in the form of term loans can be obtained from chartered banks, private sources or the Federal Business Development Bank.

The most common source of this financing is through the chartered or commercial banks. Banks usually permit loans of this nature to remain unpaid for reasonable periods of time provided the company has pledged the required collateral, the interest payments are made on time and the amount of the loan is reduced in an orderly fashion.

Finance companies, mortgage companies, insurance companies and trust companies are other sources for medium-term financing. Collateral, as with the banks, usually is required.

Medium-term financing also can be obtained through the Federal Business Development Bank, previously known as the Industrial Development Bank (I.D.B.). It lends money to companies with good chances of success but which cannot obtain financing from other sources.

Long-Term Financing

Long-term financing takes place over a period of ten years or longer. The major sources of long-term financing are from equity and long-term debt financing. Equity financing refers to the original money invested by common and preferred shareholders plus new issues of stock as well as all profits retained in the business. This money is seldom repaid. Individuals, investment companies and pension plans are the major purchasers of preferred and common stocks.

Long-term debt financing refers to bonds or debentures issued by the lender. Insurance companies, trust companies, mortgage loan companies and pension plans are the major purchasers of long-term debt issues. Fixed interest rates are levied and must be paid with repayments of principal at specified times.

Generally, long-term interest rates are higher than medium- and short-term rates, though market conditions will influence this relationship.

PART 8: SUMMARY

The financial analysis and management of an enterprise are complex tasks. This chapter has presented only an elementary framework. In order to be used successfully in the following exercises and cases, the framework requires more than just calculations; judgment is also needed.

The overall objective of the financial manager is to determine the expected return on investment and evaluate the risk incurred to earn the return. Projected results are required to determine the expected return. Quantitative analysis (statement of changes in financial position, ratio analysis and projections) plus evaluation of qualitative factors (character and business conditions) are employed to assess the risk.

Finance Exercises

Exercise I
ABC Wholesale Co.
(Statement of Changes in Financial Position)

Assignment

From the balance sheets of ABC Wholesale Co., prepare a Statement of Changes in Financial Position for:

(a) one year ending December 31, 1966
(b) one year ending December 31, 1967
(c) two years ending December 31, 1967

ABC Wholesale Co.
Balance Sheets
(in 000's of dollars)

	December 31 1965	December 31 1966	December 31 1967
ASSETS			
Cash	$ —	$ 1	$ 3
Accounts receivable, net	57	89	110
Inventory	97	141	180
total current assets	$154	$231	$293
Fixed assets, net	6	8	11
TOTAL ASSETS	$160	$239	$304
LIABILITIES			
Notes payable	$ 32	—	—
Accounts payable	57	$137	$173
Accrued expenses	—	3	7
Total Liabilities	$ 89	$140	$180
EQUITY			
Net worth	71	99[1]	124
TOTAL LIABILITIES AND EQUITY	$160	$239	$304

[1] The proprietor invested an additional $11 000. The $11 000, plus the $17 000 in net profit in 1966 retained in the business, account for the increase in the net worth account of $28 000 in 1966.

Exercise 2
ABC Wholesale Co.
(Calculation of Ratios)

Assignment

Listed below are the income statements of the ABC Wholesale Co. and a ratio sheet. Calculate the missing ratios and evaluate the company's performance.

ABC Wholesale Co.
Income Statement for Selected Years
Ending December 31
(in 000's of dollars)

	1965	1966	1967
Net sales	$724	$862	$1 151
Cost of goods sold:			
Beginning inventory	$111	$ 97	$ 141
Net purchases	606	841	1 064
Cost of goods available for sale	$717	$938	$1 205
Less: ending inventory	97	141	180
Total	620	797	1 025
Gross profit	$104	$ 65	126
Operating expenses	38	48	73
Net profit	$ 66	$ 17	$ 53
Drawings by owner	—	—	$ 28

ABC Wholesale Co.[1]
Ratio Sheet
for Selected Dates and Periods
(360-day year)

	1965	1966	1967
PROFITABILITY			
(a) Vertical analysis			
Sales	_____	100.0%	_____
Cost of goods sold	_____	_____	_____
Gross profit	14.4%	_____	_____
Operating expenses	_____	5.6%	_____
Net profit	_____	_____	4.6%
(b) Return on investment	173.7%	_____	47.5%
LIQUIDITY			
Current ratio	_____	_____	1.63
Acid test ratio	_____	0.64:1	_____
Working capital	$65 000	_____	_____
Age of receivables	_____	37.2 days	_____
Inventory in days cost of goods sold	56.3 days	_____	_____
Age of payables	_____	_____	58.5 days
STABILITY			
Net worth to total assets	_____	41.4%	_____

	1965-1966	1966-1967
GROWTH		
Sales	19.1%	_____
Net profit	_____	211.8%
Assets	49.4%	_____
Equity	_____	25.3%

[1] Note ABC Wholesale Co. is really Clarkson Co.

Exercise 3
DEF Co. Ltd.
(Projected Statements)

1. Sales projection	$250 000
2. Gross profit	20% of sales
3. Last year's ending inventory	$100 000
4. This year's age of ending inventory	90 days
5. Other operating expenses	8% of sales
6. Income tax	20% of profits
7. Accounts payable	30 days
8. Accounts receivable	20 days
9. Taxes payable	25% of year's taxes
10. Land—at cost	$10 000
11. Building and fixtures—at cost	$30 000
12. Accumulated depreciation—building and fixtures as of end of last year	$ 7 000
13. Depreciation expense for year	$ 2 000
14. Capital stock	$40 000
15. Retained earnings (last year)	$25 000
16. Salary expense	$14 000

Assignment

A. The above data has been supplied to you by the general manager of DEF Co. Ltd., a retailing firm.

    1. Prepare a projected income statement for the next year.
    2. Prepare a projected balance sheet for the next year.

B. The sales manager disagrees with the general manager's sales projection. He believes sales will be $400 000. Does this difference of opinion make much difference in DEF's projected financial performance and position next year?

1

Canadian Plastics Concentrates

On August 22, 1973, Mr. Hans Jonckheere and Mr. Doug Lamb were reviewing the notes from their recent meeting with Mr. Alan A. Thomson, proprietor of Canadian Plastics Concentrates. Mr. Jonckheere and Mr. Lamb, graduate business administration students at the University of Western Ontario, were working for the summer in a government-sponsored program providing consultant services to small businesses in southwestern Ontario.

Mr. Thomson had contacted the program to get some advice about how to finance the proposed expansion and continued growth of Canadian Plastics Concentrates, an enterprise he started a few years earlier.

During the course of the meeting, Mr. Thomson stated that in his opinion, Canadian Plastics Concentrates would need about $168 000 to finance an expansion of plant and equipment. He also stated that he was not aware of what procedures were required to raise the capital. In fact, he was not certain whether he would require additional working capital to sustain his forecasted level of operations.

COMPANY BACKGROUND

Canadian Plastics Concentrates was established in 1971 as a proprietorship, for the purposes of providing service to the plastics industry. The next year was spent obtaining and adjusting necessary equipment, establishing the present Tank Street location in Petrolia and making as many contacts as possible with potential customers.

Canadian Plastics Concentrates commenced actual operations in February 1973. Sales to August 15, 1973, had reached $84 000. Canadian Plastics Concentrates intended to incorporate provincially in January 1974.

COMPANY MANAGEMENT

Alan A. Thomson of Sarnia was the founder and sole proprietor of Canadian Plastics Concentrates. He had thirty-two years' experience in plastics and related fields, of which twenty-five years had been in a supervisory capacity. He had spent the last thirteen years with Du Pont of Canada, Plastics Division in supervision, maintenance and design engineering. He was in charge of major projects, taking them from feasibility studies to completion.

Mr. Thomson had also maintained active involvement in management seminars including such areas as problem solving, motivation, financial analysis, project control and work evaluation. In the near future, he intended to leave Du Pont so that he could be fully active with Canadian Plastics Concentrates.

David Thomson, Alan Thomson's son, had been active with Canadian Plastics Concentrates since 1971. He was involved in both factory supervision and sales but would be more restricted to the factory when the expansion program had been implemented. David's control of operations would be aided by the hiring of a receptionist-bookkeeper in the new location.

All persons have been disguised.

DESCRIPTION OF OPERATIONS

Canadian Plastics Concentrates offered two services in the plastics industry. In the first, manufacturers of synthetic plastic resins sent shipments of raw plastic pellets to Canadian Plastics Concentrates according to an agreed upon schedule. Canadian Plastics Concentrates then processed these pellets through an extruder incorporating additives for, among other purposes, colour, protection against ultraviolet attack, or reduction of effects of static electricity.

The finished product was then returned to the customer either in packaged form or in bulk. The only investment that Canadian Plastics Concentrates had in inventory was its own additives necessary for the compounding. The second service was purchasing left-over or odd supplies of pellets from regular suppliers, upgrading and reselling them in lots of varying sizes to other members of the plastics industry. In the last six months, Canadian Plastics Concentrates had found a viable market for this service and felt that it could be retained at a gross margin approaching 50 per cent.

CHOICE OF LOCATION

In keeping with the idea that a service industry should be located close to its suppliers or customers, most existing competitors were in the Toronto and Montreal areas. Canadian Plastics Concentrates had decided to locate in Petrolia, however, for the following reasons:

1. Petrolia was about twenty miles from Sarnia, which had Canada's largest existing and projected concentration of plastics manufacturing facilities. Many of these facilities required the services offered by Canadian Plastics Concentrates, but currently dealt with Toronto and Montreal operations despite the resulting transportation costs.

2. Proximity to Sarnia also meant that technical back-up from resin suppliers was readily available.

3. There existed an ample supply of semi-skilled, trainable, manual and casual labour at rates comparable to those in Toronto and Montreal.

4. The new location in Petrolia had good access by road and rail.

5. Because of tax concessions, Petrolia offered economical land and building costs.

COMPETITION

A number of competing companies existed in both Canada and the U.S. The American firms operated primarily out of Texas and were subject to a tariff. Canadian end users, dealing with these firms, were consequently looking for local suppliers.

As previously mentioned, most Canadian competitors were in Toronto and Montreal. While they still specialized in compounding, they were much larger than Canadian Plastics Concentrates with annual volumes of twenty million pounds or one to two million dollars. The plastics market had grown faster than these firms had, resulting in backlogs of ten to twelve weeks for small orders and three to four weeks on large orders. Because of their size and the market demand, these firms and their end users would welcome the arrival of a compounder the size of Canadian Plastics Concentrates so that the pressure of the numerous orders below 25 000 pounds would be alleviated.

Canadian Plastics Concentrates planned to offer favourable delivery, competitive pricing, personalized service and high quality. In addition, Canadian Plastics Concentrates was able to offer a number of unique processes whereas most of the competition was presently restricted to colour compounding.

The second phase of Canadian Plastics Concentrates' operations was buying and re-selling odd lots of resin. Since there was expected to be a world shortage of synthetic resin for the next three years, this material resale was considered a lucrative phase of Canadian Plastics Concentrates' business.

OPERATIONS

Mr. Thomson felt that company sales for the year ended 1973 would be in the order of 1 170 000 lbs based on the first six months of actual performance. Mr. Thomson stated that he wanted to expand the present operational base from solely polyethylene compounding to all polyolefins for a wide range of end users. A great deal of interest had been shown by end users and four firm quotation requests had been received. The expanded operations would require the purchase of additional classifying, packaging, storage and material handling equipment. Canadian Plastics Concentrates would also purchase land and construct a new building tailored to its needs.

Canadian Plastics Concentrates' operations in the new location were scheduled to start in January 1974. Sales for the first six months were expected to be 1 740 000 lbs and the second six months from July to December 1974 were estimated at 2 820 000 lbs. Canadian Plastics Concentrates expected sales in pounds to be twice the 1974 level at the end of 1975.

Exhibit 2 gives the breakdown of estimated sales by product type as well as data on the revenue and raw material costs for each product type.

REQUIRED INVESTMENT

Exhibit 1 gives the opening balance sheet for Canadian Plastics Concentrates along with related assumptions for 1974/75. On incorporating, Canadian Plastics Concentrates would take $20 300 worth of equipment from Mr. Alan Thomson in exchange for capital stock.

This equipment included two used extruders with related accessories which Mr. Thomson purchased from an American source. The extruders had been technically updated by Mr. Thomson and were expected to have a ten-year life with maintenance costs comparable to those of new equipment. Replacement value of these units was estimated at $392 000.

Exhibit 3 gives a listing of all fixed assets to be purchased or taken over from the proprietorship in order to realize the expansion plans. Mr. Thomson estimated that Canadian Plastics Concentrates could handle a yearly capacity of approximately 10 000 000 lbs before requiring additional capital equipment. By January 1974, Mr. Thomson estimated that Canadian Plastics Concentrates would require loans of $22 400 from himself and $168 000 from a commercial institution.

OPERATING COSTS

Mr. Thomson estimated that he could continue with two shifts for the remainder of 1973 and half of 1974 and meet projected sales levels. This would require a labour expense of $4200 per month. In order to meet estimated sales in late 1974 and 1975, Canadian Plastics Concentrates would add a third shift, which would increase the labour expense to $7000 per month.

Regarding fixed costs, Mr. Thomson thought that his depreciation expenses would be about $1950 per month and that this would include plant and office equipment. Management and office salaries were expected to be about $35 000 per year. Maintenance and supplies were estimated at $12 000 per year and general and administrative expenses at approximately $1050 per month.

Mr. Thomson also felt that all revenue and most expense items could be maintained on a three-day basis. Salaries and labour expenses would be paid in the month incurred. Accounts payable consisting of raw materials, materials for resale, and variable costs of power, water and packaging would be paid on a thirty-day basis, as would the general, administrative and maintenance expenses.

After listening to Mr. Thomson's explanation, both Mr. Jonckheere and Mr. Lamb realized that commercial sources would be able to provide funds for Canadian Plastics Concentrates at current rates of about 10.5 per cent. However, there would have to be a more formal presentation of the information regarding Canadian Plastics Concentrates' operations and proposed expansion to ensure a successful application for funds.

Exhibit 1
Canadian Plastics Concentrates Ltd.
Projected Balance Sheet[1]
as of January 1, 1974

ASSETS			LIABILITIES	
Current assets			Current liabilities	
Cash	$20 400		Accounts payable	—
Accounts receivable	—		Advance from shareholders	$22 400
Prepaid expenses	2 000			
			Total current liabilities	$22 400
Total current assets	$22 400			
			EQUITY:	
Fixed assets			Capital	
Equipment at cost	$20 300		Capital stock	$20 300
Less: accumulated depreciation	—		Retained earnings	—
			TOTAL LIABILITIES	
TOTAL ASSETS	$42 700		AND EQUITY	$42 700

Assumptions for 1974-1975
1. Sales were expected to be evenly distributed over the year.
2. Accounts receivable would be maintained on a current basis, reflecting one month's sales.
3. Interest was expected to be paid annually.
4. The income tax rate was expected to be about 35 per cent in 1974 and 50 per cent in 1975.
5. Prepaid expenses, consisting of organizational costs, would be expensed in the first year of operations.

[1] This Balance Sheet reflects the incorporating position of C.P.C. and is not a summary of operations prior to incorporation.

Exhibit 2
Canadian Plastics Concentrates Ltd.
Assumptions on Revenue and Cost by Product Type
(Sales Forecast in Pounds[1])

Product	First Six Months 1974	Second Six Months 1974	1975	Expected Revenue	Expected Costs
Type A: All Materials Supplied	1 500 000 lbs	2 500 000 lbs	8 000 000	$0.063/lb	No Materials Cost Variable Cost[2] $0.0175/lb
Type B: No Materials Supplied	120 000 lbs	120 000 lbs	240 000	$0.336/lb	Raw Materials Cost $0.15/lbs Variable Cost[2] $0.0175/lb
Type C: Purchased for Resale	120 000 lbs	200 000 lbs	320 000	$0.14/lb	Purchase Cost for Resale $0.07/lb

1 Plant Capacity @ 10 000 000 lbs/year
2 Variable cost of power, water and packaging for processing per pound
Note: Direct Labour Expense @ 2 shifts $4 200/month
                                @ 3 shifts $7 000/month

Exhibit 3
Canadian Plastics Concentrates Ltd.
Fixed Assets Required

	Total $	To Be Purchased $	To Be Exchanged For Capital Stock $
Land	2 100	2 100	
Building	68 250	68 250	
Machinery and Equipment:			
Product screener	2 100	2 100	
Hopper loader (2)	1 400	1 400	
Platform scale	3 500	3 500	
Air compressor	1 400	1 400	
Waste grinder	2 100	2 100	
Feed hoppers (4)	4 200	4 200	
Blender	7 000	7 000	
Dryer	4 200	4 200	
Silo (bulk shipping)	16 800	16 800	
Silo loader	7 000	7 000	
Laboratory equipment	4 900	4 900	
Bagger	3 500	3 500	
Upgrade extruder	14 000	14 000	
Large extruder	12 600		12 600
Small extruder	2 100		2 100
Fork lift truck	3 500		3 500
Pallet truck	700		700
Hopper loader	1 120		1 120
Drum mixer	280		280
Moving expense	1 050	1 050	
Installation expense	7 000	7 000	
Office equipment	3 500	3 500	
	174 300	154 000	20 300

2
Clarkson Lumber Co.

After a rapid growth in its business during recent years, the Clarkson Lumber Co. anticipated a further substantial increase in sales in the spring of 1968. Despite good profits, which were largely retained in the business, the company had experienced a shortage of cash and had found it necessary to borrow $48 000 from the Suburban National Bank. In the spring of 1968, additional borrowing seemed necessary if sales were to be increased and purchase discounts taken. Since $48 000 was the maximum amount that Suburban National would lend to any borrower, it was necessary for Mr. Paul Clarkson, proprietor of the Clarkson Lumber Co., to look elsewhere for additional credit.

Through a personal friend who was well acquainted with one of the officers of a large metropolitan bank, the Northrup National Bank, Mr. Clarkson obtained an introduction to the officer and presented a request for an additional bank loan of $80 000. Consequently, the credit department of the Northrup National Bank made its usual investigation of the company for the information of the loan officers of the Bank.

The Clarkson Lumber Co. was founded in 1958 as a partnership of Mr. Clarkson and his brother-in-law Mr. Henry Stark. Six years later Mr. Clarkson bought out Mr. Stark's interest and continued the business as sole proprietor.

The business was located in a suburb of a large midwestern city. Land and a siding were leased from a railroad. Two portable sheet metal storage buildings had been erected by the company. Operations were limited to the wholesale distribution of plywood, mouldings, and sash and door products to lumber dealers in the local area. Quantity discounts and credit terms of net thirty days and net sixty days on open account were usually offered to customers.

Sales volume had been built up largely on the basis of successful price competition made possible through careful control of operating expenses and quantity purchases of materials at substantial discounts. Almost all of the mouldings and sash and door products, which amounted to 40 per cent and 20 per cent of sales respectively, were used for repair work. About 55 per cent of total sales were made in the six months from March through August. No sales representatives were employed; orders were taken exclusively over the telephone. Annual sales of $313 646 in 1963 and $476 275 in 1964 gave net profits of $32 494 and $34 131 respectively. Comparative operating statements for the years 1965 through 1967 and for the three months ending March 31, 1968, are given in Exhibit 1.

Mr. Clarkson was an energetic man, thirty-nine years of age, who worked long hours on the job not only handling management matters but also performing a large amount of the clerical work. Help was afforded by an assistant who, in the words of the investigator of the Northrup National Bank, "has been doing and can do about everything that Mr. Clarkson does in the organization."

There were nine other employees, of whom seven worked in the yard and two drove trucks. Mr. Clarkson had adopted the practice of paying union dues and all social security taxes for his employees; in addition, bonuses were distributed to them at the end of each year. Mr. Clarkson was planning to incorporate the business in the near future and to sell stock to certain employees.

As part of its customary investigation of prospective borrowers, the Northrup National Bank sent enquiries concerning Mr. Clarkson to a number of firms which had business dealings with him. The manager of one of his large suppliers, the Barker Co., wrote in answer:

The conservative operation of his business appeals to us. He has not wasted his money in disproportionate plant investment. His operating expenses are as low as they could possibly be. He has personal control over every feature of his business and he possesses sound judgement and a willingness to work harder than anyone I have ever known. This, with a good personality, gives him an excellent turnover; and from my personal experience in watching him work, I know that he keeps close check on his own credits.

All of the other trade letters received by the bank bore out the statements quoted above.

In addition to the ownership of his lumber business, Mr. Clarkson held jointly with his wife an equity in their home, which was mortgaged for $12 000 and cost $25 000 to build in 1955. He also held a $16 000 life insurance policy, payable to Mrs. Clarkson. Mrs. Clarkson owned independently a half interest in a home worth about $20 000.

The bank gave particular attention to the debt position and current ratio of the business. It noted the ready market for the company's products at all times and the fact that sales prospects were particularly favourable. The bank's investigator reported, ". . . it is estimated volume may run from $1 280 000 to $1 600 000 in 1968." The rate of inventory turnover was high and losses on bad debts in past years had been small. Comparative balance sheets as of December 31, 1965 through 1967 are given in Exhibit 2. A detailed balance sheet drawn up for the bank as of March 31, 1968, is shown in Exhibit 2.

The bank learned through questioning another lumber company that the usual terms of purchase in the trade were 2 per cent ten days after arrival. Suppliers took sixty-day notes when requested but did this somewhat unwillingly.

Exhibit 1

Clarkson Lumber Co.

Income Statements for the Years Ending December 31, 1965
through 1967 and for the Three Months Ending March 31, 1968
(in 000's of dollars)

	1965	1966	1967	First Quarter 1968[1]
Sales	$ 740	$ 880	$1 179	$ 310
Less: sales discounts[2]	16	18	28	8
Net sales	$ 724	$ 862	$1 151	$ 302
Cost of goods sold:				
Beginning inventory	$ 111	$ 97	$ 141	$ 180
Purchases	$ 611	$ 846	$1 069	$ 336
Less: purchase discounts	5	5	5	1
Net purchases	$ 606	$ 841	$1 064	$ 335
Cost of goods available for sale	$ 717	$ 938	$1 205	$ 515
Less: ending inventory	97	141	180	244
Cost of goods sold	$ 620	$ 797	$1 025	$ 271
Gross profit	$ 104	$ 65	$ 126	$ 31
Less: operating expenses	38	48	73	20
Net profit[3]	$ 66	$ 17	$ 53	$ 11
Drawings by proprietor	—	—	28	6

[1] In the first quarter of 1967 net sales were $252 000 and net profit was $13 000.
[2] Quantity discounts
[3] This item is stated before any provision for federal income tax liabilities. As distinct from corporations, no federal income taxes are levied on the profits of proprietorships and partnerships as such. The owners of a proprietorship or partnership, however, must include in their personal income their proportionate share of such profits and must pay taxes on them at the regular personal income tax rates.

Exhibit 2
Clarkson Lumber Co.
Balance Sheets
(in 000's of dollars)

	December 31 1965	December 31 1966	December 31 1967	March 31 1968
ASSETS				
Cash	$ *	$ 1	$ 3	$ 1
Accounts receivable, net	57	89	110	129
Inventory	97	141	180	244
Total current assets	$ 154	$ 231	$ 293	$ 374
Fixed assets, net	6	8	11	10
Deferred charges	—	—	—	3
TOTAL ASSETS	$ 160	$ 239	$ 304	$ 387
LIABILITIES				
Notes payable—H. Stark	$ 32	—	—	—
—bank	—	—	—	$ 48
—trade	—	—	—	66
Accounts payable	57	137	173	138
Accrued expenses	—	3	7	6
TOTAL LIABILITIES	$ 89	$ 140	$ 180	$ 258
EQUITY				
Net worth	71	99₁	124	129
TOTAL LIABILITIES AND EQUITY	$ 160	$ 239	$ 304	$ 387

* Under $500
[1] Mr. Clarkson invested an additional $11 000. The $11 000 plus the $17 000 in net profit in 1966 retained in the business accounts for the increase in the net worth account of $28 000 in 1966.

3

Confederation Sporting Goods Ltd.

In early June 1977, Gail Edwards, assistant credit manager, was reviewing the credit application of Bowhill Sport Stores Ltd. The sales manager had just called her and asked for her decision on the request of Mr. Bowhill to ship $15 000 worth of merchandise to him, to be paid over an eighteen-month period, with all replacement orders to be treated as normal credit sales.

In 1977, Confederation Sporting Goods Ltd. was one of the major manufacturers and distributors of sports equipment in Canada. The company's line included hockey, baseball, football, soccer, basketball and other team sport equipment. The company, in addition to its manufacturing activities in Canada, contracted with foreign suppliers. At the last executive meeting the president, while pointing out the progress of the company, related that the out-of-pocket costs, or variable costs, associated with producing the company's line had steadily declined, and were now 70 per cent of sales. He expected that the new facilities and production techniques planned would further reduce the cash paid directly to generate a dollar of sale. In closing his address to the executives, the president stated that if the aggressive selling activities were maintained and the expected production efficiencies realized, Confederation would have its best year on record, achieving the objective of a net profit return on sales of 5 per cent.[1]

In April 1977, Scott Bowhill had called the sales manager, Ian MacKay, to inquire if Confederation would be willing to help finance a new undertaking. Ian MacKay, an acquaintance of Mr. Bowhill, replied that while he, of course, was interested in increasing Confederation's sales, any deal would be subject to review and approval by Confederation's credit department.

Gail Edwards was given the assignment of evaluating Mr. Bowhill's credit request. In preparation for the assessment, Gail Edwards obtained the latest credit report on Bowhill Sports Stores Ltd. The credit report outlined that the company had been in business for two years in West City (population under 500 000). The credit agency had been unable to get financial data on the company: Mr. Bowhill refused to comply with the credit agency's request for such information. The agency reported, however, that the company did have a bank loan. Payments in the initial year were reported by other suppliers as slow. The payment record in the second year of operation had worsened.

After receiving the credit agency's report on Bowhill Sports Stores, Gail Edwards discussed the prospective request with Ian MacKay. The sales manager related that he had known Mr. Bowhill for a number of years. Mr. Bowhill had been a very successful salesman with a competing sports goods manufacturer, Best Equipment Inc. In fact, several years before, Ian MacKay had tried unsuccessfully to hire Mr. Bowhill. Mr. Bowhill, prior to undertaking sales activities, had been in the public relations department of Best. Mr. Bowhill had been a professional football player, and in the off-season promoted the use of Best's equipment by participating in sports clinics. Unfortunately, early in his football career, Mr. Bowhill suffered an injury that terminated his participation in professional sports. With the sudden end of his professional sports career, Mr. Bowhill sought a sales position with Best Equipment. In a matter of a few years, Mr. Bowhill had become one of Best's leading salesmen. Given his success in selling and his desire to be independent, Mr. Bowhill decided to start a sporting retail/wholesale business in 1975.

At Ian MacKay's urging, Gail Edwards arranged a meeting with Mr. Bowhill during a trip that had been arranged for her through western Canada to review other accounts and

---

[1] The difference between 5 per cent profit and 30 per cent after direct out-of-pocket costs is expenditures that are made irrespective of sales levels achieved.

sales activities. On approaching the store, Gail Edwards noted that the taxicab driver had some difficulty in finding the location of Bowhill's store and that when they arrived, all of the four parking spaces in front of the store were full and the front window was covered with signs, "Sale, 50% off." As she arrived, Mr. Bowhill was there to greet her. He apologized for the fact that he could not meet her at the airport, but explained he was needed to help organize the forthcoming sale. Inside, the store seemed spacious and well organized. Several sales people were busy pricing goods or talking to the two customers in the store. Mr. Bowhill laughed as he noted Gail Edwards inspecting his premises. He stated that this was the start of his dream to own a chain of sports stores.

After entering his office, a small cubicle set at the back of the store, Mr. Bowhill discussed his business and the opportunity he now had. He related that he had started his store with the intention of becoming a price discount leader in West City. He stated that his previous experience had taught him that if a good product was delivered on time, at a good price, sales would grow easily. Consequently, he established a retail/wholesale sports business with a dual concept: a discount operation for the general public and a focus on team equipment orders for the amateur sports associations in the region, that is, a wholesale operation. Best Equipment had agreed to stock a substantial portion of his inventory with the understanding that within two years, his payables would be normal.

As Mr. Bowhill handed the company's financial statements to Gail Edwards, he said, "Now look at the results, not the expectations." Referring to the income statement, Exhibit 1, Mr. Bowhill pointed out that he had been successful in gaining a healthy sales volume; however, profits had not been what he had originally hoped for. In reviewing the two years of hard work, Mr. Bowhill related that he may have chosen the wrong location. He had chosen his current site because of the low rent. The current location provided spacious facilities (about 2000 square feet) and allowed him to keep his overhead at a minimum, but in so doing made direct contact between his business and prospective retail customers difficult. He said that in the last year, promotion expenses had been increased in an attempt to overcome the location disadvantage. However, the retail promotion had been only marginally successful. The wholesale business had been successful from opening day. Before he started his own business, Mr. Bowhill had called on the contacts he had made in the sports clinics. He discovered that with price cuts and delivery he was able to gain significant penetration in the West City and regional wholesale market. However, the competion had responded and he expected that significant wholesale sales increases, at profitable levels, would be impossible to achieve.

While Mr. Bowhill had accepted his profit situation, he was disturbed by the financial position of the company as presented in Exhibit 2. He related that the company's cash position was such that he could not meet his original commitment with Best Equipment. In fact, they had called the other day to say they were going to cut Bowhill off, unless he made immediate payment of 50 per cent of their bill. In order to do this, Mr. Bowhill was preparing a sale.

Mr. Bowhill then became more intense as he outlined his plans for turning the operation into a success. He had been approached by the owner of a shopping mall, due for completion in early July. The mall owner was interested in obtaining a sports shop to round out the mall shopping activities. The mall owner was a personal friend of Mr. Bowhill and was impressed by the volume of business Mr. Bowhill had generated in a short time. The mall had a 1000 square feet outlet available for rent. If Mr. Bowhill agreed to move his retail business to the mall, the mall owner would grant him a lease at $10 per square foot annually or 7 per cent of gross sales, whichever was greater. The mall store would feature both individual and team sports equipment and accessories. The mall was being constructed in the fastest growing segment of West City. The surrounding neighbourhood comprised single family residential, detached, semi-detached and attached units, plus high-rise apartments. The mall would be the major shopping centre for a section of the city with 20 000 people.

Mr. Bowhill viewed the sales opportunity as excellent. In fact he expected to generate a sales volume 20 per cent higher than the current rate at a substantially higher gross margin. The increase in retail sales and the addition of higher margin products to his sales mix would yield on average, he hoped, a gross margin of 45 per cent. Mr. Bowhill mentioned that he had been wrong before but he believed sales would be no lower than 80 per cent of his current level and a minimum gross margin of 35 per cent would be achieved.

Mr. Bowhill continued that if this venture proved successful, the mall owner was planning to open similar malls in other sections of the city and in western Canada.

Mr. Bowhill's problem was a lack of cash to stock the new store. He suspected that he would have little inventory or cash left, once the current sales campaign had eliminated the inventory at his current location. The expenses associated with the move were minimal. The rent was paid monthly since the conclusion of the lease agreement in March 1977. Many of the current store fixtures could be used in the new store, with only $4000 of new fixtures being required. The mall operator had agreed to finance the leasehold improvements required to convert the space to a sports shop. Financing the inventory would be difficult. All monies and assets that Mr. Bowhill had were pledged to liquidate his current business, to provide a minimal opening cash balance in July and to purchase the additional store fixtures. Mr. Bowhill related that he had contacted Best Equipment about a financial arrangement similar to the one two years previous. Best declined, and continued its efforts to collect past due accounts. Consequently, Mr. Bowhill contacted Confederation's sales manager, Ian MacKay, about financing the original stock and future replacements for the new store. Mr. Bowhill estimated that his initial requirements for a line of credit with Confederation would be $15 000. This would be equal to three months' sales. Mr. Bowhill would make a note payable to Confederation for the $15 000 and start payments at the rate of $1000 per month, three months after the store opened and goods were received. All other shipments after the initial sale would be on normal credit terms of net thirty days. While walking Gail Edwards to her cab, Mr. Bowhill thanked her for her interest in his business and said that he would call Ian MacKay at the end of the week to find out Confederation's decision.

Exhibit 1
Bowhill Sports Stores Ltd.
Income Statements for the Years
Ending March 31
(in 000's of dollars)

	1976	1977
Sales	$278	$305
Cost of goods sold:		
Beginning inventory	$—	$ 68
Purchases	253	210
Goods available for sale	$253	$278
Less: ending inventory	68	77
Cost of goods sold	185	201
Gross profit	$ 93	$104
Operating expenses:		
Salaries and wages	$ 45	49
Rent	9	9
Selling and administrative	29	36
Interest	3	2
Total	86	96
Net profit before tax	$ 7	$ 8
Estimated income tax	2	2
Net earnings	$ 5	$ 6

Exhibit 2
Bowhill Sports Stores Ltd.
Balance Sheets as of March 31
(in 000's of dollars)

	1976	1977
ASSETS		
Current assets		
Cash	$ 1	$ 3
Accounts receivable	16	16
Inventory	68	77
Total current assets	$ 85	$ 96
Fixed assets		
Store fixtures, net	18	16
TOTAL ASSETS	$103	$112
LIABILITIES		
Current liabilities		
Bank loan	$ 23	$ 18
Note payable—Best Equipment	25	25
Accounts payable	37	47
Taxes payable	2	—
Total current liabilities	$ 87	$ 90
Long-term note due—S. Bowhill[1]	10	10
TOTAL LIABILITIES	$ 97	$100
EQUITY		
Capital stock	$ 1	$ 1
Retained earnings	5	11
Total equity	6	12
TOTAL LIABILITIES AND EQUITY	$103	$112

[1] Subordinated to bank loan and note payable.

4

Fletcher Industrial Supply

In June 1973, Mr. Fletcher was working out the financial details of a tentative plan to build an extension onto his warehouse. He was concerned as to what source of funds he should use in order to raise the $10 000 required for construction costs.

THE COMPANY

Fletcher Industrial Supply was a distributor of machine tools, maintenance parts and related equipment in Barrie, Ontario. Fifty-five miles north of Toronto and situated on Lake Simcoe, Barrie was the largest and fastest growing industrial centre in the Georgian Bay region of Ontario. In 1972 the city had an estimated population of 34 500. In addition it served the surrounding farming communities and summer cottage trade. The customers of Fletcher Industrial Supply were mostly industrial maintenance departments, but there was also some high margin retail business, principally from farmers in the surrounding area.

Mr. Fletcher purchased the business from its previous owner in February 1970. By this time he had already gained wide experience in a series of jobs. He had worked for a variety of different companies, including one of his current Toronto-based competitors. During those years, however, a persistent ambition to operate his own business dominated him. His first personal venture was a retail hardware store in Peterborough, which he sold when he acquired the Barrie Industrial Supply distributorship.

Mr. Fletcher felt pleased with the progress his company had made in the three years since he had purchased it. He had enjoyed considerable success in building up sales. In June 1973, monthly sales volume averaged over $20 000. (Exhibit 1 gives income statements for the past three years.) Mr. Fletcher was also proud of the company's reputation for dependability and integrity. He believed his success was due largely to the personalized service and engineering advice he offered his customers. He also realized that an important factor in attracting new customers and building lasting customer relationships was his success in obtaining exclusive rights to handle the products of some of the better manufacturers. Maintaining good supplier relations with those manufacturers who granted him exclusives was a key element to future success.

COMPETITION

Until late 1972, Mr. Fletcher had been the only distributor of machine tools and parts who was situated in Barrie. Competition had come from salesmen operating from out-of-town warehouses. In the fall of 1972 another distributor started up an operation in Barrie. Mr. Fletcher believed, however, that the new competitor would not conflict directly with more than a small part of his business because of the exclusive distribution rights he held and his specialized products. This new distributor also did not as yet have the reputation for dependable service that Fletcher enjoyed.

THE FUTURE

Although market information was limited, Mr. Fletcher thought that he had about 35 per cent of the machine tool and equipment market in Barrie and the surrounding region.

All persons in this case have been disguised.

Given the existing market potential, he felt that he could not expect to increase his sales beyond $400 000 without expanding his geographical market area. For the next two years he projected probable sales to be $273 000 for the year ending January 31, 1974, and $322 000 to January 31, 1975. He felt sales could fall as low as $261 700 and $297 000 for fiscal 1974 and 1975 respectively, or go as high as $300 000 and $350 000.

THE PROBLEM

In June 1973, one of Mr. Fletcher's major concerns was the cramped space in his warehouse. With his present facilities he felt he could not handle any significant increases in inventory on hand. In order to maintain his high standard of service and delivery, he wanted to add a warehouse extension as soon as possible. At the same time one of his top priorities was to reduce the age of his accounts payable to sixty days before the end of the fiscal year. If he failed to do so he feared that he would put some of his exclusive distribution agreements in jeopardy. First, Mr. Fletcher wanted to determine the amount of money he needed to carry out his plans, and then to decide which source of funds to use. Several options were available. Mr. Fletcher's preference would be to borrow either from the bank or from a private lender. He did, however, have another alternative, namely selling some of his interest in the company to a friend. He could do this either by forming a partnership or by incorporating and selling shares. At the time of his decision, Mr. Fletcher was hesitant to use equity financing. He felt he would not get as much now for a share in the company as he could expect in a year when his hard work had paid off in increased profits. He was also wondering about the company's capability to generate its own funds.

Exhibit 1[1]
Fletcher Industrial Supply
Comparative Statement of Profit and Loss
for the Year Ended January 31

	1971		1972		1973	
Sales (net)		$93 011		$159 992		$206 682
Cost of sales						
Inventory, opening	$22 651		$ 30 898		$ 34 208	
Purchases	72 666		120 486		160 939	
	$95 317		$151 384		$195 147	
Inventory closing	30 898	64 419	34 208	117 176	47 463	147 684
Gross margin		$28 592		$ 42 816		$ 58 998
Expenses						
Wages and commissions	$10 987		$ 14 555		$ 19 176	
Rent[1]	1 943		2 220		1 110	
Interest expense	2 723		2 922		3 375	
Provision for doubtful						
accounts	671		—		—	
General selling expenses	2 910		2 756		2 386	
General administrative						
expenses	7 643		10 472		13 285	
Depreciation	—	26 877	1 030	33 955	2 436	41 768
Net profit		$ 1 715		$ 8 861		$ 17 230
Drawings		$ 7 375		$ 10 836		$ 11 441

[1] With the purchase of the land and building, rent expense had now been eliminated.

Exhibit 2
Fletcher Industrial Supply
Comparative Balance Sheets as of January 31

	1971	1972	1973
ASSETS			
Current assets			
Cash	$ 8 606	$ 1 751	$ 142
Accounts receivable, net	12 850	20 167	33 869
Inventory	30 898	34 208	47 463
Prepaid interest and rent	302	302	174
Total current assets	$52 656	$56 428	$81 648
Fixed assets			
Automobiles	$ 3 435	$ 3 435	$ 4 785
Land	—	—	6 088
Building	—	—	12 294
Equipment	—	—	399
	$ 3 435	$ 3 435	$23 566
Less: accumulated depreciation	—	1 030	3 466
Total fixed assets	$ 3 435	$ 2 405	$20 100
Other assets			
Goodwill	3 000	3 000	3 000
Deferred charges	657	385	275
TOTAL ASSETS	$59 748	$62 218	$105 023
LIABILITIES			
Current liabilities			
Accounts payable	$18 464	$29 074	$50 250
Employee deductions payable	165	237	268
Sales tax payable	445	948	1 937
Accrued interest and salaries payable	969	—	1 380
Total current liabilities	$20 043	$30 259	$53 835
Long-term liabilities			
Bank loan[1]	12 690	10 170	7 650
GMAC payable[2]	3 024	1 773	521
O'Connor payable[3]	19 651	17 651	17 651
Mortgage payable[4]	—	—	17 212
Total long-term liabilities	$35 365	$29 594	$43 034
TOTAL LIABILITIES	$55 408	$59 853	$96 869
CAPITAL[5]			
Personal capital	4 340	2 365	8 154
TOTAL LIABILITIES AND CAPITAL	$59 748	$62 218	$105 023

[1] $15 000 was borrowed in 1970. Principal repayments—$210/month, interest—$58/month.
[2] Balance owing on a truck bought in 1970. It was totally repaid in April 1973.
[3] Loan from previous owner of the business, secured by inventory, incurred in February 1970 as part of the purchase agreement. Principal repayments of $1000 due in January 1971 and 1972, with repayments of 2000 due every succeeding January. Interest of 8¾ per cent to be paid half-yearly on the balance of principal owing, in January and June.
[4] Mortgage loan made in August 1972 when Mr. Fletcher purchased the property and building. Five-year mortgage for $17 500 at 9 per cent. Combined interest and principal repayments of $176 were due each month.
[5] Fletcher originally contributed $10 000.

Exhibit 3
Fletcher Industrial Supply
Loan Interest and Principal Repayment Schedules

Principal: $210/month
Interest: $ 58/month

Bank loan
O'Connor—8-3/4%

Year Ending	Principal Owing	Principal Repayments	Interest
January 31/73	$17 651		
June 30/73	17 651		772
January 31/74[1]	13 651	4 000	772
June 30/74	13 651		597
January 31/75	11 651	2 000	597

Mortgage—9%   Combined principal and interest payments: $176/month

Year Ending	Principal Owing	Principal Paid	Interest Paid
January 31/73	$17 212		
January 31/74	16 596	$616	$1 496
January 31/75	15 924	672	1 440
January 31/76	15 190	734	1 378

[1] The $2000 principal repayment due on January 31/73 was not paid, and will have to be added to the January 31/74 payment.

5

Gold Coast Marine Supply Co.

Early in April 1959, Mr. Donald Copeland, president and owner of the Gold Coast Marine Supply Co., was told by his accountant that the firm's cash balance had fallen below $1000. The accountant went on to report that his projections for the coming sixty days indicated that the collection of accounts receivable would be insufficient to handle certain trade obligations on which both men considered speedy payment to be essential. These projections, in fact, showed that the company's planned level of purchases and sales to June 1 would result in substantially greater accounts payable on that date than at present.

Gold Coast had been criticized by trade suppliers for its failure to make payment within stated terms of sale on several occasions in the past few years. These complaints had increased sharply in recent months; two important suppliers suggested that they would have to put future shipments on a C.O.D. basis unless rapid improvement in payment was made. Trade relations with several of these suppliers included valuable franchises and distributorships; consequently, Mr. Copeland was anxious to avoid any breach in these connections.

After examining the accountant's forecasts with great care, Mr. Copeland concluded that the only solution to his problem lay in obtaining, as soon as possible, an increased loan from his bank of account, the Peninsular Deposit Co. Gold Coast was currently borrowing $10 000 from this bank on six-month, unsecured, renewable notes. He disliked large-scale borrowing as a matter of principle and had hoped to be able to avoid asking for an increase, but he was confident that the growing size of his business, together with his record of increasing profits, would prevail upon the bank to increase this loan to $100 000 for a few months until matters were "squared away." He thought that this amount would enable him to clean up his balance sheet and thus make it unnecessary to spend time worrying about day-to-day financial problems such as trade payments, payrolls, etc. He was also aware that the business was losing a growing amount of prompt payment discounts and thought that it would be advantageous to borrow funds for this purpose. Accordingly, he visited Mr. Ives, a vice-president of the Peninsular Deposit Co. and made his request.

Initially, Mr. Ives expressed some surprise at the size of the projected loan increase, but after skimming the company's financial statements (Exhibits 1 and 2), he remarked that he was clearly not up to date on the firm's status and had not realized the extent of the progress which Mr. Copeland had made in his sales volumes. Periodic renewal of the modest current note, he said, had been made in a routine fashion; before granting such a substantial increase as Mr. Copeland requested, he would have to study the entire situation thoroughly. He promised to inform Mr. Copeland of his decision within a week or ten days.

The Gold Coast Marine Supply Co. was located in Miami, Florida. Mr. Copeland established the business in 1952; he had lived in the Miami area all his life except when on active duty with the U.S. Navy during World War II and the Korean emergency. In his youth he won numerous important sailing prizes and, in following years, established a widespread regional reputation as a yachtsman. After his release from active duty in 1946, he took a position as partner in a yacht brokerage and insurance firm in Miami, but after being recalled to duty in 1950 and subsequently returned to civilian life in 1952 at the age of thirty-seven as a commander in the U.S. Naval Reserve, he had decided that his real desire was to own his own boating business. Accordingly, he sold his brokerage partnership and with the proceeds of $25 000 from this sale, together with $50 000 of savings and inheritance, established the Gold Coast Co. He found a satisfactory building and storage area which he secured on a favourable ten-year lease from an individual investor, and, largely through his reputation, obtained important wholesale distributorship franchises for marine products.

The business had been profitable in each year since its establishment; sales volume had continued to grow, and Mr. Copeland had, from time to time, added new product lines which had growth possibilities. The company's staff was small, consisting mainly of clerical help and semi-skilled warehouse labour. Mr. Copeland believed that this staff could handle substantial increases in sales volume within its present size. In 1959, Gold Coast sold, as wholesale distributor,[1] a variety of small sail and power boats (not over 25 ft in length) made of wood or fiberglass as well as outboard motors, water skis, skin-diving equipment, and marine hardware and accessories. His purchase of these items was generally on terms of 2 per cent ten days, net thirty-days. In the fall of 1958, he competed for and won a valuable franchise, on a one-year trial basis, for the distribution of a line of moulded plywood boats produced by a leading European manufacturer. Purchase terms for this producer were for net amounts on thirty-day drafts with bills of lading and insurance papers attached. Since shipment time from Europe sometimes exceeded thirty days, it was necessary on these occasions to make payment prior to receipt of the shipment. In April 1959, Gold Coast had completed an extensive publicity campaign relative to this new line; dealers were just beginning to place orders, and Mr. Copeland thought that in another six months the boats would "really be moving."

Gold Coast's geographical area of distribution varied with different product lines. Some of the franchises were only for the Miami area or for the state of Florida, though a number of them, particularly the line of fiberglass boats which accounted for almost 40 per cent of dollar sales in 1958, extended throughout the southeastern United States. Although there was some seasonal variation in sales within certain franchise areas and for certain products, these tended to balance one another with the result that, for the business as a whole, there was no appreciable monthly variation in sales.

The financial condition of Gold Coast's own customers was a major problem; most of them were small, one-man businesses that were usually undercapitalized. Although Gold Coast allowed a 5 per cent discount for ten-day payment, few of these customers paid within this period. Thus while Gold Coast was forced to carry many of these dealers for weeks or even months, the manufacturers of these lines insisted that dealers' orders be promptly filled by Gold Coast; there was heavy and growing competition in all marine supply product lines at all levels and there was a constant problem of losing dealers to another distributor of a competing product solely on the basis of credit extension and speed of shipment. On the other hand, distributorships from important manufacturers were much sought after, and therefore Gold Coast was not in a position, as were its customers, of dealing at will with whatever supplier provided most liberal credit accommodation.

In 1959, Mr. Copeland was in excellent health, worked ten to fourteen hours a day and derived enormous satisfaction from his business. He withdrew only a modest salary to support his family and to pay his taxes, preferring to reinvest as much as possible of the company's profits in the business. He had noted the mushrooming popularity of boating all over the country and was convinced that the trend would continue for several years. He was prepared in every way to participate in this growth. Current indications

---

[1] Approximately 10 per cent of sales were made at retail to individual boat owners.

were that Gold Coast's sales volume would reach about $1 600 000 for 1959 and that further increases of at least $250 000 per year could reasonably be expected.

On a few occasions Mr. Copeland made additional withdrawals from the business to provide funds for outside investments of unusual promise. He had purchased, in this way, a part interest in a new, "popular-price" motel, an option on a parcel of waterfront real estate, and some stock in one of his suppliers' companies. Though these investments were not directly related to his business, Mr. Copeland felt that he owed it to his family to diversify his estate as it grew in size; furthermore, he believed in 1959 that the value of these holdings had at least doubled over the total $43 000 initially invested.

Mr. Copeland's accountant and lawyer, as well as several business associates, suggested several times that Gold Coast should be incorporated and that stock should be sold. On each such occasion, Mr. Copeland had made it clear that while he recognized that such a course of action would potentially provide more permanent capital for the business and at the same time reduce his personal liability, the time was premature. He preferred to wait until the company's profitability had become firmly established so that stock could be sold on a "decent basis"; until such a time, he argued, he would be giving away part of the business which he had worked so hard to establish and which still contained so many potential elements of growth.

Mr. Ives, the banker, contacted several other marine dealers in the Miami area and found that Mr. Copeland was highly regarded by all. He was characterized by these sources as a "real competitor," "an imaginative salesman," and as "one who knows this business backwards and forwards—a man whose basic objective is and always will be growth."

Exhibit 2
Gold Coast Marine Supply Co.
Balance Sheets on December 31, 1956-1958, and on March 31, 1959

	1956	1957	1958	1959
ASSETS				
Cash	$ 13 018	$ 9 052	$ 4 288	$ 2 722
Accounts receivable, net	112 200	153 550	199 892	254 526
Inventories, at cost	127 361	150 028	219 283	242 404
Total current assets	$252 579	$312 630	$423 463	$499 652
Equipment and supplies, net	8 225	7 774	10 026	9 882
Deferred charges	3 113	4 666	6 800	6 521
TOTAL ASSETS	$263 917	$325 070	$440 289	$516 055
LIABILITIES AND CAPITAL				
Notes payable—bank	$ 5 000	$ 10 000	$ 10 000	$ 10 000
Trade accounts payable	57 605	91 088	182 220	248 062
Accrued expenses	906	2 644	7 914	11 987
Total current liabilities	$ 63 511	$103 732	$200 134	$270 049
Proprietorship account	200 406	221 338	240 155	246 006
TOTAL LIABILITIES AND CAPITAL	$263 917	$325 070	$440 289	$516 055

Exhibit 1
Gold Coast Marine Supply Co.
Operating Statements, Years Ended December 31, 1956-1958
and Three Months Ended March 31, 1959

(in 000's of dollars)

	1956	1957	1958	3 mo. 1959
Net sales	$772	$891	$1 220	$388
Cost of sales[1]	571	677	939	303
Gross profit	$201	$214	$ 281	$ 85
Operating, sales, and administrative expense[2]	116	143	195	62
Operating profit	$ 85	$ 71	$ 86	$ 23
Add: purchase discounts taken	6	7	8	2
	$ 91	$ 78	$ 94	$ 25
Deduct: sales discounts allowed	19	21	20	6
Net profit[3]	$ 72	$ 57	$ 74	$ 19
Owner's withdrawals	45	36	55	13

[1] Cost of sales was computed for each year above as follows:

	1956	1957	1958	3 Mo. 1959
Beginning inventory	$102	$127	$ 150	219
Add: purchases	596	700	1 008	326
	$698	$827	$1 158	$545
Deduct: ending inventory	127	150	219	242
Cost of sales	$571	$677	$ 939	$303

[2] Includes rental payments on lease which in each year calls for base payment of $25 000 plus 5 per cent of gross profit.

[3] No income taxes were assessed against the profits of nonincorporated businesses such as partnerships and proprietorships; these profits were considered the personal income of the owners and as such the owners paid personal income taxes on them. Under the provisions of the Internal Revenue Code of 1954 (Section 1361), however, certain nonincorporated businesses could elect to be taxed at rates applying to domestic corporations. Mr. Copeland's accountant had advised him that such corporate rates would be lower than personal income tax rates at anticipated profit levels, and this method of taxation had therefore been selected for 1955 and for following years. The applicable corporate tax rates were a tax of 30 per cent on all corporate net income plus a surtax of 22 per cent on all corporate net income in excess of $25 000.

6
Lakeshore Fabricators Co. Ltd.

On September 12, 1973, Mr. C. W. Middleton, manager of the Belleville, Ontario, branch of the National Bank of Canada, was reviewing his file on Lakeshore Fabricators Co. Ltd. Mr. Andrew Blake, president of Lakeshore, had just called to arrange a meeting to discuss an additional loan of $125 000 to finance working capital required by the most recent expansion proposal. Lakeshore's loan from the bank had grown rapidly over the past years and was now well beyond the authorization level of a branch bank. Following his analysis, Mr. Middleton was required to submit a report to the regional office in Toronto and copies would be forwarded to the commercial loan department of Head Office.

COMPANY BACKGROUND

In 1967, Mr. Blake, after spending nearly twenty years as an executive in the textile industry, formed his own company, Lakeshore Fabricators Co. Ltd. The company was primarily involved in the texturizing of synthetic fibres using the Taslan process, whereby different synthetic fibres were fed at varying speeds into an air jet. The air jet blended and stretched the fibres, resulting in a textured effect similar to wool yarn. Originally developed by Du Pont, the Taslan process created a demand for the textured fibres by weavers[1] and manufacturers for upholstery in the automotive and furniture industries.

Mr. Blake began operations in 1967 with ten employees and a few used machines of limited capacity. Financing for the operation came from some personal savings, a bank loan and advances from prospective customers. For the first two years, Mr. Blake struggled to establish Lakeshore. Suppliers assisted by extending their credit terms on the understanding that Lakeshore would make every attempt to return to the forty-five-day terms as soon as possible. Since then, the company had enjoyed considerable success, increasing sales by 30 per cent in each of the last two years (Exhibit 2). Sales projections for the near future indicated an acceleration in the rate of growth. Profits during this period had been adequate but had not grown at the same rate as sales. In the future, Mr. Blake expected profitability to improve significantly.

At the beginning of each fiscal year, Mr. Blake projected sales and capital requirements and arranged the necessary credit with the bank. However, sales growth continually had been greater than anticipated and the bank had agreed to increase Lakeshore's credit levels.

To cope with the rapid growth of Lakeshore, Mr. Blake hired Mr. Roy Tatum, an old friend, to supervise the production of the fibres. As the company grew, Mr. Tatum took on more responsibility within the company. At present, he held the title of Vice-President of Sales and shared a small, cluttered office with Mr. Blake.

The management style of the company was quite informal. Decisions regarding policy were often negotiated between Mr. Blake and Mr. Tatum as problems arose. Decisions regarding pricing, purchase and/or delivery of orders were sometimes made between the two men while the interested party waited on the telephone. Although both men carried full workloads in the sales, purchasing and administrative activities of the company, they were not above taking wrench in hand when production delays occurred due to machine breakdown.

---

[1] These organizations were generally large producers of varied types of woven materials who sold their products to other manufacturing concerns for use in their own production process.

RECENT COMPANY DEVELOPMENTS

In 1972, Mr. Blake began an expansion program designed to increase production of fibre by the Taslan process from 80 000 lbs per month to 150 000 lbs per month. This expansion would require significant capital outlay because the last quoted price on one 24-position machine was approximately $18 000 and, in addition, each machine required an air compressor. Compressors were valued at approximately $8000 each.

Mr. Blake had successfully offset a significant amount of the cost of the Taslan expansion by purchasing used machines in good condition. However, because the only manufacturer of the new machines had recently gone out of business, the actual rate of expansion of this line was restricted by the uncertainty of a continued supply of used equipment.

As well, Mr. Blake had added the "Knit de Knit" line to produce a yarn which was used in the manufacture of double knit garments. This line was successful but put additional strain on Lakeshore's capital position. Each new spinning head cost approximately $1500 and by the end of 1973 Mr. Blake expected to have forty heads in operation. Mr. Blake and Mr. Tatum had drastically reduced the capital cost of the line by engineering and modifying spinning machines to make them suitable for the "Knit de Knit" line. Even so, Mr. Blake had been forced to lease some air compressors because he could not raise sufficient funds internally or externally to purchase all the equipment he desired.

In addition to the capital equipment program, Lakeshore Fabricators had purchased the land and building from which the company operated early in 1972. Although the company leased only one-quarter of the building, Mr. Blake thought that the purchase of a site in an industrial mall close to the business section of the city would be a sound investment. He maintained that it would insure Lakeshore's ability to expand and industrial land would appreciate in value. The purchase, which cost $375 000 in total, had been financed largely by the Industrial Development Bank and Montreal Trust.

As a result of this expansion program, the capital structure of Lakeshore Fabricators was altered significantly (Exhibit 1). The company had borrowed $57 000 from the National Bank of Canada to purchase equipment and had negotiated a $100 000 line of credit for working capital requirements. At the end of 1973, $49 000 of the line of credit was outstanding. Lakeshore expected to repay the term loan at the rate of $1500 per month. The company also owed $110 000 to the I.D.B. and $250 000 to Montreal Trust, both of which were secured by mortgages on the building. The principal of the I.D.B. loan was repayable in ten installments of $12 000. Annual principal payments of $11 000 would be made to Montreal Trust.

THE EXPANSION PROPOSAL

Mr. Blake's most recent proposal called for an additional line of credit of $125 000 for working capital to allow Lakeshore Fabricators to produce and market false twist yarns from polyester fibres. The market for false twist polyester yarns was estimated by textile industry sources to be about 75 million pounds per year in Canada.

Mr. Blake had negotiated the purchase of the most advanced machines available from an English company. The British government would provide the financing for the $275 000 deal. The contract terms were 10 per cent down on the machines at the time of ordering, 10 per cent on arrival of the machines (expected to be January 1974) and the remainder to be paid over 36 months, with an annual rate of 8 per cent interest charged on the outstanding balance.

The new machines would run continuously and allow Lakeshore to produce about 1.5 million pounds of false twist yarn per year. Although the operation of the new machines did not require substantial supervision, Mr. Blake proposed to hire a plant manager who would take on all production responsibilities of the day-to-day polyester production. The new man would also supervise the 110 production workers currently employed by Lakeshore on the other product lines.

The major suppliers of polyester fibre were Du Pont and Celanese and these companies were also the main producers of false twist yarn. Mr. Blake had approached both of the potential polyester fibre suppliers to gauge their reaction to his entering the false twist yarn market as a competitor.

Du Pont had indicated that they would like to see Lakeshore become a licensee of Du Pont whereby Lakeshore would produce for and sell to them at a negotiated volume and margin. Celanese had indicated that they would supply Lakeshore with polyester fibre and Lakeshore could produce at whatever volume and price they could negotiate with users of false twist fibres.

Although the Du Pont offer was attractive in that there was a degree of guarantee against the cyclical nature of the industry, Mr. Blake had decided to take the Celanese offer because of its potential for higher profits.

Under the proposed expansion, the new line would come on stream early in 1974. Mr. Blake had already made contracts with certain accounts which would, if confirmed, take all the false twist fibres Lakeshore could produce. As part of the expansion, Lakeshore would take up one-quarter more of the building to house new equipment and offices. Arrangements were currently being made with the present tenants and Mr. Blake did not foresee any difficulty.

Mr. Blake expected total company sales to be about $3.125 million for the year ending April 30, 1974. There would be no appreciable increase in sales from the polyester false twist yarn until the next fiscal year. He felt that there would be no significant change in the overall profitability of Lakeshore in the year ending April 30, 1974. He foresaw sales of $6.25 million in 1975, with the polyester false twist yarn line accounting for about $2.5 million of total sales. Purchases were expected to be $1.82 million in 1974 and $3.38 million in 1975. It was anticipated that the addition of the false twist yarn line together with improved operating procedures in the Taslan and "Knit de Knit" lines would increase the overall gross profit margin to 25 per cent in 1975. Mr. Blake also expected that selling, general and administrative expenses would remain constant as a percentage of sales. Other income would decrease to about half the 1974 figure since Lakeshore would be taking up more of the premises in 1975 and consequently receiving less rental income.

Exhibit 1
Lakeshore Fabricators Co. Ltd.
Balance Sheet as of April 30
(in 000's of dollars)

	1970	1971	1972	1973
ASSETS				
Current assets				
Cash	$ 24	$ 17	$ 50	$ 16
Certificates of deposit	13	13	13	55
Accounts receivable	79	109	139	217
Returnable bobbins[1]	1	—	4	1
Inventory	150	154	227	220
Prepaids	4	3	12	8
Deposit on machines	—	—	—	28
Total current assets	$271	$296	$ 445	$ 545
Fixed assets				
Land	—	—	$ 63	$ 63
Building (net of depreciation)[2]	—	—	321	305
Machinery and equipment (net)[2]	116	109	149	157
Total fixed assets	$116	$109	$ 533	$ 525
Other assets				
Securities	$ 8	$ 8	$ 8	$ 5
Kingsway Textiles[3]	—	65	33	33
Swiss Yarns	—	—	—	—
Other	—	—	1	1
Total	8	73	42	39
TOTAL ASSETS	$395	$478	$1 020	$1 109

[1] Purchases of raw material yarn included the winding core or bobbin which was returnable to the supplier for credit.
[2] The building was depreciated at the rate of 5 per cent per year. The machinery and equipment were depreciated at an annual rate of 15 per cent.
[3] Kingsway Textiles was an operation similar to Lakeshore Fabricators, located in Durham, North Carolina. Kingsway was started by Mr. Blake and some American associates in 1969 and appeared to be stabilizing after a period of rapid growth. Sales were expected to be over $15 million at year end. Mr. Blake personally held an interest in this company. Additionally, Lakeshore Fabricators Co. Ltd, owned an interest in the American company. Together, Mr. Blake and Lakeshore held about 40 per cent of the outstanding shares of Kingsway Textiles.

Exhibit 1 (continued)
Lakeshore Fabricators Co. Ltd.
Balance Sheet as of April 30
Liabilities and Shareholders' Equity
(in 000's of dollars)

	($000's)			
	1970	1971	1972	1973
LIABILITIES				
Current Liabilities				
Working capital loan	$ 14	$ 33	$ 39	$ 49
Accounts payable	144	125	210	269
Royalty payable[4]	5	10	24	34
Accrued expenses	5	20	12	18
Miscellaneous liabilities	18	4	16	—
Total current liabilities	$186	$192	$ 301	$ 370
Long term Liabilities				
Bank term loan[5]	$ 13	$ 50	$ 49	$ 57
Mortgages payable				
I.D.B. 10½%	—	—	122	110
Montreal Trust 7%	—	—	262	251
Deferred taxes	9	7	11	10
Total long-term liabilities	22	57	444	428
TOTAL LIABILITIES	$208	$249	$ 745	$ 798
Shareholders' equity				
Capital stock	$ 23	$ 23	$ 23	$ 23
Retained earnings	164	206	252	288
Total shareholders' equity	187	229	275	311
TOTAL LIABILITIES AND SHAREHOLDERS' EQUITY	$395	$478	$1 020	$1 109

[4] The Taslan process was patented by Du Pont and texturizers were required to pay a royalty for use of the process. The royalty amounted to approximately 1 ½ cents per pound per month.
[5] This bank loan had been negotiated for purchase of equipment. A lien against all the machinery and equipment owned by Lakeshore provided security for the loan.

Exhibit 2
Lakeshore Fabricators Co. Ltd.
Profit and Loss Statement
for Years Ending April 30
(in 000's of dollars)

	1970	1971	1972	1973
Sales[1]	$881	$1 028	$1 359	$1 935
Cost of goods sold[2]	705	829	1 091	1 582
Gross profit	$176	$ 199	$ 268	$ 353
Selling expenses	$ 58	$ 77	$ 105	$ 165
General and administrative expenses	38	47	54	73
Total operating expenses	96	124	159	238
Operating profit	$ 80	$ 75	$ 109	$ 115
Less: other expenses[3]	14	20	65	105
Plus: other income[4]	12	8	17	38
Net income before taxes	$ 78	$ 63	$ 61	$ 48
Provision for income tax[5]	30	21	15	12
Net income	$ 48	$ 42	$ 46	$ 36

[1] Lakeshore was started in 1967. Sales and profits for the years 1967 through 1969 were as follows:

	($000's)		
	1967	1968	1969
Sales	$465	$806	$1 009
Profits (after tax)	$ 34	$ 48	$ 34

[2] Cost of goods manufactured included direct and indirect labour, depreciation and overhead as well as purchases plus freight-in. Purchases for the years 1970-73 inclusive were:

($000's)			
1970	1971	1972	1973
$539	$611	$853	$1128

[3] Other expenses included interest incurred to service investments made by Lakeshore. Other expenses for 1972 and 1973 included respective losses of $11 250 and $41 250 on a retail fabric outlet undertaken by the company. The venture had been terminated but would account for a further loss of approximately $27 500 in 1974.

[4] Other income included interest and investment income but consisted principally of rental income from the company property.

[5] The income tax rate was expected to be about 20 per cent on income up to $50 000 and 40 per cent on income above this level.

7

Pioneer School Furniture Co. Ltd.

Gerry Wig, manager of the downtown branch of the Dominion of Canada Bank in London, Ontario, had to make a decision regarding a loan proposal in time for a meeting Monday morning. It was now late Friday afternoon. Mr. Schmidt, president of Pioneer School Furniture and a long-standing customer of the bank, had visited Mr. Wig the previous week with a plan for an expansion of Pioneer's facilities. Mr. Schmidt needed money for working capital and for the construction of the plant addition. He had gone to a mortgage company, which had agreed to lend him the money needed for the plant addition. He was asking Mr. Wig to increase Pioneer's line of credit to cover his increasing need for working capital. Mr. Wig knew as he reviewed the Pioneer file that he would have to evaluate the proposal as objectively as possible especially in view of a recent memo received from the bank's head office (Exhibit 1).

COMPANY HISTORY

Mr. Schmidt was fifty-two years of age. He and his wife had immigrated to Canada in 1948 from Europe. For several months he worked in Montreal as a labourer, then moved to London in response to an advertisement for trained machinists. Since Mr. Schmidt had both excellent qualifications and experience he was given a position in the newly formed school and institutional furniture division of a large Canadian metal fabricating company.

The division grew rapidly, enjoying the benefits of the expansionary postwar economy. Mr. Schmidt advanced within the company on the basis of his own skill and determined nature. Eventually he was made plant superintendent of the division and his responsibilities included meeting production requirements, maintaining plant efficiency through a system of standards and supervising a staff of over one hundred men, most of whom were highly trained. Mr. Schmidt was expected to select, train and supervise foremen. As well, he participated in the industrial relations procedures in the plant. As plant superintendent he earned a reputation for his product knowledge, his ability to solve problems and the exacting standards he set for himself. These attributes resulted in Mr. Schmidt's increasing participation in the design of new products and the capital budgeting for the plant.

Late in 1966 Mr. Schmidt's company merged with another large company and he learned that the new management had decided to phase out the metal furniture division. But he wanted to remain in the school furniture industry and the company's decision prompted him to enter into business for himself.

In 1967, Mr. Schmidt began operating Pioneer School Furniture Co. Ltd. The company's financing was provided primarily by Mr. Schmidt's own savings and a bank loan secured by his personal assets. The first years were extremely difficult ones. Mr. Schmidt worked long hours with little help and with limited facilities. During this period he withdrew only $2000 to $3000 a year from the company for the support of his family. Gradually, however, the company began to grow, producing a quality product at a price which made Pioneer highly competitive. Mr. Schmidt maintained that high product quality and guaranteed service combined with a fair price would be a successful combination for the school furniture market.

Producing school furniture exclusively in the years 1967-1970 created certain problems for Pioneer. It was necessary to bid for contracts in January and February for delivery in September. Most school boards purchased significant quantities of furniture by tender only once a year. Consequently, this required skillful bidding as contracts missed due to noncompetitive bids could not be easily replaced. Nor could contract estimates be adjusted to offset rising costs. This tender system also necessitated the production of virtually all of the required furniture over the summer period for delivery in the fall. In addition, school boards and government agencies, who were Pioneer's principal clients, were traditionally slow in settling their accounts. In most instances these customers took from 60 to 120 days after delivery to complete payment.

In 1971, Mr. Schmidt purchased the A & B Co. Ltd. in order to partially offset the seasonal production problems of Pioneer. A & B was a small, specialized operation which produced a high quality line of metal office furniture. A drafting table which A & B had manufactured and marketed as a licensee was redesigned by Mr. Schmidt and became a very profitable product for Pioneer School Furniture.

In 1972, the company moved from its rented quarters in an old building to a more modern plant in an industrial area of the city. At that time, Mr. Schmidt's lawyer and accountant advised him that for estate and tax management purposes, Pioneer School Furniture should not purchase the new building. They advised Mr. Schmidt to form a second company called H. Schmidt Ltd. which would buy the plant and then rent it to Pioneer School Furniture. Acting on behalf of H. Schmidt Ltd., Mr. Schmidt convinced the Dominion Bank to loan it $137 000 to finance the building. The loan was secured by a mortgage on the property. Pioneer paid a monthly rental for the use of the facility. The rent had been established by an appraiser at fair market value.

INDUSTRY SITUATION

Until the 1950s and early 1960s most school furniture was made from wood. However, during the 1960s the sharp increase in the cost of wood and labour resulted in significant price increases. School boards, in an attempt to comply with budget constraints, began to buy furniture made from combinations of metal and plastic. The trend toward metal furniture provided an opportunity for new and existing metal fabricating companies to expand their sales by entering the school furniture market. In these early years competition was intense, but the market for metal furniture expanded sufficiently to allow most companies to earn adequate profits.

Towards the end of the 1960s, the education system faced continued pressure to reduce costs in view of levelling student enrollment. Pressure was felt among the suppliers to the education industry as competition for contracts increased. Some manufacturers of metal school furniture, particularly those with other related product lines or those which were divisions of large established companies, began to cut prices. Industry participants viewed this as a move to force small and inefficient operators out of the industry. The price-cutting policy intensified through 1970, 1971 and 1972. Pioneer School Furniture was able to compete in these years due to its low overhead, company reputation and contacts already developed by Mr. Schmidt through his years in the industry. In 1973, with the sharp increase in material costs and continued price competition, the outlook looked bleak for industry participants. From the dozen or more Ontario manufacturers who had been in the industry in 1966, only six major competitors remained. Midway through 1973, a year which promised to be difficult for Pioneer, three major manufacturers announced their withdrawal from the market. Each of these Ontario-based operations was a division of a large company and each cited inadequate returns as the major reason for quitting the school furniture industry.

EXPANSION PROPOSAL

Mr. Schmidt assessed this turn of events in 1973 as an opportunity for the makers of school furniture to pass increased raw material costs, previously absorbed by the manufacturers, on to the school boards. There was also the chance for enterprising companies to increase their market share significantly.

In order to compete during the recent lean years, Pioneer had been forced to restrict capital expansion. Lack of plant facilities now posed a severe impediment to any expansion plans. Even at present levels of production raw materials and finished goods were stacked in the aisles on the production floor. The blocked aisles restricted the workers' ability to perform their jobs, limited productive capacity and increased costs.

In early 1973, Mr. Schmidt purchased from Global Manufacturers the manufacturing rights to a new line of metal shelving for school and institutional use. This product's earnings potential, based upon market response to date, was limited by the lack of plant capacity. Mr. Schmidt wished to build a 7000 sq ft addition to the present plant, which would increase the plant area by approximately one-third and provide ample storage for Pioneer products and for raw material. Mr. Schmidt, acting on behalf of H. Schmidt Ltd., had asked the bank to give him additional funds to finance the addition to the plant. The bank had changed its lending policies and wished to withdraw from that area of financing so they suggested that H. Schmidt Ltd. approach a mortgage company for the money. Mr. Schmidt negotiated with a mortgage company, which agreed to provide the $103 000 needed to finance the plant extension. In addition, the mortgage company agreed to take over the existing mortgage currently held by the bank on the original plant. The mortgage company had agreed that the mortgage on the property including the plant and the addition would provide adequate security. The cost of the addition would be reflected in increased rent charged to Pioneer by H. Schimdt Ltd. This arrangement with the mortgage company pleased the bank since it relieved the bank of its mortgage commitment, which was consistent with its expressed desire to withdraw from that area of financing.

In presenting his request for the bank to extend Pioneer's $225 000 line of credit to handle the expected increase in working capital needs, Mr. Schmidt had indicated that effective immediately, prices on existing products would be raised on an average by 5 per cent. The price increase would reflect the higher cost of materials and labour. Most school board representatives to whom he had spoken did not object to price increases reflecting increased costs. These individuals had indicated that they were more concerned that quality and service remain the same. Mr. Schmidt felt that the price increase would do much to improve his profitability (Exhibits 2, 3, and 4).

Mr. Schmidt projected Pioneer's future total sales volume to increase by 20-25 per cent in 1974 in addition to the price increase and by a further 20 per cent in 1975 if the expansion could be financed. He also felt that working capital requirements would increase in direct proportion to sales increases but that expenses would remain constant as a percentage of the new dollar sales figure. Income taxes were expected to rise to a 40 per cent rate. With regard to capacity, Mr. Schmidt projected that current equipment would be adequate to handle the proposed increases in sales and that any further capital expansion could be put off until late in 1975.

Exhibit 1

MEMO: DOMINION BANK OF CANADA
FROM: VICE-PRES. COMMERCIAL SERVICES, AUG. 16, 1973.
TO: BRANCH MANAGERS

In view of the recent forecasts by our economists on the movement of interest rates, the shortage of raw materials, the tightening of the money supply and the general business outlook for the upcoming quarter, I would like to remind all managers that in periods of economic uncertainty our standards for quality and risk factor should be weighed even more heavily in investigating alternative commercial placements.

The growth of loans outstanding at the branch level should not exceed 2 per cent. Similarly, as loans are repaid every effort should be made to place available funds with the proposals offering the highest return and least risk.

Exhibit 2
Pioneer School Furniture Co. Ltd.
Income Statement
for the Years Ending September 30

	1970	1971	1972	1973
Sales[1]	$1 264 426	$1 083 965	$1 058 659	$1 564 389
Cost of goods sold[2]	969 185	863 659	844 256	1 278 314
Gross profit	$ 295 241	$ 220 306	$ 214 403	$ 286 075
Operating expenses				
Office salaries	$ 29 497	$ 30 900	$ 33 216	$ 50 054
Freight	33 690	30 450	28 652	43 924
Advertisement	4 770	7 047	9 141	10 465
Telephone	3 681	3 941	5 242	7 066
Car & truck	20 820	20 000	19 839	26 357
Office	2 562	2 936	2 139	4 246
Fees & dues	710	229	284	1 503
Legal	1 925	2 247	3 436	3 884
Interest	3 798	2 819	6 472	13 801
General	967	782	715	743
Sales commission	39 445	33 228	31 759	46 931
Depreciation	6 401	12 675	9 560	23 810
Management bonuses	99 325	25 208	—	—
Total expenses	247 591	172 462	150 455	232 784
Net operating profit	$ 47 650	$ 47 844	$ 63 948	
Less: extraordinary expenses[3]	—	—	16 320	—
Earnings before income tax	$ 47 650	$ 47 844	$ 47 628	$ 53 291
Provision for income tax	11 694	10 555	11 540	12 666
Earnings after tax	$ 35 956	$ 37 289	$ 36 088	$ 40 625

[1] Pioneer was incorporated in 1967. Sales and profits for the years 1967 through 1969 were as follows:

	1967	1968	1969
Sales	$320 022	$686 793	$856 429
Profit (after tax)	$ 2 052	$ 21 256	$ 28 851

[2] Cost of goods manufactured included raw materials, rent, direct labour, indirect labour, depreciation and plant overhead. Purchases of materials for the years 1970-73 respectively were

1970	1971	1972	1973
$730 056	$428 244	$764 747	$908 089

[3] In 1972, Pioneer experienced non-recurring expenses as part of its relocation to a new plant site.

Exhibit 3
Pioneer School Furniture Co. Ltd.
Balance Sheet
as of September 30

	1970	1971	1972	1973
ASSETS				
Current assets				
Cash	$ 1 549	$ 1 111	$ 275	$ 384
Accounts receivable	298 560	247 111	241 135	297 654
Inventory	62 500	108 827	114 262	211 920
Prepaid expenses	2 371	2 603	4 300	3 804
Total current assets	$364 980	$359 652	$359 972	$513 762
Fixed Assets				
Equipment	$ 52 202	$ 66 913	$118 801	$156 150
Vehicles	23 069	23 069	37 535	41 571
Tooling1	—	—	—	40 473
Subtotal	$ 75 271	$ 89 982	$156 336	$238 194
Less: accumulated depreciation	34 075	46 750	56 310	80 120
Total Fixed Assets	41 196	43 232	100 026	158 074
Other Assets				
Due from H. Schmidt Ltd.2	—	—	50 249	23 775
Patents	$ 274	$ 274	$ 274	$ 274
Goodwill	13 700	13 700	13 700	13 700
Incorporation expenses	274	274	274	274
TOTAL ASSETS	$420 424	$417 132	$524 495	$709 859

	1970	1971	1972	1973
LIABILITIES				
Current liabilities				
Bank loan	$ 52 060	$ 82 200	$116 450	$219 200
Accounts payable	116 809	74 229	145 302	169 510
Wages payable	125 882	58 088	42 869	35 241
Notes payable A & B Co.	—	—	—	2 364
Taxes payable	5 214	204	—	262
Total Current Liabilities	$299 965	$214 721	$304 621	$426 577
Long-term liabilities				
Lien notes payable3	—	9 459	23 577	17 406
Due to shareholder4	$ 18 502	41 882	23 227	16 940
Notes payable A & B Co.	—	11 824	2 364	—
Notes payable Global Co.	—	—	—	36 867
Deferred income tax	—	—	2 118	2 856
Total long-term liabilities	18 502	63 165	51 286	74 069
Total liabilities	$318 467	$277 886	$355 907	$500 646
SHAREHOLDERS' EQUITY				
Authorized				
2600, 6% non-voting redeemable preferred, par value $10.				
10 000 common no par value				
Issued				
Preferred5	$ 13 700	$ 13 700	—	—
Common	141	141	$ 141	$ 141
Retained earnings6	88 116	125 405	168 447	209 072
Total Equity	101 957	139 246	168 588	209 213
TOTAL LIABILITIES AND SHAREHOLDERS' EQUITY	$420 424	$417 132	$524 495	$709 859

[1] In previous years tooling had been expensed in the year purchased. Changes in the tax act required that tooling be capitalized and depreciated. Mr. Schmidt felt purchases of tooling would remain at the 1973 level for the next two years. Mr. Schmidt intended to depreciate all tooling at the rate of 30 per cent per year on a declining basis.
[2] Pioneer had lent H. Schmidt Ltd approximately $50 000 in 1971 to be used for improvements on the plant. The amount was to be repaid over two years.
[3] Purchases of tooling and equipment were financed through suppliers and finance companies using lien instruments. Mr. Schmidt felt that the lien notes payable would remain relatively constant over the next two years.
[4] For tax purposes this money was considered to be distributed to the shareholders (principally Mr. Schmidt). However, to accommodate Pioneer's working capital requirements, the account was set up as a liability.
[5] The preferred shares were retired for tax purposes in 1971.
[6] Retained earnings were readjusted for tax purposes in 1972.

Exhibit 4
Pioneer School Furniture Co. Ltd.
Sales Breakdown by Product Line in 1973

	SCHOOL FURNITURE	A&B PRODUCTS	GLOBAL SHELVING	CUSTOM WORK	TOTAL
Sales	$1 127 236	$177 844	$152 628	$106 681	$1 564 389
%	72.1	11.4	9.8	6.8	100.0
Material Cost					
%[1]	57.9	41.0	42.0	46.9	53.7
Labour Cost					
%[1]	10.5	17.9	21.6	15.8	14.6
Overhead Cost					
%[1]	11.8	21.7	30.7	18.9	13.4
Gross Profit	$ 223 192	$ 34 525	$ 8 721	$ 19 637	$ 286 075
%[1]	19.8	19.4	5.7	18.4	18.3

Note: detail may not add to totals because of rounding as a per cent of sales.

8
James W. Saxton Co.

The James W. Saxton Co., manufacturer of fine home furniture in Rocky Mount, North Carolina, distributed its products directly to department stores, independent home furnishing retailers, and a few small regional furniture chains. Early in April 1951, the credit manager of the Saxton Co., Mr. Frank Preston, received from his assistant, Mr. Richard Rossi, pertinent information on two accounts in Missouri—Bauman's Inc. of St. Louis, and Vardon's Emporium of Kansas City. Mr. Rossi believed changes in these companies warranted Mr. Preston's attention.

Bauman's retailed quality home furnishings from four locations, one in the downtown section of St. Louis and the others in nearby suburban areas. The company also manufactured custom upholstered furniture on special order. Since Bauman's handled a complete line of home furnishings, sales were fairly steady throughout the year and were approximately 75 per cent for cash and 25 per cent by thirty-day charge or twelve-month installment terms. Installment terms called for 25 per cent down and the balance in equal monthly payments over a twelve-month period.

The store had been established in 1915 as a partnership and was incorporated in 1946. In June 1950, two of the four original partners sold their shares in the company to the two remaining owners.

Bauman's had been a customer of the Saxton Co. since 1918 and had previously handled its affairs in a most satisfactory manner. Vardon's Emporium was a comparatively new customer of Saxton's, having been sold since 1946. A medium-sized department store in downtown Kansas City, it was well known for its extensive lines of home furnishings. Its account with Saxton's had been satisfactory through 1950.

Both accounts were sold on terms of 1/10, net thirty and, although not discounting, had been paying invoices promptly until December 1950. Mr. Preston had previously established a $10 000 limit on Bauman's and a $15 000 limit on Vardon's.

The Saxton Co. advertised its lines nationally and attempted to maintain intensive coverage of trading areas by distributing through stores strategically located within a particular marketing area. Beginning in 1949, activity in the furniture market had become sufficiently spotty that quality of product and service were not the only bases for competition among manufacturers for outlets. Credit terms and financing of dealers became equally important; thus, the Saxton Co., in Mr. Preston's words, was "backed into the position of supporting numerous customers in order to maintain adequate distribution for its products."

Because of this requirement for the extension of fairly liberal credit, Mr. Preston had since 1949 adhered strictly to a policy of obtaining current reports on the financial status of customers. These reports, obtained as annual balance sheets and profit and loss statements, for customers that were considered satisfactory risks, were supplied directly by the customers. Under certain circumstances, wherein Saxton's was working very closely with a particular customer who was trading actively on a small investment, Mr. Preston received quarterly and at times monthly statements in order "to keep on top" of the credit situation.

In early April 1951, Mr. Richard Rossi, assistant credit manager of the James W. Saxton Co., received the annual reports of Bauman's Inc. and Vardon's Emporium. After reviewing these statements and checking the accounts receivable ledger for both customers, Mr. Rossi felt that the accounts should be reviewed by Mr. Preston. Accordingly, he furnished Mr. Preston with the information found in Exhibits 1 through 5.

When receiving the accounts, Mr. Rossi kept in mind that 1950 had not been a particularly good year for retail furniture stores. It was generally known that stores such as Vardon's, carrying low-priced furniture lines, were the first to suffer the declines which had come in the late summer and early fall. This situation was followed by signs of a relaxing demand for furniture of higher quality and higher price toward the end of 1950. The drop in volume and the subsequent price cutting hit the profit margins of some retailers to such an extent that their losses in the latter part of the year equaled or more than offset profits gained in the earlier part of the year.

In the early months of 1951 the "softness" of the furniture business continued. Although there was no severe drop in the buying of furniture at the retail level, there was an indication that "scare" buying and purchasing in anticipation of potential shortages had been curtailed. Accordingly, retail stores reduced orders of new lines and reorders of established lines in February, March and April. Throughout the country, orders for shipment in April were down about 30 per cent from March; March had itself shown a drop of about 10 per cent from February. Thus, credit managers among furniture manufacturing concerns were placed in the unhappy position of trying to please sales managers who wanted to maintain volume while they were aware that the shipment of furniture to customers who had already overextended their financial positions was potentially dangerous in such a period.

Exhibit I
James W. Saxton Co.,
Bauman's Inc. Balance Sheets as of January 31, 1949-1951
(In 000's of dollars)

	1/31/49	1/31/50	1/31/51
Assets			
Cash	$ 14	$ 11	8
Accounts receivable, net	231	261	268
Inventory	304	303	304
Total current assets	$549	$575	$580
Land	59	59	59
Buildings, fixtures, and equipment	225	228	263
Less: reserve for depreciation	31	48	66
Net buildings, fixtures, and equipment	$194	$180	$197
Investment	11	11	11
Due from stockholders	—	36	48
Deferred charges	7	3	3
TOTAL ASSETS	$820	$864	$898
LIABILITIES			
Accounts payable	$144	$145	$154
Notes payable—employees	12	13	13
Estimated federal income tax	11	—	—
Current maturities on long-term debts	26	60	37
Miscellaneous accruals	36	34	11
Total current liabilities	$229	$252	$215
Notes payable—bank[1]	91	150	145
Mortage notes payable	376	375	438
Preferred stock—5% noncumulative	32	32	32
Common stock	60	60	60
Capital surplus	—	—	19
Earned surplus	32	5[2]	11[2]
TOTAL LIABILITIES AND EQUITY	$820	$865	$898

[1] Secured by pledged accounts receivable
[2] Deficit

Exhibit 2
James W. Saxton Co.
Income Statements of Bauman's Inc. for Years Ended January 31, 1949-1951
(in 000's of dollars)

	1/31/49	1/31/50	1/31/51
Sales	$1 945	$1 583	$1 502
Less: Returns and allowances	175	186	122
Net sales	$1 770	$1 397	$1 380
Cost of goods sold	1 077	854	859
Gross profit	$ 693	$ 543	$ 521
Less: Operating expenses	595	515	498
Operating profit	$ 98	$ 28	$ 23
Other income	67	11	14
Net after other income	$ 165	$ 39	$ 37
Other deductions	40	41	43
Net profit (loss) before tax	$ 125	$ (2)	$ (6)
Dividends paid	$ 35	$ 35	—

Exhibit 3
James W. Saxton Co.
Vardon's Emporium—Balance Sheets as of January 31, 1950-1951
(in 000's of dollars)

	1/31/50	1/31/51
ASSETS:		
Cash	$ 123	$ 79
Notes and accounts receivable[1]	917	884
Inventory	895	821
Tax carryback claim	—	74
Total current assets	$1 935	$1 858
Fixed assets, net	244	221
Leasehold improvements, net	598	577
Cash value life insurance[1]	47	46
Investments	9	9
Notes receivable—officers and employees[1]	18	23
Prepaid and deferred items	25	26
TOTAL ASSETS	$2 876	$2 760
LIABILITIES:		
Notes payable—Industrial Finance Corporation	$ 885	$ 717
Accounts payable	407	443
Miscellaneous accruals	98	113
Total current liabilities	$1 390	$1 273
Common stock	570	570
Surplus	916	917
TOTAL LIABILITIES AND EQUITY	$2 876	$2 760

[1] Pledged to secure thirty-day renewable notes to Industrial Finance Corporation.

Exhibit 4
James W. Saxton Co.
Vardon's Emporium—Income Statements for Years Ended January 31, 1950-1951
(in 000's of dollars)

	1/31/50	1/31/51
Gross sales	$5 210	$4 828
Less: Returns and allowances	478	369
Net sales	$4 732	$4 459
Cost of goods sold	2 975	3 064
Gross profit	$1 757	$1 395
Operating expenses	1 499	1 630
Operating profit	$ 258	$ 235[1]
Adjustments:		
Elimination—reserves for inventory losses	—	135
Reduction—bad debt reserve	—	18
Tax carryback	—	84
Federal income tax	108	—
Net before dividends	$ 150	$ 2
Dividends paid	100	1
Net to surplus	$ 50	$ 1

[1] Deficit

Exhibit 5
James W. Saxton Co.
Aging of Accounts Receivable Balances as of March 31, 1951

Due from	Prior	Dec.	Jan.	Feb.	Mar.	Totals
Bauman's Inc.		$5 803.14	$ 913.30	$3 524.37	$1 028.01	$11 268.82
Vardon's Emporium	$380.84[1] (October)	4 883.96	1 025.55	4 352.00	9 124.77	19 767.12

[1] Represents invoice on disputed shipment; customer claimed damaged merchandise.

9

The Village Variety Store

In the fall of 1973, John McGee received $40 000 as an inheritance from his father's estate. John, forty-two years old, had been a wholesale company sales representative for fourteen years. Now, with his home paid off he wished to satisfy a lifelong ambition to run his own business. With the help of his longtime friend Tony Marshman, John sought out many small retail business opportunities in southwestern Ontario. Early in 1973, Tony received a call from a London, Ontario realtor who advised him that the establishment of a variety store—The Village Variety Store—in Stratton, Ontario was for sale. Stratton was a community of approximately 12 000 people located some thirty miles northwest of London. The Village Variety Store was established in 1934 as a general store by David Goldback. In 1956, when Mr. Goldback died, his son Larry took over and changed it to a variety store. The store was located at the main intersection in Stratton.

John had a professional appraisal done of the business. In addition, he and Tony went over all the past business records of the firm and made personal appraisals of its value as a going concern. With these figures, John negotiated a sale price of $50 000 for the business including equipment and inventory. A cash settlement was arranged for March 1, 1974.

All the time John was looking for a good buying opportunity, Tony continually stated that he wished to work for him. "John, I think this store could turn into a small gold mine. Goldback has been resting on his reputation and hasn't taken nearly the advantage of that location or the type of products that will move there. With some reshuffling of shelf space and little work, sales could be increased by 50 per cent by the end of the year. I only wish I could help you with the money end." John realized that Tony had had difficulties making ends meet. With four children and a wife to support, Tony had not saved any money. In spite of this, John realized that without Tony's assistance and expertise he would not have considered buying the variety store alone.

Tony Marshman, age forty, was the son of a tailor and had worked in his father's store after finishing high school until he married at the age of twenty-two. Then, Tony moved to Toronto where he joined a major department store. He served with this store as a salesman, department manager, and assistant accountant. After twelve years, Tony found Toronto very expensive and moved to London, where he was assistant store manager in a grocery chain. After six years in the same position, Tony realized that the company had no plans for advancing him. Thus, when John McGee approached him for help, he was more than eager to become involved.

John discussed the purchase of the variety store with David Stone, his lawyer. Mr. Stone explained over the telephone that there were a number of possible ways to establish the new business. He followed his telephone conversation with the following letter:

All names and places have been disguised.

David M. Stone, LLB
Barrister and Solicitor
London, Ontario
February 22, 1974

Mr. John McGee
Box 188
Stratton, Ontario

Dear John:

This letter is a follow-up of our conversation on the telephone last week. As I mentioned at that time, there are three ways to establish ownership in the Village Variety Store. Most smaller stores are operated as proprietorships. Under this form of ownership, you would own the store and have entire control over its operation. From a legal standpoint, your only requirements are to obtain a vendor's permit and establish yourself with the retail sales tax people. The simplicity of establishing a proprietorship must be weighed against the risk. You are liable not only to the extent of your investment in the business but also your personal assets are liable if you cannot meet your debts from assets of the business. When you leave the business, it is legally dissolved. The profits from operations can either be retained by you or distributed to other employees. Any distribution does not constitute a partnership unless the parties agree to share both profits and losses.

If you choose to form a partnership, you and your partner(s) continue to have unlimited personal liability. The new tax act states that each activity of the partnership will be viewed as being carried on by the partnership as if it were a separate person resident in Canada. Income and capital gains amounts, as calculated for the partnership, are shared by the partners in the manner agreed on by them and each partner declares his share of each such item in his tax return. A legal partnership agreement is required to define the initial investment and the division of income. Any partnership is dissolved when any partner dies or any change is to be made in the partnership agreement.

Your third alternative would be to form a limited company. The most significant difference between the sole proprietorship and the partnership on the one hand and the corporation on the other is that in law the company is regarded as an entity, with an existence of its own quite separate from that of the people who own it. Property acquired by the corporation does not belong to the shareholders of the corporation, but to the corporation itself. The corporation may, subject to certain restrictions, contract with its owners as would a separate person. It may also sue or be sued—just like a person. However, unlike a person, it has indefinite life until terminated by bankruptcy or voluntary dissolution. Its whole character depends on the grant of life which it receives from the government and upon such legislation and law as may have developed in the jurisdiction where it is chartered.

To incorporate a company in Canada, an application must be made to the government department designated by the Provincial Legislature or the Canadian Parliament to have jurisdiction in such matters. The petition sets out the proposed name of the corporation (which must not conflict with an existing name), the purposes and objects which it is intended that the company shall pursue, the amount of capital to be authorized, the number of directors and the names of the provincial (temporary) directors. Assuming that the application is found to be in order, a charter will be issued in the form of "Letters Patent" (provincially—articles of incorporation). The company is deemed to exist from the date of its charter.

The word "corporation" most often takes the place of "company" in the company's name and under Dominion Company Law. In the law of some provinces the word "limited" must be added. Changes in a company's charter may be obtained by application to the authority granting the charter, which upon approval, will incorporate the changes by the grant of "Supplementary Letters Patent" (provincially—articles of amendment).

Through the right to vote at the annual meeting and special meetings, the shareholder exercises his right as an owner to control the destiny of the corporation. Here, he elects his representatives, the directors, who guide and control the business operations of the company through its officers. The matters upon which the stockholders must be consulted are found in the law of the jurisdiction of the incorporations (federal or provincial) and in the charter.

Under the usual methods of voting, each common shareholder has one vote for each voting share owned. Under this system, one or more shareholders controlling one share more than half of the total number of voting shares can carry every question and elect every director on the board. The result is rule by those holding a majority of the voting stock and not necessarily by the majority in number of shareholders.

Profits from the company accrue to the shareholder(s). Profits must be paid out in the form of dividends or retained to finance future growth. The allocation of the profits is the responsibility of the directors elected by the shareholders.

Total cost of incorporation for a business such as yours would be approximately $900, which includes all registration costs.

I trust this letter will help you in establishing your business.

Sincerely,

David Stone, LLB

John was concerned about the tax implications of his new operation. After a thorough examination of the past operations of The Village Variety Store, John and Tony determined that it could reasonably expect a profit of $32 000 before any wage payments. It would take two full-time people to operate the store since it was to be open fourteen hours a day, seven days a week. To better ascertain the financial implications of the business, John contacted the Toronto chartered accountant firm of Wiley and Company. Jim Wiley, the senior partner of the company, sent him the following letter explaining the relative tax considerations of each of the forms of ownership John was considering.

Wiley and Company
Chartered Accountants
April 10, 1974

Mr. John McGee
Box 188
Stratton, Ontario
Dear Mr. McGee:

In regard to your inquiry concerning the effect of current Canadian tax laws upon expected income of $32 000 before taxes or salaries, I will outline the tax considerations which apply to your new business.

Under a proprietorship or partnership, all earnings are treated as personal income and taxed accordingly. The proprietorship income is distributed at the discretion of the proprietor while the partnership income is divided by a prearranged formula established in the initial partnership agreement.

As a corporation, the earnings for 1973 would be taxed at the rate of 25 per cent on the first $50 000 and 49 per cent on amounts above $50 000. The 49 per cent rate on amounts over $50 000 decreases 1 per cent per year until reaching a rate of 46 per cent in 1976. Any dividends are distributed after corporate tax and are taxed as personal income. Dividends receive a preferred rate of tax due to dividend tax credits. All salaries of corporate officials are expenses before tax and are taxed as personal income only.

There is an additional consideration. Provincial governments also levy their own corporate income tax.[1] In Ontario this amount would be 12 per cent of taxable income. To make room for these taxes, the federal rates of corporation income tax indicated above are abated in all provinces by 10 per cent. This would make the total corporate tax payable on earnings of less then $50 000 in the amount of 27 per cent (25 + 12 − 10 per cent) of taxable income.

To determine taxable income for an individual taxpayer, the income from employment, business, property investments and capital gain must be determined. If the business is unincorporated, the net income of the enterprise will be taxable in the owner(s) hands as business income. If the business is incorporated, the employees/owners will probably receive wages (employment income) and dividends (property income). The business income of the corporation will be taxed in the hands of the corporation at the rates quoted above. A couple of points should be noted. You are allowed to deduct from employment earnings only 3 per cent of gross employment income, up to a maximum of $150, whereas with business and property income, all reasonable expenses incurred to earn business and property revenues may be deducted to determine net income. On your tax form, "total income" is the sum of the net incomes. To calculate "taxable income," Canada Pension Plan contributions (maximum $90 for employed taxpayers, $180 for self-employed), registered retirement savings plan contributions, and personal exemptions are deducted from "total income."

To calculate your federal tax, apply the applicable rate as outlined in Exhibit 1. Ontario provincial income taxes are 30.5 per cent of the federal tax.

The taxation of dividends is complex: first, the taxable amount of dividends is not the dividend received, but the dollar receipt plus one-third of the receipt. This additional one-third is called a tax credit and is partially used to reduce your federal tax liability. The fed-

---

[1] See Appendix A for provincial corporate income tax rates.

eral tax credit is 20 per cent of the taxable dividend amount. An example may aid your understanding: if your federal personal tax rate was 35 per cent and you received a dividend of $300 from a taxable Canadian corporation, the taxable amount of the dividend would be $400—$300 plus one-third of $300, $100 (the tax credit). Your gross federal tax liability would be $140, 35 per cent of $400. However, your *net* federal tax liability would be less because you would deduct $80, 20 per cent of the taxable dividend amount, $400, from the gross liability, leaving a net federal tax liability of $60 ($140 − $80). Your provincial tax then is calculated in the normal manner, as a per cent (.305 in Ontario) of the federal tax liability, or $18.30 (.305 × $60).

If I can be of any further assistance, please call.

Sincerely,

J. W. Wiley

For 1974, John found that he would have total personal exemptions of $3838 while Tony Marshman would have total exemptions of $4478. He was considering the following alternatives:

1. An individual proprietorship under which he would pay Tony Marshman a salary of $12 000 per year and the remainder would go to himself.
2. A partnership in which he and Tony Marshman would share all profits and losses on the basis of 60 per cent for himself and 40 per cent for Tony.
3. A corporation in which the common stock was owned by himself. The corporation would pay Tony Marshman a salary of $12 000 per year and himself a salary of $16 000 a year. The remainder would be retained in the business.
4. As (3) above, except that the remainder would be paid out in the form of dividends to himself.

Exhibit 1
The Variety Village Store
Personal Federal Income Tax Schedule

TAXABLE INCOME	TAX	
$533 OR LESS	12%	
In excess of:		
$ 533	$ 64 plus 18% on next	$ 533
$ 1 066	$ 160 plus 19% on next	$ 1 066
$ 2 132	$ 362 plus 20% on next	$ 1 066
$ 3 198	$ 576 plus 21% on next	$ 2 132
$ 5 330	$ 1 023 plus 23% on next	$ 2 132
$ 7 462	$ 1 514 plus 25% on next	$ 2 132
$ 9 594	$ 2 047 plus 27 % on next	$ 2 132
$11 726	$ 2 622 plus 31% on next	$ 3 198
$14 924	$ 3 614 plus 35% on next	$10 660
$25 584	$ 7 345 plus 39% on next	$15 990
$41 575	$13 581 plus 43% on next	$22 386
$63 960	$23 207 plus 47% on remainder	

Appendix A
Provincial Tax Rates

	PROVINCIAL PERSONAL INCOME TAX MULTIPLIER APPLIED TO FEDERAL TAX	PROVINCIAL CORPORATE INCOME TAXES (% OF TAXABLE INCOME)
	(%)	
Newfoundland	38.0[1]	13
Nova Scotia	38.5	10
Prince Edward Island	36.0	10
New Brunswick	41.5	10
Quebec	N.A.[2]	12
Ontario	30.5	12
Manitoba	42.5	13
Saskatchewan	40.0	12
Alberta	36.0	11
British Columbia	30.5	12

[1] Payable at 40 per cent rate after July 1, 1974, 36 per cent before July 1, 1974.
[2] Quebec collects its own tax on a different tax schedule.

SECTION IV
An Introduction to Management of Human Resources

To be effective, every manager must be able to accomplish tasks through the efforts of others. The ability to win the willing effort of others is not a widespread trait. Thus, many who are placed in managerial positions fail miserably even though they possess the technical skills required for the task. For example, many organizations have experienced the misfortune (after promoting their top salesman to the position of sales manager) of losing a good salesman and gaining an inept manager. Knowledge of the task is not sufficient for accomplishing that task when one is dependent upon the efforts of others.

People vary in their capacity to direct the efforts of others. Some managers possess a seemingly innate ability to gain the unflinching loyalty of their subordinates. Such managers' requests are fulfilled by subordinates with vigour and enthusiasm in an atmosphere of cooperation. Interpersonal difficulties that do arise are relatively short lived, and thus cause a minimum of disruption because the trust relationship created by the manager allows him to deal with such difficulties head-on. Other managers' efforts to get things done are met with hostility and resentment on the part of their subordinates. Indeed, the lack of cooperation is sometimes so extreme as to result in subordinates' deliberate sabotage of their superiors' efforts to accomplish the task.

A manager is the head of two organizations: an economic one and a social one. Unfortunately, most managers tend to concentrate their efforts on the economic organization and fail to see that an understanding of the social organization is essential to achievement of economic goals. What distinguishes good managers from bad ones more than anything else is their feeling for, and understanding of, human behaviour. Managers who possess an understanding of human behaviour are able to create an atmosphere of trust and respect, thus allowing them to deal effectively with the individual and interpersonal problems that occur in their organizations and, moreover, to motivate their subordinates to achieve higher levels of performance.

The purposes of this chapter are as follows:

1. To assist you in identifying human resources (HR) problems.
2. To assist you in understanding the nature, sources and extent of HR problems.
3. To assist you in formulating action alternatives, deciding among those alternatives and designing specific action plans to remedy HR problems.

HUMAN RESOURCES PROBLEMS AND PROBLEM-SOLVING APPROACHES: AN OVERVIEW

The list of HR problems managers have confronted is seemingly endless; here are a few of the common issues that continually arise:

- Recruiting and selecting competent employees
- Orienting (training, etc.) new employees
- Motivating the poor performer (and improving productivity in general)
- Deciding on appropriate compensation schemes
- Handling promotions, transfers and dismissals
- Dealing with complaining workers (and "conflicts" in general)
- Delegating responsibility
- Dealing with rule infractions, absenteeism, turnover, etc.

- Conducting performance appraisals
- Communicating effectively

The most difficult human resources management problems relate to change: initiating change, overcoming resistance to change or resisting change. In this regard, the tools and values of human resources management are applicable to management situations in general, not just to what some individuals term personnel management or human relations.

A combination of managerial experience and psychological research has taught us a number of valuable lessons which help us deal in general with HR problems:

1. Begin by identifying the problem clearly. What is the behavioural performance that is not as desired? How often has it happened? How severe a problem is it? Is it a symptom of more serious problems? Is the problem defined properly: not too narrowly and not too broadly? How much time have you got to remedy the problem?
2. Next, try to understand what caused the problem. What factors in the individual, the task, the organization and the environment outside the organization contributed to the undesirable performance outcomes? In short, operate on the assumption that "all behaviour is caused." Your job is not to describe the behaviour or the situation, but to *explain* it so that you can identify ways to alter the behaviour towards more desirable outcomes. In effect, you go through two steps:
   (a) What caused the observed behaviour?
   (b) What new "causes" will result in the desired behaviour?
3. There are generally three factors which the manager may be able to alter in order to obtain new behaviour: the nature of the task (job to be performed), the conditions of work (a very broad catch-all) and the people involved (e.g., replacement of personnel). As manager, you must decide (a) whether (and to what extent) any of these can be altered (those factors which cannot be changed become constraints to be considered) and (b) which of the possible changes gives the most "leverage" on the problem at a reasonable "cost" (money, time, impact on others, etc.). Some solutions may be short-term and some may be long-term. Does the solution you propose fit the real problem? For example, dismissing a complaining employee may be short-term if the task and work conditions are such to lead all replacements to complain as well.
4. All of the analytical tools do not work all of the time. You must be selective in the tools you use and flexible in your method of use. The analytical models (to be discussed later) tend to represent situations as black and white. In fact, HR problems are grey. Further, many of the models lead aspiring managers to think behaviour can be easily explained with a single "cause" or two. In fact, behaviour is nearly always the result of multiple causes, interacting with one another.
5. Action recommendations can be evaluated in much the same way managers assess financial, marketing or production proposals. We have found that a pictorial "decision tree" is often useful with HR problems. Suppose you have an employee that is a poor performer and a complainer too. Your options might be as follows:

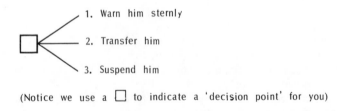

(Notice we use a ☐ to indicate a 'decision point' for you)

As a manager, as you weigh these options, you are concerned with what will happen *if* you follow any one of these courses of action. You can diagram that too as a set of ''consequences'':

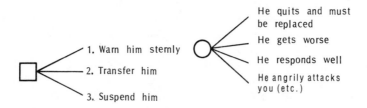

(Notice we use an ○ to indicate a consequence point —— after your action, these are the events you think could happen).

You have two tasks at this stage: first to decide what consequences are possible for *each* alternative you have and, second, to decide which consequences are most likely. The first task is based on your understanding of the individual involved. If you can figure out *why* he acted as he did in the past, you have a reasonable (not perfect) way to predict what he might do in the future given various sorts of stimulation. The second task involves pushing this a bit further. If you had to place bets on that employee's behaviour, what is he most likely to do?

You may do this for all of the alternatives you feel can reasonably be expected. Clearly, the trick is to confine this approach to a plausible set of options based on the value of your analysis of past behaviour. The better your analysis, the easier this ''decision tree'' approach becomes.

Such analysis is only useful if extended to the stage when the problem is resolved, the ''dust has settled.'' For example, it may involve a rather ''bushy'' tree:

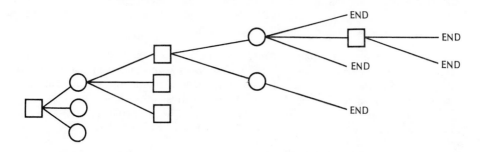

Here, after facing a set of consequences (reactions by individuals and groups involved), another set of decisions must be faced and so on. Diagram until you reach ''equilibrium'' or what we call ''end'' on our diagram.

6. Action recommendations must be specific in terms of what to do, who's to do it, when and how. Naturally, a complete job will include provisions for monitoring behavioural outcomes to see if they are as expected and as desired.

LEADERSHIP: FINDING AN APPROPRIATE MANAGEMENT STYLE

In this chapter, we will use the term leadership to refer to the way in which a manager chooses (explicitly or otherwise) to relate to his subordinates, that is, his management style. There are a number of ways to describe management style: we will look at two, the managerial grid and McGregor's Theory X and Theory Y.

The managerial grid, developed by Dr. Robert Blake and Dr. Jane Mouton, portrays five basic styles of management. Each style of management is a combination of varying degrees of concern for two managerial functions: concern for production (or task) and concern for people. For example, a management style characterized by lowest concern for production and highest concern for people was labelled as "country club management."

Blake and Mouton have developed elaborate profiles of the management style of each of the five management styles and have offered a detailed strategy for managers to learn how to reach the style of simultaneous highest concern for production and for people. While the model appears to suggest an "optimum" style, research for some time has shown clearly that there is no one best style of leadership for all occasions. In fact, the astute manager varies his style according to circumstances. The best style in any situation depends on (a) the task to be performed, (b) the characteristics of the leader, (c) the characteristics of the followers and (d) most probably on the other situational factors as well. The grid offers us a framework to classify and examine management style closely along two dimensions, thus helping us make judgements about the appropriateness of management style in particular circumstances. Notice that this assessment may be done from varying perspectives: a manager's, a subordinate's and an outsider's.

Another approach—based more on explanation of behaviour than classification of behaviour—was formulated by Douglas McGregor. After much observation and thought, McGregor concluded that the particular management style a manager adopts is determined by the kinds of assumptions he holds about human nature. McGregor did not "prove" his conclusions and some people dispute them; however, they provide us with a spectrum of possible assumptions managers may make which, in turn, will influence their choice of management style.

McGregor believed that traditional management approaches tend to frustrate the needs of mature people because the entire basis for such management is founded upon what he termed "improper assumptions." He said that the typical management approach is based upon the following assumptions regarding the adult personality:

1. The average human being has an inherent dislike for work and will avoid it if he can.
2. Because of the human characteristic of dislike for work, most people must be coerced, controlled, directed and threatened with punishment to get them to put forth adequate effort toward the achievement of organization objectives.
3. The average human being prefers to be directed, wishes to avoid responsibility, has relatively little ambition and wants security above all.

These assumptions, taken together, were termed "Theory X" by McGregor. He believed that managers who use them are grossly underestimating the interest and capacities of their subordinates. He postulated the opposing "Theory Y" which, he argued, states a more realistic assessment of the capabilities of people. It is based upon the following assumptions:

1. The expenditure of physical and mental effort in work is as natural as play or rest.
2. Man will exercise self-direction and self-control in the service of objectives to which he is committed.
3. Commitment to objectives is a function of the rewards associated with achievement.

4. The average human being learns, under proper conditions, not only to accept but also to seek responsibility.
5. The capacity to exercise a relatively high degree of imagination, ingenuity and creativity in the solution of organizational problems is widely, not narrowly, distributed in the population.
6. Under conditions of modern industrial life, the intellectual potentialities of the average human being are only partially utilized.

McGregor believed that the thinking represented by Theory X, because of its narrow and limited set of assumptions about human behaviour, is less capable of being used in a wide variety of situations or with varying types of employees. Adaptability he saw as one of the major differences in a management approach that results from the use of Theory Y versus Theory X assumptions. Management strategies evolving from Theory X assumptions tend to be *rigid,* implying that control be imposed from outside the individual, whereas those evolving from Theory Y require *flexibility* on the part of management. Theory Y implies that people are internally controlled and thus challenges management to deal with people as individuals with varying characteristics. McGregor emphasized this notion of flexibility versus rigidity:

> Assumptions like those of Theory Y open up a range of possibilities for new managerial policies and practices. . . . If, however, we accept the assumptions like those of Theory Y, we will be challenged to innovate, to discover new ways of organizing and directing human effort.[1]

Theory X and Theory Y have been widely misinterpreted. First, as McGregor emphasized, the theories embody assumptions about the nature of man; they do not provide a ''cookbook'' on how to manage. The theories are not managerial strategies; they are sets of assumptions. The management style (or leadership pattern) evolves on the basis of the assumptions selected. Secondly, McGregor *suggests* that people are capable of exercising creativity, self-control and integration of personal and organizational goals; he does not say they will. Employees, he said, will exercise self-direction and become involved in working toward organizational objectives *only to the degree that they are committed to those objectives*. Many things may get in the way of an individual's becoming so committed. One important variable is the need level at which he is motivated. A second consideration is the nature of the work itself. A third is the employee's perception of the manager's style, such as the nature of interpersonal relationships that the manager maintains in the organization. A fourth consideration is the degree and nature of the individual's own involvement in the management process. If, as a result of these or other factors, commitment is minimal, only a minimal amount of self-control will result and external control will be required. Theory Y, then, does not imply that external control need never be used. It does, however, suggest that in the presence of strong commitment conventional controls are unnecessary and possibly self-defeating.

McGregor wished to encourage managers to adopt a more flexible set of assumptions about human nature in order that they might release the true potential of their subordinates. Adoption of Theory Y assumptions does not imply the abdication of management, the absence of leadership, the lowering of standards or other characteristics usually associated with ''soft'' management approaches. Theory Y does not imply soft management any more than Theory X implies hard management. What it does imply is a *creative* approach to the management of human resources. By emphasizing the impact which managerial assumptions have upon managerial strategies, McGregor has made us more sensitive to the importance of choosing a management strategy congruent with the needs, aspirations and perceptions of the particular individuals involved.

---

[1] Douglas McGregor, *The Human Side of Enterprise* (New York: McGraw-Hill Book Company, 1960).

UNDERSTANDING INDIVIDUALS

The basic unit in an organization's human resources is the individual, so we'll begin with that unit of analysis. There are a few points we wish to make in this section:

1. We can "model" a behavioural situation based on some "assumptions." This will usually enable us to structure our analysis.
2. One of the useful concepts available is called "self-theory" based on personality theories.
3. A range of useful insights is provided under the heading of "motivation theory."
4. As we talk about an individual, you'll realize that we cannot analyze him effectively in a vacuum but rather we must think in terms of an individual in a particular situation in a particular organization.

In the previous section we discussed assumptions that managers may make about people. You probably have your own feelings about which assumptions are warranted and which are not in particular situations. We caution you to remember that the principal difficulties encountered in HR management stem from one simple source: taking things for granted, rather than trying to understand how people differ one from another on such dimensions as perceptions and aspirations.

A useful starting place in understanding individuals was offered by H. J. Leavitt in his text *Managerial Psychology,* 1958. He stated that behavioural analysis may begin with three basic assumptions:

1. All behaviour is caused (by conditions or situations outside the individual).
2. All behaviour is motivated (by forces which are internal to the individual).
3. All behaviour is goal-directed (towards that which will neutralize the prior cause and motivation).

These assumptions are illustrated in this model:

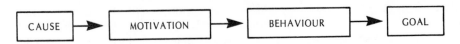

Behaviour, as represented in this model, is the overt, or observable, response to an external stimulus (cause) and to internal needs (motivation). Behaviour may consist of activities, expressed feelings, expressed expectations and/or expressed perceptions. Because behaviour is observable, there is a temptation to make judgements about people on this basis alone. The model forces us to consider the cause(s), underlying motivation and goals(s) sought. By so doing, we should be able to make better judgments about individual behaviour and, where necessary, take more appropriate action to deal with it.

All Behaviour Is Caused

The individual operates in an environment which gives him certain beliefs, values, customs, factual information, etc., which, in turn, causes or stimulates him to behave in certain ways. Moreover, these external forces are always coloured by the individual's perception of them. Thus, in looking at causes for behaviour, we must be careful to consider stimuli in terms of how the individual perceived them if we are to deal intelligently with the behaviour that resulted.

An individual's perception, or the way in which he sees things, is part and parcel of that which we term "personality." Dale S. Beach defined personality as follows:

> Personality is the sum total of the physical, mental, emotional and social characteristics
> of a person. It is the integrating process by which all of the physiological and psychologi-
> cal components of man are combined into the whole.[2]

There are a number of different approaches to an understanding of a personality. An approach known as "self-theory" lends itself readily to discussion and analysis of problems
related to individual and organization behaviour. Theorists associated with this approach
equate personality with the "self" or "self-concept." They see the *self-concept* as being
composed of two distinct parts: the "I" and the "me." The "I" is the personal view an
individual takes of himself; that is, the person he believes he is and strives to be. The
"me," on the other hand, is the way a person believes he appears to others.

This view a person takes of himself and the role he believes he must play in the external environment is a function of a vast number of variables. Many behaviourists consider
the strongest influence to be one's home during the formative years. Therein, the standards set by parents, reasons for and methods of discipline and interaction with siblings all
come into play. As the child moves outside the home, other authority figures such as
friends, school teachers, clergymen and so on become instrumental in shaping his self-
concept. Beach suggests that gradually the child "gains a view of his personal worth on
the basis of the way others respond to him and on the basis of his achievements" and that
"as maturation takes place, the individual acquires rather definite beliefs about what his
behaviour, values and goals ought to be."[3]

McGregor maintained that the dependence relationship of subordinate-superior (that
is, the dependence of the subordinate on the superior for satisfaction of his needs for continuity of employment, compensation, promotion, etc.) is an absolutely critical aspect of
industrial human relations. Since subordinates "will struggle to protect themselves
against real or imagined threats to the satisfaction of their needs in the work place," according to McGregor, and since the way in which that dependence relationship is perceived and handled determines the nature and extent of perceived threat, it is important to
understand how parties to the relationship view themselves and one another on the dimension of dependence. According to McGregor:

> The adult subordinate's dependence upon his superiors actually reawakens certain emo-
> tions and attitudes which were part of his relationship with his parents and which ap-
> parently have long since been outgrown. The adult is usually unaware of the similarity
> because most of this complex of childhood emotions has been repressed.[4]

Deeply ingrained views about oneself (the self-concept) are difficult to change,
sometimes impossible. Even discovering what another person's self-concept is can be a
difficult task. Most people have not thought about it much and those that have probably
won't tell you, fearing that you will use the information against them. So, you have to
speculate based on whatever information you have. Here is an incomplete list of some of
the adjectives you might find useful in describing someone's self-concept.[5]

---

[2] Dale S. Beach, *Personnel, The Management of People At Work,* second edition, (New York: Macmillan company, 1970) p. 443.

[3] Dale S. Beach, *Personnel, The Management of People at Work,* second edition, (New York: Macmillan Company, 1970) p. 443.

[4] Douglas McGregor, "Getting Effective Leadership in the Industrial Organization," *Journal of Consulting
Psychology,* 1944, 8(2).

[5] Adapted from Milton Rokeach value study, 1967.

ambitious	independent
broad-minded	intellectual
capable	logical
cheerful	loving
clean	obedient
courageous	organized
forgiving	polite
helpful	responsible
honest	self-controlled
imaginative	

Another notion in self-theory is *concept of other*. This may refer to one's description of other people (e.g., how John perceives Mary) or of the external situation in general. Great care must be exercised when using this notion to specify which "other" is being referred to.

All Behaviour Is Motivated

According to Webster's dictionary a motive is "something (as a need or desire) that causes a person to act," and further it "implies an emotion or desire operating on the will and causing it to act." Our understanding of human behaviour is greatly dependent upon an understanding of the underlying wants, needs or desires that impel an individual to action. The earliest philosophers in their study of human nature recognized that man functioned in response to needs or drives and that, while man held certain needs in common with the lower creatures (food, water, sex and so on), he was different in that he had so-called higher needs. While this was a break-through in their efforts to understand human nature, it tended to produce as many problems as it solved; they became bogged down with lengthy, unwieldy and sometimes ludicrous lists of "needs." Nevertheless, the recognition that man is a "wanting" creature, acting in his own interest, as he sees it, is critical to our understanding of human behaviour.

The early psychologists advanced understanding still further by classifying the multitude of needs into two broad categories—primary and secondary. The primary needs are considered innate while the secondary needs are thought to be learned. The primary needs are those concerned with self-preservation and preservation of the species (e.g., hunger, thirst, sex). They are also termed "physiological needs." The secondary or acquired needs, broken into two subcategories (social and egoistic) are much less tangible than are the primary needs and appear to vary in intensity from one person to another. The social need category includes the need for companionship, love, affection, belonging, safety and security. They are related to man's desire for, acceptance by and affiliation with others. The egoistic needs, on the other hand, are concerned with the preservation and enhancement of one's self-identity. Satisfaction of these needs tends to strengthen one's view of oneself. Egoistic needs include the need for self-significance, self-respect, respect of others, self-accomplishment and so on. Categorization into primary and secondary needs and recognition that man is driven by needs other than those of self-survival did much to enhance understanding of human nature.

This conceptualization was advanced still further by the observations of psychologist and behavioural scientist Abraham H. Maslow. As a result of his studies, he postulated that there is a definite rank order priority or "hierarchy of needs." Schematically, Maslow's hierarchy appears as follows:

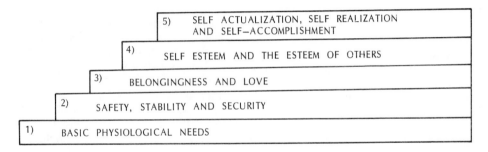

1. Man's first priority according to Maslow is his need to survive and thus his need to satisfy his basic physiological needs. The physiological needs, in that they are concerned with survival of the individual and the species, include the need for food, shelter, water, clothing, sex and so on. Only after this highest priority need has been reasonably satisfied do other needs become operational (i.e., motivate the individual).

2. Maslow suggests that, given reasonable satisfaction of the physiological needs, man next becomes aware of the need for safety and security. These needs are reflected in man's desire for job tenure, an orderly society, insurance, religion and the like. In a sense, man's safety and security needs are satisfied by an assurance that his physiological needs will continue to be met.

3. Once the necessities for continued existence have been reasonably met and there is reasonable assurance that they will continue to be, the three "higher" needs are activated. The need for belongingness and love, or the social needs, refer to man's need for affection and his desire for association with others. Such needs are satisfied by membership in formal and informal groups, satisfactory marital and family relationships and so on.

4. The esteem, or ego, needs include the drive for social approval and self-respect. Gratification of these needs contributes to a feeling of self-confidence, worth and capability.

5. Finally, the highest need level, according to Maslow, is that of self-actualization. Self-actualization refers to man's desire for self-fulfillment and achievement. It encompasses not only the ability to accomplish but also the need for actual achievement of something in life. Self-actualization is a very personal thing in the sense that satisfaction is internally generated. External plaudits are not sought by individuals operating at this need level and, if received, are superfluous. It is a complicated concept and it appears few of us are primarily motivated by this need level.

The hierarchial arrangement of needs in the model stems from Maslow's central assumption that "higher" needs may not be activated until "lower" needs have been reasonably satisfied. Needs that cannot be activated, or aroused, do not result in motivation. Thus, before we can hope to gain cooperation from people by way of stimuli designed to arouse higher level needs (such as self-esteem), we must ensure that lower needs (such as job security) have been reasonably satisfied. There isn't much merit, for example, in a professor's attempting to entice a student to devote more time to his studies with the promise of a higher grade if, in order to do so, it means that the student must give up a part-time job, which spells the difference between security and starvation. In this case the esteem needs cannot be aroused until the student has some reasonable assurance that he will continue to satisfy his physiological needs. Maslow's hierarchy of needs may be looked upon as a "first things first" approach to human motivation.

Next, Maslow advises us that people are motivated by unsatisfied needs, in the sense that these needs have been aroused but have not been satisfied. Conversely, he stated that people are not motivated by needs that have been gratified. In this context, he suggests that an average North American might be eighty-five per cent satisfied in his physiological needs, seventy per cent in his security needs, fifty per cent in his love needs, forty per cent in the esteem category and ten per cent at the self-actualization level. Thus, in our society, since the physiological and security needs are reasonably satisfied for most people, they cannot be used as effective motivators. Rather, it is the higher need levels that hold potential for motivation. Regrettably, most of our traditional reward/punishment systems are geared to the lower, not higher, need levels. The successful manager of human resources is one who, in recognizing the existence of higher need levels, is able to exercise the necessary creativity to assure that the pursuit of these needs is not frustrated but, rather, is associated with desired work behaviour.

Yet another approach to motivation was provided by Frederick Herzberg. Concerned with the role that work and working conditions[6] play in the lives of people, Herzberg conducted research directed toward determining the factors that lead to employee satisfaction. He and his research team interviewed employees in a variety of occupations and organizations about the effect on job satisfaction of a host of factors (pay, working conditions, supervision, status, work itself, and so on). It was assumed that for each of these factors a location could be plotted on a continuum ranging from job dissatisfaction on one end to job satisfaction on the other:

JOB   ●————————————————————●   JOB

DISSATISFACTION   SATISFACTION

Thus, the research might show that people are generally satisfied by their working conditions, status and supervision but dissatisfied by such things as pay and the nature of the work itself. The results of the research were different from what was expected.

On the basis of the data that were gathered, Herzberg concluded that there were two continuums, not one, because there were two significantly different classes of factors. The first class, which he termed "hygiene" or "maintenance" factors, make up a continuum ranging from job dissatisfaction to no job dissatisfaction,

JOB   ●————————————————————●   NO JOB

DISSATISFACTION   DISSATISFACTION

It includes the following:

- Company policy and administration
- Supervision
- Working conditions
- Interpersonal relations
- Salary
- Status
- Job security
- Personal life

Herzberg contends that these factors do not serve to promote job satisfaction but, if deficient, they can lead to job dissatisfaction. In other words, the provision of good working conditions, competitive salaries and job security only serves to reduce dissatisfaction. Provision of such factors does not result in satisfaction.

---

[6] Working conditions generally refer to all aspects of the work situation, both physical (such as the type of facilities) and emotional (such as atmosphere or mood). In short, it is the work environment.

The second class of factors Herzberg terms "motivators" because his findings suggest that these are effective in motivating employees to greater performance and productivity. Included in this class are such factors as:

- Achievement
- Recognition
- Responsibility
- Advancement
- Opportunity for growth

Motivators make up a continuum ranging from no job satisfaction to job satisfaction.

NO JOB   JOB

SATISFACTION   SATISFACTION

The motivators are concerned with the work itself rather than its surrounding physical, administrative or social environment. Motivation, therefore, evolves from the sense of achievement, recognition, opportunities for advancement and growth and the responsibility inherent in the job itself. All of the other factors serve only to "clean up" the environment and prevent dissatisfaction.

The motivation/hygiene approach to employee satisfaction rests on two assumptions concerning the nature of man:

- The need to avoid pain
- The need to grow

Hygienic factors prevent dissatisfaction and pain by providing a good work environment. Motivation factors enable growth and movement toward some degree of self-actualization. While he emphasizes the importance of the latter in terms of motivation, Herzberg is not de-emphasizing the importance of hygienic factors in successful management. These factors constitute an essential base on which to build. If management neglects to provide such a base, employees will become dissatisfied with their jobs and antagonistic toward the organization. Motivation, of course, is not possible in such an environment. Herzberg does try to impress on management, however, that provision of a comfortable work place, competitive salaries and other such hygienic factors will not, in themselves, result in motivation or increased effort.

Modern industrial societies offer new challenges for the management of human resources because the traditional tools are no longer fully appropriate. The social welfare system assures that no one will go without adequate food and shelter. Unions and the competition between organizations for qualified personnel assure reasonable compensation and job security for those who wish to work. Thus, the promise of a job and salary, in themselves, are not adequate incentives for increased effort on the part of subordinates. Such an environment demands creativity in management. This creativity can evolve only from a manager's willingness to understand human nature.

All Behaviour Is Goal Directed

An individual's actions are goal directed in the sense that they are aimed toward the satisfaction of aroused needs. Pinpointing what an individual's goals are can be very difficult. One may attempt to draw conclusions on the basis of observed behaviour, the apparent need level, the work situation and so on. Seldom will people tell you explicitly what they are after. The more specifically you are able to identify a person's goals, the more likely you will be able to understand and deal with specific behaviour patterns of that individual.

For example, "prosperity" is too vague a goal to offer much useful insight into behaviour whereas "an income level of at least $25 000 per year" is more likely to be useful goal information. Sometimes we have difficulty understanding how some particular behaviour could possibly be goal directed. It seems counter-productive to goal achievement, sometimes even "neurotic." By adding to our model we can explain much of that kind of behaviour. In short, we did not previously take into account those occasions when attempts to attain a goal were blocked by some obstacle or barrier. Such situations result in what is called "frustration" and in behaviour that does not neatly fit the previous model. An expanded model appears as follows:

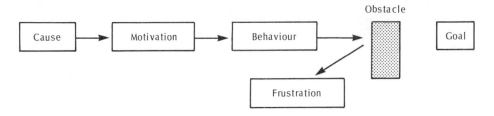

Before moving to a discussion of the forms of behaviour that are a consequence of frustration,[7] it is useful to differentiate between the types of obstacles. Obstacles may be either overt (external, physical) or covert (internal, psychological). The most difficult obstacles to surmount are covert obstacles because their solution often demands an altering of one's self-concept.

All of us are faced with a multitude of obstacles, real or imagined, as we go through life. Most often, when faced with an obstacle, we are able to adopt a problem solving form of behaviour. Sometimes it is simply a matter of substituting an alternative, and more realistic, goal. Other times we need only try harder. Or, it may require that we change our perception of the problem, such as discovering that the door wasn't stuck, it was locked. In these and other ways, we are able to face up to most obstacles presented to us and surmount them with a minimum of frustration. This is called "coping behaviour."

While as reasonable "well-adjusted" people we are often able to approach our problems in this manner, frustration sometimes triggers "defence mechanisms" in an individual. These mechanisms serve to protect the "self" but often do so at the price of distorting reality or causing more problems than existed at the outset. There are many such mechanisms but they may, for simplification, be categorized into the following three types: aggression, withdrawal and fixation. The particular form of reaction which an individual adopts depends upon his personality, the situation and how he perceives the barrier.

Aggression is forceful, attacking behaviour, either constructively self-assertive and self-protective, or destructively hostile to others or to oneself.[8] The physical form of this mechanism is more readily recognizable but it is not the only form. In fact, "education and training have taught most adults in most situations to channel their aggressive impulses into non-violent forms."[9] The non-violent forms are more subtle: rumour spreading, ostracism from a work group, work slowdowns and so on. Being more subtle, they are more difficult to prove, are more socially acceptable and are less susceptible to retalia-

[7] This analytical approach was significantly influenced by lectures and lecture notes provided by Professor A. Mikalachki, School of Business, University of Western Ontario.

[8] *Webster's New World Dictionary, Second College Edition,* Nelson, Foster and Scott, 1970.

[9] Dale Beach *op. cit.*

tion. To slam another person in the teeth may result in an equal and opposite reaction. To spread suspicion as to another person's honesty is less apt to result in retaliation and, in the long run, is more damaging. Sometimes a person finds it inadvisable or impossible to attack the real source of his frustration (especially if it is himself); therefore, he picks on an innocent person or object. This form of aggression, known as displacement, is exemplified by the individual who cannot retaliate when his boss has proven to be a source of frustration and, therefore, goes home and makes life miserable for his family.

Withdrawal refers to physical or mental retreat as a means of avoiding an obstacle. Physical withdrawal may involve resignation from a job position while mental withdrawal may involve fantasy or even a nervous breakdown.

Fixation refers to a continuation of the particular behaviour that has already proven inappropriate to goal attainment. Unlike aggression and withdrawal, fixation behaviour increases rather than decreases tension in the individual. As an example, suppose a foreman is trying to improve the quality of production output, but his workers are angry with company disciplinary procedures and are deliberately reducing quality as a means of protest. The foreman has tried threats of disciplinary action to improve quality, but this has only aggravated the situation. Continued, even escalated, threats of disciplinary action (when this behaviour clearly would not result in goal attainment for the foreman) would constitute fixation behaviour.

An individual, when faced with an obstacle preventing attainment of a desired goal, may assume a coping, or problem-solving approach to his difficulty. Should such an approach prove impossible, as it often does when the obstacle is covert, the individual may resort to defensive behaviour. Recognition of the symptoms of defensive behaviour can help us deal with problems related to individual behaviour. Sometimes it is possible to remove such barriers; at other times the solution can only lie in helping the individual surmount the obstacle by forcing him to face up to the situation and altering that aspect of his behaviour, motivation or goals that is creating his problems.

Another way of looking at frustration situations is as a conflict between the way we see ourselves (self-concept) and the way in which we see our environment or the people in it (concept of other). When the information an individual receives from his environment conflicts with what he believes he can and should have, he is said to be in a state of emotional disequilibrium. He will devote all of his energies to restoring equilibrium. Let us look at the ways in which an individual might attempt to eliminate a conflict between his self-concept and his concept of other:

1. Take action to change the environment. One solution to the conflict might be to take action to change the facts in the real world and in so doing create a more acceptable concept of other. Thus, if the poor grades a student receives are not consistent with his self-concept, he might put forth more effort or seek assistance from his instructor or classmates.
2. Change the concept of other. It is possible to alter the concept of other without changing the real world. In this case an individual reorganizes his perception of the real world into something more acceptable. Sometimes this entails creating a more realistic perception of the real world, such as when a student recognizes the failing grade to be a function of less than earnest effort. At other times it becomes a distortion of reality, such as when a student decides that the poor grade is a result of the instructor's dislike for him.
3. Change the self-concept. A third method of eliminating the conflict is to alter the self-concept so that the concept of other is no longer a threat. This is possible when that aspect of the self-concept which is in conflict with the environment is not critical to the whole. A student who performed poorly on the finance section of this book may eliminate any conflict by deciding that ''he isn't very good with numbers.''

4. Neurotic reaction. Sometimes the individual is thrown into such a state of anxiety that he is incapable of eliminating the conflict by fair means or foul. Instead, he suppresses the conflict in his subconscious, usually by substituting a new problem at the conscious level. Thus, the student with a failing grade might decide to slug the teacher who awarded the grade (aggression) or go off some place to drown his sorrow in strong ale (withdrawal). These neurotic reactions, you can see, are equivalent to what we termed "defensive mechanisms" in our earlier discussion of frustration and adjustment.

Summary

It is important to recognize that human behaviour is caused, motivated and goal directed. Only by making these "assumptions" and by taking the time and effort to identify each of these aspects of the behavioural situation can we expect to deal effectively with problems related to individual behaviour. To take action without such identification is analogous to writing a prescription for pain killers instead of trying to uncover the underlying cause of the headache in an attempt to eliminate it. Similarly, bawling out an uncooperative employee, while producing a desired short-run effect, may not be the long-run solution to the problem. The behaviour in this instance, like the headache, is merely a symptom. It is the effective manager who recognizes this and is able to uncover and deal with the underlying cause and motivation.

UNDERSTANDING INTERPERSONAL AND GROUP BEHAVIOUR

To this point we have treated managing HR primarily as the interaction between an individual and the formal organization. Managing HR often is more complicated because of the influence of the social environment of the organization. The actions, attitudes and the general deportment of individuals are frequently conditioned by the groups to which they belong or aspire to belong. We will approach the matter of groups via a discussion of interpersonal problems.

From a management standpoint, the most difficult task in managing interpersonal relationships is dealing with interpersonal conflict. For example, two individuals, A and B, who are expected to cooperate in a work situation are in conflict with one another. Many of us are tempted to view such a situation as a "personality conflict" and leave it at that. Clearly, we need to probe deeper into the reasons for interpersonal conflict if we are to deal with it effectively.

For example, we can build on the self-theory approach described previously. If A and B are not hitting it off, perhaps it is because of differing perceptions of each other or of the situation. For example, one possibility is that A's self-concept is at odds with B's concept of A (or vice versa). Thus, B may be asking A to act in ways A does not consider congruent with his self-concept:

Such a conflict can be resolved in several ways: (a) removing A or B from the situation, (b) changing A's self-concept, (c) changing B's concept of A's self-concept, (d) changing the situation so the conflict doesn't occur or doesn't matter.

Such "incongruencies of perception" have received a lot of attention, but we have found that the most useful approach to them is via "role theory." A role refers to a set of expected behavioural activities and attitudinal expressions in a particular situation. We have all been in role situations: student, brother or sister, girlfriend or boyfriend, teller, bag-boy at a grocery store, high school senior, defenceman on a hockey team, etc. In each case, the role may have been easy to perform or very difficult. Difficulties arise when the individual is:

1. Technically unable to fulfill the role (e.g., not a good defenceman).
2. Not sure what is expected of him (e.g., no one explained clearly what a teller is supposed to do and not supposed to do).
3. Faced with too many roles to play at the same time (e.g., dating too many "steady girlfriends" at the same time).
4. Supposed to play a role incongruent with his self-concept (e.g., deferring to the boss when you know you are right and think of yourself as one who stands up for his beliefs).
5. Trying to play a role someone else is playing too, and there is only room for one to play that role in that situation (e.g., both professor and student trying to direct the class at the same time).

Often interpersonal conflicts are the direct consequence of these role problems. The cause of such problems may be in the individual or the situation:

- Inadequate skills (poor fit of role and individual)
- Inadequate communication of expectations
- Excessive expectations
- Conflicting beliefs about appropriate behaviour
- Conflicting need satisfaction (goal fulfillment) attempts

Sometimes resolution may be achieved via improved communication (e.g., clear definition of the teller's job) and sometimes via changes in expectations, people involved, etc.

Another approach to interpersonal behaviour problems is to focus on the interpersonal relationship itself as it is evidenced in behaviour. One species of this approach is generally known as "transactional analysis." Primarily advanced by psychologists and psychiatrists, transactional analysis deals with the "balance of trade" between individuals under the assumption individuals, over a period of time, will only interact with other individuals who satisfy certain needs. In short, A will deal with B, giving satisfaction to B only if A gets back roughly equal satisfaction from B. The theory has been considerably embellished (by Eric Berne, Thomas Harris and others) with types of transactions, a unit of exchange ("stroke"), intrapersonal components ("child, parent, adult"), trading situations and methods ("games," rituals," etc.). For our purposes, the important point is this: if A and B are not getting along, what is each getting (or not getting) from the other. Look at the trading behaviour from each participant's point of view to see if a reasonable "balance of trade" can be re-established.

Individuals frequently join groups and these groups can add more complexity to HR management. This complexity occurs because membership in a group often entails changes in individual behaviour: productivity of individuals may increase or decline, morale may increase or decline, etc. That is, the emergent behaviour of group members is often different from the behaviour one might expect of the members individually. Managers must therefore understand why individuals join groups, how groups operate and how groups affect individual behaviour patterns.

For the purpose of this discussion, groups may be small and informal (e.g., your preclass study group) or large and formal (e.g., unions).

Why do people become members of groups? Think about some of the groups to which you belong or have belonged. Think further as to why you joined the groups. Your first thoughts will no doubt centre on the benefits you acquired, or expected to acquire, from membership in the group. People join groups because they see membership as yielding benefits that are in their self-interest to acquire. The following are some examples of these benefits.

1. *Fellowship*   Membership in a group may provide an individual with a sense of belonging. Abraham Maslow rated social needs as being very high on the average individual's priorities. We all require the opportunity to interact with others. This is never more evident than when you find yourself in a strange city far from family and friends. We seek membership in some groups in order to interact with others. The fact that others are willing to interact with us is an indication that we are accepted. Critical to self-acceptance is acceptance by others. Thus, one possible benefit derived from membership in a group is satisfaction of social needs.
2. *Protection*   Of even higher priority is man's recognition that banding together to present a united front against common enemies has been essential to the survival of mankind. Similarly, membership in a group is sometimes essential to an individual's survival in the modern industrial setting. The group protects its members by closing ranks to speak up for those who find themselves in trouble with management, by covering up for mistakes made by members or even by doing the work for members who are having a bad day.
3. *Prestige*   Some groups hold a reputation which makes membership attractive to an individual. In becoming a member of a prestigious group, the individual inherits some of that prestige. Thus, a boy in the slums wishes to become a member of the "toughest gang." Certain fraternities and sororities are more attractive than others because of the reputations they have established. Similarly, in the work place an individual might pride himself in being a member of "the loading dock crew" because of some perceived prestige that such a group carries with it.
4. *Effect Change*   Presenting a united front often allows people to change conditions that they find undesirable. Unions, for example, are often able to increase wage rates or improve working conditions because the members act in unison. Similarly, other interest groups have held mass demonstrations to call attention to conditions they wish improved as in the case of marches on Parliament Hill. In these instances people recognize that a united group stands a much greater chance of achieving a desired goal than do individuals operating independently.
5. *Assistance with a Task*   Often an individual requires the assistance or advice of others in accomplishing a task. Isolating himself from neighbours at home or from fellow employees in the work place can place him in dire straits when the task requires skills or strength beyond his capacity.
6. *Communication*   In the industrial setting the informal organization provides a communications network. This network, known as the grapevine, keeps members informed of what is going on. Moreover, it generally does so more quickly than do the formal channels of communications. In one organization it became a standing joke that if one wanted to keep advised of possible promotions or transfers he should keep in touch with the company's truck drivers. These drivers had established a grapevine that spanned Canada from coast to coast. Generally, they had news of an individual's promotion or transfer, among other things, at least three weeks in advance of that individual's immediate supervisor. Membership in the informal organization, then, is often essential to keeping informed of developments in the formal organization.

In return for the multitude of benefits that can accrue from membership, the group is able to exact certain tributes from its members:

1. *Pre-eminence of Group Goals*   In return for membership the individual must be prepared to forfeit his personal goals in deference to those of the group. Thus, the individ-

ual may find himself engaged in activities contrary to his personal goals because the group so demands. A student may find himself, for example, at a party rather than his desk on the eve of an exam because the group has placed the party on its agenda.

2. *Norms of Behaviour* The group establishes certain standards of behaviour to which members must conform. One boy's street gang adopted black leather jackets as its accepted uniform. A member's parents were opposed to their son's wearing such apparel because of the unpleasant connotation it presented to them. He compromised by purchasing a red leather jacket but was immediately ostracized by the gang. Thereafter, that boy's name became synonymous with breaking the group norm. Anyone who dressed, or in anyway acted, differently from the perceived group norm was termed a "Dexter." The term carried with it the threat of ostracism and served as a means to enforce group norms. Similarly, trade unions are able to enforce group solidarity in a strike by threats of the term "scab." Some work groups are able to restrict production by enforcing certain standards, or norms, of production. A member who over-produces or, as it is termed, "kills the job" finds himself in difficulty. The penalty may take more severe forms than simple ostracism, such as when a deviant is beaten up or any "mistakes" he makes on the job are reported to management. Individuals are generally willing to make these kinds of sacrifices in return for group membership. The extent to which they will engage in behaviour they do not like depends on the importance of the group to the individual's need satisfaction.

Groups can be analyzed on several dimensions: roles played by group members, decision-making processes, sanctions to enforce group norms and so on. One useful approach is the relationship between group cohesion ("stick togetherness" of group members), management control approaches and the productivity of the group's members.[10]

Productivity and Cohesion

Focus of Integration

		Task	Social
Means of Control	Rights and Duties	**High Output** Task Cohesive	**Low Output** Social Cohesive
	Punitive Sanctions	**Restricted Output** Protective Task Cohesive	**Output Not Related to Situation** Protective Social Cohesive

---

[10] This section is based upon A. Mikalachki, *Group Cohesion Reconsidered*, 1969 (published by the School of Business Administration, U.W.O.).

Highly cohesive groups (wherein members act together, engage in egalitarian behaviour, and have a positive attraction to the group) can aid in boosting output if the focus of the members' cohesiveness is on the task and if the members are motivated by positive sanctions. If the focus of the members' cohesiveness is the satisfaction of social needs rather than getting the task completed, management probably will not get the productivity hoped for no matter what it tries. Low cohesive groups have a precarious existence: members are not attracted to the group, behaviour is not coordinated and it is probable that the group will ultimately fragment or dissolve entirely.

The important point to remember is that when you are dealing with a cohesive group, you must be careful: find out what the focus of cohesion is before attempting to change behaviour—otherwise your efforts may backfire.

UNDERSTANDING ORGANIZATIONS

A few issues related to the management of human resources in a complex organization remain to be discussed. The manager of the overall organization has two major tasks to perform: first, designing the overall "organization structure" and, second, designing the "operating mechanisms" to reinforce the intent of the organizational design.

Design of the organization structure doesn't mean simply drawing up an organizational chart with boxes and arrows. Instead it means deciding what tasks must be performed, grouping similar tasks together, setting up appropriate organizational units to handle these task groupings, staffing the organizational units with "specialists" and finding ways (and people) to achieve cooperation and collaboration among the separate units. This is all easy to say, but it requires involved consideration of job functions, the number of individuals a manager can control, communication networks, authority and responsibility networks and the trade-offs between centralization and decentralization.

Operating mechanisms may encompass a variety of factors, but we intend it to refer to the reward-punishment system, the communication system, the control system and the development system. Each of these can be broken down into components (the control system, for example, is comprised of performance evaluation, feedback methods, etc.). The important questions for you to answer, however, are whether these operating mechanisms:

1. are internally consistent, that is, work together to reinforce the organizational structure and achieve organizational goals;
2. are consistent with the organizational task, the people involved, environment, etc., in order to realize organizational goals.

As a manager, you must be able to understand the nature of your organization: what it is, how it works and what factors influence what factors. The more you understand it, the more likely you will be able to guide it to achieve your objectives. The following diagram summarizes where we are to this point:

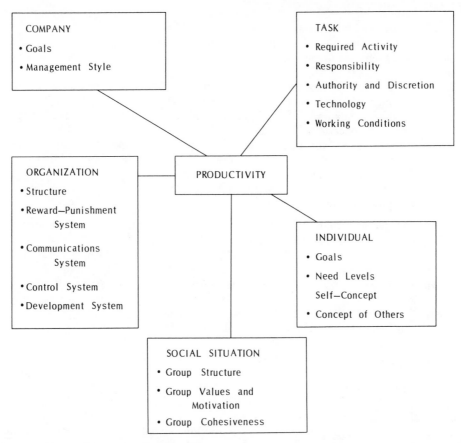

If these five aspects of HR management fit together, then productivity and organizational growth will be supported as much as possible.

THE MANAGEMENT OF CHANGE

One big topic remains. Assuming we now are able to identify problems and formulate desirable solutions, how do we implement changes when we "know" people tend to resist change in general?

First, we must be able to anticipate such resistance. When does it occur? Most often when it is unexpected or undesired. Why does it occur? For several reasons, including

- Change is perceived as a threat to economic security.
- Change introduces uncertainty and inconvenience.
- Individuals feel a sense of loss when required to give up familiar ways.
- Change is perceived as a threat to the competence or status of individuals.
- Change entails a shift in personal relationships.
- Change was unexplained and/or unanticipated.

Second, we must be able to formulate ways to deal with change management. The first step here is to realize that resistance to change is a signal that something has gone wrong. You must find out what. Then, there are some general ways to ease the pain that you may be able to adapt to the particular situation:[11]

---

[11] Based upon Ralph Hirschavitz, "The Human Aspects of Managing Transition" in *Personnel,* May-June, 1974.

1. Tell those involved the reasons for change.
2. Involve those affected in the design of the change process.
3. Be especially sensitive to their needs for reassurance and recognition during the transition stage.
4. Provide help in learning new tasks, new roles and establishing new relationships.
5. Be more available for discussions, questions, etc., than usual.
6. Encourage them to talk about the change, the "old days" and their feelings of frustration, anxiety and concern.
7. Be sensitive to the need for patience and clarification. The change process may cause "shock" temporarily, so re-statement of information may be necessary before an employee fully comprehends it.
8. Be enthusiastic and hopeful by demonstrating frequently and constructively that the transitional problems can be overcome.

If individuals perceive the change as a threat to their economic security, this aspect of the resistance to change must be dealt with first before the other factors on the above list. Notice that resistance to change shows itself in ways understandable in our frustration model discussed previously.

Seldom, if ever, is it wise to impose change by "decree," expecting sheer power will win the day. People and organizations need time and help in order to adjust to change. As a manager you will find that deciding how to implement changes, no matter what their size, is just as important as deciding what to change.

CONCLUSION

The purpose of this chapter is to provide you with some generally recognized "tools" with which you may approach human resources problems. Our treatment has by no means been exhaustive as you will discover when you read more about "human relations," "managerial psychology," "personnel administration" and the like. It is extremely important for you to realize that the mechanical use of these tools of analysis will not make you a good manager of people. What we cannot provide for you is a set of values, an orientation with which you put these tools and human resources problems into perspective. Only with this set of values can you tailor your decision-making skills and analytical tools to the circumstances in which you find yourself. Effective management of human resources, in the final analysis, is a creative approach to people and circumstances. Creativity in leadership means thoughtful action by a concerned person who has an understanding of the whole situation.

10

Ajax Distributors

In April 1974, the sales manager of Ajax Distributors, Ltd. received a letter from his field supervisor urging that consideration be given to the rehiring of a former employee of the company, Mr. Rod Adams, who had left the company three years earlier.

COMPANY HISTORY

Ajax Distributors was organized in 1936 to act as wholesaler and exclusive agent for products used in concrete construction. The main product distributed by the company was material used for hardening concrete. In conjunction with this, the company distributed iron rods and mesh, wire, light structural steel, and other allied products. The chief customers were industrial concerns, building supply outlets and construction companies. During the past ten years the company had been transformed under new and progressive management, and a number of valuable agencies and rights had been secured from United States and European firms.

Basically, Ajax Distributors was à sales organization with warehousing as a key function. Since it was necessary to develop the market for the new product lines, a group of well-trained, energetic salesmen was required. In 1974 these salesmen were considered well paid: on a salary and commission plan, the average salesman drew $15 000, with top salesmen earning slightly over $20 000. While a successful salesman was appreciated, the company executives at this time were also looking for potential management ability, since they planned to expand the general office sales department and to open new branch offices. In 1971, there were fourteen such branch offices in Canada with plans for an additional twelve to fifteen to be opened within five years. Five had been opened by 1974. At each branch warehouse, the manager was in charge of one to ten salesmen, depending upon the size and potential of the area served, as well as responsible for the warehouse staff.

The head office of the firm was in Hamilton, Ontario, where the sales manager and his field supervisor were located.

EXPANSION PROGRAM

The company's policy was to promote from within but, when this was not possible, salesmen were recruited from placement agencies, competitors, colleges, allied businesses, etc. In view of the expansion program the sales manager was instructed to step up his efforts to get good men. He realized that this could not be done entirely at a central location since salesmen sent out to the branches would not be completely acceptable to the branch managers who wanted a hand in choosing those who worked for them. Also, such a policy would, in effect, confine the company's source and contacts for new men to one geographic area. To help the branch managers hire intelligently, specifications were prepared for the type of salesman they thought might later become part of management. The specifications were compiled by a committee that studied some of the star salesmen and analyzed the job to be done.

The branch manager held two interviews with candidates (where possible, someone else from the branch was also present), then made a specific recommendation and forwarded the application to the sales manager for a final decision.

ROD ADAMS

During the course of recruiting in 1971, the Hamilton branch manager, whose office was in the head office of the company, drew to the sales manager's attention an interesting application submitted by a Mr. Rod Adams. This application (Exhibit 1) indicated that Adams was thirty-seven years of age, was married and had two children. He had the minimum educational requirements that the company desired, Grade 13. He had no previous selling experience but had been with the Hamilton Police Department for a number of years, where he had moved ahead and was well regarded by both his superiors and the men with whom he worked. Mr. Adams pointed out in his application that he had gained wide experience in the field of public relations while employed with the Police Department, where he had handled all types of people, from irate employers whose men he had had to arrest, to the offenders themselves. The branch manager had secured former job information by contacting the Police Department. Rod Adams also submitted the names of a bank manager and a minister as character references and they had supplied positive feedback.

Rod Adams had resided in Hamilton for fourteen years but stated he was willing to go elsewhere for the company. The credit reports showed that he had a good equity in his home and owned his car. He had a reasonable amount of life insurance and was believed to have a savings account that was increasing at a slow but steady rate.

The sales manager and the branch manager decided to hire him on the basis of his favourable impression on several people at head office. They thought he would do very well in their business because he was "a big, likeable chap." The general manager had questioned the decision since his previous positions showed "lack of initiative." Nevertheless, he was willing to accept the opinion of the sales manager and the branch manager.

TRAINING PERIOD

Rod Adam's training record was most satisfactory. He began the training program which the company had established for salesmen at a starting salary of $800 per month. This program involved one month in the office learning policies and procedures, two weeks in a warehouse becoming familiar with the products and the warehousing system and four weeks in sales training which included travelling with other salesmen and a branch manager, and a formal selling course involving lectures, role-playing, etc., that was put on by a sales training organization.

The branch manager in Hamilton in charge of Rod Adams during his training became well acquainted with his wife and family. He discovered that the couple were keenly interested in the welfare of their oldest son, a third-year high school student, who planned to enter the medical profession. The family physician was already very interested in the boy and promised to help with his education in terms of getting enrolled in university and financially, if necessary.

At the end of the training period, Adams was given a good sales post at the company's Thunder Bay, Ontario, branch which served approximately 150 customers. The branch sales volume had averaged $900 000 over the past three years and it was felt that the sales potential in this territory was increasing rapidly. Upon completion of the training period, salesmen began selling on a basic salary of $600 per month, plus a car and an expense account, and the opportunity to earn an additional $500 to $600 per month on commissions. The basic salary was increased to $650 per month after one year, to $700 after the third year, and so on in accordance with a sliding scale.

Adams seemed very enthusiastic about this move, but mentioned that he was very ambitious and wanted to advance to a larger branch and eventually to the head office. He was told that if his record was good, he might expect a move in three years, depending on conditions and his progress.

While in Thunder Bay completing his preparatory training with the older salesman he was replacing, Adams seemed worried about whether he could handle the job, how much money he would make, and particularly whether the older salesman felt he might be able to get back to western Ontario. This anxiety reached the point where Adams was not sleeping at nights and seemed physically ill during certain periods of the day. He finally asked permission of the Thunder Bay manager to call the sales manager. He agreed since he felt that it might be the way to get Adams straightened out. The sales manager talked with Adams and reassured him he was experiencing the bewilderment common to some new salesmen. Finally, Adams asked flatly to be brought back to Hamilton and be given a territory there, since he felt he needed more training. Since he was due to return to Hamilton on the weekend, he was urged to discuss the matter then. He did so and at this point, the real source of trouble was revealed: Mr. Adams's wife did not want to go to Thunder Bay.

The sales manager, who was forty-eight years old, could think of similar instances that had taken place, and it had been his experience that in the majority of these cases it was just a matter of getting used to the new location. He recalled one recent case in which a salesman had objected strongly to a move to another northern Ontario location but within two years had become so well established among new friends and business acquaintances that he did not want to leave.

The sales manager suggested Mrs. Adams go to Thunder Bay at the company's expense to look over the situation. Mrs. Adams made the journey, but stayed less than twenty-four hours. Adams then wrote the sales manager and explained that he felt the real trouble was that his wife felt leaving Hamilton might affect the future of their boy, who would be entering the premedical course in two years. The Hamilton branch manager, who had been taking a close interest in Mr. and Mrs. Adams, pointed out to them that this would be just as possible from Thunder Bay, but they remained unconvinced.

ADAMS'S RESIGNATION

Adams seemed not only disappointed, but embarrassed, since he had stated on his application that he would be willing to go anywhere the company wished to send him. His only suggestion, however, was that he be given a territory in Hamilton or its vicinity. Adams felt that he could do a good job there and be contented, and that eventually his wife might decide that they could move elsewhere. He reluctantly stated that he would be forced to tender his resignation if this were not possible.

Rod Adams had made several friends within the Head Office, and serious consideration was given to his case, which, like all other matters involving a policy decision, was discussed at a general executive committee meeting. The sales manager, arguing against accepting Adams's conditions, stated that there were many other salesmen's wives who would like to choose where their husbands were employed. His experience while building the business had been that salesmen who stayed on in one place got into a comfortable rut, and were not suitable for advancement. He felt quite strongly that an employee should be willing to go wherever the company wished to send him. He also raised the question about Adams's sincerity since in his application for employment he had specifically agreed to go wherever the company sent him. The company had gone to considerable expense to train him and while accepting this training and the offer to have his wife visit Thunder Bay, Adams must have had some indication that he would eventually be unable to accept the conditions of such a move.

The field supervisor, whose opinions were held in high regard by all members of the executive, argued the other side of the case. He said that he had come to know Rod Adams and his family well and was confident that Adams had been sincere but that the move did impose some special hardships on his family. In his view, the sales staff could be strengthened by such men as Rod Adams even if they remained in one location.

In spite of his satisfactory record in training and other obvious attributes, it was finally decided that Rod Adams's resignation must be accepted, although the decision was reached most reluctantly by only a small majority of the executive committee.

Subsequently, Mr. Adams secured a job with a firm selling hospital supplies and was given a territory near Ottawa, where he lived in a small apartment. Mrs. Adams and the children remained in Hamilton. He was promised that as soon as an opportunity opened up closer to Hamilton he would be transferred, but three years later, no other had opened up, nor had he been promoted, although his record had been an excellent one. As Ajax Distributors was continuing to expand and having difficulty in finding suitable salesmen, the Hamilton branch manager, with whom Adams had kept in contact, decided to sound out Adams's feelings with regard to his present position. Mr. Adams stated that he was about to resign the hospital supply job since his wife was still adamant over the Hamilton location, and the situation at home was becoming strained. His son was now attending the local university and hoped to be admitted to the Medical School when his science courses were completed.

Although no basic changes had occurred in the company's personnel requirements regarding staff mobility during the three-year interval, the Hamilton branch manager urged the sales manager to hire Adams in Hamilton and recommended that later, when conditions at his home had changed, he might be moved elsewhere.

Exhibit 1
Application For Position
Ajax Distributors Ltd, Hamilton, Ontario

Date—April 17, 1971

NAME—Rod Adams
PRESENT ADDRESS—424 Elm Avenue
    Hamilton, Ontario
PREVIOUS ADDRESS—217 William St
    Hamilton, Ontario
POSITION APPLIED FOR? Salesman

HOME TELEPHONE NO 477-4386
HOW LONG HAVE YOU LIVED
THERE? 14 years
HOW LONG DID YOU LIVE
THERE? 5 years
EARNINGS EXPECTED (as discussed)

Personal

DATE OF BIRTH—Sept. 12, 1934

HEIGHT—6'2" WEIGHT—210 lbs
NATIONALITY OR COUNTRY OF ALLEGIANCE—Canadian
NO OF OTHER DEPENDENTS—0
BIRTHPLACE—Acton, Ontario
(Town & Province)
DO YOU OWN YOUR HOME? x RENT?
WOULD YOU BE WILLING TO WORK ANYWHERE IN CANADA? YES x NO
DO YOU OWN FURNITURE? YES x NO
IS YOUR WIFE EMPLOYED? NO x YES PART TIME   YES FULL TIME
DO YOU CARRY LIFE INSURANCE?   NO   YES x
WHAT PHYSICAL DEFECTS DO YOU HAVE?   None
DATE LAST MEDICAL—Feb, 1970
DO YOU WEAR GLASSES?   NO x   YES, ONLY FOR READING   YES, ALL THE TIME

SINGLE MARRIED x SEPARATED
WIDOWED DIVORCED
NO OF CHILDREN—2 AGES 10 & 15

NAME AND ADDRESS OF
NEAREST RELATIVE—Mrs. C. R. Adams
Acton, Ontario

Education

Type of School	Name and Address of School	Courses Majored in	Check last yr Completed	Graduate Give Degrs	Last Year attended
Public	Acton P. School		5 6 7 8 x	Yes x No	1948
High S.	Acton High		1 2 3 4 5 x	Yes x No	1953
College	N/A		1 2 3 4 5		

COLLEGE STANDING? HONOURS PASS
EXTRACURRICULAR ACTIVITIES IN H.S.?—Football, baseball, student assembly
WHAT OFFICES DID YOU HOLD IN THESE GROUPS?
EXTRACURRICULAR ACTIVITIES IN COLLEGE?   OFFICES HELD?

Work History

List positions held commencing with the most recent	Time Employed	Nature of Work	Starting Salary	Salary at Leaving	Reasons for Leaving
1. Hamilton Police Department	June/63	Police Constable	$350/mo	$1100/mo	Present Employer
2. Hamilton Fabrication	Apr/57 May/63	Labourer	$300/mo	$ 350/mo	More appealing work with Police Force
3. Acton Cooperative	June/53 Apr/57	Attending customers and some delivery	$150/mo	$ 250/mo	Sought work with more opportunity to get ahead

MAY WE REFER TO ABOVE EMPLOYERS?   YES x   NO
HAVE YOU EVER BEEN REFUSED BOND?   YES   NO x
HAVE YOU ANY RELATIVES IN OUR EMPLOY?   YES   NO x
REFERENCES (Not employers or relatives) ADDRESS

                                                  POSITION
  1. Rev A. S. Bessinger, Acton United Church   Minister
  2. Mr R. A. Turner, Hamilton   Bank Manager
  3. Sgt Blossenz, Police Department, Hamilton   Sgt

WHY DO YOU WISH TO WORK FOR THE AJAX DISTRIBUTORS LTD?
  I like meeting people. Have handled all kinds of groups in police work. Have heard Ajax is progressive and I want to get ahead.
WHEN CAN YOU START WORK IF EMPLOYED?—2 weeks' notice

11
A Salary Dispute

JoAnn Burns and Nancy Carr were bank tellers at the Goderich Branch of the Ontario Bank. (See Exhibit 1 for the organization chart.) JoAnn, the more senior of the employees, had been with the organization for more than twenty years while Nancy had several years' experience. JoAnn's position in the organization was that of head teller. Although her formal job description did not indicate it, she handled in the order of sixty to eighty thousand dollars cash per day. She was also responsible for all incoming and outgoing money parcels in the branch. Consequently, she had a high degree of responsibility and was normally quite a complacent individual. Her day-to-day work was adequately done from a customer relations point of view and she had produced well on various deposit campaigns in the past.

Nancy on the other hand was a very outgoing individual with an attractive appearance and personality. She was considered highly productive and a good company employee. According to John White, the assistant manager (credit), her productivity and selling capabilities appeared to entitle her to a higher salary than JoAnn. Her job was to run the cash. She assumed no responsibilities equal in degree to JoAnn's. She worked well with the rest of the staff.

Unfortunately, one day after work JoAnn discovered that Nancy was making considerably more money than she. (See Exhibit 2 for backgrounds of the employees.) This upset her and an argument took place over the matter. The argument, in turn, upset Nancy and she told JoAnn, "It is none of your damn business," and later, "I'm not going to apologize for the way I'm speaking to you." Both employees left the office upset over the argument.

That evening JoAnn phoned John White. She was crying and very distressed over the whole incident. Prior to this JoAnn and Nancy had appeared friendly and had had no trouble getting along.

The next morning while opening the mail John White said to Bill Fox, the accountant trainee of the branch, "We're going to straighten this thing out this morning. If JoAnn is going to behave this way, she can get the hell out of the branch. We don't need that kind of behaviour in this office."

As Bob French, the manager, wouldn't return from a trip for several days, John White knew he had to make a decision. He was especially concerned about the tension that was spreading throughout the whole office because of the incident. He wondered how to solve the problem.

Exhibit 1
A Salary Dispute
An Organizational Chart

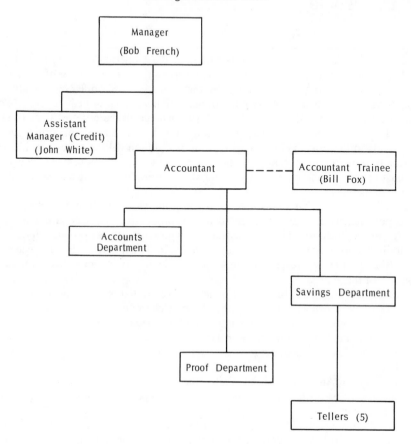

Exhibit 2
A Salary Dispute
Background of Employees

	Nancy Hawkins	Nancy Carr	JoAnn Burns	Clara Williamson	Betsy James	Sylvia Purne
Length of service in years	1/2	3	23	N/A	3	2
Salary approximately/year	$4000	$4800	$4500	—	$4400	$4200
Attitude toward Nancy Carr	+		—	Neutral	+	+
Attitude toward JoAnn Burns	Neutral	—		+	—	—

Exhibit 3

A Salary Dispute

Staff Report — Worksheet

NOT TO BE RETAINED AFTER
REPORT IS COMPLETED

APPRAISAL OF PERFORMANCE — REFER TO PERSONNEL MANUAL

	EXCELLENT	VERY GOOD	GOOD	IMPROV REQUIRED	NOT ACCEPTABLE	NOT APPLICABLE	REMARKS		EXCELLENT	VERY GOOD	GOOD	IMPROV REQUIRED	NOT ACCEPTABLE	NOT APPLICABLE	REMARKS
ACCEPTANCE OF RESPONSIBILITY								ORAL EXPRESSION							
ACCURACY								ORGANIZATION							
ATTITUDE								PERSONAL NEATNESS							
CAPACITY								STAFF RELATIONS							
CUSTOMER RELATIONS								STAFF SUPERVISION							
INITIATIVE								STAFF TRAINING							
JUDGEMENT								SUCCESS IN SOLICITING BUSINESS							
KNOWLEDGE OF DUTIES								WRITTEN EXPRESSION							
MENTAL ALERTNESS								OVERALL PERFORMANCE _____							

ASSESSMENT OF POTENTIAL — REFER TO PERSONNEL MANUAL

1 PROMOTABLE	2 DOMINANT STRENGTHS	3 AREAS FOR IMPROVEMENT	NOW	FUTURE
☐ 1. AS SOON AS THERE IS A SUITABLE OPENING				
☐ 2. WITHIN A YEAR OR TWO	A.	A.		
☐ 3. LIKELY TO QUALIFY FOR FURTHER PROMOTION TIME UNCERTAIN	B.	B.		
☐ 4. LATERAL TRANSFER				
☐ 5. NOT LIKELY TO QUALIFY FOR FURTHER PROMOTION	C.	C.		

4	5 ASSIGNMENT PREFERENCES	6	7	RELUCTANT TO ACCEPT	YES	NO
IF THE EMPLOYEE HAS ANY SKILLS OR APTITUDES WHICH COULD BE USED MORE EFFECTIVELY BY THE BANK PLEASE SPECIFY UNDER COMMENTS SECTION	A. B.	IF THERE ARE ANY CIRCUMSTANCES WHICH RESTRICT THE MOBILITY OF THE EMPLOYEE IN ANY WAY PLEASE INDICATE AND SPECIFY UNDER COMMENTS SECTION. YES ☐ NO ☐	INDICATE AND EXPLAIN UNDER COMMENTS SECTION IF DURING THE NEXT TWELVE MONTHS THE EMPLOYEE WOULD BE RELUCTANT TO ACCEPT THE DEMANDS INHERENT IN HIGHER LEVEL POSITIONS.	A. MORE RESPONSIBILITY B. TRAVEL C. GREATER SOCIAL DEMANDS	☐ ☐ ☐	☐ ☐ ☐

8 IF THE EMPLOYEE IS INTERESTED IN AN ASSIGNMENT IN ANOTHER COUNTRY PLEASE INDICATE YES ☐ NO ☐	10 GEOGRAPHIC PREFERENCES	11 COMMUNITY SIZE PREFERENCE
	A.	☐ 1. NO PREFERENCE
9 IF THE EMPLOYEE IS INTERESTED IN AN ASSIGNMENT IN ANOTHER DISTRICT PLEASE INDICATE YES ☐ NO ☐	B.	☐ 2. LARGE (OVER 100,000) ☐ 3. MEDIUM (10,000 – 100,000)
	C.	☐ 4. SMALL (UNDER 10,000)

12 PARTICIPATION IN WORTHWHILE COMMUNITY ACTIVITIES?	13 COURSES COMPLETED BY THE EMPLOYEE WITHIN THE LAST THREE YEARS				
	COURSE NAME	DURATION	COURSE NAME	DURATION
☐ ACTIVE	A.		D.	
☐ MODERATE	B.		E.	
☐ LIMITED	C.		F.	

COMMENTS (ELABORATE ON QUESTIONS 1 TO 3 AND 5 AND IN ALL OTHER CASES WHERE APPLICABLE   CONTINUE ON REVERSE IF NECESSARY)

12

Glencoe Manufacturing Co.

Jean Talbot was hired in March by the Glencoe Manufacturing Co. to operate a multilith machine. The company was an old established firm. It had a factory and a sales office in a large industrial city in eastern Canada. The sales office was located in the business centre; the factory was on the outskirts of the city, some distance from the sales office.

Miss Talbot was a very attractive girl with a pleasing personality. She was a high school graduate, but when she was hired by the Glencoe Manufacturing Co., she could not type and did not have shorthand. After leaving high school, Jean Talbot worked in the office of a small company as a filing clerk and receptionist. At the time she was employed by the Glencoe Manufacturing Co., she was twenty years of age.

Most of Jean Talbot's work consisted of operating the multilith machine. However, she also sorted, distributed, and collected mail. In addition, she served as a relief for the switchboard-receptionist. Jean had a good speaking voice and was courteous on the phone. Customers commented very favourably about her pleasant telephone manner. After three months' service with the company, Jean began to practise typing.

Six months after Jean began with the Glencoe Manufacturing Co., she became quite unhappy about doing multilith work. She disliked having the special ink used in the machine on her hands. It irked her to wear a smock to protect her clothing when she operated the machine. She was annoyed with the necessity of putting a special lotion on her hands to prevent the ink from getting in the pores of her skin.

Shortly after Jean had indicated to some of the other employees that she was unhappy at work, the company hired a part-time multilith operator. This action was taken because the work load had become heavier on the mail and switchboard-reception desk. The part-time multilith operator worked about three hours a day, sometimes in the morning and sometimes in the afternoon. The addition of the part time operator to the office staff resulted in an improvement in Jean's morale because she now was given opportunities to do typing and filing. After the part-time multilith operator had been with the company for about six months, Jean asked the office manager, Mr. Ronald Bowman, for a chance of advancement. She wanted to get away from the mail work entirely. She told the office manager that she disliked being known by the people in the office as the mail girl.

After approximately one year at the Glencoe Manufacturing Co., an opportunity came for Jean to work at the factory. The factory office needed a switchboard-receptionist with some typing experience; shorthand, however, was not required. She discussed the new job with Mr. Bowman, then was transferred to the factory. She was not too keen about going to the factory as it was some distance from the centre of the city and transportation was difficult. She accepted the job at the factory, however, as it got her away from the mail job; and, furthermore, her salary would be slightly better at the factory office. She had accepted the position at the factory with the understanding that, if an opening occurred at the sales office, she would be given the first opportunity to apply for it. Since such an opening would require stenographic skills, she started to study stenography at night school.

Within two months after she had transferred to the factory office, an opening for a stenographer came up at the downtown sales office. She was then transferred back to the sales office with the understanding that she would bring her stenography up to standard requirements. The transfer back to the sales office took place in June, at which time she had 15 months of service with the company.

In September, Jean had not made any favourable progress in developing her stenographic skills to the required standard. Her excuse was that there was no night school during July and August. This, of course, was quite true. However, Mr. Bowman, who had foreseen the possibility of this condition, had gone to considerable trouble in selecting some regular and special types of letters for Jean to use for practice purposes. He suggested that she have someone read these letters to her for a period every evening, taking them down in shorthand and then reading them back. Jean had not taken the office manager's suggestion seriously.

The office manager learned that the night school commenced on October 1 and about that time, he told her that he would give her until the end of December to bring her shorthand up to standard. He also warned her that her personal popularity with the office staff would not be sufficient to put her across with him and the company. He told her that if she could not produce work as required, there would be no other alternative for him but to find competent stenographic help.

Jean Talbot worked for three men in the office. These men had cooperated with the program to give Jean time to improve her shorthand. First of all, they had used dictaphones during June and July. By August, the men had been asked by the office manager to give Jean some dictation for practice. The men tried this briefly, but nearly all such dictation had to be retyped as she could not transcribe her notes. By September, the three men had returned to using the dictaphone in order to get their work out in time.

In November, Mr. Bowman again asked the three men to start giving Jean some dictation. They did so but soon found that she could not get the work done in time. Thus, the efficiency of the three men was affected to a marked degree. Towards the end of December, the office manager reviewed this phase of Jean's work with her. She claimed that she got out all the work she was given. Upon checking this claim, Mr. Bowman found that the three men had only given Jean a relatively small amount of their work. Instead of writing letters, they had been using teletypes, telegrams, and long distance phone calls.

Toward the end of January Mr. Bowman decided to dismiss Jean and told her his reasons:

1. She had failed to bring her stenography up to the standard required.
2. She had not been able to get the work out for the three men in time.
3. She had not been prompt enough in getting out the teletypes.
4. She had spent too much time in the rest room.

Mr. Bowman had this discussion with Jean after work, and asked for her resignation within two weeks.

That very evening, Jean telephoned several of the members of the office staff. She told them that she had not been given a fair chance by the company and that Mr. Bowman had given her a dirty deal. The next morning, Jean's mother phoned the district sales manager, Mr. Richard Black, and was rather abusive about the treatment given her daughter by the Glencoe Manufacturing Co. Mr. Black told Jean's mother that he was completely in accord with the action taken by Mr. Bowman. Next Mrs. Talbot phoned Mr. Bowman to tell him that Jean would not come in to the office any more. Mr. Bowman terminated Jean's salary immediately.

That day was a difficult one for Mr. Bowman. He soon found that he had a minor mutiny on his hands, because Jean had been very popular with all the staff. He was aware of this, but had not fully appreciated its intensity. First of all, Jean's best friend, Nancy Turner, came in to see him and pleaded with him for some time. The next day Miss Thompson, secretary to the president, handed in her resignation. Later that day, one of the salesmen told Mr. Bowman: "I hear that Miss Thompson has resigned and that several of the other girls are looking around for other positions. You had better watch out or you won't have any office staff here."

13

Hovey and Beard Co.

PART 1

The Hovey and Beard Co. manufactured wooden toys of various kinds: animals, pull toys, and the like. One part of the manufacturing process involved spraying paint on the partially assembled toys. This operation was staffed entirely by girls.

The toys were cut, sanded, and partially assembled in the wood room. Then they were dipped into shellac, and afterwards painted. The toys were predominantly two-coloured; a few were made in more than two colours. Each colour required an additional trip through the paint room.

For a number of years, these toys had been produced entirely by hand. However, to meet tremendously increased demand, the painting operation had recently been re-engineered so that eight girls who did the painting sat in a line by an endless chain of hooks. These hooks moved continuously past the line of girls and into a long horizontal oven. Each girl sat at her own painting booth, specially designed to carry away fumes and to backstop excess paint. The girl would take a toy from the tray beside her, position it in a jig inside the painting cubicle, spray on the colour according to a pattern, then release the toy and hang it on the hook passing by. The rate at which the hooks moved had been calculated by the engineers so that each girl, when fully trained, would be able to hang a painted toy on each hook before it passed beyond her reach.

The girls working in the paint room were on a group bonus plan. Since the operation was new to them, they were receiving a learning bonus that decreased by regular amounts each month. The learning bonus was scheduled to vanish in six months, by which time it was expected that they would be on their own—that is, able to meet the standard and to earn a group bonus when they exceeded it.

PART 2

By the second month of the training period, trouble had developed. The girls learned more slowly than had been anticipated, and it began to look as though their production would stabilize far below expectation level. Many of the hooks were going by empty. The girls complained that they were going by too fast, and that the time-study man had set the rates wrong. A few girls quit and had to be replaced, which further aggravated the learning problems. The team spirit which the management had expected to develop automatically through the group bonus was not in evidence except as an expression of what the engineers called "resistance." One girl whom the group regarded as its leader (and the management regarded as the ringleader) was outspoken in making the various complaints of the group to the foreman: the job was a messy one, the hooks moved too fast, the incentive pay was not being correctly calculated, and it was too hot working so close to the drying oven.

The Hovey and Beard case from *Money and Motivation*, edited by William F. Whyte. Copyright © 1955 by Harper and Row. Reproduced with permission.

14

Jack McGraw

For three months Jack McGraw had been president of the Central Hamilton Chapter of Squires International, a voluntary community service club. During that time he had become increasingly concerned about the problems facing the chapter, and questioned his own effectiveness as chief executive in handling those problems.

NORTH YORK CHAPTER EXPERIENCE

There were local chapters of Squires International throughout Canada and the United States. While many of these chapters were becoming involved in community service projects in general, most of the organization's effort was directed toward youth work. The chapters organized team sports, provided recreational facilities, and planned events such as hockey tournaments and bicycle rallies. The money for these activities was provided through the chapters' various fund-raising projects such as bingo, raffles, dances, and exhibitions. Many of the chapters had received commendation from local governments and police forces for their efforts in combatting and reducing juvenile delinquency.

Before joining the Central Hamilton Chapter, Jack had been a member of the North York Chapter for five years. During two of those years, he had served as vice president in charge of external activities. Chairmen in charge of such activities as community service, fund raising, and youth work were responsible to him. His counterpart was a vice president in charge of internal activities who worked with chairmen involved in membership, finance, and program activities. The organization was typical of all Squires International chapters. Jack had gained a great deal of personal satisfaction from his association with the North York Chapter, and he was anxious to join a chapter in Hamilton when he was transferred there by his company.

The North York Chapter was a highly successful club in spite of a very weak beginning. In retrospect, members attributed its success to a single member, Roy Wizowski. Roy had joined the chapter during its second year and the following year was elected president. He recognized that this triumph was a dubious honour since he had run unopposed. Nevertheless, he treated the post with utmost respect. Roy was described by members as a tireless, enthusiastic individual who could easily instill his own enthusiasm in others. The chapter's fortunes were reversed with Roy's pet project: the establishment of a hockey league in North York. The hockey league required an arena and thus the chapter found itself suddenly committed to two large projects.

Some members thought Wizowski was striving too high, but he soon had fund-raising projects under way as well as a high-powered membership drive. Jack was among the men introduced to the club during that drive. He had been hesitant about joining the club because at twenty-two he was considerably younger than the majority of members who ranged in age from late twenties through early forties. Roy was insistent that the chapter *needed* Jack, his help would be invaluable in dealing with young people. Jack, like all members of the chapter, learned that it was impossible to say "no" to Roy Wizowski. Even after his term of office Roy remained the driving force behind the success of the group.

ESTABLISHMENT OF CENTRAL HAMILTON CHAPTER

Jack was employed as a manager of the Hamilton branch of a national chain of department stores. After his transfer to the city, he attended meetings of various local chapters of Squires International. All of these were long established clubs. Each had its pet project around which most of its efforts were centered. None seemed anxious to branch into anything new. For some, this attitude predicted disaster as established members became apathetic and the club had difficulty in attracting new members.

At one of these meetings Jack met the district coordinator of Squires International who described a new chapter that was being organized. This new chapter, to be chartered as the Central Hamilton Chapter, was a new concept in Squires clubs. First, the club would be made up predominantly of younger men between twenty and thirty years of age. More importantly, there was a fundamental difference in the group's emphasis. It was to deal with problems, such as drug abuse, which were common to all areas of the city. At the same time, the district coordinator hoped that the members would establish organized recreation for young people in the previously neglected core area of the city. Jack was excited by what he heard and agreed to attend an organizational meeting.

Jack joined the Central Hamilton Chapter and was elected vice president in charge of internal activities. The president of the club was a young lawyer and the external activities vice president, an insurance salesman. Both appeared to share Jack's enthusiasm for the new club.

The membership of the club numbered forty-five on charter night early in October; everyone seemed very enthusiastic. Included in the group were twelve university and community college students, four high school teachers, two social workers, eight salesmen, three private businessmen, and two lawyers. A notable plus, the members felt, was the inclusion of two city aldermen in the chapter. Jack was the only member who had prior experience as a Squire, but help was promised from the sponsoring chapter.

During the months immediately before and after the charter was received, a large number of social events were held. Other Hamilton chapters invited the men to their meetings to welcome them as new Squires. The Central Hamilton Squires themselves organized several parties for the men and their wives. Both Jack and his wife were impressed with the conviviality and enthusism of the group.

The social gatherings resulted in the initiation of a few projects. One weekend about eight of the members and their families took a group of children from a local orphanage on a camping trip. Most of the members volunteered to supervise boy's basketball and floor hockey games in a church basement in the core area. One of the social workers had initiated a "help" program for reformed drug abusers. Two raffles held before Christmas provided the funds for these projects and others. The club seemed to be off to a successful start.

After Christmas, however, there were some foreboding signs. Attendance at the twice-monthly dinner meetings fell off. Some members would wait until after dinner to arrive claiming that they could not afford the meal. Similarly, the club had difficulty in collecting membership dues. In March, the group was forced to locate its meeting in another, less attractive setting because attendance had not been sufficient to meet the minimum cover charge for the room. The excess had been taken from the dues kitty; but the kitty was dwindling. Meanwhile all efforts at fund raising had ceased, thus limiting community service projects.

In April the president-elect was badly injured in an automobile accident that forced him to remain in the hospital for an extended period of time. During the third week he phoned the president of the chapter to notify him of his resignation from the club. He said that he would have a great deal of work to catch up on when released from the hospital and would not be able to spare any time.

As a result, Jack was named president-elect. He welcomed the opportunity since he was still very optimistic about the club's future.

THE RECREATION CENTRE

In May, Phil Whalen, a member of the chapter, came forward with a proposal from his uncle, Mr. Henry Jenkins. Mr. Jenkins owned an abandoned factory in the core area of the city. He had planned to tear the building down and sell the property, but now offered the Squires the use of the building as a recreation centre if they would agree to pay the taxes on it. Alternatively, he would sell them the property for $10 000, which represented one-half its appraised value *if* they agreed to use it for youth work.

Jack and other members of the executive visited the site the following day. They were impressed by the size of the building and by the opportunities it presented. It was located in the older section of the city, an area with few recreational facilities. The high concentration of juvenile crime in the area had often been attributed to the lack of organized recreational activities. Jack saw this as the answer to the club's problems, likening it to Roy Wizowski's hockey league.

Jack's enthusiasm seemed to carry over to the other members of the club. The next meeting of the Squires was held at the factory. Attendance was almost 100 per cent. The members toured the factory, each making suggestions on how to utilize the rooms and commenting on the work that had to be done. They agreed unanimously to take over the building and convert it into a neighbourhood community centre.

Almost immediately, teams of the club's members started tearing down interior walls, sweeping, washing, repairing, and painting. This early industry, however, did not continue. By late June there was little indication of progress. Often the work teams spent more time playing basketball at the rear of the building than they did working. Oddly enough these men blamed the lack of progress on others who were not coming out as often. There had been a very big clash between two members who argued over who was "in charge of the building." Jack was able to settle the disagreement, but the friction had already broken the spirit of a few members. The summer broke up many of the work teams as members left for vacation. In mid-July the president of the chapter announced that he would be out of town until September. He suggested that Jack take over as president immediately instead of waiting until September. Jack agreed. He and a few other dedicated members continued to work at the factory a couple of nights a week, but their enthusiasm, too, was waning.

FUND-RAISING PROBLEMS

Meanwhile, in their excitement over the factory, the members had forgotten about fund raising. Plans which the fund-raising chairman had put forth were rejected with little discussion. Jack saw that the members were reticent about it. He had hoped their enthusiasm for the opportunities presented by the factory would carry over to fund raising. Some members were frank and admitted that they didn't like to ask anyone for money, even if the cause was right. Jack suspected that most members felt this way.

In August, Jack received the first municipal tax bill for the factory property. It was payable within ten days and an emergency meeting was called. The members voted to borrow the money from the bank; each signed a promissory note for a portion of the loan. They discussed possible fund-raising projects and agreed that "something" had to be done, but no one agreed on a specific course of action.

One night after Jack and three of the members had finished some work at the factory, the subject of fund raising came up again. The four decided to run a raffle and to have tickets printed without the approval of the group as a whole. Once the tickets were printed, they felt the members would feel obliged to sell them.

Details of the raffle were explained and the books distributed at the next dinner meeting. No one expressed any opposition to the raffle or dissatisfaction with the way it had come about. Jack emphasized that it was important that the group sell the tickets since the bank would soon be asking for repayment of the loan. The members agreed to *try* to sell the tickets. Tickets were delivered personally to the large number of members not at the meeting that night.

Jack took over much of the responsibility for this fund-raising project. Each week he phoned or visited each of the members to encourage them to sell the tickets and to get a tally on the number sold to date. On each occasion he warned that the failure of this project would result in loss of the factory. Many of the members said the tickets were too difficult to sell.

By October, Jack knew that the raffle was not going to be a success. In fact, a tally taken at a meeting showed the club would actually *lose* money when the draw took place. The members present agreed to try to sell more tickets so that the club would at least break even. The fund-raising chairman did not think this was enough. He said there was no sense in going through all this effort simply to break even. Furthermore, he felt that because he had been able to sell more than his quota others should do the same. The discussion became an argument and many harsh statements were shouted in anger. Jack calmed everyone down and the meeting ended with no further incidents. Afterwards the fund-raising chairman apologized to Jack, but resigned from the club. He said that he had better things to do with his time than sit on a sinking ship.

OTHER PROBLEMS

It was not the first resignation he had received, and Jack had learned not to try to convince anyone to stay. In fact, membership had fallen to twenty-eight in spite of the introduction of five new members. Jack hated to lose the resignees who were hard workers, but efforts to convince them not to quit were unsuccessful. Losing members was not unusual, but inductees were expected to at least balance the outflow. The small number of inductees was partially due to the lack of a recruiting effort by the individual members. Where members had brought prospective members to meetings, the membership chairman had failed to follow up with a letter inviting them to join. This simple procedure had proved a valuable tool for other Squires chapters in recruiting new members, yet it wasn't being done in the Central Hamilton Chapter.

Jack wondered if the fund-raising chairman had been accurate in describing the chapter as a "sinking ship." The club's difficulties were not limited to fund raising; dues collection, meeting attendance and membership were also problem areas. The chapter's program chairman had been remiss in his duties too, and the club had not had a guest speaker at many meetings.

The chairmen in charge of community service and youth work were both energetic and had initiated some worthwhile projects. Unfortunately, they often worked alone because they were tired of begging people to come out to help. Jack felt that once members were exposed to the worthwhile kinds of projects these men had instigated they would want to help. He knew it was necessary to push the members into projects but considered it up to the individual chairmen to provide this push even if it was a hard, frustrating job.

Fred Mathers, publicity chairman, also presented a problem for Jack. Fred was the fourth person to take over this position and the first who had managed to get the biweekly news bulletin out on time. Under earlier chairmen it often did not get out at all. Fred's bulletins were thorough, imaginative and interesting. Unfortunately, Fred tended to get carried away with his enthusiasm for producing an entertaining bulletin. Some of the language and cartoons had proved offensive to some members and definitely to the president of Squires International, who received copies of all chapters' bulletins. He reminded Jack that the bulletin was sent to the members' homes so that the whole family could read it. Jack agreed but did not know how to approach Fred. He feared that his criticism might dull Fred's interest. Thus, Jack found that even the bright spots in the organization presented difficulties for him.

To compound his troubles, Jack's workload at the department store was expected to be heavy due to an upcoming store-wide sale. This would leave him with little time to do Squires work. Furthermore, his wife had been urging him to resign from the club because it took up so much of his time and paid off only in frustration for him. Initially, Jack had promised himself that he would give the club a full year as president during which he would try his utmost to make it a success. Now, after only three months, he wondered if he shouldn't give up the presidency to someone who might handle it better.

15

La Femme Fashion Boutiques (B)

"Our first boutique is scheduled to open in eight weeks," said Dean Marshall, "so we have a relatively short period of time in which to hire a manager. Since she will control our major source of revenue, which is the sale of products, as well as the fact that we will spend approximately $1500 to train her, it is extremely important that we select the right person for the position."

Dean went on to say, "We have put all of our own money into the company so we are forced to draw some salary. We are also obligated to make monthly payments on the money we borrowed. Since the company is incurring operating expenses and expected revenues are uncertain, it is crucial at this stage of our corporate development that we do not make any decision which could jeopardize our present or future working capital position."

After graduating from university, Dean Marshall and Vince McClain incorporated Marshall and McClain Ltd. Their initial capital was approximately $100 000, over two-thirds of which was borrowed and personally guaranteed. They purchased from a Chicago company the Ontario franchise for La Femme Cosmetic Boutiques. The contract they signed allowed them complete freedom to adapt the concept to suit the Canadian market.

McClain and Marshall demanded this type of contract because they were not satisfied with the American design for the interior of the boutique and had decided to change its general atmosphere to give it a very modern, intimate and personalized image. In addition to these changes, they also wanted to expand the product line to fit the new atmosphere. They would search for, screen and select new products that would appeal to their defined major target market—women from fifteen to thirty-five years of age. The product line would include high fashion "mod" clothing as well as jewellery and other accessories. In other words, the original concept of a cosmetic boutique was completely changed to one of a fashion boutique.

During the first three months of incorporation, Vince had contacted various suppliers of merchandise and put together a complete product mix. Dean found a location in a large mall suitable for their first boutique with floor space of approximately 1000 square feet (40 ft by 25 ft, roughly comparable to the size of an average classroom).

The mall was situated in North Toronto near a major expressway and was adequately serviced by public transportation. The surrounding market area was almost entirely residential with a population of 425 000. The mall had eighty-five stores, two of which were major department stores. All of the services usually provided by a mall to ensure customer convenience and satisfaction were available. This was the type of location that was planned for all future boutiques.

Vince commented concerning the type of person required for the job. "Because of the product and service we are offering to our consumer group, I feel we must hire a manager with whom our customers can identify. Age and physical appearance is therefore very important. Such a person will be expected to dress according to the current fashions and know how to wear and match her clothes and cosmetics for best effects.

"We intend to give the woman we hire almost complete freedom and flexibility in the operation of the boutique. However, she will not be directly involved in the purchasing of merchandise for the product line. Dean and I will concentrate our efforts in this area as well as the overall expansion of the company so we will not have time available to become involved in the day-to-day managing of each boutique."

Part of the manager's responsibilities would include hiring, training and supervising additional part-time sales personnel. Since the boutique was required to be open from

10:00 A.M. to 10:00 P.M., six days a week, it was estimated that two temporary sales girls would be necessary.

Part-time sales girls could expect to earn $2.65 an hour. They would be required to work during the busy times at the mall, which included Wednesday, Thursday, and Friday evenings and all day Saturday. The manager was also expected to be at the boutique during these hours.

One part-time sales girl could be left alone at the boutique during slow periods at the mall. Such periods were usually Monday, Tuesday and Wednesday mornings and Saturday evenings.

The manager would keep up-to-date on modern style changes and colour combinations for various types of clothing by reading modern fashion magazines and attending major local fashion shows. She would also do most of the selling in the boutique. In addition, the manager would be responsible for keeping a very simple bookkeeping system, paying all bills under fifty dollars, compiling weekly sales reports, balancing the cash account, paying the part-time sales girls, and making daily cash deposits at a nearby bank. Since cooperative promotion and sales were customary among location owners in large mall complexes, the manager would work in conjunction with other store managers in the mall to promote the sale of La Femme products.

Regarding the manager's salary, Dean commented, "Initally we cannot afford to pay whomever we hire a great deal of money. We plan to pay her a basic salary of $125 a week which is comparable to an average secretary's salary. This will be supplemented by a 4 per cent commission on net sales and we expect the average daily sales volume to reach $275 once the store is established. We will also, of course, have to pay the employee's portion of various compulsory fringe benefits. In addition to monetary remuneration, she will spend two weeks in Washington, D.C., at our expense where she will receive excellent training at a leading fashion school in the various aspects of coordinating styles, colours and accessories to complement the physical appearance and personality of the customer."

Since Dean and Vince had developed a new and unproven approach to merchandising this type of product and service, they realized it would be difficult to accurately predict the future success of their company. Because of their limited financial resources, they estimated they had sufficient working capital to last only eight to ten months if their target market did not accept the products and services offered in the boutique. Therefore, it was imperative to get the boutique open, keep overhead low, and generate as much revenue as possible.

An advertisement briefly describing the job and the requirements of the position was placed in the job opportunities section of a daily Toronto newspaper (Exhibit 1). All replies were by letter. Exhibit 2 contains three letters typical of those received. Vince and Dean planned to personally interview the better applicants. Not only did they have to decide which applicant was best suited for this particular manager's position, but they also wanted to develop their selection and hiring process since their objective was to open three more boutiques during the first year of operation and this would mean hiring three new managers.

Exhibit 1
La Femme Fashion Boutiques (B)

Actual Size of Advertisement

The advertisement as it appeared in the job opportunity section of a daily Toronto newspaper.

POSITION AVAILABLE

POSITION	Manager of a women's fashion boutique in a centrally located, large shopping mall.
THE JOB	Selling very modern, high fashion women's clothing and accessory items. Managing the operation of the boutique.
REQUIREMENTS	Attractive, well groomed, sales ability and experience necessary, management experience desired. Willing to accept responsibility and use own judgement. Reply giving brief personal history to: La Femme Fashion Boutiques, c/o Marshall and McClain Ltd., P.O. Box 201, Station B, Toronto, Ontario.

Exhibit 2

220 Holt Road,
Etobicoke, Ontario.
June 10, 1973

La Femme Fashion Boutiques,
c/o Marshall and McClain Ltd,
P.O. Box 201, Station B,
Toronto, Ontario.

Dear Sirs:

I would like to apply for the position as offered in your recent advertisement. I am thirty-three years old, married and do not have any children.

I have worked in the Toronto area for the past three years as a consultant for Helena Rubenstein. My duties include visiting retail outlets, showing the buyers our new products and explaining the aspects of our products to the salesgirls. I am also responsible for setting up displays for our products.

Before working at my present position, I was a saleslady for a women's sporting goods store in Montreal. I was in the clothing section and for three years received a great deal of sales experience.

Prior to this position, I was a secretary for a large law firm in Toronto. I had general secretarial duties as well as responsibilities for collection of accounts receivable. I also acted as receptionist.

I have my senior matriculation as well as a diploma from a secretarial school. I have also taken two modelling courses from a large and reputable modelling school.

My personal interests are painting, modelling, tennis and reading. My husband is a salesman for a large company that manufactures air conditioners.

If I received the position you are offering, I would have to give two weeks' notice to my present employer. I would like the opportunity to discuss the job further.

Sincerely,

Edith Martin

1201 Langsdown Crescent,
Scarborough, Ontario.
June 8, 1973

La Femme Fashion Boutiques,
c/o Marshall and McClain Ltd,
P.O. Box 201, Station B,
Toronto, Ontario.

Dear Sirs:

I was really happy to see your ad in the paper. I have been looking for a job like this for a while now.

My name is Laura McDermott. I'm forty years old but a very modern thinker. I'm married and have three children. Two are in public school and one is in high school. My husband also has a good job.

I'm not working now. The canning company I had a position with had a lay-off and I got laid off. That was a few months ago but I was going to quit anyhow. Before that job, I worked for four years as a hairdresser. I really enjoyed that sort of thing but then I got pregnant again.

Before I worked for Helen's Beauty Shop, I worked for Eaton's selling. I got a lot of experience selling and I liked it. They are after me to come back but I would sooner have your job. I like to work with people and sell things. Eaton's said I was a good saleslady.

I read fashion magazines all the time and I make a lot of my own clothes. I go to Eaton's fashion shows all the time and the K-Mart near our home asked me to wear some of their clothes in a fashion show two weeks ago but I couldn't make it.

I know I can sell and my experience has helped me to know how to manage. I will be looking forward to hearing from you. Give me a call at 722-9600. I am usually home everyday but Wednesday afternoon.

Sincerely,

Laura McDermott

1240 Riverside Drive,
Apt. 1402,
Toronto, Ontario.
June 9, 1973

La Femme Fashions Boutiques,
c/o Marshall and McClain Ltd,
P.O. Box 201, Station B,
Toronto, Ontario.

Dear Sirs:
I am replying in regard to your recent advertisement concerning the position of manager of your fashion boutique. I will attempt to relate my personal background and general experience.

I am twenty-nine years old. I have been divorced for two years and do not have any children. I am currently employed as a saleslady for Diest Fashions. I have worked for this company for 1-1/2 years. During this period of time, I have been responsible for supervising three salesgirls.

Previous to this position, I was employed for five years by Fayette's Modelling School where I was an instructor. I terminated my employment here because I was offered a managerial position with Diest.

I have a Grade 13 education with sales and modelling experience during the summer. The sales experience was with a large merchandising chain in the women's clothing department.

The reason for my willingness to terminate my present employment is due to the fact that I am presently one of three supervisors and I do not see any chance for immediate advancement and increase in responsibilities. Remuneration is not a prime objective but there must be the possibility for future growth and development.

I have attempted to briefly outline my past history. If you would like to discuss it further, I would appreciate the opportunity to meet with you at a mutually convenient time.

Yours truly,

Patricia Lemieux

16
Maintrel Ltd. (A)

On August 21, Mark Rogers returned to his office at 6:00 P.M. He found his friend Joe Kelt, supervisor of the mechanical group, waiting for him. (See Exhibit 1 for a partial organization chart.)

"Hi Joe! I don't see you here at night very often."

"No," replied Joe, "but I heard I would probably find you here after your dinner so I stopped off to see you."

"Oh, I just wanted to clear my desk of all this paper," said Mark. "During the day I'm quite busy just keeping the jobs moving. I never get enough time to clear up the paperwork within normal hours. So I come back here for a couple of hours, twice a week, to do this."

"Why do you have to be so very busy with details, Mark? Can't your people do things by themselves?" Joe asked.

"Well, yes, and no. You see, Joe, this company can't seem to find the number of experienced engineering designers we need, so we have to depend on an inflow of new graduates. These people are intelligent and self-motivated, but they don't have very much experience. So I try my best to help. And, Joe, except one, all of my people are doing well. I don't think I will have to come in at night again after, say, about two months. They will all be in good shape by then."

Joe: Mark, I know you don't like beating around the bush, so I will come right to the point. I want to tell you something before you hear it from rumours and gossip. But, please, don't lose your cool after hearing what I have to say. Your report on the Calgary Project caused quite a stir. In fact, Bert Phillips called a meeting for 3:30 this afternoon to discuss the report.

Mark: Well! I wasn't asked to attend.

Joe: No, but don't forget that Bert is the project manager, and he explained to the rest of us that he didn't think you should be there, but he neglected to say why. Anyway, the report literally got thrown out of the window. Except for two of us, the majority decided to ignore the report.

Mark: Well, it's Bert's problem now. I did my part. Jack Manning asked me to review the Calgary Project, with emphasis on engineering design. He wanted me to find out if everything was all right. And I think I did just that. Bert's approach to the project boils down to "well, it's the client's money, so what the hell." I don't agree with that. You know, this company had been out in the cold for a few years with Felicity Ltd. They never got over the engineering and financial mess our company got them into when we put in their first automatic labelling machine in Regina. Jack knew this, and when we got our second chance we underbid everybody to the extent that we almost didn't get away with the shirts on our backs. But we got what we wanted. We managed that project so well from both technical and management points of view that Felicity now feels that we proved our worth and gave us the Calgary Project on a cost-reimbursable-plus basis. Do you think we should screw it all up now? Oh, well, I have done my share, and my responsibility ended with the report.

Next morning, Thursday, at 8:00 A.M., Mark Rogers was in Jack Manning's office. He had in his pocket two letters of resignation. One giving the company one month's notice, and the other requesting to be released at 5:00 P.M., Friday.

Manning: And how's Mark today?

Mark: O.K. Well . . . I have to talk to you for a few minutes, Jack.

Manning: Give me a couple of minutes will you, Mark. I will be right back.

Mark placed the second letter down on Jack's desk. Manning glanced through the letter and shouted, ''I won't have it. I knew it. I knew I was going to have trouble today. No, I won't accept it.''

He tore up Roger's resignation and threw it into the trash can.

Manning: You go back to your office and settle down. It's not going to happen. I won't accept it.''

Mark: Well, what's that going to do? If you don't accept it, I just have to keep going higher and higher until I reach the president's door. Then where are you going to be? The cat is really going to be out of the bag then. Think about it.

Rogers went back to his office.

In his office, Mr. Manning sat and pondered.

One year ago, Mark Rogers came to Canada from England. He came to Maintrel Ltd. as a freelance mechanical designer through an employment agency. He seemed like a loner to most of the supervisors he worked with. But within the first month of his employment, everybody concerned agreed that he was one of the best designers they had ever had. He never seemed too talkative, never wasted his own or anybody's time, and in fact whenever a job was given to him, he never needed to discuss any problem with his supervisors. Mark Rogers was an engineer with about seven years' experience in design and two further years' experience in project management. With this information, and personal knowledge of his capability, Mr. Manning offered him a substantial salary, more than Rogers was earning as a freelancer, if he would join Maintrel full time. When he explained that the position was permanent with unlimited potential for advancement, Rogers took the job.

Manning noticed a change in Rogers' attitude within about two months after he started with Maintrel. In fact, he became a sort of father confessor-cum-advisor to most of his co-workers. It was apparently never too troublesome to him to lend a hand to less experienced men with problems, even when he was most heavily loaded with work himself. He was not regarded as a bosom pal by everybody, but he was thought of as a man one could go to for help, if needed.

Seven months later one of the three engineering supervisors quit the company for a better job. An immediate replacement to fill the vacancy could not be found because of a general shortage of experienced talent in the industry. Manning decided then to use Rogers as a temporary replacement in this position. When he asked Rogers if he would like to try the job out, Mark accepted it without any outward show of emotions, but Manning had a feeling that Rogers was pleased.

During the next six months Rogers functioned in that position quite successfully, Manning thought. In fact, quite a few of the designers came to see Manning, especially to tell him how well they liked working with Rogers, and requested that they not be transferred to any other group. They indicated that their daily work-problems did not seem like problems at all. They were mostly young designers, and probably liked working with a young supervisor, Manning thought. These events led Manning to consider seriously offering Rogers the position permanently. At about this time the company's manager of construction requested Mr. Manning to consider a Mr. Hugh Horton for the position Rogers was holding temporarily. The interdepartmental relationship between the engineering and construction departments had always been in a state of hostility. Mr. Manning felt that the construction manager's request was well worth considering, since ''a favour done is a favour returned.'' Furthermore, Mr. Horton's supervisory ability seemed to be outstanding and he appeared well qualified in all respects, including the fact that he had spent a couple of years in Engineering Design at the start of his career. He was reasonably young, and commanded high praise from the construction manager, who more than hinted that he would like to see Mr. Horton advance. Upon considerable deliberation, Mr. Manning decided to offer Mr. Horton the position, and acted upon it.

He realized that Rogers could be upset on hearing this news, but decided to promise Rogers the next vacancy that occurred. He called Rogers into his office and informed him of the changes. He carefully noted Rogers's reaction to this news and felt relieved when Rogers left his office, laughingly saying, ''Well, it was pretty good while it lasted, but don't worry about it, the job was a temporary one to me anyway.''

About a month after Mr. Horton took over the group a major contract was awarded to Maintrel by a very large diversified company, Felicity Ltd. Some years ago Maintrel had a project to design and construct an automatic product labelling unit for Felicity Ltd., and because of certain organizational problems within Maintrel, coupled with lack of experienced supervisory staff, Maintrel failed to satisfy its client. This resulted in Felicity's declaring it would not consider giving Maintrel any further business. Maintrel management was concerned about this problem, and decided to ''buy'' a project under Public Tender by bidding deliberately low, so that Maintrel could get a chance to restore a good relationship with Felicity. In fact, this course of action proved successful, since Maintrel's board of directors issued a definite directive to all related departmental heads that the talent employed in this particular project must be the best Maintrel could offer. The client was so pleased with the marked quality of work that sometime later Felicity awarded a further contract to Maintrel, which not only ran into several millions of dollars, but also was at no financial risk to Maintrel as it was on a cost-plus basis. This was known as the Calgary Project.

About three quarters of the way through the engineering stage of this contract, Mr. Manning became concerned about any potential foul-up of the project, similar to that experienced by the company before. He wanted a thorough and independent analysis of his department's handling of the job before it went to the client, so that any problems uncovered could be erased at source. Since Mark Rogers had been involved in the last successful contract with Felicity Ltd., and was not associated with the current contract, Mr. Manning decided he was the most suitable man for the job.

On August 20, 1970, after spending three whole weeks independently investigating all design feasibilities associated with the project, Rogers produced a report which was highly critical of the design features of some very crucial parts of the project. Mr. Manning passed it on to Mr. Bert Phillips, project manager, expressly warning him of the possible consequences that might follow should contents of the report prove to be correct. A meeting was called on that day to discuss the report, and by a majority vote, coupled with assurances from Mr. Phillips that the project was going well, they decided to ignore the report.

At this time, Mr. Manning personally felt that Mark Rogers was correct in his assessment of the state of the project, but he felt Mr. Phillips, as project manager, must be given a free hand to decide upon his own affairs. But now, with Mark Rogers's letter of resignation in the trash can, he felt a little uncomfortable. He collected the pieces carefully and taped them together. He felt worse now than he felt when he first looked at it, and he pondered his problem.

Exhibit 1
Partial Organization Structure of Maintrel Ltd.

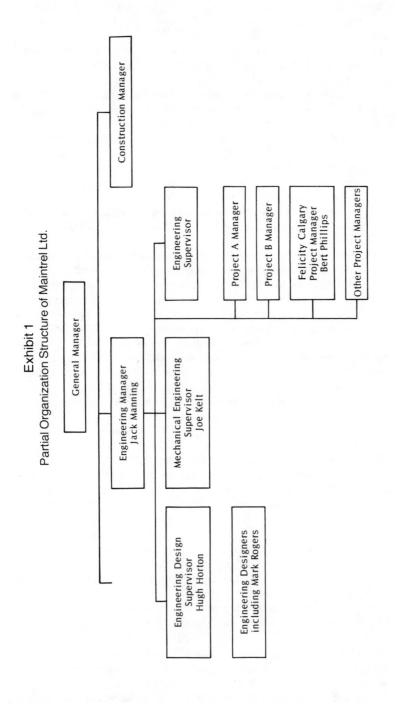

Maintrel Ltd. (B)

After considering his problem with Mark Rogers briefly, Mr. Manning decided to telephone Mr. Phillips.

Manning: Bert, I want a copy of Rogers's report.

Phillips: You sound pretty upset. What's the matter? Is there anything I can do?

Manning: Look, I am not in any mood for social chats right now. As a matter of fact, I don't like the idea of losing Rogers today, he's my best designer.

Phillips: Has he resigned?

Manning: Yes—and has given us two days.

Phillips: The damn fool. Has he got a job to go to or something?

Manning: What do you think?

Phillips: He always did seem pretty arrogant and irresponsible to me. Does he realize that his family is going to be in a lot of trouble financially if he leaves like this?

Manning: Never mind, just send me that report. And I want you to get in touch with Felicity and get their opinion on our situation with the project. Make out you are looking for an answer to a very hypothetical question. Don't, repeat don't, raise their suspicion, about the kinds of problems Rogers foresees, but I want to check out Rogers ideas and I want it fast, Bert.

At 3:00 the same afternoon Mr. Manning had a call from Mr. Phillips.

Phillips: I'm sorry Jack, I guess I have to eat my hat this time. Felicity's answer to my inquiry was, in summary, what Rogers said. I guess I have to go along with his recommendations under the circumstances.

Manning: You haven't helped my stomach any by that, Bert, but get on with the changes now. Leave me to wrestle with my problems.

Maintrel Ltd. (C)

Mr. Manning called Mark Rogers into his office late Thursday afternoon. He told him that the changes he recommended had been considered and found justifiable and were being effected immediately. He thanked Rogers for being so capable, and for saving the company from a situation of disastrous consequences.

Manning: Look, Mark, I am sorry this ever happened. I promise I will make it up to you for saving my skin.

Rogers: That may be so, Jack, but I am still leaving tomorrow. It's nicer to retreat in victory than in defeat. Thanks, but I don't think I have any alternative.

Manning: Think it over, Mark. I can assure you that you have a great future with the company. Let's get together again tomorrow morning.

Maintrel Ltd. (D)

Early Friday morning, before seeing Mark Rogers, Mr. Manning had a visit from Maintrel's personnel manager, Mr. Richard Howel.

Howel: I just had a call from a friend of mine in the personnel department of Felicity Ltd. I think you ought to know.

Manning: You might as well get it over with if it is bad news of any kind. I think I can take another ounce over the pound I have had so far.

Howel: Did you know Mark Rogers has had an offer to go to Felicity as contract coordinator?

Manning: No. When?

Howel: It seems they know of him quite well. Somehow or other some of the members of their senior management group learned about Rogers leaving us, so they asked their personnel man to get hold of him right away. He did and met Rogers last night. Well Jack, apparently they couldn't care less even about interviewing him. So, in short, they hope Rogers will start there on Monday to handle mainly their major capital projects. I think you know what that means.

    Mr. Manning looked very worried and wondered what, if anything, he ought to do next.

17
Pollockk Emergency Vehicle Sales Ltd.

On June 1, a meeting had been held between Peter Dekker, production foreman, Jim Devanie, the fiberglass mould maker, and Dan Patterson, general manager, to make final arrangements for the new fiberglass headliner, required for a new class of ambulance, the SBS74. It was agreed that Jim would have the new mould completed and the first headliner ready for installation by July 31. After a conversation with the first SBS74 customer, Dan decided a few changes should be made in the headliner. The customer felt that having a storage cupboard in the headliner would be useful. On June 15, Dan instructed Jim to make several design changes. Two days later, Peter noticed the changes and instructed Jim to change the work back to the original specifications. To carry out Peter's instructions, Jim would drop a week behind schedule unless he worked a considerable amount of overtime. This was not the first time that Jim had been forced to work weekends because of a mix-up between Peter and Dan. Outraged, Jim demanded that Peter find out who was boss or he was quitting that afternoon.

The Ambulance Division was engaged in custom designing and building ambulances. The basic process involved the modification and conversion of existing vehicles. Production orders would be received from the customer by Peter. He would estimate completion dates and schedule the completion of the preliminary vehicle work. Wood and fiberglass products would be brought directly to the vehicle for installation on schedule. Preliminary work usually took one day and the entire production five days, once the wood and fiberglass parts were available. A lead time of two weeks was required for the wood and fiberglass shops.

Peter Dekker was forty years old. Prior to joining Pollockk's, he was employed as a foreman for a local furniture plant. With five children, Peter had been forced to moonlight as a cab driver. The increased wage at Pollockk's enabled him to give up the cab job. Within a year after joining Pollockk's, Peter had started work on a new five-bedroom house. Peter believed that it was best to treat his men as friends. He was always reluctant to assert authority. If a man was slacking off, Peter would assign the work to someone else rather than disciplining the worker.

The general manager, Dan Patterson, previously had been the sole owner of the Ambulance Division for twenty-seven years. Stiff competition and a need for future capital forced Dan to merge with Pollockk's. Prior to going into business, Dan had spent five years as an officer in the navy. Exhibit 1 shows the organizational structure before and after the merger.

Jim Devanie was forty-five years old. He had been in the mould-making trade for twenty-two years. Previously, Jim had worked for a large mobile home manufacturer as head of the fiberglass department, where he had been in charge of new mould preparations and repairs to the old ones. Fabricating moulds was a painstaking task which required a great deal of experience. Jim was highly regarded by the mobile home manufacturer's management. He said that he quit there to come to Pollockk's because the pressures of having more than one boss hindered his workmanship.

Jim was periodically absent because of a drinking problem. His attendance was very irregular, but when he was on the job he did excellent work. Under most circumstances management wouldn't have kept him on, but his skills were such that he was worth the trouble. Jim took great pride in his moulds. He had made it quite clear to Peter that he wanted to know who his boss was and that he would only report to that one boss.

Peter was unsure what to do. He felt that Jim was just blowing off steam, but a confrontation with Dan might be necessary.

Exhibit 1
Organizational Structure of Ambulance Manufacturing Division

Before Merger

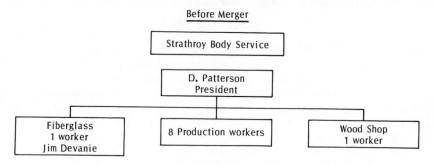

After Merger

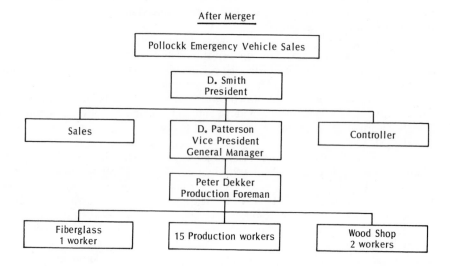

18

Queon Textile Mills Ltd.

Allan Bulmer, general foreman of the Queenstown plant of Queon Textile, had just received a call from Mrs. Floyd Woods concerning the disciplinary action taken against her husband during the night shift.

Allan Bulmer was fifty-two years old. He was born and raised in Queenstown, and had known the Woods for as long as he could remember. Mr. Bulmer had been with Queon Textile for over twenty-eight years, having joined them as an unskilled worker. His willingness to undertake difficult assignments had led to further opportunities in the Queenstown mill. Mr. Bulmer had done almost every job there was in the Queenstown plant, and was promoted to assistant foreman, then foreman and finally general foreman. As general foreman, Mr. Bulmer reported to the plant superintendent and was responsible for the scheduling of men and machinery. Under his direct supervision, he had seven operating foremen and one foreman responsible for maintenance.

Floyd Woods was fifty-five. He was born in Queenstown and had joined Queon Textile twenty-five years ago. He joined the company as a skilled tradesman, assigned to the repair and maintenance department. Mr. Woods's skills were highly regarded in the Queenstown mill, and he had proven to be the most able maintenance man in the mill. Several times, Mr. Woods had been offered a promotion to assistant foreman but had declined. Three years ago, however, the opening of assistant foreman was posted on the employees' bulletin board, before being offered to Mr. Woods. Immediately after the notice was posted, Mr. Woods went to the personnel manager and asked why the job had not been offered to him first. The personnel manager replied that, given his continual refusals, he had assumed he was not interested in the job. Mr. Woods responded that he could do the job and that he was the best man in the department. After further discussion, Mr. Woods applied for, was offered and accepted the position of assistant foreman.

Mr. Woods undertook the assignment with relish. The foreman of maintenance, Gerry Clarke, was a man Mr. Woods had trained several years before and he was glad to have him as his assistant. Mr. Woods was given the task of managing the night shift maintenance schedule, which was a change because previously he had worked the prime shift from eight to four.

For several months after the change, things seemed to go well, and Mr. Clarke was satisfied. Maintenance schedules were kept, and the work done was of acceptable quality. However, some eighteen months after Mr. Woods's appointment as assistant foreman, the performance of the night shift work crew began to deteriorate. Consequently, Mr. Clarke approached Mr. Woods about the problem. Mr. Woods said he had not realized that the work was sloppy, and that he would talk to his crew that night. The talk between Clarke and Woods seemed to have some effect. The quality of work returned to its past level.

Several weeks before, Mr. Woods had shown up for the night shift intoxicated. When discovered, a warning was given and Mr. Woods was sent home. Thereafter, it was not obvious that Mr. Woods was drinking, though his speech and movements became awkward as the night shift passed. Concurrently, the level of performance of the night shift maintenance group again deteriorated. Several of the night shift men complained to Mr. Clarke about Mr. Woods.

In response to the complaints, Mr. Clarke returned to the plant in the middle of the night shift and found Mr. Woods asleep. Mr. Clarke awakened Mr. Woods with difficulty and told him he was suspended. An argument followed which ended with Mr. Clarke stating that Mr. Woods's days as an assistant foreman were over, and about all Mr. Woods was good for was pushing a broom, "if he could ever find the right end of the handle." Mr. Clarke, with the help of a few night shift workers, was able to get Mr. Woods into a taxicab and on his way home.

The next morning, Mrs. Woods called Mr. Bulmer and asked him to rescind Mr. Clarke's decision to demote her husband. Mrs. Woods stated that she was concerned about any change in Mr. Woods's status that would affect him and make his situation worse. Upon questioning, Mrs. Woods admitted that her husband did have a drink or two before going to work, but "nothing that would cause any problems." In concluding her call Mrs. Woods stated she could not understand how the company could treat a loyal employee this way.

19
Sturbridge Electric Corp.

Personnel of the Sturbridge Electric Corp. were entering the final stages of running acceptance tests on a computer they had contracted to supply to the armed services. One of the stipulations in the acceptance test was a demonstration by the contractor that the computer would function correctly and reliably under actual operating conditions with the special program prepared by Sturbridge Electric's chief programmer, Al Abrams. Several days prior to starting this test Abrams submitted his program to his immediate superior, Bill Eden, who was computer project engineer (see Exhibit 1). Eden had to determine that the equation was in proper form so that when it was run through the computer with predetermined inputs, the solution could be checked against hand-calculated values. It was not intended that Eden check the correctness of the translation from mathematical symbols to the computer ''language'' since the forthcoming operational tests would confirm that fact. In the course of the check, Eden found that Abrams had taken some liberties in one of the terms of the equation. When asked about it, Abrams replied that he was aware of the discrepancy but that it would make no difference in the end result. Eden discussed the matter with Charlie Small, another computer engineer for Sturbridge, and they agreed that the program was not acceptable as presented. When Abrams learned of their decision he became enraged and made some very caustic remarks about their ability to pass judgement on his work. His closing comments were:

''I'm not going to have my work checked by everyone! I've been working on this program a long time and I'm the only one that can say whether or not it's okay! You guys have made my life miserable from the very start! You sneak around behind my back and pull all sorts of stunts. I deserve to know that's going on around here. Eden, you've driven me like a common labourer since you were assigned to this job. You've never given me any help—I've been all alone on this job. I don't know what to expect next! As far as I'm concerned this is the finish. I quit!''

With that he walked rapidly from the computer room. Harris Johnson, supervisor of the field test facility, who had heard the last part of the conversation, finally caught up with him at the door. Abrams tried to turn in his badge.

Johnson: I won't take your badge now. Take a minute to relax and calm down.
Abrams: Damn it! Take it!
Johnson: No! Go on home and cool down. If you still want to quit in the morning, I'll accept your badge then.
Abrams: I don't want to be mollified! I don't want to cool down! If you won't take my badge, I'll leave it with the guard at the gate!

Sturbridge Electric was a large manufacturer of electrical equipment for industry, the armed services and the consumer. Their industrial electronics operations specialized in radar and all types of communications equipment. One of the subdivisions of this operation was engaged in the development of missile guidance equipment. Their field test facility at the Special Weapons Test Center in Florida had been in operation for fourteen months; its purpose was to conduct performance tests on the missile guidance system designed and built by the company. Although on a military base, the test facility operated as an independent entity insofar as the direction of its activities were concerned, and it relied on military personnel and supply for support only. For instance, although the buildings were within a classified area guarded by Military Police, the company retained responsibility for security of the project and could give or withhold permission for entrance to the area. When shipments had to be unloaded it was done under the direction of company personnel but with the help of military personnel and equipment. (The military also supplied certain types of vehicles which were in turn driven by Sturbridge employees unless some specialized skill was required. In general, the relationship was such that to preclude unnecessary duplication the armed forces provided the needed services and facilities that might be common to Sturbridge and the various other contractors with test facilities on the base.)

The Sturbridge Electric test facility supervisor reported directly to the manager of the missile control department at headquarters in Allentown, Pennsylvania. Harris Johnson had been placed in charge of the operation when it was first set up and took with him from Allentown several key people who would form the nucleus of the field organization. Technicians and others from the local area in Florida were added to the group. These personnel lived either in their own homes or in apartments nearby. The work day for the test facility staff, which numbered approximately fifteen, began at 7:00 A.M. with a coffee break at 8:00 A.M. when the Post Exchange coffee wagon made a stop at their building. The lunch period extended from 11:15 until 11:45 but, because of the nature of their work, the personnel took the half hour when it was convenient rather than observing a strict schedule. The staff members were very congenial and enjoyed many outside activities together like beach parties and fishing trips. The work day ended at 3:30 P.M. except when overtime was scheduled.

The bulk of the missile control equipment was built by the company in its Allentown plants. As it began to arrive in Florida, additional technical assistance was sent from Allentown on a temporary basis. These people reported to Johnson for administrative purposes while in Florida, although any technical direction specifically relating to their grouping of equipment was given by their respective supervisors at headquarters.

The large digital computer was the only major piece of equipment not designed and built by Sturbridge, although the company prepared the performance specifications for the machine. When it was delivered to Florida there was still a great deal of work to be finished, hence a large number of computer contractor personnel came also. To this group were added the several members of the Sturbridge computer group who had been dividing their time between Allentown and the contractor's plant in Concord, Massachusetts. The group, comprised of Bill Eden, Al Abrams, and Fred Smith, although considered temporary personnel in Florida, stayed on indefinitely while the visits of other temporary personnel rarely exceeded a week. The group, with their families, occupied adjoining two-room motel apartments at a tourist court not far from the military base. Although their wives saw each other daily and their children played together, the families did not share many common social activities. The apartments consisted of one bedroom, a large living room that made up into a bedroom, and a combination kitchen and dining area which opened off the living room and a bath. The motel was located on the ocean and, while reasonably comfortable, did not constitute luxurious accommodations by any means. Transportation to and from work was generally by company car, although all three families brought their own cars to Florida.

The fact that there were still many unresolved problems in the computer when it was delivered made the work day rather hectic. The computer contractor's personnel had first priority, since they were vitally interested in completing their work as rapidly as possible. The headquarters' interest in completing the contract and the ever mounting costs associated with the installation and check-out operation provided added pressure to the daily work. Coupled with this was the necessity for Al Abrams to begin checking out portions of the computer program as soon as the machine was in operation. It was necessary for Sturbridge to have a completed program before the computer could be put through its acceptance tests, yet work on the program, by necessity, required machine time to complete. This made it mandatory to utilize any time when the contractor's employees were not performing work which interfered with machine operation for programming work. However, much of this time was lost due to Abrams's inability to interrupt abruptly his efforts on one phase of the program and place other parts of the program, which he may have mapped out several weeks before, in the machine, run them, and evaluate the results.

Bill Eden's purpose in Florida was to represent Sturbridge on installation questions with the contractor, make preparations for the acceptance tests of the machine, and generally keep track of progress on the program. He did not have a great deal to keep him busy since the work day soon settled down and became rather routine. Much of the time he merely stood by in the computer room observing the work being done by the contractor's personnel. He was always willing to take on special jobs suggested periodically by Mr. Johnson and relished the opportunity to do something tangible. Fred Smith was kept busy running the many detailed computations on an electric calculator since it was necessary to prove each part of the program as Abrams completed it. In this way the hand-calculated results could be checked against the computer results to indicate the validity of the computer program.

Al Abrams was forty-five years old and had worked in three distinct fields: accounting, teaching and engineering. His undergraduate college training had prepared him primarily for teaching but his interest in mathematics led him into graduate work preparatory for a master's degree in that field. Al's search for further knowledge carried him into electronics and he completed in excess of 150 semester hours of undergraduate and graduate study in radio engineering.

He began his business career in the tax department of New York State, but left it after two years to take a position as test planning engineer for Northern Electronics, Inc. While there he also began teaching electronics for the Army Air Force. Following this he ventured back to accounting and served for a year as agent-in-charge for a bureau of Internal Revenue office making examinations of the tax returns of individuals, corporations, estates and trusts. During this period he also began teaching freshman and sophomore engineering physics at a New York College and continued there for seven years. Concurrently, he operated his own business, preparing financial statements and tax returns, until mid 1955. During an eight-month period he also tried various positions with four different companies in which he reviewed tax reports, gave advice on items that might invite examination by the B.I.R., audited books and prepared financial statements. In late 1952 he accepted a position as a circuit and applications engineer with Erie Tube Corp. and remained with them until he came to work for Sturbridge in April 1954.

Upon arriving at Sturbridge he was assigned to the missile control project, where he assisted in the preparation of the purchasing specification for the computer. During the time lag while the contractor was beginning production of the machine, he assisted the analysis group at headquarters on the solution of mathematical problems. Following this he was sent to the computer contractor's plant in Concord, where he attended their school for programmers as well as filling a minor capacity in the coordination of the equipment manufacture. It was during this period that he also began work on programming the actual equations to be used in Florida. It was also during this period that the original Sturbridge computer project engineer, McAlpin, was promoted and Eden was assigned the technical responsibility for the computer.

Al Abrams had spent two months at the computer contractor's school for programmers. He learned the logic of the computer he was to work with, that is, the characteristics of the various sections of the machine, how they functioned in relation to one another, the forms in which data were placed in and taken from the machine, the speeds with which computations could be handled and many other factors which provided him with the basic tools of programming. From there on the work of translating a complex mathematical equation into electrical impulses that could be fed to and acted upon by the machine was up to the ingenuity of the programmer. This required a high degree of proficiency in math and the type of mind that could, in an orderly systematic fashion, juggle a vast number of factors, until the desired result was obtained. The programming process began with the break-down of the equation into its basic elements, i.e., the solution for the sine of an angle, the taking of a cube root, or a multiplication, addition or subtraction. Generally, provision had to be made to store various bits of information and the solution of some of the elements in either the electrostatic or magnetic drum storage sections of the machine since the value was to be used later in the solution of a subsequent step. Particular attention had to be given to the amount of time taken to perform each operation since the problem was being solved in "real time," that is, the time required for the performance became an integral part of the problem and affected the final answer. Because of the close interlocking relationship between computation time and sequence of operations it was possible to have several days' programming work prove worthless because of an incongruity which suddenly appeared. When a particular element of the program was completed and proved, it was then pieced with a number of other elements to form a larger part of the entire sequence of computations, in effect pyramiding the complications that could arise from incompatibility. Each element was like a building block and it was not uncommon to find misfits, hence many painful and time-consuming repeats. In absolute magnitude the job may have hundreds of separate and distinct operations that had to be considered and could require several man years of work to complete. Al Abrams was the only member of the Sturbridge computer staff who had been through the entire programming school, although Eden and Smith had been exposed to portions of it.

One day following lunch Al Abrams walked into Johnson's office with a look of disgust on his face.

Abrams: I'm sorry, Harris, I just can't take it any longer. I've talked it over with my wife and she agrees that my health is more important. I want to resign, effective immediately. I've never had to take the kind of guff that I'm getting around here.

With this, Bill Eden walked into the office, obviously disturbed.

Abrams: I don't know what this guy (pointing to Eden) expects of me. I've never taken the kind of treatment he's been giving me off of anyone—even during the Depression when jobs were tough to find. He hounds me all day long. I just can't be driven and I can't be paced by that machine!

Eden: Al, you know I do no such thing. I try to be as considerate of you as I possibly can. We've got a job to get done and you've got to work on the machine when it's free.

Abrams: I don't work that way! When I get on a train of thought at my desk, I've got to follow it through. When you interrupt me I lose the train and it means I have to repeat the entire mental process that led up to it. I just can't stop in the middle of a programming sequence and run back to that damn computer just because it's free for a couple of minutes. I've been on a milk and crackers diet for the past two weeks because my ulcers are acting up again and it's all because of this work. You're driving me crazy!

Eden: That's not so, Al. You know damn well that I try not to aggravate you. You're so doggone touchy, it's pitiful!

Johnson: Hold on now! It's not going to do either of you any good to get hot under the collar. Let's try to get at the root of the trouble without all the fuss.

Abrams: Just take today for instance. You call me down to the machine this morning because it's going to be free for an hour. What happens? The damn thing isn't working and all my efforts were wasted. It took me two hours to retrace the steps up to the point at which you interrupted me.

Eden: It wasn't the machine, Al, your program had a mistake in it. The machine was okay.

Abrams: That's not so! You know damn well the computer was consistently failing to meet the maintenance routine splatter test limits for the electrostatic storage. How in the hell do you expect me to test part of my program with an unreliable E.S.U.?

Eden: The program checks you were making didn't involve the E.S.U.

Abrams: How the hell do you know what I was checking?

Johnson: All right, come on back to earth!

Abrams: This business had me so upset this morning that I called my wife and asked her to meet me at the PX right away so we could discuss it in private. I left here on the 11:00 A.M. bus. We decided that it just wasn't worth it. My health is more important than this job. I know I'm not doing myself any good professionally by quitting, but it's the only answer. And that's not all; I got back here at 12:00 and the first crack out of the box this guy says, "Where the hell have you been?" in a nasty tone of voice.

Eden: I did not use a nasty tone of voice! You'd been gone for an hour and a half and you didn't even have the courtesy to tell me when you left or where you were going!

Abrams: It was none of your damn business! I don't have to tell you every time I want to walk away from my desk. And for your information I told Mary[1] when I left and when I'd be back.

Johnson: How about it Bill, did you check with Mary? You know she keeps pretty good track of us.

Eden: No.

Abrams: Harris, I didn't have any trouble working in this group until Bill took over from McAlpin. Mac and I got along fine. And I don't want to put the company in an embarrassing spot by walking off before the program is complete. But I've got to think of myself.

The conversation continued along these lines for another half hour. Eden walked out after a while and Johnson and Abrams discussed in detail some of the factors behind the blowup. It became evident that Abrams had been stewing over the interruptions to his work at the desk for several weeks. A previous incident that had occurred in Allentown was also rehashed. At that time Abrams had mistakenly interpreted Eden's request for the name of one of the computer contractor's programmers as an indication that the company was out trying to hire a replacement for him and that he was going to be fired. Eden simply asked the question and gave no explanation. After Abrams thought about it for an hour or so he became so incensed that he marched into the manager's office, broke up a meeting, and asked if they wanted him to quit. Johnson assured Abrams that the company did not operate in that fashion and that if they were dissatisfied with his work, the fact would be discussed completely with him. The conversation drew to a close with an agreement that Abrams would continue work on the program until it was finished. Johnson promised to try to arrange a transfer to another department as soon as it was completed and also to attempt to find a solution to his difficulties with Eden. With this Johnson called Eden back into the office.

---

[1] The office stenographer.

Johnson: Bill, Al has agreed to finish up on the main program. I hope you two will try
           to keep in mind the other fellow's feelings and try to be a little more tolerant
           and considerate. You know Al is doing the sort of work that involves uninter-
           rupted concentration, so make sure that the free machine time is really worth
           breaking in for. And, Al, you know that Bill's chief concern is the schedule
           and that he is afraid that we won't meet it. Understand that when he becomes
           apprehensive over your progress he is not being critical but just wants to know
           where we stand. One thing more, I want it understood that neither of you has
           prejudiced your position by what has been said here today. You have honest
           differences and we'll try to resolve them, but we'll need the cooperation of
           each of you.

With this Abrams left, but Eden stayed behind.

Eden: You know, Harris, I bend over backwards with that guy. I'm just as nice as I
           can possibly be. I never go near him unless it's absolutely necessary. I leave
           him completely free for the program and screen out all of the little detailed
           matters. But he's so damn suspicious of everything you do. Why one day the
           boss asked me to check on the name of a programmer. The Concord crowd
           owed us some instruction time under the terms of the contract and since the
           fellow in question was familiar with our machine, the boss felt we might col-
           lect the time by sending some work up there. All I did was ask Al for his
           name, nothing more, and darned if he didn't think we were going behind his
           back and trying to hire someone to take his place. After he blew up and
           learned the whole story he changed his tune to the effect that he wasn't being
           consulted on such matters as he should be.

Bill Eden, age forty-two, had graduated from college following World War II,
during which he served as a first-class petty officer in the U.S. Navy. He was fortunate in
not being required to take the labs associated with his major field, electrical engineering,
at a large midwestern university, because his full-time forty-hour-per-week job, which he
maintained in addition to class preparation and attendance, was in the university's research laboratory.

In spite of the tremendous workload, he managed to complete the requirements for a
bachelor's degree in three years. His wife, whom he met and married while they were in
the Navy, also obtained her degree. Following graduation Bill continued on as an engineer
in the research laboratory, working on basic development work for the defence effort. A
year later he accepted a position with a large west coast aircraft manufacturer where he
was placed in charge of a group preparing technical manuals. He left their employ in 1953
to accept a position with Sturbridge Electric Corp. as project engineer in the Systems Section. Bill had been dissatisfied with the prior job, in part because of a golfing friendship
that had developed between one of his subordinates and his boss. The subordinate's professional loyalty appeared to be open to question and Bill felt that he used the golf course
to further his own cause.

With Sturbridge, Eden did an excellent job of coordinating the many system functions assigned to him. Prior to his coming, the entire design department had grown very
rapidly. This, coupled with the new personnel's lack of familiarity with system concepts
and requirements, the steady progress in design of the many hardware components of the
system, and the pressure of early design and dates, had created impetus for assigning the
detailed coordinating responsibility to one person who could work with all of the design
sections and gather, sort, analyze and evaluate data and design considerations. With the
help of two assistant engineers, Eden accomplished the desired results. He continued in

this capacity until the promotion of the former computer project engineer created the vacancy into which he moved.

When Johnson had occasion to leave the office for several days he made it a practice to designate one member of the permanent staff responsible for the operation of the activity. On one such occasion Jerry Franklin, who generally filled this spot, was playing bridge with several other members of the staff as was the lunch-time custom. As the group was completing the final hand, Bill Eden walked over to the group and observed for a minute or two. He cleared his throat a couple of times and finally said, "Don't you fellows think it is about time that you all got back to work?" When the group did break up he followed Al Abrams over to his desk. "Say, Al, I'd like to get a progress report from you. Would you let me have the parts of the program you have completed?"

Abram's reply was to the effect that none of the work was in such a form that it would mean anything to Eden. He maintained that he had a series of notes in his file which contained the rough outline of the sequence in which the various computations were to be performed and some finalized operations. He stressed that, in their present form, they would be valueless to Eden and were more than likely subject to change in any event. Bill was nevertheless insistent and the level of their voices rose. After several heated exchanges in which charge and countercharge were hurled, Eden stalked off. When Johnson returned the following day Eden stopped in to see him.

Eden:	If you've got a minute there's something I'd like to discuss with you.
Johnson:	Sure thing, pull up a chair.
Eden:	Well, I had another run-in with Al the other day and frankly I'm worried. He just will not give me anything concrete in the way of a progress report. He maintains that he is making satisfactory progress and will tell me if he feels he is getting behind. You will recall that when he made his original estimate of how long it would take him to do the job, I made a point of letting everyone know that I didn't agree that he had allowed sufficient time. Now with his reluctance to let me see what he has done, I'm more convinced than ever that we will not finish on time and that he is hiding the fact. Every time I try to find out where we stand he gets temperamental on me and if there's anything I can't stand it's a prima donna! When he finds that time has run out he'll probably up and quit on us.
Johnson:	Ouch! That's all we'd need! I hope you are misjudging Al.
Eden:	I hope so, too, but the fact remains that I have no means of measuring his progress and have only his word for assurance that we are on schedule. You know the blood will be on my hands if we miss our dates and I'm plenty worried.
Johnson:	Well, for peace of mind, if nothing more, we have to determine the program status. After all, our schedule for the entire test facility is based to a large extent on Al's end date. If you had his file on the program could you do a sufficiently comprehensive analysis on the contents to establish our position?
Eden:	Possibly, but I doubt it. Ed Hall up in Allentown would be in a much better position to do it since he has had a great deal of general programming experience. But I know if you call in Hall for that purpose it'll make Al mad.
Johnson:	You're certainly right about that! However, if Hall would come down for a visit on a related matter, the progress report might be obtained as a by-product. With his work on system simulations, there should be plenty of common ground on which the two of them can get together.
Eden:	That's a thought.
Johnson:	Suppose I discuss the matter with the boss and see what we can cook up.

A visit for Hall was arranged. As a result of some rescheduling at headquarters it was convenient to shift some programming work associated with the test phase of the Florida activity. It had originally been planned for Abrams to do this after completion of the main program. The stated purpose of Hall's visit was to coordinate this shift. After it had been arranged Johnson called Abrams into his office and informed him of the plan and the reasons. Abrams thought it was a good idea and promised to help in any way possible. After the visit, Hall assured everyone that Abrams appeared to be making satisfactory progress and that for the present, at least, he had every chance of meeting the schedule.

On a Friday, several weeks following the scheduling controversy, Abrams stopped Johnson in the lab.

Abrams: Say, Harris, Bill wants Smith and me to work tomorrow and I don't see the need for it. I'm keeping up with the schedule I've set for myself and until I get behind I see no reason for putting in overtime. Besides, I'd like to spend some time with my family.

Johnson: Can't say I blame you for that. Why does Bill feel that it's necessary?

Abrams: He just said that we should make use of every available minute now as a cushion against missing our schedule. I'm being very careful to be sure I maintain a progress rate consistent with our dates and I feel that overtime now is a needless imposition. If I find myself falling behind in any week, I'll certainly tell you and request overtime.

Johnson: From what you've told me I've got to agree with you. Suppose I talk it over with Bill and see what he has in mind.

Abrams: Okay.

On his way back to the office, Johnson stopped by Bill Eden's desk and asked him about the overtime situation.

Eden: The two fellows from Concord who are experts on the electrostatic storage section are leaving for home on Sunday. So far this week we haven't gotten in more than two hours of actual operating time on the machine and I figured that if we worked Saturday we could get in a solid eight hours with these boys standing by in case of trouble. In fact, they suggested that we do it so that they could be sure that the reliability of that section of the computer was up to par. Besides, it won't do any harm to get in all of the time we can now. I know Al is sore about it because he had planned to take off for Miami with his family tonight to spend the weekend with relatives.

Johnson agreed that they should work Saturday under the circumstances and walked back to the computer room to find Abrams. When Johnson related Eden's full story, Abram's quickly agreed to work. His closing remark was, "If Bill had only said something about the fellows leaving for Concord there wouldn't have been any argument in the first place."

Two months later, just prior to the beginning of acceptance tests, Al Abrams blew up over the questioning of his modification to the equation and Mr. Johnson was again faced with the problem of how to handle an administrative situation over which he had no direct line of responsibility. Abrams and Eden worked for the systems section head, and although Johnson had kept him informed on all developments in Florida, the geographical separation seemed to Johnson to make him the one who had to cope with the problem on the spot. There was always a question as to what lengths he could go to in handling the matter because of his inability to make any commitments which would be binding on the section head.

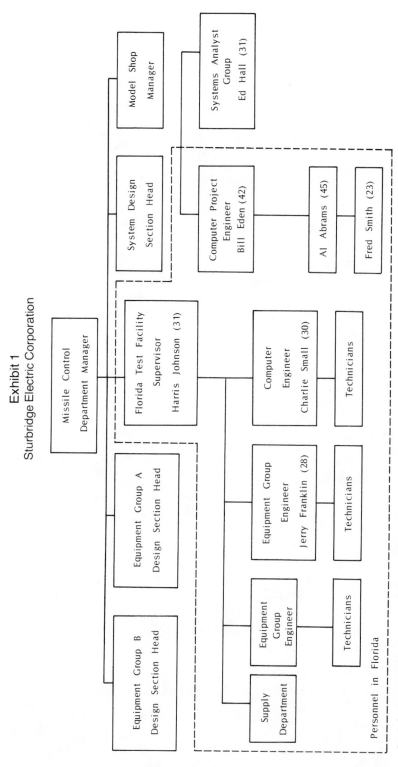

Exhibit 1
Sturbridge Electric Corporation

Partial Organization Chart — Missile Control Department

SECTION V
An Introduction to Industrial Relations

Since the early 1800s, organized labour has played an increasingly important part in the Canadian economy. The union movement has grown to the point where more than one in every four Canadian workers is a union member. In spite of this growth, many of us do not understand the union movement. Much of what we think about organized labour comes to us through the media and we tend to think that strikes, violence and militancy are the major characteristics of unions. And while it would be naive to deny that irresponsibility, violence and hostility exist in the union movement, media coverage of these sensational facets of union activity has tended to distort the true nature of organized labour in Canada.

Our labour movement originated in times when exploitation of people for profits was commonplace. The motivation to organize into united groups was, in the early days, more a question of survival than an attempt to gain higher wages. Conditions which many of us take for granted—the forty-hour (or less) work week, equitable wages, protection against unsafe conditions—were fought for and won from capitalists who tried hard to maintain their almost feudal control over workers. It was in these early struggles for decent conditions and for the right to organize that the prevailing adversary stance of labour and management originated.

A real understanding of industrial relations must start from the most objective viewpoint possible. Such a viewpoint must be based upon an understanding of organized labour's origins, structure and function. We will present an overview of Canadian industrial relations, including:

1. A brief history of Canadian industrial relations.
2. Union organization and certification.
3. The union-management relationship.
4. Dispute-handling mechanisms.
5. The contemporary Canadian labour movement.

A BRIEF HISTORY OF CANADIAN INDUSTRIAL RELATIONS

Union organization in Canada began in the early 1800s. During the first half of that century the union movement came under two direct influences: domination by skilled trade organizations and the impact of British and European tradesmen. The majority of early union activities centred on the skilled trades: the earliest organizing activity occurred among tradesmen in Saint John, N.B., in 1812. Many tradesmen in Canada were immigrants and they brought with them the traditions of the older British and European labour movements. Although this connection rapidly diminished during the second half of the nineteenth century, it put an international focus on the Canadian labour movement. Today this international orientation is one of the major aspects of industrial relations in Canada.

Organization by crafts and trades dominated the movement until the 1930s and 1940s. The change to "industrial" organization is the subject of much of what follows in this section.

Early organization was encumbered by two legal concepts which had been inherited through British common law. The Masters and Servants Act discouraged, under penalty

---

Preparation of this chapter was significantly influenced by Professors Peach and Keuchle, authors of *The Practice of Industrial Relations* (Toronto: McGraw-Hill Ryerson, 1975).

of imprisonment, a worker's moving from one job to another. Such action was liable to charges of breach of contract. Also, the Criminal Conspiracy Doctrine maintained that it was a criminal activity for workers to combine to seek collective rewards. These two legal constraints were used repeatedly in the early 1800s to discourage labour organization.

The first major turning point in Canadian labour history occurred in 1872. The initial impetus for the changes that followed was a strike in April by Toronto printers, members of the Typographical Society. The issue was singular: the printers wanted their working day reduced from ten to nine hours. The employers, led by George Brown, rejected their demands and the strike ensued. In Canada's first real demonstration of labour solidarity, the Toronto Trades Assembly, which represented twenty-four unions in the city, showed its support for the printers in a mass rally on April 15. Brown then secured the arrest of the leaders of all affiliated unions under the conspiracy doctrine. The men were arrested, tried and convicted on April 17. News of this resulted in another mass meeting calling for political action. Action came in the form of the Trade Union Act of 1872, which said that, henceforth, combining to bargain collectively would not be considered criminal conspiracy.

The impetus behind the Trade Union Act is interesting. Similar legislation recognizing labour's right to organize had been passed in England in 1871. However, the immediate reasoning behind the Canadian legislation was more political than historical. John A. Macdonald, the Conservative Prime Minister, secured passage of the Act on April 18 in order to embarrass his political opponent, the Liberal George Brown. Regardless, the legislation resulted in victory for the striking workers; their work day was reduced to nine hours. By the end of the year, many major industries including the railroads, had adopted the nine-hour work day.

While the Act theoretically opened the way for labour to organize actively, such was not the case for many years, primarily because of the passage in the same year of the Criminal Law Amendment Act which provided penalties for violence or intimidation during strikes and also established that a union-management contract was not legally binding. Therefore, although the conspiracy doctrine was theoretically dead, union organization was still considered in practice to fall into the criminal conspiracy realm and was treated as such until the mid 1900s. It was not until 1943 that Ontario finally did away with the conspiracy doctrine.

Out of the success of the printer's strike, Canada's first union combination was formed. In May 1872, union members from Toronto, Brantford and Montreal met to discuss common problems. The result was the formation of the Canadian Labour Union (CLU) in September. However, despite the successes of 1872, the labour movement did not grow significantly; by World War I, less than 10 per cent of Canadian workers were organized.

In the period leading up to 1918 the labour movement became increasingly dominated by American unions. In 1886, the Knights of Labour, an industrial organization originally founded in Chicago, combined with a number of Canadian craft unions to form the Trades and Labour Congress (TLC). In addition to the international aspect of this merger, it also represented the first time a merger had combined industrial and craft unions, which led to further trouble in the labour movement.

Under pressure from the American Federation of Labour (AFL), a predominantly craft union combination, the TLC in 1902 expelled the Knights from its ranks because they competed in the U.S. with AFL affiliates. Further, at its 1902 convention the TLC elected as its president a paid officer of the international union. Thus, Canada's largest union organization clearly opted for U.S. domination and organization along craft or trade lines.

Following World War I, the 1918 TLC convention demanded a shift towards industrial organization and greater Canadian control. Western delegates who had spearheaded the demand for change met in March 1919 and formed the One Big Union (OBU). They resolved to cut their affiliation with international organizations and to organize along industrial lines.

Concurrent with this development was the Winnipeg General Strike. Workers, dissatisfied with their economic lot in light of their contribution to the war effort, demanded an eight-hour day, double pay for overtime and recognition of the newly formed metal trades council. With 35 000 workers on strike, the city of Winnipeg was paralyzed, support spread throughout the labour movement across Canada, and as a result, all three levels of government joined to end the disruption. When Winnipeg policemen and firemen joined the strike, the Royal Canadian Mounted Police, supported by "irregulars," entered the city. One month after the strike began, its leaders were arrested and in the riot which resulted during a protest rally, two demonstrators were killed, thirty injured and over one hundred persons arrested. Winnipeg was placed under military control. Forty-one days after it started, the General Strike was broken.

Little was gained from the strike. Some concessions were made concerning the length of the working week. However, the image of radicalism it fostered tainted the union movement for years to come and led to the deterioration of the OBU; by 1921 it had ceased to be a major force.

In 1938, U.S. domination of the labour movement was again confirmed when the AFL-controlled TLC expelled members affiliated with the newly formed Committee for Industrial Organization (CIO). The CIO was an AFL competitor, formed from dissident unions including the United Auto Workers (UAW) and the United Mine Workers. As had been the case in 1902 when the Knights of Labour posed a threat to the AFL, so the CIO in its three-year history did the same. However, the expelled CIO unions combined in 1940 to form the Canadian Congress of Labour (CCL) which, because of its drive to organize along industrial lines, continued to grow at a faster rate than the predominantly craft-oriented TLC.

By the end of World War II, the AFL had softened its line on industrial organization and the two U.S. organizations and their Canadian counterparts staged bitter fights for members throughout the late 1940s. Because their efforts were proving to be counter-productive, the AFL and CIO merged in 1955 to form the AFL-CIO; in 1956, the TLC and CCC followed suit, merging to form the Canadian Labour Congress (CLC).

Legislative developments during the first half of this century focussed primarily on dispute-settling measures and federal-provincial jurisdiction. The Conciliation Act of 1900 allowed the Minister of Labour to supply mediators to disputing parties if they requested such help. In 1903 the Railway Labour Disputes Act provided for compulsory mediation and arbitration for disputes involving railway workers. The arbitrator's recommendations, however, were non-binding and the Act provided no constraint on strikes or lockouts. The inadequacies of both the 1900 and 1903 legislation were compensated for in 1906 with the Conciliation and Labour Act which was revised in 1907 and called the Industrial Disputes Investigation Act (IDI). The Act called for compulsory conciliation of disputes and prohibited any activity beyond that of conciliation until the dispute had been fully investigated. Further, conciliation boards were given power to make recommendations concerning the outcome of the dispute. The Act, however, failed to provide penalties for employers who actively fought against union organizing drives. Regardless, the IDI remains as one of the keystone pieces of industrial relations legislation in Canada.

The jurisdiction of federal legislation was challenged in 1925 with the case of the Toronto Electric Commission v. Snider. The courts ruled that the IDI applied only to enumerated industries of a national nature. With the exception of Prince Edward Island, all provinces then either passed enabling legislation to make the IDI applicable or passed their own IDI-type legislation. As a result of the Snider case, the provinces have become the principal makers and enforcers of labour law in Canada.

A strike by Ford Motor Co. workers in 1945 demanded, among other things that their plant become a "union shop"; that is, employees had to be union members. In a precedent-setting decision, Justice Ivan Rand suggested and got agreement to a compromise which is now known as the Rand Formula or "agency shop." Under this arrangement, workers represented by a union must pay dues to their local but they do not have to become members. This decision further advanced union security and has played an important part in the growth of organized labour in Canada since 1945.

The passage in 1967 of the Public Service Staff Relations Act was significant because it recognized that government employees had the right to organize and bargain in the same manner as private sector employees. The unionization of public employees represented the latest major growth in union ranks. Unionization of white collar workers has occurred, but so far has not been as widespread as had been projected in the 1960s.

Developments during the 1970s will be discussed later in this chapter.

UNION ORGANIZATION AND CERTIFICATION

Union organization begins with the local unit or bargaining group. Generally, this unit will comprise the employees of a single plant location or identifiable work group within a plant. The local unit may be a member of a national union or it may be independently chartered. National unions and independents combine to form large groupings of unions such as the CLC and the AFL-CIO.

Union locals are formed in one of two ways. Either a group of disgruntled employees seeks out a large established union and asks its help or a field worker from a union contacts an employee of a non-union shop and persuades him to help in an organizing drive.

After determining if organization is feasible, organizers invariably set about to sign up (saying they want representation) over 65 per cent of the employees in a still undefined unit. The objective is to work as quickly and quietly as possible in order to avoid possible management retaliation. In spite of the law against discrimination against workers seeking union representation, it is obvious that such discrimination can occur and is often difficult to prove.

The onus falls on the organizer to prove that 50 per cent or more of the employees want representation and further, that the future unit is appropriate. Although an application can be made to the Labour Board with only 35 per cent of employees signing cards, the law states that a local is automatically certified if 65 per cent of employees sign up and all other procedural matters are correct. Obviously, organizers try for 65 per cent or more and at a minimum 50 per cent.

The bargaining unit is generally agreed upon by the union and the company. If an agreement cannot be reached, the Labour Board will decide at a later hearing. General guidelines for assessing appropriateness are as follows:

1. Is the unit distinguishable by geography, skill or craft?
2. Has the unit ever been agreed upon previously?
3. Is there a "community" of interests among members of the unit?
4. Are typical lines of advancement/demotion found in the unit?
5. Is the proposed unit typical?

The union must file an application for certification with the Labour Board along with documented proof of desire (sign-up cards, etc.). The application must be specific, that is, exclusionary descriptions are unacceptable. For example, an application could not say, ". . . all employees except . . ."; rather it must state exactly whom the application covers.

The employer is asked to comment on the application and must conspicuously post a copy for all to see. At the same time, the employer must provide the Board with a list of all employees in the proposed bargaining unit along with specimen signatures for verification of the sign-up cards.

A hearing is held approximately three weeks after the application is filed. A terminal date is set for one week prior to the hearing up until which time evidence regarding membership, etc., can be filed with the Board.

The hearing will do four things:

1. Determine appropriateness of the unit;
2. Determine number and percentage of employees indicating a desire for membership;
3. Entertain objections to certification from outside parties (e.g., competing unions); and
4. Indicate subsequent action.

This action may be either an order for automatic certification, denial of certification, or request for representative vote on the question under the auspices of the Board. In 1971, over 60 per cent of all hearings resulted in an order for automatic certification.

THE UNION-MANAGEMENT RELATIONSHIP

We find that a clear understanding of industrial relations requires some way of thinking about the union-management relationship. Traditionally, the relationship has been one of union challenge and management response. Considering the varied stances unions can adopt in their challenge and the equally varied stances management can adopt for its response, we find a model useful for studying the relationship. The varying types of relationships can be shown on what has been called the spectrum of union-management relations. Any particular union-management relationship will fall somewhere in this spectrum:[1]

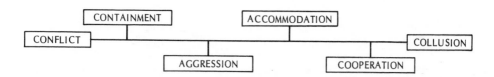

Conflict relationship

Both parties are highly militant and communication or cooperation is non-existent. The evolution of labour law has all but eliminated this particular posture.

Containment-Aggression relationship

Both parties working under this relationship, while acting within the legal letter of their collective agreement, actively work to increase their degree of power. This stance is characterized by a sense of militancy and little cooperation or communication.

Accommodation relationship

Both parties work within the bounds of their collective agreement while actively seeking to increase mutual trust. This posture is characterized by a degree of cooperation and communication above and beyond that demanded by the agreement. It is productive because it lessens the chance of disruptions and strikes.

---

[1] Benjamin Selekman *et al.*, *Problems in Labor Relations*, 3rd ed. (New York: McGraw Hill, 1965) pp. 1-11.

Cooperative relationship

Management considers labour as full partners in the business and the relationship is characterized by a very high degree of cooperation and communication, profit sharing and participative management.

Collusive relationship

Union acts in concert with management to the detriment of the membership. For example, a union fearing a raid might agree with management that in return for a high wage settlement (which would protect the incumbent against the raid) it would not fight technological changes which would reduce the work force.

The point at which any union-management relationship falls on the spectrum is dictated by a series of internal and external influences. Internally, a union's stance toward management evolves from the following:

1. Its history and tradition,
2. The nature of its leadership,
3. The current union political scene,
4. Its policies regarding the collective agreement.

External influences cannot be controlled by either party and obviously a complete list would be lengthy. Some major influences are:

1. The specific characteristics of the industry (elasticity of demand, degree of unionization, intensiveness of labour content, cyclicability of business),
2. The state of technology and the degree of automation in the production process,
3. Legislation,
4. Government policy and administration,
5. The judiciary,
6. Socio-economic conditions.

DISPUTE-HANDLING MECHANISMS

There are two ways of handling disputes in industrial relations before resorting to strikes or lockouts. These are mediation and arbitration.

Mediation

Mediation, or as it is sometimes called, conciliation, is the intervention by a third party into negotiations to help produce an agreement. It is an extralegal process and is generally carried on in an informal manner. In Canada, parties must submit their dispute to a mediator before a strike can legally occur. However, this is a formality since mediators have no power to enforce either their suggestions for settlement or those of the disputing parties. The success of mediation, therefore, depends first upon the disputing parties having an honest desire for agreement and second, upon the persuasiveness of the mediator.

Arbitration

Arbitration is the resolution of any industrial relations dispute by an impartial person or by a board. The decision of the arbitrator is final and binding, although it can be appealed through the courts in certain instances.

Two forms of arbitration are found in Canadian labour relations. The most common type is *rights* arbitration; that is, disputes over the application or interpretation of a collective agreement. Often, this process is known as grievance arbitration. Grievance arbitration, with the exception of Saskatchewan, is compulsory in Canada.

The second, less common form is *interest* arbitration, which deals with impasses in contract negotiation. This process is only compulsory in a few sectors of the economy, notably public service employees.

GRIEVANCE ARBITRATION PROCESS

Most disputes concerning the contract are settled before going to arbitration. Arbitration is the final step in the appeal process and as such is generally required only when a dispute relates to significant changes in policy on either party's side. Grievances of a routine nature are nearly always resolved by the foreman or personnel manager and union steward.

Before a dispute can be submitted to arbitration it must be first judged arbitratable. The criteria for an arbitratable dispute vary enormously depending upon the industry, the jurisdiction and the terms of the contract. One general rule states that a dispute is arbitratable if it directly concerns the interpretation, application, administration or violation of the contract. Thus an employee complaint, in order to be submitted to arbitration, must directly relate to a specific violation of some term of the agreement.

Actual arbitration is usually carried out by boards of arbitration in Canada. Boards are comprised of three persons: one representative chosen by each of the two parties and a neutral chairman. Rulings are based on majority votes.

Arbitration is quasi-judicial in nature and although informal, it is conducted according to general legal protocol (cross-examination, summation, etc.). Arbitration differs from judicial procedure significantly in its treatment of evidence. Hearsay evidence, allegations, circumstantial evidence and insinuations are generally admissible although treated according to their merits. Further, arbitration is not subject to precedent to the same degree as judicial proceedings and appeal is not justified on the basis of precedent.

INTEREST ARBITRATION

Resorting to interest arbitration is growing. Already compulsory for areas of vital public concern (nurses, policemen, etc.), trends indicate a willingness on the part of other sectors of industry to submit to binding interest arbitration. Some countries, Australia for example, require an impasse in any collective bargaining process to be settled by arbitration.

Because individual party interests are at stake, interest arbitration is much more complex and criteria for decision are ambiguous. It is less legalized and occasionally contradictory.

Some efforts have been made to establish standards for contract settlement; the most notable are those contained in the Public Service Staff Relations Act.

THE CONTEMPORARY CANADIAN LABOUR MOVEMENT

Industrial relations in Canada exhibit certain characteristics, many of which have come from its history and many of which are a result of the changing economic environment.

Size

Contrary to popular opinion, the majority of Canadian workers do not belong to unions. Overall, less than a third of the total work force was unionized in the early 1970s. Membership in various industries, however, varies dramatically. While 99.5 per cent of agricultural workers are not unionized, 100 per cent of workers in the brewing industry are unionized. With the exception of significant growth in public employee unions and some growth in white collar unions, union growth has been relatively stable since the late 1950s.

Composition

There are over 400 separate unions in Canada ranging in membership from fewer than ten members (for example, the International Association of Siderographers) up to huge international unions with membership in the hundreds of thousands. Twenty unions comprise over 50 per cent of total union membership. The four largest are the Canadian Union of Public Employees, the United Steelworkers, the Public Service Alliance of Canada and the United Auto Workers.

The majority of unions in Canada are affiliated with two federations of unions—the CLC and the Confederation of National Trade Unions (CNTU). The major difference between the two federations is that the CLC is national, comprising international, national and independent unions across Canada. The CNTU is a federation of Quebec unions only. One large union, the Teamsters, has no affiliation with either federation. Although neither federation has strong constitutional power, both are important in the development of inter-union cooperation and the overall development and growth of the union movement.

Control and Leadership

Over 60 per cent of Canadian union members belong to international unions; that is, unions based in the United States. In general, there is little difference between international unions operating in Canada and truly Canadian unions.

Some positive results have accrued to the Canadian labour movement from this American domination. In general, the labour movement has developed more rapidly in Canada through the greater resources and experience of the American-based unions. In addition, American affiliated unions have enjoyed greater bargaining power simply because of their connections. Finally, Canadian unions have gained some measure of respectability and acceptance from their affiliation with the U.S. unions.

There are also a number of negative consequences of the U.S. domination. The most serious is that policy and control of finances, to a large extent, rest with headquarters outside of Canada. The strong ties between unions have resulted in calls for Canadian wage parity with equivalent American industries, parity which many claim we cannot afford. Greater rationalization of national unions has been retarded by the growth and dominance of international unions. And, according to many, this domination has resulted in occasional infringement on Canadian economic sovereignty.

Power

The Canadian labour movement is parochial. The strength of the movement lies in its grass roots nature. The local is the main unit of power.

Even the enormous growth of some unions has failed to produce a significant centralization in any executive committee which any local would hesitate to challenge. Many tentative agreements have not been ratified by union membership recently, indicating the power usually lies with the members on such major issues as contract settlement.

Political Affiliation

The Canadian labour movement is conservative in comparison with the European movement. Both Canadian and American unions support and work for the continuation of the capitalist economy. Unions, both in Canada and the United States, support, to some degree, political parties financially and in other ways. In this sense, the Canadian movement is less politically active than the European labour movement.

Union Management

Union management is becoming more sophisticated. The giant unions now have support staffs of lawyers, economists and administrators which match many large corporations. Increasingly, training of union administrators is being done professionally. A prime example is the CLC's labour relations school hosted by McGill University.

Union's Role in Industry

A subtle but sure shift in the attitude of some major union leadership toward labour's part in the economy is evident. This shift encompasses a number of important areas. For instance, some major unions are now actively seeking significant changes in industrial work environments. In line with this concern for issues other than financial reward, unions are taking an active interest in the future of their respective industries.

WHAT A UNION MEANS TO HUMAN RESOURCE MANAGEMENT

So far in this chapter, we have described industrial relations, but unlike earlier chapters, we have not said much about making industrial relations *decisions*. We will conclude with a brief discussion of decision making.

   We believe there are two ways to think about industrial relations decisions. First, there are a host of decisions that have to do with a union-management relationship, including:

1. Should we encourage or discourage union certification in our company? (This may not be a choice.)
2. What basic posture do we want to take with union leaders and members?
3. What bargaining strategies will we employ during contract negotiations?
4. How willing are we to strike?
5. To what extent will we back other members of management in disputes with union leaders and members? (This is especially a problem when we think such managers are in the wrong.)

Second, there is a set of decisions that have to do with overall personnel relationships, including:

1. How will we treat non-unionized employees as compared with our unionized employees on issues such as pay, seniority, promotion, dismissal, etc?
2. How technical (or legal) do we want to be in interpreting contract provisions? For example, if an employee lets us down, will we "throw the book at him" or will we use some of the principles we've learned about human resources management?

   There are both advantages and disadvantages to having a unionized work force. For example, it becomes difficult for a manager to be flexible in his treatment of employees when the union contract requires equalized treatment. This characteristic prevents manipulative managers from dividing and conquering their employees on such issues as compensation and termination. In fact, specified expectations of what employees must do and what management must do can make human resource management in a unionized firm much easier to achieve than in a non-unionized firm, provided the firm and the union are on good terms. On the other hand, legal rules and regulations for human resource management often make it difficult for management to recognize unequal performance, ability instead of seniority, and so on. We challenge you to prepare your own list of advantages and disadvantages of the unionized work force from both the management and employee points of view.

20

International Equipment Co.

On August 10, 1973, the general manager of International Equipment Co. received notice of application for certification of his office employees (see Exhibit 1). He was undecided as to whether he should permit the application to go through without contest by management, or try to influence his employees to reject the union.

The International Equipment Co. was a wholly owned subsidiary of the International Manufacturing Co., an American corporation, with its principal offices in Minneapolis, Minnesota, and with plants in various cities in the United States. There were two Canadian manufacturing plants of International Equipment, located at Magog, Quebec, and Brampton, Ontario.

The products manufactured at the Brampton works included heavy-duty machinery controls, such as hydraulic systems. It was anticipated that other lines of manufacture would be undertaken in Canada on a scale similar to that in the United States. It was noted in this connection that while the Brampton plant presently occupied less than three acres, the company had purchased approximately fifty-five acres at Brampton for future expansion.

The parent company maintained an industrial and community relations division, which was created in 1957 for the purpose of coordinating the industrial relations policies at the various company plants and of maintaining a cordial relationship between the company and its employees and the community in which particular works were situated. Another purpose of the division was to keep the company informed of variations in factors affecting industrial relations and to anticipate and facilitate adjustments where the company deemed it advisable. This ability to survey wages and working conditions on a company-wide basis assisted in determining fair and reasonable working conditions in the particular plant concerned.

On August 2, 1973, there was a total of 246 employees at the Brampton plant, who were classified by type of work as follows:

Production and maintenance employees		180
men	168	
women	12	
Office employees		32
men	14	
women	18	
Supervisory and other		34
production	13	
office	21	

The production and maintenance employees were organized by the United Automobile Workers (UAW-AFL/CIO), which had been their certified representative since October 5, 1952. The current two-year agreement which expired December 20, 1974, was the ninth between the company and the union. Since the Brampton plant had no industrial relations or personnel office or officers, these agreements had been negotiated by the plant manager with the help of the Magog and Minneapolis offices.

Even though the company had 246 employees, the general manager was reputed to know every employee by first name. The relationship between the union and the company was said to be excellent. The union was obtaining satisfactory rates and benefits for its members. One of the consequences of this was that a production worker at a comparable level to an office worker and with comparable skill was earning a higher salary. The company recognized the need for a revised salary plan and was in the process of formulating a program which was slated for installation on September 1, 1973. The employees were unaware of this plan.

The office employees were all located in one large L-shaped room with rows of desks touching each other except for one aisle in the centre of the room. There was considerable non-work interaction among the office employees and they were regarded by management as a tightly knit group.

On August 10, 1973, the Brampton works received by mail a notice of certification of the office employees from the Ontario Labour Relations Board (see Exhibit 1). The union involved was the same one that was certified to represent the production and maintenance employees. The notice came as a complete surprise to management. Through initial inquiries the company learned that the majority of the eligible office employees had signed union cards. If certified, it would be the first office union to gain representation in the entire International Manufacturing organization. Upon receipt of the notice of certification the Minneapolis industrial relations office was contacted immediately and given full details on the situation. A labour relations specialist was sent to Brampton to deal with the matter on a first-hand basis.

The general manager assembled his management team to discuss the various courses of action. It was apparent that there was no general agreement. The comptroller was very disturbed. He visualized many problems in dealing with a union that involved all of the office and clerical workers with the exception of the general manager's secretary, the department heads, and engineers.

"It will be impossible to keep anything confidential with my assistant, my secretary, and the telephone operators in the union. People will want to do only one job and no overtime. Our best policy is to fight this certification. If we tell the employees that they are really members of management, and that we have a new salary plan which can be installed immediately, I believe they will reject the union."

The engineering department manager agreed with the comptroller that there could be many problems, but he believed that it was too late to do anything about it.

"Apparently about 60 per cent of the employees want the union and have signed membership cards. The Labour Relations Act states that we cannot interfere [Exhibit 2]. I think it would be better in the long run if we accept certification now. This will enable us to negotiate a better contract and help us develop a more satisfactory working relationship for the future."

The plant manager reported that relations with this particular union had been satisfactory at the shop level; however, he was of the opinion that it might be wise to ask the Labour Relations Board to conduct a vote by secret ballot to make certain that the employees had really signed cards without duress. Regardless of the Board's action on the vote, the plant manager believed that the company should file a reply to the Board listing management's idea of what jobs should be in the bargaining unit. He stated that it should be possible to exclude people who were performing managerial functions and also any persons handling confidential matters relating to industrial relations.

The head office labour man said, "The plant manager is correct. We must file exclusions immediately. However, the additional action is not clear at this moment. I suspect that salary inequities are a major part of the employee dissatisfaction. Legally, management can announce and implement the plan immediately. The company can carry on business as usual. It can discipline, make improvements, talk to its employees individually or collectively, but it must carefully avoid any reference to the union; however, while management has the legal right to institute the salary plan, I can recall many instances where the union has successfully turned this kind of action into a union victory by stating that merely the threat of a union has brought rewards to the employees.''

After listening to the various points of view, the general manager was still undecided about which course of action to follow. He realized that the notice (Exhibit 1) had to be posted immediately. It was possible also that a group of employees might have second thoughts, withdraw from the union, and intervene at the hearing on August 19.

Exhibit 1
THE LABOUR RELATIONS ACT
NOTICE TO EMPLOYEES OF FILING OF APPLICATION
BEFORE THE ONTARIO LABOUR RELATIONS BOARD

Between: International Union, United Automobile Aircraft and Agricultural Implement Workers of America, Affiliated with the American Federation of Labour and Congress of Industrial Organizations
Applicant,

— and —

International Equipment Co. Ltd., Brampton Works
Respondent.

TO THE EMPLOYEES OF

International Equipment Co. Ltd., Brampton Works

TAKE NOTICE that the applicant, International Union, United Automobile Aircraft and Agricultural Implement Workers of America, Affiliated with the American Federation of Labour and Congress of Industrial Organizations, on August 7, 1973, filed with the Ontario Labour Relations Board an application, a copy of which is attached, for certification as bargaining agent of the employees of International Equipment Co. Ltd., Brampton Works in a unit described as

All office and clerical workers of the respondent company, save and except engineers doing engineering work, private secretary to the manager, department heads and all those above the rank of department head.

AND TAKE NOTICE THAT any employee, or group of employees, affected by the application and not desiring the applicant to be certified as the bargaining agent, whether or not that desire has been indicated in any other manner, may so inform the Board in writing not later than the 17th day of August, 1973.

AND TAKE NOTICE of the hearing of the application by the Board at its Board Room, 125 Harbour Street, Toronto, Ontario on Monday, the 19th day of August, 1973, at 9:15 o'clock in the forenoon (D.S.T.).

AND FURTHER TAKE NOTICE THAT any employee, or group of employees, who has informed the Board in writing of his or their desire may attend and be heard at the hearing; and that upon failure to attend, the Board may dispose of the application without further notice and without considering his, or their, desire in writing filed with the Board.

The desire shall be signed by the employee or each member of a group of employees.

An employee, or group of employees, may attend and be heard at the hearing by a representative.

DATED this 7th day of August, 1973.

(A. M. Brunskill)
  Registrar

(Note: Address all communications with respect to this application to
  The Registrar
  Ontario Labour Relations Board
  125 Harbour Street
  Toronto, Ontario.)

Exhibit 2
Excerpts from the Labour Relations Act
Revised Statutes of Ontario, 1970
Chapter 232

UNFAIR PRACTICES

56. No employer or employers' organization and no person acting on behalf of an employer or an employers' organization shall participate in or interfere with the formation, selection or administration of a trade union or the representation of employees by a trade union or contribute financial or other support to a trade union, but nothing in this section shall be deemed to deprive an employer of his freedom to express his views so long as he does not use coercion, intimidation, threats, promises or undue influence. R.S.O. 1970, c. 232, s. 56.

57. No trade union and no person acting on behalf of a trade union shall participate in or interfere with the formation or administration of an employers' organization or contribute financial or other support to an employers' organization. R.S.O. 1970, c. 232, s. 57.

58. No employer, employers' organization or person acting on behalf of an employer or an employers' organization,

(a) shall refuse to employ or to continue to employ a person, or discriminate against a person in regard to employment or any term or condition of employment because the person was or is a member of a trade union or was or is exercising any other rights under this Act;

(b) shall impose any condition in a contract of employment or propose the imposition of any condition in a contract of employment that seeks to restrain an employee or a person seeking employment from becoming a member of a trade union or exercising any other rights under this Act; or

(c) shall seek by threat of dismissal, or by any other kind of threat, or by the imposition of a pecuniary or other penalty, or by any other means to compel an employee to become or refrain from becoming or to continue to be or to cease to be a member or officer or representative of a trade union or to cease to exercise any other rights under this Act. R.S.O. 1970, c. 232, s. 58.

59. (1) No employer, employers' organization or person acting on behalf of an employer or an employers' organization shall, so long as a trade union continues to be entitled to represent the employees in the bargaining unit, bargain with or enter into a collective agreement with any person or another trade union or a council of trade unions on behalf of or purporting, designed or intended to be binding upon the employees in the bargaining unit or any of them.

(2) No trade union, council of trade unions or person acting on behalf of a trade union or council of trade unions shall, so long as another trade union continues to be entitled to represent the employees in a bargaining unit, bargain with or enter into a collective agreement with an employer or an employers' organization on behalf of or purporting, designed or intended to be binding upon the employees in the bargaining unit or any of them. R.S.O. 1970, c. 232, s. 59.

60. A trade union or council of trade unions, so long as it continues to be entitled to represent employees in a bargaining unit, shall not act in a manner that is arbitrary, discriminatory or in bad faith in the representation of any of the employees in the unit, whether or not members of the trade union or of any constituent union of the council of trade unions, as the case may be. R.S.O. 1970, c. 232, s. 60.

61. No person, trade union or employers' organization shall seek by intimidation or coercion to compel any person to become or refrain from becoming or to continue to be or to cease to be a member of a trade union or of an employers' organization or to refrain from exercising any other rights under this Act or from performing any obligations under this Act. R.S.O. 1970, c. 232 s. 61.

62. Nothing in this Act authorizes any person to attempt at this place at which an employee works to persuade him during his working hours to become or refrain from becoming or continue to be a member of a trade union. R.S.O. 1970, c. 232, s. 62.

21
Primo Electric Co. Ltd.

In May 1975, Local 54 of the United Electrical, Radio and Machine Workers of America (UE) and Primo Electric Co. Ltd. met with a Board of Arbitration to settle Grievance No. 230, which read as follows:

> The unjust discharge of Richard Stevens, a layout man and boring mill operator, based upon company reasons of refusing to obey orders, poor work record, and using abusive language to a foreman.

The Primo Electric Co. had several plants in a large city in western Ontario which turned out a wide variety of products from major appliances, such as stoves and refrigerators, to heavy electrical apparatus, such as motors and generators. The incident causing the grievance took place in department D-1 of the power products division of the company's plant No. 1. The work performed in this department was generally of a machining nature, utilizing various types of machines to process material for use throughout all three plants. The grievor had worked in this department first as a boring mill operator and later, since August 1968, as a layout man.

Richard J. Stevens, age twenty-eight, the grievor, was an extremely active union steward in Local 54. He had worked for the company since September 1967, and had been appointed union steward in April 1973. For eleven months after his date of hiring, he had been a vertical boring mill operator, and from then until August 1974, he had been employed as a second-class layout man.[1] On company work histories, his attendance, application and skill were reported as good. However, his general deportment was described as poor; he was a chronic complainer. In his foreman's opinion, Stevens was considered to be a very aggressive union steward who was often inclined to be quite unreasonable in his dealings with management.

Two unfavourable incidents stood out on Stevens's record. One involved a charge of obstructing police in a picket line disturbance. This had occurred in October 1973 when Stevens and two other Primo employees had been absent from work without leave because they were serving on a picket line which the UE had thrown up around another local company. The company laid them off for a period of three days. The lay-off was later interpreted by a Board of Arbitration to have been an unjustified suspension.

In addition to the lay-off which Stevens received in October 1973, he also received a suspension in December 1973 for leaving his work station without permission. This was in connection with a complaint by a number of employees regarding the scheduling of alternate work days over Christmas. On this occasion, Stevens refused to return to his work station when told to do so. As a result, he was suspended for four days, but a Board of Arbitration subsequently reduced the suspension to one day.

Because of a work shortage in department D-1 in August 1974, the foreman, Donald Jackson, deemed it necessary to transfer Stevens back to a vertical boring mill. Stevens had asked to be allowed to exercise his plant-wide seniority to bump[2] onto a layout job in another department, but Jackson required him to exercise his departmental seniority first as provided in the Collective Agreement.

---

[1] Working from blueprints, this man outlines the various cuts on work pieces to guide operators who are doing the machining.

[2] Bump—to displace another person with less seniority.

Donald Jackson was the general foreman in department D-1 and had worked for the company for twenty-nine years; eleven years as a supervisor and nine years as a supervisor in department D-1. He was a rough-and-ready sort of man who sometimes caused strained relations with his employees.

Jackson contended that even a month after Stevens had bumped onto the boring mill he was not doing a satisfactory job or making a real effort to raise his performance. The major point of annoyance was Stevens's continual moving back and forth between his layout table and the boring mill to obtain tools from the former location. Stevens refused to take his personal tools to his new work station on the grounds that there was not a satisfactory place in which to lock them at the boring mills.

Jackson considered this to be nonsense as other operators had stored their tools at the boring mill without difficulties. Both the foreman and subforeman repeatedly told Stevens to move his tools to his new work station, but Stevens continually refused and began stating that he was promised a new tool cabinet which would be built by the carpenter shop.

It was the opinion of some management people that Stevens's real reason for resenting the boring mill job was that it did not allow him to move around in the department on union business. The layout job had facilitated his contact with the workers as he had to show each one how materials were to be machined. It was known that a cabinet at his layout table contained union documents and files relating to departmental time studies.

Supervision also surmised that Stevens's appointment as a union steward had given him an exalted opinion of his own importance and the feeling that his duties as a steward were more important than his work for the company. It also seemed apparent that Stevens felt his position gave him a degree of immunity from any effective supervision by his supervisors.

On October 12, 1974, at approximately 3:30 P.M., an incident occurred which ultimately resulted in Stevens's dismissal by the company. Jackson's account of the episode was as follows:

"I went to the grievor while he was at the layout table and asked him what he was doing there. He replied that he came up to get some tools. I again told him to get all his tools up to the boring mill and I was not going to tell him again. He said there was not room at the boring mill and I told him there was plenty of room. At this point he became annoyed and as we started back to the boring mill he said, 'Jackson, you're an s.o.b.; you want to hang your cross with those other bastards in labour relations.' I told him to watch his language or be fired. To this, he retorted, 'You damned s.o.b., fire me if you want to—I don't care—I know that's what you want to do.' He persisted in his abusive language and I finally told him to pack up his tools and be out by five o'clock, and not to report until I sent for him. I doubt whether anyone in the vicinity heard our conversation but at no time did I use abusive language."

The following day, Stevens was telephoned and told to report to the employment office. A meeting was held between the supervisor of labour relations, the plant superintendent, and Mr. Jackson for the company, and Mr. Stevens and Mr. Robertson, the president of Local 54. The grievor was told by Mr. Jackson that he was being discharged for: (1) use of profane and abusive language, and (2) repeated refusal to obey his supervisor's orders with respect to moving his tools.

The same day, Richard Stevens submitted his grievance (Exhibit 1). This grievance, No. 230, was processed through the various stages as provided for by Article XVI of the Collective Agreement.

Throughout the processing of this grievance, the company steadfastly maintained that Stevens had been justifiably discharged (Exhibit 2). Finally, on October 27, 1974, the union informed the company that it was posting the grievance for arbitration, and at the same time named their choice of representative for the Board of Arbitration.

The chairman was appointed on May 16, 1975. During the six-month interval that had expired due to the time taken to obtain a suitable chairman for the Board and to schedule a date for the hearing, Richard Stevens had applied for unemployment insurance. He had subsequently terminated it when he took another job with a local radio and television store. Stevens had received unemployment insurance after the Unemployment Insurance Commission court of referees heard his case and ruled that his discharge was unjust as the order to move his tools to the boring mill was an unreasonable one. This ruling was not accepted as union evidence by the Board of Arbitration.

At this hearing, and at the arbitration, Richard Stevens's account of his actions contradicted that of the foreman. It was Stevens's contention that he had an understanding with supervision that he did not need to move his tools until such time as space was provided for them at the boring mill. He claimed that the foreman of the carpenter shop had been to his work station to obtain measurements for the construction of a new tool cupboard. Stevens admitted that he had not conversed with the foreman but had been right beside him when plans for the new cupboard were discussed. Management stated that this new cupboard was to be used to store clamps used for work on a number of machines in Stevens's area, and that it would contain no space for tools as there was already a cupboard available for tools used by the boring mill operator.

Stevens also stated that he needed all his tools for the boring mill job and they were locked in drawers at the layout table. (Management steadfastly maintained that very few tools were needed for a boring mill as compared with layout table work.) The grievor maintained also that profanity was common in his conversations with Jackson and that a few words such as damn or hell might have been spoken in the particular altercation in question. A number of workers who had witnessed the altercation between the two men corroborated Stevens's statements, and one stated the exchange of words seemed only a normal argument.

Stevens's account of the October 12, 1974, episode differed considerably from that of Jackson. He related that, while at the layout table getting a tool he required for boring mill work, Jackson stormed in and bellowed: "Get those goddamned tools up to the place you work!" A heated discussion followed, which ended with the foreman telling him to go home at five o'clock and not return until called.

In addition to the grievor's reasons, the union listed a number of items of provocation which would justify a considerable resentment by the grievor for his foreman. These items were:

1. A previous five-day suspension of the grievance by the company (the agent of which was Mr. Jackson) which was later reduced to a one-day suspension by a Board of Arbitration (although the exercise of discipline was upheld as justified).[3]
2. A three-day suspension later cancelled by a Board of Arbitration. (Stevens and three others involved here.)
3. Mr. Jackson's placing of the grievor on the boring mill which the grievor found uncongenial, unpleasant, and dangerous, as well as a form of demotion. (No evidence of this.)
4. The boring mill in question was considered by the grievor to be the worst one in the plant. (Company evidence to the contrary.)
5. Mr. Jackson's broken promises to the grievor. (Denied by Jackson.)
6. Mr. Jackson's excessive watching and besetting the grievor at his work on the boring mill. (Denied by Jackson.)
7. Mr. Jackson's misleading the grievor about his intention to build a secure cupboard for the grievor's tools at his boring mill. (Company denied that any such cupboard was planned.)

---

[3] Company rebuttal in brackets.

Exhibit 1
Primo Electric Co. Ltd.
Grievance Report

Plant—East
Date—October 13, 1974

Name—Richard J. Stevens   Male   x
Address—108 East 13th Street   Female
Department—D1 Operation—layout boring mill
Length of Service—Seven years   Clock No.—3707
Nature of grievance—I feel that I have been unjustly discharged. Request immediate reinstatement and
    full reimbursement for lost wages.

....
....
....
....
....

                                                Richard J. Stevens
Copy for Foreman

Exhibit 2
Primo Electric Co. Ltd.

cc: D. Jackson

October 22, 1974

Business Agent, Local 54
United Electrical, Radio & Machine
Workers of America

Dear Sir:

Re: Grievance #230—Third Stage
    Unjust Discharge—R. Stevens
    Department D-1

As pointed out at the third stage hearing, the griever was discharged due to his refusal to obey orders of supervision, and his use of abusive language to his foreman. This action was taken after careful consideration of the griever's previous record including warnings and suspension.

Evidence submitted by the Union at the third stage hearing in no way justifies any change in the Company's position.

This discharge, therefore, stands.

Yours truly,

Supervisor,
Labour Relations,
Industrial Relations Dept.

22

Unemployment Insurance Commission

Late in the fall of 1971, Mr. Erin Scott had brought the following grievances against his employer, the Unemployment Insurance Commission: "The Unemployment Insurance Commission has wrongfully refused to compensate me for overtime work performed, for the period 5:45 P.M. to 8:45 on October 28, 1971. This refusal of compensation constitutes a misapplication or misinterpretation of Articles 27.01 and 27.03 of the relevant collective agreement."

The grievance, however, had not been dealt with to Mr. Scott's satisfaction and he appealed it to the adjudication stage. The adjudicator, Mr. David Toland, heard the grievance on May 2, 1972.

Section 91 of the Public Service Staff Relations Act provided that:

1. Where an employee has presented a grievance up to and including the final level in the grievance process with respect to
   (a) the interpretation or application in respect of him of a provision of a collective agreement or an arbitral award, or
   (b) disciplinary action resulting in discharge, suspension or a financial penalty, and his grievance has not been dealt with to his satisfaction, he may refer the grievance to adjudication.

Section 92 of the Act stated:

1. The Governor in Council, on the recommendation of the Public Service Staff Relations Board, shall appoint such officers, to be called adjudicators, as may be required to hear and adjudicate upon grievances referred to adjudication under this Act.
2. The Governor in Council, on the recommendation of the Board, shall designate one of the adjudicators appointed under this section to be chief adjudicator to administer, subject to any regulations of the Board, the system of grievance adjudication established under this Act.
3. An adjudicator shall be appointed for such period, not exceeding five years, as may be determined by the Governor in Council but may be removed by the Governor in Council at any time on the unanimous recommendation of the Board.

Excerpts of section 96 of the same Act stated:

1. Where a grievance is referred to adjudication the adjudicator shall give both parties to the grievance an opportunity of being heard.
2. After considering the grievance, the adjudicator shall render a decision thereon and
   (a) send a copy thereof to each party and his or its representative, and to the bargaining agent, if any, for the bargaining unit to which the employee whose grievance it is belongs; and (b) deposit a copy of the decision with the Secretary of the Board.
3. Where a decision on any grievance referred to adjudication requires any action by or on the part of the employer, the employer shall take such action.
4. Where a decision on any grievance requires any action by or on the part of an employee or a bargaining agent or both of them, the employee or bargaining agent, or both, as the case may be, shall take such action.
5. The Board may, in accordance with Section 20, take such action as is contemplated by

that section to give effect to the decision of an adjudicator on a grievance but shall not inquire into the basis or substance of the decision.

At the time of the grievance, Mr. Scott was employed as a full-time officer at the level of S.A.-3 by the adjudication section of the Unemployment Insurance Commission in Victoria, British Columbia. His normal or scheduled hours of work were from 8:15 A.M. to 5:00 P.M. These winter hours had been set by the agreement between Scott's bargaining unit and the Unemployment Insurance Commission and were matched by shorter summer hours.

Mr. Scott's responsibilities were of a clerical nature. However, he was periodically assigned the task of delivering and explaining various forms and other materials to Unemployment Insurance Commission agents located in a number of places in British Columbia outside of Victoria. During Scott's performance of one such delivery assignment, the situation giving rise to the grievance arose.

Prior to the week of October 27, 1971, Mr. Scott had meetings with both his immediate supervisors, Mr. Jackson and Mr. Roy Jameson. The purpose of the meetings had been to discuss in detail the new Unemployment Insurance Commission material to be delivered the following week. Mr. Jackson and Mr. Jameson agreed that the job probably would require two full working days to complete. On the basis of his own experience in doing a similar task, Mr. Jameson felt that doing the job in two days would require a very tight schedule. Besides delivering the material, Scott would have other responsibilities during the week of the 27th. His supervisor, Mr. Jackson, planned to be absent on a training course and Scott would have to assume some of Jackson's supervisory duties in addition to his own day-to-day duties. He would not be able to devote two full days to the delivery of the material since his other responsibilities would require his presence at the Victoria office for at least part of each day.

During another meeting prior to the week of October 27, the following conversation occurred between Scott and Jackson:

Jackson: Erin, it's rather important that these UIC forms be delivered while I'm away next week.
Scott: Will do, Jack, although next week is going to be a rather hectic one for me. I have to do some of your job, all of mine, plus deliver these forms.
Jackson: I agree, but I'm sure you'll manage.
Scott: It's quite possible that the delivery thing might take beyond 5:00 o'clock.
Jackson: Yes, it may.
Scott: Anyway, have a successful trip next week, eh!
Jackson: Thanks, Erin.

On October 27, 1971, Mr. Scott left the Commission offices in Victoria at 10:15 A.M. and had finished delivering some of the Unemployment Insurance Commission forms by 5:00 P.M. However, he stayed at the office after 5:00 P.M. to clear up some of the extra paperwork that had accumulated during his absence and to load his automobile with the material to be delivered the next day.

On the 28th, the day in question in the grievance, Scott left the office at 10:00 A.M. Throughout the day he delivered and explained the various forms and other material to the Unemployment Insurance Commission officials in such communities as Courtenay and Port Alberni. (Exhibit 1 shows the locations of these communities). His last scheduled delivery had been to Nanaimo and was completed at 4:15 P.M. However, instead of returning to Victoria, Scott decided that since he was relatively close to Vancouver, he should make one further delivery to Mrs. Stewart, an Unemployment Insurance Commission official who worked in that city. He thought that if he did not make the delivery to Mrs. Stewart, then another trip on another day would have been necessary in order to make only this one delivery. This would obviously be a waste of time. On the way back to Victoria after making the delivery in Vancouver, he stopped for dinner, for which he spent $4.

Scott finally arrived back at his office at 8:45 P.M. The trip had taken longer than expected because he had to wait for the ferry in travelling both to and from the mainland. The travelling time on the mainland was also longer than he anticipated, although the ferry trip had taken most of the time.

Scott was reimbursed for the $4 expenditure for his dinner. The $4 reimbursement appeared to have been paid in accordance with Part IV of the Treasury Board Travel Directive which provided for the payment of various allowances to persons in "travel status." Travel status was defined in the Directive as "absence of the employee from his headquarters on government business with the approval of the employer." The Unemployment Commission felt that the pause for dinner had been justified.

Scott, according to the Travel Directive, also received thirteen cents per mile for the use of his own vehicle. Payment was made only for "authorized official use of a private car."

Furthermore, he received compensation for forty-five minutes of overtime, for the period of 5:00 to 5:45 P.M. on October 28. This time span included a fifteen minute period of travel time from the ferry dock on the mainland to Mrs. Stewart's office in Vancouver.

However, the Commission refused to compensate Mr. Scott for the other three hours, 5:45-8:45 P.M. The primary reason they gave was that Scott's last trip to Vancouver had not been explicitly "authorized" by his superiors, and also that the *travel time* which Scott took between Nanaimo and Vancouver did not constitute work within the definition of "overtime" in Clause 27.01 of the Collective Agreement. The relevant sections of the agreement are listed below.

27.01 in this Article:
(a) "overtime means"
    (i) in the case of a full-time employee, authorized work performed in excess or outside of his scheduled hours of work

27.03 subject to Clause 27.05:
(a) An employee at Level S.A.-1, 2, 3 who is required to work overtime on his scheduled work days is entitled to compensation at straight time for the first two and one-half (2½) hours per work week and at time and one-half (1½) for all hours worked beyond the first two and one-half (2½) hours in each work week;

27.04, Subject to Clause 27.05:
(a) An employee who is required to work on a day of rest is entitled to compensation at time and one-half (1½) for all hours worked.

27.05:
(a) An employee is entitled to overtime compensation under Clauses 27.03 and 27.04 for each completed period of one-half (½) hour of overtime worked by him:
    (i) When the overtime work is *authorized* in advance by the Employer, and
    (ii) When the employee does not control the duration of the overtime work.

After his request for overtime compensation had been denied, Scott filed the grievance which ultimately reached Adjudicator Toland.

During the adjudication session, the following arguments were made by Mr. Andrew Callus, the representative of the Unemployment Insurance Commission.

First of all, at no time prior to October 27, 1971, and also October 28 had Mr. Scott been given explicit authorization to work overtime on the task of delivering and explaining the forms and other material. Therefore, since the work had not been expressly authorized, it did not qualify as overtime under Section 27.01 (a) (i) and Scott was not eligible for compensation.

Secondly, Mr. Callus argued that "travel" and "work" were terms which did not include one another. He pointed to the distinctions made in the same collective agreement between "travel" on a day of rest and "work" on a day of rest (Clauses 27.01 and 27.04). He also pointed out that Clause 27.03 provided for overtime compensation for work which was overtime work on scheduled work days but that there was no provision for travel on scheduled work days. From these provisions, Callus believed that work and travel were two different activities and that travel did not constitute "work" within the definition of "overtime" in Clause 27.01. Therefore, Scott again did not qualify for compensation.

On the other hand, Mr. Charles Knight, representative for Mr. Scott, argued that although *explicit* authorization to work overtime had not been given to Mr. Scott, he had been *implicitly* authorized to do so by his superior. He pointed out the fact that in neither of the conversations between Scott and his superiors, Messrs. Jackson and Jameson, had any time limit been set on the job. Also, Jackson had responded affirmatively when Mr. Scott suggested that the job would possibly take beyond 5:00 P.M. Furthermore, Jameson had stated that "it would be a tight schedule to perform it in two days, starting from Victoria around 8:15 A.M. and returning to Victoria each afternoon." Scott's counsel said that the facts showed that his client did not have two full working days to perform the task. Rather, he only had parts of each of two days, because during the week when the job was performed, Scott was required to perform some of the day-to-day supervisory duties of Mr. Jackson. Overtime work had therefore been implicitly authorized.

In regard to Callus's second argument, Mr. Knight said that management's previous actions had indicated that "travel" and "work" were terms which in fact did include one another. Scott had been compensated for the period of 5:00 P.M. to 5:45 P.M. However, this time span, as was indicated before, had included a fifteen-minute period of *travel time* from the ferry dock on the mainland to the place where Scott had made his delivery and explanation. From this it seemed that "travel" indeed constituted "work" for which overtime compensation was due, at least in the view of Mr. Scott's employer.

Exhibit 1
Unemployent Insurance Commission

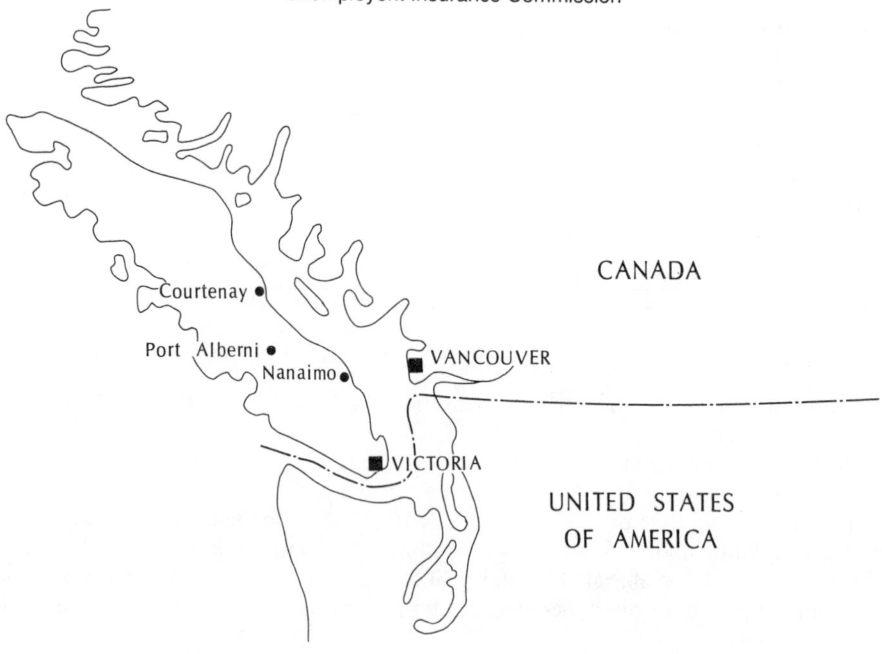

SECTION VI
An Introduction to Marketing Management

The purpose of this chapter is to provide you with an understanding of the fundamental concepts and techniques of marketing decision making. Although we will begin with a discussion of individual elements of a marketing program, our ultimate goal is the improvement of your ability to integrate these individual elements into a well-reasoned and practical marketing plan. Such a plan connects the organization's aims and abilities with the customers' needs and wants in the context of an environment. Several of these terms merit classification at the outset.

There have been innumerable definitions of marketing management—no individual phrasing has captured universal acceptance. Most contemporary definitions include the following notions:

1. Marketing management is purposeful—those engaged in it are attempting to accomplish organizational objectives such as dollar profit, share of market, political candidate's success, charity donation goals, etc. The most common goal is profit, but it is not the goal in all situations.
2. Marketing management is designed to satisfy the needs and/or wants of *constituencies*; for management to achieve organizational goals, some constituency (hereafter referred to as customer group or consumer group) must buy a product, service, or idea from the organization.
3. Marketing management involves trade-offs—an organization's resources (dollars, skills, location, costs) impose limits on how well it can meet the requirements of its customers. No organization can be all things to all people. Thus, marketing managers must decide upon a specific customer group to whom to cater (called the market target) and decide what, of the several alternative possibilities, it will offer to that group.
4. Marketing management is competitive—with rare exception, organizations must compete for the attention, initial patronage, and continued patronage of their customers. Sometimes the competition is very direct (one shaving cream versus another) and sometimes very indirect (the relative share of milk versus other beverages in individuals' daily fluid intake). Usually, there is a spectrum of competitive offerings a manager must "better" to obtain and maintain customer patronage.
5. Marketing decision making can be improved via a combination of experience and academic discipline; while only a few would maintain marketing management is a science, most knowledgeable individuals would agree that there are some conventional wisdom and "fundamental concepts."

The above five points are all essential to an understanding of what modern marketing management entails. Marketing does not equal selling, nor does it equal advertising. Marketing is an approach to improving the relationship between an organization and its existing (or sought-after) clientele. Most business observers can cite countless examples of successful marketers and unsuccessful ones. In our opinion unsuccessful marketers always make one or more of the following mistakes:

They did not understand or ignored the first principle of marketing management, which is: "know the characteristics of your clientele." They tried to *sell*, rather than *market* their product, service, or idea. Marketing begins with establishing the existence of a market and learning what the market wants. One can sometimes peddle products without knowing much about the market, but the chances of success, especially over time, are much slimmer. It's easier to determine what is wanted and then try to provide it in terms of the product, price, method of distribution, and so forth.

They did analyze the characteristics of their clientele, but either did it poorly or did not use what information they had to design the best possible marketing program. This is an extremely common shortcoming that results from going through the motions of decision making rather than understanding the point of it all.

They underestimated the competition. In short, if someone else offers a better package of benefits, in time, customers usually discover it.

They were overly ambitious or optimistic. Many marketing failures are the direct result of marketers with big plans, little patience, and inadequate resources.

There are other reasons that may contribute to failure in the marketplace, but the point of this discussion is that the odds are against the marketer who does not do his or her homework.

If we define the critical task of a marketing manager as the determination of the most appropriate marketing program for the organization, several questions arise. First, what is a marketing program? Second, how do we formulate a marketing program? And finally, how do we know whether it is the most appropriate? The remainder of this chapter is a discussion of these three questions.

MARKETING PROGRAM CHARACTERISTICS

A marketing program consists of a selection of activities that will be performed by or for the organization (hereafter referred to as company) to attract the patronage of its target group of consumers and in turn, to achieve its marketing objectives. The usual decisions to be made in establishing an integrated marketing program include:

- What product (or service) will be offered?
- At what price?
- Through what distribution channels?
- With what communications effort?

This list can be expanded by breaking down issues such as communications into the elements of advertising, personal selling, packaging, publicity and sales promotion. In any particular situation, a marketing manager has some discretion as to what combinations of policies along these dimensions will constitute the marketing program. Hence, the ingredients of marketing programs may be mixed according to an enormous variety of recipes. One often hears of these variables referred to as the ''marketing mix.'' The trick is to find the particular recipe that is consistent with both the consumer's needs and the goals of the company.

PRODUCT POLICY DECISIONS

Product policy decisions relate to the number, type, style and quality of products or services to be offered as well as production quantities and schedules. Consumers buy total ''packages of benefits'' that have both physical and psychosocial dimensions. For example, a product may be characterized in terms of what it is or does (physical attributes) or in terms of how the consumer perceives it (benefits). To many adults, a Corvette is more than a mechanical means of conveyance. The same toothpaste may mean prevention of cavities to one consumer and enhancement of sex appeal to another. The basic question under the heading of product policy is: What package of benefits should we offer?

Many firms offer more than one individual product in a particular product category. Related products are referred to as a product line; related product lines are referred to as product groups. For example, an electrical goods firm may offer several lines including toasters, irons, and blenders and organize its marketing management under the heading of electric housewares group. Clearly, decisions such as *number* of product lines, *depth* of product line (number of sizes, colours), and *brand* names are also major product policy decisions.

Products may be classified by a variety of dimensions. Two common dimensions are product life duration and type of buyer. Using the former, products may be durable goods (automobiles and refrigerators) or non-durable goods (deodorants and food). Using the latter dimension, products may be consumer (breakfast cereals), industrial (tractor trailers), or government (military equipment). These two dimensions may also be combined. For example, breakfast cereals are classified as consumer non-durable products. Such classifications are often used to generalize experience with one product to another comparable product. Many of the principles in shampoo marketing are useful in deodorant marketing.

PRICING POLICY DECISIONS

The answer to "what price should be charged for Product A?" is seldom simple. Legal considerations aside, there are a number of issues to consider: (a) cost, price, volume, (b) margin, and (c) overall strategy.

First we must examine the relationships between cost, price and volume. For example, suppose we knew a ballpoint pen could be produced at 75c per unit and that we had two choices: sell the pen at $1.50 per unit or at $3.00 per unit. Without some indication of the number of units that might be sold at each price level, a decision amounts to a guess. Suppose further that an experienced ballpoint pen salesman estimated that on a monthly basis 1500 units could be sold at $1.50 and only 500 units at $3.00. What would the best decision be then? We would obtain more revenue per month at the lower price ($2250 versus $1500). At the same time, 1500 units would cost $1125 while 500 would cost $375. Profit per month at the lower price would be $1125—the same as at the higher price. If profit is our goal, it does not matter which route we choose in this example. Clearly, such calculations may become much more complicated:

- Production costs may vary with volume (suppose 1500 pens could be produced at 60c per unit instead).
- Marketing costs may vary with volume (suppose we had to hire more salesmen to handle higher volume).
- We may not have very good estimates of the sensitivity of consumers to different price levels and thus be forced to calculate a variety of possible outcomes (an optimistic and pessimistic forecast).

One technique developed to simplify such calculations is called break-even analysis. The purpose of break-even analysis is to determine the minimum acceptable relationship among cost, price and volume to make a venture worthwhile. For example, returning to the pen, suppose we had the following information:

- Cost per unit—$.75
- Plant cost in order to produce—$5000 (per year)
- Salaries and other administrative expenses—$10 000
- Expected selling price per unit—$1.50
- Advertising expense planned—$2000

Suppose, further, management has decided it will not proceed unless enough pens are sold this year to cover all the costs. How many pens must we sell at least to break even?

The arithmetic in this example is not very difficult, so an answer may be achieved in a variety of ways. Here is a general approach to this type of problem:

- Separate costs into two categories, fixed and variable. Fixed costs do not change with volume (at least not over some range of volume) while variable costs change directly with volume.

Fixed costs

plant	$ 5 000
salaries	10 000
advertising	2 000
	$17 000

Express variable cost on a per unit basis:
Variable cost
$.75/unit

Notice that sometimes this separation into categories requires judgement or is done according to some particular industry tradition.

- Calculate unit contribution. Unit contribution refers to the difference between selling price per unit and variable cost per unit.

(Selling price—cost)   = contribution
($1.50 − $.75)   = $.75

- Calculate break-even unit volume.

$$\text{B.E.} = \frac{\text{total fixed costs}}{\text{unit contribution}}$$

$$\frac{\$17,000}{\$.75} = 22\ 667 \text{ pens}$$

Thus, we learn that given these cost figures, 22 667 pens must be sold per year to break even. Each pen that is sold contributes $.75 towards the $17 000 fixed costs. After 22 667 pens are sold, each additional pen would contribute $.75 toward profit. How many pens must be sold to achieve a profit of $1000? (24 000, or 22 667 to break even and 1333 to make the $1000 more). In short, to test profit targets, add the dollar amount of profit to the total fixed costs and divide by the contribution per unit. Remember, most businesses are seeking profit, not break even.

Break-even analysis does not reveal how many we *will* sell, only how many we *must* sell to reach a certain relationship among cost, price and volume. Using the pen example again, the experienced salesman predicted a sales level of 1500 units per month (18 000 pens per year) at $1.50 selling price. If this is correct, not enough pens will be sold to reach break even. With this approach we may change any or all of the variables. Suppose prices were increased or unit cost was reduced.

A second pricing consideration involves margins. Margin refers to the difference between cost price/unit and selling price/unit. Some people like to express margin as a percentage of selling price and others as a percentage of cost. For example, suppose an item cost the seller $1 and it sold for $2.:

Margin as a percentage of selling price $= \dfrac{\$2.00 - \$1.00}{\$2.00} \times 100 = 50\%$
    (Markon)

Margin as a percentage of cost $= \dfrac{\$2.00 - \$1.00}{\$1.00} \times 100 = 100\%$
    (Markup)

This difference in approach can be confusing when it is not specified which method is being used. When in doubt we suggest you use the margin-as-a-percentage-of-selling-price method. You may encounter the term markdown, especially in the context of items on sale. Markdown is the reduction in selling price, expressed as a percentage of selling price. For example, if an item which ordinarily sold for $2 was marked down to $1.80, the markdown is 10 per cent:

$$\frac{\$2.00 - \$1.80}{\$2.00} \times 100$$

Each business has "customary" margin levels and ways of expressing those margins. We urge you to be flexible about this, and to be careful you discover what method of margin calculation is being used in any particular situation.

Finally, in addition to the above considerations, companies usually have overall strategies regarding price. Some believe in low price—high volume (called penetration strategy, for example, MacDonald's hamburgers) while others believe in high price—low volume (called skimming strategy, for instance, Joy perfume). Some companies like to set the price for a product category (price leader) while others like to imitate (price follower).

DISTRIBUTION POLICY DECISIONS

In most instances, a marketer may change prices frequently and with little difficulty. Changes in methods of distribution are much more difficult to implement. All marketers have to decide how their goods will physically reach the ultimate consumers, be they householders, industrial users, or government. The major decision is whether to perform the tasks involved oneself, or pay someone else to help out. Distribution involves skills often quite different from manufacturing and a great variety of middlemen has developed to perform specialized distribution tasks. Often, such specialized middlemen can reach consumers more effectively and more efficiently than manufacturers could directly. Some common channels (distribution routes) are as follows:

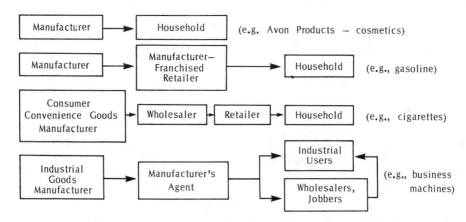

Sometimes, there are no reasonable alternative channels to consider. For example, liquor can only be sold for home consumption through the government retail network in Ontario. At times, however, there are a variety of options to consider that involve issues such as:

- Who performs what tasks (stocks the retail shelves, does warranty work, etc.)?
- Who bears what costs (has to hold the finished inventory)?
- Who makes decisions on selling methods, advertising, amount of stock to carry, etc?
- Who gets what share of the final sales dollar?

To complicate matters, distributive institutions are changing constantly in character. Some of the relatively new retail types include discount department stores, catalogue showrooms, and warehouse outlets. As channels change, opportunities for improved distribution methods are presented to alert marketers.

One generalized way to categorize types of distribution was developed many years ago. Products and outlets are classified as either "convenience", "shopping", or "specialty." Convenience goods are those which the consumer wants readily available. Such items are bought usually at the nearest outlet. Cigarettes are a convenience item. Shopping goods are those which cause the consumer to compare prices and other features in different outlets. The usual examples are automobiles and home appliances. Specialty goods are those for which the consumer will go far out of his or her way. For example, one may be willing to drive across town to buy a certain kind of stereo receiver. Convenience goods generally require mass distribution (many outlets), shopping goods selective distribution (not so many outlets, but well-situated ones), and specialty goods exclusive distribution (one or very few dealers in any particular region). In short, one distributes products according to their physical characteristics, their image among consumers, and the types of outlets available.

MARKETING COMMUNICATIONS POLICY DECISIONS

Marketing communications refers to those methods a marketer may use to inform and persuade consumers to buy a product or service. The methods include:

- Advertising—print (newspapers, magazines)
            —broadcast (radio, television)
- Sales promotion—coupons, premiums, contests
- Publicity—editorials, news articles, interview shows
- Personal selling—door-to-door, telephone, mail order
- Packaging—boxes, cans, bottles

Each of these methods may be used to (a) give information about the product and its availability, (b) influence attitudes as to the product's superiority, (c) cause action (purchase or repeat purchase). While each method of communication may be examined separately, it is important to recognize the similarities among them, hence the concept of the communications (or promotion) mix to refer to the right blend of the five methods into an overall communications strategy.

In each instance, the marketer must ask the following questions:

- What message will be most appropriate for the target audience to achieve the communications objectives (which may include awareness of the product, favourable attitudes toward the product, persuasion to try the product)?
- What methods of transmitting this message are most appropriate (reach the target at reasonable cost with high impact)?
- When should communications occur (scheduling)?
- How much money should be spent (budget)?
- How will results of the communications campaign be evaluated (effectiveness)?

If the marketer cannot answer each of the above questions specifically, any communications program implemented may be insufficient. An enormous amount of money is wasted on ill-conceived communications programs. A cost-benefit analysis, however rudimentary in form, is mandatory for effective communications decision making.

MARKETING PROGRAM FORMULATION

The preceding brief discussion of the elements of a marketing program and the need to fit these elements into a coherent package should make it clear that marketing decision making generally is a challenging task requiring information and judgement. In this section we will examine the types of information most useful to program formulation, including:

- Consumer analysis
- Competitive analysis
- Environmental analysis
- Corporate capabilities analysis

In addition, we will make a few comments about judgement and the use of marketing research to improve decision making.

CONSUMER ANALYSIS

Many students of marketing quickly latch onto the fact that a consumer analysis is essential to marketing decision making, go through the motions of such an analysis, and then proceed to make decisions without any reference to the analysis. The only point of consumer analysis is to enable you to make better decisions as to the characteristics of your marketing program. Any analysis that does not contribute to improved decisions may be interesting, but definitely is useless to us in this context.

Experience has shown that there are six simple questions which serve well as an outline for consumer analysis:

- Who are existing and potential customers?
- What do these customers want?
- How do these consumers make buying decisions?
- Where do these consumers shop?
- When do these consumers shop?
- Why do they behave as they do?

Answers to these questions serve to guide marketing program formulation. For example, some of the implicatons are as follows:

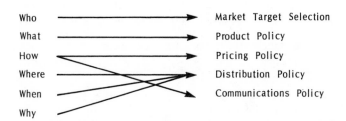

The usefulness of the analysis is greater than can be simply diagrammed here. Further, the answers to these questions frequently overlap with one another. The point is not to fill out a check list, but rather to make sure you understand your customers.

Who

Except in the case of a very large volume buyer (large industrial concern, government agency), it is seldom worthwhile to examine each individual consumer or buyer in detail. Each will have different characteristics: age, sex, income, life style, attitudes, needs and wants. It is important, however, to see if there exist groups of consumers with similar characteristics. Such groups of consumers are called *market segments*. The principle of market segmentation is to find groups of consumers that are similar within groups and different across groups. There are many dimensions that may be used to segment a market and the choice of which dimensions to employ depends on the specific situation. Perhaps age and income are most important for distinguishing among high potential and low potential users of perfume, while amount of consumption may be important for distinguishing among types of breakfast cereal customers. Sometimes the most useful dimensions are demographic (age, sex, income, stage in life cycle,), sometimes psychological (status, peer group pressure, self-image) and sometimes a combination of both, known as psychographic.

The major reason for examining a market for segments is that it is difficult to be all things to all people. We use segmentation to select a target audience to whom we will cater in particular. In this way, we tailor our marketing program to the segment or segments we believe will be most responsive to us. If a segment is described in ways that do not allow us to reach it, then the segmentation method is useless. For example, one might say "blue-eyed, left-handed Anglicans who were born in July represent our best market for Product A," but clearly in this absurd instance, how would we use this information?

Another outcome of this analysis is an estimate of the size of the relevant market. For example, there is obviously an important difference between "all Canadian malt beverage drinkers" and "Ontario males under thirty who drink a case or more of ale per week." A five per cent share of market of the former is clearly different in size for a company than a five per cent share of the latter. In short, is the segment big enough to justify the marketer's efforts?

What

In order to design an appealing marketing program, we must have some idea as to what our target market wants. People buy packages of benefits that include product characteristics, price, service promises, status feelings, delivery convenience, etc. To use one famous example, "People buy ¼-inch holes, not a ¼-inch drill." What characteristics of the package of benefits are most important to consumers? We need a sense of balance in this area: a package of benefits too narrowly conceived leaves a firm open to rigidity, obsolescence, and inability to compete; a package of benefits too widely conceived leaves a firm open to excessive dilution of efforts and, again, inability to compete. In short, what business is the firm in?

How

The question "How do consumers buy?" may seem simple, yet the implications of more than superficial answers are far reaching. Do consumers compare features and prices, do they respond to advertisements or to the advice of friends, do they buy on impulse or only on a carefully preplanned basis, do they want credit or prefer cash? Do consumers buy cars the same way they buy cigarettes?

We attempt to find out how the consumer buys in order to see what, if anything, we can do to predispose the consumer to our offering. If consumers want to compare deals, perhaps we will locate close to our competition so the consumer will include us in the set of stores considered. For example, clothing and automobile outlets are usually found in groups. If the consumer seeks a great deal of product information, we may hire knowledgeable salesmen and keep product literature at point-of-purchase. For example, better household furnishing stores employ expert salesmen to assist consumers in demystifying the differences among furniture.

Two other concepts are useful in answering the "how" question. First, is there a distinction between who influences the purchase, who makes the purchase, and who uses the purchase? If so, how do these persons interact? For years, cereal marketers have operated on the principle that although the mother buys the cereal (and must be reassured there is some food value in it), it is the child who determines which brand will be selected (and must be convinced Cheerios are better than Captain Crunch). Second, there appears to be a generalized process consumers go through at varying speeds in making a purchase which may be simplified as follows:

- Awareness of the product
- Knowledge of the product characteristics
- Favourable attitudes toward the product
- Purchase
- Post-purchase experience and feelings
- Repeat purchase

If these steps are necessary before a sale (or repeat sale) is made we should be interested in ensuring consumers do move through the process. Do they know about the product and where to get it? Will advertising or personal selling influence their attitudes toward the product? Application of this process model helps us understand why the consumer buys (or does not buy) our product and, in general, why consumers have certain purchase behaviour patterns.

Where

Where do potential buyers shop or want to shop? The emphasis recently has shown a trend toward convenient, one-stop shopping. Shopping malls with easy parking facilities have prospered based on this "need." Location is also critical for the industrial purchaser as it has implications for costs and delivery time. A wholesaler who carries a full line of industrial goods may be preferred over more limited wholesalers by an industrial purchasing agent.

The location of a product or service often has a crucial effect on its image. There would probably be a negative effect on the potential consumer of $300 Paris originals if they suddenly became available at a discount department store. Similarly, where do consumers expect to find certain products? Despite the trend towards "scrambled retailing" (stores carrying all kinds of unrelated products), consumers expect to find hardware items in certain stores and not in others, and so on. Having the right product in the wrong location can be disastrous for any marketer.

When

When do potential consumers buy? Daily? Weekly? Monthly? Yearly? Seasonally? Morning? Afternoon? Evening? Holidays? Currently, many downtown merchants are being adversely affected by the fact that with the exception of one or two nights a week, their hours are basically 10 A.M. until 6 P.M., whereas shopping malls are often open until 9 or 10 P.M. every night. As more and more women pursue full-time careers, dramatic changes are occurring in purchasing time for many products, such as groceries.

The consumer life-cycle dimensions are also critical here. For example, marriage involves a whole new buying process from the engagement ring to the retirement home. Companies also have different purchase needs as they grow and develop. It is important for us to be aware of these changing needs and purchase patterns in order to plan production and distribution activities. Sometimes special incentives can alter when consumers buy (e.g., the pre-season sale), but usually it is the marketer who must adapt to the consumer's pattern of behaviour.

Why

The more we know about a consumer, the better able we are to gain that consumer's business. It is one thing to know that women between the ages of forty-five and sixty with reasonably high income prefer one product and buy it in department stores; it is another to know why. For example, DuBarry cosmetics discovered that its customers had aged with the company (and both were dying), that they preferred a cosmetician's help in purchase selection, that price was an indicator of quality to its patrons, that the company had an old-fashioned image, and that skin treatment was their major concern. DuBarry suddenly realized it was not reaching the large group of young, fashion-conscious single girls who preferred self-service outlets and sex-oriented advertising, had more limited budgets, and wanted colour and style more than creams and lotions. Subsequently the company drastically revamped its marketing program. For a long time, management knew what was happening to sales and profits, but they did not look at the consumer to find out why.

SUMMARY

The development of insightful consumer analysis is seldom an easy task. Some statistical evidence is often available, but frequently judgements must be based on experience, educated guesses, and observation. Marketing writer Philip Kotler put it this way: "Customers are neither so simple that they do not require study nor so complex that there are no rewards from study."

COMPETITIVE ANALYSIS

A comprehensive and continuing study of our competition is obviously important. We may and should study our competition in the same depth as we study our target market. A successful marketing program both satisfies the needs and wants of a target audience and does so better than the marketing program of the competitors. The following questions usually assist in an analysis of the competition:

1. Who are relevant competitors?
2. Are they now after the same target market? Could they be after the same target market in the future?
3. What are their marketing programs (product, price, distribution, communication) and how successful have they been?
4. What competitive stance are they likely to take either in anticipation of or reaction to your own marketing program?
5. How strong are the competitors? In a head-to-head battle, who would likely win? What implications does this assessment have for your own marketing strategy?

One way of characterizing competition in product categories is referred to as the product life cycle. It refers to the pattern all products seem to follow at varying speeds from birth (introduction) through adolescence (growth) through adulthood (maturity) to death (decline and withdrawal). In general, the concept is diagrammed as follows:

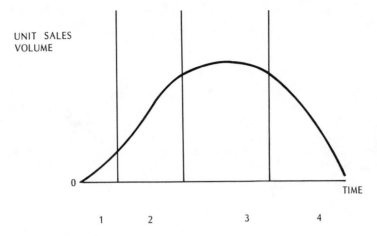

1 : Introduction

2 : Growth

3 : Maturity (and market saturation)

4 : Decline

This curve can be prepared for an individual product or service, a product line, or even a product category. It varies in shape across product types. For example, the product life cycle for hula hoops was very peaked (fast up, fast down) whereas the product life cycle for commercial airplanes is usually quite flat (longer product life). This concept is important for several reasons:

- The overall shape gives us clues as to an appropriate time horizon. For example, short product life means we must recoup and exceed our investment in a short-time period. This usually means higher initial prices and more agressive marketing. For example, consider fashion and fad items. What will the product life be for this year's most popular clothing style?
- The current or anticipated position of a product in its cycle gives us clues as to the likely marketing activities of our competitors. For example, price cutting is frequently very prevalent as unit sales begin to slip in the decline stage.

The product life cycle is clearer in retrospect than in prospect for most products; however, by examining the history of comparable products and how other marketers behaved at various points in time, we may derive considerable insight as to an appropriate marketing program to combat competition.

Environmental Analysis

The external environment (here meaning the context in which the firm or organization operates) presents a host of dynamic, largely uncontrollable problems and opportunities for marketers. Some of the most important areas to monitor are as follows:

- Political
- Economic
- Social
- Technological

In brief, we must analyze other aspects of the situation in addition to the consumer and the competition.

Political

Recent groundswells of consumer discontent with marketing practices and institutions (referred to as consumerism) have spawned a raft of new regulations and restrictions at all political levels that marketers must now consider in the formulation of marketing programs. Legislation has resulted in restraints on advertising, merchandising, pricing, labelling, interest rates, etc. The trend towards more government involvement in marketing seems inexorable and irreversible.

Economic

As a marketing decision maker, you should also evaluate the current economic situation and try to predict its future direction. How will a recession affect the sale of your products? Inflation? Wage and price controls? Does the value of the dollar affect overseas sales or the supplies which are brought in from other countries? Are there any economic indicators, housing starts, GNP, for example, which will aid in forecasting the problems or opportunities the economy might bring to bear on your plans?

Social

Studies have shown that consumers are changing drastically. Most of the buying power is now in the hands of the younger part of the population. Some of their characteristics include:

- Transience (home and job)
- Fewer children and at a later age
- Husband and wife both work
- Increasing interest in leisure-time activities
- Alternative life styles

How will such changes affect the demand for our product or service? Will marketing programs need to be changed to achieve greater impact?

Technological

The unprecedented acceleration in the rate of technological development in the twentieth century has shortened product life cycles, accelerated changes in distribution, moved more information to more people faster, and so on. Marketing has become faster paced, more complex, more interesting, more expensive, and more risky.

Summary

An analysis of the environment reveals both opportunities and problems. Makers of small economy cars saw and exploited the opportunity to capture a large share of the automobile market. Inflation and spasmodic food supplies have made a mockery of the public relations efforts of large supermarket chains. Marketers must keep their eyes and ears open and be flexible in their marketing stance.

CORPORATE CAPABILITIES ANALYSIS

Analysis of consumers, competition, and the environment enables you to determine what your company might do to realize marketing objectives. Analysis of your finances, people, equipment, and other corporate resources enables you to determine what your company could do to realize marketing objectives. What resources are needed? What are now available? What are potentially available and at what cost? Can the existing distribution network handle the new product? Can new salesmen be found and trained in time? Can production provide the product in time and in sufficient quantity? Will finance provide the funds to finance inventory and accounts receivable increases? The list of important questions is lengthier than this, but perhaps the point is clear.

MARKETING RESEARCH

Information may be classified as follows: that which we have and is useful; that which we have and is useless; that which we want and can get at a reasonable cost; that which we want and cannot get at a reasonable cost.

All marketing decision makers operate in a situation that is less than perfect, that is, we do not have all of the useful and necessary information at hand. Sometimes, it is worthwhile to seek more information; at other times, it is futile. There are several ways to collect information: sales reports, trade magazines, government statistics, telephone and mail surveys, interviews, observation of competitors, and so on. The management of this information collection, analysis and dissemination is usually called marketing research.

Marketing research is a service function—it exists to make better marketing decisions. Marketing research activities should only be undertaken if there will be a direct payoff in improved marketing program decisions. As a decision maker seeking research information, you should be able to state:

- What specific information is wanted
- How that information will result in better decisions
- How much the information is worth in dollar value

Marketing research may involve learning more about consumers or about competitors. For example, marketers frequently test their new products, test new advertising campaigns, experiment with price levels. There are a host of data collection methods and analytical techniques. You must be careful never to lose sight of the basic purpose of marketing research—some techniques and some researchers are seductive, but inappropriate for the problem at hand.

THE APPROPRIATE MARKETING PROGRAM

It is important that you develop your own approach to marketing decision making which, through experience, proves most helpful. We all can analyze a problem thoroughly, seeking logical approaches and the best marketing program. The test comes in the marketplace. You can tell if your program is successful by monitoring several performance criteria, such as the following:

- Dollar sales
- Unit sales volume
- Share of market
- Sales growth rate
- Profitability (several measures including return on investment)
- Number of consumers who have heard of the product
- Number of repeat customers

The following diagram may help you remember the points made in this chapter.

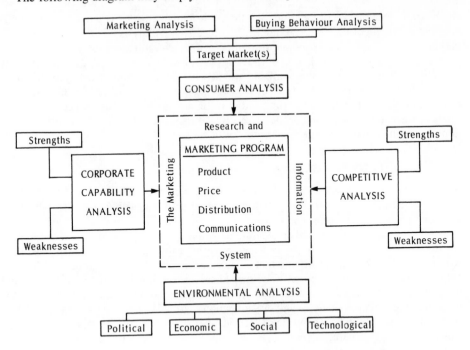

23

The Birds, the Bees, and the Bugs

> When I came home, though, then came sorrow. Too, too plain was Signor Gonorrhea. I rose very disconsolate, the poisonous infection raging in my veins and anxiety and vexation boiling in my breast. What, thought I, can this beautiful, this sensible, and this agreeable woman be so sadly defiled? Can corruption lodge beneath so fair a form? And yet these damn twinges, this scalding heat, and that deep-tinged loathsome matter are the strongest proofs of infection.
>
> *Boswell's London Journal*
> *1762-1763*

In the spring of 1973, Mr. Tony Cosgrave presented an action plan to alert the people of Saskatchewan to the dangers of and the treatment for venereal disease. Mr. Cosgrave had been asked to prepare a complete promotional program by Dr. W. G. Davidson, M.D., D.P.H., the Provincial Epidemiologist (epidemics) for Saskatchewan. Dr. Davidson considered venereal disease no longer just a medical problem, but a social problem as well, and believed a major effort was necessary to curb its increase in Saskatchewan. Mr. Cosgrave presented his plan to the advisory Committee on the Venereal Disease Control Program (A.C.V.D.) and that committee was presently evaluating his proposals.

VENEREAL DISEASES[1]

Gonorrhea

Gonorrhea has been a frequent complication of lovemaking throughout the ages. The first record of gonorrhea was in Scriptures, Book of Leviticus (about 1500 B.C.) where symptoms were described in detail. The Greek physician Hippocrates (400 B.C.) stated that gonorrhea resulted from "excessive indulgence in the pleasures of Venus," the goddess of love. In 1793, the French general Carnot wrote that venereal disease, transmitted by the 3000 prostitutes serving his army, "killed ten times as many men as enemy fire." The problem of gonorrhea had apparently worsened since the Viet Nam conflict because many of the strains of the infection had become penicillin resistant.

The bacteria that cause gonorrhea, the "gonococcus," are some of the most sensitive of all bacteria which cause human disease. Outside the human body the gonococcus dies within a few seconds because it does not survive sunshine, drying or soap and water. Thus, doctors believe it is almost impossible to catch gonorrhea from toilet seats, cups, towels, etc., that have been used by an infected person. The only prevalent way the gonococcus can survive the transfer from one person to the other is through very close physical contact such as vaginal, anal or oral-genital sexual intercourse.

---

[1] Gonorrhea and syphilis are the most prevalent and dangerous venereal diseases, but there are other venereal diseases such as chancroid, grandloma, and lymphogranuloma venerium. Only gonorrhea and syphilis will be discussed in detail in this case. The information provided in this case on these medical problems is not intended to be fully complete, so it should not be relied upon for personal medical care.

Most men with a gonorrhea infection of the penis first notice symptoms three to five days after becoming infected. Swelling of the meatus (the opening at the end of the penis), burning pain upon urination and a thick yellowish green discharge from the meatus are common symptoms. Basically, when someone has been infected, they know it! Even without treatment, these symptoms might disappear on their own a few weeks after infection. Untreated, gonorrhea may result in sterility in both men and women, arthritis, meningitis or peritonitis (inflammation of the joints, brain or membrane lining of the abdomen, respectively).

Fifty to 80 per cent of women infected with gonorrhea typically do not notice any discomfort or symptoms of their disease for the first few weeks or even months. Even then, the coloured discharge is difficult to detect. Other parasitic infections also tend to have the same type of discharge and make accurate diagnosis difficult. However, those who do experience symptoms have pain on walking or sitting, tenderness in the genitalia and heavy pus discharge.

Prevention of Gonorrhea

Tuesday, 17 May. . . . We went down a lane to a snug place, and I took out my armour, but she begged that I might not put it on, as the sport was much pleasanter without it, and as she was quite safe. I was so rash as to trust her, and had a very agreeable congress.

Wednesday, 18 May. . . . Much concern was I in from the apprehension of being again reduced to misery, and in so silly a way too. My benevolence indeed suggested to me to put confidence in the poor girl, but then said cool reason, ''What abandoned, deceitful wretches are these girls, and even supposing her honest, how could she know with any certainty that she was well?''

Boswell's London Journal
1762-1763

The use of the condom, the intestine of a sheep in Boswell's day, had been promoted for years as a means of preventing the transmission of social diseases, but this was not always 100 per cent effective as a preventive measure. United States Army experience had shown a 60 per cent reduction in the incidence of gonorrhea from 625 cases per 1000 to 35 per 1000 population through enforced use of the condom. There had been some experimentation with vaginal foams, but these had not been very satisfactory.

Many myths existed about prevention. Soap and water washing after contact might help somewhat, but birth control pills, contrary to opinions held by many people who visited clinics, did not prevent disease, only pregnancy. Therefore, part of the program had to deal with the promotion of a change in, or additions to, present contraceptive practices. Mr. Cosgrave thought this topic might well provoke a much more unfavourable public reaction than contraceptive information campaigns mounted previously.

Treament of Gonorrhea

An individual could get treatment for gonorrhea or another venereal disease by visiting his or her regular doctor or by going to a VD treatment centre. Four of these centres, public health clinics specifically designated for VD, had been established in Saskatchewan to provide quick, simple, free medical treatment and advice for walk-in patients. Most visitors to these centres found their way there by word-of-mouth, referrals from doctors or by reading signs posted in washrooms in some public buildings, such as the Post Office. According to a clinic worker, many people preferred the treatment centres because they would be embarrassed to have their own doctor find out or they were worried the doctor would tell their parents or spouses about the situation. Dr. Davidson noted that as the incidence of venereal disease increased, the proportion of patients being treated by physicians decreased. ''Many people are sensitive about venereal disease,'' he added. ''Being middle class, they feel VD isn't a middle-class disease and shouldn't have happened to them.''

Treatment at a VD clinic was relatively quick, on average about 20 minutes. Lab samples were taken, antibiotics administered if it seemed appropriate, and some vital statistics gathered (such as age, address, occupation and any known contacts). The situation was supposed to be strictly medical with no moralizing discussions. There was some disagreement as to the success of these clinics, but most criticism centred on claims of inhospitability and poor locations.

There was also criticism of the way in which private physicians treated venereal disease. For example, Dr. J. D. Wallace, secretary-general of the Canadian Medical Association in 1973, claimed most Canadian doctors did not take venereal disease seriously enough and that until they did, the incidence of VD would remain at epidemic levels. According to Dr. Wallace, often doctors would not report VD cases to public health offices, would not check on possible contacts and did not engage in adequate follow-up treatment.

Dr. Davidson believed every case of VD had to be considered the source of a potential epidemic. Since no case existed in isolation, it was vitally important to locate and examine all relevant sexual contacts as soon as possible to prevent further spread of the infection in the community. There was a major problem in getting infected individuals to name their contacts, despite the fact the name of the informant was never disclosed. Because the symptoms in males were much more obvious, most of the patients treated were males. In 1972, about 90 per cent of the patients at the VD centres were male. Dr. Davidson stressed to Mr. Cosgrave that something had to be done not only to convince women who had had relations with strangers or near-strangers to have a check-up, but more importantly, to convince the public that naming contacts was a thoughtful and considerate act.

Syphilis

Syphilis is a rare bacteria which has evolved successfully alongside man. Early syphilis in Africa was called yaws, and appeared as large, moist sores on the skin. As man moved from a moist environment into more northern, drier climates, the disease retreated to the moist areas of the human body (the mouth, nostrils, under arms, crotch and anus) and was known as endemic syphilis. The introduction of better sanitation began to make a significant impact on prevention of endemic syphilis, as the bacteria, which was passed by touch, was weak, fragile and often cured by simple cleanliness. In response to the challenge, syphilis has adapted, surviving in parts of the body which remain moist but which are rarely exposed to the outside world (the sexual organs and the anus).

The bacteria are transferred at any point where there is contact with an open sore, the most usual contact being intercourse. Wearing a condom does not prevent transfer, as the organisms can be transmitted to the area at the junction of the penis and the rest of the body, the part not covered by the prophylactic. The bacteria can then work their way right through the skin, and, within a few hours of entry, can reach the bloodstream and be carried to all parts of the body.

As early as three days or as long as three months after sexual intercourse with an infected person, the primary sore of syphilis, called the chancre, appears at the spot where the bacteria invaded the body. Generalized symptoms include enlarged and tender lymph nodes, headaches and nausea. Usually quite visible in men, the chancre of primary syphilis is often not visible in women, as it usually appears on the cervix or inner vaginal walls. If left untreated, the chancre heals within one to five weeks of its appearance.

Within two weeks to six months after the primary chancre disappears, a secondary syphilitic stage appears, a generalized skin rash with secondary lesions (sores). The appearance of this rash is extremely variable; the only factor common to most cases is that syphilitic rashes do not itch or hurt. Most commonly, the rash is seen as cherry-coloured, raised bumps of different sizes. In warm, moist areas of the body, the rash might form broad-based rounded growths. Dull red at first, they develop a greyish white surface that eventually breaks down to reveal a dull red surface oozing a clear liquid containing large numbers of syphilis bacteria, extremely contagious to other people. Without treatment, secondary stages might disappear two to six weeks after their appearance. Yet this stage may reappear at intervals up to two years after.

If secondary syphilis is not treated, it progresses to a stage called latent syphilis, in which there are no symptoms at all. About two-thirds of untreated people live the rest of their lives without any further disturbance from the disease. However, the remaining one-third may suffer from (a) *benign late syphilis,* a large destructive ulcer on the skin, muscles, digestive organs, liver, lungs, eyes or endocrine glands, which develops three to seven years after infection; or (b) *cardiovascular late syphilis,* which appears ten to forty years after infection, and affects the heart and major blood vessels and often leads to death; or (c) *neurosyphilis*, a fatal attack on the spinal cord and brain, which strikes ten to twenty years after the onset of the infection. Paralysis and insanity precede death. Syphilis can also be passed to a fetus if the mother has been infected but not treated, or to a breast-fed infant.

Prevention of Syphilis

Unfortunately, there was little that could be worn or used to prevent syphilis. Thorough washing before and after intercourse might have helped kill the fragile bacteria before they could enter the body. Like gonorrhea, the major prevention of the spread of the disease was ensuring that infected persons listed their contacts so that those infected could be treated.

Treatment of Syphilis

In order to combat syphilis, doctors used to administer weekly injections of arsenicals and other heavy metal drugs for a period of twelve to eighteen months, sometimes longer. In 1943, when penicillin was discovered, doctors found it an effective combatant against syphilis. Doses of penicillin were injected into the buttock of the patient (as for gonorrhea) for a period of one to three weeks depending on the stage of the disease. Dosage levels were a matter of controversy, but the cure for early syphilis was considered to be 80 per cent effective. There was some difficulty establishing the effectiveness level because reinfection was possible and often common for many individuals who had suffered early infectious syphilis.

In Ontario, the law stated that females had to have three negative tests, while males had to have two negative tests. By regulation, anyone who refused to come in for a test once named as a contact, and notified as such, could be jailed. This was not the case in Saskatchewan.

EXTENT OF THE VD PROBLEM AND SOME ATTEMPTS TO SOLVE IT

Both syphilis and gonorrhea were increasing in frequency according to the number of notifications received by the Saskatchewan Department of Health from doctors and clinics. Between 1972 and 1973, syphilis (all stages) had increased from 164 to 189 cases (15 per cent increase) and gonorrhea from 3162 to 3637 cases (15 per cent increase). The following table provides some statistics on the incidence of gonorrhea in Saskatchewan between 1968 and 1973.

Table 1: Incidence of Gonorrhea

	1968	1969	1970	1971	1972	1973	% Change 1968-1973
A. Total notifications of gonorrhea	2 094	2 373	2 267	2 797	3 162	3 637	+ 73.4
B. Number of notifications in 15-19 year age group	354	424	475	681	857	1 071	+202.5
C. Percentage of notifications in 15-19 year group (B ÷ A = C)	16.9	17.8	20.9	24.3	27.1	29.4	
Population between 15-19 years	93 276	95 776	97 109	98 857	100 636	98 945	
Rate per 100 000*	379.2	442.7	489.2	688.8	851.9	1 082.3	

* For the total population of Saskatchewan. For further information about Saskatchewan, please see Exhibit 1.

The Advisory Committee on Venereal Disease (A.C.V.D.) noticed that the fifteen to thirty age group had the highest incidence of VD, was the fastest growing population segment, had experienced the fastest growth in VD infections over the past five years and had a high repeat treatment rate. Accordingly, they decided this group would be the main target of their new campaign.

Previous attempts to curb VD in Saskatchewan included some educational efforts in the high schools and a requirement for a syphilis test before receipt of a marriage licence. The school programs had faltered apparently because the materials provided teachers were considered inadequate and because teachers felt uncomfortable discussing the topic. The school boards were receptive to outside help, but had received little. The Saskatchewan Marriage Act stipulated that all applicants for a marriage licence had to have passed a blood test for syphilis. Although gonorrhea was far more prevalent than syphilis, tests for gonorrhea infection were not required under the Act.

GONAX

In addition, a self-testing kit had been developed to enable women to check for gonorrhea infection at home. One thousand kits were being planned for production, and awaited only a decision from the A.C.V.D. on what budget would be available for them. They were to be distributed to university campus health centres, public health centres, doctors' offices, and by mail. The kits cost $.50 each (Exhibit 2 illustrates the instructions received with the kit), and advertising their availability would add to the cost. (See Exhibit 3 for sample newspaper ad.) In a pilot test, the kits proved to be an effective means of testing for disease, provided they were properly used.

THE ADVISORY COMMITTEE ON THE VENEREAL DISEASE CONTROL PROGRAM

The Saskatchewan Minister of Health, on recommendation by Dr. Davidson, established the A.C.V.D. in 1973 to create a complete program to combat one of Saskatchewan's worst health problems. The A.C.V.D. comprised eight members of the Health Department and concerned citizens and met frequently to exchange statistics and ideas on what to do. Most A.C.V.D. members were concerned about the moral and political implications of trying to educate the public about VD preventive measures—they anticipated much more antagonism by some groups than the controversial sex education programs in the schools. Exhibit 4 contains a sampling of opinions of A.C.V.D. members and others on approaches to the VD problem in Saskatchewan.

The A.C.V.D. had a budget of approximately $100 000 to $150 000 per year for the next two years. There was considerable disagreement among committee members as to how to spend that money. The doctors and the Health Department favoured putting most of the money into clinics, with more staff and drugs. Other members of the A.C.V.D. favoured upgrading physician education in areas where clinics did not exist and instigating a media campaign to educate the public about VD. Each new clinic would cost approximately $9000 to establish plus staffing costs of approximately $25 000-$40 000 per year depending on circumstances. Existing VD clinics could be expanded with part-time staff at a cost of about $5000 per year for each additional public health nurse. Another related proposal was the expansion of the VD detection program at the provincial laboratory. Such expansion was thought by some to be necessary if the Gonax kit was successful. Preliminary estimates for this expansion were in the neighbourhood of $5000.

An information campaign directed at physicians and nurses had not been thought through. One suggestion was a series of information booths at medical conferences. A rough guess of $1000 per booth per conference was mentioned in the meeting.

A brochure had been prepared by the Saskatchewan Department of Health entitled "Bodyguards and Self-Defence: Your VD Protection Manual." These brochures cost $.10 each to print. Staff members of the department advocated a production run of 1000 copies to be distributed to schools, doctors' offices, libraries, clinics, hotels, motels, bars and occupational health centres. The following gives an idea of the contents of the brochure:

Bodyguards

For the male:
- Applying a condom before sexual contact.
- Urinating immediately after sexual intercourse.
- Washing the genital area with soap and water immediately after sexual intercourse.

For the female:
- Insisting that your male partner use a condom.
- Gentle vaginal douching with a mild soapy solution after sexual contact.
- Washing the genital area with soap and water immediately after sexual intercourse.
- The use of some vaginal contraceptive gels and creams. These may kill venereal disease germs.

On the back of the brochure was the statement "Should you require any further information, telephone _____." The idea was to establish a telephone hot line to provide information on venereal diseases and to suggest a visit to the nearest VD clinic if the situation seemed to warrant it. One proposal involved counsellors answering the phones from 8:00 A.M. to 9:45 P.M. each day. Another proposal involved an "electronic secretary," a tape message receiver that would operate twenty-four hours a day. Each morning a clinic staff member would answer the messages of the previous day. Cost of the tape machine was $20.50 per month. Preliminary cost estimates for a telephone system, including INWAT long distance service adequate to handle calls from the entire province, were $300 connect costs and $730 per month equipment rental.

THE PROPOSED MEDIA CAMPAIGN

Dr. Davidson had not given Mr. Cosgrave a specific budget figure for an advertising campaign. As he examined various alternatives with the help of advertising agencies and the Department of Health staff, Mr. Cosgrave received several varying suggestions on how much to spend. He had not decided on an appropriate budget, but hoped the A.C.V.D. meeting would result in a consensus on the amount to be spent.

Mr. Cosgrave prepared a statement of objectives for the campaign, as shown in Exhibit 5. In addition, he laid before the A.C.V.D. a number of alternative media ideas for their evaluation. These ideas involved the use of print advertising, television advertising, radio, and "shorts" at drive-in movies.

Print Advertising

There were four daily newspapers and about seventy weekly newspapers in the province. One agency suggested to Mr. Cosgrave that three one-eighth page ads (two of which are shown as Exhibit 6) be produced at a cost of $882 and run ("placed") at a cost of $5184: $2020 to dailies, $2874 to weeklies, and $290 to other periodicals. Another group suggested one-quarter page ads at a production cost of $4000 (two of which are shown as Exhibits 7 and 8). They estimated that for "saturation provincial coverage" each insertion would cost $4800.

Television Advertising

There were eight television stations in the province. An animated thirty-second spot with voice-over was proposed. Production cost would be in the neighbourhood of $4000. One thirty-second commercial on the eight stations at prime time would cost a total of $718. Health Department staffers recommended twenty announcements for twenty days' exposure during August and September, one spot per day, for a total cost of $14 360.

Radio Advertising

There were nineteen radio stations in the province. One thirty-second spot during prime time on the nineteen stations would cost a total of $250, a sixty-second spot would cost $306. Ratio audience data are shown as Exhibit 9. One agency had prepared some sixty-second spots for VD in 1972 which Mr. Cosgrave felt might be appropriate. Production costs for four commercials were estimated at $300.

Drive-in Movie Shorts

A drive-in movie short was somewhat like a T.V. commercial and was shown before each movie at the drive-in. A 35 mm live action spot would cost approximately $2000 to produce. Placement costs varied greatly as shown in Exhibit 10.

As Mr. Cosgrave finished his presentation, he added his suggestion that $5000 be set aside to evaluate the effectiveness of the campaign. Dr. Davidson then asked the members of the A.C.V.D., "What do you think we should do?"

Exhibit 1
The Birds, the Bees, and the Bugs
Demographic Data: Province of Saskatchewan*

AREA 220 182 square miles
POPULATION 1971, 4.2 per square mile

June 1, 1966	June 1, 1971
955 344	926 242

Average annual change 1951-1971—0.5%
1971 — 53% urban, 22% rural non-farm, 25% farm
1971 — 470 720 males
        455 515 females

1971 —	Male	Female
10-14 years	51 500	49 400
15-19 years	49 700	47 600
20-24 years	36 700	35 000
25-34 years	49 800	49 000
35-44 years	48 600	46 600

Cities		
Regina	140 000	
Saskatoon	125 000	
Moose Jaw	32 000	
Prince Albert	28 000	
Swift Current	15 000	
North Battleford	13 000	
Yorkton	13 000	

Source: *Canada Year Book,* 1973

Exhibit 2
The Birds, the Bees, and the Bugs
The Gonax, a Self-Test Kit for Gonorrhea

- A kit designed to allow a woman to collect a specimen in the privacy of her own bathroom that can be tested by the laboratory for gonorrhea.

Contents of Kit

- Small jar with brown jelly, plastic bag and twister.
- Tampax tampon.
- Instruction sheet with address label.
- Paper wad with chemicals (when wad is dampened with water, it slowly releases gases needed to help germs multiply so that the laboratory can find them).
- Metal mailing cylinder

How to Collect the Specimen

- Read all the instructions first. Locate the address label at the end of these instructions. Cut out the address label along the broken lines. Answer all the questions on the address label so that a report can be sent to you.
- Unwrap the tampon and adjust its length to expose about one-quarter inch of cotton.
- Insert the tampon as far as possible into the front passage. Leave it in for at least three minutes.
- Remove the tampon, and gently rub or dab the cotton end onto the chocolate jelly in the jar. Do not break the surface of the jelly.
- Throw away the tampon.
- Screw the top of the jar snugly. Then loosen the top about one-quarter turn so that the air can get in.
- Dampen the paper wad with water by passing it swiftly under a running tap. Do not soak. Put the water-dampened wad into the plastic bag.
- Drop the jar into the plastic bag on top of the paper wad. Press out the air from the plastic bag.
- Knot the plastic bag tightly to seal it or use the twister.
- Put the plastic bag with contents and your address label into the metal mailing container.
- Screw the lid onto the mailing container and put $.20 postage on the address label.
- Mail the container in an indoor mailbox (severe heat in summer or frost in winter may spoil your specimen).
  You may expect the report about a week after mailing your specimen.

What Is Gonorrhea and How Do You Get It?

Gonorrhea or clap is an infection of the vulva, vagina, urethra or penis which may develop a few days after sexual intercourse with an infected partner. The risk of infection increases with the number of sexual partners that either the man or the woman has had.

What Are the Symptoms in a Woman?

About one-third of women who become infected develop burning or itching upon urinating, tenderness, visible sores or a vaginal discharge. Any woman with any of these symptoms should visit her doctor or a public health clinic.

About two-thirds of women who become infected do not develop any signs or symptoms of the infection, but their reproductive system and general health may be seriously damaged.

Who Should Take the Test?

A woman who has no symptoms, but fears that one of her sexual partners may have infected her, should take the test.

Will the Findings of this Test Be Kept Confidential?

Yes. The report will be mailed to your given address as shown on the address label. A copy of a positive report will be sent to the physician named to inform him that he might proceed immediately with the necessary treatment.

Does a Negative Report Mean That You Do Not Have Gonorrhea?

Only if you do not have any symptoms! A single negative test is only 80 per cent reliable. If you have symptoms, you should repeat the test—or better still—see your physician.

Exhibit 3
The Birds, the Bees, and the Bugs
Sample Newspaper Advertisement for Gonax (Actual Size)

A Self-Test Kit for Gonorrhea Available FREE to Women

The kit is an easy way to test yourself for Gonorrhea (VD). Instructions on how to use are enclosed in the kit.

TO RECEIVE YOUR KIT, FREE OF CHARGE, JUST DIAL YOUR DIRECT DISTANCE DIALING ACCESS CODE NUMBER THEN THE TOLL FREE NUMBER

800-667-0681

or write: GONAX, 1328 College Avenue, Regina

Saskatchewan Dept. of Public Health

Exhibit 4
The Birds, the Bees, and the Bugs
SAMPLE OF OPINIONS EXPRESSED ABOUT VD BY CONCERNED OFFICIALS

1. "Schools cannot be expected to replace the social functions of the family, nor can the burden of transmitting a coherent and unitary value system properly be placed on a government."
2. "Can we treat those under eighteen without their parents' consent? Experience in Toronto shows that legislative constraints force those under eighteen to turn to black market drugs, most of which do not cure but simply suppress the symptoms."
3. "The problem with present pamphlets is the tone of moral condemnation which is inappropriate, and indeed counterproductive, in today's society. By implying that women who have VD are easy "pick ups," they inhibit women from seeking treatment for fear of having themselves branded as such. By describing premarital relations as illicit (i.e. unlawful) and suggesting physical exercise as an alternative to sexual relationships they "turn off" young people who find this advice "Victorian" and inane.

   "The new publications have, in my estimation, overcome these faults. The information transmitted is more accurate and rather than running counter to prevailing sexual behaviour patterns, they attempt to insert into those patterns a willingness to name sexual contacts out of respect for and responsibility to sexual partners."
4. Jack Migowski ed., Maple Creek News Ltd.

   ". . . in many rural areas a very small percentage of the people actually receives daily newspapers, and the only real effective way to get to those people is through the medium of the weekly press.

   "I am sure you realize that, also due to density of population, there is a larger problem in the cities than in the rural centres. However, we wonder what the percentage would be in the two situations. And because of the reluctance of the affected people to come forward that will always be an unknown factor.

   "However, I am sure that you also realize and appreciate the old saying of 'out behind the barn.' And where are the barns?????"

5. TO: Hon. A. E. Blakeney & Cab. Min.
   FROM: Min. of Pub. Health
   RE: VD Control Program 1973
   I would like the support of my cabinet colleagues to markedly step up our attempts to control the spread of syphilis and gonorrhea in the province. VD is now the most prevalent infectious disease in the province and Canada. My reasons for this request are:
   (a) The steadily mounting incidence of venereal disease, especially in the fifteen to nineteen year age group.
   (b) Some of the innovative and unorthodox steps suggested may provoke public criticism; in particular, the necessity to detect a large part of affected but symptomless female carriers in the fifteen to nineteen year age group may create significant problems.

6. TO: Administrators of all Sask. Hospitals
   FROM: Dr. J. D. Berry, Director
         Regional Health Services Branch
   That some of the present VD clinics are inadequate is apparent to anyone visiting the premises of, for instance, the Saskatoon facility which is in no way conducive to the type of operation which the Committee believes desirable. It is desirable that all clinics induce a willingness to attend on the part of those at risk. Access and appearance are factors which affect attendance. Space, furnishings and equipment are necessary for successful operation by the nurse in charge.

7. Dr. J. T. Y. Chiao, Medical Health Officer
   "My contention is that when teenagers who have contacted a venereal disease come into a clinic they require more than a therapeutic injection of a drug."

8. "Inserts should be placed in the 300 000 Saskatchewan Health Insurance Plan circulars which are distributed every year."

9. "A special pamphlet for the "Gay Society" is available from B.C. at $.10 each, minimum order of 500. Strong interest has been expressed by the Gays for such a publication."

10. "Community involvement is essential."

11. "How do we measure success of the new program? If we have a dramatic rise in the statistics because people are now coming in for treatment, and these statistics get into the press nationally, Saskatchewan will look like a hotbed of disease."

12. "Saskatchewan has been part of the 'Bible Belt' for years. How do you bring things like this to the people without having open hostility which will force the politicians to kill the project?"

Exhibit 5
The Birds, the Bees, and the Bugs
The Proposed Campaign: Phases and Objectives

A Sure Cure for VD

We can't promote celibacy. We can't encourage condom use. And we aren't going to limit promiscuity.

Venereal disease is a disease. There is nothing "wrong" with it.

What is wrong is that some people who have contracted it are not getting treated.

Our ability to prevent VD depends upon our ability to:
1. Educate the public as to its nature and symptoms, and
2. Motivate people who have it to get treated.

Within these parameters we have created a three-phase campaign with a twofold objective.

Phase I Awareness

The initial phase of our campaign deals with awareness.

We want to advise people of the high levels of incidence and of the seriousness of untreated VD.

The stance we will adopt for this communication is reasonable and mature. We would like to encourage a thoughtful examination of personal attitudes towards VD and hopefully, to create a more tolerant social environment.

VD is a by-product of the new sexual mores. And while the thought of sex and VD still makes many people uncomfortable, the thought of someone going untreated because of social inhibitions has to be worse.

Phase II Education

There's no point in hitting a hornet's nest with a baseball bat, unless you know what you're doing.

So if we don't have a good follow-up educational program there's no reason to create an awareness.

Consequently, we recommend the creation of a new VD booklet tailored to the Saskatchewan experience.

We propose to call it "Everything you wanted to know about VD but were afraid to ask."

In our opinion the booklet is the most important feature of the entire campaign.

If it's unfeasible, because of economics, to do a new one we would suggest using the book created in Ottawa. It's at least competent and contains the right tone and information.

The key to the education program is distribution. People, even when they're interested, will only commit so much energy to acquiring information. Therefore, the booklet should be effortlessly available.

We would like to investigate the possibilities of placing it in places like high school bathrooms, central government outlets, including liquor stores and drug stores. It's imperative that anyone who wants one can get one.

We should also advise people of the additional resources that are available. Like speakers for groups, clinic numbers, places for private consultation.

The booklet would carry the burden of communicating the physical symptoms of the disease. We really don't think this can be done effectively in an ad. And anyone who is motivated to get the booklet will read it and get a lot more out of it.

Phase III Motivation

Phase III is designed to get people who have or suspect they have VD to see a doctor.

The highest reported incidence of VD exists among people fifteen to thirty (71 per cent).

This also means that the highest unreported incidence exists here too.

Phase III consists of specific communications to people fifteen to nineteen and one to people twenty to thirty.

Besides being the statistically largest segment these people are also the easiest to reach and influence. (Anyway, what can you say to someone over thirty who refuses to be treated?)

The biggest problem perceived here is a social stigma and fear of parental reactions. Consequently, the discretion of the clinic personnel is stressed. We realize, of course, that this is an awkward and delicate line to walk. But our position is that it's better to be treated than not be treated.

Through the use of our headlines we create an immediate empathy with our market by stating, in their own words, the problem of VD as it exists in their surroundings. So, we achieve communication, but even more importantly, we form a basis for honest discussion of the problem between parent and child by pointing out their obvious barriers.

We would also like to stress this as an educational ground and explore ways to saturate the schools with the book and any additional resources we have.

Besides lowering the levels of incidence here we will have given them a solid base and understanding for dealing with VD in the future when they have grown into other age segments.

How It Works Together

We see the various components of this campaign working together to fulfill an immediate and a future need.

By creating a more tolerant social environment and talking directly to the most sensitive area we'll reduce the present levels of incidence.

And by a massive educational program we will be able to control future levels.

Exhibit 6
The Birds, the Bees, and the Bugs
Newspaper Ads, One-Eighth Page

You can get it

An information booklet on VD, its symptoms, treatment, and long-term effects if untreated, is available from libraries, doctors' offices, Metis Society offices, and hospitals, or the Saskatchewan Department of Public Health.

For more information, phone VD
Information Centre
Regina residents 523-9694
Out-of-Regina residents 800-667-0681

All information is kept confidential

Venereal Disease.
What You Don't Know *Can* **Hurt You.**

Saskatchewan Department of Public Health

The forgotten fact of life

A program has been set up by the Department of Public Health to make everyone aware of a high increase of VD throughout the province.

VD is Saskatchewan's fastest growing communicable disease; in the first half of this year there was a 20% increase in treated cases, which means an increase in untreated cases.

The most common venereal diseases are Gonorrhea and Syphilis. If left untreated they may lead to:

Gonorrhea: sterility and arthritic conditions. Women infected during pregnancy can transmit the disease to their unborn children.

Syphilis: untreated syphilis can cause blindness, insanity, sterility, and death.

Cure occurs only with proper medical treatment. All personal information is known only to your Public Health nurse or doctor.

Public Health Clinics

General Hospital
Regina, Sask.
Phone: 522-5467

Regional Health Care
1257-1st Avenue East
Prince Albert, Sask.
Phone: 763-7276

Wing "G" Ground Floor
University Hospital
Saskatoon, Sask.
Phone: 343-5323

53 Stadacona Street West
Moose Jaw, Sask.
Phone 692-4523

Venereal Disease.
What You Don't Know *Can* Hurt You.

For Further Information

Call (Direct and toll free)
V.D. Information Centre
Regina residents . . . 523-9694
Out of Regina residents . . . 800-667-0681

Saskatchewan Department of Public Health

Exhibit 7
The Birds, the Bees, and the Bugs
It's also a state of mind

To a lot of people VD still carries a social stigma. That's a state of mind.

Venereal disease is transmitted through sex. So it's very often hard to talk about it.

But it is time to talk. Because VD has become the fastest-growing communicable disease in Saskatchewan. Greater than mumps, measles and chicken pox put together.

The first half of this year alone has brought a 20% increase in reported and treated cases.

And that means an increase in untreated cases. That a lot of people who have VD, or suspect they have it, aren't doing anything about it.

Because they're embarassed and worried about what people may say or think.

Which is tragic.

Because an untreated venereal disease, such as gonorrhea, can lead to sterility, arthritic complications and congenital defects in unborn children.

But cure is not possible without proper medical treatment. Symptoms are often hard or impossible to detect without a professional examination. And an untreated venereal disease spreads with further sexual contact.

And yet medically, VD is like any other infection. As such it can be quickly treated and cured. Properly and discreetly.

If it's diagnosed in time.

Protect yourself, your family and your friends. Find out the facts about VD. Now.

Because despite what anyone may say there's nothing worse than untreated VD.

VENEREAL DISEASE. WHAT YOU DON'T KNOW *CAN* HURT YOU.
FOR FURTHER INFORMATION CALL (Direct & Toll Free) VD Information Centre. Regina Residents 523-9694—Out of Regina Residents 800-667-0681
The Booklet "Everything You Always Wanted To Know About VD. But Were Afraid to Ask" is available "FREE" at ● Libraries ● Doctors' Offices ● Health Region Offices ● Hospitals

Exhibit 8
The Birds, the Bees, and the Bugs
The forgotten fact of life

If the facts about venereal disease came with the facts of life, VD wouldn't be quite the problem it is today.

But very often, they don't.

The facts are, that venereal disease is transmitted through sex. That symptoms are often hard or impossible to detect without a professional examination. That cure occurs only with proper medical treatment. And that an untreated venereal disease spreads with further sexual contact.

And today, venereal disease is Saskatchewan's fastest-growing communicable disease.

Greater than mumps, measles and chicken pox put together. The first half of this year alone has brought a 20% increase in reported cases. Which also means a significant increase in untreated cases.

That means a lot of people who have VD, or suspect they have it, aren't doing anything about it.

And that's tragic.

Because an untreated venereal disease, such as syphilis, can lead to blindness, insanity, sterility and even death.

And yet medically, VD is like any other infection. As such it can be quickly treated and cured. Properly and discreetly.

If it's diagnosed in time.

But the people who have VD, or may be susceptible, must have the facts. And a bit of understanding.

Because the final fact remains, there's nothing worse than untreated VD.

It's something no one can afford to forget.

VENEREAL DISEASE. WHAT YOU DON'T KNOW *CAN* HURT YOU.
FOR FURTHER INFORMATION CALL (Direct & Toll Free) VD Information Centre, Regina Residents 523-9694—Out of Regina Residents 800-667-0681
The Booklet "Everything You Always Wanted To Know About VD But Were Afraid To Ask" is available "FREE" at ● Libraries ● Doctors' Offices ● Health Region Offices ● Hospitals

Exhibit 9
The Birds, the Bees, and the Bugs
Radio Audience Data*

TEEN AUDIENCE—12-17 YEARS

Station	Peak Time Periods	Day	Average Audience	Adult Audience (18+)
*CKCK Regina	8-8:30 A.M.	M-F	6 550	54 350
	10-11 P.M.	M-F	4 333	5 200
	3-4 P.M.	Sat.	3 000	8 500
	11 P.M.-mdnt.	Sat.	3 800	1 800
	9-11 P.M.	Sun.	3 750	40 500
	4-5 P.M.	Sun.	3 200	14 500
CKRM Regina	7:30-8 A.M.	M-F	1 500	12 350
	6-6:30 P.M.	M-F	650	5 100
	*10 A.M.-noon	Sat.	2 350	17 650
CFMC-FM Saskatoon	No appreciable teen audience			
*CFQC Saskatoon	7:45-8:15 A.M.	M-F	3 900	36 950
	9 A.M.-noon	Sat.	2 666	30 800
	5-6 P.M.	Sat.	2 400	6 900
	10-A.M.-noon	Sun.	4 950	49 900
CJUS-FM Saskatoon	Data not available			
*CKOM Saskatoon	7:30-8 A.M.	M-F	3 750	6 800
	10-11 P.M.	M-F	2 066	1 700
	7-8 P.M.	Sat.	1 900	2 100
	7-8 P.M.	Sun.	2 200	2.100
CHAB Moose Jaw	8-8:30 A.M.	M-F	600	6 200
	4:15-5 P.M.	M-F	400	2 050
	9-10 P.M.	M-F	300	650
	7-9 P.M.	Sat.	600	300
*CKBI Prince Albert	7:30-8:30 A.M.	M-F	2 125	26 525
	4:15-5:15 P.M.	M-F	875	3 925
	10-11:30 P.M.	M-F	700	1 425
	9-10 A.M.	Sat.	900	5 400
	8-9 A.M.	Sat.	800	2 200
	10-11 P.M.	Sat.	900	3 100
CBK Regina	8:15-9 A.M.	M-F	1 633	13 566
CFMQ-FM Regina	9-10 A.M.	Sun.	400	2 300
*CJME Regina	7:30-8:15 A.M.	M-F	5 200	10 366
	4-5 P.M.	M-F	3 350	2 675
	7-8 P.M.	M-F	2 400	2 300
	10-11 P.M.	M-F	3 200	2 267
	1-4 P.M.	Sat.	3 700	1 250
	1-5 P.M.	Sun.	3 500	3 442
	10-11 P.M.	Sun.	3 600	2 700
*CJGX Yorkton	7:30-8:15 A.M.	M-F	9 666	13 833
	10 P.M.-mdnt.	M-F	7 402	860
	9-11 A.M.	Sat.	1 250	10 850

Prepared by J. A. C. Struthers and Associates, 1960 Albert Street, Regina, Saskatchewan, 525-9566.

Exhibit 10

The Birds, the Bees and the Bugs
Saskatchewan Drive-in Movie List

Regina	—	Cinema	For 3, $250
		Queen City	
		Starlite	
Saskatoon	—	Skyway	For 4, $320
		Starlite	
		Sundown	
		Sutherland Park	
Prince Albert	—	Norlite	For 2, $100
		Pines	
Moose Jaw	—	Golden West	$ 60
North Battleford	—	North Park	$ 40
Meadow Lake	—	Northland	$ 30
Nipawin	—	Skyview	$ 30
Yorkton	—	Crest	$ 50
Fort Qu'Appelle	—	Twilite	$ 25
Melfort	—	Sunset	$ 33.50
Lloydminster	—	C + H	$ 40
Kamsack	—	Sunset	$ 30
Unity	—	Twilite	$ 27

24
Castrol Oils (Canada) Ltd.

In the words of its recently appointed marketing manager, Mr. Douglas Taylor, Castrol Oils (Canada) Ltd. had been operating in Canada for over forty years, but had done little more than "show the flag" of the world-wide Castrol organization. Then, starting in January 1968, the company embarked on an ambitious program to become a significant force in the marketing of oil and lubrication products in Canada. Mr. Taylor's own appointment was a result of that program. He joined the Canadian firm in 1968 with the assignment of improving Castrol's marketing policies and practices.

Castrol's principal product was motor oil, and the most difficult problem Mr. Taylor found confronting him was the unwillingness of major Canadian oil companies to stock Castrol products in their service stations. To improve distribution and to spur oil sales in general, Castrol launched a special $75 000 promotional campaign in the spring of 1969. Its focal point was a new product, Castrol GTX motor oil and a consumer advertising campaign directed at automobile owners. Trade advertising and sales promotional material supplemented the consumer campaign. A special selling effort was launched to establish new independent dealer outlets for Castrol products. A Castrol-sponsored Formula A racing car participated in major Canadian competitions, and Mr. Taylor made personal sales calls on senior executives of major Canadian oil companies.

In June 1969, the marketing manager was reviewing the progress of the GTX promotional campaign in an effort to evaluate its effectiveness to date.

THE COMPANY

Castrol Ltd., a British firm, was founded in 1899 for the purpose of marketing railway oils. The company entered the motor oil market in 1909 and, over the years, evolved into a world-wide conglomerate specializing in manufacturing and marketing all types of lubricating oils. By 1966, Castrol controlled over forty companies operating throughout the free world.

In October 1966, Castrol Ltd. merged with The Burmah Oil Co., a British firm whose interests were concentrated in petroleum exploration and refining. One result of the merger was an increasing concern with the operations of subsidiary companies. Castrol Oils (Canada) Ltd. (hereafter referred to simply as Castrol) was one of the subsidiaries found to be yielding an unsatisfactory return. In January 1968, a new president was appointed to the Canadian firm and assigned the task of improving its ROI performance. Mr. Taylor joined the company as its new marketing manager in September 1968.

Castrol was referred to as a "lubricating oil company," a term used to refer to firms who specialized in manufacturing and marketing their own brand of oil and lubricating products. Lubricating oil companies did not sell gasoline, and did not have their own service stations or refineries in Canada. In addition to Castrol, other lubricating oil companies included Veedol Oil Co. (Canada) Ltd., Quaker State Oil Refining Co. (Canada) Ltd., Kendall Refining Co. of Canada Ltd., and Valvoline Oil Co. of Canada Ltd. Veedol was estimated to sell about two million gallons of lubricating oil products a year, Quaker State about one million gallons, and Kendall and Valvoline approximately one-half million gallons each. Castrol's own sales volume was exceeded only by that of Veedol.

Virtually all Castrol products were manufactured in Canada from ingredients purchased from Canadian suppliers. Company sales were not disclosed, but were estimated by trade sources to be in the vicinity of $4 million. These sales were divided into three general classifications:

1. *Aviation and marine products* sold directly to large air and shipping lines;
2. *Private brand products* sold directly to leading manufacturers of snowmobiles, outboard motors and power chain saws;
3. *Motor oils and lubricants* for a wide range of general and special purpose applications, sold to consumers on an indirect basis.

Aviation and marine products accounted for 8 per cent of Castrol's dollar sales volume. These special oils and lubricants were sold under long-term contracts negotiated between Castrol and individual large users. Castrol was a leader among lubricating oil companies in this field. Its customers, for example, included Air Canada and Cunard Shipping Lines.

Private brand products accounted for 10 per cent of Castrol dollar sales, and were also sold to manufacturers on a contract basis. Each of the company's three major customers was the leader in its field. A line of snowmobile oils and lubricants, packaged under the Ski-Doo brand name, was sold to Bombardier Ltd. Outboard motor products bearing Evinrude and Johnson brand names were sold to Outboard Marine Corporation, and a line of private-brand chain saw lubricants was sold to the Pioneer Chain Saw Co.

The remaining 82 per cent of company sales was made up of a broad mix of motor oils and lubricants marketed under the Castrol name. These products, a partial list of which is shown in Exhibit 1, included motor oils, fluids, racing oils, motorcycle oils, gear oils, greases and two-stroke lubricants. All were distributed to ultimate users through Castrol's network of company salesmen, exclusive distributors and dealers.

DISTRIBUTION OF MOTOR OILS AND LUBRICANTS

Castrol motor oils and lubricants were sold by a company sales force, or by exclusive distributors, to approximately 3000 dealers across Canada. Dealers were independent service stations (that is, those not affiliated with major oil companies), automobile accessory stores, repair garages and new car retailers who resold Castrol products to ultimate users. Independent service stations accounted for 9 per cent of Castrol's dollar sales of motor oils and lubricants. Automobile accessory stores and repair garages accounted for 10 and 38 per cent respectively, while new car retailers made up the remaining 43 per cent. As was common practice in the automotive trade, dealers received an approximate markup of 100 per cent.

In the region of Canada's three largest metropolitan areas, motor oils and lubricants were sold to dealers by a company sales force. Castrol had sixteen salesmen—nine operating within a 100-mile radius of Toronto, five in the Montreal area and two in Vancouver. Each salesman had an assigned geographic territory consisting of about 150 customers. The salesman's job was to call on existing customers, or on potential new customers, in an effort to sell Castrol products. Salesmen were paid a base salary of $6000-$7000 plus a commission of approximately three cents a gallon. A regional sales manager in each of the three major cities was responsible for salesman supervision.

Outside the regions of the three major cities, Castrol products were sold to dealers through a network of sixteen automotive distributors. Distributors were located throughout the country; each was granted an exclusive territory. Markups for distributors were in the vicinity of 20 per cent. It was the job of the three regional sales managers to call on distributors, solicit sales and assist distributors in the overall marketing of Castrol products.

COMPETITION FOR MOTOR OIL AND LUBRICANT SALES

In 1968, almost 164 million gallons of motor oils and lubricants were sold in Canada. Approximately 60 per cent of this total was consumed in Ontario and Quebec, as indicated by the provincial sales data shown in Exhibit 2.

Motor oil and lubricant sales were dominated by eighteen major Canadian oil companies. These large companies operated their own service stations through which they sold only their own brands of motor oil and lubricants. Major oil companies would not stock products of the lubricating oil companies, including Castrol.

Selected information on service station outlets in Canada, as shown in Exhibit 3, highlights the market dominance of major oil companies. Of 43 600 retail gasoline outlets in Canada, over 80 per cent were controlled by major oil companies. Four majors—Gulf Oil, Imperial Oil, Shell and Texaco—operated on a national scale. Together, these four controlled over half of Canadian retail gasoline outlets. The remaining fourteen major oil companies operated on a regional basis only.

There were approximately 7000 "independent" service stations in Canada. These were small, independently owned chains usually consisting of one to twenty service stations, although a few independent chains had as many as eighty or ninety stations.

Lubricating oil companies including Castrol, competed for dealer outlets and sales through independent service stations, automobile accessory stores, repair garages and new car retailers. Sales to new car retailers were usually made on an exclusive contract basis. The lubricating oil company helped a new car retailer to finance the cost of lubrication equipment in return for an agreement to stock only the products of that company. Other types of dealers had no such exclusive agreement, and often carried two or three competing brands of motor oils and lubricants.

Further competition for Castrol came from tire, automotive, and service specialty chains. In 1969, as shown in Exhibit 4, there were about thirty such chains in Canada representing, in aggregate, over 1400 retail outlets. Tire, automotive, and service specialty chains often sold their own private brands of motor oil and lubricants, or sold the brands of lubricating oil companies at discount prices. Castrol policy was not to sell its products to these chains, or to manufacture private brands for them.

THE GTX CAMPAIGN

GTX was a new, multigrade motor oil developed at the research laboratories of Castrol Ltd. at Bracknell, England. Introduced to the British market in 1967, the new oil had at least two distinct competitive features. It was the only oil with an SAE 20W/50 viscosity range, and contained a patented anti-friction, anti-wear additive called Liquid Tungsten. Laboratory and field tests showed GTX to be highly effective in minimizing oil consumption, preventing sludge formation in cold and stop-start driving conditions, and in preventing ringsticking and cylinder wall corrosion.

When plans were formulated to introduce GTX in Canada, Mr. Taylor realized that the new oil provided an ideal opportunity to build a promotional campaign for *all* Castrol products. GTX was particularly appropriate for addressing the distribution problem. To gain distribution in major oil company outlets, Mr. Taylor felt it was necessary to offer these companies a product they did not have. GTX, with its viscosity range and Liquid Tungsten additive, was thought to be such a product.

For 1969, Castrol had budgeted to spend $210 000 on promotional activities. From this amount, a sum of $75,000 was set aside to launch a special promotional campaign coinciding with the introduction of GTX on May 1, 1969. The stated objectives of the GTX campaign were to make the public aware of Castrol and GTX, to arouse the attention of major oil companies, and to assist in securing new dealer outlets for Castrol products.

Because of budgetary constraints, the GTX campaign was limited to the metropolitan Toronto and Vancouver markets. Montreal, an attractive market area, was omitted from the campaign because of the high cost of bilingual advertising. However, if the initial campaign proved successful, it was to be expanded to Montreal and other areas at a later date.

The different activities involved in the GTX campaign could be broadly classified into five major areas: consumer advertising; selling efforts directed at independent dealers; trade advertising; racing sponsorship; and selling efforts directed at major oil companies.

CONSUMER ADVERTISING

A total of $47 000 was allocated for GTX consumer advertising in Toronto and Vancouver. Its target audience was young married and family drivers, aged eighteen to fifty, among whom Castrol hoped to build product loyalty. The budget was evenly divided between two periods, May-June and September-October, with approximately two-thirds of the total being spent in Toronto. Radio and outdoor media were chosen, divided as follows:

	May-June	*September-October*
Radio	$11 000*	$13 000
Outdoor	$12 000**	$11 000

* Eighty-six one-minute spots on CFRB, Toronto, and seventy-two one-minute spots on CKNW, Vancouver.
** A "full-showing" of seventy-two billboards in Toronto and forty billboards in Vancouver, each for a four-week period.

Both radio and outdoor advertising utilized a well-known radio personality as their central figure. Wally Crouter of CFRB was chosen in Toronto, Jack Finlay of CKNW in Vancouver. Only one station was used in each city, and the same announcer read all radio advertisements. The central theme of the consumer advertising was best exemplified by the copy of an outdoor advertisement:

YOUR SERVICE STATION DOESN'T
HAVE THE WORLD'S BEST
MOTOR OIL. FIND IT.
CALL "CROUTER" 426-5511

A facsimile of a can of Castrol GTX appeared beside the copy. In response to the advertisement, it was hoped that consumers would call the listed telephone number. An answering service operator gave the caller the name of the nearest GTX dealer, and the consumer's name and address were passed along to the dealer. A radio advertisement, using a similar theme, is reproduced in Exhibit 5.

Radio advertisements were scheduled to run in the early morning commuting hours. Wherever possible, billboards were selected adjacent to a service station of one of the major oil companies.

SELLING EFFORTS TO INDEPENDENT DEALERS

To tie in with the consumer advertising, a "blitz" selling effort was directed at what Mr. Taylor referred to as the "unsold potential." These were independent dealers not currently carrying Castrol products. In Toronto, for example, 320 dealers were called on by

Castrol salesmen in the month of April. The basic selling message delivered was that, by stocking Castrol products, the dealer could be one of those mentioned by Wally Crouter in response to consumer enquiries.

Eleven hundred dollars was spent in preparing salesmen's vinyl folders designed specially for the GTX campaign. Other GTX sales promotion material was purchased for use in both the blitz and subsequent selling efforts. Leaflets, decals and posters cost $5000, point of sale display pieces cost $4000, and 20 000 GTX key rings were bought at a cost of $2000. A typical dealer poster is illustrated in Exhibit 6.

TRADE ADVERTISING

A total of $8000 was budgeted for magazine advertising to dealers. Advertisements appeared in the April and May issues of such magazines as *Canadian Automotive Trade, Track and Traffic, Auto Relations,* and *Wheel Spin.* A typical trade advertisement appears in Exhibit 7.

RACING CAR SPONSORSHIP

Mr. Taylor offered that, at one time, he had mixed feelings about sponsoring racing car drivers. Such publicity, he had felt, reached only hard core enthusiasts who knew about Castrol products anyhow. But more recently he realized that auto racing was becoming a mass-audience sport—40 000 people attended meets at Mosport, 20 000-30 000 attended Ste. Jovite, while substantial numbers were found at Harewood and similar tracks. Further, these people tended to serve as "opinion leaders" for others who sought advice on automotive matters.

In Europe, the Castrol name was well-known in automotive racing circles. Over the years, Castrol-sponsored cars had been highly successful in Grand Prix racing, at Le Mans and other famous races. No real effort at racing sponsorship had been undertaken in Canada, however. With the launching of the GTX campaign, Mr. Taylor decided the company should enter racing sponsorship in Canada. Bill Brack, Canada's champion Formula A driver, was contracted to drive for Castrol. Brack's Lotus car was emblazoned with "Castrol GTX" in the company's white, red and green colours. His mechanics wore Castrol colours. A team of four Castrol employees attended all racing meets in a Castrol station wagon and trailer. These men handed out promotional literature and provided a hospitality centre for the press. Bill Brack appeared in company advertisements endorsing GTX.

The cost of racing sponsorship was about $20 000, plus a fee to Bill Brack that was partly contingent on his performance in races. Since the contract with Bill Brack ran for the full racing season, only $5000 of this amount was allocated to the GTX campaign budget.

SELLING EFFORTS TO MAJOR OIL COMPANIES

In Mr. Taylor's view, the most important single task of the GTX campaign was to secure new dealer outlets for Castrol through service stations of the major oil companies. The marketing manager assumed personal responsibility for this aspect of the program.

During the months of May and June, Mr. Taylor called on key executives in each of the major oil companies. He delivered a basic selling argument. GTX was an outstanding product with unique qualities. In Great Britain, where government regulations forced major oil companies to carry competing brands of oil, Castrol outsold all other brands. It had an estimated 30 per cent of the total motor oil market, including the brands of major oil companies. By stocking Castrol in Canada, a major oil company would find that customers who sought out the Castrol brand would also buy gasoline.

Mr. Taylor was also aware that some service station operators for major oil companies were presently stocking Castrol, even though not permitted to do so. They could not display Castrol, but kept it available out of view. The attraction to a dealer was higher profit on Castrol products. GTX, for example, sold at a suggested retail price of $1.25, as compared to $.90-$1.10 for the top line, multigrade oil of a major oil company. Percentage margins for the dealer were slightly higher on Castrol products.

To impress the dealer's point of view on major oil company executives, Mr. Taylor had his salesmen administer a short questionnaire to about 200 dealers of these companies. The dealer was asked if he now stocked Castrol, and if not, would he do so if permitted. Virtually all replied that they did not now stock, but would do so if allowed. This information was communicated in sales presentations to major oil companies.

SITUATION AT THE END OF JUNE 1969

As Mr. Taylor reviewed the progress of the GTX campaign at the end of June 1969, he was encouraged. Consumer advertising had resulted in a total of seventy-six enquiries in Toronto and Vancouver. The marketing manager reasoned, however, that a far greater number of consumers had become aware of the Castrol name and what it stood for.

The blitz selling effort and trade advertising campaign resulted in about a dozen new independent dealers for Castrol. Mr. Taylor felt that the full effects of this effort were yet to be realized. Establishing new dealers was an ongoing selling job, and with further efforts, it was probable that many more would eventually take on the line.

It seemed unlikely that negotiations with any of the four "national" major oil companies would prove fruitful. But there was cause for optimism in the case of those operating on a regional basis. Murphy Oil Co. had just agreed to stock Castrol in all of its 400 service stations in Quebec and Ontario. Pacific Petroleums was to conduct a test of Castrol products in six of its Vancouver stations, and Golden Eagle Co. had agreed to a similar test in the Maritimes. Negotiations with another regional company with over 1500 stations had progressed to the point where a successful conclusion appeared imminent.

In Mr. Taylor's view, radio advertising in Toronto had proved particularly effective. In fact, he was considering an allocation of additional funds in order to continue radio advertising through the months of July and August. This would "fill in the hole" between the end of June and September/October (where more radio advertising was already planned and budgeted for). Further, it seemed to Mr. Taylor that the original objective relating to the creation of consumer awareness of Castrol had now been accomplished in Toronto. A change to a new theme emphasizing the scope of the world-wide Castrol organization seemed appropriate.

As he pondered the possibility of expanding and changing the radio advertising, Mr. Taylor jotted some notes to send along to his advertising agency for consideration:

> Are you using Castrol Motor Oil. If not—why not?
> Air Canada keep their turbo-prop fleet flying on Castrol. Cunard keep the most modern passenger liner in the world, the QE II, cruising on Castrol. B.M.C. uses it for their racing team and recommend Castrol in their specification books. Ford use it in their 1969 Trans-Am Mustang winning team. The Queen uses it! Dan Gurney would not drive anywhere without it.
> So if Castrol Motor Oil is good enough for all these people, it should be good enough for you. For cruising, flying, racing—even riding like the Queen of England—rely on Castrol, the world's best motor oil. I do!

Exhibit 1
Castrol Oils (Canada) Ltd.
Partial List of Motor Oils and Lubricants, June 1969

ENGINE OILS

Castrol GTX
A new high-performance, multigrade motor oil containing Liquid Tungsten additive to reduce engine wear. The only brand of oil with an SAE 20W/50 viscosity rating. Castrol GTX Winter grade with 5W 30 viscosity rating.

Castrol Super SAE 10W/40
Castrolite SAE 5W/30
Castrol XL SAE 20W/40
A line of multigrade motor oils containing Liquid Tungsten additive.

Castrol HD Motor Oils
Monograde detergent motor oils, all containing Liquid Tungsten, available in SAE 10 to SAE 50 viscosities.

Castrol CRD Oils
A line of oil for use in diesel engines operating under severe conditions.

Agricastrol Multi-Use
Multigrade oil for use in all types of tractors.

AUTOMOTIVE SPECIALITIES

Castrol TQ Automatic Transmission Fluids
A line of various types of fluid, each to meet the requirements of a specific automobile manufacturer.

Hydraulic Oil
A special high viscosity oil for use in hydraulic lifts and hydraulic systems of fork lift trucks.

Castrol M
A castor-based oil for use in racing two-stroke motorcycles, racing outboard engines and model aircraft engines.

Castrol Girling Brake and Clutch Fluids
Castraulic Heavy Duty Brake Fluid
Castrol LHS-2
Castrol Girling Shock Absorber Oil Thin
Fluids designed for hydraulic systems, some for racing and competition. LHS-2 is a special synthetic oil for hydropneumatic systems of Citroen cars.

Castrol Racing Oils
A line of castor-based motor oils designed especially for continuous performance at high speeds.

Castrol Grand Prix Motorcycle Oil
The only brand of oil designed especially for motorcycles, available in SAE 20 to SAE 50 viscosities.

GEAR OILS

Castrol ST SAE 80/90
Castrol D SAE 140
Castrol Hypoy B
Castrol Hypoy LS SAE 90
Castrol Outboard Gear Oil
A line of multi-purpose and specialty minerals oils for lubrication of various types of gears.

GREASES

Castrol MP Grease
Castrol LM Grease
Castrol LMZ No. 1 Grease
Multi-purpose greases, as well as a grease for use in extreme temperature ranges.

TWO-STROKE LUBRICANTS

Castrol Super 2-Cycle Motor Oil
Castrol Two Stroke SAE 3/40
Castrol Chain Saw Lubricants
A full line of oils recommended for use in two-stroke air and water cooled engines in chain saws, power motors, motor scooters, snowmobiles and off-road vehicles.

Exhibit 2
Castrol Oils (Canada) Ltd.
Motor Oil and Lubricant Sales in Canada, 1968

Province	*Sales in 000's of Gallons*
Newfoundland	3 200
Maritimes	8 800
Quebec	33 900
Ontario	66 100
Manitoba	6 900
Saskatchewan	10 100
Alberta	16 600
British Columbia	17 500
Yukon and N.W.T.	700
Total	163 800

Source: Dominion Bureau of Statistics.

Exhibit 3
Castrol Oils (Canada) Ltd
Selected Data On Service Stations In Canada, 1968

Company	Total Retail Outlets	Provinces in which Retail Outlets Located									
		Nfld.	N.S.	N.B.	P.E.I.	P.Q.	Ont.	Man.	Sask.	Alta.	B.C.
BP Canada Ltd.	1 810	•	•	•	•	×	×	•	•	•	•
Champlain Oil Products Ltd.[1]	660	×	•	•	•	×	×	•	•	•	•
Golden Eagle Co. Ltd.	346	×	×	×	•	×	×	×	×	×	×
Gulf Oil Canada Ltd.	4 702	•	•	•	×	×	•	×	×	×	×
Home Oil Distributors Ltd.[1]	335	•	•	•	•	•	•	•	•	•	•
Husky Oil Canada Ltd.	350	•	•	•	•	×	×	×	×	×	×
Imperial Oil Ltd.	6 668	•	×	×	×	×	×	•	•	•	•
Irving Oil Co.	3 000	×	×	×	×	•	•	×	×	×	•
Mohawk Oil Co. Ltd.	125	•	•	•	•	×	•	•	•	•	×
Murphy Oil Co. Ltd.	400	•	•	•	•	×	×	×	×	•	•
Pacific Petroleums Ltd.	294	•	•	•	•	×	×	•	•	•	•
Petrofina Canada Ltd.	1 754	•	×	×	×	•	×	×	×	×	×
Royalite Oil Co. Ltd.[2]	1 203	•	•	•	•	×	×	×	×	×	×
Shell Canada Ltd.	6 278	•	×	×	×	•	×	×	×	×	×
Standard Oil Co. of B.C. Ltd.	601	•	•	•	•	•	•	•	•	•	•
Sun Oil Co. Ltd.	1 100	•	•	•	•	×	×	•	•	•	•
Supertest Petroleum Corp. Ltd.	1 540	•	•	•	•	×	×	×	×	•	•
Texaco Canada Ltd.	5 000	×	×	×	×	×	×	×	×	×	×
Total retail outlets of 18 major companies	36 166					Not Available					
Total retail outlets in Canada[3]	43 603	841	1 808	2 005	335	12 967	13 273	2 547	4 366	3 596	1 867

1 Subsidiary of Imperial Oil Limited
2 Subsidiary of Gulf Oil Canada Limited
3 Excluding Yukon and N.W.T.

Source: National Petroleum News, 1969 Factbook Issue.

Exhibit 4
Castrol Oils (Canada) Ltd.
Tire, Automotive, and Service Specialty Chains in Canada 1969

	Nfld.	N.S.	N.B.	P.E.I.	P.Q.	Ont.	Man.	Sask.	Alta.	B.C.	Total
Associated Tire Centres										10	10
Cal-Van Auto Supply Stores										7	7
Canadian Tire Stores	5	18	10	2	40	156	3				234
Carling Muffler Ltd.					4						4
Clark's Gamble Ltd.						1	6				7
Dunlop Stores		2	2		5	13	2	2	7	11	44
Econo Drive-In Stores										6	6
Finacentres Ltd.		1		1	13	4					19
Firestone Stores	Atlantic Prov.			3	21	58	9	8	15	10	124
General Tire Stores			1		3	5	1	1	2	1	14
B. F. Goodrich Stores		1	2		2	16	1	2	2		26
Goodyear Service Stores		3	1	1	23	46	4	4	10	10	102
Handy Andy Stores	13	9	4		112	5					143
Imperial Oil Ltd.		3			12	16	3	3	4	6	47
K-Mart-Jupiter		2	2			9	2		2	1	18
MacLeod's Ltd.						5	52	90	78	9	234
Midas Muffler Shops					4	15				4	23
Miracle Mart					15	7					22
Motorcade Stores Ltd.			2			135					137
Mister Muffler Ltd.					11	2					13
O.K. Tire Stores				1				2	16	24	43
Penner Tire & Rubber Co. Ltd.							4	3	4	2	13
Simpson's-Sears Ltd.	1		2		2	15	1	3	5	4	33
Speedy Muffler King					6	26					32
Uniroyal Centres			2		5	24	3	2	2	2	40
Western Tire & Auto Supply Ltd.	Atlantic Prov.			26	47	44					117
Woodward Stores (Automotive)									4	9	13
Woolco Auto Centres	1	1	1		3	11	1	1	5	2	26
Zeller's Ltd.					6	1			1		8
TOTAL	20	40	29	34	324	623	93	121	157	118	1559

SOURCE: *Petroleum, Automotive and T.B.A. Marketer—1969* (Toronto: Fullerton-Weston Publishing Limited, 1969), p. 37.

Exhibit 5
Castrol Oils (Canada) Ltd.
Sample of a Castrol GTX Radio Advertisement

Copy   **BRADLEY-VALE ADVERTISING LTD.**

CLIENT Castrol Oils COPY CA-R60-241 Medium Radio #3
RUNNING DATE_____DATE TYPED Mar. 7/69 DATE OF REVISION _____

This is Wally Crouter. Ever heard of Castrol? Castrol probably sells more quality oil than anyone else in the world. So it's no small fry. And Castrol has just come out with a new high-performance oil—Castrol GTX. The first of its kind in Canada, tests have proven Castrol GTX to be superior in performance to ordinary oils. It has Liquid Tungsten to radically reduce frictional wear on moving parts; a special ingredient to inhibit rust and corrosion; and a full-bodied 20W-50 viscosity which goes on protecting your engine like no oil has before. You may never see Castrol GTX in your service station. Most only carry ordinary oils with their own names on the can. Which leaves you with two choices. You can put your car's life in the hands of your service station. Or you can make the small effort to get the best engine protection money can buy. Just call me, Wally Crouter, at 426-5511, and I'll tell you where your nearest Castrol GTX dealer is. There are 1300 in Ontario, so you won't have to go far. It's a matter of your car's life: more, or less. 426-5511.

Exhibit 6
Castrol Oils (Canada) Ltd.
Sample of a Castrol GTX Dealer Poster

Exhibit 7
Castrol Oils (Canada) Ltd.
Sample of a Castrol Trade Magazine Advertisement

We believe in giving our customers the best. How about you?

You've stocked some great Castrol oils.
But never one like GTX.
There's a matchless combination
of laboratory research and racing
experience behind GTX.
It's a 20W-50 that stays a 20W-50.
No shearing off into 20W-30 or worse.
So it cuts consumption without losing
anything in engine protection.
GTX body maintains pressure, too.
Protects against corrosion (vital for
cars left standing out overnight).
Ensures quick starting and
low-drag during warm-up
We confidently tell you - our customers
- that GTX is today's finest motor oil.
Pass it on.

25

Duncan Hardware and Auto Parts Co. Ltd.

In early October 1976, Mr. F. P. Duncan, owner of Duncan Hardware and Auto Parts Co. Ltd., was considering a purchase of toy tow trucks in preparation for Christmas sales. The tow truck was a well-designed, durable toy that operated on two 1.5 volt dry cells. The truck, without batteries, had retailed for $9.95 the previous year in his store and in the local department store. A local discount department store had sold the trucks "on special" the week before Christmas for $8.95. Batteries varied in retail price according to their length of life and brand name, but Mr. Duncan estimated that on average a consumer spent $1 per truck for batteries.

Duncan Hardware and Auto Parts was located in the downtown section of a city of 265 000 people. The firm was founded in 1925 by Mr. Duncan's uncle, who subsequently turned the business over to him in 1950. In the early 1960s Mr. Duncan had joined a fifty-store group of retail hardware outlets in his province. This group purchased its hardware lines almost exclusively from one wholesaler. The Handi Hardware group of stores, as they became known, received store layout, record keeping, inventory planning, promotion and merchandising help from the wholesaler. The member stores used the Handi Hardware ensigns on all their advertising and signs and participated in the total store group special sales programs, which were supported by shared cost advertising programs. The member stores were billed for all purchases at regular wholesale list prices and at the end of each year received a percentage rebate on their total purchases from the wholesaler. Although member stores were not required by contract to purchase any or all of their requirements from the Handi Hardware wholesaler, the percentage rebate formula did increase at higher purchase levels and thereby encouraged them to purchase as much as possible from the one wholesaler.

Duncan Hardware and Auto Parts was the only Handi Hardware store which operated a retail auto parts supply business in conjunction with the hardware business. As a result, the product line in Duncan's store ranged from mufflers, tires, tachometers, spark plugs and car radios to hockey sticks, toys, hammers, saws, piping and small appliances.

Duncan's total sales in 1975 amounted to $500 000. His total store profit after tax amounted to 3 per cent of sales. He stocked toys heavily only at Christmas. In 1975 he sold $15 000 worth of toys: $11 500 in November and December.

During a recent visit to the Handi Hardware wholesaler's warehouse in September 1976, Mr. Duncan noticed a stock of 400 toy trucks left over from the 1975 season. He mentioned the stock to the wholesaler and found that the line had not moved as well as expected last year. Each truck had been imprinted with the Handi Hardware insignia and thus could not be returned to the manufacturer. The wholesaler stated that they had sold 350 toy trucks the previous year and did not intend to reorder any more. They hoped to move the stock in bulk and offered the complete stock to Mr. Duncan at $3.25 per unit, or half the stock at $4 per unit. Mr. Duncan requested a day to think it over.

On the way back to his store, he stopped in at a local department store and saw that they were offering the same truck, without the insignia, at $9.95 again. When he returned to his store, he looked up his records. Last year he had ordered and sold fifty trucks in the two and a half months before Christmas. His cost had been $6 per truck. He decided he would not buy any trucks unless he was reasonably confident that he would at least double the total gross profit he made last year on the sale of the trucks.

As he thought about likely price levels, Mr. Duncan reasoned he could sell fifty trucks at $9.95, seventy-five trucks at $8.95 and one hundred trucks at $7.95, all without any advertising support. He also figured, based on other toys he had carried that about $250 advertising support would increase sales by fifty trucks over the no-advertising support sales levels and that about $350 advertising would increase sales by one hundred trucks over the no advertising support sales levels. Mr. Duncan's son, who was second-in-command at the store, disagreed with Mr. Duncan's estimates. "Last year we left money on the table because we did not take a big enough risk by having inventory right up to the end," he said to his father. "I think we can sell 100 trucks at $8.95 without advertising support. I would prefer to sell them at $8.49. We would sell 150 trucks easily without advertising and at least 200 if we spent about $200 on advertising."

He did not envisage any other costs associated with buying and selling the toy tow trucks, unless he was stuck with trucks at the end of the Christmas buying season. As a general rule, Mr. Duncan figured it cost him 5 per cent of inventory cost to carry Christmas seasonal items from one year to the next.

With these thoughts in mind, Mr. Duncan wondered whether he should buy the toy tow trucks for the upcoming Christmas season.

26

General Cigar Co. Ltd. (A)

Since 1955, the growth and profitability of General Cigar Co. Ltd. had resulted primarily from the success of its Old Port brand. The mild Old Port blend of tobacco, rum-flavoured and wine-dipped, was first introduced in 1955 as a plain end cigar. Later, in 1964, a cigarillo shape was introduced using the same blend of tobacco and, in 1966, a plastic-tipped cigarillo was added to the Old Port line. From sales of 10 million cigars in 1956, demand for Old Ports grew to 104 million cigars and cigarillos in 1966 and was expected to exceed 130 million in 1967.

The fastest growing item in the Old Port line was the tipped cigarillo. By mid-1967, one year after introduction, Old Port tipped cigarillos accounted for about 10 per cent of all cigars and cigarillos smoked in Canada. Old Port plain end cigarillos and plain end cigars accounted for a further 14 per cent and 5 per cent respectively.

In the summer of 1967, Mr. Robert Alexander, vice-president and general manager of General Cigar Co., was considering the development and introduction of an entirely new brand of flavoured tipped cigarillos. At this time, Old Port remained as the only significant *flavoured* Canadian cigar and cigarillo brand on the market. Mr. Alexander was concerned that Old Port's unique position in the flavoured segment of the market was extremely vulnerable to potential challenge by new products from competitive cigar manufacturers. He wondered whether a new brand of flavoured tipped cigarillo, patterned after the Old Port tipped cigarillo in size, price and market target, would protect and improve General Cigar's position in the flavoured market segment.

THE CANADIAN CIGAR INDUSTRY

The Canadian cigar industry was dominated by two firms, General Cigar Co. Ltd. and Simon Cigar Co. Ltd. Collectively, the various brands marketed by General Cigar accounted for about 60 per cent of the cigar and cigarillo market in mid-1967, while Simon Cigar's brands comprised an approximate 30 per cent market share. Two additional companies, Allied Cigar Corporation and Ontario Tobacco Co. Ltd., held market shares of 6 per cent and 4 per cent respectively.

Industry sales for 1967, as shown in Exhibit 1, were expected to reach 453 million units in 1967, an increase of 5 per cent over the previous year. On this basis, Canadian per capita consumption in 1967 would remain at the 1966 level of 22.5 cigars/cigarillos per year. This compared with an annual per capita consumption of 48 cigars/cigarillos in the United States. The retail value of the 1967 Canadian production was expected to be in the vicinity of $32 million at manufacturers' prices, or $40 million at retail—both figures including federal and provincial taxes.

Between 1949 and 1966, Canadian manufacturers were able to offset increasing federal and provincial taxes on tobacco with cost-saving improvements in production technology. During this period, there were virtually no increases in cigar and cigarillo prices at the manufacturer level. By 1966, federal and provincial taxes accounted for almost one-quarter of the retail sales value of cigars and cigarillos, and a price increase at the manufacturer level was passed on to the Canadian consumer. Most cigar manufacturers felt that they would only be able to keep up with any further tax increases by additional price increases.

Following the 1966 price increase, sales of cigars in the $.09-$.13 retail price range declined seriously. Industry sales of cigars (not cigarillos) were projected at 195 million in

1967, a drop of 16.5 percent from the 1965 level. At the same time, sales of cigarillos were growing. Cigarillos, both plain and tipped, increased from 52 per cent of total cigar/cigarillo sales in 1965 to 54 per cent in 1966. Industry officials predicted a 9 per cent increase in 1967.

Tipped cigars and cigarillos, which for a long time were not generally popular, began to grow in Canada in 1966. Tipped cigarillos had been increasingly successful in the United States after the introduction of the Tiparillo brand in 1953. In 1967, tipped products were expected to account for close to 30 per cent of total cigar/cigarillo sales in Canada. Tipped cigarillo sales increased from 22 per cent of total cigarillo sales in 1965 to 26 per cent in 1966. Indications in 1967 were that tipped cigarillos would increase to 37 per cent of total cigarillo sales that year.

Imported cigar products (complete products, not raw materials) had less than 2 per cent of the total Canadian market in 1966. Cuban cigars were in the high price bracket and had only a fraction of one per cent of the market, while most of the remainder of imported sales were accounted for by Dutch products.

Canadian manufacturers marketed cigar products in a wide variety of shapes, sizes, tastes, smoking durations, packages and prices. For example, in 1967, General Cigar Co.'s product mix included forty-seven different shapes, eighteen brands and seventy-seven different types of packages. A selection of General Cigar's various brands is illustrated in Exhibit 2. Exhibit 3 shows the major competitive brands of Canadian manufacturers, together with examples of retail prices at which each brand was most commonly sold.

In the opinion of Mr. George Patrick, cigar product manager of General Cigar Co., there were many different ways in which a marketer could segment the Canadian cigar market. "Up until about 1965," he noted, "all our decisions and analysis of cigar products were based on price and size differences. For example, we would compare the market for the $.09 cigar versus the $.17 cigar; the panetela versus the corona; or the cigar versus the cigarillo. However, in 1965, we began to feel that taste was also an important factor that could be used to segment the market. Thus, we thought of Havana, traditional domestic, and flavoured as additional segments cutting across size and price considerations. We've found that the Havana blend has been holding steady, the traditional domestic blend (whether cigars or cigarillos) has been declining, and the flavoured blend (meaning some taste element other than tobacco added—there was only the Old Port line) has been growing."

GENERAL CIGAR CO.

Incorporated in 1920, General Cigar Co. was created by the merger of three established Canadian cigar manufacturers. In 1930, the company was acquired as a wholly-owned subsidiary of Imperial Tobacco Co. of Canada Ltd., a large Canadian holding company known predominantly as a cigarette producer. General Cigar's production facilities were located in the nearby head office of Imperial Tobacco, also in Montreal.

General Cigar utilized tobacco and confectionery wholesalers in the distribution of its products and did not sell directly to retailers. A sales force of seventy called on the wholesalers, and also helped wholesalers by doing missionary work at retail establishments. These salesmen sold General Cigar products plus tobacco products of the parent corporation, Imperial Tobacco. Salesmen were compensated on a straight salary basis.

As a convenience purchase item, cigars were sold in a very large number of retail outlets. In Ontario, for example, there were over 17 000 retail establishments licensed to sell tobacco products. Company officials felt that 20 per cent of the retail outlets sold 60-80 per cent of all tobacco products. General Cigar suggested retailers take a 13 per cent margin on the recommended retail price, while it suggested wholesalers take margins equivalent to an additional 7 per cent of the recommended retail price.

The wholesale and retail margins of competitive cigar manufacturers were almost identical to those of General Cigar. Unlike General Cigar, competitive manufacturers also distributed a small proportion of their total sales on a direct basis to larger retail establishments. In such instances the retailer received a total trade margin of 20 per cent.

General Cigar's advertising and sales promotion budget amounted to approximately $2.70 per 1000 cigars. About half of this amount was spent on sales promotion, mostly for point-of-purchase material because of the impulse nature of a cigar purchase. The other half of the budget was devoted to media advertising. Approximately $80 000 of the media advertising budget was allocated to advertisements for the House of Lords brand in selected magazines such as *Time* and *Actualité*, while the remainder was spent in television advertising of the Old Port brand.

An independent audit company reported that media advertising by General Cigar's principal competitor, Simon Cigar, amounted to $406 000 in 1965 and $268 000 in 1966. It was expected that Simon Cigar would spend about $300 000 in 1967. Most of Simon Cigar's advertising was allocated to its El Producto brand, a traditional cigar. Radio was the principal medium employed. Media advertising by Allied Cigar and Ontario Tobacco was negligible.

There was no practical method of auditing competitor's expenditures on sales promotion. Simon Cigar was known, however, to spend heavily on this activity—probably as much as General Cigar. Allied Cigar and Ontario Tobacco also utilized sales promotion.

Dominion Bureau of Statistics data for all manufacturers of tobacco products indicated that $16 189 000 was spent on media advertising in 1965. This was equivalent to 5.08 per cent of sales at the manufacturer level before the addition of federal and provincial taxes, or 2.14 per cent of manufacturers' sales when taxes were included. There were 43.6 billion cigarettes sold in Canada in 1965 with a value at manufacturers' level, including taxes, of $657.7 million. On the same basis, cigar and cigarillo sales in 1965 were valued at $31.5 million.

INTRODUCTION OF THE OLD PORT LINE

In the early 1950s, General Cigar held close to 70 per cent of the domestic cigar and cigarillo market. In 1953, however, Consolidated Cigar Corporation of the United States, the largest cigar manufacturer in the world, purchased Simon Cigar, General Cigar's major Canadian competitor. Subsequently, Consolidated Cigar proceeded to introduce its "big gun" brands from the United States into Canada. This move precipitated an erosion of General Cigar's market share which continued for nine years and reduced the company's share of the Canadian market to a low of 45 per cent in 1962. For example, the volume of White Owl, the company's major brand at that time, declined from 60 million to 20 million per year.

The company's declining market share made it sensitive to any competitive activity. Thus, in 1954, when a small importer began distributing Wolf Brothers Crooks, a rum-flavoured "crooked" cigar manufactured in the United States, General Cigar immediately began work to produce a competitive product. Production constraints made it impossible to manufacture a crooked cigar, so the emergent product was straight. Hence, the name Old Port Straights was given the new rum-flavoured, wine-dipped cigar. It fitted into what was then the most popular segment of the cigar market, the $.09-$.10 panetela shape.

Prior to launching the new product, it was tested by a panel of cigar smokers and was summarily rejected. Nevertheless, the company's continuing decline in market share prompted General Cigar to introduce the brand "in an uncharacteristic flash of irreverence for the scientific method.'' Over the next nine years, the new brand captured 6 per cent of the total market.

The conflict of sales results with the pessimistic consumer research projections was explained by Mr. Patrick: ''In hindsight, we should have gone to cigarette smokers for the research. We went to the traditional cigar smoker, the only market we knew. Research subsequently revealed to us that Old Port smokers were a different breed from those who smoked traditional cigars. In fact, they bore a close resemblance to cigarette smokers.''

OLD PORT CIGARILLOS

In 1963, work began on developing a cigarillo shape for Old Port, a ''cigar'' with the same taste as Old Port Straights, but which had half the smoking duration and sold for half the price. Other cigarillos on the market at that time—such as William Tell, Trump, and Simon's—were enjoying moderate sales success. General Cigar executives hoped to tap this market segment with a successful blend of mild tobacco combined with an increasingly popular shape. In 1964, just as the United States Surgeon-General was releasing his widely publicized report on smoking and health, General Cigar introduced the Old Port Cigarillo. Within two years, it was sold nationally and had captured 16 per cent of the total Canadian market for cigars and cigarillos.

OLD PORT TIPPED CIGARILLOS

''During the health scare,'' said Mr. Patrick, ''sales of all small cigars increased. However, as it died down, the sales of traditional unflavoured products fell right back to their previous levels, while Old Port slipped only a little. We knew, then, that we had an acceptable taste.

''About this time (1965), we were looking for new Old Port products. The success of the Tiparillo brand (a tipped cigarillo in the United States) got us thinking about an Old Port tipped cigarillo. This presented problems, however, because the polyethylene from which tips are made is a blah-tasting material, whereas Old Port was becoming known for its taste sensation. We decided that we would have to duplicate the Old Port flavour in the tip itself.

''Our research and development people felt that we could develop a way of impregnating polyethylene with a flavour compound. A project was started in conjunction with Du Pont of Canada and, within about ten months, we found it could be done and that it was a patentable process. We applied for the patent on flavour impregnation. Next, we conducted consumer tests at various levels, finally selected one, and moved into the market with Old Port tipped cigarillos in Toronto in June 1966.''

No promotion accompanied the Old Port tipped cigarillos launch. In the six months of 1966 for which the product was on the market, almost 13 million Old Port tipped cigarillos were sold. For the calendar year 1967, demand was expected to exceed 45 million cigarillos.

The introduction of Old Port tipped cigarillos had a significant impact on total Old Port sales. Sales of all items in the Old Port line, as shown in Exhibit 4, were expected to exceed 133 million cigars/cigarillos in 1967. This compared with 104 million and 113 million sold in 1966 and 1965 respectively.

''For tipped cigarillos,'' continued Mr. Patrick, ''we had expected to win over 50-60 per cent of existing Old Port plain end smokers, plus pick up some new smokers. Instead, contrary to our belief, we got a whole bunch of relatively young guys smoking tipped cigarillos on a very occasional basis—for example, at a social function around a billiard table. We were naturally happy about this because the total Old Port franchise grew to almost 30 per cent as a result. Nonetheless, it led us to realize that Old Port was in a very vulnerable position.''

Consumer research indicated that the Old Port tipped cigarillo smoker was very different from the traditional cigar smoker. Nearly 17 per cent of all cigarette smokers also smoked cigars or cigarillos. Approximately 80 per cent of all Old Port smokers also smoked cigarettes. The following age profiles were observed in the consumer research:

	Traditional Cigar Smoker	*Old Port Tipped Cigarillo Smoker*	*Regular Size Filter Tipped Cigarettes*
Less than 25 Years	9%	42%	41%
25-39 Years	23%	31%	32%
40 or Over	68%	27%	27%
	100%	100%	100%

OLD PORT RAPIERS

Old Port Rapiers were a traditional, untipped cigar made with the same flavour and blend of tobaccos as the rest of the Old Port line. Their shape and packaging, however, were intended to create the impression of a ''high class'' cigar. First introduced in January 1967, Rapiers were very long and thin in shape and were sold in a distinctive gold foil package at a suggested retail price of $.15 a cigar. As of June 1967, the product had not yet expanded to national distribution and it was considered too early to predict its eventual sales level.

ADVERTISING THE OLD PORT LINE

In one of the company files on the Old Port brand, General Cigar's advertising strategy for the brand was summarized as follows:

Advertising strategy has been to emphasize the difference between Old Port and traditional cigars thus appealing to the cigarette smoker who is interested in varying the type of tobacco he smokes but distrusts traditional cigars because of the properties, real and imagined, commonly attributed to them. Also, primary importance has been attached to creating a high level of consumer awareness.

Three major factors support this approach to Old Port advertising:

1. The rum-flavoured, wine-dipped tobaccos in Old Port produce a smoking taste significantly different from cigarettes and traditional cigars;
2. This taste difference, generally characterized as ''sweeter'' and ''milder,'' has proved to be very popular among Canadian smokers (80 per cent of Old Port smokers also smoke cigarettes);
3. Market research shows that young male cigarette smokers frequently like a change. They are attracted to cigars but are inhibited by the characteristics—particularly size and aroma—traditionally attributed to them.

Campaigns have been built around mass television exposure and supporting exposure in university publicatons as well as strong point-of-sale displays emphasizing the rum-and-wine taste and mildness of Old Port products. Reach is given precedence over frequency to gain maximum brand awareness among prime prospects.

PROPOSAL FOR A NEW BRAND OF FLAVOURED TIPPED CIGARILLO

Mr. Alexander, the company's vice-president and general manager, stated that he had long believed the prime growth segment in the Canadian market was the mild, flavoured, tipped cigarillo aimed at the near twenty-five age group. As early as the beginning of 1966, members of the General Cigar marketing group had thought about flavoured cigars and cigarillos other than Old Port. However, nothing progressed beyond the discussion stage for a number of reasons. There were no imminent competitive challenges to Old Port, and a fear that any new brand would only cannibalize Old Port's position. Also, the company's production capacity was overtaxed meeting the demands for the Old Port brand. Finally, General Cigar's research chemists knew little about what other flavouring agents could be added to a polyethylene tip.

Between 1966 and mid 1967, a number of developments occurred which made Mr. Alexander re-examine the idea of a new flavoured brand. These developments included a substantial increase in production capacity at General Cigar and the threat of new competition from other cigar manufacturers.

In 1966, General Cigar began investigating a new German cigar manufacturing machine known as the "KDS." This machine produced tipped cigarillos at a rate of 550 per minute (approximately 110 million per year), as opposed to General Cigar's existing equipment rate of 15.5 cigarillos per minute. A complete machine group—including the KDS, conveyors, packers and other equipment—was priced at $250 000. Mr. Alexander expected the contribution towards marketing costs, overhead and profits per thousand cigarillos would increase with the KDS from $6.25 to approximately $13.75.[1]

In January 1967, General Cigar ordered a KDS and expected delivery within one year. Shortly after placing the first order, a second system was ordered.

Increasingly, General Cigar was expecting a competitor to enter the lucrative flavoured market. Simon Cigar, backed by the extensive resources of Consolidated Cigar, seemed a likely entrant. If Old Port's sales success was to be diluted, Mr. Alexander preferred it was by another General Cigar product.

Mr. Alexander roughly calculated the out-of-pocket cost of developing and launching another flavoured tipped cigarillo at $24 000. This included consumer research at $4500, package design at $3500, point-of-purchase displays at $10 000, and a mould for the plastic tip at $6000. The other costs would be covered by normal operating costs for marketing and research and development activities. As of the summer of 1967, Mr. Alexander was seriously considering developing a new brand of flavoured tipped cigarillos for the Canadian market.

Exhibit 1
General Cigar Co. Ltd. (A)
Total Canadian Cigar/Cigarillo Market, 1963-1967

Year	Total Number of Cigars and Cigarillos Sold	Percentage Change Over Previous Year	Consumption per Capita
1963	393 004 000	—	20.4
1964	476 949 000	+21.2%	24.0
1965	488 664 000	+ 2.4%	24.3
1966	436 555 000	−10.7%	22.5
1967 (projected)	453 000 000	+ 3.9%	22.5

Source: Company records based on Dominion Bureau of Statistics Data (32-225)

[1] Disguised figures.

Exhibit 2
General Cigar Co. Ltd. (A)
General Cigar, Major Cigar and Cigarillo Brands in 1967

Exhibit 3
General Cigar Co. Ltd. (A)
Major Canadian Cigar and Cigarillo Products and Retail Prices

	Brand	Description	Usual Retail Price*
General Cigar	House of Lords	plain end cigars	$.94 and $1.19
	Reas	plain end cigars	$.94 and $1.19
	White Owl	plain end and tipped cigars	.71
	Marguerite	plain end cigars	.71
	Marguerite	plain end cigars	.40
	La Palina	plain end cigars	.94
	Tiparillo	tipped cigarillos	.35
	Old Port Straights	plain end cigars	.71
	Old Port Cigarillos	tipped cigars	.35
	Old Port Rapiers	plain end cigars	.75
	Ricardo	tipped cigarillos	.30
Simon Cigar	El Producto	plain end cigars	.71
	El Producto	tipped cigars	.71
	Muriel	plain end cigars	.71
	Muriel	tipped cigars	.71
	Tueros	plain end cigars	1.19
	Trump	plain end cigarillos	.35
	Trump	tipped cigarillos	.35
	Simon's Cigarillos	plain end cigarillos	.35
	Simon's Cigarillos	tipped cigarillos	.35
Allied Cigar	William Tell	tipped cigarillos	.35
	Pedro Montero	plain end cigars	.71
Ontario Tobacco	King Edward	plain end cigars	.64
	King Edward cigarillos	tipped end cigarillos	.35
	Topper	plain end cigarillos	.28

* Based on a five pack or five single cigars.

Exhibit 4
General Cigar Co. Ltd. (A)
Old Port Sales, 1965-1967

Year	Total Old Port Line	Old Port Cigars Plain	Old Port Cigarillos Plain	Tipped
1965	112 528 000	26 554 000	85 974 000	—
1966	104 239 000	22 103 000	69 253 000	12 883 000
1967 (projected)	113 500 000	24 400 000	63 600 000	45 500 000

All figures are expressed in terms of numbers of cigars and/or cigarillos.

General Cigar Co. Ltd. (B)

"We began developing our new coffee-flavoured cigarillo in the summer of 1967. In July 1968, we began test marketing in Toronto. Two years earlier our launch of Old Port tipped cigarillos in Toronto, without any supporting media advertising, met with immediate success. We didn't use media advertising for our coffee-flavoured cigarillo either. However, our sales results by April 1969 were very discouraging. I don't know what we did wrong. This new product is important to us to maintain our position in the flavoured market segment, but we can't seem to get it off the ground."

Mr. Robert Alexander, vice-president and general manager of General Cigar Co. Ltd. was perplexed. As of April 1969, the company's newest product, a coffee-flavoured tipped cigarillo, had failed to live up to expectations. Consumer research on the product during its year of development was encouraging. Yet in ten months of test marketing, sales in Toronto had not reached a 2 per cent minimum market share objective. A second test market, with advertising support for the new product, had been underway for six months in London, Ontario. There, sales had failed to achieve 4 per cent share objective. Mr. Alexander was uncertain as to what steps to take next with regard to the new cigarillo product.

GENERAL CIGAR'S MARKETING ORGANIZATION

Imperial Tobacco Co. of Canada was a holding company with extensive interests in tobacco, food and beverages. Imperial Tobacco Products Ltd. (ITPL) was the "tobacco wing" of the parent corporation. As a subsidiary of ITPL, General Cigar's marketing organization was nominally integrated into the overall marketing organization of ITPL, as shown in Exhibit 1. Thus, marketing activities of General Cigar were the ultimate responsibility of ITPL's vice-president, marketing. Mr. Alexander, as vice-president and general manager of General Cigar, reported directly to the ITPL vice-president, marketing, on matters relating to marketing. Other marketing executives who reported to the vice-president, marketing, of ITPL included a national sales manager, two cigarette group brand marketing managers, a manager of marketing administration, and a manager of marketing services.

Although the vice-president, marketing of ITPL had line authority over the activities of General Cigar's marketing group, he seldom exercised this prerogative. Consequently, Mr. Alexander enjoyed almost complete autonomy. From time to time, Mr. Alexander was asked to submit budgets to obtain resources, and to make presentations to ITPL showing how he was utilizing his resources. For example, prior to luanching a new product, Mr. Alexander was expected to make a formal presentation to the senior management group (including the president) of ITPL. This management group made the final "go—no go—hold" decision on a new product launch.

General Cigar's own marketing organization consisted of relatively few men. The profitable market development of General Cigar's products was the responsibility of Mr. George Patrick, product manager, and Mr. Jack Caron and Mr. Ray Paradis, both assistant product managers. Mr. Patrick largely concerned himself with cigars and cigarillos while Mr. Caron and Mr. Paradis worked mainly on pipe tobacco and fine cut tobacco respectively (fine cut tobaccos were used for making "roll your own" cigarettes). Mr. Alexander, whose background was in sales, took an active interest in the day-to-day activities of his product managers. Although all three product managers were usually considered part of General Cigar, they could conceivably be called upon at any time to work on problems relating to cigarettes or any other kinds of activities within the total ITPL organization.

Selling General Cigar products was carried out by ITPL's national sales force. Seventy salesmen in this sales force were specifically designated to concentrate their attention on General Cigar Products—cigars, cigarillos, pipe tobacco, and roll-your-own tobacco.

Most of the staff marketing services in the ITPL organization were available to serve General Cigar. ITPL's marketing services included departments specializing in consumer research analysis, forecasting and sales research, product design, product development, promotion, display, systems planning, information control and media. The parent corporation charged General Cigar an annual amount which included the use of these services and other head office overhead.

NEW PRODUCT DEVELOPMENT AT GENERAL CIGAR

New products were regarded by General Cigar to be extremely important to its future, although the company was not considered large enough to justify its own organizational department to advise on new product matters. The Product Development Department of ITPL devoted its time entirely to cigarettes. Consequently, Mr. Alexander and the three product managers assumed responsibility for new product development with Mr. Patrick responsible for new cigar product development.

Mr. Patrick and Mr. Alexander enjoyed a close personal relationship. In fact, most new product decisions were usually the result of joint discussions, argument and ultimate agreement between the two men. "It's really never a matter of seeing Bob about a project on an occasional basis," said Mr. Patrick. "He's usually in on everything all the way."

Despite active involvement by Mr. Alexander, the product managers were held responsible for coordination of new product development projects. In this capacity, they worked closely with other personnel from General Cigar, staff specialists at ITPL and external organizations such as the company's advertising agency and commercial marketing research firms. Mr. Patrick judged that a great deal of his time, and that of the two other product managers, was taken up with new product development matters. Many of these activities simply involved telephoning different persons or departments as they were needed, or chasing after these people to get their part of a project done.

THE INITIATION OF PROJECT CINDY

In July 1967, Mr. Alexander made the decision to proceed with the development of a new brand of flavoured tipped cigarillos. Responsibility for coordinating various activities in the new product development project, known as "Project Cindy," was undertaken by Mr. Patrick, the Cigar Product Manager.

As a first step in getting Project Cindy underway, Mr. Patrick set out the principal activities that would need to be carried out, together with an assessment of who should be responsible for each activity. He then proceeded to prepare a written "booklet" on Project Cindy, the contents of which were as follows:

- An introductory section outlining the rationale for General Cigar's decision to develop a new brand of flavoured tipped cigarillos.
- A memorandum stating Mr. Patrick's own responsibilities for coordinating Project Cindy, as well as participating in some aspects of its development.
- A memorandum stating the responsibilities of General Cigar's Manufacturing Department for developing a recipe (blend of tobaccos) and wrapping material (outer surface of the cigarillo) for the new product, as well as ensuring availability of adequate production capacity.

- A memorandum stating responsibilities of Package Design and ITPL staff department, for designing a cigar band, package, shipping container and point-of-purchase display materials.
- A memorandum stating responsibilities of General Cigar's Purchasing Department for acquiring a mould for plastic tips, for participating in package design and for purchasing packaging materials.

The purpose of the booklet was to facilitate coordination of Project Cindy. A complete copy was sent to each department that would be involved in the project in any way, excepting ITPL's Marketing Research Department which, it was anticipated, would be called in as needed throughout the project. A copy of Mr. Patrick's booklet is shown in Exhibit 2.

PROJECT CINDY ACTIVITIES TO THE END OF 1967

In the period July-December 1967, a number of activities got underway simultaneously. They could be broadly classified as: recipe development; development of the plastic tip (including impregnation of flavour); product name; package design; and point-of-purchase display material.

Recipe Development

There were two elements in the smoking taste of the Old Port tipped cigarillo: the tobacco recipe "up front" and the flavour impregnated in the plastic mouthpiece. Mr. Alexander and Mr. Patrick felt the leaf mixture in the Old Port cigarillo was extremely popular. Therefore, they decided to alter the mild, somewhat sweet Old Port blend only slightly for the new product. The key difference, they decided, would be the flavour in the plastic tip. Accordingly, the Recipe Department (who became involved in recipes whenever additives other than tobacco were concerned) worked together in the development of a tobacco blend for the new cigarillo.

Development of the Plastic Tip

Prior to formally commencing Project Cindy, Mr. Alexander and Mr. Patrick discussed a number of flavour ideas for a new tipped cigarillo. These possibilities included drambuie coffee, cherry, apricot brandy and hickory barbecue. Prior to the summer of 1967, the Research and Development Department had done little more than a preliminary investigation of these flavour ideas. Technical difficulties had been encountered with all of the flavours but, among the alternatives, the Research and Development Department reported that coffee might be the easiest to mix with polyethylene. By the time Mr. Patrick sent out his original Project Cindy booklet, he and Mr. Alexander had decided on a coffee flavour. They felt coffee and smoking were a natural, everyday combination. Therefore, they asked the research chemists to develop an acceptable coffee-flavoured polyethylene mouthpiece.

By the fall of 1967, the Research and Development Department was able to overcome the technical problems of impregnating a coffee flavour into the polyethylene tip. The resulting mouthpiece was brown in colour. Two additional decisions remained to be resolved—the level of coffee concentration and the level of sweetness in the flavour.

To assist in the concentration decision, a panel of Old Port flavour testers composed of fifty to one hundred General Cigar employees tried four mouthpieces with different levels of coffee flavour concentration. A level of concentration was selected on the basis of their reactions. By December 1967, no decision had yet been reached on the level of sweetness to be incorporated in the tip of the new product.

Product Name

Toward the end of July 1967, Mr. Alexander and Mr. Patrick, having decided on the coffee flavour, selected the name Columbia Tips for the new tipped cigarillo product. ''In retrospect,'' said Mr. Patrick, ''we really didn't seriously consider a number of names. We had an old established cigar brand called Columbia. We were so intrigued with the Colombian coffee connotations of the name Columbia that it seemed a natural. We also hoped the consumer might associate the new product with our old brand.''

Package Design

Mr. Alexander gave the Product Design Department a broad directive for the development of a package for Columbia Tips: ''The prime prospect for Columbia Tips will be similar to that for Old Port tipped cigarillos; that is, primarily males, under forty years of age, somewhat sophisticated, and centred on the socio-economic scale.'' The Product Design Department, working in conjunction with an outside designer, created several packaging alternatives, some of which are shown in Exhibit 3. Package design Number Six was selected by Mr. Alexander.

Point-of-Purchase Display Material

Since Mr. Alexander and the product managers believed cigars and cigarillos were largely impulse purchase items, the company relied heavily on point-of-purchase promotion. The Product Design Department was asked to prepare a suitable point-of-purchase counter display for the new product's introduction to the market. The final display, chosen by Mr. Alexander, held 200 cigarillos in forty five-packs. Two thousand of these displays, shown in Exhibit 4, were ordered in anticipation of test market at a price of $3 each.

THE DAVID WATERS STUDY[1]

As of December 1967, work had progressed on Project Cindy to the point that General Cigar had a name, a tobacco recipe, a flavoured mouthpiece (the final level of sweetness was yet to be determined), a package and a point-of-purchase display. At this point, both Mr. Alexander and Mr. Patrick judged that it would be advisable to verify some of the decisions they had made through consumer research. ITPL's Marketing Research Department was therefore called upon and after a review of activities in Project Cindy to date, the Marketing Research Department hired an outside marketing research firm, David Waters Consultants Ltd.

The Waters Study, begun in December 1967, had the general objective of evaluating consumer attitudes toward the point-of-purchase display for Columbia Tips. In addition, the research attempted to explore the potential conceptual acceptance of a coffee-flavoured cigarillo and the avenues that could be used to promote and market the product. These included evaluation of tip colour for the cigarillo, aroma, the name Columbia Tips, the package design and so forth.

Three group sessions with cigarette- and cigar-smoking males (about twenty-five persons in total) were conducted by David Waters. The groups were composed of university students, young working men, and older men. The participants ranged in age from eighteen to fifty and had an income anywhere from ''being a student to $15 000 per annum.'' Respondents were drawn from various areas of Metropolitan Toronto. The Waters Study described the research method as follows:

---

[1] Disguised name.

The interview conducted in each session was open ended. It was designed to permit a free response from the subjects rather than responses limited to stated alternatives. The task of the interviewer in each case was to encourage the respondents to talk freely and fully in response to the questions. A loose general outline sequence was followed. The discussions were first centred on the concept of coffee flavour, then the package design and finally, the point-of-purchase display. After this, the topics ranged far afield.

Exhibit 5 contains excerpts from a summary of the Waters Study, as prepared for Mr. Alexander by the Marketing Research Department.

Based on this study, Mr. Alexander selected a dark brown colour, close to the brown on the package, for the plastic tip. "I think the brown will make people think of good healthy coffee," said Mr. Alexander. "The idea of a lighter colour, supposedly representing coffee with cream, can wait until some later time. Right now, two colours would unnecessarily complicate things. Waters's study makes me feel we're on the right track, so we'll carry on. We haven't decided on a level of sweetness for the tip yet, so we'll have to do some further consumer research."

THE RONALD SEARS STUDY[2]

To determine an acceptable level of sweetness for the flavoured plastic mouthpiece, Mr. Alexander and Mr. Patrick once again called on the Marketing Research Department. Accordingly, in April 1968, the Marketing Research Department commissioned the Ronald Sears Co. to test consumer reaction to the product.

Ronald Sears located a total of 161 smokers of tipped cigarillos by door-to-door interviewing in Metropolitan Toronto. Each respondent was given two five-packs of Columbia Tips identifiable only by the digits 38 and 53 and differing only in the level of sweetness in the flavoured plastic tips. In May 1968, the Marketing Research Department reported to Mr. Alexander and Mr. Patrick. The following summary was included in the report:

> There was significant preference by all the subgroups of the sample for the sweeter of the two products. It was preferred for strength/mildness, tobacco flavour, and coffee flavour. Both No. 38 and No. 53 were given an average rating for the amount of strength/mildness and quality of tobacco flavour. Almost half the sample thought the concept was a good idea, less than one-quarter felt it a poor idea, and the remainder had mixed feelings.

At the same time the results of this study were being tabulated, the Manufacturing Department was preparing for production of Columbia Tips. From the outset, the physical specifications of the product were limited to the capabilities of the new KDS machines. Mr. Alexander was encouraged by the research and anxious to get Columbia Tips to test market. ITPL top management agreed with Mr. Alexander's proposal and gave their approval to a test market launch of Columbia Tips. Production of Columbia Tips began in late May 1968 in anticipation of test market launch in July 1968.

PREPARATION OF THE SALES ORGANIZATION FOR TEST MARKET LAUNCH

General Cigar sold its products through the ITPL sales organization. In this sales organization, shown in Exhibit 6, a national sales manager was responsible for administering and supervising all selling activities. Each of five regional sales managers was responsible

---

[2] Disguised name.

for all cigarette and General Cigar product sales in a region. These regional managers reported directly to the national sales manager and received their instructions from him. Under the regional sales managers were branch managers who directly supervised the activities of the salesmen. Cigarette salesmen handled cigarettes exclusively. The Cigar and Tobacco salesmen (known as the C & T force) concentrated on General Cigar Products, although they were often asked to assist with cigarette sales, especially on a new product launch. "All-products men" sold both cigarette products and General Cigar products. They were located in areas where Imperial Tobacco felt there was insufficient justification for a separate C & T force. In total, there were seventy salesmen handling General Cigar products as of July 1968.

General Cigar's main contact with the sales force was through Mr. Alexander and the national sales manager. Although General Cigar product managers maintained informal contact with the regional sales managers and in some cases the branch managers, all important matters were conducted through Mr. Alexander and the national sales manager.

Salesmen for General Cigar products (hereafter referred to simply as General Cigar salesmen) sold to tobacco and confectionery wholesalers across Canada. In turn, these jobbers served the retail outlets. In Ontario alone, there were 17 000 government-licensed retail tobacco outlets. It was strict ITPL policy that no sales were to be made directly to a retail outlet, even though ITPL's competitors often sold on a direct basis.

The principal task of the General Cigar salesmen was selling and servicing cigar and tobacco jobbers. However, since these salesmen were responsible for ensuring that General Cigar products had the best possible opportunity for retail sale, they customarily helped the jobbers in any way possible. For example, a General Cigar salesman would "drop ship" product into a retail store, arrange the retailer's shelves, exchange fresh stock for dry stock, and do any other missionary work required. Nevertheless, all billing was done through the appropriate wholesaler.

For purposes of sales analysis and sales force deployment, retail outlets were classified into four categories—A, B, C and D—on the basis of sales volume and level of product turnover. The A accounts were the lucrative high volume/high turnover tobacco outlets. These naturally received most of the sales attention since 60-80 per cent of tobacco products sold through 20 per cent of the outlets. Nevertheless, General Cigar salesmen covered 70 per cent of their retail outlets at least once every twelve weeks on a rotating basis. This percentage would be higher except that many of the outlets were seasonal, such as summer concession stands.

Mr. Alexander was quite optimistic about Columbia Tips, but believed success in a test market was necessary before launching the product nationally. He therefore decided to test the new product in Ontario's "Golden Triangle" area (Toronto, Hamilton and Niagara) where Old Port tipped cigarillos had been launched very successfully approximately two years previously. The area represented a large market and, in Mr. Alexander's opinion, a reasonably representative one for most of Canada. Also the company had a Toronto warehouse from which the test market could be readily supplied. Quebec was not considered for a test because, in Mr. Alexander's judgement, it represented a unique kind of market.

In early June 1968, Mr. Alexander and Mr. Patrick arranged a sales meeting in Toronto to brief all the Ontario C & T salesmen on the Columbia Tips launch scheduled for July, as well as on a pipe tobacco launch scheduled for three weeks before Columbia Tips. Although the Columbia Tips test market immediately concerned thirteen salesmen—ten in Toronto, two in Hamilton, and one in Niagara—all the Ontario salesmen were present at the meeting on Columbia Tips in order that they would know what the company was doing with the product. "We told them what the market situation seemed to be and why we were introducing Columbia Tips," said Mr. Patrick. "Also we showed them the point-of-purchase material available, the date of the launch and area of launch. After that, we left the planning of specific activities in the territories to the discretion of the individual managers. After all, they've been through this kind of thing before.''

Each C & T salesman in the test area was told Columbia Tips was his number one priority. That is, his prime task during the launch was ensuring Columbia Tips were placed in the retail outlets. This meant that if he visited a retail store, he would first deal with Columbia Tips and then check on the other General Cigar products. The C & T salesmen began a launch by isolating the A accounts and calling on them first. Subsequently, they began the B, C and D accounts.

Plans were made to send each jobber at least one case of Columbia Tips prior to launch in order that his salesmen would have the product to sell. These wholesalers, however, were not to receive any point-of-purchase displays. Each C & T salesman was asked to visit the retail outlets in his area, discuss Columbia Tips with the store managers, give them display units filled with stock and sufficient inventory, and bill through the appropriate jobbers. If a C & T salesman discovered a jobber salesman had been in a store before him, he was to place a counter display unit in the store and put the previously placed stock in the display.

The C & T salesmen were also asked to audit the activities of the jobbers to ensure Columbia Tips was receiving proper attention. For example, often a jobber would run out of stock on a new item yet fail to reorder. This was usually attributed to the jobber's unfamiliarity with the new product and poor warehousing techniques. If the salesmen discovered a stock-out situation they were asked to ''reintroduce'' the product.

PUBLICITY ACCOMPANYING THE GOLDEN TRIANGLE TEST MARKET

In further preparation for the launch in the Golden Triangle test market, a publicity campaign was developed. Mr. Alexander and Mr. Patrick decided to rely on publicity and point-of-purchase material for promotion. Similar to the introduction of Old Port tipped cigarillos, no media advertising support was planned.

Mr. Patrick prepared a publicity kit which he mailed to media representatives (for example, newspapers), the Coffee Institute, and coffee producers. This kit included a number of press releases. Some featured the female research chemist Denise Blondin, who figured prominently in the development of the flavoured mouthpiece. ''After all, it's unusual for a woman to be working on cigars,'' said Mr. Patrick.

Exhibit 7 presents one of the press releases which described the support General Cigar gave to the Canadian Olympic Association in Toronto. Also in each kit was a burlap ''coffee bag'' containing five Columbia Tips cigarillos. Exhibit 8 presents the letter Mr. Patrick sent by way of explanation with the kits.

In early July, General Cigar held a cocktail party/press conference in Toronto. The purpose of the party—complete with Colombian decorations—was to ɔain publicity for Columbia Tips. Mr. Patrick invited all the major Ontario cigar wholesalers, news reporters, and the Colombian Consul General. Despite these efforts, publicity was not as heavy as had been anticipated.

RESULTS OF THE GOLDEN TRIANGLE TEST MARKET

Mr. Alexander and Mr. Patrick decided on a ''crystal ball'' minimum market share objective of 2 per cent, based on total cigars and cigarillos sold in the area. This was equivalent to about 50 000 cigarillos per week. If sales of Columbia Tips in the Golden Triangle test market exceeded the 2 per cent market share, Mr. Alexander intended to make a proposal to ITPL that the product be moved into national distribution immediately. Both Mr. Alexander and Mr. Patrick expected that Columbia Tips would quickly surpass the target figure.

Columbia Tips were launched in test market in early July 1968. Approximately 900 point-of-purchase displays were placed throughout the market area. The suggested retail price was $.35, the same as Old Port tipped cigarillos. This allowed retailers a margin of 13 per cent of suggested retail price. Wholesale margins were equivalent to an additional 7 per cent.

In Mr. Patrick's judgement, the best available means for measuring Columbia Tips' performance in the test area was a count of withdrawals of cigarillos from the Toronto warehouse for shipment to various tobacco jobbers in the Golden Triangle area. These data provided an approximation of product movement from jobbers to retailers and sales at the retail level. Both jobbers and retailers tried to keep their inventories to a minimum and, in Mr. Patrick's experience, there was a close correlation between warehouse withdrawals at a given time and retail sales about three weeks later.

Sales of Columbia Tips, as measured by withdrawals from the Toronto warehouse, were disappointing. The withdrawal figures, shown in Exhibit 9, reflected an initial surge in July attributable to filling the distribution pipeline. Thereafter, withdrawls peaked in September, and began to show a slight decline in October. By the end of October, the minimum sales objective of 2 per cent had still not been reached.

Problems were encountered in the timing of the launch. In retrospect, Mr. Patrick reasoned that General Cigar had picked the worst possible time for a new product launch. ITPL was introducing Cortina Cigarettes at the same time in the same area, and the C & T salesmen were asked to assist in the cigarette launch as well as introduce Columbia Tips. During the summer months, salesmen took their one-month vacations, and many of the jobbers were also on vacation.

By the fall it was clear that there was a problem with Columbia Tips, but neither Mr. Alexander nor Mr. Patrick knew what it was. The only apparent thing was that the brand was not moving as they had thought it would.

TELEPHONE AWARENESS STUDY

In October 1968, Mr. Alexander asked the Marketing Research Department to determine why sales were below their expectations. After investigation, the Marketing Research Department hypothesized that the problem was that the level of awareness for Columbia Tips was below what it should be, although they added they had no idea what the level of awareness should be for a new product at this stage.

Accordingly, the Marketing Research Department contracted a commercial marketing research firm, Webster Research Ltd.,[3] to conduct a telephone survey in order to assess the situation quickly. Webster Research Ltd. referred to a survey of this kind as an ''overnight telephone awareness study.'' Its objective was to measure level of consumer awareness of Columbia Tips, extent of trial of the product and intention to retry. Results for Columbia Tips were to be compared to those for other new brands of cigarillos. A total of 628 male smokers were interviewed in Toronto, 50 per cent of whom claimed to be cigar or cigarillo smokers. The remainder smoked cigarettes.

The first question asked was designed to test unaided awareness: ''Can you name any new brands of cigarillos or cigars off hand?'' In response to this question, 2 per cent mentioned Columbia Tips, 2 per cent mentioned Simon's Extra Long Tipped Cigarillos, one per cent mentioned Willem II, 8 per cent mentioned other brands, and 87 per cent could

---

[3] Disguised name.

not think of any. Simon's Extra Long Tipped was introduced prior to Columbia Tips without any advertising. Willem II was an imported Dutch brand.

The unaided recall question was followed by: "Have you happened to have heard about a new brand called Columbia Tips (Simon's Extra Long, Willem II)?" In response to this aided recall question, 18 per cent knew of Columbia Tips, 28 per cent knew of Simon's Extra Long, and 11 per cent knew of Willem II.

The study then dealt with trial and retrial intention. Three per cent had tried Columbia Tips, 8 per cent had tried Simon's Extra Long, and 2 per cent Willem II. When questioned about their intention to try again, 2 per cent said they probably would try Columbia Tips again versus one per cent who said they would not. In the case of Simon's Extra Long, the figures were 6 per cent and 2 per cent respectively. For Willem II, it was one per cent and less than one-half per cent.

Finally, in an attempt to test the recall about Columbia Tips, respondents were asked for points they remembered about Columbia Tips. The following table shows the results:

Recall of Points about Columbia Tips
Based on 110 Respondents—All Those Aware

	Percentage
Coffee flavoured	8
Flavoured mouthpiece	1
Coffee-flavoured mouthpiece	1
Coloured mouthpiece	2
Mild/milder	6
Any reference to package	4
Other	11
Nothing or vague	70

The results of the telephone survey led Mr. Alexander and Mr. Patrick to speculate that the problem with the Toronto test market was the exclusion of media advertising support. Therefore, they decided to try Columbia Tips in another area with the same program plus media advertising.

THE LONDON TEST MARKET

London, Ontario, was chosen because it was easy to service through the General Cigar Toronto warehouse and its size and geographical location made it economically feasible to test the effect of media advertising. Since the London area accounted for 2½ per cent of the total Canadian cigar market, Mr. Patrick thought spending $5000 on media advertising in London would be roughly equivalent to spending $200 000 nationally.

General Cigar's advertising agency suggested a $5200 six-week campaign in London employing newspapers and radio from the first week in November 1968 until the second week in December. Exhibit 10 presents excerpts from the agency's recommendations. Exhibit 11 shows a sample newspaper advertisement.

Columbia Tips were launched in London in November 1968. There were two regular C & T salesmen in London. They were joined by a third to assist them in the introduction of Columbia Tips. This product was their number one priority until two weeks before Christmas and again immediately after Christmas. As of April 1969, Columbia Tips were still top priority in the London area.

As 4 per cent minimum market share objective was established by Mr. Alexander and Mr. Patrick for the London test market. This was equivalent to about 10 000 cigarillos per week. By April 1969 this objective had not been reached. Although performance of Columbia Tips in London was somewhat better than was experienced in the Golden Triangle, Mr. Alexander was not convinced that advertising would solve the brand's problems.

Exhibit 12 shows monthly warehouse withdrawals from the Toronto warehouse to jobbers in the London area during the period November 1968 to March 1969. Also shown are comparable withdrawals to jobbers in Toronto, and to all jobbers in the combined London/Golden Triangle test market areas.

THE SITUATION AS OF APRIL 1969

Mr. Alexander calculated General Cigar had incurred approximately $30 000 in out-of-pocket expenses on Columbia Tips since Project Cindy began in July 1967. These expenses included package design, consumer research, point-of-purchase displays, media advertising and sales promotion. They did not include costs that would have been incurred whether the project was underway or not—for example, charges made by ITPL to General Cigar for use of its staff marketing services.

Mr. Alexander was perplexed: "I have numerous alternative courses of action. I suppose I could recommend we go national with Columbia Tips. I've had calls for the product out West and from people in Montreal, but I haven't made any promises. We could discontinue Columbia Tips and start all over with something else. Maybe we're using the wrong appeal in our promotion, or perhaps we haven't put it in the right test markets. I don't know."

Mr. Patrick summed up the situation as he saw it: "We really haven't had any feedback that anything's wrong, so how do we know what to change, if anything?"

Exhibit 1
General Cigar Co. Ltd. (B)
Marketing Organization of Imperial Tobacco Products Limited

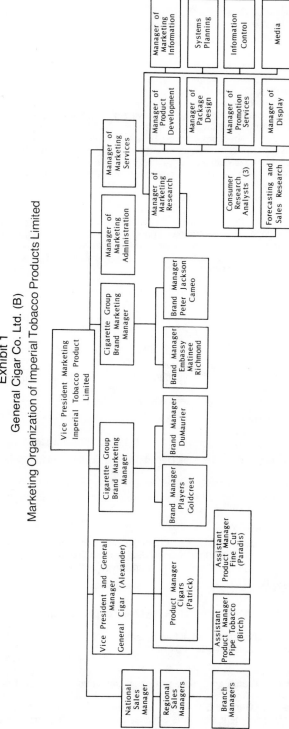

Exhibit 2
General Cigar Co. Ltd. (B)
Booklet Prepared by Mr. Patrick
at the Outset of Project Cindy

INTRODUCTION

The marketplace consists of people who use one or more categories of smoking products. The traditional segmentation has been: (1) cigarettes, (2) cigars, and (3) pipes. Within each of these segments or categories, there have been various subcategories based on difference in size, strength, flavour, etc. More recently, a further two distinct categories (not subcategories) have emerged from what was generally referred to as the cigar segment: cigarillos and flavoured cigars.

Initial research has validated that cigarillo and cigar smokers have little or nothing in common. In fact, there may be far more rapport between cigarillo and cigarette smokers. The same conditions apply to the consumer who uses flavoured cigars; he is rejected by "real" cigar smokers. If we combine the two—the cigarillo and the flavoured product—we have Old Port cigarillos and tipped cigarillos, but Old Port is the only major entry. We are vulnerable! It can be deduced that if "real" cigar smokers reject Old Port, the growth of the flavoured cigar/cigarillo segment will come from cigarette smokers, cigarillo smokers, or non-smokers.

Therefore, it is in our best interests to develop a new entry at cigarillo size which is flavoured and, because of the volume and growth of the tipped cigarette market, should have a holder (not for filtering purposes, but to keep the consumer's mouth from direct contact with the tobacco). We should also take advantage of our ability to flavour mouthpieces, thus offering the consumer a unique product appeal. When developed, it is recommended we test market the product.

MARKETING DEPARTMENT—G. A. PATRICK

1. Coordinate project.
2. Prepare product information sheet.
3. Submit to executive committee.
4. Develop trade circular.
5. Brief field managers in launch area.
6. Work with agency on development of communications program.
7. Work with Consumer Research Department on testing various levels of coffee flavour in mouthpieces.
8. Develop statistical feedback program with Marketing Research Department.

MANUFACTURING DEPARTMENT—F. CORBEIL

1. Work in conjunction with Leaf Department and Research and Development Department in development of recipe.
2. Work with Purchasing Department and Technical Services Department in development of physical specifications of wrapping material.
3. Ascertain sufficient production capacity. Initial launch quality estimate 50 000 and 50 000 per month. Ultimate net sales increase will be calculated on figures obtained from test market. It is assumed Cindy will eat into sales of Old Port tipped cigarillos.

PACKAGE DESIGN DEPARTMENT—L. A. MACY

1. Work in conjunction with outside design house to design cigar band, pocket pack, introductory display container, regular display container, and shipping container. Bear in mind that this product will not be a cigar—most of our smokers will be persons who normally smoke cigarettes.

PURCHASING DEPARTMENT—J. F. RYAN

1. Acquire mould for mouthpieces.
2. Work with Technical Services Department and supplier on development of physical specifications on packaging material.
3. Work with Package Design and supplier on graphics of packaging material.
4. Purchase quantities of packaging material to cover 500 000 cigars.

NOTES

(a) The Consumer Research, Marketing Research and Package Design Departments were staff departments of ITPL's Marketing Division.
(b) The Marketing Department was the three General Cigar Product Managers.
(c) Manufacturing, Leaf, Research and Development, Technical Services and Purchasing were departments within General Cigar's manufacturing organization.
(d) All of the departments listed in (a), (b) and (c) received copies of the booklet, with the exception of Marketing Research.

Exhibit 3
General Cigar Co. Ltd. (B)
Some Packaging Suggestions for Columbia Tips

Exhibit 4
General Cigar Co. Ltd. (B)
Point-of-Purchase Display

Exhibit 5
General Cigar Co. Ltd. (B)
Excerpts from Marketing Research Department's Summary of the David Waters Study

—There is little rejection of the concept of a coffee-flavoured cigar. Those who dislike coffee or who find coffee bitter are not impressed. The product will have appeal for those people who like the taste and the aroma of coffee.

—There is no doubt that the coffee flavour idea has considerable appeal. The expected aroma upon opening the package is the key factor. If a coffee aroma was released when the cigar was smoked, this would be a major incentive to smoke them.

—The expectations with respect to coffee flavour are that it would not be overly strong. They expect to taste the coffee when the cigar is initially put in the mouth. After one or two puffs, they expect to smoke a regular cigar. They note that this is what happens with Old Port. Their expectations have been conditioned by their experiences with Old Port.

—The coffee-flavoured cigar is noted as being one for different occasions, as opposed to Old Port. Old Port is identified with status and sophistication. Columbia Tips is seen as an outdoor, easy going, earthy cigar.

—The burlap bag has contemporary, masculine, rugged associations. It identifies the product as warm, rugged, modern and progressive.

—The burlap bag is the highlight of the display. It is a conversation piece. It is unexpected. It is a toy that many men would like to have on their desks or on a bar.

—The package is noted as being attractive and unique. Most men would not feel uncomfortable with it. They see it as a warm masculine package. The outstanding feature is the burlap association. Burlap is identified as a modern, young, masculine, comfortable fabric.

—The name Columbia Tips is not identified as old-fashioned. It is associated with quality coffee and Colombia. It is noted as being a simple, easy to remember name.

—There may be good reason to market the brand with two different-coloured tips for people who like their coffee with cream and for people who like their coffee black. This gives the individual an opportunity to identify his choice with his coffee preference. If one tip is to be used, the most popular is the dark tip.

—The coloured tips are novel and attract attention. Some say that they give the cigar a better overall appearance.

Exhibit 6
Sales Organization for Imperial Tobacco Limited

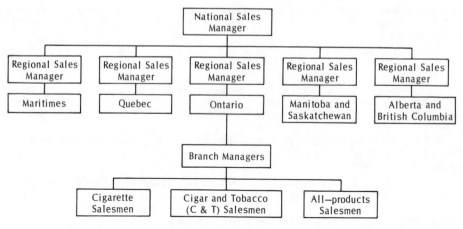

Source: Company Records

Exhibit 7
General Cigar Co. Ltd. (B)
Sample Press Release for Columbia Tips
Toronto Test Market

FOR RELEASE: Wednesday, July 3, 1968
ISSUED FOR: General Cigar Co. Ltd.

Cigar Company Launches New Product with
Olympic Fund-Raising Drive

Toronto, July 3, 1968: At a reception here, today, James Worrall, chairman of the finance committee of the Canadian Olympic Association (C.O.A.), invited Torontonians to "take a coffee break for Canada's Olympic Team."

Supported by the General Cigar Co. of Montreal, the C.O.A. will attempt to raise $1 500 between 12 noon and 2 P.M. at the Colonnade on Bloor Street on Friday, July 5. General Cigar will distribute samples of the world's first coffee-flavoured cigarillo, Columbia Tips, and will donate $1 to the Canadian Olympic Association for every cigarillo band deposited in a central receptacle outside the Colonnade.

The money has been earmarked for the purchase of "Olympic pins" for Canadian athletes participating in the 1968 Olympic Games in Mexico City. "Olympic pins" are carried by representatives of all countries and swapped for the pins carried by athletes representing other countries. "We have never been able to give our team members a large enough supply of these items in past years," Mr. Worrall said. "This year we will do the job properly".

Exhibit 8
General Cigar Co. Ltd. (B)
Promotional Letter Sent by Mr. Patrick
Toronto Test Market

General Cigar Co. Ltd.
P.O. Box 6500
Montreal, Quebec

June 27, 1968

Sir:

The coffee cup is on the way out.

Museums of the future will display it behind thick glass and caption it, "Cvp Vsed in Ancient Tymes to Partake of the Liqvid Coffee."

Those born before 1968 may fondly reminisce about the old days when coffee was served in cups. Tears may be shed for the idyllic ease of that bygone era.

But we have grounds for believing the end will justify the beans. Corporation executives and efficiency experts will be seen to smile again, indeed laugh out loud, as the controversial coffee break dies. The nation stands to prosper!

With pride, we announce another pinnacle scaled in man's traumatic quest for Utopia and submit for your appreciation a new coffee product. It is a highly concentrated blend requiring no cream or sugar. It is heated simply by the application of a match. Its taste is without equal.

For the betterment of all mankind, we offer the world's first coffee-flavoured cigarillo, Columbia Tips, samples of which are enclosed.

Thank you for your attention.
Sincerely,

G. A. Patrick,
Product Manager,
General Cigar Company Ltd.

P.S. I know I'm no Stephen Leacock, but it's fun and I hope you enjoy the Columbia Tips.

Exhibit 9
General Cigar Co. Ltd. (B)
Warehouse Withdrawals of Columbia Tips
July 1968-October 1968

	Withdrawals to Jobbers in Toronto Only	Withdrawals to Jobbers in the Entire Golden Triangle Area
July	186 350	302 050
August	9 500	13 700
September	42 800	70 900
October	29 450	32 050

Source: Company records.

Exhibit 10
General Cigar Co. Ltd. (B)
Excerpts from Agency Recommendations for
an Advertising Campaign in London

It was felt that a short schedule of advertising could be scheduled in one Ontario market to determine whether advertising could generate increased awareness of the brand and subsequent increase in trial. London was selected as the market for advertising. Toronto was to be used as a control market.

OBJECTIVE OF TEST

To measure the effect of advertising on sales on Columbia Tip cigars in Ontario. Sales out of the Toronto warehouse to wholesalers in Toronto and London would be tabulated to serve as the method of test measurement.

ADVERTISING STRATEGY

Advertising for Columbia Tips will increase awareness among prime prospects that it is the world's first coffee-flavoured tipped cigarillo offering a unique taste sensation and mildness.

PRIME PROSPECT

The prime prospect for Columbia Tips will be similar to that for Old Port Cigarillos tipped (i.e., primarily males under forty years of age, somewhat sophisticated and centred on the socio-economic scale).

BUDGET

Newspapers:	
1000 line × 4 columns	
4 insertions = $840 each	$3 360
Radio:	
30-second breakfast rotation	
6:00-10:00 A.M.	
15 spots week 1	458
10 spots weeks 2-6	1 350
Total Media Cost:	$5 168

Exhibit 11
General Cigar Co. Ltd. (B)
Sample Newspaper Advertisement
Columbia Tips London Test Market

Exhibit 12
General Cigar Co. Ltd. (B)
Warehouse Withdrawals of Columbia Tips
July 1968-March 1969

1968	Withdrawals to Jobbers in London	Withdrawals to Jobbers in Toronto	Withdrawals to all Jobbers in Combined London/ Golden Triangle Area
July	—	186 350	302 050
August	—	9 500	13 700
September	—	42 800	70 900
October	—	29 450	32 050
November	91 350	31 850	130 500
December	11 500	13 700	40 850
1969			
January	23 750	28 200	94 200
February	34 450	39 250	131 300
March	28 800	65 100	173 800

Source: Company records.

27
General Packaging Ltd.

In January 1970, General Packaging Ltd., a medium-size packaging and manufacturing firm located in St. Catharines, Ontario, purchased all the assets of R. B. Barnes Ltd., a manufacturer and marketer of a wide range of horticultural dusts, sprays and fertilizers for home gardeners. These were sold under the brand name, Gro-Aid. (See Exhibit 1 for a partial list of products.)

For some time prior to January 1969, the management of General Packaging Ltd. had been searching for a line of consumer products which offered potential for growth and which would pick up some production, packaging capacity slack that occurred with their present line of products in the January to June period.

R. B. Barnes Ltd. had been established in 1965 by Mr. Roy Barnes and by 1969 all products manufactured by Barnes were marketed under the Gro-Aid brand name through six wholesalers, located in Ottawa, Kingston, Toronto, Hamilton, London and Windsor. There was no contractual arrangement with these wholesalers but traditionally Barnes had only one wholesaler in any market. The wholesalers supplied approximately 300 hardware stores, department stores and nursery outlets throughout southern Ontario. Sales had shown steady increases over the years (actual sales for 1968 and 1969 are outlined in Exhibit 2).

As a general rule, demand by retailers for the Gro-Aid line was highest during late winter and spring, declined in the late summer and was virtually non-existent during the fall and early winter period. Mr. Barnes had devoted his full time to the company and two years previously had hired Mr. Robert C. Smith on a full-time basis. Casual labour was hired as required during the production period. Mr. Barnes devoted his time to selling activities and overseeing the general operations. Mr. Smith acted as production manager as well as handling incoming orders, billing and some general office work.

Mr. Barnes had leased manufacturing space in a building formerly occupied by a St. Catharines automobile dealer. The lease expired as of January 1, 1970, and could not be renewed. His difficulty in locating comparable low-cost space, the thoughts of relocating coupled with his declining health had prompted Mr. Barnes to contact a friend who was a vice-president of General Packaging Ltd. regarding the possible purchase of his company.

Under the terms of the purchase Mr. Barnes had contracted to work with General Packaging Ltd. for a period of six months. Mr. Smith had also been hired as assistant production manager for the total plant, a position General Packaging Ltd. was attempting to fill at that time. Since the manufacturing of the Gro-Aid line was essentially a mixing and packaging operation comparable to other products handled by General Packaging Ltd, integration into the General Packaging Ltd. plant presented no problems.

Immediately following the purchase of R. B. Barnes Ltd., Mr. C. B. Kennedy was appointed product manager with responsibility for the Gro-Aid line. He was to operate as a profit centre with the budget outlined in Exhibit 3. Mr. Kennedy had been an assistant product manager with General Packaging for the past three years and was considered most capable. It was expected that he would work very closely with Mr. Barnes on marketing activities during the six months of Mr. Barnes's employment.

In the past Mr. Barnes had spent the major portion of his time doing missionary sales work, calling on his wholesalers and retailers. Any orders he received from retailers he would turn over to the nearest wholesaler for delivery and billing. For 1970 Mr. Kennedy intended to follow this approach.

Mr. Barnes attributed his past success to the high quality of his products and the fact that the Gro-Aid line was sufficiently broad to enable the retailer to offer customers a complete range of garden chemicals by purchasing only one line. Mr. Barnes was a chemical engineer and he personally had developed the formulations for the various Gro-Aid products. Retailers generally took a 40 per cent markup on the retail price of the product line while the wholesaler margin averaged 20 per cent of suggested retail. Although a number of other brands of garden chemicals were marketed throughout southern Ontario, Gro-Aid prices were competitive and no other manufacturer offered as wide a range of products.

Late in February 1970, Barnes and Kennedy learned that Bill Lockhart, one of the largest Toronto retail dealers, was no longer interested in carrying the Gro-Aid line. They discovered that the dealer had just been appointed the Ontario distributor of a Quebec-manufactured line of horticultural chemicals to be marketed under the brand name of Surgro.

Upon learning of this appointment, Barnes and Kennedy were able to determine from some of the other retail dealers that Lockhart had appointed three manufacturers' agents to promote the Surgro line to hardware stores, department stores and nursery outlets throughout the province at dealer cost prices averaging 5 per cent lower than Barnes had traditionally sold Gro-Aid products. All wholesalers were to be offered the new line. Orders for ten cases or more could be placed directly by retailers with Lockhart and they would be billed at wholesaler prices. The Surgro line included only slightly fewer products than the Gro-Aid line.

Barnes and Kennedy learned that the company which manufactured Surgro planned to support the introduction of the line with a one-quarter page newspaper advertisement in ten major markets in May, and would offer dealers an attractive wire display stand free with an initial $50 order.

In the past, Barnes had not felt it necessary or wise to invest in advertising Gro-Aid products. Although during the past two years he had packed a simple, combined display and price card into each case of products, Barnes found the dealers generally had not made extensive use of these since the products were usually stocked on shelves in the retail outlets.

In order to determine the quality of the new competitive lines, Kennedy decided to purchase and analyze samples of the Surgro products. Chemical analysis revealed that in all instances Surgro samples were inferior in quality to Gro-Aid products. On March 1, Kennedy sat down to examine all the information he had been able to gather about the new competitive development and to consider what, if any, adjustments in marketing strategy were required. In making his decision, Mr. Kennedy knew that he would have to consider the financial implications as well.

Exhibit 1
General Packaging Ltd.
Gro-Aid Product Line Types (Partial List)

	Size	*Suggested Retail Price*
Lawn Fertilizer	gallon	$5.99
	24 oz	1.89
Plant & Shrub Fertilizer	gallon	5.69
	24 oz	1.69
	8 oz	.99
Rose Protector (Aphids)	24 oz	2.29
(Fungicide)	24 oz	1.98
Lawn Weed Killer	gallon	8.70
	24 oz	2.49
	8 oz	1.49

Exhibit 2
General Packaging Ltd.
Profit & Loss Statements
Years Ending December 31, 1968 and 1969
For R. B. Barnes Ltd.

		1969		1968
Sales		$90 000		$72 000
Cost of Goods Sold		54 000[1]		45 050
Gross Margin		$36 000		$26 950
Operating Expenses				
Mr. Barnes's salary	$7 000		$7 000	
Selling Expenses	7 000		6 000	
Delivery Expense	1 800		1 400	
Office Expense	4 000[2]	19 800	3 800	18 200
Net Profit before taxes		$16 200		$ 8 750
Income Taxes		3 564		1 914
Net Profit after taxes		$12 636		$ 6 836

[1] Including $5 000 of Smith's salary.
[2] Including $2 000 of Smith's salary.

Exhibit 3
General Packaging Ltd.
Budget for the Gro-Aid Division 1970

Sales		$120 000
Cost of Goods Sold		72 000[1]
Gross Margin		$48 000
Operating Expenses		
Kennedy's salary	$12 000	
Other selling expenses	7 000[2]	
Delivery Expense	2 400	
Overhead Allocation	6 000[3]	
		27 400
Budget Divisional Contribution		$20 600

[1] Transfer price of finished product from the manufacturing division to the Gro-Aid Division.

[2] Travelling expenses, etc. No charges for payments to Mr. Barnes were allocated to the Gro-Aid division since for internal budgeting purposes they were considered as part of the original purchase price.

[3] Five per cent of sales which was allocated to all product divisions to cover administrative and other costs.

28

Gerry's Service Station

On July 17, 1972, Gerry Bradley, a service station operator, was trying to decide what action he should take in view of the competitive price situation on gasoline which had developed in his area. The twelve closest service stations to his outlet had recently dropped their prices in line with the majority of service stations in the city (price survey presented in Exhibit 1), and in doing so, were undercutting Gerry's prices on regular and premium grades of gasoline by four cents per gallon.

Gerry had been a service station operator since November 1966 when he had leased an outlet from the Fantom Oil Co., one of the five largest major oil companies in Canada. The station was located on the southeast corner of Spruce Street and Oak Avenue in Rineville, Ontario (population 280 000). Spruce Street was the main access route into the city from Highway 401, a major throughway. Spruce Street was a typical strip development complete with motels, restaurants, and service stations. Oak Avenue was a paved road which continued for a number of miles into the rural area. Residential construction in the immediate area of Spruce Street and Oak Street had not begun in earnest until 1970 with the greatest activity occurring in late 1971 through 1972. An industrial park was taking shape to the north in the area bordering the highway. A map of the area as it appeared in 1972 is presented in Exhibit 2.

The residential and industrial growth in the immediate area, however, did not eliminate the Spruce Street service station operators' dependence upon transient trade for the major portion of their volume. Downtown and suburban service stations with a very large local following were much less dependent on gasoline sales for their profitability since such a clientele brings with it the more profitable parts, accessories, and repair sales. Gerry estimated that 70 per cent of his gasoline sales were from people who did not live in the immediate area, but this was just a guess and it could have been 60 or 80 per cent. Gerry's profit and loss statements (Exhibit 3) were typical of the gasoline to other product sales ratio of operators in comparable locations. The ratio had been improving over the years and 1972 appeared to be no exception with the first six months' sales for non-gasoline products amounting to $35 000, compared to $26 000 for the same period in 1971. Gasoline gallonage had increased by 59 000 gallons to 497 000 gallons for the same period. Gerry attributed about 19 000 gallons of the increase to the fact that in the past three months he had increased his hours of operation to twenty-four hours a day as opposed to sixteen. The 11 P.M. to 7 A.M. shift sales amounted to six to seven thousand gallons per month.

In March 1972 most of the downtown and suburban dealers of the Beach Oil Co., another major supplier, reduced their retail prices of gasoline by four cents per gallon. Their per gallon prices on regular and premium grades became 49.9 cents and 54.9 cents respectively as compared to other dealers at 53.9 and 58.9 cents. It was rumoured that this was an attempt to combat the growth in sales by unbranded gasoline outlets which retailed gasoline at two to five cents below the price of the majors. Most of the major oil company dealers in the city followed the example set by Beach dealers; however, initially the two Beach dealers on Spruce Street did not drop their prices, and there the prices remained stable at 53.9 and 58.9.

Early in May, the Beach dealers on Spruce Street did drop their prices by four cents, and all the other outlets with the exception of Gerry's followed suit. One Spruce Street dealer then reduced his prices by an additional cent and displayed a sign advertising regular grade gasoline at 48.9 cents per gallon. The following day the Beach dealers on Spruce

Street raised their prices to the former level and again the other dealers followed their lead. Prices on Spruce Street were down for little more than a week.

On Monday, June 26, prices at the Beach stations on Spruce Street returned to the 49.9 and 54.9 cents per gallon level. Within a couple of days all Spruce Street service stations, save Gerry's, were at these prices complete with large signs announcing their lower price. Gerry had hoped this was a temporary situation as had been experienced in May; however, on July 17 the lower prices remained.

The Fantom Oil Co. sales representative, Phil Rupp, had called on Gerry a number of times over the three-week period. On each occasion he had explained the company policy of guaranteeing dealers who requested assistance a 7-cent per-gallon margin in meeting competitive prices.[1] Gerry felt this was unacceptable as it meant his taking a 3-cent-per-gallon margin reduction while the company absorbed a penny of the 4-cent reduction. Phil indicated that the company's offer was acceptable to other Fantom Oil dealers in the city, most of whom had reduced their prices, but Gerry felt the other dealers could better afford to take a cut in gasoline margins as they were not as dependent for their profits on gasoline sales. In Gerry's situation he was just now beginning to generate these types of sales and could not afford to lose his gasoline margins.

Phil called on Gerry again on July 17. It appeared his whole purpose in making the call was to point out that while Gerry's gallonage was not dropping, it had ceased to increase at the rate which it had in the past. He called Gerry's attention to the 3000 gallon increase for the first two weeks of the month and warned Gerry that it was just a matter of time before sales of other products would decrease. After Phil left, Gerry pondered the situation. He, too, had noticed that sales were not up to expectations and feared further reductions. Although no one had complained about the prices Gerry couldn't help but notice that a few cars each day were leaving as soon as they were within viewing distance of the prices on the pumps. To further confuse the situation, he had heard one rumour that prices were probably going to drop even further because the unbranded dealers sales were still high, and another to the effect that prices were going to go up because the service station operators were all feeling the effects of the reduced gasoline margins.

---

[1] Competitive prices generally meant the prevailing prices by other major oil company outlets in the immediate area of the dealer in question (in this case the competitive price would be 49.9 cents on regular grade gasoline).

Exhibit 1
Gerry's Service Station
Gasoline Price Survey—Urban Rineville—July 14, 1972

Price columns shown as Regular / Premium:

Brand	54.9 / 59.9	53.9 / 58.9	52.9 / 57.9	51.9 / 56.9	50.9 / 55.9	49.9 / 54.9	48.9 / 53.9	47.9 / 52.9	46.9 / 51.9	45.9 / 50.9	44.9 / 49.9	43.9 / 48.9	Totals
Fantom	2	1				21							24
Beach						22							22
Major #3	3	2	1			12							18
Major #4	5	2	1			26	3						35
Major #5	3		1	2		25	2	3					36
Major #6	11	4				21	2	1	2	3			44
Major #7	2	2				11							15
Major #8						6	2	3		2			13
Minor #1					1	3		6	4	8			22
Miscellaneous Minors									2	9		2	13
Mass Merchandisers						3			2	3			8
Totals	26	10	2	3		150	6	16	10	25		2	250

Exhibit 3
Gerry's Service Station
Comparative Income Statements
(1967-1971)

	1971	1970	1969	1968	1967
Sales:					
Gasoline—Gallons	1 085 000	956 000	874 000	752 000	659 000
—Dollars	$598 377	$517 674	$464 531	$382 768	$332 465
Other Sales	61 033	46 114	35 061	28 810	21 221
Total	$659 410	$563 788	$499 592	$411 578	$353 686
Cost of Goods Sold					
Gasoline	$490 962	$423 030	$378 005	$308 320	$267 224
Other	41 502	31 357	24 192	20 743	14 854
Total	$532 464	$454 387	$402 197	$329 063	$282 078
Expenses:					
Wages	$ 52 543	$ 44 091	$ 40 321	$ 35 872	$35 244
Rent[1]	16 614	14 256	12 678	10 840	8 238
All Other	21 749	19 378	17 457	13 675	12 716
Total	$ 90 906	$ 77 725	$ 70 456	$ 60 387	$56 198
NET PROFIT BEFORE TAXES	$ 36 040	$ 31 676	$ 26 942	$ 22 128	$ 15 410

[1] Rent: Money paid to Fantom Oil as per terms of lease. It was calculated partly as a fixed sum per gallon of gasoline and partly as a percentage of the sales on other products.

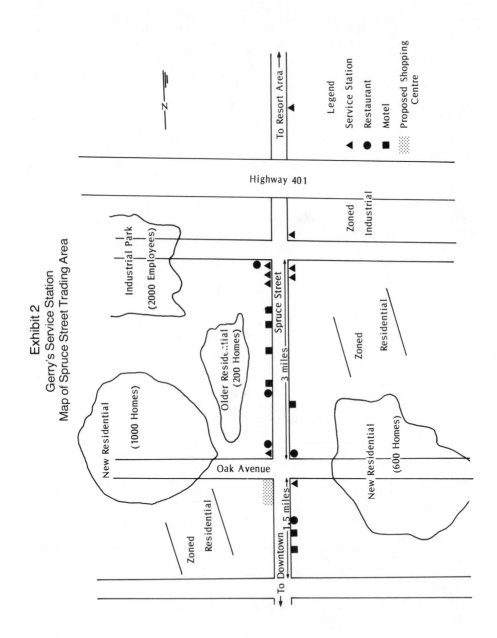

Exhibit 2
Gerry's Service Station
Map of Spruce Street Trading Area

Legend

▲ Service Station
● Restaurant
■ Motel
▨ Proposed Shopping Centre

29

Lambton Road Cash and Carry

Early in August 1969, Mr. Don Barlow, manager of Lambton Road Cash and Carry, a retail lumber and home improvement supply centre located in Sarnia, Ontario, learned the Beaver Lumber Co. had acquired a property directly across Lambton Road from his location. Mr. Barlow also understood plans for the establishment of the Beaver outlet, which would focus on retail sales, were well advanced and construction was to begin soon. Beaver Lumber had operated in Sarnia for some time. Their main emphasis had been wholesaling (sales to tradesmen, contractors, industries, etc.) from a yard located in an older industrialized section of Sarnia.

Lambton Road was a main thoroughfare in the northeast part of the city. Two nearby shopping malls built in the last year, whose stores were open from 10 A.M. to 10 P.M., guaranteed a reasonable flow of traffic past the Cash and Carry store.

The premises on Lambton Road were purchased in 1952 by the owners of Lambton Lumber and Builders Supply Ltd., a long-established company in the Sarnia area. Until early 1961, the Lambton Road location was used as a wholesale service yard. Prior to the time, all retail sales had been made through Lambton Lumber's predominantly wholesale yard, which was located on a main thoroughfare in an industrial area close to the downtown area.

In April 1961, the main emphasis of the Lambton Road store became retail business. It was felt the establishment of a separate, retail-oriented outlet, operating on a cash and carry basis, would relieve the main yard of the expensive and tedious process of filling, billing and delivering many small orders from wholesale inventory. Prices on retail orders could be reduced since costs would be lowered and the product line could be diversified and better merchandised in a retail-oriented outlet.

The city of Sarnia was located in Lambton County at the southern end of Lake Huron, directly across the St. Clair River from Port Huron, Michigan. Sarnia was sixty-two miles west of London and sixty-two miles northeast of the Windsor-Detroit area. The city's population in 1969 was 57 699; Lambton County, including Sarnia, had a population of 110 786 in 1968. Due to the high concentration of petrochemical manufacturing in the area, the St. Clair basin was known as "Canada's Chemical Valley." In the Sarnia area there were three large oil refineries, a synthetic rubber plant and a dozen allied chemical plants. In addition, two large plants manufactured auto parts. Many of the chemical and petrochemical plants called for continuous process manufacturing. As a result, three-shift operations were common, with shift changes usually at 8 A.M., 4 P.M. and midnight. In other industries, the usual plant working hours were 8 A.M. to 4:30 P.M.

Appendix I shows additional selected statistics on the Sarnia area taken from an Industrial Survey prepared by the Sarnia and District Chamber of Commerce.

The product line carried by the Lambton Road Cash and Carry outlet was very diverse. It included such items as household hardware, tools, bathroom fixtures, tile and floor coverings as well as basic lumber products and building supplies. Sales at the Lambton Road store were $400 000 in 1968, gross margin was 28 per cent, and net profits before taxes amounted to $18 000.[1] Almost all sales were "cash only."

The Lambton Road store was open six days a week, from 8 A.M. to 5 P.M. and was staffed by experienced personnel, most of whom were originally transferred from the downtown yard of Lambton Lumber. Home delivery of purchases was not encouraged but could be arranged on a fee basis.

Lambton Road Cash and Carry had used local radio stations as their main advertising medium on a regular basis. The table below shows the stations used, the programs currently sponsored, and the type of commercial message employed.

Station	Program	Time	Frequency	Type
CKJD	Newscast	8:00 A.M.	Daily	60-second spot
CHOK	Sports	12:40 P.M.	Daily	60-second spot
''	Regular	10-12 A.M.	Saturday	Remote

The Saturday morning program was broadcast from the Lambton Road location and had run for the past five years. The program featured music, interviews and announcements of up-coming area events. Although the regular commercial time for this broadcast period was also sold to other sponsors, throughout the program the announcer stated where he was broadcasting from and often conducted interviews with store personnel and customers. At $50 per program, the Saturday morning time was considered by store personnel as a "good buy." In addition to regular radio advertising, Lambton Road Cash and Carry occasionally used a local daily newspaper, *The Sarnia Observer,* to announce special sales and promotions. The annual cost of newspaper advertising was approximately $300.

The company also participated in the Sarnia "Hi Neighbor" service. This service was designed to welcome new residents to Sarnia through personal visits by a hostess who gave general information about the city and presented gifts and samples from local businesses. Lambton Building Supply provided personalized key chains which were mailed to new arrivals after the visit of the hostess. Annual cost of this service was roughly $150 plus $150 for key chains. Annual advertising in the telephone directory "Yellow Pages" added $1200 to the promotion budget.

Lambton Road Cash and Carry, through Lambton Lumber and Builders Supply Ltd., was a member of the Allont Federation of Building Material and Supply dealers. In 1969 Allont had approximately 135 dealer-members throughout Canada and was organized to give its members the adverntages of centralized, high-volume buying.

Allont also provided promotional help through the publication of illustrated colour catalogues for distribution by Allont dealers to their customers. The standardized format of these full-colour, eighty-page catalogues allowed the dealers to purchase the catalogues each year at the low price of $.11 per copy. Mr. Barlow estimated that as of August 1969, over 18 000 of the 1969 catalogues were in the hands of his customers and prospective customers. Exhibit 1 is a reproduction of the index page from an Allont catalogue, showing the products offered by Allont dealers. Twice a year Allont also published four-page "flyers" which described special bargains and cost dealers one cent each. Delivery costs for the catalogues and flyers totalled $1400 in 1969.

Soon after he heard of the planned Beaver outlet, Mr. Barlow attempted to learn more about their method of operation. In checking other centres, he found that Beaver stores often stayed open until 9 P.M. each weekday evening, and closed at 6 P.M. on Saturdays. Beaver offered a thirty-day, no-interest credit facility to customers on purchases over $50 as well as an interest-bearing time payment plan for major purchases. Delivery services were available free of charge on virtually all purchases.

The Beaver Lumber chain had ninety-five member yards in Ontario and about 263 in the western provinces. The size of this membership meant that the Beaver outlet on Lambton Road could be expected to have buying power comparable to that enjoyed by Lambton Road Cash and Carry. In checking over a Beaver catalogue, Mr. Barlow found the products and prices offered were generally comparable to, and competitive with, those in the Allont catalogue. Beaver Lumber's promotional program appeared to rely heavily on newspaper advertising.

April, May and June had traditionally been the biggest selling months for the Lambton Road Cash and Carry, with December, January and February relatively slow months. Sales fluctuated through the week, with Saturday by far the busiest day. Monday was usually the second biggest volume day of the week. Mr. Barlow also found the average weekday purchase in the Lambton Road stores was $10.50, whereas the average purchase for generally comparable stores in the United States (the only data available) was $15 to $17, with 15 to 35 per cent of sales for these same U.S. stores being credit sales. In studying his Saturday volume, Mr. Barlow found the average sale was $8.50 with 80 per cent of the total day's sales made between 10 A.M. and 2:30 P.M.

Mr. Barlow felt the competition posed by the establishment of the new Beaver outlet warranted a thorough appraisal of his marketing approach. In addition, the other four lumber and building supply centres in Sarnia, although still "wholesale oriented," were continually becoming more aggressive in their efforts to develop retail volume. He was particularly concerned with the amount of money he should commit to advertising and promotion as well as the selection of advertising media and the timing and content of the advertising message. Very little information was available to help him, although he understood some dealers used 1.5 per cent of gross sales as a rule of thumb to establish their promotional budgets. To aid him in his planning, Mr. Barlow assembled the cost and coverage data for Sarnia media as shown in Exhibit 2.

Exhibit 1
Lambton Road Cash and Carry
Your Allont Index To Big Values in Building Materials

A

Accessories,
　bathroom 52, 53,
　　　　　　　　54, 55
Acoustic Tile 11, 12, 13
Adhesives 45, 60, 62
Aluminum Doors 42
Aluminum Insulation 31
Aluminum Ladders 58
Aluminum Windows 41, 43
Antiquing 59
Appliances, kitchen 50
Arborite 47
Arbours and Trellises 70
Asbestos Siding 26, 27
Asphalt Roofing 23, 24

B

Bar, plans 17
Basement Paint 62
Bathroom
　accessories
　.................52, 53, 54, 55
　bathtubs 55
　caulking 60, 62
　fans 49
　medicine cabinets 52
　mirrors 17, 52
　showers 55
　shower doors 53
　sinks 54
　soap dishes 54
　tile 53
　toilet seats 55
　toilets 55
　towel racks 54
Bathtubs 55
Bifold Doors 35
Blinds 37
Brushes, paint 57
Budget Plans 21

C

Cabanas, wood 71
Cabinet Hardware 77
Cabinets 51
Cafe Doors 34
Canopies 72

Carpets 46
Carpet Tiles 46
Carports 74
Caulking
　Compounds 60, 62
Cedar
　closet lining 16
　siding 26
　sundecks 71
Cedar Sundecks 71
Ceilings,
　suspended 12, 13
Ceiling Tile 11, 12, 13
Cements and
　Glues 45, 60, 62
Cement Paint 62
Ceramic Tile 54
Chain Link Fences 64
Chimes 72
Chimneys 76
Closet Rods 76
Concrete Mixes 69
Concrete Patch 69
Corrugated
　Plastic Panels 65, 72
Cottages 75
Counter Tops 49
Cove Base 45
Cupolas 31, 39
Custom Kitchens 51

D

Decorative
　Plastic Panels 15
Dishwashers 50
Disposer, garbage 50
Door
　aluminum 42
　bells 72
　bifold 35
　cafe doors 34
　chimes 72
　decorative panel ..33, 35
　folding 34
　garage 73
　grills 43
　hardware 42, 77

louvred 34, 35
moulding 22
screen doors 34, 42
shower 53
shutters 37
sliding glass 36, 38
weatherstripping 16
wood exterior 33, 34, 35
wood interior 33, 35
Door Locks 36
Drawer Pulls 77
Driveway Sealer 69
Drywall 21

E

Eavestroughing 76
Electrical Fixtures 63

F

Fans
　bathroom 49
　kitchen 49
　range hoods 49
Farm Buildings 78
Fences
　chain link 64
　plastic panel 65, 72
　wood 66, 67
Filigree, hardboard 15
Fillers
　concrete 58, 60, 69
　plaster 58, 60, 62
　wood 58
Fixtures, bathroom ..52, 54
Floor Paint 57, 59, 62
Floor Tile 44, 45
Flooring
　adhesives 45
　carpets 46
　seamless 59
　tiles 44, 45
Folding Doors 34
Formica 48
Foundation Coating 60

G

Garages 74
　doors 73

Garbage Disposer 50
Garage Doors 73
Garden Hose 70
Garden Items
　arbours 70
　cedar sundeck 71
　picnic tables 71
　plastic panel 65, 72
　storage sheds 68
　tools 80
　trellises 70
　hedge trimmer 80
　wheel barrows 70
Garden Tools 70
Glues 60, 62
Gypsum Wallboard 21

H

Hardboard Filigree 15
Hardboard
　Panels 8, 9, 10, 19
Hardboard Siding 27
Hardware
　cabinet 77
　door 77
　kitchen 77
　shelf 14, 15
Hose, garden 70
House Paint 57, 61

I

Idea Booklets 34, 75, 78
Indoor/Outdoor Carpet .46
Insulation
　aluminum foil 31
　caulking 60, 62
　fibre glass 30
　louvres 31
　mineral wool 29
　poylthene sheet 32
　polystyrene foam 29
　tackers 11
　weatherstripping 36
　zonolite 32

J

Joist Hangers 25
Jack Post 76

Exhibit 1 (continued)

Exhibit 2
Lambton Road Cash and Carry
Sarnia Media

RADIO

	Station CHOK	*Station CKJD*
Broadcasting power	10 000 watts	1 000 watts
Basic format	Standard-pop	Standard-pop
Special daily features	Open line 9-11 A.M.	Telephone show 9:05-10 A.M.
	Women's shows 1-3:30 P.M.	Teenage 6:10-11 P.M.
	Teenage 6:30-9 P.M.	
	Farm segment 6-6:30 P.M.	
Time classifications	'AA' 6:30 to 9 A.M.	'AAA' 6 to 9 A.M.,
	Mon. to Sat.	12 to 2 P.M.,
		4 to 7 P.M. daily
	'AA' 9 A.M. to 1 P.M.	'A' 9 A.M. to 12 noon,
	4 to 7 P.M.	2 to 4 P.M.
	Mon. to Sat.,	
	all Sunday	
	'B' all other times	'A' 7 P.M. to 1 A.M.

Rates:

		AA	A	B	AAA	AA	A
(approximate;	60 sec	$18.00	$15.00	$12.00	$15.00	$12.00	$10.00
no discounts	30 sec	16.00	13.00	11.00	12.00	10.00	8.00
shown)	15 sec	14.00	11.00	10.00	N.A.	N.A.	N.A.

NEWSPAPERS

Newspapers	*Circulation*	*Line Rate**	¼ Page*	½ Page*	Full Page*	Page Size
Sarnia Observer	18 274	$.18 (b/w)	$110	$215	$430	23½ × 16½
Sarnia Gazette	12 500	.10 (b/w)	18	35	69	16½ × 11½
London Free Press	29 597 [1]	.50	347	693	1386	22 × 16½

* Approximate, no discounts shown.
[1] Lambton County
Source: Canada Advertising Rates and Data, June 1970.

Appendix 1
Industrial Survey of Canada's Chemical Valley

1. POPULATION

Sarnia (1969)—57 699
Lambton County (1968)—110 786
Households in Sarnia (1969)—19 055
Current population growth rate—19 per cent per decade

Population Growth	*Population Forecast*
1961—51 000	1970—58 100
1966—53 900	1975—62 700
1967—56 000	1980—66 700
1968—56 600	1985—70 100
1969—57 700	

2. COMMUNICATIONS

Radio

Station CHOK—10 000 watts day and night.
Station CKJD— 100 watts day and night.

Television

Stations: London—Channel 10
        Windsor—Channel 9
        Detroit—Channels 2, 4, 7, 35, 50
Huron Cable T.V. Ltd.: Channels 2, 4, 5, 7, 9, 10, 11, 15, 50, 56

Newspapers	Frequency	Circulation
Sarnia Observer	daily	18 274
Sarnia Gazette	weekly	12 500
St. Clair Gazette	weekly	2 500
Windsor Star	daily	3 451
London Free Press	daily	6 447 (city)
London Free Press	daily	29 597 (county)

3. RESIDENTIAL AND BUILDING

Housing

(a) Apartments:
    Availability — Fair
    Type   — Wide range from ultramodern with pool to older homes.
    Rentals — Modern two bedroom—$160 average
             — Older homes, two bedrooms—$150 average

(b) Houses:
    Availability — for sale—fair
                — for rent—poor $160 up
    Average cost new 5-6 room—$25 500
    Average cost new exec. home—$35 000
    Down payment—new—$6000-7000 average

Building Statistics—1968

186 new dwellings valued at $5 377 380
  14 permits for schools, churches, etc. $2 230 600
104 permits for commercial and industrial $2 877 670
161 permits for repairs and alterations $197 235
159 permits for private garages $110 675

Total number of permits issued in 1968—684
Total value of permits issued in 1968—$10 829 485

4. RETAILING

Stores in Metro Sarnia Area

7 Department stores	81 Salons and barbers
68 Food	43 Home decorating
43 Variety	43 Building material
75 Apparel	109 Gas stations
32 Furniture and household	23 New car dealers
29 Drug stores	27 Used car dealers

Retail sales (1968)—$88.2 million
Per Capita Sales—$1520 (25 per cent above National Average)

5. PERSONAL INCOME

Personal disposable income (1968)—$185.5 million (per capita income—$3200)
Average income per taxpayer—$5778 (43 per cent above National Average)

Income Statistics

Income Class	Taxpayers
Under $3 000	9 001
3 000-5 000	5 681
5 000-7 000	5 621
7 000-10 000	6 886
10 000-20 000	3 236
over $20 000	335

6. LABOUR

Labour Force (1961) Census	Male	Female
Managerial	1 325	131
Professional, technical	1 998	959
Clerical	769	1 586
Sales	729	592
Service, recreation	962	1 431
Transport, communication	1 019	116
Primary	132	6
Craftsmen, etc.	5 246	200
Labourers	838	60
Total	13 018	5 081

Average Weekly Wages and Salaries (August 1969)

Sarnia	Windsor	Oshawa	St. Catharines	Sault Ste. Marie
$155	$142	$139	$133	$127

7. INDUSTRIALIZATION

Manufacturing (1966)

	Establishments	Employees
Sarnia	47	7 779
Lambton Co.	110	10 742

Distribution by Employees (Major Companies)

No. of Employees	No. of Companies
1-100	5
101-200	3
201-500	3
501-1000	3
1001-2000	1 (Dow Chemical)
2001 and over	2 (Imperial Oil, Polymer Corp.)

30
Latimer Tool Co. Ltd.

In January 1975, Paul Desmarais, a dealer who had been selling the Latimer line of industrial tools in the Milltown area for about four years, approached Mr. A. W. May, general sales manager for the Latimer Tool Co., and requested that in the future he be considered as a territorial distributor and thus qualify for an additional discount on his purchases from the Latimer Tool Co.

At the time of request, the Latimer Tool Co. had distributorship arrangements with only two firms, both national distributors. Several executives in the Latimer Co. were opposed to granting any territorial distributorship, since this would, in effect, mean a complete change in the distribution policy of the company. However, it was recognized that the parent company in the U.S. had traditionally distributed its products through territorial distributors, and that this method of distribution had much to recommend it.

The Latimer Tool Co. was the largest Canadian manufacturer of cutting tools for metal working. These cutting tools ranged in sized from delicate watchmaking tools to large-scale cutting tools used by manufacturers of heavy industrial equipment such as large electrical generators and turbines.

It was the policy of Latimer to concentrate on maintaining high and uniform quality in its products. The company felt that long-lasting uniform tool wear enabled the user to produce a better, more consistent finish on his manufactured goods.

The Latimer company was one of five major producers of cutting tools in Canada, and in 1975 had over one-third of the total Canadian market. Imports accounted for about 15 per cent of total cutting tool sales in Canada, and of these imports 60 per cent came from the United States while the rest were divided between England and Sweden.

Latimer executives said that, in their experience, sales of cutting tools tended to closely follow industrial development. A wide range of industries used cutting tools in manufacturing their products, the total market from British Columbia to Newfoundland containing roughly 7500 cutting tool users. The largest users were manufacturers of heavy apparatus, automobile parts manufacturers, and other firms operating large machine shops.

Mr. May said that, from the customer's standpoint, the three most important elements in the sale of cutting tools were: (1) prompt service on the part of suppliers; (2) the quality of the products; and (3) the relationship of the seller with the buyer. He said that most cutting tool users maintained about a 60-day inventory of their cutting tool requirements, although on standard tools where delivery could be obtained within a week, only a ten-day to two-week stock might be kept. Special items took from four to six weeks for delivery. Some larger companies like General Motors, the Steel Co. of Canada and the Ford Motor Co. of Canada made cutting tool purchases almost daily in order to maintain their inventory at minimum levels.

Mr. May felt the customer's purchasing agent was a very important factor in the sale of cutting tools, and it was Latimer policy that he be the first person contacted in the company. With the purchasing agent's permission, the Latimer salesman would work down the line to shop superintendents, foremen, master mechanics and tool room superintendents, pointing out the quality and reliability of Latimer cutting tools.

To ascertain their relative position in the industry, the Latimer Co. computed the percentage of Latimer sales to total cutting tool sales for Canada as reported by several trade and association journals. This percentage was called "normal." To break sales figures down further, executives established a potential for each industrial area, such as Milltown, by using salesmen's estimates, local trade directories and Chamber of Commerce figures on industries and production.

Mr. May said one of the big problems facing the cutting tool industry was the lack of standards. In the Latimer Co. alone there were about 4000 standard items, varying in type of steel used, size of tool and shape of cutting edge. When three to five customers used the same type of cutting tool it was usually added to the list of standard items and a stock kept. More than half of the orders received by the Latimer Co. were filled from stock, but a large number were special-purpose tools for which no stock was kept.

In the general line of cutting tools, the company employed eight salesmen, whose main function was to give technical assistance to the distributor's salesmen, but who also attempted to find new business. Technical assistance generally involved specifying the proper cutting tool to use on any specific metal and type of material. Latimer salesmen were located in Hamilton, Windsor, Toronto (2), Montreal (2), Welland, and one in Calgary, whose territory was from the head of the lakes west. In providing technical assistance, the Latimer salesman might accompany the distributor's salesman on his calls, or he might try to find new customers for the Latimer Co. and the distributor.

Salesmen were compensated on a guarantee-and-incentive basis. A basic part of their salary was guaranteed, and the incentive was based one-half on the total company sales and one-half on the sales in each salesman's own territory.

Typically, the salesman was expected to make from four to five calls a day either on tool users or distributors. The sales manager believed if the salesmen made more than this number of calls they were not doing their job properly. If a salesman obtained an order from a new customer he was not under any circumstances to recommend one distributor over another.

In the Latimer Tool Co.'s terminology, a ''dealer'' was any outlet which bought direct from Latimer for resale, but which was not an authorized distributor of Latimer products. Mr. May said that distributors were expected to carry certain basic stocks, depending on the industries and area serviced, while dealers usually purchased infrequently and often on a customer's special order.

Dealers received a somewhat smaller discount on purchases than did distributors. For example, on the typical tool, the price list would be as follows:

List Price	$4.60
Price to Dealers	2.25
Price to Distributors	1.98

A few large users of cutting tools purchased directly from Latimer. These accounts would be charged $2.42 in the case of the cutting tool described above. The pricing tables, as well as freight charges, were designed to encourage large purchases and thus discourage direct buying. Latimer would prepay freight on any purchase weighing over 100 lbs, thus making small purchases uneconomical in most cases. The sales manager said he would prefer to sell only through distributors, but direct selling was continued because some large users preferred to purchase in that manner, and dealer sales were continued because they gave Latimer a substantial profit.

Competition in the cutting tool business came mainly from four Canadian companies. In all cases these companies sold through distributors, although one competitor made more use of dealers, since their product range included many items which would appeal more to the home market.

Since its founding in 1919, the Latimer Tool Co. had used Jackson-Dowling Ltd. as the sole national distributor for Latimer products. Jackson-Dowling handled a tremendous number of products in the industrial field, including a great deal of heavy machinery. They employed some 160 salesmen working out of 15 sales offices and warehouses located in Halifax, Saint John, Quebec City, Montreal, Ottawa, Toronto, Windsor, Thunder Bay, Winnipeg, Regina, Saskatoon, Calgary, Edmonton, Vancouver, and Victoria.

In 1965, a second national distributor was added, following a drop of approximately 7 per cent in Latimer's total share of the industry sales. Executives believed that the dip was due in part to the fact that Jackson-Dowling was handling too many lines to give Latimer products the time and sales effort needed. The new distributor, Canatool Ltd, had only twenty lines, all non-competing, and eighteen salesmen operating from sales offices and warehouses located in Toronto and Montreal. When Canatool Ltd was taken on, Latimer stressed that it was employed to solicit new business and not to take existing business away from Jackson-Dowling. However, Mr. May said this had not always been the case.

Mr. May said that Jackson-Dowling was unhappy at the addition of another distributor, but after he explained the situation to them they began working to recover sales lost to Canatool Ltd. In 1975, Jackson-Dowling was doing a greater volume in those areas of competition with the new distributor than before. Mr. May said competition like this was desirable because it increased the overall business for Latimer and "kept everyone on his toes." In 1974, Canatool added new warehouses in Edmonton, Thunder Bay, and St. Thomas, Ontario, and a sales office in Hamilton. With the addition of each of these new outlets, Jackson-Dowling expressed dissatisfaction, but in each case Mr. May said he could show them where total Latimer sales increased after addition of the outlets. In 1975 the big bulk of sales were still made through Jackson-Dowling.

In 1971, neither of the Latimer Tool Co.'s national distributors had a warehouse located in Milltown, Quebec. Milltown was a medium-sized industrial city located in the centre of an area where, within a seventy-mile radius, close to four hundred industrial manufacturers were situated. Until 1967, these accounts were serviced by Jackson-Dowling through their Montreal warehouse, located 150 miles from Milltown. The company's participation in this industrial area was only one-third normal, and in an attempt to improve on this showing Mr. May had for some time been trying to persuade Jackson-Dowling to build a warehouse in Milltown to service the area. He was convinced that the poor showing in Milltown was due in considerable part to the lack of any nearby source of supply for goods.

In 1971, Mr. Desmarais, owner of a local industrial supply house servicing the Milltown area, approached the Latimer Tool Co. and asked to handle the line as a distributor. Latimer executives rejected the request for a territorial distributorship. However, they did agree to accept the firm as a dealer with the understanding that the Latimer Tool Co. would provide the technical assistance through Latimer's salesmen. The Milltown supply house agreed to these terms.

This Milltown supply house had at that time two salesmen who called on the various industrial accounts in the area. Their lines covered virtually every major type of industrial hardware, and included grinding wheels, pumps, motors, materials-handling equipment, screws, nails, and hand tools, along with a wide variety of other items.

After a period of approximately four years, Latimer sales in the Milltown area had increased more than 10 times. Virtually all of this increase had resulted from the efforts of the local supply house. According to participation or share of market figures of the Latimer Co., the Milltown area in 1975 was the most productive area in Canada in relation to its potential. The dealer had at this time four salesmen whom he had sent to the Latimer plant to receive training courses, and an office staff of eight people. He was servicing over three hundred accounts and was billing approximately $220 000 for the Latimer Co. The dealer carried a full line of standard Latimer products in stock, which meant he stocked an inventory valued at between $25 000 and $30 000. Eighty-five per cent of the dealer's total sales were made by only ten lines that he carried. Latimer products were one of these lines.

At this time, 1975, Mr. Desmarais again asked Mr. May for a distributor's discount for the following reasons: (1) he had increased Latimer's business in the area by over ten times in the last four years, (2) he was performing a warehousing and service function in the area comparable to a distributor's operations; (3) his salesmen were highly trained and, he said, serviced the area better than either of the national distributors; (4) he was now servicing over 75 per cent of the accounts in the area; and (5) the company's total participation in this area was the highest in Canada.

The dealer pointed out that under a territorial distributorship his net profit would be twice that obtained under a dealer's discount. He would at the same time be able to extend more attractive bids to industrial users of competitive products. He claimed that, if given the extra margin, he would be able to increase his participation in the area to almost 90 per cent.

Most of the Milltown dealer's success in promoting the line lay, Mr. May believed, in the fact that the dealer carried extensive stocks and was able to provide quick delivery and service where necessary. Local Milltown industrial firms therefore preferred to order locally for this reason, and because the dealer was part of their community. Latimer equipment was otherwise available from the two national distributors, whose nearest warehouses were located in Montreal. This usually meant a waiting period of from four days to six weeks in filling orders by these distributors, whereas the local dealer filled the order the same day or in a maximum of four weeks if the desired product had to be produced to special order by the Latimer Co. Also, the dealer's qualified salesmen were able to carry out tests on certain products to the customer's specifications at any time they were desired. The national distributors had specialists who would have to be contacted by the company and a suitable time arranged to make the tests.

Mr. May felt that the Milltown dealer deserved a distributor's discount, but he realized that in granting such a discount he would be setting a precedent, in effect, by establishing a territorial distributor. Mr. May knew that the addition of a territorial distributor would endanger the company's relationships with the national distributors. On the other hand, territorial distributorships seemed to be the best method of increasing sales in areas where the participation was low, although good local distributors were not always available. He was undecided as to what action he should take with regard to the Milltown dealer's request, particularly since continued refusal to grant the special discount might well mean loss of the dealer's business to a competitor.

31
Lineman Promotions

On February 1, 1976, Fred Lineman went to see his brother-in-law, Bill Drake, with the intention of asking Bill to lend him $6000 so that Fred could arrange his first concert.

Fred Lineman had recently graduated with a B.A. and had established himself as a booking agent for musical groups under the name LINEMAN PROMOTIONS. With his savings he opened an office in London, Ontario, on December 1, 1975. From this office he planned to establish his career in the booking field.

"It was a gas to book the bands at school when I was social convener. I knew the groups' agents were taking 10 per cent of the groups' gross. Most good agents had fifteen to twenty-five $1000 per week bands booked steadily. At 10 per cent, that's a lot of beans!"

Up until late January, Fred had only earned $300 while his expenses were close to $600 per month. Over half the $1200 was for rent. Because Fred had used all of his savings to establish his agency, he could not afford to run at a $450 per month deficit much longer. In order to generate some quick cash and at the same time put his musical knowledge to work, Fred decided he would try to put on a concert. He knew that London concerts in the past had grossed up to $28 000 for one night and had lost as much as $12 000. He felt that with his knowledge of music and his need for cash, it would be a good opportunity for him to put his knowledge to the test.

Fred hoped that if he came up with a good plan for his concert, his brother-in-law, who owned a profitable business, would agree to lend him the money needed to finance the concert.

After Fred arrived at Bill Drake's house, he discussed with Bill the process he had gone through to put his plan together.

"I started phoning around to check out the various big name groups including *Guess Who, Eagles, Average White Band*. They all wanted about fifteen grand for a forty-five-minute set and at that they still wanted a nine-week notice. No way!"

Fred started seeking alternative solutions. He discovered that over the past six months, seven discotheques had opened in the London area. Discos were a new concept in nightclub entertainment where, instead of live bands, records were played through very sophisticated sound systems. Also, these types of clubs usually had light shows and some had illuminated dance floors. The discotheque was a place to go if you wanted non-stop music and dancing. There were two basic types of discos. One catered to the eighteen to twenty-four group, the other catered to the twenty-five and over group. The type of music offered made the difference.

"In going to these discos, I got to meet the disc-jockeys who play the records there. They told me that the fourteen to eighteen year olds were the ones who really liked and purchased the majority of the disco records from the stores. [The difference between a disco record and a regular record is that the former type lends itself easily to dancing the latest types of disco-style dances—the 'Bump', the 'Hustle.' There is a strong emphasis on the beat so that the dancers can easily follow it. These types of records are played constantly at the discotheques.] Since there was an age limit to nightclub admittance, only those that could prove they were at least eighteen years of age were able to patronize these clubs. The disc-jockeys also told me that the disco scene was just starting to 'boom' in London in spite of the fact that they had been growing in popularity in the United States for over two years. Consequently, I drew up a list of all the groups which produced disco records and was on my way."

On January 29, Fred was able to get a lead on *Kool and the Gang,* a twelve-piece group from New York. During 1974, this group had had three big disco hit records in the U.S. market: "Funky Stuff", "Jungle Boogie" and "Hollywoods Swinging." Because some of these records had been popular in London discotheques during the disco boom, Fred was eager to follow up the lead.

"They were playing in Detroit, February 16, and in Buffalo, February 20. We were right in the middle between these two cities. They normally charged $9500 for one hour but I could pick them up for $7500 on the 18th if I promised to arrange the following items:[1]

1. Seventeen separate rooms to be reserved at the nearest luxury hotel/motel;
2. Three cases of red wine to be supplied to the troupe upon arrival;
3. A minimum of 6000 watts RMS (10 000 watt peak) system would have to be provided—twenty-four microphone capacity;
4. Seven set-up men and stage crew to be available;
5. "Star" billing to be provided for the group;
6. $3500 to be paid on signing the contract, the balance of the payment to be made to the group leader *before* they perform their one-hour show;
7. Transportation to be arranged to and from the airport, hotel and arena;
8. Newspaper and/or television coverage to be conducted through and by the group's manager *only*;
9. Ten dressing rooms to be reserved."

To further add to his concert, Fred decided to start the show with two new Toronto groups, *Crack of Dawn* and *Sweet Blindness*, each with a newly released disco record on the hit charts—"Keep the Faith" and "Cowboys to Girls."

"I could get both acts for $1500. I knew they needed the exposure for their new records, plus Wednesdays are off-nights for local bands since weekends are the prime time for concerts."

A place for the concert had to be chosen. In London there were four arenas that were used for local concerts. Bus routes serviced all but the London Gardens. The bus line stopped approximately 5000 ft from the Gardens and the last one departed from this stop for the downtown area at 11:30 P.M. Exhibit 1 outlines, in more detail, information about the four arenas. In outlining the data, Fred stated he preferred the London Gardens because it offered the greatest chance to make a substantial gain.

"In Toronto tickets sell for up to $10 per person for two acts. In London they range from $4.50 to $6 for a similar show. I've got to cover my costs, (Exhibit 2) but I also want to make a pile of money. If I charge $5 per ticket the only place I can go to make any money is the Gardens."

To promote his concert, Fred estimated $1500 should be sufficient for radio advertising, his primary promotional media. Using the schedule in Exhibit 3, Fred made up the radio coverage advertising plan outlined in Exhibit 4. The stations chosen would cover a substantial portion of southwestern Ontario.

"I couldn't find any data on CHLO's audience, but it's a great station, cheap, and all the other concerts use it—so why not? Also two weeks should be enough, everyone does it the same way."

During this same period, Fred was aware that several other concerts had been planned. Two rock and roll groups, *Rush* and *Thundermug,* would be performing at the

---

[1] Failure to provide *any* of these items could result in the cancellation of the concert by the group. Any prepaid deposits would then be forfeited in the group's favour. Most concert contracts included a mutual cancellation clause. This allowed either party to cancel the concert, but *only* within a mutually determined time span—usually three weeks prior to the concert.

London Arena on February 7. The world-famous jazz drummer Buddy Rich and his fifteen-piece band were playing at Centennial Hall on February 17. Bruce Cockburn, a top Canadian folk singer, would be appearing in Alumni Hall on February 15. Tickets for these concerts ranged in price from $4.50 to $6.50 per person and were available at all regular ticket outlets. The student market for the concerts in the London area included 30 000 students from grades 7 to 13, 5000 students from Fanshawe Community College, and 17 000 university students. Because this would be a "big" event during the middle part of the week, Fred did not think that alternative forms of entertainment such as night clubs, movies and sports events would offer the concert any notable competition.

"Sure there'll be other concerts before mine, so what. Mine will have three disco groups, 11 inch by 14 inch posters, and super radio ads using the groups' songs as background while the announcer talks." (Exhibit 1).

Fred decided that the best way to distribute the tickets and posters would be to use all the regular outlets, plus the box office of the arena chosen for the concert.

"I will use all the regular places uptown, a few malls in London, and one out of town. Some friends of mine will distribute the posters and tickets to these spots. I've printed 200 complimentary tickets which my friends will give to the managers and staff of these retail outlets in return for selling our tickets and displaying our posters. My friends can keep whatever tickets and posters are left."

Fred knew that the other concerts before his would also have posters in the ticket outlets and the general rule was to leave them up until the night of the concert.

"Since mine are shocking pink people will see ours first, no matter where they are put up in these stores."

In completing the presentation of his plan, Fred tried to convince Bill to lend him up to $6000 to pay for the preliminary start-up expenses. Crucial to this whole plan was the fact that Fred had to sign the final contract on or before February 3, 1976. Following the presentation, Bill promised to give Fred an answer within the next two days.

Exhibit 1
Lineman Promotions
Copy of Proposed Concert Radio Ad

1. 60-SECOND AD

   Produce with music from groups mentioned in selected spots (bracketed), approximately 10 seconds for each song.

   Announcer: (Arena chosen) becomes Canada's largest Discotheque—8:00 P.M.—Wednesday, February 18. It's CRACK OF DAWN ("Keep the Faith"), SWEET BLINDNESS, ("Cowboys to Girls") and special guest stars, KOOL AND THE GANG ("Hollywood Swinging"). One show only. Advance Tickets available at Sam's, Bluebird, Mister Sound, The Disc Shop in the Sherwood Forest Mall, Fig Leaf, The Disc Shop in Northland Mall and St. Thomas's Elgin Mall and the (arena chosen) box office.

2. 30-SECOND AD

   Mention group's name only.
   Only use "Hollywood Swinging" music for background.
   The rest of the copy will be the same.

Exhibit 2
Lineman Promotions
Arena Information

	London Gardens	London Arena	Centennial Hall	Alumni Hall
ARENA	London Gardens	London Arena	Centennial Hall	Alumni Hall
CAPACITY	6000	2800	1500	2400
PARKING	Excellent	Poor	Good	Good
BUS	1 mile away (approximately)	1/2 block away	2 blocks away	to the door
LOCATION	Southeast section of the city adjacent to Highway 401 (a major provincial four-lane expressway)	Downtown, industrial section	Downtown, commercial and residential area	Northcentral section of the city, in the middle of the university campus
EVENTS	Hockey, rock and western concerts, Ice Capades	Bingo, roller skating, wrestling, indoor soccer, concerts	Local symphony, band and popular music recitals, dances	Concerts, basketball
AGE	10 years	45 years	8 years	12 years
RENT[1]	Greater of $1000 or 10% of gross	$1000	$950	$1000

[1] Minimum rent to be prepaid.

Exhibit 3
Lineman Promotions
Budget Items

Entertainment		$9 000[1]
Sound system rental		500[1]
Arena	— rental	?
	— security, stage and light facilities	700[1]
	— insurance	75[1]
Promotion	— radio	1 500[1]
	— newspaper	450[2]
	— posters	100[1]
	— tickets, printing	200[1]
Miscellaneous		200

[1] To be prepaid
[2] This would be sufficient for thirteen small box insertions in the entertainment section of the only local daily paper. The paper went to a high percentage of London residences and had significant coverage throughout southwestern Ontario.

Exhibit 4
Lineman Promotions
Radio Coverage Data

	CKSL	CJBK	CFPL-AM[1]	CFPL-FM
Evening Coverage based on 1/4 hour averages, Fall 1975	8:00-12 P.M.	7:00-1 A.M.	6:00-12 P.M.	8:30-12 P.M.
Monday-Friday				
Teens 12-17	800	2 400	400	200
Adults 18-34	2 700	2 800	1 300	400
Saturday				
Teens 12-17	1 200	3 100	300	100
Adults 18-34	3 500	8 000	1 700	1 600

Source: Broadcasting Board Members (BBM) Journal, Fall, 1975

[1] CFPL-AM did not have advertisements after 6:00 P.M.

* *Note:* CHLO was not a BBM member and therefore no data was available. However CHLO's market manager suggested that average weekly coverage was approximately 60 000.

Rates: All day Sat. & Sun., Mon.-Fri. 10:00 A.M.- 2:00 P.M. 30 sec=$27   60 sec=$38
Mon.-Fri. 6:00 A.M.-10:00 A.M. 30 sec=$57   60 sec=$83
Mon.-Fri. 2:00 P.M.- 6:00 P.M. 30 sec=$17   60 sec=$22

Exhibit 5
Lineman Promotions

1. Radio Advertising Budget

CHLO	29X30 sec	@ $ 6	$174		
	15X60 sec	@ $ 9	135	$309	
CJBK	9X30 sec	@ $16	$144		
	4X30 sec	@ $20	80		
	1X30 sec	@ $24	24		
	4X60 sec	@ $25	100		
	22X60 sec	@ $20	440		
	3X60 sec	@ $30	90	878	
CKSL	9X30 sec	@ $16	$144		
	13X30 sec	@ $12	156	300	$1 487

2. Radio Coverage Plan
   (Number of commercials by commercial size)

		Station				
		CHLO		CJBK		CKSL
Date (February 5 to 18)		30 sec	60 sec	30 sec	60 sec	30 sec
Friday	4 P.M.- 7 P.M.					1
	7 P.M.-12 A.M.	1	1		2	1
Saturday	7 P.M.-12 A.M.				2	1
Sunday	7 P.M.-12 A.M.	1	1			1
Monday	4 P.M.- 7 P.M.					1
	7 P.M.-12 A.M.	1	1	1		1
Tuesday	4 P.M.- 7 P.M.					1
	7 P.M.-11 A.M.	1	1	1		1
Wednesday	4 P.M.- 7 P.M.					1
	7 P.M.-12 A.M.	1	1	1		1
Thursday	4 P.M.- 7 P.M.					1
	7 P.M.-12 A.M.	4	2	2	5	1
Friday	4 P.M.- 7 P.M.					1
	7 P.M.-12 A.M.	4	2	2	5	1
Saturday	7 P.M.-12 A.M.	5	2	2	2	1
Sunday	7 P.M.-12 A.M.	5		2		1
Monday	4 P.M.- 7 P.M.	1				1
	7 P.M.-12 A.M.	2	2	1	5	1
Tuesday	4 P.M.- 7 P.M.	1				1
	7 P.M.-12 A.M.	2	2	1	5	1
Wednesday	4 P.M.- 7 P.M.			1	3	1
(Concert)	7 P.M.-12 A.M.					1
Total		29	15	14	29	22

32
Marketing Arithmetic Exercises

1. A ballpoint pen manufacturer had the following information:

Plastic tubes: top and tip	$.06/pen
Ink	.01/pen
Direct labour	.01/pen
Selling price	.20/pen
Advertising	$ 40 000
Managerial & secretarial salaries	$100 000
Salesmen's commissions	10% of selling price
Factory overhead	$60 000

Total ballpoint pen market is 10 million pens

Calculate:
   (a) Unit contribution
   (b) Break-even volume in units
   (c) Share of total market required to break even
   (d) Total profit of the company if 3 million pens are sold.

2. Hector MacDonald, a farmer in Nova Scotia, was considering manufacturing lobster traps during the winter months. In previous winters, Mr. MacDonald had cut pulpwood, earning a profit of at least $2500 per season. He found an unused building on the waterfront which he could rent for the season at $1200. Heating, light and power would cost an extra $10 per week. A good supply of raw materials was available locally. He learned that a former boat builder would rent to him all the necessary tools and equipment for a seasonal rental fee of $200.

   Mr. MacDonald decided to employ two high school students who would work Saturdays and part-time for $30 per week each. After talking to a relative who manufactured lobster traps elsewhere in Nova Scotia, he became confident that he could sell all the traps he could make. The going price for a trap was $5.95, including rope and marker. Mr. MacDonald estimated that he could turn out about 100 traps per week and he planned to operate for 20 weeks.

   The costs of raw materials (wood, netting, nails, etc) would be $2.85 per trap plus $1.30 for the rope and buoy.
   (a) How many lobster traps will Mr. MacDonald have to sell during the season in order to do as well as he had done in the past, cutting pulpwood?
   (b) Should he proceed with his plans? Why or why not?
   (c) Mr. MacDonald discovered that he could obtain a discount of 20 per cent on the cost of his raw materials, excluding rope and buoy, by using another supplier located 65 miles away. He thinks that he would prefer "inside work" in the winter and is willing to proceed with the project if he can earn a minimum of $75 per week.
      i What must his break-even sales dollar volume be in order to earn $75 per week?
      ii What would the net profit be, after Mr. MacDonald's drawings of $75 per week, if he achieves his projected production figure of 2000 traps?

3. Richard Miller was preparing a new product analysis for Brand A. He had decided Brand A would sell at $10 at retail, based on his market research. Retailers customarily

expected a 40 per cent margin and wholesalers a 20 per cent margin (both expressed as a percentage of their selling price). Brand A's variable costs were \$2/unit and estimated total fixed costs were \$28 000. At an anticipated sales volume of 9000 units, would Richard's Brand A make a profit?

33
Oland & Son, Ltd.

Early in 1965, Mr. Victor Oland, President of Oland & Son, Halifax, Nova Scotia, had to determine whether he should introduce Oland's Schooner beer and ale into the Greater Boston market. The prospect of limited growth in existing markets had prompted company executives to seek new markets.

If he decided to enter the Boston market, and if the Boston experience proved successful, Mr. Oland was considering entering other United States metropolitan markets. Therefore, he regarded the Greater Boston market, whose population in 1964 was approximately 3.2 million, not only as a possible source of increased sales and profits, but also as a test market.

THE COMPANY

Oland & Son, Ltd. was founded in 1867 by John Oland. The company grew by acquiring other breweries located in the Maritime provinces.[1] In 1957, they operated two breweries in Halifax and one in Saint John, New Brunswick. The Saint John brewery was to be replaced with a larger facility to be completed in the fall of 1965.

The company brewed Schooner beer and ale, and Oland's Porter and Stout.[2] Beer and ale together accounted for 99 per cent of the company's sales, typical for Canadian brewers—Oland's ale accounted for nearly 80 per cent of the company's sales. Although beer and ale were brewed by essentially the same process, slight differences in the yeast used imparted different tastes to the two products. Since 1952, Schooner ale had taken four prizes in the British Commonwealth competition among bottled beer and ale.

Oland & Son was the largest of seven Canadian regional breweries, that is, breweries whose products were sold in some but not all of the provinces and territories of Canada. In 1964, Oland's sales were about $10 million,[3] nearly twice the company's sales in 1954. Earnings after taxes averaged about 4 per cent of sales. A balance sheet as of December 31, 1964, is shown in Exhibit 1.

Although the company's common stock had been traded publicly since 1950, management and ownership still rested largely with the Oland family. In 1964, the five directors occupied the chief management positions within the company; all the directors were also members of the Oland family. Victor Oland's son, Sidney, a recent graduate of the Harvard Business School, was also active in the management of the company.

The company's marketing activities were the responsibility of the vice-president for administration. The marketing department itself consisted of the general sales manager (who reported directly to the vice-president for administration), the assistant sales manager, the clerks who kept sales records, and three men who serviced the draught beer dispensing units in bars and restaurants that served Schooner draught beer and ale. The general sales manager was responsible for routine customer-contact activities, for liaison with the company's Halifax advertising agency, and for supervision of any special sales promotional activities.

---

[1] Nova Scotia, New Brunswick, and Prince Edward Island.
[2] Porter and stout are brewed in a manner similar to that used for ale, but include additional ingredients which impart a taste which differs from that of ale.
[3] All figures are in United States dollars.

OPERATIONS IN THE MARITIME PROVINCES

In 1965, total Canadian consumption of beer and ale exceeded 11 million barrels. About 90 per cent of this amount was sold by the three national brewers who operated throughout Canada: Canadian Breweries, Molson's, and Labatt's. The remaining 10 per cent, about 1.1 million barrels, was accounted for by regional breweries, such as Oland & Son.

Over 95 per cent of Oland's sales came from the three Maritime provinces of Nova Scotia, New Brunswick, and Prince Edward Island (Exhibit 2). In 1963, sales of beer in these three provinces amounted to 454 000 barrels,[4] or about 4.4 per cent of total Canadian consumption. By 1965, total consumption in the three provinces was estimated at almost 500 000 barrels, of which 45 per cent was consumed in Nova Scotia, 50 per cent in New Brunswick, and 5 per cent in Prince Edward Island.

Oland & Son held slightly over 50 per cent of the Maritime market. Over 80 per cent of Oland's sales came from Nova Scotia, where the company's home office and plants were located, and where Oland held more than two-thirds of the total market. Oland's major competitor in the three provinces was Moosehead Breweries, which held about 40 per cent of the three-province market. The vast majority of Moosehead's sales came from New Brunswick, where its offices and plants were situated. The remaining 5 per cent to 10 per cent of the three-province market was accounted for by the three national brewers.

The marketing of beer in Nova Scotia, New Brunswick and Prince Edward Island was subject to strict federal and provincial government regulation. Prices were set by provincial governments. Beer for "off-premise" consumption was sold only through government-owned liquor stores, and only limited sales promotion activities were permitted.

In Nova Scotia, the price at which a brewer could sell a case of 24 11½-ounce bottles of beer to government-owned stores was set at $3.12. Brewers were responsible for delivering their products to the stores at their own expense. The price to the consumer was set at $5.13 for a case of 24 11½-ounce bottles.

More than 60 per cent of Oland's sales were made through government stores. The remainder was made to bars, restaurants and clubs that served beer on the premises. More than half of the sales to "on-premise" outlets were of bottled beer. The balance of the beer sold to on-premise outlets was sold in barrels for serving as draught beer. Beer sold to bars and restaurants for on-premise consumption was also priced at $3.12 per case of 24 11½-ounce bottles, or $43.37 per barrel.

Most of Oland's sales of packaged beer were made in 11½-ounce glass bottles. Although Oland had been one of the first brewers in Canada to introduce aluminum snap-open cans, only a small (but increasing) percentage of the company's packaged beer was sold in cans.

Advertising of beer, although allowed, was very strictly regulated. In describing the regulations, Mr. Sidney Oland said, "Each advertisement must be cleared through a government office. Mentioning or showing pictures of bottles, glasses, or people drinking beer are all forbidden. In fact, there are so many prohibitions that we really have to negotiate with the government for permission to run each series of advertisements. Point-of-purchase advertising is completely prohibited.

"The amount of advertising we may do is also restricted. For example, we cannot run more than three-eighths of a page of newspaper advertising in any one week; expenditures in other media are similarly restricted."

All advertisements were prepared and scheduled, subject to government approval, by a local advertising agency. The company imposed no direct control on the agency, other

---

[4] All measurements of beer volume are in United States units of measurement. One barrel of beer contains approximately 13.9 cases of 24 11½-ounce bottles.

than approving the budgets proposed by the agency, and held the agency responsible for all its advertising activities. Because of the government restrictions on the amount of advertising which the company could do, the company's annual promotional budget was less than a dollar per barrel, compared to an average of substantially more than a dollar per barrel for brewers in the United States.

Sidney Oland described the company's other selling activities as follows:

Brewery representatives are not allowed to call on liquor stores or on-premise outlets. The only service which a brewery may provide to an on-premise outlet is a serviceman for the draught beer dispensing units. Any conversation between this serviceman and the tavern owner which does not directly relate to the function of the dispensing unit is strictly forbidden.

Brewers are allowed, however, to sponsor local teams, to give trophies, and to engage in public relations activities. We have built the *Bluenose II* for this purpose. *Bluenose II* is a replica of the famous fishing schooner *Bluenose* which is pictured on the Canadian dime. The original *Bluenose* was famed throughout Canada, for she had never lost an official international racing series. We sail *Bluenose II* throughout the Maritime provinces during the summer, taking groups of people for short excursions.

Company executives believed that exporting beer to markets other than the United States offered Oland & Son scant opportunity for growth. More than 98 per cent of the beer exported from Canada by all brewers in 1963 was shipped to the United States. Most of the beer exported to the United States was brewed by the three largest breweries, Canadian Breweries, Molson's and Labatt's; Oland & Son did not export beer to the United States.

Apart from exporting, the company had considered two other methods of expansion: entering additional markets in Canada, or acquiring a brewery located in the United States. Because of high freight costs and strong provincial loyalties to local beers, company executives did not look with favour on expansion to Canadian markets outside the Maritime provinces. Furthermore, the company had entered the Quebec market and then withdrawn from it in 1960, after trying unsuccessfully for several years to penetrate it.

Both Molson's and Labatt's, the second and third largest brewers in Canada, had recently called off merger negotiations with large regional brewers in the United States. One reason given for discontinuing negotiations was the fear of prosecution under the United States antimonopoly laws. Moreover, many local or small regional brewers in the United States had already been acquired by larger domestic brewing firms; as a result, few if any, brewers were available for sale.

THE GREATER BOSTON MARKET

In the fall of 1964, the company had engaged a Boston advertising agency to make a survey of the Greater Boston market. The Greater Boston market, like the entire Massachusetts market, was dominated by 10 large domestic brewers whose brands accounted for more than 90 per cent of sales. Exhibit 3 shows the sales in Massachusetts for the 20 brewers with the largest sales. In 1963, sales in Massachusetts of beer and ale brewed outside the United States came to less than 18 000 barrels. Sales of major foreign malt beverages in Massachusetts are shown in Exhibit 4.[5]

---

[5] Greater Boston was one of 10 metropolitan areas which together consumed 71 per cent of all the beer imported into the United States. The New York market consumed 29 per cent, Chicago 13 per cent and Los Angeles 9 per cent. Each of the seven other metropolitan areas consumed 2 per cent to 4 per cent of the total: San Francisco, Cleveland, Philadelphia, Boston, Detroit, Miami and Washington, D.C. Total sales of imported beer in the United States amounted to less than six-tenths of one per cent of total United States beer consumption of 93.8 million barrels in 1963. Imports of foreign beers into the entire United States, by country of origin are shown in Exhibit 5.

Of all the malt beverages consumed in Massachusetts in 1964, beer accounted for more than 80 per cent of the total. Ale had less than 20 per cent of the market and for the past several years its share had been declining steadily.

Eighty-five per cent of the total market was accounted for by packaged beer (bottled or canned). Draught beer accounted for the balance of 15 per cent. It was almost all consumed in on-premise outlets. In greater Boston draught beer accounted for only 11 per cent of sales.

The Greater Boston market consumed about a third of the estimated 2.99 million barrels of beer and ale sold in Massachusetts in 1964. Neither total Massachusetts consumption nor the relative importance of the Greater Boston market had changed significantly during the past ten years.

THE CONSUMER

Research studies performed by individual brewers and the American Brewers Association indicated that about half of the adult population were beer drinkers. Eighty per cent of these adults were men. In fact, 25 per cent of these men drank 80 to 90 per cent of all the beer consumed in the United States.

According to trade studies, consumption patterns in the Greater Boston market differed little from the national market. In Greater Boston, the highest per capita consumption was found to be among men between twenty-five and fifty-five years of age who had completed high school, and who were earning from $5000 to $8000 in blue-collar jobs. This group was primarily of Irish or Italian origin. Industry sources estimated that consumption of imported beer by these men was negligible.

Although no quantitative data were available, it was widely assumed that imported beers were popular primarily among professional and higher income groups. To obtain some idea of the consumption habits and preferences of such consumers, Oland & Son authorized exploratory consumer research, at a cost not to exceed $1000. Taste preference tests and interviews were conducted among two small groups of married couples. Most of the men and women were between twenty-five and thirty years old; all of the men had white-collar or professional occupations.

This research indicated that half of the men and half of the women purchased malt beverages. Most of the consumption occurred in on-premise outlets, such as bars, restaurants or clubs. The couples interviewed typically visited a bar or restaurant about twice a month. The men indicated that they would order malt beverages once in every four to six such occasions; the women indicated that they would order beer or ale once in every five to eight occasions. The research report indicated, however, that respondents might have overstated the frequency of beer-drinking occasions, because of the manner in which the research was conducted.

One-third of the men reported that they consumed more than one bottle of beer or ale on many of the occasions on which they drank malt beverages. One-fourth of the women occasionally drank more than one bottle.

In order to determine how respondents reacted to the country of origin of foreign beers, persons interviewed were asked to indicate which of eight beers (German beer, Danish ale, etc.) was best described by each of twenty-four adjectives. Both men and women said that over 85 per cent of the words were appropriate for the six European beers and ales, while fewer than 15 per cent were appropriate for Canadian beer and Canadian ale combined. Such words as smooth, distinctive and satisfying were used to describe European beers. Both men and women described Canadian beer as light, thin and mild, and Canadian ale, as sharp and bitter.

In a separate test, men and women were asked to taste Budweiser beer and Schooner beer, and to state their preferences. Both beers were presented in unidentified glasses. Half of the men and half of the women preferred Schooner; the other half preferred Budweiser. There were no differences in the words used to describe the two beers.

A third test explored the preference for Schooner beer relative to Schooner ale. A group of eighteen couples was asked to sample both the beer and the ale, which were presented in glasses marked only *w* and *x* and to indicate their preference. In order to test the consistency of their preferences, they were asked to repeat the procedure about half an hour later, with malt beverages identified *y* and *z*. Between the tests, respondents were asked to complete questionnaires about their beer-drinking preferences and habits.

Only twenty-one of the thirty-five respondents (one woman did not complete the study) preferred, on both the initial and final taste preference tests, either Schooner ale to Schooner beer, or Schooner beer to Schooner ale. Preferences of these twenty-one persons are shown in Table 1.

Table 1

Number of Men and Women Who Preferred Schooner Beer or
Schooner Ale on Both Tests

Preferences	Men	Women	Total
Preferred Schooner ale to Schooner beer on both initial and final test	6	2	8
Preferred Schooner beer to Schooner ale on both initial and final test	3	10	13
TOTAL	9	12	21

Among the twenty-one showing consistent preferences, only seven indicated a strong preference for either Schooner beer or ale. Five of the seven preferred Schooner beer to Schooner ale; two preferred Schooner ale to Schooner beer. The fourteen others had consistent, but slight, preferences for one Schooner beverage over the other.

When the "consistent respondents" were asked to identify their preferred drink as either beer or ale, they experienced considerable difficulty. Only one of the six men who had a consistent preference for ale was able to identify the beverage correctly. Two of the six identified the beverage as beer, and the other three were unable to make a choice. The ten women who preferred Schooner beer to Schooner ale all identified their preferred beverage correctly. The two women who preferred ale, however, identified it as beer.

DISTRIBUTION

Of the malt beverage outlets in Massachusetts, 1700 were retail "package stores" (including some grocery stores). They sold malt beverages exclusively for off-premise consumption. Beer for on-premise consumption was sold at 7300 outlets, such as bars, restaurants and clubs.

In Greater Boston, of the approximately 2500 malt beverage-dispensing outlets, 68 per cent or 1700 were on-premise outlets, and 32 per cent or 800 were off-premise outlets. Sales, however, were divided almost equally between on-premise sales and off-premise sales.

The pattern for foreign beers was somewhat different. Industry sources estimated that 85 per cent of all foreign beer was consumed in on-premise outlets. One industry source estimated that 99 per cent of all imported beer consumed on-premise within the Greater Boston market was consumed in 900 taverns, cocktail lounges and restaurants. Of these

900 on-premise outlets, 500 were informally rated ''AAA'' or ''highest prestige'' accounts; 200 were rated ''AA'' or ''high prestige'' accounts; and 200 were rated ''A'' or ''prestige'' accounts. These ratings were based on (1) general appearance of the on-premise outlet and its clientele, and (2) industry ''guestimates'' of the sales of imported beer. Clientele of all three classes of outlets were judged to be professional people, as opposed to workingmen.

Although most off-premise outlets carried six or more of the popular domestic beers, a few large package stores accounted for most of the off-premise sales of imported beer. A great many off-premise outlets carried no imported beers at all. Those which did offer foreign beers usually stocked two or three brands, but a few outlets stocked more than six different imported beers.

Each of the two dominant Canadian imported beers, Molson's and Labatt's, was sold in only 30 to 35 per cent of the total (on-premise and off-premise combined) retail outlets. Although precise figures on the distribution of European beers in Massachusetts were not available, it was known that Lowenbrau had a national goal of gaining distribution in about 25 per cent of the total outlets in markets in which it was distributed.

All on-premise and off-premise outlets purchased most of their beer from wholesalers who were primarily beer distributors. They made weekly deliveries. Some beer, however, was sold by distributors whose primary business was in wine and hard liquor. These distributors usually called every two to four weeks. Typically, only one distributor for any one brand of beer called on a particular on-premise or off-premise outlet.

Most Boston beer distributors carried only one major brand of beer, but some distributors carried additional ''non-competing'' brands as well. For example, the Schaefer distributor in Boston carried Lowenbrau. Both foreign beers and smaller volume domestic beers were often handled by wine and hard liquor distributors. In a few instances, large package stores imported some foreign beers directly.

PERSONAL SELLING

Personal selling efforts were carried out both by distributors' driver-salesmen and ''missionary'' salesmen employed by the brewers. Each of the Boston distributors of the major brands of beer employed between fifteen and thirty driver-salesmen, who called on on-premise and off-premise outlets. These driver-salesmen made weekly calls in distributors' trucks to check inventory, to take orders, to make delivery, and to set up displays. Distributors' driver-salesmen typically made about fifteen calls per day.

Although distributors' driver-salesmen were supposed to set up displays and push the brands of beer they carried, most brewers supplemented their efforts with missionary salesmen. These men, who were employed by the brewer, visited package stores to persuade clerks to push their particular brands and to obtain favourable shelf displays. These displays ranged from cardboard displays which cost the brewer less than $5, to large and elaborate fixtures which cost from $35 to $100 each.

In the on-premise outlets, the objectives of missionary salesmen were both to provide customers with ''samples'' of a particular brand of beer and to encourage bartenders and waiters to recommend that brand to customers. Missionary men usually bought drinks for customers. In addition, they tipped bartenders and waitresses generously. This technique was employed generally, but discreetly, throughout the industry. Missionary salesmen also sought permission in the on-premise outlets to set up displays such as counter and table-top point-of-purchase material. Occasionally they obtained permission to check the stock on hand of their brand of bottled beer in the bar's refrigerator. Bars would sometimes sell out their refrigerator stock and neglect to replace it with the bottles kept in the storeroom. The ''refrigerator check'' also sought to place the missionary's brand near the front of the refrigerator, where the bartender was able to reach it easily when he was busy.

Most missionary salesmen were men who knew the beer business. They were on friendly terms with the owners and employees in the outlets they visited. On average they made about ten calls per day. Their salaries varied from $7000 to $12 000 annually. Expense accounts, which included tips to waiters and bartenders and drinks for customers, averaged around $20 per day, but could run as high as $30.

In 1964, most major domestic brewers had two to three missionary men assigned to the Greater Boston market. Among the importers, Lowenbrau had two men covering Massachusetts, while Heineken assigned two men to cover the six New England states. Labatt's employed one man to cover Massachusetts and portions of two other states.

Other sales promotion activities in which all brewers engaged were providing "give-away" items to on-premise and off-premise outlets, and providing entertainment and incentives for distributors' salesmen. Common give-aways were ash trays valued at $2 per dozen and up, and beer glasses valued at $.35 to $1 each. Incentives varied considerably. One European brewer flew distributors' men to its main plant. Another offered colour television sets as prizes in a Boston area sales contest.

ADVERTISING

Beer advertising expenditures in the Greater Boston market were estimated at more than $4 million in 1964. This figure included radio, TV, newspaper and outdoor advertising. Exhibit 6 shows traceable advertising expenditures for nine months of 1964 for some, but by no means all, of the major brands of beer sold in Greater Boston. Exhibit 7 contains illustrative advertising rates of Greater Boston media.

Boston consumers were also exposed to beer advertisements in national magazines. Domestic brewers typically spent less than 10 per cent of their advertising budgets on national magazine advertising. Some foreign brewers, however, spent a large portion of their total United States advertising dollars in magazines such as the *New Yorker*. Exhibit 8 shows national advertising expenditures for each of three years for magazine and newspaper space for selected imported beers. Industry sources estimated that 1965 expenditures for European beers might be double those of 1962. As of 1965, foreign brewers had used almost no radio or TV advertising.

PRICING

Massachusetts law required that each brewer charge a uniform price to all distributors (wholesalers), and that each distributor charge a uniform price on any particular brand of beer to all his retailers. Although package stores were free to set whatever prices they wished, prices of the major brands were similar throughout Greater Boston (see Exhibit 9). On-premise outlets charged from $.25 to $.75 a bottle[6] for most domestic beers. Imported beers were usually sold from $.65 to $1 per bottle, but were occasionally priced at $1.25 a bottle.

Margins for both wholesalers and package stores ranged from about 15 per cent to about 25 per cent (see Exhibit 9). Margins of retailers were often increased and margins of distributors were often reduced by quantity discounts granted by distributors to retailers. For example, distributors of major domestic brands often gave retailers discounts of one per cent on 100-case lots. Discounts granted by distributors could, however, run up to 2 per cent of the distributors' selling price. Almost all distributors of foreign beers gave a

---

[6] Bottles of domestic beers usually contained 11½ to 12 ounces. Bottles of foreign beers usually contained 11½ ounces.

2 per cent discount on orders of five or more cases. Many of them offered the 2 per cent discount on orders of only one case.

COSTS

Although individual brewers did not release data on their production costs, industry sources agreed that the total cost of brewing, bottling, and packaging for shipment of a case of 24 11½-ounce throw-away bottles was approximately $1.26. Industry sources further estimated that the components of this figure were as follows:

	$/case	% of total cost
Brewing materials	.17	13.5
Packaging materials	.72	57.2
Direct labour: brewing	.09	7.2
manning packaging lines	.13	10.3
warehouse and maintenance	.07	5.4
Overhead	.08	6.4
Total brewing and packaging expense	1.26	100.0%

Although beer consumption during the peak summer months could be as much as 200 per cent of winter consumption, brewers reduced the number of unskilled labourers employed in the operations.

In addition to the costs shown above, brewers were responsible both for paying the cost of shipping their products to distributors and for paying U.S. federal tax and import duty. Freight from Halifax to Boston amounted to 30 cents per case in carload shipments. U.S. federal tax was 65 cents per case; import duty, $.28 per case.

Mr. Oland knew that the company would incur some additional expenses if he decided to enter the Greater Boston market. In addition to possibly hiring a missionary salesman who would discharge some management duties, Mr. Oland estimated that he would have to pay either an advertising agency or someone located in Boston between $300 and $500 per month to coordinate promotional campaigns and to assume other managerial responsibilities. He also realized that both he and his son, Sidney, would have to make frequent trips to Boston, sometimes for several days at a time.

OTHER CONSIDERATIONS

From initial examination of the Greater Boston market, executives of Oland & Son had concluded that, if the company decided to enter the Boston market, existing distributors should be sought to carry Schooner products. The alternative was to establish a wholly owned distributor for which an investment of $50 000 would be required. Both this investment and annual operating expenses of as much as $75 000 were considered prohibitive.

Regardless of whom he employed as a distributor, Mr. Oland thought that it would be necessary to work out with the distributor a plan to replace any beer not sold within three months of delivery to the retailer. If bottled beer was stored longer than three months, it might lose its original flavour and freshness.

Although some imported beers were sold in draught as well as packaged form, Mr. Oland had tentatively decided not to sell draught beer in Boston until sales of packaged beer reached a fairly high volume. Once a barrel of draught beer was opened, it had to be consumed within a few days, or the beer would become stale. Consequently, Mr. Oland believed that sales of Schooner beer or ale through any one on-premise outlet would have to exceed fourteen cases per week before he would consider selling draught beer to that outlet.

Associated with the problem of freshness was a decision on the type of container for Schooner beer and ale. The company could package Schooner beer and ale either in brown or green disposable bottles, or in aluminum snap-open cans, in order to preserve its original taste. On the other hand, Mr. Oland knew that most European beers were packaged in green bottles, even though green glass offered less protection from light, exposure to which accelerated the loss of the original taste and freshness of packaged beer. Mr. Oland thought that the cans had been well received in the Maritime market, but he did not know whether the cans would be accepted in New England, where bottles were preferred to cans.

If bottles were used, each bottle could be capped with gold- or silver-coloured foil. Such a foil cap would cover the top 1½ inches of the bottle. Although the cost of the foil was insignificant, the machinery necessary to add this feature would cost in the vicinity of $20 000. Mr. Oland did not plan to add foil caps to bottles distributed in the Maritime provinces.

Mr. Oland believed that a large potential market for Schooner products existed in the Boston and eastern Massachusetts area. He guessed that emigrés from Nova Scotia and their descendants currently numbered 750 000 of a total population of approximately four million. This emigration had begun in the early 1900s. According to Mr. Oland, almost all of the original emigrés had come from rural Nova Scotia to Massachusetts hoping to better themselves economically. He also believed that some of these emigrés—especially those who returned occasionally to Nova Scotia—still had strong ties to their home province, and would welcome the opportunity to purchase Schooner beer and ale.

An executive of the Boston advertising agency which Oland & Son had retained commented: "There's a real opportunity for a Canadian beer in Massachusetts. Molson's and Labatt's have sold in Massachusetts for years without any sales promotion to speak of. If we really do a good selling job, we should easily be able to match their performance."

Trade reaction to the possibility of introducing Schooner beer and ale to the Boston market had been favourable and, in some cases, enthusiastic. The advertising agency had approached a number of both beer and liquor distributors who were eager to discuss the possibility of adding Schooner beer and ale to their lines, particularly if the products were given strong promotional support. One liquor distributor who carried a number of imported beers indicated immediate willingness to carry Schooner beer and ale.

If he went ahead with his plans, Mr. Oland hoped to be able to introduce Schooner beer and ale into Boston in time for the summer months, which accounted for up to 40 per cent of total annual consumption. Since distributors had to post prices a month in advance, all marketing plans would have to be completed by May 1, in order to begin sales on the first of June, 1965.

Exhibit 1
Oland & Son, Ltd.
Consolidated Balance Sheet
December 31, 1964
(in 000's of dollars)

Assets	*1964*	*1963*
Cash and negotiable paper	$ 945	$ 878
Accounts receivable	1 258	1 398
Inventories	989	867
Prepayments	8	9
Total current assets	$3 200	$3 152
Investment in subsidiary company	311	268
Net fixed assets	2 789	2 722
TOTAL ASSETS	$6 300	$6 142
Liabilities and Net Worth		
Accounts payable	$ 464	$ 451
Other current liabilities	1 506	1 586
Total current liabilities	$1 970	$2 037
Total shareholders' equity	4 330	4 105
TOTAL LIABILITIES AND NET WORTH	$6 300	$6 142

Source: Annual report

Exhibit 2
Oland and Son, Limited

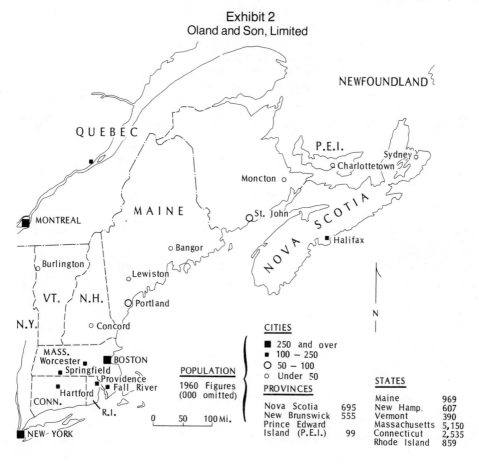

NEWFOUNDLAND

QUEBEC

P.E.I.

Sydney

Charlottetown

Moncton

MAINE

St. John

NOVA SCOTIA

MONTREAL

Halifax

Burlington

Bangor

Lewiston

VT. N.H.

Portland

N.Y.

Concord

N

MASS.

Worcester

BOSTON

Springfield

Providence

Hartford

Fall River

CONN.

R.I.

NEW-YORK

CITIES
- ■ 250 and over
- ▪ 100 — 250
- ○ 50 — 100
- ○ Under 50

PROVINCES

POPULATION
1960 Figures
(000 omitted)

Nova Scotia	695
New Brunswick	555
Prince Edward Island (P.E.I.)	99

STATES

Maine	969
New Hamp.	607
Vermont	390
Massachusetts	5,150
Connecticut	2,535
Rhode Island	859

0   50   100 Mi.

Exhibit 3
Oland & Son, Ltd.
Sales in Massachusetts of Top Twenty Massachusetts
Brewers plus Malt Beverages Imported
into Massachusetts from Other States
(000's of barrels)

Brewer	1964	1963	Per Cent Changes[2]
Jacob Ruppert	532	516	+ 3 %
Narrangasett Brewery[1]	503	455	+ 10
Anheuser-Busch, Inc.	345	299	+ 15
Carling Brewing Co.	252	288	− 13
F. & M. Schaefer Brewing Co.	251	233	+ 8
Jos. Schlitz Brewery Co.	175	169	+ 3
P. Ballantine & Sons	163	186	− 13
Piel Bros.	151	145	+ 4
Pabst Brewing Co.	119	68	+ 75
Haffenreffer & Co.[1]	92	152	− 39
Miller Brewing Co.	89	74	+ 21
Rheingold Breweries	83	81	+ 2
Dawson's Brewery	73	68	+ 7
Diamond Spring Brewery	48	50	− 2
Eastern Brewing Corp.	13	8	− 66
Hans Holterbosch, Inc.[3] (Lowenbrau)	10	7	+ 32
National Brewing Co.	9	1	+880
Genesee Brewing Co.	8	10	− 18
The Old Reading Brewery	7	7	− 3
C. Schmidt & Sons	6	7	− 8
TOTAL	2 929	2 824	+ 3.6%

1 Narragansett acquired Haffenreffer brands as of October 2, 1964.
2 Based on exact gallonage.
3 Lowenbrau was the only beer among the top twenty which was not brewed in the United States.

Source: Massachusetts Wholesalers of Malt Beverages.

Exhibit 4
Oland & Son, Ltd.
Malt Beverages of Non-U.S. Origin Imported into Massachusetts
(barrels)

Brand	Greater Boston	12 months 1963			First 9 Months 1964
		Other Mass. Areas	Total Mass. Imports		Total Mass. Imports
Lowenbrau					
(German Lager)	2 774	4 473	7 247		7 146
Wurzburger					
(German Lager)	279	485	764		598
Heineken					
(Dutch Lager)	2 329	1 648	3 977		3 638
Tuborg					
(Danish Lager)	Nil	953	953		744
Carlsberg					
(Danish Lager)	285	60	345		611
Guinness Stout					
(Irish)	887	116	1 003		N.A.
Harp					
(Irish Lager)	Not sold in Massachusetts until July 1965				328
Labatt's					
(Canadian Ale and Lager)	452	555	1 007		708
Molson's					
(Canadian Ale and Lager)	224	288	512		418
Moosehead					
(Canadian Ale and Lager)	N.A.	N.A.	365 (est.)		114
Miscellaneous Brands	N.A.	N.A.	N.A.		454

Source: Massachusetts Wholesalers of Malt Beverages

Exhibit 5
Oland & Son, Ltd.
United States Imports of Malt Beverages, by Country of Origin 1954-1964
(000's of barrels)

Country of Origin	1954	1955	1956	1957	1958	1959	1960	1961	1962	1963	1964
Canada	82	91	90	104	108	111	115	115	114	114	123
Mexico	6	5	5	5	6	6	8	8	11	12	N.A.
United Kingdom	2	8	7	10	11	8	6	6	6	8	N.A.
Ireland	1	3	3	2	4	8	9	9	10	14	N.A.
Denmark	6	9	10	12	18	21	24	25	33	35	44
Netherlands	27	33	42	51	63	75	83	95	105	107	126
Germany	50	67	80	97	104	135	135	160	183	186	232
Sweden	1	1	1	1	1	1	1	2	2	4	N.A.
Norway	1	1	2	4	4	5	4	5	15	37	52
Other Europe	1	1	1	2	4	3	3	4	4	5	N.A.
Japan	2	2	2	3	4	4	4	5	5	5	N.A.
Philippines	3	3	2	2	3	4	4	6	8	13	N.A.
TOTAL	182	224	245	293	330	381	396	440	496	540	N.A.[1]

[1] Although gallonage figures were not available, it was known that the declared dollar value of all imported malt beverages at the port of entry was $23.7 million in 1964 against $19.4 million in 1963.

Source: Trade periodicals.

Exhibit 6
Oland & Son, Ltd.
Traceable Advertising Expenditures in Greater Boston
for Selected Brands of Beer[1]
January 1-September 30, 1964

Brand	Radio	TV	Newspaper	Outdoor	Total
Ballantine	$136 370	$130 780	$22 679	$ —	$289 829
Carlings	84 160	161 720	6 650	16 800	269 330
Heineken[2]	—	—	2 474[4]	—	2 474
Lowenbrau[3]	—	—	1 091[4]	—	1 091
Narragansett	176 664	647 606	33 850	—	860 120
Ruppert	110 640	177 710	—	88 200	376 550
Schaefer	165 945	136 024	—	11 112	313 081

[1] Does not include coverage of Boston provided by national media.
[2] Heineken was advertised exclusively in Sunday newspapers in 1964.
[3] Lowenbrau was advertised exclusively in morning and evening newspapers in 1964.
[4] January 1-December 31, 1964.

Sources: *Beer Distributor Magazine*
 Television Advertising Bureau
 Printer's Ink
 Advertising Age
 Mediascope
 Simmons Report

(The Canadian beers sold in Boston, Molson's and Labatt's, did virtually no local advertising in Boston in 1964.)

Exhibit 7
Oland & Son, Ltd.
Illustrative[1] Media Rate for Greater Boston Media[2]

	Full Page	1/2 Page	1/4 Page	1/8 Page
NEWSPAPERS (black and white rates)				
Morning or evening edition	$1500	$ 750	$375	$190
Sunday edition	3350	1675	840	420

RADIO
Spot announcements (20 seconds): $30 per announcement
Five-minute news/weather program: $70 per broadcast
 (maximum length of advertising message: 60 seconds)

TELEVISION
Spot announcements (20 seconds): $350 per announcement
Five-minute news/weather program: $650 per telecast
 (maximum length of advertising message: 60 seconds)

OUTDOOR
Combinations of 5 to 100 billboards within 75 miles of Boston: $60 to $100
per board per month, depending upon size and location.

[1] Rates could vary as much as 50 per cent above or below these figures, depending upon the exact amount and kind of space or time purchased. These figures exclude production costs.
[2] These media served an area whose boundaries sometimes extended as far as 75 miles from Boston.

Exhibit 8
Oland & Son, Ltd.
National Advertising Expenditures for Magazine and
Newspaper Space for Selected Imported Beers
1962-1964
(in 000's of dollars)

	1962	1963	1964
LOWENBRAU (GERMANY)			
Newspapers[1]	$ —	$ 59.3	$ —
Magazines	118.3	167.4	127.4
Total	$118.3	$226.7	$127.4
HEINEKEN (NETHERLANDS)			
Newspapers[1]	$113.1	$ 55.3	$ 79.7
Magazines	57.4	129.2	114.0
Total	$170.5	$184.5	$193.7
LABATT (CANADA)			
Newspapers[1]	1	1	$117.4
Magazines	N.A.	N.A.	16.1
Total			$133.5
MOLSON (CANADA)			
Newspapers[1]	1	1	$ —
Magazines	N.A.	N.A.	3.5
Total			$ 3.5

[1] Includes expenditures for space in widely circulated newspapers such as *The New York Times* as well as expenditures for space in the locally circulated newspapers.

Source: Media records.

Exhibit 9
Oland & Son, Ltd.
Prices for a Case of 24 12-Ounce Bottles

Brand	Brewer to Distributor	Distributor to On- and Off-Premise Outlet[1]	Off-Premise Outlet to Consumer (Typical Prices per Bottle)
IMPORTED BEERS			
Lowenbrau	$6.50	$8.60	$.38-.50
Bass Ale	6.00	8.00	.45
Heineken, Harp, Guiness, Tuborg, Carlsberg	5.75-6.00	7.25-7.50	.40-.43
Labatt's	4.85	6.30	N.A.
Molson's	4.41	5.60	N.A.
Thor (Scandinavian)	3.55	4.50	.25
Sköl (Scandinavian)	2.59	4.14	N.A.
DOMESTIC BEERS			
Budweiser, Miller, Schlitz	3.10	3.69	.21[2]
			.21
Schaefer, Ballantine, Carlings, Piel, Rheingold	2.25	2.86	.17[2]
Harvard	2.00	2.60	.15[2]

[1] These prices are before any quantity discounts.

[2] Prices shown apply particularly to beer sold in cases of 24 bottles. Some stores charged slightly higher prices for individual bottles.

Source: Massachusetts Wholesalers of Malt Beverages.

34

Purple Patches

"I had a small speaking part in this year's production, *Anything Goes,* but other than that, I haven't had any experience with Purple Patches," said Mr. Tom Lewis. "I guess I'm really starting from scratch, although I have worked in many aspects of student theatre and radio at McGill University during my undergraduate years. Purple Patches will be my first attempt at producing a musical show."

Purple Patches was a voluntary theatrical organization of students at the University of Western Ontario. Its activities were devoted to the production of an annual musical show in February of each year. Mr. Tom Lewis, a Master of Business Administration student at the university, was selected in March 1969 as Purple Patches' new producer. In this position, he was fully responsible for the show that would be staged by the organization in 1970. In April 1969, Mr. Lewis was reviewing the progress of his first month as producer, and wondering what action to take on several important decisions confronting him.

"I want to produce a highly successful show. I'm going to make sure that we're organized and produce everything in good taste consistent with a high quality standard. Although the show is still ten months away, the hardest part of my job is right now. This is when the key decisions must be made and the planning set into motion. I've got to choose a show, decide on a location, and get the marketing, finance, production, and staffing well under way. This show will be won in the planning."

THE UNIVERSITY OF WESTERN ONTARIO

"The Western University of London, Ontario" received its charter from the Legislature of the Province of Ontario in 1878. Its first classes graduated in arts and in medicine in 1883. In 1923, the name of the university was formally changed to "The University of Western Ontario."

Growth in the university's early years was relatively slow. By 1963, total enrollment was 5714 students. The decade of the 1960s, however, brought substantial growth. By the 1968-69 academic year, slightly over 10 000 full-time students were enrolled at Western. Of this total, 8814 were undergraduates—including a freshman class of approximately 2200—and the remaining 1327 were graduate students. During the fall and winter months, a further 2477 were enrolled as part-time students in night courses offered by the Extension Department. Full-time enrollment was expected to be about 11 000 in 1969-70. Approximately 3000 faculty and staff were employed by the university.

Degree programs offered at Western included, arts, divinity, engineering, law, music, science, business administration, medicine, dentistry and nursing. The university was situated on spacious grounds near the northwest edge of London. There was frequent bus service between the campus and the city's main shopping area, located about three miles away. About 1492 of the 6342 males enrolled as full-time students lived in men's residences on the campus. Women's residences on campus accommodated 837 of the total female enrollment of 3848.

About 24 per cent of the full-time students at Western were natives of the city of London. Most of the remainder came from cities and towns located within a 75-mile radius. The city of London was a prosperous community of 200 000. Approximately 4300 Western alumni resided in London as of 1969. Per capita income ranked among the highest of all cities in Canada. London was generally regarded as the financial, commercial, and cultural capital of the western Ontario region.

PURPLE PATCHES

Purple Patches was established in 1946 by students at Western. Its purpose was to present a campus variety revue organized and performed by the students. Patches continued in a variety revue format until 1963 when *Bye Bye Birdie,* a Broadway musical, was performed. From 1963 to 1969, Patches presented Broadway musicals. The musicals in those years are shown in Exhibit 1.

According to the producer, the objectives of Patches were threefold. The show was to provide a means for students to obtain experience in all aspects of popular musical theatrical production. It was to provide entertainment for the university community in particular, and the city of London audience in general. Finally, the show had to break even financially.

Typically, 150 to 200 students were involved either as cast or supporting staff in a Patches' production. Patches was composed and managed almost entirely by Western students, but some "outside talent" was often employed. The outside talent might be a director, set designer, musical director and/or a choreographer.

The organizational structure of Purpose Patches varied from year to year. For *Anything Goes* in 1969, the organization that developed is represented in Exhibit 2.

Key jobs in the organization were usually filled in the spring of the year. Usually, the producer's first task was to select a director. Thereafter, working in consultation with the director, he selected a musical director, choreographer, set designer and business manager. Together, this group could loosely be thought of as constituting the "executive" of a Purple Patches show.

Managers were responsible for recruiting their own supporting staff, customarily in September. Auditions for cast members were usually held in October. Both supporting staff and cast members did not have much to do until Christmas. According to Mr. Lewis, there were no prerequisite qualifications required for these positions other than "enthusiasm, willingness to work hard, and creativity."

Before coming to Western, Mr. Lewis worked with student organizations at McGill University in Montreal. He wrote, worked on publicity and served as general administrator for the McGill Red and White Revue, a student variety show. Subsequently, he was production manager for Radio McGill.

Immediately after being chosen as the 1970 producer, one of Mr. Lewis's first steps was to look for a director. He approached Mr. Don Fleckser, an alumnus of Western and the Director of Speech for Catholic Schools in London. Mr. Fleckser was a professional director who regularly did musicals for the London Little Theatre, a local community theatrical group. He also directed two previous Purple Patches shows—*South Pacific* in 1967 and *A Funny Thing Happened on the Way to the Forum* in 1968.

Mr. Fleckser agreed to return to Purple Patches as director, providing that he and Mr. Lewis could agree on a show. As of April 1969, no other members of the executive had been selected.

AUDIENCE COMPOSITION

Ticket sales data for Purple Patches shows in recent years revealed that 80 per cent of the tickets sold for a production were distributed through outlets located on the campus. Mr. Lewis decided that this meant approximately 80 per cent of Patches' audiences were university students.

Purple Patches also maintained a mailing list of university alumni located in the London area. Each year, direct mail advertisements were sent out to those on the list who had purchased tickets to Patches in the previous year or two. Mail order sales to alumni declined from $4100 in 1967 to $1400 in 1968, and to $900 in 1969.

In the fall of 1968, a group of undergraduate business administration students undertook a course project to assist in the marketing of the 1969 show, *Anything Goes*. Included in the report of this project were the results of two consumer surveys that the group conducted in December 1968. The first survey was designed to find out what students knew about Purple Patches. A total of 125 students were randomly selected for interviews during lunch hours, 25 in each of the university's five cafeterias. Some results of this first survey are shown in Exhibit 3.

The second survey was designed to assist in the selection of future shows. Its stated purpose was to compare current students' preferences for the shows performed in the past by Patches with historical attendance figures. A total of 50 students were surveyed in four cafeterias during the same week in December 1968 that the first survey was conducted. The completed report contained the table shown in Exhibit 4.

SELECTION OF A SHOW FOR 1970

There were no set guidelines for selection of a Patches show. Usually the producer consulted with the previous year's producer, the director and any other of the current executive selected. The producer made the final decision. In general, it was Mr. Lewis's opinion that a Patches show should meet the following criteria:

1. Utilize a good size cast to allow many students to participate;
2. Be suitable for the age group of university student actors;
3. Appeal to the university student market;
4. Provide reasonably undemanding roles; and
5. Be suitable technically for the facilities available.

According to Mr. Lewis, Patches, over the period 1966-1969, presented two modern classics, a current Broadway hit, and a revival. He felt that *Anything Goes* was less than successful and that, according to the business students' report, Patches' reputation was not high. He hoped to produce a quality, prestige show that would help rebuild the organization. A quality show meant good music direction, superb sets and costumes, and a strong cast performing a good story. Mr. Lewis decided that there was not enough apparent student writing talent on campus to merit attempting a student revue. Therefore, he decided to look at Broadway shows.

In their final discussions, the alternative shows considered by Messrs Lewis and Fleckser were *Hello Dolly, Cabaret, Camelot, The King and I* and *Sweet Charity*. Subsequent investigation revealed that *Hello Dolly* and *Cabaret* had not been released for production by amateur theatrical groups. Selected information on the three remaining plays under consideration is shown in Exhibit 5.

"Whichever we choose," said Mr. Lewis, "I realize this will be the most ambitious show Patches has tried in recent years. But I'm confident that, with a professional set designer and good costumes, we can make a success of it. We must, however, find a suitable location to stage the show."

LOCATION

Until 1966, Purple Patches shows were performed in the Grand Theatre located in downtown London. But in 1965, *Fiorello* lost approximately $2000 and the executive of that time began to look for new ways to economize on costs. Through lower rental charges and other savings, it was estimated that a move to the newly built Althouse College Theatre just off the west end of the campus would save approximately $2400 per year.

Purple Patches performed in Althouse College from 1966 to 1969. However, each year Patches' technical staff complained about the lack of adequate technical facilities.

Mr. Lewis was considering the possibility of moving the 1970 show to a different location. The alternatives under consideration were the Grand Theatre, Alumni Hall, and finally, remaining at the Althouse College Theatre.

The Grand Theatre was an old, well-known theatre in London that sat 1100 people. It was located on a bus route in the city's downtown area, two blocks from the main street and central shopping district. Patches could rent it at $350 a night plus $200 a night for union stagehands (students were not allowed to do their own stagework in the Grand). The Grand's stage facilities and acoustics were very good. It could be available for Patches from January 24 to 30.

Alumni Hall, on campus, held 2300 people in seats and bleachers. It was used for a variety of functions ranging from visiting full orchestras to basketball games. Despite its size, no microphones would be required for a Patches production. Alumni's technical facilities were considered poor, especially since no sets could be hung from the ceiling over the stage. Alumni Hall was available to Patches at $500 a night.

Althouse College was located about one-half mile away from the main campus of the university. Its theatre accommodated 650 people and rented for $125 a night. Stage facilities and acoustics were considered poor. In previous years, no bus service was available to Althouse. Thus, persons going there had to travel by car or walk the half-mile distance from the nearest bus stop on the campus. However, the London Transportation Commission recently announced that a new bus route which included service to Althouse College would begin operation in September 1969.

An additional consideration on location was a suggestion by the director that, if *Camelot* was selected, consideration be given to playing it "in the round". That is, the play would be staged in the centre of the audience similar to the Shakespearean theatre. Seats would surround the stage on all sides or on "three sides." Alumni Hall was the only one of the three locations where this could be attempted. Bleacher seats could be erected on the existing stage and around a raised platform on the floor that would serve as a stage. *Camelot* was produced in the round in the United States in 1968. The director was intrigued with the idea. He envisaged a large set surrounded by 1200 seats and 1000 bleachers.

FINANCE

Purple Patches was a self-supporting student activity. Its financial structure was restricted only by its ability to generate income because one of its objectives was to break even financially. Since most of its income was realized long after the majority of the expenses were incurred, Patches relied on the University Students' Council for working capital loans. The Council made loans on the basis of budgets submitted by Patches in the spring and early fall, but would not support any losses incurred by Patches.

The Patches' business manager, usually a Western business student, was responsible for all of the financial affairs of the organization. In the past, the Patches' business manager had required that he approve personally all expenditures over $10. During the spring, he composed a preliminary budget based largely on past results. Over the summer as more detailed plans were made, more accurate estimates of expenditures were possible. A revised budget was prepared in September and submitted to the Students' Council. Exhibit 6 shows the financial records available in the Patches files at the beginning of April 1969. A 1970 business manager was not chosen at that time. Therefore, Mr. Lewis began to prepare a preliminary budget himself.

Royalties would cost $1500. Lighting would be in the neighbourhood of $800 to $1000 depending on the adequacy of the facilities of the theatre chosen. Orchestra costs would approximate $400 a night. The set designer estimated sets would cost close to

$2000 for a top quality job. Outside talent costs were expected to be near $1600. For planning purposes, the Patches' costume manager estimated each cast member would require an average of two and one-half costumes for the shows under consideration. Costumes would cost about $15 each. Tickets and programs would be near $1000.

PROMOTION

The task of marketing traditionally fell to the producer. To assist him, usually a Publicity and Public Relations Committee was established to publicize the show. There was no set job definition for this committee—whatever jobs they did not perform the producer took upon himself. The committee usually became involved in attracting Patches' staff members in September, attracting cast to auditions in October, and publicizing the show through posters, radio, newspaper advertisements, press releases and so on.

Although it seemed somewhat premature to formulate specific plans for publicity and promotion. Mr. Lewis realized he needed some idea of what was involved in these areas, if only to prepare his preliminary budget. There were no historical records of promotional efforts for previous shows, but Mr. Lewis was able to reconstitute events for the 1969 show, *Anything Goes*.

In 1969, roughly $1000 was allocated to the Publicity Committee to do with as they thought appropriate. In September 1968, some posters were prepared to attract staff members to work on sets, makeup, etc. Approximately 700 more posters were printed in October to advertise the show itself. Of these, almost 350 were used. Also, October auditions were publicized in the weekly university student newspaper, *The Gazette*.

During November and December, members of the twenty-eight-person committee canvassed local businesses for contributions towards a cooperative advertisement in the *London Free Press*—London's major daily newspaper. Money for a half-page advertisement was collected. At the same time, letters were mailed to alumni who attended the previous year's show by buying tickets by mail. To mail to alumni on a larger scale would involve sending to every Western alumnus since the only mailing list was alphabetical. No other mail orders were solicited.

In January 1969, the cooperative advertisement appeared in the *London Free Press*. Three weeks prior to Friday, February 7—the opening night of the eight-night run for *Anything Goes*—a quarter-page advertisement appeared in *The Gazette*. Two weeks prior to the opening night, the cartoon-style full-page advertisement shown in Exhibit 7 appeared in *The Gazette*. No radio or television was used at all throughout the campaign until the last moment when radio was used in an attempt to booster the small sale of tickets.

On February 1, several of the Patches' cast donned costumes and visited campus cafeterias at noon hour. They sang one song and announced when the show was starting, where, what it was about, and where to buy tickets. About this time, a banner appeared over the Thames bridge in the centre of the campus advertising the show. The banner only lasted one night.

On Friday, February 7, opening night, *The Gazette* printed a preview story describing the show. In the same issue of this weekly newspaper, an advertisement announced opening night. Helen Wallace, an entertainment critic for the *London Free Press* also published an article previewing the show in the London newspaper.

On February 8, Helen Wallace wrote a review in the *London Free Press*. The Publicity Committee was so pleased with it that they ordered 2000 reprints at a cost of $14, and distributed copies in cafeterias throughout the campus. A copy of this handout appears in Exhibit 8. The committee was also pleased with the review that appeared in the university newspaper, *The Gazette*. However, the review did not appear until *The Gazette* issue of Friday, February 14, one day before the final performance of *Anything Goes*.

A summary of publicity and promotional expenditures for *Anything Goes* is shown in Exhibit 9. Also shown are comparable figures for the 1968 show, *A Funny Thing Happened on the Way to the Forum*.

SALES

The producer traditionally delegated ticket sales to the Publicity and Public Relations Committee, but retained the prerogative of setting ticket prices. When in the Grand Theatre, Patches sold tickets at $1.50, $2, and $3. With the move to Althouse College in 1966, Patches set a price level of $2.50 on all seats. In both theatres, all seats were reserved. Mr. Lewis was considering raising the price to $2.75.

Past policy was against anything but cash sales. Mail orders were solicited and accepted only from alumni. Tickets were sold on campus in the Somerville House ticket office—the building housing the main cafeterias—beginning three weeks before opening night from 11:30 A.M. to 1:30 P.M. Monday to Friday. In addition to this advertised outlet, tickets were available on campus anytime in the Purple Patches office in Somerville, although this fact was not widely known or publicized. Cast members were not given tickets to sell unless in exchange for cash. Because the Patches executive felt that the university market would not support the show and in light of their objective of reaching the London audience, they obtained and advertised a ticket outlet in downtown London. Starting two weeks before opening night, Patches tickets were available at Words and Music—a book and record store that also handled tickets for many other kinds of entertainment functions. Words and Music received a ten-cent commission on every Patches ticket sold.

Little information was available on past sales trends. Monday night attendance was consistently the lowest of the eight nights. Friday and Saturday nights were usually capacity audiences. The closing night, Saturday, was always the first to sell out. The heaviest weekly sales volume occurred in the week before the show, especially after a preview was published.

In 1969, with one week left before opening night, less than 50 per cent of the tickets for *Anything Goes* were sold. The Patches executive launched a "panic campaign" using radio, making personal selling visits to faculty offices, attempting to get into secondary schools to sell high school students, and offering half-price seats to high school students who presented their student cards. After the show opened, reprints of the Helen Wallace review of opening night were used. The direct results of the campaign were uncertain. For example, very few high school students took advantage of half-price tickets. As of April 1969, sales results for *Anything Goes* were not final. However, it appeared that the 1969 production would realize revenue of approximately $10 000.

ADDITIONAL CONSIDERATIONS BY MR. LEWIS

Mr. Lewis was uncertain as to the extent Patches was in competition with other university events and other theatrical productions in London. The Gilbert and Sullivan Society, a university student group, performed Gilbert and Sullivan operettas for eight nights each winter. In 1969, the Society performed in Talbot College Theatre on campus for eight nights in early January. The Society planned to present its next show in early December, 1969. Tickets sold at $2 for weeknights and $2.50 for weekends. For the first time in its history, the Society broke even financially in 1969.

Another student theatrical group, Players' Guild, presented modern drama. Although Players' Guild had no set policies on the type or number of shows presented, it tended to have one major and one minor production each year, and to sponsor numerous other theatrical activities such as visiting groups and noon-hour theatre.

The London Little Theatre Group performed a series of diverse productions throughout the year at the Grand Theatre in downtown London. The Group performed one Broadway musical in the fall of every year. Since 1960, the Group had performed the musicals listed in Exhibit 10.

The musical was always filled to capacity. London Little Theatre sold tickets on a subscription basis only. Either eight plays at $14 or six plays at $12 were available. Students could buy eight play subscriptions at $7. Approximately 6000 persons attended the run of each show.

Mr. Lewis continued: "I think we can attract about 6000 people to the 1970 show—if we make good plans and market it properly. I'm working on that now."

Exhibit 1
Musicals Presented by Purple Patches
1963-1969

1963	*Bye Bye Birdie*
1964	*L'il Abner*
1965	*Fiorello*
1966	*Oklahoma*
1967	*South Pacific*
1968	*A Funny Thing Happened on the Way to the Forum*
1969	*Anything Goes*

Exhibit 2
Purple Patches Organization – 1969

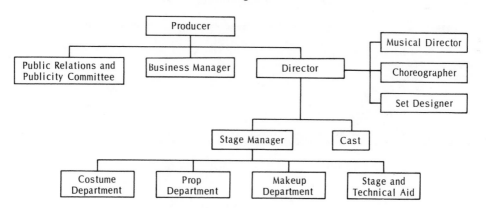

Exhibit 3
Survey of Student Knowledge of
Purple Patches, December 1968

1. What year are you in?
   First   12%
   Other   88

2. Have you ever heard of
   Purple Patches?
   Yes   96%
   No   4

3. Do you prefer musical
   comedies or straight musicals?
   Comedies   72%
   Straight   20
   Either   8

4. Did you go to Patches last year?
   Yes   24%
   No   76

   If not, why not?

   Price   4%
   Musical disliked   0
   Lack of time   25
   No tickets   25
   No date   46

5. How did you hear of the Patches
   production last year?
   Campus paper   40%
   Posters   56
   Campus talk   38
   Radio   12
   Friends in show   25

Exhibit 4
Survey of Student Preference for Plays
Previously Staged by Purple Patches, December 1968
and
Purple Patches Attendance Records,[1] 1963-68

	Play	Survey Rank	Per cent of Capacity Attendance
1963	*Bye Bye Birdie*	1	80
1964	*L'il Abner*	2	98
1965	*Fiorello*	6	59
1966	*Oklahoma*	4	not available
1967	*South Pacific*	5	86
1968	*A Funny Thing Happened on the Way to the Forum*	3	86

[1] Between 1963 and 1965, Purple Patches was performed in London's Grand Theatre, (capacity of 7700 for a 7-night run). In years after 1965, Patches was performed in a theatre at the university's Althouse College (capacity 5200 for an 8-night run).

Exhibit 5
Selected Information on Musical Comedies
Under Consideration by Purple Patches
for 1970

CAMELOT

Musical in two acts, based on *The Once and Future King* by T. H. White. Book and lyrics by Alan Jay Lerner, music by Frederick Loewe. Story is set in the legendary court of King Arthur, and concerns two themes: King Arthur's dream of a peaceable world where might serves right and the ill-fated romance between Queen Guenevere and young Lancelot.

Camelot opened at the Majestic Theatre in New York on December 3, 1960, with Julie Andrews, Richard Burton and Robert Goulet in leading roles. Cast of 22, plus 41 supporting singers and dancers. Closed on January 5, 1963, after 873 performances. Ranks 46th in terms of all-time longest runs on Broadway.

Musical numbers include: "I Wonder What the King Is Doing Tonight?" "The Simple Joys of Maidenhood"; "Camelot"; "Follow Me"; "C'est Moi"; "The Lusty Month of May"; "When You May Take Me to the Fair"; "How to Handle a Woman"; "The Jousts"; "Before I Gaze at You Again"; "If Ever I Would Leave You"; "The Seven Deadly Virtues"; "What Do Simple Folk Do?"; "The Persuasion"; "Fie on Goodness!"; "I Loved You Once in Silence"; "Guenevere"; "Camelot" (reprise).

THE KING AND I

Musical in two acts, based on *Anna and the King of Siam,* by Margaret Landon. Music by Richard Rodgers, book and lyrics by Oscar Hammerstein, II. The story is set in and around the King's palace, Bangkok, Siam, in the early 1860s and concerns the educational and romantic trials and triumphs of an English schoolteacher retained for the royal Siamese family.

The King and I opened at the St. James Theatre in New York on March 29, 1951. Yul Brynner and Gertrude Lawrence played the leading roles of the King and Anna. Cast of 13, plus approximately 30 singers and dancers. Closed after 1246 performances. Ranks 21st among all-time longest runs on Broadway.

Musical numbers include: "I Whistle a Happy Tune"; "My Lord and Master"; "Hello, Young Lovers!"; "The Royal Siamese Children"; "A Puzzlement"; "The Royal Bangkok Academy"; "Getting to Know You"; "We Kiss in a Shadow"; "Shall I Tell You What I Think of You?"; "Something Wonderful"; "Western People Funny"; "I Have Dreamed"; "The Small House of Uncle Thomas"; "Shall We Dance?".

SWEET CHARITY

Musical based on the screenplay, *Nights of Cabiria* by Federico Fellini, Tullio Pinelli and Ennio Flaiano. Book by Neil Simon, music by Cy Coleman, lyrics by Dorothy Fields. Set in present day New York City, and concerns a warm-hearted dance hall hostess who goes from man to man, looking for the right one. She is always the loser, even at last when she thinks she is finally winning.

Sweet Charity opened at the Palace Theatre in New York on January 26, 1966, with Gwen Verdon in the leading role. Cast of 24, plus 19 singers and dancers. Closed in June 1967 after approximately 600 performances.

Musical numbers include: "Charity's Wish"; "You Should See Yourself"; "The Rescue"; "Big Spender"; "Charity's Soliloquy"; "Rich Man's Frug"; "If My Friends Could See Me Now"; "Too Many Tomorrows"; "There's Gotta Be Something Better Than This"; "I'm the Bravest Individual"; "Rhythm of Life"; "Baby, Dream Your Dreams"; "Sweet Charity"; "Where Am I Going?"; "I'm a Brass Band"; "I Love to Cry at Weddings".

Exhibit 6
Historical Records of Purple Patches
Costs, Actual and Budgeted

	Anything Goes (1969)		A Funny Thing Happened on the Way to the Forum (1968)		South Pacific (1967)		L'il Abner (1964)	
	Budget	Actual	Budget	Actual	Budget	Actual	Budget	Actual
ADMINISTRATION								
Royalties	$ 1 800	$1 100	$1 700				$ 970	
Orchestra	2 100	1 650	1 400				2 114	
Outside Talent Costs	1 700	1 450	1 200				675	
Theatre	600	650	1 000				2 000	
Stage hands	—	—	—				1 161	
Other	—	—	—					
TOTAL	$ 6 200	$4 850	$5 300	$5 559	$5 680	$5 645	$6 920	$8 065
EXPENSES								
Sets	$ 1 000	$ 958	$ 800	$ 956	$1 200	$ 926	$1 500	$2 813
Costumes	800	362	500	602	500	1 015	550	372
Publicity	1 000	945	1 000	1 049	1 200	1 002	1 085	1 205
Office	250	15	250	365	150	140	325	428
Make-up	70	50	—	—	50	204	85	179
Program	600	635	400	428	475	644	550	688
Props	100	70	100	92	100	105	125	153
Tickets	300	67	300	294	400	297	148	276
Transportation	200	40	200	94	150	242	100	97
Lighting	600	485	450	790	100	436	—	—
Parties	—	—	—	—	—	—	40	119
Misc.	250	360	250	689	240	335	—	—
Contingency	—	400	250	—	—	—	—	—
GRAND TOTAL	$11 370	$9 237	$8 900	$10 918	$10 245	$10 991	$11 428	$14 395

Exhibit 7
Purple Patches

Exhibit 8
Purple Patches
Review of *ANYTHING GOES*
By Helen Wallace
of the *London Free Press*

Purple Patches Friday night took a dead horse of a musical and flogged it with so much life that the Cole Porter antique *Anything Goes* beat all odds and came in a winner.

There's little to recommend the musical except a few nostalgic songs that now rank as classics, but the production was so strong, well-conceived and energetically performed by a first rate cast that it survived despite a sagging and trite script.

This year's annual University of Western Ontario production at Althouse College Theatre was a triumph of production over content.

It did take some time getting used to, and there were moments when the production with its mod setting and contemporary references seemed to waver uncomfortably between the psychedelic and vaudevillian. This wasn't helped by a first act which took time gaining steam or a sharp contrast between musical numbers which lifted the production to a peak, and bouts of dragging dialogue which let it sag.

These contrasts, however, are built-in-flaws of the script, which is liberally laced with dead jokes and blue corn. Director E. A. Peyroux obviously saw the traps and introduced enough innovations to keep the production moving at a reasonable clip.

Set on a ship sailing from New York to England, *Anything Goes* tackles both a star-crossed romance, as a young man tries to break up his girlfriend's engagement to an English lord, and the underworld as a Runyonesque thug tries to evade the law by disguising himself as a minister. The songs are all standbys now, includ-ing, "You're the Top", "It's Delovely", "Friendship", "I Get a Kick Out of You" and "Blow, Gabriel, Blow".

Choral work, directed by Phil Murphy and choreography by Sue McIlroy were excellent and once the second act opened with "Public Enemy Number One", only to be topped by "Blow, Gabriel, Blow", the musical never lost speed.

But perhaps the strongest element of the evening was the lead performances, all exceptionally well cast and highlighted by four solid cameo characterizations.

It's a toss-up as to who gets the most honours: the gravelly voiced Mae West of a nightclub singer, Reno Sweeny, as played by Ricarda Randall; the bug-eyed, timid and shrill Sir Evelyn as played by Gordon Watkin, or Eric Sanderson's sly but harmless conman Moonface. The trio, whether clowning, singing or dancing all exhibited good comic potential and created some of the best moments. They were ably supported by Moonface's naive and amply endowed girlfriend, Bonnie, as played by Marian Botsford.

Pete Fitzgibbons as Billy Crocker, Martha Sadler as the domineering mother, Mrs. Harcourt and Mavis Kerr as her daughter, Hope, also provided solid support.

Anything Goes, which continues until February 15, is strictly entertainment. The plot may prompt groans, but the production is spirited enough to justify the revival.

London Free Press, February 8, 1969.

Exhibit 9
Publicity and Promotional Expenditures
for Purple Patches, 1968 and 1969

	A Funny Thing Happened on the Way to the Forum (1968)	Anything Goes (1969)
Posters	$187.00	$176.00
Radio	125.00	175.00
Newspaper—*Gazette*	282.00	293.00
London Free Press	365.00	256.00
T.V.	65.00	—
Miscellaneous	124.00	95.00
TOTAL	$1 148.00	$995.00

Exhibit 10
Musicals Presented by the London Little Theatre
1960-69

1960	*Carousel*	1965	*My Fair Lady*
1961	*The King and I*	1966	*West Side Story*
1962	*Brigadoon*	1967	*Music Man/Oliver*
1963	(not available)	1968	*Showboat*
1964	*Kiss Me Kate*	1969	*How to Succeed in Business Without Really Trying* (planned)

35

The Slater Co. Ltd.

In 1965, Mr. William M. Slater organized The Slater Co. Ltd. and through it took over the sole ownership and operation of the assets of a small, nearly bankrupt manufacturer of a line of light air compression equipment which had been sold primarily for use in spray painting. After the takeover, Slater expanded this line to include small compressors which were used by service stations and garages to operate pneumatic tools and tire changers.

In July 1967, Salter was successful in obtaining the Canadian rights to distribute a U.S. line of spray guns and supplies. Subsequently, he developed a special "undercoating gun" to supplement the American line.

In mid 1967, the Tobin Co. of Chicago, Illinois, placed an advertisement in the *Financial Post* announcing that they were interested in appointing Canadian companies to manufacture and distribute their line of light welding equipment. Slater answered the advertisement and was awarded a five-year agreement under which he would manufacture and distribute the Tobin line in Ontario and Quebec on payment to Tobin of a 10 per cent royalty on sales. He also agreed to purchase and install the $13 000 worth of equipment necessary to manufacture the products. Tobin supplied the necessary dies and designs. Sufficient manufacturing space was available in Slater's existing plant so no additional plant investment was required.

Prior to the Tobin agreement, Slater had employed one salesman to call on garages, service stations, painting contractors and light manufacturers in Ontario. In discussions with the Tobin Co., he agreed to add another salesman and extend his sales coverage into the province of Quebec. As a result, one salesman covered Ontario and the other covered Quebec, each carrying all the products Slater sold. Both salesmen were paid a flat salary.

Early in October 1972 Slater received notice from the Tobin Co. that they had decided to establish their own manufacturing facilities and marketing organization in Canada and did not intend to renew the licensing agreement which would expire on the following December 31. In their notice, Tobin offered to purchase all the inventory of finished goods and supplies of Tobin products which Slater might have on hand at the year end at 20 per cent above his full factory cost. Slater was disappointed when he heard this news since, during the past five years, sales volume of the Tobin line had increased to the point where it was now contributing 40 per cent of Slater's total sales revenue of $600 000.

In the process of determining the effect the loss of the Tobin business would have on his company, Slater noted that profits on the Tobin line had been extremely favourable, contributing approximately 55 per cent of the 1972 gross profit.

Slater spent considerable time attempting to locate or develop a line to replace the Tobin business. He examined and discarded a number of products largely because potential volumes were too small, margins were too slim to permit profitable manufacture or because the products were not compatible with the existing Slater lines of air compression and spraying equipment.

Three possibilities did look promising, however, and, early in December, Slater sat down to give serious consideration to (1) undertaking the manufacture of his own line of light welding equipment, (2) entering into an agreement to distribute a line of electronic automotive engine testing equipment which was manufactured in Germany and (3) accepting an offer to act as a sub-contractor, manufacturing components parts for a large local valve and plumbing supplies producer.

MANUFACTURING WELDING EQUIPMENT

Over the years, Slater had recommended to the Tobin Co. a number of improvements in their welding equipment line. The nature of the improvements suggested by Slater would permit adjustment of the point of the torch flame to allow for welding of small parts more neatly and effectively. These improvements would increase the cost of the product about 35 per cent. Tobin executives had repeatedly refused to permit their incorporation into the Tobin equipment line, believing that the required increase in the selling price would reduce the competitive effectiveness of the lines.

The two Slater salesmen had repeatedly mentioned requests from light manufacturers for such an improvement. Slater was confident the improved equipment could be developed and ready for the market in four months. Development costs were estimated at $12 000, largely for new designs and equipments.

If no improvements were made, direct material and labour costs to manufacture a Slater line very similar to the present Tobin line would run 5 per cent above current costs (before royalty charges). This cost increase was felt to be the value of the dies and other assistance provided by Tobin. If the improvements were incorporated into certain models manufacturing costs on these models only would be from 35 per cent to 40 per cent higher than for basic equipment.

DISTRIBUTING GERMAN TESTING EQUIPMENT

Through the Department of Trade and Commerce listings, Slater had learned of a German electronics manufacturer of high-quality automotive engine testing equipment who was interested in obtaining distribution throughout Canada. A representative of the manufacturer expressed considerable interest in Slater's inquiries about the possibility of his company distributing the line insofar as Slater salesmen were already calling on a large number of potential customers for the equipment. The manufacturer's representative estimated the total Ontario and Quebec market for auto engine testing equipment at approximately $3 million per year and suggested that Slater should be able to obtain 10 per cent of this volume during the first year.

The German product was comparable in quality to similar products being sold in Canada and would be priced to sell at prices 15 to 20 per cent lower than similar equipment of the two large manufacturers located in Canada, who currently dominated the market. As part of an agreement, Slater would have to stock a $30 000 inventory of the equipment and supplies, purchased on six-month terms for the original order, and sixty-day terms thereafter. Slater's markup on the product line would average 25 per cent. Individual prices of equipment ranged in price to users from $100 to $2500. A complete installation would be in the range of $4000.

SUBCONTRACTING

In discussing the loss of the Tobin line with a friend of his, the friend advised Slater that the company for which he was purchasing agent, Dundee Plumbing, a large valve and plumbing supplies manufacturer, had been unable to locate a satisfactory second source of supply for a line of machined components for one of its most important industrial valve products. The friend pointed out that the present supplier was located 300 miles from the plant and, as purchasing agent, he was interested in obtaining a local supplier to manufacture a portion of the components and to provide emergency deliveries. Investigating further, Slater learned that the Dundee Co. purchased these components at prices which would permit Slater to earn a 15 per cent manufacturing margin (before depreciation) on volumes over 5000 units per year. The purchasing agent estimated that Dundee's requirements from Slater would amount to approximately $375 000 or 25 000 units, in the best years, dropping to a minimum of $75 000, or 5000 units, in the poorest years. His 1973 estimate of requirements from Slater was $200 000. As the components could not be manufactured in Slater's existing equipment, a $40 000 investment in new equipment would be required.

The company's balance sheet and profit and loss statement to their year end at September 30, 1972 are shown as Exhibits 1 and 2.

Exhibit 1
The Slater Co. Ltd.
Balance Sheet
as of September 30, 1972

ASSETS		LIABILITIES	
Cash	$ 25 500	Bank loan	$ 22 500
Accounts receivable	57 000	Accounts payable	27 000
Inventory			
Tobin equipment	18 000	Advances from	
Slater & other		shareholders	15 000
equipment	31 500	I.D.B. loan	30 000
	$132 000		
		TOTAL LIABILITIES	$ 94 500
		EQUITY	
Plant (net)	75 000	Capital stock	75 000
Equipment (net)	42 000	Surplus	79 500
		TOTAL LIABILITIES	
TOTAL ASSETS	$249 000	AND NET WORTH	$249 000

Exhibit 2
The Slater Co. Ltd.
Profit and Loss Statement
for Year Ended September 30, 1972

Sales		
Tobin equipment	$240 000	
Slater and other equipment	360 000	$600 000
Cost of goods manufactured		
Direct costs to manufacture		
Tobin equipment including		
10% royalty	150 000	
Slater & other equipment	277 500	
	427 500	
Manufacturing overhead	22 500	
		$450 000
Gross Profit		$150 000
Operating expenses		
Selling expense	42 000	
Transportation expense	12 000	
Office expense	18 000	
Executive salary	18 000	
Other expenses	4 500	$ 94 500
Net profit before taxes		$ 55 500

36
The Stereo Shop

In May 1973, Mr. Angelo Lorelli was reviewing data he had gathered about the feasibility of establishing a new stereo component retail outlet in London, Ontario. To date, a variety of information had been collected covering such topics as the stereo component industry, the potential market in London, existing competition, supply sources, and projected capital requirements and operating costs. At this point, it was Mr. Lorelli's responsibility to recommend whether he and his two partners should proceed with the proposed venture and, if so, on what basis.

Mr. Lorelli had recently graduated from a well-known Canadian business school. As graduation neared, he realized that he was not enthusiastic about working for a large corporation. Forming his own business was an alternative Angelo had seriously pondered and stereo components, his principal hobby, was a natural area to consider.

With a promise of family financial support, Mr. Lorelli had entered into an agreement with two friends to form a company to retail stereo components. Their plan was to open an outlet that would specialize only in stereo components, and only those of better quality. Mr. Lorelli, who would have a controlling interest in the firm, would be the only equity holder active in its operations. The agreed plan called for him to prepare a feasibility study by no later than May 1973, at which time a final go/no go decision would be rendered.

THE STEREO COMPONENT INDUSTRY

Almost no information was available concerning the Canadian market for stereo components. Statistics for the U.S. market, however, were published by the trade magazine *Merchandising Week*.[1] These data indicated that the U.S. industry was in a period of substantial growth. Retail sales in 1972 were estimated at $500 million, up from $300 million in 1967. With the anticipated future growth of quadrasonic sound, which required more speakers (four, versus two in the stereo systems) and more elaborate components, industry experts were anticipating a $2 billion market by 1975.

The average price paid for a stereo component system was $500-$600 as compared to $300-$400 in 1967. The increase was thought to be due to increased popularity of better quality components, since price levels of comparable equipment had remained almost stable during this period. An estimated 27 per cent of all component sales were replacement, trade-up, or add-on purchases.

In part, growth of the component industry had come at the expense of console sales, in which all components of the stereo system were built into a single piece of furniture, a console. In 1972, console sales totalled $296 million at retail, compared to $437 million in 1967. Average retail price paid for a console in 1972 was $310, an increase of approximately 6 per cent over 1967. Replacements of existing consoles accounted for 28 per cent of 1972 sales.

Mr. Lorelli suspected that Canadian experience mirrored the U.S. growth trends, although lagging in development by a year or two. He estimated Canadians paid retail prices 15-30 per cent higher than in the United States.

Stereo components were sold in a wide variety of outlets. Specialty stereo shops were

---

[1] Data in this section were taken from selected tables and articles in *Merchandising Week*, issues of January 29, 1973, and February 26, 1973.

the strongest single class of outlet, but appliance stores, radio and TV outlets, department stores, discount stores and mail order houses also accounted for significant proportions. With the industry experiencing rapid growth, mass merchandising outlets had been particularly active in giving added emphasis to stocking, displaying, and promoting components.

THE LONDON MARKET FOR STEREO COMPONENTS

The city of London was generally regarded as the financial, commercial, and cultural centre of western Ontario. Its metropolitan area, defined as Middlesex county, had a 1971 population of 286 000. This represented an increase of 58 per cent over the past decade, an average growth rate for a Canadian urban centre. The city's retail sales of $1650 per capita ranked eighth among twenty-two Canadian cities of 100 000 or more population, and were 16 per cent above the Canadian average. Financial institutions and light manufacturing industry formed the principal base of the regional economy. The University of Western Ontario, with a student population of over 14 000, was situated in London.

Data on stereo component sales for London were not available. Census statistics were available, however, indicating 1966 total sales of the following classes of retail establishments in Middlesex County:

1. Furniture, television, radio and appliance stores, defined as those in which not one of the four lines exceeded 50 per cent of total sales;
2. Household appliance stores, defined as those in which appliances exceed 50 per cent of total sales;
3. Television, radio and hi-fi stores, in which these three lines accounted for over 50 per cent of total store sales.

Mr. Lorelli used his own judgement to estimate that stereo sales (component and console) accounted for 20 per cent, 15 per cent, and 35 per cent of total sales of the respective store classes. On this basis, he arrived at an estimate of $3.3 million for 1966 Middlesex county total stereo retail sales. Next, using available data on past U.S. experience, Mr. Lorelli developed a simple regression equation to represent industry growth trends. Applying the equation to Middlesex county, the 1966 figure of $3.3 million was projected to a comparable 1973 total of $5.7 million.

Competition for stereo sales came from a number of sources. The 1972 London telephone directory, for example, listed over forty retailers under the "High Fidelity and Stereophonic Equipment" section of its yellow pages. Further, these listings did not include either of the city's two major downtown department stores, nor the suburban outlets of major variety chains such as Woolco, K-Mart, Zellers or Horizon.

In Mr. Lorelli's opinion, however, many of the existing outlets did not represent direct competition for his proposed store. Their lines were of cheaper quality and low price. Others carried stereo components only as a minor sideline to a principal emphasis on television sets and/or consoles. On this basis, only three stores were judged to be direct competitors: the Hi-Fi Stereo Shop, Schneider's, and The Audio Centre.

All three direct competitors carried well-known, quality brands in the component industry, and in some instances had exclusive territorial rights to these brands. Display at both Schneider's and The Audio Centre was arranged so that a customer could listen to any speaker from any set in the store, although this was not conveniently possible at the Hi-Fi Stereo Shop. All three offered a listening room where the set would be heard free of other noise distractions. In Mr. Lorelli's view, however, the attractiveness of display and listening room features in all three stores was not what it could be.

The Hi-Fi Stereo Shop was located on the basement level of Heintzman's, a musical instrument retailer situated on the main street in the downtown London shopping area.

Schneider's also had a downtown location, but was one block removed from the main street. The Audio Centre was approximately two miles east of the downtown shopping area. The Audio Centre also sold television sets. Both The Audio Centre and Schneider's were particularly active in advertising in the local newspaper, often featuring a sale item in their advertisements.

THE CONSUMER SURVEY

Because of the limited available information, Mr. Lorelli felt it would be appropriate to conduct a consumer survey. Budget was limited, so it was decided that a telephone survey would be most appropriate. The questionnaire shown in Exhibit 1 was designed by Mr. Lorelli for this purpose.

A random sample of 216 names was drawn from the London telephone directory. Because univeristy students were thought to be a prime market for quality stereo components, a further 108 names were drawn randomly from the University of Western Ontario's Student Directory. Execution of the survey resulted in 167 usable responses from the city population, 81 from the student population. Selected results from the survey are reproduced in Exhibit 2.

OPERATING COSTS FOR A PROPOSED OUTLET

The stereo components industry was characterized by a large number of potential suppliers. Thus, while some well-known lines were held by competitors on an exclusive basis, Mr. Lorelli contemplated no difficulty in obtaining a line of products suitable to his requirement of selling only quality components. Gross margins of manufacturers varied widely, and competitive pressures frequently forced retailers to sell at less than recommended list prices. After allowing for these factors, Mr. Lorelli anticipated the realized gross margin would average approximately 30 per cent.

Capital requirements were estimated at $150 000. This sum included an inventory requirement of $70 000, working capital needs, and the necessary store fixtures for a rented outlet capable of projecting a quality image.

Rent for a store of 3000 square feet would amount to $18 000 per year for a non-central location, or as high as $25-30 000 per year for a downtown location. Other annual operating expenses would include wages ($35 000), insurance ($6000), delivery expenses ($2500), bad debt allowances ($3000), and telephone, supplies and miscellaneous ($7000). Interest on borrowed capital would be charged at a 10 per cent rate. An initial projection of $27 000 per annum for advertising was assumed.

Exhibit 1
The Stereo Shop
Questionnaire Used in Telephone Survey

1. Do you own a stereo? What brand is it?
2. Is it a component or console set?
3. Are you considering a purchase (repurchase)?
   When? —within one year
         —from two to three years
         —from four to five years
         —longer than five years
   Price range? $100-399
          400-599
          600-799
          800-999
          over $1000
4. What type of store would you go to to make this purchase?
   —furniture
   —appliance
   —TV store
   —specialty store
   —department store
5. What was (is) important to you in purchasing a stereo?
6. Would you return to the same store for a repurchase?
7. How important is brand name? —very important
                            —moderately important
                            —not important at all
8. Do you know the service arrangements that you have with the store at which you made your purchase?
9. If you make a repurchase, would you trade up to higher price and quality?
10. Would you consider a trade-in service an important feature of a retail stereo shop?
11. What is your age? under 25
                 26-34
                 35-50
                 over 50
12. Are you married?

Exhibit 2
The Stereo Shop
Selected Results of Telephone Survey

1. OWNERSHIP OF STEREO

	City Population	Students	Total
Own a console	46%	32%	42%
Own a component set	32	47	37
Don't own a stereo	22	21	22
Total	100%	100%	100%
	(n = 167)	(n = 81)	(n = 248)

2. PLANNING TO PURCHASE OR REPURCHASE A STEREO

	City Population	Students	Total
Plan to purchase			
within 1 year	17%	12%	16%
in 2-3 years	24	43	30
in 4-5 years	11	11	11
in more than 5 years	7	16	10
Do not plan to purchase	41	16	33
Total	100%	100%	100%
	(n = 167)	(n = 81)	(n = 248)

3. PRICE PROSPECTIVE PURCHASERS EXPECT TO PAY

	City Population	Students	Total
Less than $400	25%	20%	23%
$400-599	27	38	31
$600-799	26	20	24
$800-999	13	9	11
$1000 or more	9	13	11
Total	100%	100%	100%
	(n = 98)	(n = 68)	(n = 166)

4. TYPE OF STORE RESPONDENT WOULD ENTER FOR STEREO PURCHASE

	City Population	Students	Total
Furniture	23%	12%	20%
Appliance	13	14	13
TV	16	15	15
Specialty	23	47	31
Department	14	9	12
Don't know/no answer	11	4	9
Total	100%	100%	100%
	(n = 167)	(n = 81)	(n = 248)

Exhibit 2 (continued)

5. FACTOR(S) REGARDED AS MOST IMPORTANT IN PURCHASING A STEREO

	City Population	Students	Total
Sound	28%	40%	31%
Style	11	12	11
Construction	11	7	10
Price	11	9	10
Brand name	2	1	2
Style and price	9	0	6
Sound and price	8	20	12
Style and quality	4	5	4
Don't know/no answer	17	6	13
Total	100%	100%	100%
	(n = 167)	(n = 81)	(n = 248)

6. KNOWLEDGE OF SERVICE ARRANGEMENT (FOR STEREO OWNERS ONLY)

	City Population	Students	Total
Know service arrangement	49%	75%	59%
Don't know service arrangement	51	25	41
Total	100%	100%	100%
	(n = 108)	(n = 64)	(n = 172)

7. AGE AND MARITAL STATUS OF RESPONDENTS

Age	City Population	Students	Total
25 or less	27%	68%	40%
26-34	35	19	29
35-50	17	4	13
Over 50	11	1	8
No answer	10	9	10
Total	100%	100%	100%
	(n = 167)	(n = 81)	(n = 248)

Marital Status	City Population	Students	Total
Single	19%	75%	37%
Married	59	21	46
Other	10	1	7
No answer	13	2	9
Total	100%	100%	100%
	(n = 167)	(n = 81)	(n = 248)

SECTION VII
An Introduction to Production/Operations Management

To many of us, the word "production" seems to mean large numbers of blue-collar workers doing uninteresting jobs in a monstrous assembly plant. Very few of us associate production with the problems of health care delivery, university management, supermarkets, Air Canada, or McDonald's. Our purpose in this chapter is to show you what production can mean by illustrating some important production tasks and decision situations that are common to all organizations that attempt to provide goods or services. The title, "production/operations," is our attempt to convey to you the wide variety of circumstances encompassed by this material. If you have trouble thinking in terms of the production problems of a hospital, perhaps you'll find it useful to think in terms of its operations problems. We'll alternate between the two terms in this chapter.

Most writers define production as a kind of transformation process: inputs (such as labour and materials) are *transformed* into outputs (such as hamburgers, healthy people, cars, etc.). Viewed this way, production involves four basic inputs: labour, material, equipment and technology; four basic transformations: physical, locational, exchange, storage; and a wide variety of outputs. Personally, we have found this approach easy to put on a blackboard, but not very instructive to students. Instead, we prefer to think of production under three headings:

1. What production/operations tasks are to be performed?
2. What is the appropriate system to perform those tasks effectively and efficiently?
3. Once designed and set up, how do we ensure the system actually delivers what it is supposed to?

Using these headings you can probably anticipate the kinds of decisions a production manager may face:

- Product or service characteristics
- Location
- Layout (physical arrangement of facilities)
- Maintenance of quality standards
- Quantity within a time period
- Equipment
- Materials
- Management of in-process inventory
- Job allocation
- Scheduling

Obviously, the list could be quite lengthy. It is not our intent to cover these topics exhaustively, but rather to suggest an approach that will enable you to deal with production/operations situations as you encounter them. The first principle of this approach is always to begin with a clear understanding of the production task.

UNDERSTANDING THE PRODUCTION/OPERATIONS TASK

In general terms, the production/operations task refers to what an organization must do to ensure that the product is manufactured or the service performed in a manner that both meets the needs of the customer and allows the organization to realize its overall objectives. For example, we might say that in an organization manufacturing automobiles, the production task includes transforming steel into shaped pieces then assembling these pieces into automobiles that meet the style, price, and safety requirements of consumers. Similarly, in a service organization such as a railroad, we might say the production task includes transporting passengers and freight from one place to another as quickly as possible without endangering the safety of either in the process. More specifically, the production task in all organizations is to deliver the right product (or service), at the right price, in the right place, at the right time, and in the right quantity. To understand this, we have to consider the "environment" of the production manager.

First, marketing is the liaison between production and the firm's customers. Marketing should help translate customer needs and wants into terms of sales volume forecasts, product features, delivery schedules, and so on. Second, personnel is the liaison between production and its sources of employees. Personnel should help to locate, train and keep records on the workers production needs. And third, finance is the liaison between production and the company treasury. Finance should help production make investment decisions and measure the costs incurred in the production process. The production manager needs to deal with these three aspects of his internal environment, but he also must keep up with technological developments (changes in equipment and technique), material developments (such as shortages), and competitive developments (such as changes in industry capacity). This is all easier said than done.

Based on all of these aspects of the internal and external environment, the production manager can specifically define the production/operations task under five headings:

- Quantity
- Design
- Cost
- Quality
- Delivery

We'll use our examples of the railroad and the automobile manufacturer to illustrate these.

Quantity

The railroad must ensure that enough "transport" is available for all passengers and freight. Too few locomotives or cars would lead to a loss of business to other forms of transport. However, too many locomotives or cars implies that the railroad will incur higher costs than necessary.

Design

The automobile manufacturer must ensure that the design of its cars will appeal to the consumers who are expected to buy them. A company which is slow in responding to changing consumer tastes will suffer low sales. By the same token, radical design changes may lead to sales to only a limited group of consumers.

Cost

The cost of freight service must be comparable to that of competing transport services such as truck or air. If railroad costs are too high, shippers will switch to alternative services.

Quality

The automobile manufacturer must ensure that the cars produced meet minimum safety standards and do not suffer undue wear after short use. Otherwise, potential customers will switch to other firms' products. However, if the quality is too high, costs may be excessive and sales correspondingly low.

Delivery

Clearly, if the railroad is always late delivering freight or passengers to a destination, or delivers them to the wrong destination, then both shippers and passengers will switch to alternative forms of transport.

The role of the production/operations manager is to accomplish these tasks as effectively and efficiently as possible.

- Effectiveness refers to the extent an objective is realized.
- Efficiency refers to the extent the desired objective is achieved with a minimum of cost, effort, and waste.

Looked at in the simplest way, for the railroad, efficiency can be described as carrying goods to a destination using as little fuel, labour, and equipment as possible. Effectiveness is delivering all goods to the right place at the right time, and moreover, remaining flexible to changes in future demand. Therefore, it is possible for a railroad to be efficient and not effective (low cost, but late and unreliable), effective but not efficient, or neither. The ideal, of course, is to be both effective and efficient, but these two goals often conflict. The relative importance of efficiency and effectiveness depends on the task. For instance, in medical care the importance of effectiveness is much greater than efficiency, and consequently, medical costs tend to be high. Once we have a good understanding of the production/operations tasks, we can design, establish and operate the system required to accomplish them.

SYSTEM DESIGN AND OPERATION

You have undoubtedly seen several different kinds of production systems ranging from large assembly plants to someone preparing dinner in a crowded kitchen. How do we design an appropriate system to perform the required production tasks? One of the very first considerations is the degree of flexibility or specialization required in the production facility. This is determined by (a) market volume (both at the moment and in the future) and (b) product standardization. Depending on the size of the volume required and the extent to which the product is standardized, we may select a system design somewhere along a spectrum:

continuous	job	project
process ←———————————	shop ————————————→	process

Continuous Process

When a market is large with relatively certain present and future demand expectations, and when the product variation is small, the production process will generally be most efficient and effective if it is very specialized (and thus not flexible). This is referred to as *continuous process* and is exemplified by oil refineries, chemical plants, large automobile assembly lines, and air freight between Vancouver and Montreal. The characteristics of continuous processes are:

1. A limited variety of output,
2. The movement of each unit of production through the same sequence of operations,
3. No designation of the process to a particular customer,
4. Product dedication—that is, the operations or machines are *specialized* and cannot easily be transformed to perform different tasks.

Job Shop Process

The *job shop* is a more appropriate form of organization when the market is, relatively speaking, somewhat smaller, or has a less certain future or if there is a large possible variety of products. This system is characterized by:
1. The potential for an extensive product line,
2. A variable routine of jobs—not all units of production go through every operation,
3. Production for individual customers,
4. *General purpose* facilities, machines and skills.
Examples are machine shops, auto service centres, hospitals, or transport to communities in the far north.

Project Process

For those instances when the market for a product is very small (possibly for only one customer, on one occasion), or when the product is very complex and/or unique, a *project* approach to production will be most efficient and effective. Here economies of scale and specialization do not apply. The organization is normally "product-dedicated," with the job characteristically stationary, and production resources brought to it. Examples are space vehicles, bridges, repair of large machinery and air rescue missions.

We must emphasize that these three types of production processes are points on a spectrum of process. Often you may encounter difficulties describing a particular production system as one form rather than another because it is a mixed type. These three classifications are useful, however, because:
1. They emphasize the importance of designing a system in accordance with the production tasks to be performed,
2. They represent very different kinds of production systems, each of which has certain critical characteristics that must be managed carefully, and
3. They help us diagnose production problems by distinguishing between issues of production *design* and production system *operation*.
     In order to set up a production system we need to do more than just select the general type of process we will use. Here are a few of the kinds of choices you might face if you were designing a production system:

- Location. Near source of supply or new customers? (Why are Stelco and Dofasco in Hamilton?)
- Layout. By machine groups, by production steps, etc.? (How would you design the kitchen of a McDonald's restaurant?)
- Purchasing. Infrequent big orders or frequent little orders? (What purchasing and inventory policies do you have for your apartment food supply? Why?)
- Equipment. Rent or buy; specialized or general purpose, etc.? (What equipment decisions would you make if you were starting a landscaping and gardening service?)
- Maintenance. When needed or preventative? (When would you change the light bulbs in a large factory?)
- Job Design. Specialization; rotation; etc.? (Would you make cars on an assembly line

where every worker repeatedly performs a small task—like General Motors—or would you use teams of workers who do major portions of cars together not on an assembly line—like Volvo?)

- Scheduling. Which jobs get priority—first in, shortest, emergency, etc? How far ahead do you plan? (How would you schedule an automobile repair garage?)
- Subcontracting. Do it yourself or hire someone else? (Suppose you had limited funds but wanted to put in a backyard swimming pool. What jobs would you subcontract to someone else?)
- Research and Development. Do your own or buy someone else's? (Why does Imperial Oil have such a large Research and Development department?)

All of these decisions must be made with appropriate consideration of the production tasks and the internal and external environment of the production/operations group. Many choices may be constrained by available company resources while others will be constrained by the type of output desired. In the clothing industry, for example, a large producer of off-the-rack ladies' wear will probably opt for a form of continuous process which would imply specialized machinery and relatively unskilled labour. In countries were labour is expensive, the initial investment in equipment may be very high. Alternatively, in Hong Kong, the production of clothing is labour intensive because the cost of skilled craftsmen is very low. An entirely different production strategy would be followed by a small producer of custom clothing where design and quality are of paramount importance and volume is low. In this case, mechanization would be low and the people hired would have to be fairly skilled.

Some of these system design decisions represent long-term commitments (such as location), others are medium-term (such as equipment investment), and yet others are short-term (such as purchasing policies). When making longer term decisions in particular, we must bear in mind both the current circumstances and our anticipation of future developments. Changing major decisions such as plant location and layout of primary machinery is always expensive and disruptive, sometimes to the point where it cannot be done without jeopardizing the future of the firm.

Once the system is in place—the employees hired and trained, the equipment operating, a management group established, etc.—the job of operations management is the control of the process. Often some of the five production tasks are rigidly defined for the production manager, leaving little discretion. For example, quantity and quality are usually expected to be provided to the customer as ordered. Design and those elements of quality that are inherent to it involve discussion and negotiations between marketing and production during the planning stages; they are relatively fixed once production begins. On the other hand, the production manager may have much more freedom in affecting cost and delivery since they are rarely defined in absolute terms. Customers normally just ask for the least cost and the shortest possible delivery time. In order to explore the concept of production/operations control further, we'll look at each of the three process types in turn because the critical aspects to watch differ among them.

Continuous Process Management

In this type of process, all units of production normally go through the entire sequence of operations in an identical order. Thus, the critical element to be controlled is the smoothness of the flow-through. A break in production at one point could cause the entire line to be idle. The first thing to be done, then, is to ensure that the rate of movement of a unit of production through each step in the sequence is even. This is normally referred to as "line-balancing" and ensures the absence of bottlenecks. To give you an idea of a bottleneck, suppose three people were washing dishes: one washing, one drying, and one putting away. If the person drying is slower than everyone else, the whole system will be bottlenecked at the drying stage: the washer will run out of places to put wet dishes and the one putting them away will be waiting for something to do. One way to handle the problem of small aberrations in the rate of flow through any part of an assembly line and to lessen the interdependence of two adjacent operations is through the use of a "decoupling" or "buffer" inventory. This means that the output from step one does not move directly to step two. Rather, it goes into a "waiting" inventory, and only when the second step is ready to accept it will it be processed. If a stockpile of waiting units of production is available at step two, then any unusual delay at step one does not interfere with overall production, at least as long as waiting inventory remains. Naturally, there are costs associated with having units of production sitting waiting for processing. The trade-off must be made between the cost of the investment in waiting inventory and the cost of idle production facilities. Sometimes, changes in equipment or personnel must be made to correct continuing line-balancing problems.

Implicit in the foregoing is proper maintenance of the line. One loose bolt could shut down an entire production line. It also implies that inputs, be they raw materials or subassemblies, (the product of another line) should be waiting for their turn on the line, and not the production process waiting for input. The scheduling questions then relate to the relative timing of inputs from the purchasing process or from different production operations. Once the basic scheduling has been done, it usually will not require constant overhaul.

Job Shop Management

Job shop processes are more product and customer oriented than continuous processes. With a wide variety of potential products, no one set sequence of operations can usually exist. This means that purchasing, inventory planning, manpower planning and scheduling cannot be established in isolation from daily sales. The incoming order is the trigger for all of these activities to begin interacting.

The incoming order might come from either inside the company or from a customer. For example, custom manufacturers or automobile repair facilities are job shops which are entirely customer bound. Indeed, these processes resemble project-type production very closely in that every unit of production is at all times associated with a particular customer. They are still basically job shops, however, because the individual orders are not highly complex and there will be similarities over different jobs. Tuning an engine, for example, is not a process that has to be redesigned in its entirety for each car brought in to a service station.

On the other hand, some job shops do not appear to be so strictly customer bound and have certain similarities to continuous flow in that the demand for the many different products can be forecasted. For example, in a restaurant which offers five standard dinners and a number of à la carte items, the kitchen is a job shop. However, the cook does not have to wait for customer orders before starting. In this case, a special type of decoupling inventory, namely finished goods inventory, may be established. Thus, if Irish stew is on the menu, the cook may prepare a quantity in advance based on forecasted demand. The costs that have to be traded off are those associated with poor forecasting (which would result in waste) and those associated with inefficient production (it is more expensive, more difficult, and more time-consuming to make any individual pots of stew rather than one large pot). The decision to establish a decoupling or finished goods inventory means that the process is no longer dependent on the final customer. In this sense, the "finished goods department" becomes the customer, who "orders" certain products at certain times in certain quantities. A parallel situation exists at the other end of the process. A custom manufacturer may not purchase supplies until a customer makes an order. A kitchen, however, has a raw material inventory of potatoes, flour, salt, and so on, which becomes the inhouse "supplier" from which "purchases" are made. For both raw material and finished goods inventory the trade-off between the benefits accrued (in the form of better customer service, independence from suppliers, and improved efficiency of production) and the costs incurred (cost of tying up cash in inventory) must be balanced.

If we describe a "continuous-type" job shop as having in-house customers and suppliers, then it resembles a "custom or project" job shop quite closely, and both can be discussed together.

Given fairly set quantity, quality and design objectives, the main task will be to optimize the trade-off between minimizing delivery time to customers and maintaining a low-cost operation through high facilities utilization and low in-process inventory. The operations manager's problem is to juggle the conflicting objectives of the system. In order to minimize delivery time, it would seem best to process each order through each operation (or job station) as soon as it appeared. This, unfortunately, would imply the need for extensive production facilities in order to handle periods of peak demand. These facilities would then stand idle at periods of lower demand, and unnecessarily increase cost. However, if capacity is designed for the average load, periods of heavy demand will result in backlogs of jobs at different job stations. These jobs must then be scheduled. To complicate this problem, since different jobs will require different operations and in varying sequences, a scheduling decision for any given station should include consideration of all the jobs in the shop, their process requirements, and the current backlog at all job stations. No perfect scheduling system has yet been developed. With the use of computers, great headway has been made in tackling this problem. Unfortunately, sometimes the cost an elaborate system exceeds the value. Some useful, though certainly imperfect rules of thumb do exist. First come, first served is one example, and it is applied rigorously in banks where various employees in different departments service a variety of customers with myriad demands. Another rule of thumb gives the job with the shortest process time precedence. Automobile repair garages use a judicious mix of the two rules.

Quite another problem arises when we again try to minimize delivery time to customers. One of the characteristics of a job shop is that it utilizes general purpose rather than specialized facilities. Thus, a job station would need to be adjusted differently for each job it works on. The set-up time is non-productive and hence is costly. For that reason, costs can be minimized through better facilities utilization if jobs are "batched" into groups with similar characteristics. A printing press, for example, needs to be adjusted for paper size, thickness, and ink colour. It would be preferable, then, to do all printing jobs of one type at the same time and eliminate as many change-overs as possible. Naturally, this can greatly magnify the scheduling problem.

On the other hand, the cost of maximizing facilities usage is not just the inconvenience to the customer of longer delivery time. The longer a given job is part of the operation the larger the investment in work-in-process inventory. For the company producing industrial boilers, it is obvious that the longer the time between the purchase of steel and the sale of a completed boiler the larger the financial cost to the company. Similarly, in an auto repair shop, the longer it takes to complete a task, the greater the investment of the garage owner (bills for replacement parts and mechanics' wages must be paid independently of when the customer pays his bill). For those job shops with raw materials inventory and finished goods inventory, poor forecasting of demand (and hence of materials requirements) will also unnecessarily increase costs.

The most difficult task for the manager of a job shop, however, is not the decision at a given moment of the optimum "batch size" job station schedule, or size or mix of inventory. Rather, management must watch for changes over time in customer demands along the five basic facets. As these demands change, the manager must be prepared to adapt his process.

Consider, for example, an automobile repair shop doing a variety of jobs. Over the years it becomes known for good, fast muffler repairs. At the same point the manager might find that the mix of products ordered has changed so that the shop is now faced with a high proportion of muffler repairs, and that requests for this product come in on a steady basis. The *quantity* of these jobs has increased, the expected *delivery* time is probably shorter than for most jobs, and inefficiencies of scheduling these jobs around larger jobs might well be increasing overall cost. Adjusting the operation from a straightforward custom-type job shop to one where at least muffler repairs are done with a more continuous-type job shop flow may well be important to future profitability.

Project Management

In some ways, a project resembles a job shop handling custom orders. It obtains its unique character from the size and complexity of the job. Here, the key component in cost is the investment in materials and human resources. Thus, early completion of a project is of as much interest to the producer as it is to the customer. The main task, then, is normally to minimize overall completion time, and, by the same token, to minimize investment in the components of the project by ensuring they are not produced before they are required. Scheduling the various parts of the project is usually the critical task: to ensure that each component is ready exactly when required (and thus that its component parts or raw materials are made or ordered at the appropriate time).

There are more management issues than those we've discussed under each of the three system types, but we will leave the rest for you to solve as you encounter them.

SOLVING PRODUCTION OPERATIONS PROBLEMS

The difficulty of production/operations problems varies. For example, if you need more output, the problem may simply be too little machine capacity or too few workers. On the other hand, if you have persistent quality control problems, it may be more difficult to uncover the cause of the problem, and even more troublesome to solve it. The persistent problems General Motors has had with its Vega production lines are a vivid case in point. Generally speaking, we suggest you approach production/operations problem analysis as follows:

1. Specifically, what is the nature of the required production tasks? Which of the five dimensions are relatively more important? Why?
2. How well is the production system performing these tasks now?
3. If not satisfactorily, is it a system design problem and/or an operating problem? (A system design problem could be trying to run what should be a continuous process as a job shop. An operating problem could be poor control of raw materials inventory.) If the problem seems to include system design and operations, begin with the system design issues first.
4. Within each area—system design and system operation—what specifically seems to be the problem? How do these problems relate to nonsatisfactory production performance?
5. What alternatives appear to exist to improve the effectiveness and efficiency of the system?
6. What are the advantages and disadvantages of each alternative? (View these in terms of the costs involved, the likely impact on performance, the problems of implementation and the reactions of other areas in the firm such as finance.)
7. What recommendations do you have either for improving the existing produc-

tion/operations system or changing to a new system? How will you know if they were worthwhile?

We've attempted to summarize the material in this chapter in a diagram, Exhibit 1. This diagram, on p. 342, shows the major aspects of production/operations management to consider when examining any production/operations system, regardless of its size or complexity.

Exhibit 1
Production/Operations Management

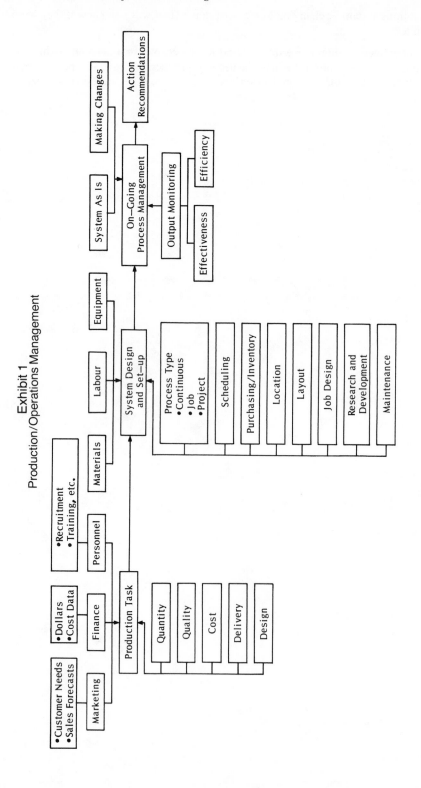

37

Bankruptcy

Bob Wilcox had just been assigned a new job, production manager—Games and Toys, for the Exemplar Manufacturing Co. Previously, Bob had worked as a foreman in another division of Exemplar for seven years. Exemplar had several well-established product lines and was beginning to diversify into new areas. Bob's superior, the general production manager, asked him to work with the new products manager on the latest new product, code-named *Bankruptcy*. *Bankruptcy* was a new adult game that marketing seemed to think would be an immense success, competing with board games such as *Diplomacy* and *Monopoly*. Bob would be responsible for designing and controlling the manufacturing of *Bankruptcy*.

An Exemplar staff member, John Duncan, informed Bob that the basic tasks to be performed were assembling components purchased from other manufacturers. In repeated attempts John was able to assemble completed versions of *Bankruptcy* in fifteen minutes. He also found that if three workers performed only two assembly operations each, instead of all six, each operation could be completed in half the time shown below. Thus, while one person working alone could produce thirty-two games a day, a team of three people working together could produce 192 games of *Bankruptcy* per day. The assembly operations could be performed in any order. The time required and material costs of the various components for each operation were given to Bob as follows:

Assembly Operation	Time Required For One Man Working Alone	For a Three-Man Team	Material Cost
A	1 minute	½ minute	$ .50
B	4 minutes	2 minutes	1.25
C	2 minutes	1 minute	.25
D	2 minutes	1 minute	.50
E	3 minutes	1½ minutes	2.50
F	3 minutes	1½ minutes	5.00
	15 minutes	7½ minutes	$10.00

All materials could usually be obtained within one week of being ordered. On occasion, materials could take up to two weeks to be delivered. The vice-president of finance recently had sent around a memo to managers asking that all inventories be kept at minimum sizes since costs for the company had risen substantially. He asked to be informed of all investment needs exceeding $10 000

Plenty of semiskilled personnel were available in the Exemplar area at a starting rate of $3 per hour (including benefits). Normal hours at Exemplar were 7:30 A.M. to 4:00 P.M. with thirty minutes for lunch. Thus, each worker was paid an average of $24 per day. Considering that on average there were twenty working days in a month, this worked out to $480 per month. Bob was told he could hire as many workers as he thought he needed and pay them on whatever basis he wished so long as he did not exceed the plant average of $4.50 per hour regular time for semiskilled labour. Overtime, if used, was calculated at time and a half.

Bob was allotted space in the plant of 50 ft by 20 ft and told he could arrange his operations as he saw fit. The department would be charged $2.40 a sq ft per year for the entire space allotted. Additional space required beyond the 1000 sq ft was also available, but would be charged to his operation at $3.60 per sq ft per year. The raw materials inventory (at $10 per unit) and finished goods inventory (valued at material cost plus labour cost) required roughly the same amount of cubic space. As the boxes were fairly bulky, he could store the equivalent of only six units of *Bankruptcy* on each square foot of floor space, assuming he piled them as high as possible. John Duncan told Bob he figured they would need 500 sq ft for assembly operations including tables, work stations, lockers, etc. Other fixed manufacturing overhead costs associated with *Bankruptcy* were estimated to be $2060 per month.

The new products manager told Bob that the marketing department forecasted a demand of 3600 units per month for at least the first year. This could vary from 3000 to 4000 in any given month. He also stressed that as *Bankruptcy* was basically an impulse purchase, stock-outs were considered very costly and said he would be after Bob to avoid such situations. The intended selling price was $12 per unit. Marketing fixed costs (mostly for packaging design, advertising, and point of purchase displays) were estimated at $20 000.

Bob was also told that one of his suppliers, Hutchison Ltd., had sent in a quotation of $11 per completed unit to produce the year's requirements of *Bankruptcy* for Exemplar. Their quality was not considered as good as Exemplar's, but they said they were prepared to provide units on any schedule desired. Unfortunately, they added, the delivery time could vary from one to four weeks depending on how busy they were.

38
Canadian Cards Ltd.

Mr. Paul Haskins, general manager of Canadian Cards Ltd., sat back after reading the company's operating statement for July 1974. It showed that the company was still not realizing the profit forecast for its counter line of cards and invitations. Although sales for the year to date were in line with the 1974 sales forecast, and prices had remained firm in spite of increasing competition, the line was producing little profit. Mr. Haskins realized that he had to take action to improve performance in this product area. However, he was not sure whether his problems lay with the work force, inventory, flow of materials, or the nature of the whole production system for the counter line.

RECENT COMPANY HISTORY

Although originally foreign owned, the company had been bought in 1962 by three Canadians who were determined that the firm would remain Canadian owned and grow into a printing industry leader. From its plant in Peterborough the company shipped cards and invitations to a chain of 200 retail dealers all over Canada. Prior to 1972 all sales were of custom printed, personalized stationery, but in 1972 a new line was introduced of eighteen standard items to be sold over the counter by the retail dealers. Sales of the counter line currently accounted for about 10 per cent of the firm's total annual sales of $3 000 000.

CUSTOM STATIONERY PRODUCTS

The major product line marketed by Canadian Cards Ltd. was custom personalized wedding, Christmas and anniversary cards and invitations. There were over 300 items in this line. Retail dealers displayed a catalogue of all the designs available from Canadian Cards Ltd. Customers ordered cards and invitations from the retailer, and left with the retailer the personal message to be printed on the card or invitation. Most orders were for between twenty and one hundred cards of any one item. The retail store forwarded the order to Canadian Cards Ltd. for printing and delivery within seventy-two hours. The company was proud of its order turnaround, which was the fastest of any Canadian firm.

In the Peterborough factory the operations performed to fill a customer order were:

1. Receive order and establish delivery date.
2. Make out work order, and note on card design and customer message.
3. Set type for printing customer message.
4. Select card from raw materials' stock.
5. Print the message on the cards.
6. Inspect and count (done by pressman).
7. Box and address for dispatch.

The layout of the Peterborough plant is shown in Exhibit 1. The custom stationery product line occupied most of the space in the plant. Raw material stocks of cards were purchased from stationery suppliers and stored on shelves next to the printing presses. Supervision in the plant was the responsibility of Mr. Jessel, the plant manager, and his two foremen, one for day shifts and one for nights. These two foremen were responsible for all operations in the plant. The factory management had never set standards of performance for the personalized stationery printing operations since Mr. Jessel felt that each order could be unique, and the printers themselves were skilled and took great pride in their own work.

THE COUNTER LINE BUSINESS

In 1972, Mr. Knowles, the sales director, saw an opportunity for the firm to expand its product line. Young people appeared to want cards and invitations that had space provided for writing in messages and invitations, rather than going to the expense of custom printing. Mr. Knowles decided that the company should market a line of eighteen standard items for weddings, Christmas parties and birthday parties that the retail sales outlets could stock and sell over the counter. He called the line of standard items the "counter line."

Mr. Haskins decided to install a small production line in the Peterborough plant to produce these items. For the first time the company cut and printed its own cards from blank stock. The new line was installed at the end of the factory opposite the main offices. The management of the line was still handled by Mr. Jessel and his two foremen, but a press man and six new girls were hired to operate the line. The average hourly wage rate for the girls was $2.47; the press man could earn up to three times as much.

The procedure for printing and packaging the cards were as follows:

1. An order was initiated when the retail dealer noticed that his counter line stocks needed replenishing. He sent in an order to Canadian Cards stating the items required and the expected delivery. An average order consisted of four counter line items, each for two boxes. A box of counter line cards contained 144 packages. One package contained either twelve or twenty cards, and cost the retailer $.75.

2. The Peterborough sales office noted the required order delivery and made up a work order for the items on the order. This work order was then filed under delivery date.

3. Each day orders were issued to the factory on the basis of delivery date.

4. The work order travelled first to the cutter. The cutter selected the blank card stock from the shelves and cut it to the required order size and quantity.

5. From the cutter the items passed to the printer. Each set-up took approximately half an hour, but varied somewhat depending on the complexity of the colours and the type. The printer then ran each order individually and passed the printed cards through to the counting station. Exhibit 2 shows the work sheet for the printer for the week of July 15, 1974.

6. At the counting station the operator folded the cards and counted them into piles of twelve or twenty. They were then placed on trays and passed to the packaging machine.

7. At the packaging station the cards were placed between two parallel sheets of plastic film. This film was then automatically heat-sealed and cut. The packages dropped into a box behind the machine. A typical work sheet for the packager is shown in Exhibit 3.

8. It was the job of the girl operating the heading machine to pick up the boxes of packages from the packaging station and carry them to her own machine. On the heading machine a paper label was attached to the top of the package which identified the type of card, and the number in the package.

9. From the heading station the cards were carried to the dispatch section, where they were neatly boxed and prepared for shipping.

Initially, the operators experienced some difficulty in making the machines on the line operate correctly. The maintenance man was unfamiliar with the new machines and took longer than normal to repair breakdowns. The girls were unfamiliar with the process of setting the machines up for new package sizes and the packaged cards frequently had to be torn apart and repackaged. However, after several months these problems appeared to be well under control.

After the line had been operating for a year it became apparent to Mr. Jessel that the new line did not perform up to its capacity. Retailers complained that their orders were delivered late and they were losing sales due to stockouts. The foremen reported to Mr. Jessel that the packaging and heading machines were operating at only half their rated capacity. Mr. Jessel and Mr. Haskins discussed the problem and agreed that the time to set up for customer orders was consuming much potential operating time. Mr. Haskins approached Mr. Knowles to see if customers would order in larger quantities, and therefore cut down on the number of orders. Mr. Knowles told Mr. Haskins that the retailers were highly adverse to holding more stock of the counter line.

At the end of 1973, Mr. Haskins instituted a second shift on the counter line in an attempt to cut down on the order backlog. Production from this new shift was very slow and he received several complaints of shortages in the packets of cards from retailers. Often there were twenty envelopes and only eighteen cards in a package.

Mr. Haskins realized that to increase the profitability of the line some action would have to be taken to increase output without increasing costs. Several courses of action appeared to be available. One was to put full-time supervision on the line in an attempt to increase the rate of work and reduce the counting errors. Alternatively, he could ask Mr. Jessel to study ways of speeding up delivery of customer orders although he was not clear how this could be done. Nevertheless, he thought that a study of the counter line business might indicate ways of improving the line's operations.

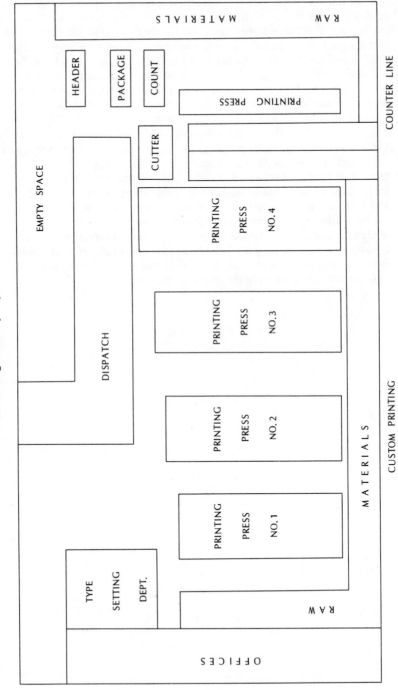

Exhibit 1
Canadian Cards Limited
Peterborough Factory Layout

Exhibit 2
Canadian Cards Ltd.
Work Sheet

Press No. 5—Counter Line—Morning Shift
Week Beginning Monday July 15, 1974

	Order No.	Quantity	Item No.	Time on	Time off	Comments
Mon. 15	74/1225	1300 cards	CL17	8:00	8:50	Part Lot
	74/1361	2880 cards	CL10	9:30	10:50	
	74/1281	1750 cards	CL4	11:30	12:20	
	74/1311	2880 cards	CL16	1:25	3:00	
	74/1312	2400 cards	CL12	3:45	4:00	Part Lot
Tue. 16	74/1410	1750 cards	CL10	8:40	9:35	
	74/1375	2800 cards	CL11	10:00	11:30	
	74/1376	1750 cards	CL1	12:05	2:15	
	74/1380	2050 cards	CL15	3:00	4:00	Part Lot
Wed. 17	74/1292	2150 cards	CL8	8:00	9:15	Part Lot
	74/1327	1750 cards	CL10	9:40	10:40	
	74/1355	1950 cards	CL1	11:05	12:00	
	74/1356	1750 cards	CL16	1:00	2:15	
	74/1420	2880 cards	CL2	2:35	4:00	
Thur. 18	74/1409	300 cards	CL5	8:00	8:15	Part Lot
	74/1412	1000 cards	CL7	8:35	9:20	*Rush* Part-Order
	74/1346	1750 cards	CL4	9:50	10:45	
	74/1342	2900 cards	CL9	11:15	12:25	
	74/1414	2900 cards	CL12	1:20	3:00	
	74/1400	1400 cards	CL13	3:20	4:00	Part Lot
Fri. 19	74/1390	2900 cards	CL16	8:15	10:10	
	74/1391	800 cards	CL10	10:30	11:00	*Rush* Part-Order
	74/1436	1750 cards	CL3	11:15	12:15	
	74/1323	1750 cards	CL7	1:10	2:00	
	74/1324	1000 cards	CL1	2:15	2:45	*Rush* Part-Order
	74/1350	1750 cards	CL2	3:10	4:00	
	74/1350	1750 cards	CL2	3:10	4:00	

12:30-1:00 Lunch
Time on is start-up time

Exhibit 3
Canadian Cards Ltd.
Packager—Counter Line—Morning Shift
Week Beginning Monday July 15, 1974

	Order No.	Quantity	Item No.	Time on	Time off
Mon. 15	74/1250	144 pkg.	CL10	10:10	10:40
	74/1241	144 pkg.	CL6	11:00	11:15
	74/1266	144 pkg.	CL2	11:25	11:50
	74/1267	288 pkg.	CL17	12:00	1:20
	74/1270	144 pkg.	CL18	1:40	2:00
	IDLE	—	—	2:00	4:00
Tue. 16	74/1325	288 pkg.	CL17	8:00	9:00
	IDLE	—	—	9:00	10:20
	74/1306	144 pkg.	CL4	10:20	10:45
	74/1311	144 pkg.	CL16	10:55	11:20
	74/1312	144 pkg.	CL12	11:30	11:45
	74/1313	288 pkg.	CL4	12:00	1:10
	74/1281	133 pkg.	CL4	1:10	1:30
	74/1410	144 pkg.	CL10	1:45	2:10
	IDLE	—	—	2:10	4:00
Wed. 17	MAINTENANCE	—	—	8:00	10:30
	74/1380	288 pkg.	CL15	10:40	11:40
	74/1381	288 pkg.	CL16	11:50	1:20
	74/1375	144 pkg.	CL11	1:35	2:00
	74/1376	144 pkg.	CL1	2:10	2:25
	74/1377	288 pkg.	CL6	2:35	3:25
	74/1378	144 pkg.	CL7	3:30	4:00
Thur. 18	74/1327	144 pkg.	CL10	8:05	8:25
	IDLE	—	—	8:25	9:00
	74/1292	144 pkg.	CL8	9:05	9:20
	74/1355	144 pkg.	CL1	9:35	10:00

Exhibit 4
Canadian Cards Ltd.
Organization Chart

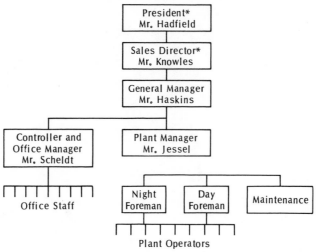

* Founder

39
Difton Cleaners Ltd.

In the beginning of 1957, Difton Cleaners had just finished its second year of unprofitable operation, and a worse year lay ahead. Located in a major Ontario city, Difton Cleaners had been a highly profitable operation until the founding manager's death in 1951. Since then sales and profits had declined. In 1957 David Barnes, a grandson of the founder, became interested in taking over active management of the firm when his mother was unable to sell it. David knew that the cost of wages in the plant was about 50 per cent of manufacturing cost and that the industry average for plants similar to Difton's was 33 per cent. He hoped that changes could be made in the plant to bring the cost of wages down to the industry average.

David Barnes had worked eight summers in the plant at almost every job and knew the operations well. He summed up the company's main problem as follows:

"The company has been losing money for the past two years. Its current ratio is 1:0 and the bank manager has already expressed his concern about a $4000 loan the company is not able to pay off. The company is three or four months overdue on the bills of some supplies at the same time. The main source of funds, incoming orders, are decreasing. Competitors are offering same-day and one-day service while Difton offers three-day service. And to add to our problems manufacturing costs are continually rising. The only way this company can survive is to have some drastic changes made which will reduce costs and increase sales."

SUMMARY OF DIFTON OPERATIONS

Buildings and Grounds

The main plant was built around 1930. This 60 ft by 80 ft brick exterior, building block interior, building had a main floor and basement floor of equal size. It stood on the northwest corner of a valuable 130 ft by 140 ft corner lot on a main thoroughfare. The building was in a good state of repair, but the interior walls in the plant had never been cleaned or painted. The centre of the main plant was used as a storage area for unclaimed orders. A store was located in the northwest corner of the building. Apart from this main store in the plant four other stores were rented near supermarket areas to receive and return customers orders.

Machinery

Most of the machinery in the plant was about thirty years old. An exception was the shirt-finishing machine, purchased in 1954. Although most machines were old, their physical condition was fairly good. An old coal-burning boiler was used for supplying steam: it created a lot of dust and needed to be warmed up for two hours before it could generate the required pressure. Three trucks, each three or four years old, were used for picking up and delivering orders. These trucks appeared to be rusty and dented and looked as though they were in poor condition. David Barnes was afraid he might have to buy at least two new trucks within the next year.

Staff

The company employed thirty-four people, five in outlying stores, and twenty-nine in the main plant and main store. The casewriter's conception of what an organization chart would probably look like is shown in Exhibit 1.

The accountant looked after payroll, the payment of bills and the checking of all customer receipts. David Barnes said, "He is a good man, but is generally busy only 30 per cent of the time." The steam engineer tended the boiler, a job which occupied about 10 per cent of his time. Provincial safety regulations specified that for this type of boiler a certified steam engineer, Grade 4, was required. There was one man occupied in miscellaneous tasks. He could do any job in the plant and was, therefore, valuable as a substitute in case other employees became sick or were absent for other reasons. The plant superintendent hired and laid off staff, supervised operations and at busy times often helped with the pressing of men's clothes. He usually was busy about 20 per cent of his time in the plant.

About ten key employees were paid a straight salary for the whole year with the understanding that they could go home early when finished their work during the slack season (see Exhibit 5) and that they must work overtime at no extra pay during the busy season. They usually worked overtime for about ten days each year. The remainder of the staff worked for hourly wages. Take-home pay varied from about $20 per week for the lower paid girls to $45 per week for pressers. In 1955 and 1956 payroll amounted to 50 per cent of total operating cost. Most of the labour force was of non-Canadian origin and lived in working-class sections of the city. Many of them had at least a few years of service with Difton. David Barnes thought that labour costs at Difton were far too high, since the industry average of labour cost was 33 per cent of operating costs.

Layout and Work Flow

The plant layout is shown in Exhibit 3. Exhibit 4 gives a summary of the flow of dry cleaning through the whole plant. The following paragraphs, describing the movement of a typical customer's order from the moment it is received in the main store until the customer picks it up again, serve as a further clarification and an elaboration of Exhibits 3 and 4.

Invoicing and Marking

David Barnes explained the plant operation and included his own opinion of each operation and the people who performed them. "Assume for illustrative purposes," he said, "that a customer comes into the main store one Monday morning and brings the following items to be cleaned and pressed:

1 wool suit (dark, coat and pants)
1 overcoat
2 cotton dresses (light)
1 white nylon scarf
2 shirts

"One of the three girls who look after the counter writes out an invoice with the name and address and itemized account of the order. She tears off the thin strip at the top of the invoice bearing the invoice number C784 326[1] and gives it to the customer and tells him he can come on Thursday to pick up his order. She ties the shirts together and also bundles the dry cleaning order in the overcoat with the invoice in the pocket. Both bundles are put behind her. The counter girls just stay at the counter, which most of the time is not busy. Just the 8:00 A.M. and the 5:00 P.M. rush require their full time. One of the girls

---

[1] C784 326 designates main store or origin of the order. The other stores and truck routes have similar letter and number combinations. Each invoice also has the name of the store printed on it.

marking in picks up the dry cleaning bundle and carries it to the marking bench. There she registers the whole order in a ledger in duplicate. She also writes the invoice number C784 326 on as many small cards as there are pieces of dry cleaning, six in this particular order. On the two tags for the suit she writes coat and pants to facilitate identification during final assembly of the order. She then pins each card with a small safety pin in a predesignated place on each piece of clothing (on the back of trousers, inside pocket of the coat, back of the collar of the dresses). Finally, she checks all pockets, removes buttons which could be damaged and puts them in a small envelope which she sends to the sewing girl. She also wraps leather buttons with tinfoil. She takes the invoice and puts it in a box on the wall marked Thursday. And then she throws the clothes in a bin on small wheels or on the floor. (These two girls are busier than the counter girls, but each still is idle about one-quarter of the time.)''

Prespotting and Dry Cleaning

''The prespotter takes the bin of clothes to his spotting board. There he attempts to remove the worst stains and spots, using special solvents. He then dumps the prespotted clothes into piles of heavy clothing, one pile of pants, one of jackets, one of overcoats, and into one or two piles of light clothing, cottons in one, synthetics in another. The original order C784 326 is probably now separated into five piles. There are three dry cleaning machines with capacities of 100 lbs, 55 lbs, and 35 lbs. One of the cleaning room workers puts in the right weight for a load in each machine as it becomes available. After a cleaning period of half an hour the clothes are moved to the extractor to extract the cleaning solvent, and then to the tumblers to dry. When a batch is removed from the tumblers the worker examines each piece for spots and if any spots still show, the piece may be respotted and/or recleaned. The batch of lights or heavies is then taken to the finishers or the pressers, where it is dumped on a table, a sawhorse, or on the floor. (The prespotter is usually busy all the time. The cleaning room crew is usually free for the first half hour in the morning, and throughout the day at least one man is usually idle).''

Pressing or Finishing

''Most of the girl pressers finish women's clothes while the man pressers work mainly on men's clothes. Each presser picks up a piece of clothing, places it on a press or ironing board, positions it carefully and presses it. The piece of clothing is repositioned and pressed again until completely finished. The presser examines each piece for buttons, stains or minor repairs. If repairs need to be made the piece is taken to the sewing girl, who makes the repairs. The floorlady inspects the work of the sewing girl and the pressers to make sure that good quality work is being performed. She also helps at busy times with any task. The presser hangs the finished piece of clothing on an overhead rail made of hollow tubing. After having completed five or six pieces the presser carries them to the 'well' rail and lets them slide downstairs. (One of the men pressers works very slowly and one of the girl pressers does a lot of poor-quality work which she has to do again. The floorlady does not really inspect each piece produced.)''

Assembling

''Downstairs three girls assemble the orders on a number of overhead rails. From the tag of each piece coming down, the assembler finds out the number of the original invoice. She hollers the number to one girl sitting at a desk with the duplicate pages of the ledger used for marking in. This girl crosses through, for example, the pants of order C784 326.

This first piece of the order to come down is then hung on the unfinished order rail. The original invoice, found in the box marked Thursday and emptied the day before, is attached to it. As more pieces come down they are added until the whole order is complete. The order is by then completely crossed out on the duplicate ledger page and is moved to the finished order rail for the main store.

"Other orders have in the meantime been handled the same way. The trucking supervisor takes an armful of finished orders, removes the invoice, puts a paper bag over the whole order and attaches the invoice to the paper bag. He then returns the bagged order to the finished order rail. Finished orders for the truck routes or the outlying stores are taken up the back stairs to the ramp by the truck drivers. Main store orders are taken up the centre steps to the storage area opposite the marking-in bench where they are hung in numerical order. (This assembly of orders is a real headache, the girls are busy practically all the time, they get flustered and combine the wrong orders. This is easily done. I've done it myself. If some way could be found to eliminate this confusion I would go for it.)"

Shirts

"One of the four girls working on shirts takes the bundles of shirts from behind the counter to the downstairs washing area. There she records the order in a ledger, marks each shirt with a small tag through the third buttonhole and puts six shirts in a nylon bag. If any shirts need not be starched they are kept in a separately tagged nylon bag. She puts about ten bags of shirts in a washer and removes the tagged bags before starching the remainder of the washer. She then removes the bags from the washer, takes out the shirts and takes them upstairs. Two girls work on a shirt-finishing machine upstairs and one girl puts the shirts in a bag, and attaches the invoice to the bag. When a number of orders are complete, she takes the bags to the front store where she puts them under the counter and in shelves along the wall. (All of the shirt girls do a good job and work hard. I wish the rest of the plant worked as efficiently as this group.)"

Checking Out

"When the customer comes on Thursday to pick up the order, he hands in the top of the invoice and the shirt receipt. The counter girl hands him the orders, receives payment and removes the invoices and puts them on a pin. The invoices are checked against receipts the following morning by the accountant and the counter girls' supervisor. (This supervisor is a wonderful girl. She has personality, and is always willing to work. She can do the accountant's job just as well as the accountant can do it. A customer who has lost a receipt creates many problems because all orders are hung numerically according to invoice number. And the customer who comes in a day or so early and for special reasons wishes to hurry up the order or wants to take the clothes out may well start a three-hour search through every pile of clothing in the plant.)"

Financial Situation

Exhibit 2 shows sales, costs and profit figures for Difton Cleaners from 1951 to 1957. David Barnes explained the financial situation in few words, "The current ratio is 1.0, Difton has a bank loan of $4000 and is unable to meet the monthly $400 installments. Some supplies bills are three and four months overdue. The bank manager is concerned and I am too."

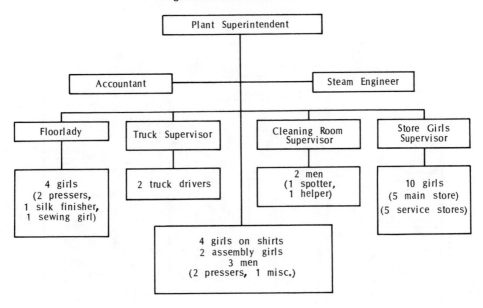

Exhibit 1
Difton Cleaners Limited
Organization Chart March 1957

Exhibit 2
Difton Cleaners Ltd.
Sales, Costs and Profit Figures
Base: 1951 Sales = 100 = $150 000 (approx.)

	Sales	Costs	Profits			Sales	Costs	Profits
1951	100	80	20		1954	95	94	1
1952	97	86	11		1955	94	98	−4
1953	96	91	5		1956	93	98	−5

Exhibit 3

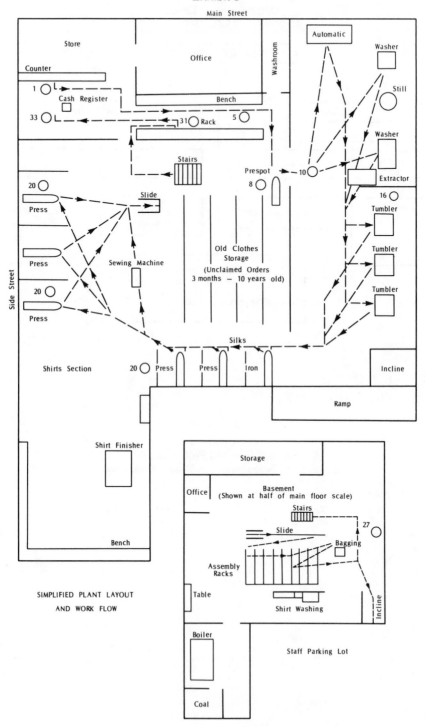

Main Street

Store

Counter

Office

Washroom

Automatic

Washer

1

Cash Register

Bench

Still

33

31 Rack

5

Washer

Stairs

Prespot

10

Extractor

8

16

20

Press

Slide

Tumbler

Side Street

Press

Sewing Machine

Old Clothes
Storage

(Unclaimed Orders
3 months — 10 years old)

Tumbler

20

Press

Tumbler

Silks

Shirts Section

20

Press   Press   Iron

Incline

Ramp

Shirt Finisher

Storage

Office

Basement
(Shown at half of main floor scale)

Stairs

27

Slide

Bagging

Assembly
Racks

SIMPLIFIED PLANT LAYOUT
AND WORK FLOW

Table

Shirt Washing

Bench

Incline

Boiler

Staff Parking Lot

Coal

Exhibit 4
Difton Cleaners Ltd.
Process Chart, Main Store and Plant
March 1957

Distance in feet	Symbol	Description	Time	Performed by
	1 O	Invoicing of order	1-3 min	3 counter girls
	2 D	Wait to be moved	5-60 min	2 marking girls
25	3 M	To marking in area	30-60 sec	
	4 D	Wait to be marked	5 sec-6 hrs	
	5 O	Marking in	1-5 min/order	2 marking girls
	6 D	Wait to be moved	5 min-3 hrs	
22	7 M	To prespotting	30 sec-2 min	prespotter
	8 O	Prespotting	10 sec-5 min/garment	prespotter
	9 D	Wait on floor	10 min-6 hrs	
	10 O	Separating into piles	5 min-15 min/pile	cleaning room foreman
	11 D	Wait in piles	10 min-14 hrs	
10-20	12 M	To washers	15-16 sec	2 helpers
	13 O	Washing	20-30 min Auto Cycle	
	(13a)	(If washing was not done in the automatic machine, clothes were moved to the extractor, where most of the cleaning fluid was extracted before tumbling.)	Wash 1.5 hrs Extract—15 min	
15-40	14 M	To tumblers	1-5 min	2 helpers
	15 D	Wait for tumblers	1 min-30 min	
	16 O	Tumbling	45-55 min	
	17 I	Removal and inspection	5-15 min/load	2 helpers
20-60	18 M	To finishers (pressers)	15 sec-3 min	2 helpers
	19 D	Wait for pressing	5 min-4 hrs	
	20 O	Press and inspect	2-20 min/garment	6 finishers
12-20	21aM	To sewing girl for repairs or/and then	1 min-2 min garment	6 finishers
10-20	21bM	To downstairs	1 min-2 min/load	6 finishers
	22 O	Wait to be assembled	5 min-1hr	2 assemblers
15-20	23 M	To assembler rail	30 sec-2 min/garment	2 assemblers
	24 D	Wait for rest of order	1 hr-12 hrs	
8-20	25 M	To finished order rail	15 sec-3 min/order	trucking supervisor
10-30	26 M	To bagging	10-30 sec/load	trucking supervisor
	27 O	Bagging	10-30 sec/load	trucking supervisor
10-30	28 M	To finished order rail	1 hr-12 hrs	
	29 D	Wait to be moved	1 min-3 hrs	
30-70	30 M	Moved to store or truck	15 min-2 hrs	2 truckers
	31 O	Hung in numerical order	1 hr-1 day	3 counter girls
	32 D	Wait for customer	2-4 min/order	
	33 O	Return to customer and receive payment		3 counter girls

Explanation of Symbols

O Operation   D Delay
M Move   I Inspection

Exhibit 5
Difton Cleaners Ltd.

Notes on the Dry Cleaning Industry

Dry cleaning is the process of cleaning wearing apparel, household furnishings and other articles made of wool, silk, rayon and related fabrics. Dirt, stains and spots are removed by the chemical action of organic solvents and special detergents, as contrasted with laundering in soap and water.

The industry is recognized for its low wages and high labour turnover. Cleaning room operators, spotters and pressers could be roughly defined as semiskilled workers and the remainder of the work force as day labourers. Increased mechanization in the past few years has resulted in a high percentage of female employees. A great deal of steam is required for the various operations and consequently the term "sweatshop" literally applies to the dry cleaning plant. Air cooling systems are in use in many plants but do not seem to be totally effective in dealing with this problem.

In the past, the practice of stealing employees was very common. Whenever one dry cleaner was short a presser or silk finisher, for example, he would stand outside his competitor's door and offer a nickel an hour more to one of the pressers or silk finishers. The competitor would be outside the first dry cleaner's door with the same pitch the next night. This practice not only led to higher wages, but also ended up with all the dry cleaners in a particular area on unfriendly terms with each other. The recently formed Dry Cleaners Association has done much to prevent this practice and to promote the industry.

Demand for dry cleaning varies considerably throughout the year in Canada. January, February, June and July are slack months and sales in the months of May and September are usually double the sales in January and February.

40
Fish Forwarders

A. THE SITUATION

Fish Forwarders supplies fresh shrimp to a variety of customers in the New Orleans area. It places orders for cases of shrimp from fleet representatives at the beginning of each week to meet a demand from its customers at the middle of the week. The shrimp are subsequently delivered to Fish Forwarders and then, at the end of the week, to its customers.

Both the weekly supply of, and demand for, shrimp are uncertain. The *supply* may vary as much as 10 per cent from the amount ordered, and, by contract, Fish Forwarders must purchase this supply. Fish Forwarders has determined that the probability of this variation is as follows:

-10 per cent from amount ordered : 30 per cent of the time
0 per cent from amount ordered : 50 per cent of the time
$+10$ per cent from amount ordered : 20 per cent of the time

Similarly, the *demand* for shrimp varies as follows:

600 cases : 5 per cent of the time
700 cases : 15 per cent of the time
800 cases : 60 per cent of the time
900 cases : 15 per cent of the time
1000 cases : 5 per cent of the time

A case of shrimp costs Fish Forwarders $30 and it sells for $50. Any shrimp not sold at the end of the week are sold to a cat food company at $4 per case. Fish Forwarders may, if it chooses, order the shrimp "flash-frozen" by the supplier at dockside, but this raises the cost of a case by $4, and hence costs Fish Forwarders $34 per case. Flash freezing enables Fish Forwarders to maintain an inventory of shrimp, but it costs $2 per case per week to store the shrimp at a local icehouse. The customers are indifferent to whether they get regular or flash-frozen shrimp. Fish Forwarders figures that its shortage cost is equal to its markup; that is, each case demanded but not available costs the company $50−$30 or $20.

B. OBJECTIVES

To manage inventory and purchasing policies to make the maximum possible gain.

C. PROCEDURE FOR IN-CLASS EXERCISE

This exercise will be conducted in class. *Prior to class,* you are expected to study this situation and formulate some decision rules to maximize your gain. The instructor, using a random procedure, will tell you what supply you received and what demand you faced each week. There will be short pauses "each week" during the exercise, but you should be prepared to make reasonably quick decisions. You will have to decide how many cases to order of regular shrimp and flash-frozen shrimp each week and enter orders and results in Exhibit 1. The order quantity of each may be any amount. Assume that there is *no opening inventory* of flash-frozen shrimp.

Reprinted with permission from Chase and Aquilano, *Production and Operations Management,* Revised Edition (Homewood, Ill: Richard D. Irwin. Inc., 1977 c.).

Steps in the exercise:

1. Decide on the order amount of regular shrimp and/or flash-frozen shrimp and enter the figures in column 3 of Exhibit 1.
2. The instructor then will tell you what variation there was in the supply received. The same variation applies to both regular and frozen shrimp orders. For example, if you ordered 1000 regular and 100 frozen, and were told the variation was −10 per cent, you would receive 900 regular and 90 frozen shrimps. You enter the amount received in column 4 of Exhibit 1.
3. Add the amount of flash-frozen shrimp in inventory, if any, (as shown in column 2) to the quantity of regular and frozen shrimps just received and enter the total in column 5. This shows how much is available for sale that week.
4. The instructor will then tell you what the demand for shrimp was that week. Enter this amount in column 6.
5. Determine the amount sold. This will be the minimum of column 5 (amount available) or column 6 (amount demanded). Enter this quantity in column 7.
6. Determine the excess. The amount of excess is simply that quantity remaining, if any, after demand for a given week is filled. Always assume that regular shrimp are sold before frozen shrimp.
7. Determine shortages (unfulfilled demand). This is the amount demand exceeds quantity available for sale each week and it occurs only when demand is greater than sales (column 6 greater than column 7). Since all customers use the shrimp within the week in which they are delivered, back orders are not relevant. Enter the amount of shortages in column 9.
8. After repeating this procedure for the specified number of weeks, determine your economic gain using Exhibit 2 as a guide.

Exhibit 1
Fish Forwarders
Worksheet

(1) Week	(2) Flash Frozen Inventory	(3) Orders Placed		(4) Order Received		(5) Available For Sale		(6) Demand	(7) Sales (Min. of Col.5 and Col.6)	(8) Excess		(9) Shortages (If Col.6 Exceeds Col.5)
		Regular	Flash Frozen	Regular	Flash Frozen	Regular	(Col.2 + Col.4) Flash Frozen			Regular	Flash Frozen	
1												
2												
3												
4												
5												
6												
7												
8												
9												
10												
Total												

EXHIBIT 2
Fish Forwarders
Economic Gain

Revenues

    1. From sales: _____ cases (Col. 7) × \$50   = \$_____

    2. From sales: _____ cases (Col. 8, Reg.) × \$4   = \$_____
       (to cat food)

    3. Total   (1 + 2)   \$_____

Costs

    4. Regular purchases: _____ cases (Col. 4, reg.) × \$30   = \$_____

    5. Frozen purchases: _____ cases (Col. 4, froz.) × \$34   = \$_____

    6. Holding frozen
         shrimp in
         inventory: _____ cases (Col. 8, froz.) × \$2   = \$_____

    7. Total   (4 + 5 + 6)   \$_____

    8. Net profit   (3 − 8)   \$_____

    9. Less: Economic loss
        from shortages: _____ cases (Col. 9) ×\$20   =   \$_____

  10. Net economic gain   (8 − 9)   \$_____

41

Haitian Rebar Co. (A)

In January 1968, five months after the start of a melt shop at Haitian Rebar, Mr. John Duncan, plant manager, received a request from Mr. Lord, melt shop superintendent, to purchase two additional ladles.

COMPANY BACKGROUND

In 1964 Mr. Lawrence Murray and two friends studied the feasibility of producing reinforcing steel in Port-au-Prince, Haiti. Haiti, population five million, covered one-third of the island of Hispaniola; the Dominican Republic occupied the remainder. Following independence from France in 1804, the Haitians fought a long and bitter struggle for political stability and economic independence. Haiti had developed its major industries of coffee, sugar, cotton and citrus products. In 1952 a Canadian and an American firm established mining companies for copper and bauxite which by 1964 employed 1100 workers. Mr. Murray, a twenty-year resident of Haiti, had worked in the Canadian company since 1953. Construction of homes and office buildings increased during the 1950s and in 1964 this industry employed about 11 000 workers. Mr. Murray had followed this economic and industrial development closely and believed there was a market for locally produced construction steel. Consequently, early in 1965 the three friends founded the Haitian Rebar Company and hired an American expert to design a plant. Reinforcing steel was to be produced from scrap, converted in an electric furnace and formed in a rolling mill.

In 1966 the company obtained from government the right to operate as a monopoly. As soon as the local company became productive, the government agreed to cut off all construction steel imports and all scrap steel exports.

Plant construction was started in 1966 and completed in August 1967. The electric furnace cost $250 000 and the rolling mill $1 200 000.[1] The immediate objective was to produce quality steel for sale on the local market by January 1968.

Mr. Murray and his partners had decided on the following policies before operations were begun. All scrap deliveries from local and country vendors would be accepted on a sliding price scale depending on grading and preparation time. Minimum price per ton would be $5 and the maximum $15. On the selling side the company established a minimum order quantity of 200 tons, and promised a three-month delivery on all shipments of not less than 20 tons. Terms were cash with order, with discounts on orders over 500 and 1000 tons. Six bar sizes were to be produced. These fell into three distinct ranges: 1 in and ⅞ in; ¾ in and ⅝ in; ½ in and ⅜ in. The selling price for one ton of 1 inch bars was set at $110.

The recruitment and training of labour and staff were difficult, because no similar industry existed on the island. As a first step, Mr. Murray hired three experienced steel makers from the United States and Canada: a plant manager, melt shop superintendent and rolling mill superintendent. Mr. Murray and his management team then met to discuss hiring and training criteria for the foremen and work force. They reviewed a number of applications and passed the final selections to a doctor and a psychiatrist. Emphasis was not placed on any prior industrial experience but on literacy, past work records (attendance and job changes) and the expressed willingness and ability of the applicants to work. The

---

[1] All figures shown in this case are in U.S. dollars. The Haitian currency conversion in 1966 was 5 gourdes = $1 U.S.

company started with a skeleton force of fifty non-union labourers. A crew of fifteen men started immediately on scrap preparation. Another fifteen concentrated on melt shop start up while the remainder were assigned to the rolling mill and essential services. The wage scale was slightly above the industry average for Port-au-Prince. Wages for unskilled work averaged $.40 per hour and skilled work averaged $.60 per hour. The skeleton crew started during the equipment installation phase in the plant in order to learn about the machinery and how it operated. Just before plant completion, management and workers held discussions and seminars on steel making and practised job duties and responsibilities using simulated runs on the equipment.

PROCESS START UP

The first stage of the manufacturing process involved scrap steel preparation, furnace refining and pouring ingots. The second stage involved ingot reheating and mill rolling. The company planned to start up regular production in two steps: the melt shop first, followed four months later by the rolling mill. Before full-scale rolling could be started the melt shop had to build up an inventory of in-process ingots and the melt could only operate on a restricted hourly basis. The furnace required large amounts of electricity (approximately 575 kwh/ton), and the Haitian government restricted the company's use of the furnace to 10:30 P.M. to 6:30 A.M. Monday-Friday and on weekends from 6:30 A.M. Saturday to 6:30 A.M. Monday. Government officials promised that a new electrical substation would be built by early 1969, which would allow the company potential twenty-four-hour operation, seven days a week.

Rebar produced the first ingots from the melt shop in August 1967. Management planned to operate initially on a one-shift basis. The scrap preparation crew worked eight hours a day, five days a week and the melt shop crew worked eight hours for four nights and ten hours on Saturday and Sunday.

In the first few months the rolling mill worked eight hours a day, five days a week on experimental runs on all sizes except ⅜ in bar.

MELT SHOP PROCESS

The melt shop process involved four distinct operations: scrap preparation, refining, ladling and pouring of ingots (Exhibit 1).

Scrap preparation was divided into sorting and sizing. Sorting included separating the cast iron and high carbon content steels from the better grades of scrap. Sizing was required to bring pieces down to manageable proportions. This normally meant cutting into 3-ft lengths. The size and the quality of the scrap caused variations in the size of charging loads and melting times in the furnace. A large electric magnet operating from an overhead crane loaded the scrap into the three charging buckets. Each charging bucket weighed 7 tons, could carry 5000 lbs of scrap and was designed with a false bottom for top charging the furnace (Exhibit 2).

Refining took place in a direct arc electric furnace. The furnace occupied half of a concrete pit 30 ft by 15 ft by 6 ft. Its mounting allowed tilting to 35° for tapping[2] and 15° in the opposite direction for adding refining agents and drawing off slag. The roof swung away during charging. Three carbon electrodes arced with the metal and melted the scrap (Exhibit 3). Refining time depended primarily on the ability of the metal to conduct the heat through the furnace and ranged from two to five hours. Loads were charged successively; after the first had melted, the second was added and the third load followed the

---

[2] Tapping is the process of pouring molten steel from the furnace to a ladle.

same way. The electrodes required about twenty minutes to enter the bath with each charge accompanied by tremendous noise as arcing took place. While refining carbon, manganese, silicon, chromium and limestone were added and metallurgical analyses performed.

When the heat reached the required temperature (2900°F) and composition, a second overhead crane placed a ladle in the pit beside the furnace ready for tapping. The crane then placed the full ladle in the travelling pouring cradle on the teeming[3] line. The cradle (Exhibit 4) was a square metal structure, open both top and bottom and mounted on four railway wheels. This supported the ladle as each mould along the line was teemed using the top pouring method (Exhibit 5). The overhead crane removed the red-hot ingots from the moulds and placed them in piles. After an hour's cooling a fork lift truck carried them to the ingot storage yard in the back of the plant (Exhibit 6).

Exhibit 7 summarizes melting equipment and labour.

LADLING OPERATION

The laid-down cost of the three ladles at Rebar was $10 000. Each ladle weighed 5 tons and could hold 16 tons of molten steel. The circular cross section, tapering inwards from top to bottom, was lined with a double layer of fire brick called refractory (Exhibit 8). The inner refractory lining protected the steel shell and the outer lining expanded on contact with the melt to form tight joints during pouring. The pouring nozzle was a graphite rod inside a refractory sheath. The pouring lever moved the rod up and down, allowing the molten metal to flow through the pouring refractory into the mould.

At the start of each heat the crane operator put a ladle under the preheater. Each ladle required two to three hours of open flame preheating to reach a temperature close to 2900°F. Twenty minutes before the refining process ended, the crane operator positioned the preheated ladle in the pouring cradle where two operators inserted the preheated pouring nozzle. Placing the nozzle was a key operation in the melt shop. If the nozzle operating mechanism was not well lubricated with graphite and did not move freely, there was a high probability that the nozzle would freeze up during teeming. The crane operator then lowered the ladle into the pit beside the furnace. All personnel cleared the area as the furnace operators started rotating the furnace to tap the molten steel. The crane operator next placed the ladle back in the pouring cradle, unhooked and swung over to place another ladle at the preheater.

Total teeming time normally was fifty minutes. The crane operator removed the empty ladle from the cradle, dumped the remaining skull[4] into a skull pot and finally placed the ladle in the reconditioning area. Two of the cradle operators then burned out the pouring refractory and nozzle using an oxygen flame. Total time, starting with preheating through to nozzle burnout normally required four hours (Exhibit 9). The ladle cooled for the next four hours before a mason started chipping away the remnants of steel and refractory around the pouring hole (Exhibit 10). He then put in new fire bricks so that the pouring refractory and nozzle could be installed after preheating. At the start of Rebar melting shop operations, the mason required three to four hours to replace the pouring refractory. However, as he became familiar with the repair work, he reduced his time to the present industry average of one and one-half hours although occasionally it might take up to two and one-half hours if the ladle was in rough shape.

Normally one of the ladle operators performed the repair and masonry work but

---

[3] Teeming is the process of pouring molten steel from the ladle into ingot moulds.

[4] Skull represents unusable steel. This loss is caused by oxidation in the ladle during the pouring operation. When the nozzle operator sees a bright orange colour, he knows the pour has ended. The remaining melt is skull.

every member of the pouring crew could do this work. In North America, masons usually worked on ladles within two hours after nozzle burnout. Mr. Lord had tried to persuade his men to start masonry work sooner, but they all claimed the ladle was much too hot to work on any earlier.

Material costs for pouring refractory repairs ranged from $25 to $35. Ladle operators became skilled in noticing when the outer refractory lining was deteriorating and informed the melt shop superintendent. Mr. Lord then scheduled a major ladle overhaul (after twenty to twenty-five heats).

Good refractory outer lining was important in protecting the thin inner lining. In extreme cases, the melt could burn through the inner lining to the steel skull and make the ladle non-repairable. The mason required from eight to sixteen hours to overhaul the complete lining. Material costs for major refractory repairs ranged between $500 and $600.

On January 18, 1968, three weeks after the melt shop started two-shift operations (Exhibit 13), Mr. Duncan received a request from Mr. Lord to purchase two new ladles. Mr. Lord said that ladle delays were becoming more frequent as a result of increased furnace efficiency and an increased number of heats per week. He had already installed portable fans to assist in cooling the ladles and still the masons complained about the intense heat. He said that furnace capacity might be limited if no further ladles were purchased.

Mr. Duncan wanted to review the melt shop records (Exhibits 11 and 12) before acting on Mr. Lord's request. He expected thirty heats per week by June 1968, using the same two shifts. He knew that Mr. Murray and his partners were concerned about the amount of money already invested in the mill. Additional requests for funds would, therefore, have to be carefully substantiated. Moreover, he was not sure himself whether the melt shop superintendent had a legitimate case.

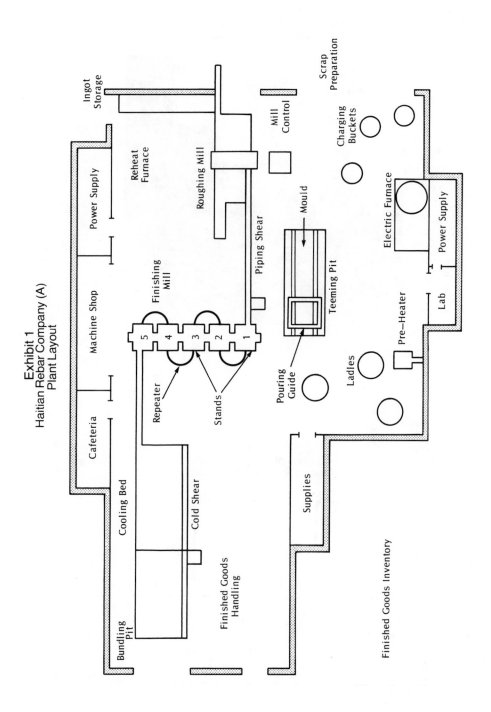

Exhibit 1
Haitian Rebar Company (A)
Plant Layout

Exhibit 2
Haitian Rebar Co. (A)
Melt Shop View Showing Scrap
Piles and Charging Bucket

Exhibit 3
Haitian Rebar Company (A)
Diagram of Arcing Principle in an Electric Furnace

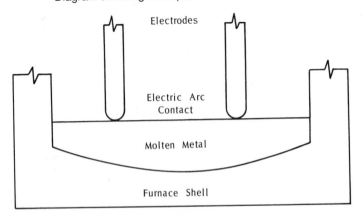

Exhibit 4
Haitian Rebar Co. (A)
Travelling Pouring Cradle and
Mould Line

Exhibit 5
Haitian Rebar Company (A)
Teeming — Top Pouring Method

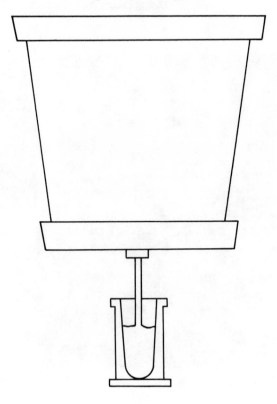

Exhibit 6
Haitian Rebar Co. (A)
Ingot Storage

Exhibit 7
Haitian Rebar Co. (A)
Melt Shop Equipment and Labour Summary

Operation	Equipment	Job Function	Number S = skilled U = unskilled
Prepare scrap	Cutting torches	Sort scrap	10 U
		Cut scrap	5 U
Charging	3 charging buckets	Operate crane	1 S
	Crane	Assist crane operator	1 U
Refining	Electric furnace	Operate furnace	2 S
Ladling	3 ladles	Operate 2nd crane	1 S
	Crane	Assist crane operator	1 U
Pouring	Pouring cradle	Teem moulds, insert hooks,	
	Moulds	prepare moulds and loosen	
		ingots	6 S
Miscellaneous	Fork lift truck	Operate lift truck	1 S
		Prepare hooks	1 U

Exhibit 8
Haitian Rebar Company (A)
Ladle Construction

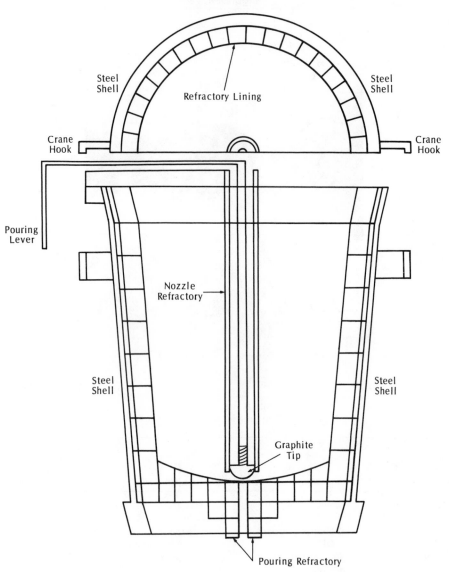

Exhibit 9
Haitian Rebar Co. (A)
Ladling Operations and Times

Operation	Time (minutes)
1. Preheat ladle	120-180
2. Move ladle to cradle and insert nozzle	20-30
3. Move ladle to furnace pit, tap and place back in cradle	20
4. Teem ladle	50
5. Move ladle to reconditioning area, burn out nozzle and pouring refractory	20-30
6. Ladle cooling	240
7. Ladle reconditioning	90-150

Exhibit 10
Haitian Rebar Co. (A)
Ladle Ready for Reconditioning Showing
Broken Pouring Nozzle Refractory

Exhibit 11
Haitian Rebar Co. (A)
Weekly Melt Shop Record—Starting August 20, 1967

Week No.	Total Heats	Ladle No.	Times Used	Charging Weight (lbs)	Melt Time Hrs	Mins	Teeming Weight (lbs) (Ingots Poured × 275)	Total Ingots Poured	Skull and Other Losses (lbs)	Melt Shop Comments
1	7	1	2	156 900	25	35	144 100	524	12 800	Electrical delay 165 min.
		2	2							
		3	3							
2	9	1	3	210 800	28	30	196 075	713	14 725	
		2	3							
		3	3							
3	12	1	4	285 000	37	15	272 255	990	12 745	
		2	4							
		3	4							
4	11	1	4	265 000	32	55	250 350	914	14 650	
		2	4							
		3	3							
5	12	1	3	301 000	37	35	284 859	1 034	16 150	
		2	5							
		3	4							
6	13	1	5	352 000	41	40	321 000	1 168	30 800	Pouring refractory froze—lost 1/3 of one heat.
		2	4							
		3	4							
7	12	1	3	336 000	40	10	296 450	1 078	39 550	
		2	5							
		3	4							
8	12	1	6	327 000	41	00	301 950	1 098	25 050	Defective coil 180 min, broken electrode 30 min, pouring refractory froze.
		2	3							
		3	3							

			1	2	3						Notes
9	16		5	6	5	421 500	41	00	398 200	1 408	34 550	Mechanical and electrode delays 120 min.
10	13		4	5	4	352 800	36	30	328 900	1 196	23 900	Lost one day's production—area power failure
11	14		5	5	4	381 400	31	10	351 725	1 279	30 675	
12	15		4	6	5	406 600	37	50	376 475	1 369	32 125	
13	14		4	5	5	374 800	35	10	330 000	1 200	41 800	Ladle delay 75 min. Furnace roof cave-in. Nozzle freeze-up lost 1/3 of one heat.
14	14		4	5	5	379 450	39	55	338 250	1 230	41 200	
15	10		3	3	4	279 400	24	35	264 275	961	15 125	Ladle delays 150 min. Bad furnace and ladle bottom.
16	18		8	8	2	534 200	51	00	500 500	1 820	33 700	Crane delay 15 min. First full week operating two shifts.
17	21		7	7	7	619 050	59	35	572 275	2 081	46 875	Broken water jacket delay 240 min, crane delay 10 min, electrode delay 30 min.
18	15		5	6	4	452 900	47	50	404 250	1 470	48 650	Ladle delays 75 min. Ladle not heated—60 min delay. Crane repair delay 60 min.

Exhibit 12
Haitian Rebar Co. (A)
Typical Daily Melt Shop Record
Week Ending October 1, 1967

Heat No.	Date		Ladle	Charging Weight (lbs)	Time Hrs	Mins	Teeming Weight (lbs)	Total Ingots Poured	Skull and Other Losses
52	Sept.	25	1	26 000	3	30	24 200	88	1 800
53	''	25	2	26 000	3	40	24 750	90	1 250
54	''	26	3	26 000	3	10	24 200	88	1 800
55	''	26	1	27 000	2	25	24 750	90	2 250
56	''	26	2	27 000	3	20	23 100	84	3 900
57	''	27	3	27 000	2	45	23 375	85	3 625
58	''	28	1	27 000	2	55	23 925	87	3 075
59	''	28	2	27 000	2	45	24 750	90	2 250
60	''	30	3	28 000	4	20	25 850	94	2 150
61	''	30	1	28 000	3	05	26 125	95	1 875
62	Oct.	1	2	28 000	3	10	25 575	93	2 425
63	''	1	3	27 000	2	45	24 750	90	2 250
64	''	1	1	28 000	3	50	25 850	94	2 150
Totals		13 Heats		352 000	41	40	321 200	1 168	30 800

Exhibit 13
Haitian Rebar Co. (A)
Melt Shop Two-Shift Schedule

Day	Production Hours	Shift One	Shift Two
Monday	8	10:30 P.M.-6:30 A.M.	
Tuesday	8	10:30 P.M.-6:30 A.M.	
Wednesday	8		10:30 P.M.-6:30 A.M.
Thursday	8	Clean-up	10:30 P.M.-6:30 A.M.
Friday	8		10:30 P.M.-6:30 A.M.
Saturday	24	6:30 P.M.-6:30 A.M.	6:30 A.M.-6:30 P.M.
Sunday	24	6:30 P.M.-6:30 A.M.	6:30 A.M.-6:30 P.M.
Total	88	40	48

Haitian Rebar Co. (B)

In January 1968, Mr. John Duncan, plant manager, was considering a request to extend the mould line in the melt shop. This followed an earlier request for more ladles (see Haitian Rebar Company (A)). Three weeks after melt shop operations had begun in August 1967, Mr. Duncan had extended the mould line 20 feet with good results. This time, the request from the melt shop superintendent seemed to be similar to the earlier situation. Mr. Duncan wondered, therefore, if the same criteria could again be applied.

MOULDS

Moulds were used to shape the ingots. Each mould weighed 400 lbs and cost $125 (Exhibit 1). Ingot weight was 275 lbs. Before a pour, two men, with the help of the overhead crane, straightened out the moulds so they were lined into three parallel rows between the railway tracks of the pouring line. The foundation of the pouring line (teeming pit) consisted of concrete covered by a 2-in layer of sand. Two rails carried the travelling pouring cradle (Exhibit 1). The cradle was constructed so that its top carriage carrying the ladle could move sideways.

Six operators worked on the pouring line. A group of three men teemed. One positioned the cradle so that the pouring nozzle lined up with each mould. One operated the nozzle lever and the third one inserted a handle bent from one-half-in reinforcing rod in each molten ingot. At the start of each pour the lever operator opened the graphite nozzle slightly. A slow initial pour formed a protective pad at the bottom of the mould. A quick pour filled the mould, followed by another slow pour to top off. Pouring time ranged from twenty to twenty-five seconds per mould.

The pouring crew started in the middle of the line and poured centre moulds for half the length. This gave maximum protection to the operators. They then travelled along one complete outside row and this finished one pour of 100 ingots (Exhibit 1).

The remaining crew of three men removed the ingots from the moulds. After about a dozen moulds had been teemed, two men began to loosen the ingots. They levered with heavy steel bars stuck under the handle in the ingot. The last pouring crew member helped the crane operator lift the loose ingots out of the moulds. The crane carried a steel bar with eight hooks chained to it. The worker inserted one hook into each ingot handle and the crane moved eight red-hot ingots to the cooling area. After all the ingots were removed, all moulds that had fallen were set up again, but not necessarily in a straight row. Three men using the empty cradle swabbed the inside of each mould with a graphite wash to prevent sticking on the next pour. Should the men have trouble loosening an ingot after several tries with the steel bar, they sprayed the mould with water and tried again. If this did not work, the ingot was considered a "sticker." The crane moved all stickers to the scrap preparation area, where it bounced them onto a steel platform. If this still did not loosen the ingot, both ingot and mould were considered scrap. If this did remove the ingot, the mould was inspected and either considered scrap or reusable. If the latter, it was marked with an *x* and placed at the far end of the teeming pit. The pouring crew kept a close eye on all sticker moulds. If sticking became too frequent the mould was sent to scrap. A mould of reasonable quality should last at least four months and might go for a year. A number of variables affected the life of a mould. During line set-up the mould had to be set vertically or the molten metal would splash and burn the shell. Burning led to small deformations (pits) in the mould, which increased the probability of sticking. The nozzle operator could burn the bottom if he started each pour too fast. The nozzle had to be well lubricated and positioned so that accurate flow control was possible. During the teeming operations, moulds reached a temperature of 1000°F and after ingot removal required three hours to cool. Shell expansion and ingot loosening seemed to be optimal if the pour was started with the mould at room temperature.

Pouring Line Start-Up

The teeming operation at Rebar was started with 240 moulds, 100 in inventory and 140 on the pouring line. Right from the beginning in August 1967, more than seventy ingots were teemed from each furnace heat. Thus every second heat some of the moulds were reused. Operators had difficulty preparing the line because of the intense heat, the number of moulds that had fallen and the number of sticker moulds that had to be replaced. After operating for two weeks, Mr. Duncan (on Mr. Lord's request), extended the pouring foundation 20 ft at a cost of $120 per ft. The teeming pit now had space for 203 moulds and could handle two heats before reusing any one mould. The pouring crew was now less rushed than before and the sticker rate immediately fell to 3.9 per cent. During the next three months the melt shop crew generally became more proficient at their tasks. The sticker rate, however, did not drop, and on February 7, 1968, Mr. Lord requested a further extension to the pit sufficient to hold another 100 moulds. Mr. Lord indicated that stickers were starting to increase again and he felt the moulds were overworked.

Mr. Duncan knew that although space was tight another 40 ft could be added to the line. He was also aware that during the first five months the company had put over 400 new moulds into service. He had difficulty assessing the cause of the high sticker rate (industry average was less than one per cent per heat).[1] The melt shop now operated two shifts (Exhibit 4) with an expected output of thirty heats per week by June 1968.

Mr. Duncan did not know how to answer Mr. Lord's request, because lately he had been primarily concerned with rolling mill operations. He was generally pleased with the melt shop start up (Exhibits 2 and 3), and he knew Mr. Lord had done an excellent job in improving the productivity of the electric furnace.

---

[1] The company did not keep records of sticker frequency. The teeming crew recalled roughly how many stickers they had on each pour and they were the source for figures and trends mentioned in this case.

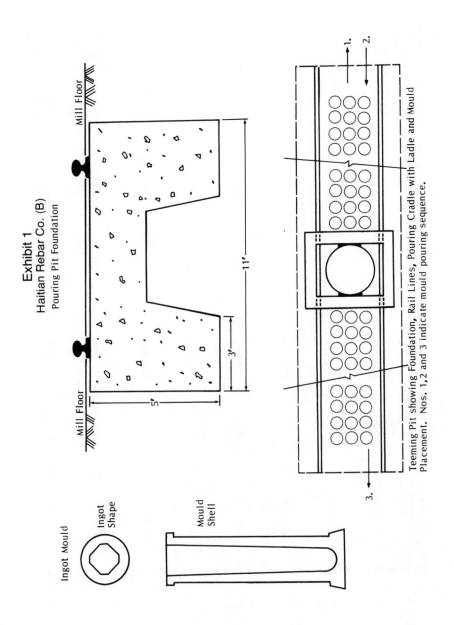

Exhibit 1
Haitian Rebar Co. (B)
Pouring Pit Foundation

Mill Floor

Mill Floor

11'

3'

5'

Ingot Mould

Ingot Shape

Mould Shell

1.

2.

3.

Teeming Pit showing Foundation, Rail Lines, Pouring Cradle with Ladle and Mould Placement. Nos. 1, 2 and 3 indicate mould pouring sequence.

Exhibit 2
Haitian Rebar Co. (B)
Weekly Melt Shop Record—Starting August 20, 1967

Week No.	Total Heats	Ladle No.	Ladle Times Used	Charging Weight (lbs)	Melt Time Hrs	Mins	Teeming Weight (lbs) (Ingots Poured × 275)	Total Ingots Poured	Skull and Other Losses (lbs)	Melt Shop Comments
1	7	1	2	156 900	25	35	144 100	524	12 800	Electrical delays 165 mins.
		2	2							
		3	3							
2	9	1	3	210 800	28	30	196 075	713	14 725	
		2	3							
		3	3							
3	12	1	4	285 000	37	15	272 255	990	12 745	
		2	4							
		3	4							
4	11	1	4	265 000	32	55	250 350	914	14 650	
		2	4							
		3	3							
5	12	1	3	301 000	37	35	284 850	1 034	16 150	
		2	5							
		3	4							
6	13	1	5	352 000	41	40	321 200	1 168	30 800	
		2	4							
		3	4							
7	12	1	3	336 000	40	10	296 450	1 078	39 550	Pouring refractory froze—lost 1/3 of one heat.
		2	5							
		3	4							
8	12	1	6	327 000	41	00	301 950	1 098	25 050	Defective coil 180 min, broken electrode 30 min, pouring refractory froze.
		2	3							
		3	3							

		Shift 1	Shift 2	Shift 3						Remarks
9	16	5	6	5	421 500	41	00	387 200	1 408	34 550	
10	13	4	5	4	352 800	36	30	328 900	1 196	23 900	Mechanical and electrode delays 120 min.
11	14	5	5	4	381 400	31	10	351 725	1 279	30 675	Lost one day's production—area power failure.
12	15	4	6	5	408 600	37	50	376 475	1 369	32 125	
13	14	4	5	5	374 800	35	10	330 000	1 200	41 800	
14	14	4	5	5	379 450	39	55	338 250	1 230	41 200	Ladle delay 75 min. Furnace roof cave-in. Nozzle freeze-up lost 1/3 of one heat
15	10	3	3	4	279 400	24	35	264 275	961	15 125	Ladle delays 150 min, Bad furnace and ladle bottom.
16	18	8	8	2	534 200	51	00	500 500	1 820	33 700	Crane delay 15 min, first full week operating two shifts.
17	21	7	7	7	619 050	59	35	572 275	2 081	46 875	Broken water jacket delay 240 min, crane delay 10 min, electrode delay 30 min.
18	15	5	6	4	452 900	47	50	404 250	1 470	48 650	Ladle delays 75 min, ladle not heated 60 min. delay. Crane repair delay 60 min.

Exhibit 3
Haitian Rebar Co. (B)
Typical Daily Melt Shop Record
Week Ending October 1, 1967

Heat No.	Date	Ladle	Charging weight (lbs)	Time Hrs	Time Mins	Teeming Weight (lbs)	Total Ingots Poured	Skull and Other Losses
52	Sept. 25	1	26 000	3	30	24 200	88	1 800
53	'' 25	2	26 000	3	40	24 750	90	1 250
54	'' 26	3	26 000	3	10	24 200	88	1 800
55	'' 26	1	27 000	2	25	24 750	90	2 250
56	'' 26	2	27 000	3	20	23 100	84	3 900
57	'' 27	3	27 000	2	45	23 375	85	3 625
58	'' 28	1	27 000	2	55	23 925	87	3 075
59	'' 28	2	27 000	2	45	24 750	90	2 250
60	'' 30	3	28 000	4	20	25 850	94	2 150
61	'' 30	1	28 000	3	05	26 125	95	1 875
62	Oct. 1	2	28 000	3	10	25 575	93	2 425
63	'' 1	3	27 000	2	45	24 750	90	2 250
64	'' 1	1	28 000	3	50	25 850	94	2 150
Totals	13 Heats		352 000	41	40	321 200	1 168	30 800

Exhibit 4
Haitian Rebar Co. (B)
Melt Shop Two-Shift Schedule

Day	Production Hours	Shift One	Shift Two
Monday	8	10:30 P.M.-6:30 A.M.	
Tuesday	8	10:30 P.M.-6:30A.M.	
Wednesday	8		10:30 P.M.-6:30 A.M.
Thursday	8	Clean-Up	10:30 P.M.-6:30 A.M.
Friday	8		10:30 P.M.-6:30 A.M.
Saturday	24	6:30 P.M.-6:30 A.M.	6:30 A.M.-6:30 P.M.
Sunday	24	6:30 P.M.-6:30 A.M.	6:30 A.M.-6:30 P.M.
Total	88	48	48

Haitian Rebar Co. (E)

The Haitian Rebar Co. was the sole manufacturer of steel reinforcing rods for the construction trade in Haiti (See Haitian Rebar Company cases A and B for company background and process notes).

The company was still in its first year of operation when the plant superintendent received the following mimeographed notice (Exhibit 1). He knew he had no choice but to try to live with the situation and wondered what action he should take to minimize potential losses.

Exhibit 1
Haitian Rebar Co. (E)
The Haitian Power Co., Port-au-Prince, Haiti

July 16, 1968
CIRCULAR TO: Schools, Hotels, Hospitals, Institutions, Government offices, Police stations, Companies, Householders, and all other users.

INTERRUPTION ELECTRICITY SUPPLY

The Haitian Power Co. wishes to advise you that beginning tomorrow, July 17, 1968, and for the next six to eight weeks or until the effect of the drought is relieved, the electricity supply will be suspended during the periods indicated below:—

Tuesdays	—	9: A.M. to 11:00 A.M.
Thursdays	—	3:00 P.M. to 5:00 P.M.
Saturdays	—	11:00 A.M. to 1:00 P.M.

The company feels that this extreme measure has become necessary due to the effect of the drought on its Hydro-Electric Stations and regrets any inconveniences that may result from these interruptions.

Jean Renaud

President

Haitian Rebar Co. (C) & (D) have not been included in this book.

42
Sunshine Builders, Inc.

In the five years since its founding, Sunshine Builders, Inc., had grown to be one of Florida's larger home builders. In the opinion of the company's management, major credit for Sunshine's growth and success was due to customer-oriented service and guarantee policies which, in combination with good construction, reasonable prices, and on-time completions, had enabled the firm to acquire an excellent reputation.

The founders of the company, Charles and Arthur Root, had come to Florida in 1953 at the ages of twenty-eight and twenty-six respectively after five years in the furniture business in Chicago. Charles Root had majored in economics at the University of Chicago and Arthur Root in chemical engineering at Northwestern. While their furniture business had been moderately successful, they felt that the potential margin of profit was becoming increasingly narrow and that the personal time and effort required was out of proportion to the return attainable.

The Root brothers were attracted to Florida as a state which offered rapid growth and above-average business opportunities. They spent their first several months becoming familiar with the metropolitan area, which included a population of nearly 500,000 within a ten-mile radius. They realized that land was appreciating in value and bought eight lots for speculation. Shortly thereafter, encouraged by their father, who had had some experience in contracting, they decided to build houses on the lots. These homes were built and sold by early 1954, subcontracting the construction work to different local contractors.

Since this operation had been profitable, population growth was accelerating, land was relatively cheap and there was some evidence of industrial movement to Florida, the Root brothers became convinced that the home construction business in Florida offered excellent prospects.

CONSTRUCTION OPERATIONS 1954-1958

Following the completion and sale of the first eight homes the Root brothers built a model home and sold forty very quickly. These homes were located on customers' lots and were entirely subcontracted. Since the customer made regular progress payments as the house progressed, beginning with an initial payment of 15 per cent, the net effect of these arrangements was that relatively little capital was required. The company was hard-pressed during 1954 and 1955 to build enough houses to meet the demand.

During this period Charles Root found that his greatest interest was in the development of land and formed a separate corporation, Root Land Development Corp., for this purpose. The elder Mr. Root took no active part in either Sunshine Builders, headed by Arthur, or the land development operations under Charles. Each brother devoted nearly all of his time to his own operations and only assisted the other as requested or when dealing with major policy issues. A third corporation, Root Associates, was established by Arthur to handle sales for Sunshine Builders. Cooperative selling arrangements were also established with local real estate firms.

From 1954 to 1958 Sunshine expanded each year. Operating data for this period and for the first four months of 1959 are shown in Exhibit 1. During the years 1954-1958, management operations had remained essentially simple in concept although they were extremely hectic and required consistently long hours on the part of both brothers. With very few exceptions, the land on which Sunshine Builders constructed homes was owned by the customer, who had purchased it from either the Root Land Development Corp., or some other source. All construction work had been subcontracted to local subcontractors who, by mutual consent, had chosen to largely concentrate their efforts on work for Sunshine Builders.

From late 1954 through 1956 Arthur Root was assisted in the job of managing the construction end of the business by Herbert Playford. Mr. Playford had known the Root brothers in Chicago and had come to Florida at their request in September 1954. He had a high school education and had worked successively as a shipping clerk, a neon glass blower and in his father's junk business. On his arrival in Florida, Mr. Playford, twenty-five, was taken by Arthur Root to visit thirteen home sites which were in various stages of construction and given immediate responsibility for their completion with the instruction: "Build them." In carrying out this assignment, he acted as superintendent, working with the various contractors, scheduling, coordinating, and supervising their various efforts.

As the business grew, four other superintendents were hired. In 1956 Herbert Playford was moved into the office to serve as an expediter and coordinator of the four superintendents and to take care of the mounting volume of paper work associated with the construction end of the business. In this capacity he set up the systems of scheduling and cost controls described later.

Mr. Playford's assumption of many of the daily details of construction left Arthur Root free for sales work, purchasing, and managing the company's finances. In late 1956 he was joined in the firm by a younger brother, Daniel Root, twenty-five, who until that time had been pursuing graduate studies in history.

On December 1, 1956, Mr. Playford resigned from the company to enter the building business for himself. He founded a new firm, Meadowlark Builders, aided with a substantial investment by the Root brothers. Meadowlark was successful from the start, building a total of 200 low-cost homes in 1957 and 1958. In December 1958 Arthur Root persuaded Mr. Playford to return to Sunshine as treasurer, assistant secretary, and manager of production and service, and the Meadowlark operation was discontinued.

By the end of 1958, Daniel Root, as vice-president and secretary, had taken up full responsibility for sales, broker relations, customer relations, advertising and the developing and merchandising of new models. Arthur Root, as president, handled all financing and purchasing. Charles Root continued to devote his time principally to the Root Land Development Corp.

The construction work, under Mr. Playford, was handled by eight subcontractors, who performed the following functions:

Plumbing	Plastering
Electrical work	Carpentry
Painting	Heating
Masonry	Cleaning

Each contractor sent in a weekly bill for the wages he had paid, plus 8 per cent for equipment. His own time was included at an hourly rate approximately 15 per cent above his highest paid man. Material was purchased and supplied by the contractor at cost. The contractor hired and fired as he felt necessary, but Sunshine Builders had the right to approve any wage increases. Arthur Root and Herbert Playford made it a practice to question the subcontractors on jobs on which their costs appeared out of line with previous cost experience. Total costs for each contractor were tabulated for each job to furnish this information. Except for the masonry crew the men were not unionized, but the wages for each trade were approximately equal to the appropriate general community average.

The contractors each had a number of crews whose activities were arranged and assigned by the four superintendents previously mentioned. The superintendents were paid about the same or slightly more than top construction craftsmen. Each superintendent covered the Sunshine Builders' homes in the geographic territory assigned to him, the bulk of which were located within a seven-mile radius.

By late 1958 Arthur Root had become increasingly concerned about the effectiveness of this entire arrangement. In discussions with his brothers and Mr. Playford, he made the following observations and criticisms of the existing operation:

1. The superintendents were spending most of their time competing with each other for crews to work on the houses in their territory. They were "high-grade expediters" but made no attempt to coordinate the crew requirements between each other.
2. Seven[1] of the contractors were personally receiving $11 000-$12 000 per year, working solely for Sunshine. In effect, they were acting not so much as independent contractors but rather as foremen, who could be hired for less to perform such work.
3. The subcontractors were not buying labour-saving equipment but tended to run old equipment into the ground.
4. It should be possible to centralize controls and scheduling and to eliminate conflicts, delays and superintendents.

After considerable discussion, a unanimous management decision was made to absorb the entire subcontractors' organizations into the Sunshine firm and eliminate the use of superintendents. As planned, the various subcontractor crews would be placed on the Sunshine payroll, and the previous subcontractors would become Sunshine foremen.

Individual meetings were held with each contractor in December 1958. The proposed changes were explained and each contractor was offered a salary according to his experience and ability. A reasonable price was to be negotiated for his equipment. In spite of the fact that the salaries offered were 10 per cent to 25 per cent below their recent annual earnings (the masonry contractor, for example, had been making $12 000 and was offered $9250), the offers were accepted by the entire group. Arthur Root felt that the offers were higher than the men could earn elsewhere and that the men realized they had been overpaid previously and that it was "a gravy train that might stop suddenly any time. They were also glad to be freed of the payroll paper work and to give up some responsibility." Under the new arrangements the foremen were to continue to do the hiring, as necessary. The foremen were also told that they would be given year-end bonuses, dependent on the company's annual operating profit.

The four superintendents were dismissed and the new method of operation was installed on January 1, 1959. Three of the superintendents were rehired as tradesmen on the various crews, and an additional eight construction workers (who had been on the payroll of certain of the subcontractors, performing on jobs other than Sunshine houses) were also absorbed, bringing the construction crew to 124.

OPERATIONS IN EARLY 1959

The Sunshine Builders' organization as of May 1, 1959, is shown as Exhibit 2. The numbers of personnel working in the various functional areas are shown in parentheses after each descriptive title. Each construction crew consisted of nearly equal numbers of skilled tradesmen and helpers with the exception of the cleaning crew, which included only unskilled general labour. The total personnel on the regular payroll at that time numbered 161. Following the organizational change, 124 were direct labour on construction. There had been no significant change in construction crew levels during the past four months.

In April 1959 Arthur Root and Herbert Playford both felt enthusiastic about results of the new organization thus far. They stated, for example, that without the superintendents there was "now a closer, more direct line of communication between the office and the crews." Further, fewer mistakes were being made now, according to Mr. Playford. The foremen appeared to be taking a broader point of view which, for example, Mr. Root

---

[1] The eighth, the cleaning contractor, had been receiving approximately $5000 per year.

pointed out was demonstrated by keeping the office better informed about their own stage of progress on each job.

Herbert Playford ran the production end of the business with an apparent assurance and good humour in spite of a constant rush of decisions and problems to solve. The basic approaches to planning and controlling production employed in April 1959 were essentially the same as those he had set up himself during the years 1955-1956.

The dispatching office and the "production boards" on two walls in that office served as a central nucleus of information in Mr. Playford's system. While no formal scheduling was attempted, the boards aided the dispatcher in keeping up to date on where each job stood. The boards themselves consisted of wallboard material on which was tacked blueprint-type paper with a two-inch grid. Across the top (along the horizontal scale) were these headings: (a) the owner's name, (b) the address where the house was to be built, (c) the model number of the house, (d) the sixty-five individual steps, operations, or phases of the construction work. These are described in Exhibit 3. The houses were then listed vertically, adding new homes at the bottom as orders were received. The board's appearance is depicted below:

	JOBS	M									
		o	1	2	3	4	5	6	7	8	9
OWNER	LOCATION	d	*Sign*	*Deliver*	*Power*	*Stake*	*Dig*	*Pour*	*Order*	*Lay*	*Fill*
		e	*Clear*								
		l	*Lot*								
E. K. Williams	14 Coral St.	69									
D. W. Onan	262 Beach Rd.	14									
A. T. Bovril	69 Hacienda	190L									

(heading above steps: CONSTRUCTION STEPS)

The dispatcher, Mabel Roark, thirty-five, posted the information to the boards. She was an active, personable woman with nearly one year of experience in her job. She placed her initials in the box after she had called the foreman requesting the performance of each construction step. The foreman, of course, knew what work was required for each step but relied on Miss Roark for instructions as to what house and which step should be his crew's next assignment. She wrote in the date when the operation had been promised for completion and noted "O.K." when the step was completed.

Miss Roark also used five coloured pins to assist in calling her attention to an operation as follows:

Black   indicated "on order"
Red   indicated "did not arrive or get
                  completed as promised"
White   indicated "crew is there, on the job"
Yellow   indicated "Mabel should call"
Blue   indicated "have a question for the
                  foreman"

From the visual standpoint, since the jobs were added at the bottom of the sheet as they were taken on and the construction steps proceeded from left to right, the completed steps made a slightly irregular diagonal line, slanting downwards from right to left. Thus, any house that had fallen behind showed up as an indent to the left in the diagonal line of completed boxes.

By and large, Mr. Playford stated that during the last twelve months all houses had been taking the same length of time to complete, namely eighty to eighty-five calendar days from the date construction work was started. Customers were promised delivery in no more than 100 calendar days from the signing of the purchase agreement. Because so many purchasers were new residents moving south and therefore had many moving details to schedule, any delays in house completions would significantly jeopardize customer relations, it was felt.

In addition to assigning the work to the foremen, Miss Roark's activity as dispatcher included maintaining the production boards and serving as a communication and recording centre for all reports and instructions. In this duty she made full use of a two-way radio system. Each foreman, Mr. Playford, and the warehouse supervisor had a two-way radio in his car or truck. The radio system had been installed in mid-1958 on a lease basis and cost the company a monthly rental of $375.

Miss Roark talked with each foreman intermittently three to six times daily or more. In a typical conversation the masonry foreman might call in and tell her that the footings operation his crew had been working on at the Kelly house was now completed, but that the iron work for the Kent job had not arrived and that Mr. and Mrs. Kent had been around that morning and asked if they could change the dimensions of their back patio from 12 ft × 15 ft to 12 ft × 20 ft. He might then ask where Mabel wanted his crew the next day and would she check her paper work to see whether the Larsen house had to have a front planter and whether the plumbers should be through with the O'Leary house so that the slab could be laid by the masons.

Miss Roark independently made the innumerable decisions as to the operations and jobs which would be done next, receiving little or no aid from Mr. Playford, whose office was next door. While he came in to see the boards once or twice a week, he did not attempt to participate in the hour-by-hour job of scheduling and directing the crews.

To prevent delays and idle crews Miss Roark had to have a clear understanding of the various operations and their interrelationships. It was essential, for instance, for her to know that the electricians could not do their rough-in until the studs were up, that the heating work could be done while the carpenters were trimming, that the electricians and plumbers could go on ahead or behind the painters on certain operations but could not work at the same time in the house with them, etc., Miss Roark stated that "I still make some mistakes but I've learned a lot about house building during this past year."

In scheduling the crews she used the guides of time and crew requirements shown in Exhibit 3. These guides had been established by Herbert Playford and Miss Roark out of their combined experience as to how many men and how much time it was necessary to allow for the completion of each step. They had learned, for example, that it was entirely reasonable to expect a crew of four carpenters to frame up an average house (Exhibit 3, Step #20) in five days working at an ordinary pace.

Miss Roark's purchasing function was confined to ordering specific items for delivery from vendors selected previously by Arthur Root. Arthur Root handled all negotiations with suppliers, arranging for prices, delivery and payment terms. This work occupied a significant portion of his time. He regularly shopped for better values in windows, fixtures, lumber, appliances, etc., and had accomplished considerable standardization of purchased items.

In late 1958 Sunshine Builders had leased a 6000 square feet warehouse in order to be able to stock various purchased materials. Five men were hired to receive, stock and deliver items stocked. A sixth employee who had previously acted as a truck driver and errand runner was also assigned to the warehouse group. The arrangement was intended to allow the company to buy in larger volumes at lower prices. It was also intended that this new approach would give Sunshine a direct and closer control over the delivery of items to building sites. Mr. Root estimated that he could negotiate volume purchases covering about 75 per cent of the material used (based on cost), which could secure for Sunshine a 4 per cent saving in cost if the company would purchase and take deliveries no more frequently than three times per year.

While Sunshine Builders did not attempt to maintain a breakdown between material and labour costs, Mr. Root pointed out that costs had been rising steadily, citing *Engineer News Record* statistics which showed that on a national basis material costs had been rising at a rate of 2 per cent over the past four years. Construction labour costs on the same survey showed increases at an annual rate of about 4 per cent.

The foremen were responsible for ordering all material from the warehouse with the exception of the staking-out material which Miss Roark ordered. The warehouse truck then delivered the material ordered to each building site.

Sunshine Builders encouraged prospective buyers to make any nonstructural changes which they desired. Daniel Root pointed out that "different models are built in each Sunshine Subdivision, making a considerable freedom of choice for the buyer which, coupled with the further variations which Sunshine offers at a nominal price, results in a low-cost house with considerable individuality." The exceptions and additions to a typical contract, shown in Exhibit 4, were not unusual either as to nature or quantity.

Miss Roark and the foremen were given copies of each customer's plans, together with the agreed-upon changes. She kept a customer detail sheet for each customer which contained this information and the frequent additional changes. Such further changes were written up and priced by the estimator at the time they were requested. A "Customer Request for Extra Work" form was filled out and signed by the customer. The original copy was sent to the office for the final bill, the customer kept the second copy, the foreman received the third copy and the fourth was sent to Miss Roark.

Before actual construction could begin on a specific house, about two or three weeks were required to complete the steps shown on the Start Chart (Exhibit 5). Commencing with the signing of the contract, Mr. Playford personally handled the preproduction phase of each job covering steps 1 through 25 on the Start Chart.

In explaining his methods of managing the production operation, Mr. Playford made the following points:

1. Two employees have been added in drafting since the first of the year in an attempt to eliminate the subcontracting of drafting work. The drafting is necessary in order to have separate plans for every house because of the large number of changes usually incorporated for each customer.
2. The major change in operations without the four superintendents is that the various foremen now have responsibility for the construction of the house at different phases. These responsibilities are as follows:

Operations	Supervisor or Foreman Responsible
1-2	Mr. Playford
3	Electrical
4	Carpenter
5-10	Mason
11	Plumber
12-18	Mason
19-23	Carpenter
24	Plumber
25	Electrician
26-30	Plasterer
31	Carpenter
32-34	Plasterer
35	Carpenter
36-37	Plasterer
38-49	Carpenter
50-51	Plumber
52-55	Electrician
56-65	Inspector

3. Low-cost construction comes from doing jobs conventionally. The only good approach to cost cutting comes from making operations fast and smooth. Sunshine has cut two

weeks off of building homes in recent years and should eventually be able to cut one or two more. I made a study at Meadowlark which showed that ideally a home comparable to Sunshine's $15 000 models could be built in fifty-two calendar days if everything worked out well.

Our men use the same methods for each step in every house. It's all pretty much standardized—the block work, slab, framing, electrical wiring, plastering—they do each house the same way as the others. We use only the most elementary common tools and equipment, such as power saws and cement mixers, and have very little else.

By and large most prefabbing does not pay unless the customer is not allowed to make any changes, and if Sunshine adopted that approach we would lose sales. For instance prefabbed roof trusses so commonly used by other construction firms are more expensive for Sunshine than on-site building of the roof structure, probably because we have so many models. We visited Levittown, Pennsylvania, in 1956 to see if we could pick up any ideas and found that they permit no changes whatever. Building houses block by block they can do more precutting and standardizing than we can since our houses are usually not adjacent.

One way we save time is to get foremen to make suggestions. For instance, our masonry foreman has learned that a mason will lay blocks faster if his helper will keep the blocks piled up ahead of him. And we have discovered that it is a good idea to supply about 10 per cent extra material to each job in order to prevent any picking and hunting for material. Any extra material left over is sent back to the warehouse. But the conventional methods of building are cheapest for us.

4. Our men are picked by the foremen. They usually hear about good men in the trade and many they hire are friends or have been sent by friends. The foreman can hire and lay off as needed. Crews work a five-day week, nine hours a day, which gives them forty-five hours of pay per week. The masons are unionized but the others are not. The men tend to work in teams, a journeyman and a helper. They also tend to specialize. For instance, on a carpenter crew the foreman has separate men for door jambs and window frames, for rafter cutting, for cornices for general framing, and a saw specialist. Helpers are paid $1.25-$1.75 per hour. We pay no overtime, just straight time. The wage structure for the craftsmen is masons, $2.75; plumbers, $3.00; carpenters, $2.45; tile setters, $3.00; plasterers, $3.00; electricians, $2.25; painters, $2.40. There is no wage progression, no future, no security, and no benefits other than those required by law, social security, etc., which add up to about 8 per cent over these rates. But we've had no major layoffs ever, and have a darn good crew.

5. Up until January, Arthur used the six charts on my office wall—which I started—to control costs. These showed the dollar-per-square-foot cost for each phase (corresponding to the foreman's areas of operations) for each house when it was completed, the point being plotted on the horizontal axis by date of completion. This would have revealed any trends and any house that was out of line. No clear trends were shown, though.

Now these charts are discontinued because they were too much work to keep up. Instead, about once a month we spot check costs by studying the accumulated costs on several completed jobs quite closely and figuring out the total cost per square foot on various operations such as electrical, plumbing, etc. Every three months I'll make a still more detailed check on twelve houses. I control material costs by controlling the amount sent out to each house, depending on its size. Arthur, of course, keeps check on supply sources.

If any costs get looking high, I talk to the foreman. Recently tile costs had moved up about 15-20 per cent and upon investigating I found that the foreman was driving twenty miles for supplies every day. I showed him how to order in advance and stock more in our warehouse. He had also guaranteed his crew ten hours of pay regardless of the actual time worked. And some of his crew were driving to our warehouse instead of getting material delivered.

As long as I'm out watching, and the men are working, and Mabel keeps things moving, the costs will be O.K.

6. We are still too lax in our attitude toward delay. I want more flow and speed, better customer relationships, lower work in process. I am getting out in the field more now that I've got things set up better here, and getting my eyes open finding jobs where no action is taking place. Mabel gets along fine with the men and they like her, but she is not firm enough with them and with outsiders. She can learn to do her job even better.

7. Crews are instructed to work an extra hour to finish up on a house and wherever possible to make moves to the next house on an overnight basis. If a house really needs only eight hours of plastering it gets nine, because we work on a nine-hour day. However, if it has what we might consider ten hours of plastering it is usually done in nine also, in order to finish it in one day.

Houses were priced by estimating construction costs (Exhibit 1) and then adding 5 per cent for expenses, and 15 per cent for selling costs and profit together. The estimating was performed by Daniel Root's assistant, who served as the company's estimator. He had had some architectural training and spent a large portion of his time working with customers on their changes from standard plans. The average house in 1959 included approximately $2500 of subcontracting. Exhibits 6 and 7 show one-page brochures on the cheapest and most expensive houses in the line. Once a price was set on a model it was not changed, though its costs tended to rise slightly as new improvements of a minor nature were gradually added. Arthur Root and Herbert Playford agreed with Daniel Root that Sunshine Builders' prices in 1959 could not be increased if Sunshine's product was to remain competitive.

Considerable emphasis was placed on customer satisfaction after the house was completed. Sunshine's policy was that during the first year they would repair any item that the customer did not consider satisfactory. As long as the request was in any way reasonable (and often where it did not appear so), they did the work at no charge and with a willing and pleasant attitude. The service department (Exhibit 2) handled this work. In the Sunshine organization it was referred to as "punch work," meaning that it was to be "punched out, without delay." In April 1959 the "punch work girl" was moved into Mr. Playford's office in order to provide better supervision of her work. The biggest single item requiring punch work was ceiling cracks. In pricing a house, about 2 per cent of the expected price was allowed for punch work and included in construction cost estimates.

On May 1, 1959, the production boards showed a total of forty-two houses listed, consisting of twelve different models in a price range of $10 990 to $18 500. Comparable figures for October 1958 and April 1, 1959, showed thirty-five and thirty-six houses under construction, respectively. Nine units of the most popular model were under way, five models showed three to six units in process, and the six other models listed three or fewer units each.

The April rise of houses in process from thirty-six to forty-two was due to a heavy influx of orders received in late March and during the month of April. The improved sales results had caused Mr. Playford to gradually increase the houses started each week from three during the first week of April to six in the last week of April. From every indication, sales prospects for the balance of 1959 appeared excellent and Mr. Playford expected to be able to continue starting five to six houses weekly. He stated that he liked to make any changes in starts on a gradual basis in order to maintain a smooth flow of work to all crews. "This approach," he said, "paces the whole operation."

Arthur Root stated five principles which he felt represented the key to Sunshine Builders' success and to its future:

1. Our houses must be completely livable.
2. They must have eye appeal.
3. As builders we must develop and hold a reputation for honesty, integrity, skill, and on-time completion.
4. We must offer exceptional value.
5. Our houses must be properly presented and promoted.

"Any one factor that is not up to standard would hurt us badly. We must do a top job on all five."

Exhibit 1
Sunshine Builders, Inc.
Operating Profit Data
(Expressed as a Percentage of Sales)

	1956	1957	1958	1959 (4 months)
Sales[1]	100.00%	100.00%	100.00%	100.00%
Construction costs[2]	85.20	86.60	83.33	84.80
Gross profit	14.80%	13.40%	16.67%	15.20%
	—	—	—	—
Expenses:				
Sales expense	5.00%	5.00%	5.00%	5.00%
Salaries and wages[3]	3.15	3.85	5.23	5.20
Sales promotion and advertising	0.63	0.27	0.78	1.38
Depreciation	0.10	0.21	0.40	0.61
First-year house maintenance ("punch work")	0.13	0.45	0.38	0.37
Auto and aircraft expense	—	0.17	0.33	0.33
Office expenses	0.37	0.18	0.18	0.32
Radio expenses	—	—	0.10	0.19
Production office[4]	0.37	—	0.16	0.70
Equipment rental	—	—	—	0.36
Maintenance of model homes	0.07	0.10	—	0.02
Maintenance of trucks, tools, and equip.	—	—	—	0.66
Legal and accounting	—	0.04	0.16	0.04
Taxes and licences	0.46	0.15	0.13	0.69
Travel and entertainment	0.10	0.08	0.20	0.34
Telephone and postage	0.08	0.09	0.10	0.14
Warehouse expense	—	—	—	0.81
Insurance	0.19	0.10	0.09	0.23
Christmas gifts to employees	0.19	0.07	0.09	0.12
Plans and designs	—	0.10	0.08	0.12
Discounts and collections fees on mortgage	—	—	0.04	0.46
Rent	0.10	0.10	0.08	0.21
Miscellaneous	0.08	0.11	0.05	0.11
Total expenses	11.02	11.07	13.58	18.41
Operating profit (loss)	3.78%	2.33%	3.09%	(3.21)%
Number of houses built	124	134	151	52 (4 months)
Average selling price	$13 500	$14 250	$15 000	$15 250
Average number of construction workers	94	114	113	124

(For the years 1956, 1957 and 1958 these figures represent the total of the subcontractors' men working on Sunshine houses. For 1959, the 124 men were on Sunshine's payroll).

[1] Based on completed houses. A sale was made only when a house was completed and construction costs were charged to work-in-process inventory until the home was completed. Expenses were charged monthly as they occurred.
[2] Construction costs include direct labour, material, subcontracting cost, and the salaries and wages of foremen, superintendents, warehousemen, draftsmen, blueprint operators, messengers and the service department, plus fringe benefits for those salaries and wages included.
[3] Includes all other salaries and wages not included under construction costs.
[4] General-purpose production requirements, such as blueprint paper, steel tapes, forms, office supplies, small hand tools.

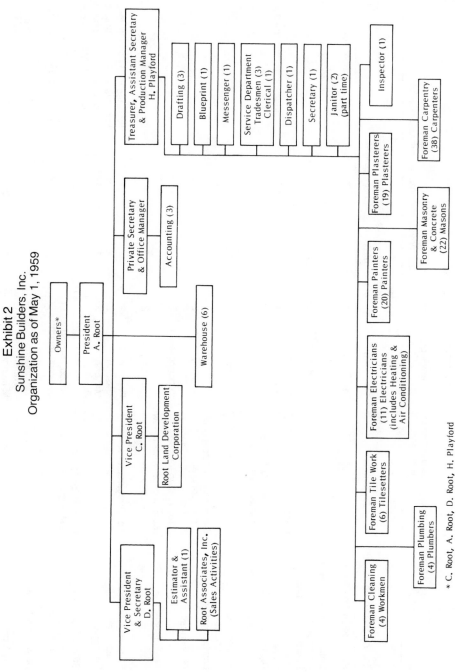

Exhibit 2
Sunshine Builders, Inc.
Organization as of May 1, 1959

* C. Root, A. Root, D. Root, H. Playford

Exhibit 3
Sunshine Builders, Inc.

Steps of the construction job as used on the company's production boards

				Manpower and time estimates for Dispatcher			
Step Number	Operation Required	Explanation	Crew	Normal Crew No. Men	Man-days of Work	Elapsed Time Allowed (days)	Remarks
1	Sign posted, lot cleared		Masonry	1	1	1	In typical subdivision lot already cleared
2	Deliver stakes, material and steel		Warehouse	—	—	—	
3	Power pole and water meter in	Done by utilities	Power Co.	—	—	—	
4	Stake out		Masonry	3	3	2	Includes a day for checking by foreman
5	Dig footing	Footings only 12"-18" below the surface	Masonry				
6	Pour footing		Masonry	2	1	1/2	
7	Order sliding glass doors		(Mabel)	—	—	—	
8	Lay foundation	Set reinforcing steel and pour concrete	Masonry	2	1	1/2	
9	Fill foundation	Fill & pack dirt within foundation for slab	Subcontracted	SC_1	—	1	
10	Tie-in foundation	Plumbing for water & sewer connections	Plumbing	2	5	—	Done during no. 11
11	Plumbing rough-in	Set plumbing for slab	Plumbing	3		2 1/2	Includes a day for city inspection
12	Grade slab		Masonry	2	2	2	Includes a day for city inspection
13	Pour slab		Masonry	3	1 1/2	1 1/2	Includes a day after pouring for slab to set
14	Strip for terrazzo	Place strips for sills or sliding doors	Subcontracted	SC	—	1	
15	Pour terrazzo		Subcontracted	SC	—	1 1/2	Includes a day for terrazzo to set
16	Deliver blocks, steel, sills		Vendor and Warehouse	—	—	—	
17	Lay block walls		Masonry	5	10	2	
18	Form and pour lintels		Masonry	2	1	1/2	Must be inspected

#	Task	Description	Responsible				Notes
19	First grind, terrazzo		Subcontracted	SC		2	
20	Carpenter's frame	Frame up interior wall studs and roof	Carpenters	4	20	5	
21	Order cabinets		(Mabel)				Included in time allowance for $20
22	Dry-in	First layer of lumber on the roof	Carpenters	4	1		Done during framing
23	Flue and/or duct work		Carpenters	2	4	2	Done during framing
24	Set tub		Masonry	SC		1/2	
25	Electrical rough-in	Place most of electrical wiring	Subcontracted	2	4	2	Done during framing (after studs in)
26	Prime cornice	Paint under overhand of roof	Painters	2	1	1/2	One day necessary for framing and elec. inspection
27	Order lath		(Mabel)			1	
28	Lath		Plaster	4	4	1	
29	Order vanity		(Mabel)				
30	Ceiling heat	Electrical radiant heating usually used	Electricians	2	2	2	
31	Roof complete	Pitch and gravel built up roof	Subcontracted	SC		2	
32	Scratch for tile	Preparation for tiling	Plaster	2	3	1/2	
33	Brown coat plaster and stucco		Plaster	4	4	1/2	
34	Second grind, terrazzo	First coat	Subcontracted	SC		1 1/2	Includes a day for drying
35	Iron work	Any decorative, iron work	Carpenters	2	1	1	
36	Tile walls	Bathrooms and sometimes kitchen areas	Tile	4	6	1	
37	Plaster and stucco complete		Plaster	4	4	1 1/2	
38	Glaze	Install window glass	Subcontracted	SC		1	Need two-day notice
39	Install sliding glass doors		Subcontracted	SC		1	
40	Insulation		Subcontracted	SC		1	Does not interfere with any other work
41	Clean and rough grade lot	Remove debris and grade	Subcontracted	SC		1	
42	Front stoop		Masonry	2	1	1/2	Usually done while framing
43	Form outside concrete		Masonry	2	2	1	

Exhibit 3 (continued)

No.	Activity	Detail	Crew				Remarks
44	Pour outside concrete		Masonry	2	2	1	Need good weather
45	Outside gravel or asphalt		Subcontracted	SC	—	2	
46	Order trim material	Mouldings, door frames, etc. (Mabel)	—	—	—	—	
47	Carpenter's trim		Carpenters	5	20	4	
48	Glaze jalousie doors		Subcontracted	SC	—	1/2	Done by vendor during trim operation
49	Install cabinets		Subcontracted	SC	—	1	
50	Septic tank		Plumbers	2	2	1	
51	Plumber's trim	Final plumbing work	Plumbers	2	2	1	
52	Heating	Install and/or complete heating system	Electricians	3	6	2	
53	Paint		Painters	4	16	4	Done while carpenters are trimming
54	Install operators & deliver screens	Window mechanisms	Carpenters	1	1/2	1/2	Must be alone in house
55	Electrical trim	Install lamps, outlet plates, etc.	Electricians	3	3	1	Now done before glazing
56	Polish terrazzo		Subcontracted	SC	—	2	Must be alone in house
57	Clean windows and interior		Cleaning	2	2	1	
58	Grass		Subcontracted	SC	—	1	
59	Install screens		Carpenters	1	1/2	1/2	
60	Painters complete, inspect		Painters	5	15	3	Incl. time for co. insp., final adjmts. & odds & ends
61	Wallpaper and mirror		Painters	2	2	1	
62	Plumbing inspection	By city inspector	—	—	—	1	City inspection
63	Electrical inspection	By city inspector	—	—	—	1	City inspection
64	Permanent electrical connection	By power company	Power Company	—	—	1	
65	Production inspection		Co. Inspector	1	1	1	Note also inspection at step No. 60

1 SC (subcontracted). In 1959 the average house required $2500 of subcontracted work.

Exhibit 4
Sunshine Builders, Inc.
Excerpt From Building Agreement With Customer

Third: All details of material and construction will be identical with those used in the model home located at

. . . Lot #4, Belle Lake Subdivision . . . with the following exceptions:

1.	Model 190L	$10 990
2.	Place wrought iron shutters with oak leaf design on kitchen windows, front bedroom windows and left side of bedroom window. Retain stucco decoration	90
3.	Substitute screen patio with terrazzo floor at house level, full foundation, 1 waterproof electric outlet, light fixture centred over sliding glass doors. Floor area 16' × 10'. Roof to extend 2' past floor area with screening to be canted toward floor. Roof to be aluminum with styrofoam insulation	740
4.	Install glass shower door in bath #2	50
5.	Substitute American Standard Bildor cast-iron tub for present steel tub	n/c
6.	Erect tile wainscot in bath #2 to 3'8" height	145
7.	Install air-conditioning aperture centre under front windows to bedroom #1, with 220V outlet on separate circuit for same	28
8.	Install tile backsplash above base cabinets in kitchen	50
9.	Install gutter and downspout over front entrance, left side of bedroom wing, kitchen and garage	50
10.	Eliminate Walltex in baths #1 and #2	
11.	Install bookshelves between living room and dinette in lieu of present planter and wrought iron. Shelves to be placed at 42", 54" and 74" height	n/c
12.	Raise 1" to 4" pressure-treated drapery hanger above sliding glass doors in living room to ceiling height	n/c

$12 143

Exhibit 5
Sunshine Builders, Inc.
Start Chart

Customer's Name _____   **Broker:** _____

Address: _____   **Legal description:** _____

Phone: _____   _____

1. Contract signed or on file
2. Detail Sheet #1 received
3. Plans ordered
4. Survey ordered
5. Detail Sheet #2 received (if there is more than 48-hr lag between #3 and #5 report to A.R.)
6. Plans returned
7. Plans inspected (if there is more than a 24-hr lag between #6 and #9 report to A.R.)
8. Plans returned for correction
9. Corrected plans returned
10. Plans inspected for correction
11. Plans sent to _____
12. Plans received from _____
13. Building permit applied for
14. Plans and letter to customer (Air Mail Special Delivery w/ enclosed return envelope)
15. Send loan plans
16. Submit plans for subdivision approval (special messenger)
17. Subdivision approval received
18. Survey received
19. Notify supervisor and production to check lot for clearing and for errors in lot line
20. Customer's approval
21. Notify accounting of loan approval and of who holds the loan
22. Construction loan
23. Add name to production chart
24. Buiding permit picked up
25. Water meter permit picked up

Exhibit 6
Sunshine Builders, Inc.
Sales Promotional Material
for a 2-Bedroom Model

'10,990 on your lot　　　With 2-car garage $11,840

- 2 master bedrooms
- 2 "decorator" baths
- cement tile roof over 2x8 rafters
- 15 ft. sliding glass wall to patio
- Sunshine kitchen; Coronet cabinets and Nu-Tone ventilating hood; Moen single-mix faucet
- General Electric wall oven, cook top, 40 gallon water heater
- radiant electric ceiling heat—silent, clean, maintenance-free, economical; individual room-thermostats
- 6" Fiberglas insulation for cooler summers, warmer winters
- Minneapolis-Honeywell tap switches; clothes dryer outlet; circuit-breakers (eliminating fuses); 200 ampere service
- Hall-Mack bathroom accessories
- spacious garage plus utility "ell"
- spot sodded lawn
- square footage: living area　　1073
  　　　　　　　　 utility　　　　 63
  　　　　　　　　 garage　　　　249
  　　　　　　　　 TOTAL　　　 1385
- Sunshine guarantee of satisfaction

Model 190

1202 Hacienda Ave. ● Minneapolis, Florida ● Phone 6-4602

it's a  home

Model Home on Poinsettia Rd. — 2 Miles South of Key Drive

Exhibit 7
Sunshine Builders, Inc.
Sales Promotional Material
for a 3-Bedroom Model

$18,500 on your lot

- **3 bedrooms**   • **3 "decorator" baths**
- cement tile roof over 2x8 rafters
- tile foyer entrance with guest closet
- spacious family room with serving bar
- sliding glass walls from living and dining rooms to
- 18 ft. screened porch
- 20 ft. free-form patio
- Coronet cabinets in solid maple or solid walnut; Nu-Tone ventilating hood; Moen single-mix faucet
- General Electric dishwasher, wall oven, cook top, 52 gallon water heater
- radiant electric ceiling heat—silent, clean, maintenance-free, economical; individual room-thermostats
- 6" Fiberglas insulation for cooler summers, winter warmth
- Minneapolis-Honeywell tap switches; clothes dryer outlet; circuit breakers (eliminates fuses); 200 ampere service
- Hall-Mack bathroom accessories; "relaxation unit" in master bath
- 2-car garage plus utility "ell"
- spot sodded lawn
- square footage:

living area	1656
porch	180
garage and utility	505
TOTAL	2341

- **Sunshine**   guarantee of satisfaction

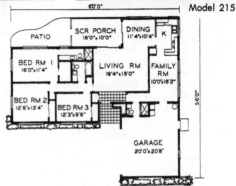

Model 215

1202 Hacienda Ave. • Minneapolis, Florida • Phone 6-4602

it's a  home

43
Willowbrook Castle

"Jim, as general supervisor on this home, you ought to be able to supply me with some badly needed information. I must know not only the expected completion date, but also the times when I can get mortgage draws from my trust company. It is imperative I have a plan because my financing will depend upon exact timing. Otherwise, I will not be able to build this house."

The request was made by Mr. Charles Talbot, the prospective owner of a new home to be constructed on a good out-of-town property site. He was speaking to Jim Fraser, who would be responsible for the home construction, although he would not be directly responsible for the hiring of the subcontractors.

Mr. Talbot also informed Jim Fraser that timing was critical because the Talbots' apartment lease would expire in 108 days. Mr. Talbot would have legal possession of the site in ten days which, according to Mr. Talbot, meant the home had to be constructed in seventy *working days* after that.

Jim had recently heard about the Critical Path Method (CPM) of scheduling projects such as house construction. This method promised to provide a clear visual aid in determining (1) which jobs or activities (sequenced in their correct technological order) were "critical" in their effect on total project time, and (2) how best to schedule resources devoted to the project in order to meet a target date at minimum cost. (See the Appendix for additional information on CPM.) With this in mind, Mr. Talbot's letter from the mortgage company (Exhibit 1) and a list of the activities that were involved in building the Talbot home, Jim decided to prepare a CPM chart for the project. He hoped it would help him answer Mr. Talbot's questions.

Exhibit 1
Willowbrook Castle

Reliable Trust Co.
395 Main Street
Littleton, Ontario

Mr. Arnold James
Branch Manager
Reliable Trust Company
395 Main Street
Littleton, Ontario

Dear Mr. James:

This will confirm that a first mortgage at current rates will be granted Mr. Charles Talbot on the proposed new home to be constructed on Lot 18, Concession 10, Township of Frontenac.

Mortgage draws will be as follows:

First Draw	—1/3 total (approx.). When house is framed.
Second Draw	—1/3 (approx.). When drywall and plastering are completed.
Final Draw	—Remainder. When home is declared completed and hydro inspected for living.

Although mortgage draw times vary slightly with different trust companies, we have found these stated times to be mutually acceptable to most of our clients. Inspection will be completed at the above specified times at the owner's request. Final mortgage paper will be closed upon final inspection and completion.

Yours very truly,

Jason Hogg
Mortgage Manager

JH:jm

Exhibit 2
Construction of Willowbrook Castle

Job Name	Description	Immediate Predecessors	Time (Days)
A	Prepare site	—	2
B	Excavate site	A	1
C	Form and pour footings	B	1
D	Pour concrete foundation	C	5
E	Lay sewer tile	B	1
F	Pour basement and garage floors	E	3
G	Backfill	D, F	1
H	Framing and rough roof	G	9
I	Rough in plumbing and vacuum system	H	3
J	Rough in wiring	H	2
K	Rough in heating	H	2
L	Shingling	H	3
M	Install windows	H	1
N	Bricklaying—interior and exterior	H	4
O	Finish roofing	L, N	2
P	Insulating	I, J, K	3
Q	Lathing and plastering	P, M, N	17
R	Finish wiring and plumbing	Q	8
S	Finish flooring	R	4
T	Trimming	S	14
U	Interior painting and varnishing	T	4
V	Install kitchen equipment	U	1
W	Install light fixtures	U	2
X	Finish exterior	O	6
Y	Finish walks, driveway and landscaping	X	3

Appendix
Willowbrook Castle

A. BRIEF INTRODUCTION TO THE CRITICAL PATH METHOD

The management of projects includes project design, scheduling, material and manpower planning, and control (e.g., completing the project on time and within budget). Increasingly complex and costly projects have taxed management abilities and have led to a variety of helpful management techniques. These techniques, differing in specifics and names, all have some common characteristics: (a) a recognition that a project can be divided into a set of identifiable independent jobs or tasks or activities, (b) a recognition that a project consists of a sequence of these tasks where some jobs must be started before others and some jobs may be performed simultaneously with others, (c) an attempt to portray the project components, in sequence, graphically, with estimates of completion time for each task indicated, and (d) an attempt to determine how long the entire project may take, what trade-offs are involved (e.g., time to change completion time or project cost). Some of the names for these techniques are PERT (Program Evaluation and Review Technique), CPM (Critical Path Method), CPS (Critical Path Scheduling), and PEP (Program Evaluation Procedure). In order to use any of these techniques, first one must master the basic tool of analysis, the network diagram.

1. *The Network Diagram*

A network diagram begins with the separation of a project into independent tasks or activities, estimation of the time required to complete each task, and determination of the technological sequence of the tasks. There are two network diagram procedures: "Activity-on Node Diagram" (AON) and "Arrow Diagram." An Arrow Diagram is the more common approach, but can become very difficult to work with. Therefore, this note will concentrate on the AON method.[1]

    Suppose the project being diagrammed was the construction of the patio. From past experience (or perhaps consultation with expert advisors), one might determine the following table:

---

[1] The complication referred to with Arrow Diagramming is the requirement in some situations of "dummy arrows." For more information, see Wiest and Levy, *A Management Guide to PERT/CPM* (Prentice-Hall, 1969.)

Job Name (Activity)	Description	Immediate Predecessor	Time Estimate (Minutes)
a	Prepare site	—	60
b	Level ground	a	90
c	Prepare concrete forms	a	60
d	Install concrete forms	c	30
e	Pour concrete	d	60
f	Level concrete and let set	e	480
g	Install lighting	b	45
h	Install barbecue	b	60
i	Complete landscaping	f, g, h	60

    Given this hypothetical example, one may construct a diagram wherein the jobs are represented by circles (hence the name "node") and precedence relationships represented by arrows. Identification of jobs and the time required for each is shown in the circles. In addition, a "start" and a "finish" circle are included. The AON diagram for this example is as follows:

Patio Project
Willowbrook Castle

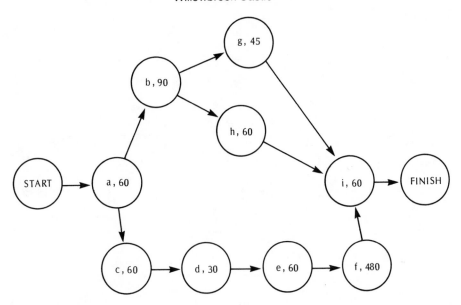

2. Determination of the Critical Path

The "critical path" is the longest sequence of connected activities through the network diagram. Its length determines the time required to complete the project. The critical path can be identified by determining the length of every possible path from start to finish. If the diagram is complex this becomes an immense job so mathematical techniques have been devised to determine the critical path. In simple diagrams, it is usually easiest to find the critical path by working through each path. The longest of these is the critical path. The point is simple: to shorten the time to complete a project one must shorten the critical path, or put differently, to affect the completion date of a project, one must affect the length of the critical path (e.g., reducing the duration of jobs not on the critical path will not shorten the duration of the project).

Returning to the patio project example, the following paths are apparent:

Path	Time
a, b, g, i	255
a, b, h, i	270
a, c, d, e, f, i	750 Critical Path

To build the patio in less time, one must shorten the path a, c, d, e, f, i. Also, if the activities on path a, c, d, e, f, i are allowed to exceed the 750 minutes planned, it will take longer to complete the patio. However, activities on the other two paths could be allowed to more than triple in duration before one of those paths becomes critical instead. For example, if installing the barbeque (h) took fourteen hours (840 minutes), then path a, b, h, i becomes the critical path (1050 minutes).

SECTION VIII
An Introduction to General Management

General management decision making requires the coordination of all aspects of business into an integrated management program. The knowledge that you have been acquiring from previous chapters—finance, marketing, production and human resources—is essential for undertaking general management problems. It will be necessary for you to relate your problem-solving skills in finance to your ability to prepare a marketing program, to your techniques in production design and your expertise in human resources, and so on. In general management you will have to evaluate objectively:

1. The company—objectives
                —strengths and weaknesses
                —analysis of performance
2. The market—existing and potential customers
                —existing and potential competitors
3. The environment—political/legal characteristics
                —economic trends
                —social trends
                —technical developments

Before we get into a discussion of the general management process, we shall examine the role of a general manager.

PART 1: THE GENERAL MANAGER

The meaning of general management varies by circumstances. In a small one-person business, the chief decision maker has to be an all-round general manager capable of longer term planning as well as daily "fire fighting" since there is no specialized staff to delegate these responsibilities. In larger firms, the general management tasks are essentially the same, although a little more complicated. However, there are usually several people who share the general management workload. Even the titles used to describe the individuals responsible for general management vary from company to company: president, managing director, vice-president: administration, and so on. In this chapter the title general manager will refer to that individual who has overall responsibility for a business or a part of one.

Suppose you were the general manager of a large firm. What would your responsibilities be? Probably they would amount to the following:

1. Finding and training competent subordinates. Your goal would be to delegate as much responsibility and authority as possible to your subordinates in finance, marketing, production and human resources to free you for the major decisions concerning the overall company.
2. Coordination. Your goal would be to ensure that the various activities of the company reinforce one another, rather than work at cross-purposes. You would act as a liaison, ensuring that coordination is sought and achieved among the various functional areas of the business.
3. Decision making. The kinds of decisions you'll save for yourself are ones that your subordinates cannot make, either because of disagreements or because they lack a sufficiently broad perspective of the issues that need to be considered.

In short, the general manager must understand all functional areas of business and be especially competent in human resources management. Based on these skills, the general manager delegates, coordinates, and facilitates decisions to the extent possible, and where necessary makes the "big" decisions affecting company welfare. To perform this demanding role adequately, the general manager must be able to appraise the company thoroughly and objectively.

PART 2: COMPANY PERFORMANCE ANALYSIS

A general manager's major concern is improving the overall performance of the company. To do so, he or she must understand what objectives are being sought, what strengths and weaknesses characterize the company, and what options there are for improvement given the operating circumstances.

Objectives

Company goals or objectives are essential, both as a guide for activities in all functional areas of the business and as criteria for evaluation. The following questions may help you understand a particular company's objectives:

1. What are we trying to do?
2. How well have we done it? Why?
3. Can we do the same thing better?
4. Should we try something different?

Objectives must be specific enough to provide useful guidelines for planning and act as benchmarks for performance. Suppose you were requested simply "to make a profit." Obviously, that does not give you much help in planning ways to achieve your performance. Suppose instead you were asked "to achieve a 10 per cent return on investment after tax next year in the original equipment radial tire market." The latter statement would obviously help.

Sometimes you may encounter difficulty in identifying what objectives have been established for a particular company, particularly in smaller companies where the owner's personal aims become intertwined with business objectives. In general, there are two common causes of apparent lack of objectives: (a) the objectives simply have not been established or (b) the objectives exist but have not been communicated clearly.

Too often managers tend to regard objectives as "written in stone" rather than reexamining them in light of changes in the company and/or its environment. The usual result, in time, is that the objectives become unsuited to the capabilities of the firm and/or to the opportunities present in the environment. Such objectives are neither good guides for business planning nor adequate criteria for performance evaluation.

As we learned in the previous sections of this book, it is often necessary to consider trade offs among objectives. Often, it is only possible to achieve one objective at the expense of another. For example, one management consultant identified the following trade offs:

1. Short-term profits versus long-term growth,
2. Profit margins versus competitive position,
3. Penetration of existing markets versus development of new markets, and
4. Related versus unrelated new opportunities as a source of long-term growth.

If you are having trouble evaluating or formulating objectives in a particular situation, we suggest you ask yourself, "What is most important to this company?" Choose your answer as the major objective. If after further consideration of the situation you feel you can add to the statement of objectives, come back to this step and do so. The important thing is not to get hung up at this stage of the analysis.

Strengths and Weaknesses

When you attempt to coordinate the various activities of your firm you must evaluate the strengths and weaknesses in each functional area. Each section of this book was designed to enable you to do this. For example:

1. In Finance we discussed management of a company's cash position, analysis of past and projected financial performance, and sources of additional funds;
2. In Marketing we tried to understand and to predict the response of consumers and competitors to changes in a company's product, price, distribution, and communications policies;
3. In Production/Operations Management we examined the various processes a company may use to produce goods and services and the techniques a company may use to improve its production efficiency and effectiveness;
4. In Human Resources we discussed ways to understand individuals, groups, and organizations in order to accomplish tasks through the efforts of other people.

As general manager, you should look at each of these aspects of the overall company in order to determine:

1. Company strengths. What can the company do, and especially, what can the company do particularly well?
2. Company weaknesses. What aspects of the company need to be strengthened in order to improve company performance?

These strengths and weaknesses are best identified by comparing what a company has or does with what is required to succeed in the particular business being examined. The prudent general manager attempts to build on strengths and overcome weaknesses.

The Market

In the marketing chapter, we outlined ways to analyze customer demand characteristics and ways to analyze the nature of competitors seeking the patronage of your target market. By using those techniques, you should be able to arrive at an assessment of (a) what market opportunities exist (e.g., size and growth rate of a market), (b) what risks are associated with pursuing those opportunities (e.g., strength of competition), and (c) what key success factors are involved in bettering competitive efforts to gain consumer acceptance. Key success factors refer to the important activities a company engages in in order to succeed in a business endeavour; for example, the key success factor in door-to-door cosmetic marketing is a very large, highly motivated sales force (such as Avon).

The Environment

Similarly, we discussed in that chapter how to examine environmental trends of importance. Until recently, most business decisions could be satisfactorily made with scant attention to the "environment of business." However, the fast-paced major changes in the political/legal, economic, social and technical features (P.E.S.T.) of our society can no longer be largely neglected. Such changes have created and destroyed major industries remarkably quickly by offering new opportunities and imposing severe constraints. Thus, astute general managers now monitor or scan the environment in order to identify and react to changes of importance to their companies.

Performance Evaluation

Analyzing corporate performance can be difficult because there are so many dimensions that can be examined and often there is not enough information or time to do a thorough job. In these circumstances, we suggest you begin with a "big picture" approach, gradually becoming more specific as circumstances warrant it. Here are three questions you might ask yourself:

1. How well has the company done in terms of its overall objectives? (This refers to profitability, market share, new product introductions, etc.)
2. How well has the company done in terms of the market opportunities it had? (This refers to the size of the market, the company's position vis-a-vis competition, environmental trends, etc.)
3. How well has the company done in terms of the resources it had to work with? (This refers to the people, finance, marketing and production resources available to the firm. Another way of saying this is corporate capabilities.)

Once you have formed some answers to these questions, you will be in a position to examine what the company might do to improve its performance, either by way of "fine-tuning" its policies and procedures or making major changes in its strategy. We'll confine ourselves here to overall strategy changes.

PART 3: STRATEGIC ALTERNATIVES

There are often several ways to achieve a particular objective. When we want to refer to the broad, overall approach a manager has taken (or may take) to satisfying the firm's objectives, we use the term strategy. Another way to think of the word is the phrase "essential plans and policies." What general strategic options might you have to achieve a certain growth objective in terms of size and profits? We think there are four major ones:

1. Market penetration—increased market share with your present product in your present market;
2. Market development—new uses and/or new geographical areas and/or new segments to expand the market for your present product;
3. Product development—new product offered to your present market;
4. Diversification—new business (new product and new market).

Each of these four broad alternatives can then be further defined. For example, if we are marketing milk and we opt for market penetration, how are we going to get our existing customers to drink more? Perhaps we might try an overall strategy of suggesting occasions when milk drinking is appropriate (essentially an advertising strategy). As you generate and evaluate different strategic options, you will probably notice that there are differences in the skills and resources required to implement these strategies. Also, there are probably differences in the degree of risk associated with these options and differences in the expected pay-off to the company. These differences are what makes strategy formulation difficult and interesting.

The choice of the "best" strategy for your company need not be an impossible task. We suggest you build upon your analysis of company performance by:

1. Identifying the past strategies of your company;
2. Assessing their success (or lack of it); and

3. Explaining why past strategies were not more successful.

In the case of a brand-new venture without past experience, we suggest you have a close look at your competitors' approaches, or if you are first into the business, have a look at experiences in comparable businesses.

Some of the questions you might ask about strategies (past or proposed) were suggested by Professor Ken Andrews of Harvard:

1. Is the strategy identifiable and has it been made clear either in words or practice?
2. Does the strategy fully exploit domestic and international environmental opportunity?
3. Is the strategy consistent with corporate competence, both present and projected?
4. Are the major provisions of the strategy and program of major policies of which it is comprised internally consistent?
5. Is the chosen level of risk feasible in economic and personal terms?
6. Is the strategy appropriate to the personal values and aspirations of the key managers?
7. Is the strategy appropriate to the desired level of contribution to society?
8. Does the strategy constitute a clear stimulus to organizational effort and commitment?
9. Are there early indications of the responsiveness of markets and market segments to the strategy?

These are tough questions. Adequate answers can only be provided after you have thoroughly investigated the firm's current and anticipated circumstances.

Once you have settled upon a major direction for your company, your job as general manager becomes one of ensuring that detailed plans for finance, marketing, production, and human resources are prepared and implemented in accordance with the overall strategy of the firm.

PART 4: COURSE OF ACTION

Obviously, to be of any use, the general manager's action plan must be specific enough to enable the general manager (or peers and subordinates) to carry out the strategy in accordance with their intentions. Such a plan should clearly specify:

1. What to do,
2. When to do it,
3. Who has the responsibility and authority to do it,
4. How results will be measured, and
5. How results will be regarded in terms of compensation, or promotion, and so forth.

A good situation analysis and a good analysis of strategic alternatives will enable you to formulate an action plan relatively easily because the action should practically "drop out" of your analysis. Remember, as a general manager it is your responsibility to see that the functional area plans (finance, marketing, production/operations, and human resources) fit together into an integrated whole, constituting your overall corporate action plan.

A good test of whether you have thought it through sufficiently is to try to persuade a skeptical person that your plan of action makes sense. If, as a general manager, you can both explain *what to do specifically,* and *why it is worth doing,* then you have reached the point we hoped you would.

44
Coffees of the World

Coffees of the World was a specialty store selling teas, coffees and coffee-making accessories, started by Tim Snelgrove and his partner, Peter Lockie, in September 1975 in a small store in a London, Ontario, shopping plaza. The plaza was located on a main road in a district that combined single family housing with a developed high-rise apartment area. The new business developed from a project Snelgrove had worked on during his MBA program. The project indicated that the venture could be successful. The operation appeared particularly attractive to the partners because only a minimum amount of capital was required, and only a part-time management committment was needed. The personal financial resources of the partners were limited, as was their time: both were embarking on their professional careers.

By March 1976, Coffees of the World was considering expansion into the Toronto market because the London location had proven successful. Snelgrove and Lockie were considering three expansion alternatives: (1) leasing mall retail locations, one at a time; (2) acquiring the firm Coffee Blender Inc., an existing chain of specialty coffee stores; or (3) franchising the Coffees of the World name and operation.

TEA AND COFFEE MARKET

Tea and coffee are two of Canada's popular beverages, with 64 per cent of the population coffee drinkers, 53 per cent tea drinkers, as opposed to only 41 per cent for juices, and 31 per cent for soft drinks.[1] Per capita consumption of coffee had increased slightly from 1.91 to 1.99 lbs per person during the period 1960 to 1970. The thirty to forty year age group drank 47 per cent more cups per day than all other age groups, and as the "baby boom" population entered this age group it was expected to have an upward effect on consumption.

In 1970 the coffee market was split in half between instant and regular coffee. Twenty-eight per cent of Canadian homes served both types of coffee. There was substantial growth in the use of domestic coffee makers such as "Mr. Coffee." It had been suggested that, with the rapidly increasing price of coffee, once the consumer was paying over $2.50 per pound of coffee, he or she would take the time and trouble to make it properly.

In 1975 the world's coffee production was low. This was expected to send the price of coffee soaring. In fact, rapidly increasing prices had been the case during the year.

Good quality fresh-roasted coffee was available through a small number of coffee specialty stores and gourmet shops. Supermarkets generally offered only low quality blends; supermarket prices were as much as 50 per cent lower than specialty shops; coffee was considered and used as a traffic builder. Rather than a blend, specialty shops featured a variety of specific growths, such as Colombian and Mocca Java. Because the shelf life of roasted coffee was only a few weeks, storing large inventories of coffee was not practical.

OPERATIONS

Peter Lockie was already located in Toronto. In early 1976, he had aquired a partnership interest in a small legal practice after receiving his "call to the bar." Tim Snelgrove was completing the final year of his MBA program in London. Tim was married and had a young family. Upon graduation, he was planning to return to an executive position in the management consulting firm he had left when he entered the MBA program. A major objective of the partners was to be able to pursue their individual careers while still running the Coffees of the World business in their spare time. All of their assets were pledged to support loans used to finance both Coffees of the World and their career development. Each had an equal number of shares in the company.

The Coffees of the World shop in London was $400 over budgeted sales for the first five months of operation and was expected to make the first year's sales forecast of $74 000. At the fiscal year end of January 31, 1976, a small profit of $1296 was realized after all start-up items, as shown in Exhibit 1. Exhibit 2 presents the balance sheet after the first five months of operation. The store was run by a manageress who hired and scheduled staff, bought merchandise as needed and prepared a weekly sales and cash reconciliation. Part-time help was used for evenings and weekends. The manageress was paid $5 per hour; all other help earned $3 per hour. Merchandise was bought from a number of Toronto suppliers on thirty-day terms. Initially, inventory turned over twelve times a year and all sales were cash so that there were no credit collection problems. Gross margins were 40 per cent on coffee, tea and accessories and 50 per cent on giftware. Recent quantity purchases of giftware had increased the margins on some items to as high as 75 per cent. The store started selling its own brand of tea and tea bags with margins over 60 per cent. Similar improvements in margins could be obtained for increased coffee purchases.

OPPORTUNITIES FOR EXPANSION

Lease Mall Locations

Tim Snelgrove was considering expanding into two leased locations in Toronto suburbs. At this time there were no locations for lease in the popular high traffic Toronto malls and no additional mall locations were being built. The two mall locations under consideration were twenty-five and fifty miles from downtown Toronto and located in single family residential areas.

Negotiations were under way for the two store locations and Snelgrove expected the mall rent would be similar to that paid in the London location of $9 per square foot for a 420 square foot store, or 7 per cent of gross sales, whichever was higher.

The Coffee Blender Inc.

In February 1976, the Coffee Blender Inc. was listed for sale with a Toronto real estate broker for $85 000. Exhibits 3 and 4 were the financial statements given to Mr. Snelgrove by the owners, Mr. and Mrs. Winstone. The Coffee Blender Inc. was Toronto's largest retailer of roasted coffee with three mall retail outlets and a Don Mills warehouse. The St. Clair and Yonge Street stores had sales of $112 000 each and the Don Mills store had sales of $49 000 for total sales of $273 000 in 1975. All of the store locations were in high rental areas. Sales had grown at the annual compound rate of 22 per cent. The firm sold only a limited amount of high margin giftware and coffee accessories, and coffee sales accounted for over 70 per cent of the store volume. In contrast, Coffees of the World sold 30 per cent coffee and 70 per cent accessories. Despite the fast growth in sales and the high volume of sales, operations were only marginally profitable in 1974. In 1975, a small loss was incurred as shown in Exhibit 3: Mr. Winstone had prematurely joined the business full time. Consequently, the firm had higher fixed costs for the $15 000 salary of Mr. Winstone. Also contributing to the low profitability was the Bloor Street store which, after opening in 1973 at an expenditure of $15 000 in fixed assets, experienced a slow growth in sales volume. The store was just becoming profitable on a monthly basis. Snelgrove felt an offer equal to the book value of the assets of Coffee Blender Inc. would be accepted, though he was uncertain as to what offer, if any, he should make.

Franchising

Tim Snelgrove had been approached about franchising the Coffees of the World concept for a location in Richmond Hill, twenty miles north of Toronto and later by a different party for a franchise in Calgary, Alberta. If any agreement was to be made, Tim Snelgrove thought the deal should be structured as following:

1. The franchisee would pay $1000 plus 5 per cent of gross sales annually for the use of the sign, merchandise bags and the use of the Coffees of the World logo;
2. A $95 per month rental charge would be levied for the coffee grinding machine, weigh scale and cash register; and
3. The franchisee would be required to buy all his merchandise from Coffees of the World, non-coffee items at a 10 per cent discount from normal wholesale prices and coffee at 5 per cent below normal wholesale prices.

As protection, Coffees of the World would agree to buy back the franchise after two years of operation if the franchisee was not satisfied. The repurchase price would be $2000, plus inventory at cost and any leasehold improvements, but not including any losses incurred. Tim Snelgrove believed that the best way to design a franchise agreement would be ''to make the franchise work so well that the franchisee doesn't want out of the agreement.'' He knew each franchise had to be successful to attract new ones.

Exhibit 1
Coffees of the World Inc.
Statement of Income and Retained Earnings
for the Five Months Ending January 31, 1976

Revenue		
Sales recorded	$37 485	
Less: provincial sales tax collected	1 011	
Net sales		$36 474
Cost of Goods Sold:		
Purchases	$27 227	
Less: closing inventory	5 178	
Cost of goods sold		22 049
Gross Margin		$14 425
Expenses		
Wages	$ 5 613	
Rent	1 885	
Utilities and maintenance	146	
Cash short	56	
Cash register rental	320	
Bank service charges and interest	198	
Miscellaneous store expenses	54	
Packaging	685	
Advertising	746	
Freight in	367	
Telephone	376	
Insurance	177	
Organization expense	541	
Administrative expense	1 273	
Depreciation and amortization	260	
Total expenses		12 697
Net operating profit		$ 1 728
Provision for income taxes		432
Net earnings		
and retained earnings, January 31, 1976		$ 1 296

Prepared by T. Snelgrove.

Exhibit 2
Coffees of the World Inc.
Balance Sheet
as of January 31, 1976

ASSETS
Current Assets
Cash	$4 245	
Merchandise inventory at cost	5 178	
		$ 9 423

Fixed Assets:
Store equipment	$ 992	
Store fixtures	1 355	
Lease improvements	780	
	$3 127	
Less: accumulated depreciation	260	2 867
TOTAL ASSETS		$12 290

LIABILITIES
Current Liabilities
Bank loan payable	$3 000	
Accounts payable	4 053	
Payroll deductions payable	148	
Rent payable	442	
Accrued expenses	146	
Accrued income tax	432	
Total current liabilities		$ 8 221

SHAREHOLDERS' LOANS AND EQUITY
Shareholders' loans[1]	2 769	
Capital issued and fully paid	4	
Retained earnings	1 296	
Total equity		4 069
TOTAL LIABILITIES AND EQUITY		$12 290

[1] Shareholder loan is subordinated to the bank loan.

Prepared by T. Snelgrove.

Exhibit 3
The Coffee Blender Inc.
Statement of Operations and Retained Earnings
for the Year Ended May 31, 1975
(with comparative figures for 1974)

	1975	1974
Revenue	$273 148	$213 572
Cost of sales		
Inventory—opening	$ 5 250	$ 6 331
Purchases	169 655	131 415
	$174,905	$137,746
Less: inventory—closing	5 664	5 250
Cost of sales	169 241	132 496
Gross profit	$103 907	$ 81 076
Direct expenses		
Wages	$ 54 009	$ 35 279
Canada pension	688	549
Unemployment insurance	692	401
Total wages and salaries	$ 55 389	$ 36 229
Advertising	2 592	1 035
Chargex costs	596	—
Store maintenance and expense	986	1 619
Store rent	23 673	19 496
Telephone	656	670
Hydro	836	691
Business taxes	604	432
Workmen's compensation	373	154
Bad debts	23	8
Depreciation—equipment	742	927
—leasehold improvements	3 598	3 598
	90 068	64 859
Contribution to profit	$ 13 839	$ 16 217
Other operating expenses		
Warehouse expenses	$ 3 513	$ 1 416
General and administrative expenses	10 516	12 092
	14 029	13 508
Profit (loss) for year, before provision for income taxes	(190)	2 709
Provision for income taxes	—	731
Net profit (loss) for year	$ (190)	$ 1 978
Retained earnings—beginning of year	11 269	9 291
Retained earnings—end of year	$ 11 079	11 269

Exhibit 4
The Coffee Blender Inc.
Balance Sheet as of May 1, 1975

ASSETS

Current Assets	1975	1974
Cash	$ 2 817	$ 7 719
Inventory—valued at lower of cost or market prices	13 248	12 113
Prepaid expenses	—	84
Corporation income tax receivable	770	1 389
Total current assets	$16 835	$21 305
Fixed assets:		
Furniture, cost	$ 7 668	$ 7 010
Automobile, cost	5 684	2 935
Leasehold improvements, cost	17 989	17 989
	$31 341	$27 934
Less: accumulated depreciation	13 440	8 481
Total fixed assets	17 901	19 453
Other assets, at cost:		
Incorporation expense	$ 537	$ 537
Goodwill	20 000	20 000
Utility deposits	110	200
Total other assets	20 647	20 737
TOTAL ASSETS	$55 383	$61 495

LIABILITIES

Current Liabilities		
Demand loan—bank	$11 000	$15 000
Accounts payable and accrued expenses	17 144	22 356
Employees withholding taxes and sales tax	1 105	808
Note payable—G.M.A.C.	1 493	—
Total current liabilities	$30 742	$38 164
Shareholders' loans	13 557	12 057

SHAREHOLDERS' EQUITY

Capital
Authorized:
36 000—6% non-cumulative, redeemable
(at par) preference shares with a par
value of $1 each. Issued, none.
4 000 common shares without par value,
not to be issued for a consideration
exceeding $4 000.
Issued and fully paid:

5 common shares	$ 5	$ 5
Retained earnings	11 079	11 269
Total equity	11 084	11 274
TOTAL LIABILITIES AND EQUITY	$55 383	$61 495

45

Extra Valu Stores

As he hung up the phone, Doug Jones, southwestern area manager of Extra Valu Stores, cursed his misfortune. The last thing he wanted on a Friday afternoon was to have to drive for two hours to check out consumer complaints about a store closing. Thirty minutes earlier the company president, Mr. Rogers, had received a telegram from a group of customers who patronized one of the two Trimball, Ontario, stores that were being closed. Apparently the group felt that their neighbourhood store should remain open. Mr. Rogers had passed the problem on to him and asked for a report by Monday morning. A call to the Trimball store manager suggested that the telegram was merely the "tip of the iceberg." The store was located across the road from a neighbourhood "action" organization and the manager expected problems. Doug decided to visit Trimball.

COMPANY POLICY

As he drove, Doug reviewed the rationale behind the decision to close the two Extra Valu Stores in Trimball, both of which he believed were still marginally profitable. During the last five years the company had been phasing out its older, smaller stores. Food retailing was highly competitive and small free-standing stores were not as profitable as large stores in mall locations. Over the past five years Extra Valu had closed forty small old stores (one-fifth of the total number in operation) and replaced them with units which were on average more than three times as large (i.e., 25 000-30 000 square feet of gross floor area versus 6000-8000 square feet). Moving to a new store was nearly always more attractive than incurring the high cost of renovation of old facilities, especially when renovations did not provide more selling space. As a result, about 30 per cent of the company's present retail capacity had come on stream in the last five years. This program of conversion to big modern outlets had improved the company's efficiency, in turn allowing it to offer better prices and generate more store traffic without a proportional increase in store personnel.

Table 1

	1974	1969	% Change	% Change Corrected for Inflation
Sales per sq ft of store space (weekly)	$ 4.90	$2.70	+81%	+16%
Sales per employee (weekly)*	$1 317	$783	+68%	+17%

* Using the ratio of two part-time employees equal to one full-time employee.

Since the labour cost and the store upkeep cost were the company's two major operating expense categories (using approximately 12 per cent and 3 per cent of every sales dollar respectively), this improvement in personnel and facility utilization was critical to profitability.

All names and places have been disguised.

The move to larger retail outlets had also allowed the company to enrich its merchandise assortment by expanding into more profitable product departments—convenience and frozen foods, delicatessens, in-store bakeries, snack bars, and so forth.

In addition, Extra Valu had set up a few prototype stores in the 40 000-50 000 sq ft size range which devoted about 30 per cent of their floor area to the display and sale of non-food items such as sewing supplies, hobby items, inexpensive children's apparel and other more traditional products (health and beauty aids, home cleaning products, tobacco and so on). These products represented inexpensive, routine purchases which an increasingly affluent society seemed to want for one-stop shopping convenience. Exhibit 1 shows the store layout for a 35 000 sq ft "superstore" in Trimball.

Doug recalled a recent report from the company's planning department which illustrated the potential impact on profitability that this expanded product mix could have. They estimated that (a) 20 per cent of a new "superstore's" volume was done in non-food items (versus 10 per cent historically); and (b) gross profit margins on non-food items would average 30 per cent of sales (versus 17 per cent on food products).

Table 2

| | Store Type | |
	Small Size	New
Food	$.90 \times 17\% = 15.3\%$	$.80 \times 17\% = 13.6\%$
Non-Food	$.10 \times 30\% = 3.0\%$	$.20 \times 30\% = 6.0\%$
Gross Profit Margin	18.3%	19.6%

This improvement in gross profit margin was very important considering that Extra Valu currently earned only about 1.5 per cent on sales (before income tax) after all operating charges. Doug's performance was evaluated on the profitability of his area so he was pleased when he could replace small stores with the more profitable superstores.

Extra Valu's policy was very successful. During the past five years their market share had risen 5 per cent, much of it at the expense of independent food merchants whose existence was founded on non-price factors such as personalized service, delivery and convenient location.

THE SITUATION IN TRIMBALL

Doug reached Trimball by 7:00 P.M. and visited the store on Hudson Street first. Large red window banners announced that the store would close in one week and offered 10 per cent off all store merchandise. There was no sign of any protest in or around the store. A few elderly ladies from the nearby senior citizens' building browsed through the discounted merchandise. The manager told him that he had not been approached by any organized groups although a city alderman had been around seeking information and some senior citizens had complained on an individual basis. This scene was in direct contrast to the situation he found at the Farnham Road store. About thirty picketers marched in a circle in front of the store carrying signs protesting the closing.

Finding a parking spot in the tiny lot proved difficult; however, Doug was not in a hurry to enter the store. He was careful to wait in his car until the television crew from the local station had finished filming. As he walked up to the entrance two elderly ladies approached him and identified themselves as working for the Farnham Road Council (FRC).

One asked him if he would like to sign their petition (Exhibit 2), while the other offered him a form letter (Exhibit 3). The ladies told him that other FRC workers were canvassing the neighbourhood getting signatures on the petition and distributing form letters. They hoped to have several thousand names by Monday morning. Doug refused politely then entered the store. It was small so there were few high margin products (Exhibit 1). Weak lighting and a wooden floor did not project the same image of Extra Valu that the larger modern stores did.

Doug was puzzled by the intense consumer reaction. The banners that announced the closing had gone up only the previous afternoon. In a little over twenty-four hours the citizens had organized this protest. They could not have had advance notice because not even the store manager had known in advance. Prior to any knowledge of consumer reaction, Doug had approved the offer of some free merchandise to customers (Exhibit 4) if they went to another Extra Valu store in town. He had no information on the extent to which customers had used this offer or how they felt about it.

Doug was eager to learn as much as he could about the group that sponsored the Farnham Road protest, the people it represented and their reasons for protesting. He decided to make some enquiries about the neighbourhood and solicited the store manager's help.

THE FARNHAM ROAD AREA

The area, which had a population of 9500, was in an older part of Trimball. The problems of this particular neighbourhood were typical of the central section of the city. Family incomes were lower, averaging $8000 compared with the city average of $10 700. Tenant/landlord problems were common and juvenile delinquency was higher per capita than in other neighbourhoods in Trimball. There were a large number of family crisis situations.

THE COUNCIL

The Farnham Road Council was an unofficial voluntary organization which met monthly in an area school. There was no charge for membership. All those who lived in the Farnham Road area were considered to be members. The executive, which was elected yearly at a public meeting, considered their role to be one of helping people to help themselves. Whenever an area resident wanted to discuss local problems he or she contacted the executive and the problem was put on the council's agenda, which was published in the council newspaper. Other interested individuals attended the meeting to meet people with similar concerns. The executive helped these interest groups form subcommittees which were responsible for their particular concerns. The executive were residents who had dealt with the various levels of government and could serve as resource persons for subcommittees.

When area residents wanted a crosswalk installed on a busy street the council helped them prepare a petition and write a successful brief to the city. Similarly, another subcommittee convinced the city to designate some undeveloped city property as a park. The council's most recent success was getting a neighbourhood improvement grant. The store manager showed Doug the FRC monthly newspaper, which had a circulation of 6500 copies. It had a front page article which asked for suggestions from the citizens on how to spend $500 000 that the government had decided to allocate to the Farnham Road area, one of two in Trimball that had qualified for grants under the Neighbourhood Improvement Program. The manager explained that the city hoped the money would help prevent further deterioration of the neighbourhood.

While the manager had been helpful, Doug wanted to get a first-hand impression of the neighbourhood and set out for the FRC meeting place in the White Library and Resource Centre, which was a short walk down the street. Wandering through the small cement block building Doug noticed offices for a full-time social worker as well as offices for a part-time public health nurse, a child management counsellor and a family benefits worker. He was intrigued by posters throughout the building publicizing various programs and activities for both children and adults. One poster reminded residents to save their Extra Valu Store cash register tapes. The poster had a photo of the new kitchenette for the volunteer nursery that Extra Valu had sent in exchange for $251 000 worth of register tapes.

Doug stopped a moment to watch a group of residents who were setting up paintings for a showing of the works of amateur artists from the Farnham Road area. The residents were talking about the good newspaper coverage the protest had received in the evening paper.

Doug left the White Centre but bought a newspaper before heading back to Valleyville. He quickly found the article which explained the citizens' protests. The major problem seemed to be the high proportion of senior citizens in the area. The apparent organizer, Elizabeth Chambers, remarked that the old people shopped two or three times a week because they could not carry heavy loads very far. Miss Chambers claimed that once the Extra Valu store was closed, the seniors would have to take the bus to the next nearest supermarket—a ride which she said would be expensive for those living on pensions and impossible for those with severe arthritis. Mr. Jones noticed that Miss Chambers did not mention the numerous small variety stores in the immediate vicinity but only referred to the supermarkets. Miss Chambers also said:

"We can appreciate the profit pinch but food supply is more than a matter of profit making. It is an essential service. Even if the store is a marginal operation, or losing a bit, we think it should stay open for humanitarian reasons. Surely a conglomerate like Extra Valu can support the odd weak link in its strong chain. . . . We are not asking it to lose money. In fact, we are not certain it is losing money. If service was cut to essentials and prices were reasonable, then we would be very happy. . . . There were a lot of good independents around here when this Extra Valu store opened twenty-five years ago, but they could not compete and went out of business. Extra Valu comes in, gets the dollar, then slips away leaving us high and dry."

As he drove back to Valleyville, he wondered what coverage was given in the local television late evening news. He suspected it would not be very favourable to the company.

MONDAY MORNING

On Monday morning Doug phoned both Trimball store managers to learn the latest developments before talking with Mr. Rogers. The Hudson Street store manager said that there had been no organized protest at his store although some residents of the nearby city-run senior citizens apartment had complained individually to him. Apparently, they had contacted their aldermen in the hope that the city would intercede on their behalf. The Hudson Street manager was unable to identify any area organizations that were strongly protesting the closing.

The manager of the Farnham Road store described that the newspaper article in Friday's paper was run again at the top of an inside section in Saturday's newspaper. The protest had received radio news coverage as well as coverage on the city's most popular open-line radio show. Senior citizens had phoned to complain publicly that they were unable to travel on buses to shop because of arthritis and that taxis were too expensive. Other people phoned to complain that they would not even be able to buy bread and milk in the neighbourhood once Extra Valu closed. Everyone seemed angry with Extra Valu.

As Doug sat mulling over the problem, a phone call from Mr. Rogers interrupted his thoughts. Mr. Rogers had received three hundred protest letters in the morning mail and although most of them were form letters he wanted Doug to hear one particularly well-written letter (Exhibit 5). He asked Doug about his progress in coming to a decision. Before hanging up he reminded Doug that he needed a decision that morning because he was receiving but not taking calls from Trimball aldermen and radio stations who wanted to know what Extra Valu was going to do.

Exhibit 1
Extra Valu Stores

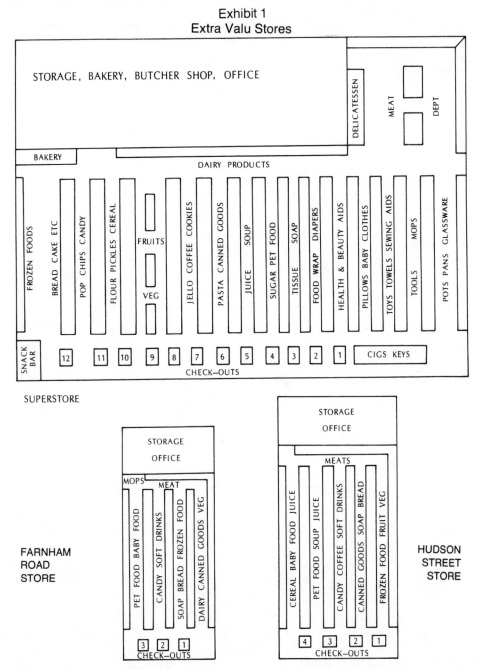

Exhibit 2
Extra Valu Stores
Petition Form

We, the undersigned, are opposed to the decision to close the Extra Valu store at Bayview and Farnham Road in Trimball. The store, which is centrally located, has served our neighbourhood for years, so that many people especially Senior Citizens (which number one in ten) have become dependent on it.

The issue is *SERVICE* to neighbourhood residents, especially our Senior Citizens, from a *LONGTIME NEIGHBOUR,* Extra Valu.

We feel strongly in our desire to have the store remain open or, as a last resort, stay open until another store can move in, thus meeting the needs of the neighbourhood.

Petition sponsored by our
FARNHAM ROAD COUNCIL

Name	*Address*	*Phone Number*
1		
2		
3		
4		
5		
6		
7		
8		
9		
10		
11		
12		
13		

Exhibit 3
Extra Valu Stores Protest Form Letter
Extra Valu Is Proud to Serve You!

Is Extra Valu Serving Us?

After years of being a part of your Farnham Road area neighbourhood, they are closing down their store! Is Extra Valu being a good neighbour of our Farnham Road area by moving out?

Who Shops at this Store?

A lot of neighbourhood people make this store their store. Senior citizens of the Farnham Road area (numbering one in ten), who have no means of transportation, are dependent on this store because of its proximity. *Where else will the seniors go?* For others, this store is a time-and money-saving convenience.

Where Will the People Shop?

Since Shoppers' World at Beach & Farnham Road closed down a year and a half ago, and if Extra Valu now closes, the nearest stores will be: Floyds' at Hudson and Beach, Shoppers' World in the Bentley Plaza and Dollar Stretcher at Bayview and Highbury, which are at the very fringe of our Farnham Road neighbourhood. Extra Valu is right in the middle of our neighbourhood.

YOU'RE AHEAD AT EXTRA VALU!	BIG DISCOUNT PRICES!
If Extra Valu leaves *who* will be ahead?	Does this mean Big Discount service too?

If you are opposed to this store closing and would like the decision reconsidered, please mail in the coupon below.

This flyer is sponsored by our
FARNHAM ROAD COUNCIL

Mr. R. Rogers, President
Extra Valu
217 Seashore
Valleyville

Dear Mr. Rogers:

I/we strongly protest the closing of the Farnham Road and Bayview Extra Valu store in Trimball and urge you to reconsider in light of the service to area residents and our long association with you as our neighbour.

Name _____

Address _____

Telephone No. _____

Exhibit 4
Exra Valu Stores
Offer to Customers

September 23, 1976

Dear Customer:

We sincerely regret to announce the closing of our branch at 500 Farnham Road, Trimball, at 6:00 P.M., Saturday, October 2.

Our appreciation is extended for your past patronage at this location, which has served the area for many years.

Our closest stores are at 1001 Farnham Road and 1350 Hudson Street East, both with ample parking facilities, and 172 River Street at Duke Road featuring a Customer Delivery Service at a nominal charge.

Your patronage is invited to any of these locations, and, as a token of our regret in closing 500 Farnham Road, this letter will be accepted by cashiers at the above stores for a free pound of our freshly ground Extrafine coffee, with assorted purchases totalling $5 and over.

EXTRA VALU MEANS TOP QUALITY AT LOW PRICES

Exhibit 5
Extra Valu Stores
A Protest Letter

September 25, 1976

Mr. R. Rogers, President
Extra Valu
217 Seashore
Valleyville

Dear Mr. Rogers:

I am again contacting you with respect to the scheduled October 2 closing of the Extra Valu store at 500 Farnham Road, Trimball.

Specifically, I draw your attention to the enclosed letter which is being distributed to your customers. This letter does *not* state why our neighbourhood Extra Valu is being closed.

We would suspect that insufficient profit is the reason, but again we really do not know what "insufficient" means. Is the store breaking even or is its profit margin too low in comparison to what you expect of your stores?

We have "heard" that profit is not the main reason for closing this store. Rather it is that the interior of the store does not fit Extra Valu's image. We would assume that if this is the case, the profit outlook for this particular store will not be sufficient to merit renovations.

We realize that, as a private corporation, we cannot force you to share with your customers the reason why you are closing our neighbourhood food store.

We can only appeal to the twenty-five years that Farnham Roaders have patronized this Extra Valu Store. That is a lot of years at being neighbours.

We acknowledge that there could indeed be a valid reason for closing this store. Could we not expect of Extra Valu the same closing policy Shoppers' World came forward with last year here in Trimball when they were planning to close their McMaster Road store? Shoppers' World gave a verbal promise not to close the store until such time that arrangements could be made for another food store to service that particular neighbourhood.

Could I again reiterate the invitation to Extra Valu to meet with area residents Wednesday, September 29, 7:30 P.M. at the White Library, 550 Farnham Road. This meeting will afford you or your representative a chance to hear first-hand our deep concerns having our only neighbourhood food store removed from our area. Also it will provide us with an opportunity to hear first-hand Extra Valu's reason for closing.

Could I kindly ask you, Mr. Rogers, to get back to me (1-653-433-1010) as soon as possible with a reply to our invitation? I thank you for dealing with this matter.

Respectfully yours,

Elizabeth Chambers
Farnham Road Council

46

Flyte Craft

For almost eight years Charles Williamson had produced power boats ranging in size from 12 to 18 feet. During that period Flyte Craft had grown from a one-man operation producing custom units to a company with a well-developed line producing in excess of forty boats a year and retailing a large variety of hardware and supplies through their factory-store outlet. However, during the years 1972 and 1973 sales volume had been static (forty-three and forty-one units respectively) dropping to twenty-nine units in 1974. Williamson felt that major changes had to be made if the company was to return to an acceptable growth pattern. Fiscal 1974 resulted in an unexpected loss of almost $12 000, accentuating Williamson's problem.

THE BOATING INDUSTRY

The pleasure-boating industry in North America had undergone dramatic change since World War II. Rapid growth, material changes, increased power options and new hull designs combined to increase the product offerings now available in the marketplace. Shorter work weeks, increased leisure, longer vacations, earlier retirement and rising income levels provided the fuel for dramatic industry growth. Individual manufacturers, however, did not benefit uniformly from the boom. Overproduction and tight money coupled with increased need for capital investment and marketing skills caused substantial industry restructuring. The trend to bigness continued, evidenced by the fact that 60 per cent of the market was dominated by ten companies. Only the producers of the larger luxury boats were somewhat immune to the fluctuations in industry operations (Exhibit 1).

There were several explanations behind the dramatic change in industry structure. Among these was a shift in materials (Exhibit 2). By 1968 the use of wood in power boats had all but disappeared. Aluminum and fibreglass made up the bulk of material used with aluminum predominant in hulls under 15 feet, and plastic dominated the medium sizes over 15 feet. Together these materials accounted for 85 per cent of all boats made. Canoes were the only major item where wood products remained dominant. Change in materials caused changes in technology. Metal fabrication techniques permitted capital investment and volume output in the smaller pleasure craft. Fibreglass technology, geared to low investment, flexibility of application, and design variety, permitted the entry of many new producers into the industry in the late 1950s and early 1960s. These characteristics prompted new entries seeking growth and profit and resulted in overproduction, inferior products, high inventories and price cutting. Profits plunged and the marginal producers disappeared. *Allied Boating Canada* reported that "of the list of 150 producers in 1959, only 50 were still in business by 1968." By 1968 some price stabilization had taken place. Smaller manufacturers had concentrated in specialized lines. Some manufacturers had closed down their Canadian operations while others had greatly expanded.

DESIGN DEVELOPMENTS

Since 1945, the sleek, fast, deep-*V* hull design dominated the powerboat industry. Its ability to handle rough water at relatively high speeds with moderate power demands made the design popular with powerboat enthusiasts. Recently, however, the "gull wing" design had appeared, offering stability and easy riding. Although this hull sacrificed rough water performance, the introduction of increased power packages had offset these disadvantages.

THE POWERBOAT CONSUMER

While over 70 per cent of all boaters were between the ages of twenty-five and fifty-four (Exhibit 3), there was a growing trend toward younger buyers. Although participation increased with income levels, middle-and lower-income buyers were having a growing impact on boat sales (Exhibit 4). Many purchasers began with an initial purchase of used equipment then traded up to new equipment as incomes increased. In general, consumer studies indicated that buyers were more interested in quality and design than price. The average buyer began with a 12-14 ft fibreglass or aluminum runabout costing approximately $2000 complete with trailer and outboard motor. Recent surveys indicated that most buyers were dissatisfied within two years and there was a constant upward movement to more space, power and luxury.

Competition was keen. Good representation was at a premium and advertising, promotion and selling were growing in professional presentation. Over the past decade the boating industry adopted a similar marketing approach as that of the auto industry. Boats were sold on appearance; purchasers were swayed by luxury, trim and interior appointments, colour and options, often to the exclusion of the technical and handling characteristics or hull designs.

The consumer had been conditioned by the automobile industry to expect discounts off list price. Thus in the peak selling season (March through July) 10 per cent discounts were normal, while in the off season (August to December) 15 per cent discounts were common.

Trade-in's were common in the industry. As a result, dealers became involved in a business complicated by inventories, service and selling that was unknown in the late 1950s and early 1960s. Such activities involved increased credit lines and the addition of the mechanical skills necessary to perform complicated service procedures on sophisticated power packages. The increase in options, growth in variations within the lines of individual manufacturers and the broad range of power equipment added substantially to the dealer investment necessary to satisfy growing customer demands.

DISTRIBUTION

Almost 20 000 dealers served the North American boating consumer. These ranged from large specialized boat stores, department stores and boat yards to the small hardware stores that carried boats as a sideline. To reach these dealers, manufacturers typically used one or more of four alternatives:

1. Manufacturers' representatives who established a force of wholesale distributors and dealers—for a fixed percentage of wholesale volume;
2. Wholesale distributor, which made use of the distributors' sales organization and often had national distribution available to the manufacturer of products with wide consumer appeal;
3. Smaller wholesalers for regional coverage;
4. In-house sales force that went directly to the retailer.

Some smaller manufacturers handled sales directly to the consumer, selling from the factory or factory outlets.

Most manufacturers by-passed wholesale channels and sold directly to retailers. Factory salesmen, familiar with local markets, provided the retailer with advertising, display and promotional help. And since good dealers were crucial, boatmakers provided financial help in the form of credit and inventory support to insure that the dealer maintained a complete stock for effective selling.

Dealers, faced with a proliferation of models in the lines of major manufacturers, began to rationalize their product policies. This often had the effect of eliminating the products of small manufacturers who offered limited product lines, and who seldom had much marketing support for the retailer.

The average dealer gained revenue from three sources: new equipment, 60 per cent; used equipment, 20 per cent; service and repairs, 20 per cent.

Typically, the dealer received discounts of 20-25 per cent on inboards and sailboats, 30 per cent on outboard boats and trailers, 32 per cent on outboard motors and 35-40 per cent on boating accessories. Often there was a further variation in these discounts based on volumes, time of purchases and boat sizes. For luxury boats, the discounts were approximately half those of standard units. In most regions the dealer buying-decision was made in late fall. Orders were confirmed between January and March and dealer sales materialized between April and July.

To finance their boat inventories dealers arranged floor plan loans with their local bankers. This type of plan covered up to 90 per cent of stock purchase price. The dealer covered the remainder plus freight, insurance and handling charges. These plans guaranteed immediate cash for the builder, allowed the dealer some financial flexibility and insured adequate stock for display and sale.

EXPORTS AND IMPORTS

In 1966, the U.S.-Canada balance of trade in the boating industry was about even. By 1970 Canada was exporting at twice the level of U.S. imports (Exhibit 5). Two major factors kept U.S. boats out of Canada: a 17½ per cent most favoured nation tariff and the devalued Canadian dollar. The latter has been erased and Tariff Board notice R-182 would soon remove the former. Canadian advantages such as lower labour costs, immigrant skills and strong competitive performances were major factors in exporting successes to date. However, lower material costs, greater efficiencies due to longer runs and a strong marketing effort by large and diversified U.S. firms raised serious questions about future trends. In the area of specialized designs and production, Canadian producers had a potentially bright future although effective marketing to these selective segments was a limiting factor.

FUTURE TRENDS

Although expenditures for recreational boating will increase they will take a declining share of total recreational spending. The major reason for this is that boating is an expensive activity and it competes for the consumer dollar with many less expensive outdoor recreational activities.

Purchases of boats will increase as a percentage of total boating expenditures, due in part to the increase in size of boats, plus the switch to costlier hull materials. Expenditures for repair and maintenance will decline as a percentage of total, since the hull materials now being used are easier to maintain and less likely to need extensive repairs.

Sales of inboard/outdrive boats, houseboats and sailboats will continue to lead industry segments in growth. Cartopper and smaller sailboats will also experience rapid growth. Shipments of inboard/outdrive engines will have the largest growth of all propulsion systems.

Aluminum has been the dominant hull material for recreational boats. However, reinforced plastics have been gaining rapidly and by 1978, 65 per cent of boat shipments will have reinforced plastic hulls. Wood hulls will continue to lose market share while thermoform plastics will find increasing application as a hull material, especially for smaller boats.

Acquisitions and mergers in the industry are expected to accelerate as both leisure-time companies (e.g., AMF, Bangor Punta, Browning Arms, Brunswick Corp., Conroy Inc., and Fugia Industries) and large diversified companies (e.g., Ashland Oil, Beatrice Foods, Chrysler Corp., North America Rockwell and Whittacker Corp.) continue to acquire smaller boat producers. After the industry shakeout eight to ten large companies will dominate recreational boating markets. The most successful companies are expected to be large firms involved mainly in producing and marketing leisure time products and services. Their presence should give the industry greater stability and offer dealers more support in terms of inventory credit and advertising.

Outside of totally new design concepts, improvements for the near future will be refinements to significantly increase quality and performance. Greater use will be made of the design freedom offered by fibreglass (e.g., modular unitized interiors instead of built-in joiner work). And there will be increasing servicing demands as glass hulls age although these requirements will vary from historical repair work.[1]

Although the boating boom was expected to continue, many industry participants doubted that the 1970s would duplicate the market growth which characterized the past decade. Increased affluence and leisure time as demand factors were expected to be supplemented by a growing replacement and second-boat market so that boating was expected to get a fair, but declining, share of the 78 billion dollar recreational market projected in North America by 1978.

THE COMPETITION

Within the region serviced by Flyte Craft there were numerous boat retailers. No official figures covering sales could be found for the region bordered on the west by Belleville and on the east by Brockville. The whole area was an important tourist region and it abounded with cottages, summer homes and private and public campgrounds. With Lake Ontario, the St. Lawrence River and many smaller lakes in the region, it was a boaters' paradise.

Charles Williamson, the president and general manager of Flyte Craft, had some information on boat sales and competition in the region but it was general. As he commented:

"It was only recently, in fact this year when our sales started to skid, that we paid much attention to the competition. In fact we always felt our products appealed to a unique market. Few of our customers were first-time purchasers. We always believed that the buyer had to know a lot about boats before Flyte Craft could sell. Now we are not so sure. In fact, I suspect that few first-time buyers ever heard of us and it is only after they get into boating that they see our wares. Because we can make minor adjustments, customizing, I guess you'd call it, our buyers tend to come looking for combinations they can't get elsewhere. But of course, first-time buyers lack the skills to do this and as a result they don't see our product or service, given its higher per foot price, as a competitive option. Our major competitors? I guess in this area the big sellers are Starcraft, OMC (Outboard Marine Corporation), and Chrysler. They have a number of dealers, wide product lines, a lot of promotion and big names.

"As I say, we really never thought of them as competition but I can certainly see how many buyers find it extremely difficult to see any difference between our product and theirs. We price about the same but they are big marketers—we've never considered that approach. It was only when I heard from some of the local dealers in the Kingston area that their sales had held up well in 1974 that this whole competition thing began to bother me—we're looking at it now but frankly, as a small company I'm not sure what we can do about it."

---

[1] *Allied Boating Canada Report* 1972.

FLYTE CRAFT BOATS LTD.

Charles Williamson had produced powerboats under the Flyte Craft name for almost eight years. Located in the Kingston, Ontario, area, Flyte Craft had grown from a part-time boat service and accessory business into a manufacturer and seller of powerboats and related equipment. With the boat manufacturing boom, Williamson had expanded the retail outlet which sold his boats. Exhibit 6 shows Flyte Craft's sales along with the sales of other equipment and accessories. Typically, about 50 to 60 per cent of sales were gained through selling Flyte Craft while the balance came from those items that Williamson sold as a retailer. Flyte Craft had only the one outlet and all boats were sold directly without the use of salesmen, agents or distributors.

FLYTE CRAFT HISTORY

Williamson had lived most of his life in the Kingston area, a region noted for tourist and boating activities. He acquired a small boating supply firm from his father. He had originally intended to sell the shop and property; however, late in 1966 he had lost his job in a temporary layoff. During this period, Williamson decided to build an 18 ft wooden powerboat that he had been planning for some time. Before he was able to complete the boat he sold it and began building a second. He never did return to his job. With the help of one full-time employee and some part-time assistance he completed and sold thirteen units in 1967. Early in 1968, Williamson had several requests for fibreglass boats. These, coupled with a dwindling demand for his wooden boats, prompted him to expand his facilities and move into the production of fibreglass powerboats. In 1968, he began to sell snowmobiles and broaden his line of accessories. These sidelines were to aid immeasurably in keeping the business afloat for the two years it took to get his boat operations up over break even. Since 1969, unit sales, revenue and profits had increased consistently until 1973. In 1974, Flyte Craft experienced a wide range of problems. Unit prices were not increased to cover increases in unit costs and the volume of sales in both boats and the other lines had declined, resulting in a net loss of $11 247 for the year. It was in this setting that Charles Williamson was reappraising Flyte Craft's future direction.

"The loss came as a complete surprise. Oh, we knew that sales were off but we also knew that 1974 revenues would exceed those of 1971 and in that year Flyte Craft's profits exceeded $8000. It's only now since the loss became evident that I've begun to worry about where this business is going. Always before we just made and sold boats and accessories and, as you can see, except for 1968 (changeover from wood to fibreglass) and 1974 the bottom line always came up right. We've never spent a lot of time managing the details, everyone around here knows his job and I've always assumed if each of us did our jobs we could avoid this type of thing."

FLYTE CRAFT ORGANIZATION

Flyte Craft, with only eleven employees, never had developed an organization chart. Exhibit 7 gives an idea of the way company responsibilities were divided. Williamson filled both the president's role and that of production manager with most of his time spent on the latter. One of the store employees, William Carrier, had originally worked in the shop with Williamson but following an accident several years ago he had returned to handle retail sales for the firm. He continued to fill this position although he now had help to maintain the store hours which had been extended to include nights and weekends during the peak seasons.

In production two individuals acted as department lead hands. Pierre Tremblay supervised the hull-layup operations while Monty Phillips, a cabinet maker by trade, supervised the finishing operations.

MARKETING

Unlike many boat manufacturers, Flyte Craft had no agency, wholesalers or dealers. All of the company's boats were sold directly to the consumer through the company's own retail operations. In-store displays of two or three units were maintained to allow the prospective buyer a view of available models. About 50 per cent of sales were made from floor or inventory units with the balance classified as custom built.[2] The company offered twenty- to thirty-day delivery on these special units with immediate delivery on inventory items.

Advertising for new and used boats was limited to classified placements in the newspapers of Kingston, Belleville, Brockville and Napanee. In addition, the company occasionally displayed boats and boating accessories in recreational equipment shows. Williamson was convinced that word-of-mouth created most sales; that, and former customers coming back to upgrade.

Flyte Craft had not gone to the trouble of designing brochures although specification sheets with sketches had been mimeographed. These were available to prospective customers who visited the shop. There were also assorted photographs of boats that could be viewed at the store to show colour combinations and trim arrangements.

PRODUCTION

Wooden moulds, capable of producing 1000 hulls, started the process. These moulds, one for each size in the line (four), formed the base for the combinations of polyester and fibreglas cloth which constituted the hull (three to six layers of fibreglas). The first layer was carefully rolled to remove bubbles and insure a smooth hull surface. Additional layers of fibreglass were added for strength with the transom and the keel reinforced to withstand the stresses of motor operations. Subsequently, the floor and ski rack were added to the hull before the boat was "blown" from the mould. The hulls were then moved to the assembly areas on dollies where the "glass" was trimmed, vinyl floor installed, front and rear sections of the hulls painted, moulded deck outfitted with hardware, deck installed, gunnel mould placed, leatherette dashboard and panels installed, steering gear and controls placed and windshield and trim installed. These operations varied somewhat where inboard or inboard/outboard power was involved. The plant layout is shown in Exhibit 8.

Inventory of marine hardware, supplies and manufacturing materials was stored in an area at the rear of the plant. No formal records were kept to monitor supplies. The lead hands from both assembly and hull layup kept an eye on these materials and advised Williamson when it was time to reorder. Special items were ordered when the sale was made and installed as the boat reached the finishing stages. Orders for store inventory were handled by Carrier.

The factory operated on a forty-hour week although the practice during busy periods was to work more than forty hours, accumulating this time for additional vacation during the slack summer months.

CONTROL

While the regular financial accounting duties were handled by the bookkeeper, Gary Robbins, little in the way of internal control was used to make operating decisions. Hours,

---

[2] Colour, trim, power, etc., to fit customer specification.

direct and indirect, materials and supplies were not assigned to a specific hull so that costs could be calculated only on an average basis from purchase order data and payrolls. Some attempt had been made to install a piecework system, but Williamson and his bookkeeper could never find time to keep up to date with the records required. Accumulating or even relating labour inputs to a particular job was complicated by a production process that constantly shifted workers from job to job—responding to urgency. During slack periods production workers shifted to maintenance jobs and repair work, and once again, no records were kept to identify this work and its cost.

The "books," as they were currently kept, consisted of a general journal, accounts payable ledger, accounts receivable ledger, payroll ledger and journal of purchases and expenses. The books were drawn together at year end by a small accounting firm which prepared the annual statement. The bookkeeper prepared a monthly operating statment which indicated sales, expenses and estimated profit; however, since inventories and work-in-process were not valued, such statements constantly over or understated the actual situation. Some additional records were kept in conjunction with tax, unemployment insurance and pension requirements but these were for government use and provided no management data for Flyte Craft.

FINANCIAL

From its inception almost eight years before Flyte Craft had suffered from under capitalization. The equity base was made up of common stock (10 per cent), preferred stock (25 per cent) and retained earnings (65 per cent). The company relied heavily on debt financing and used a combination of personal loans from friends and relatives as well as bank loans for both the working capital (factory) and floor plan (retail operations) needs. The loans were secured by plant, equipment and inventory with much of the debt being short term. The issue of broadening the equity base had never been discussed although Mr. Williamson speculated that it might become an issue when the local bank manager saw his latest statement. He was aware that debt financing had permitted the business to survive and grow but it was becoming increasingly evident that his use of short-term funds for capital expenditures had put the company in a position where working capital was strained to the limit. The financial statements are shown in Exhibits 9 and 10.

The seasonal nature of the boat business forced the cash requirement to peak over the production season between February and June. In recent years, Williamson had tended to hold off producing for inventory but this had put an upper limit on Flyte Craft's output. Inventory reductions through preseason and postseason sales (10-15 per cent reduction) had helped the cash flow but reduced profits.

Store operations were integrated into company financial statements with no specific attention paid to retail profitability. The sale of winter recreation equipment had provided a contraseasonal line to keep the store open and some part of the work force productively employed. However, in the past two years a slackening in the demand for snowmobiles in particular had prompted large discounts in order to reduce inventories and free up capital for boat operations. Repair and warranty work, accessory sales and used boat sales made a substantial contribution to Flyte Craft's operations although Williamson was not sure all of these different facets of the business were profitable.

THE CURRENT SITUATION

"We are at a turning point in Flyte Craft and I'm really not sure which way to move. We are in a lot of different businesses here and I seem to be in a position of either cutting back drastically so I can manage this thing effectively or expanding to the point where I can afford to add the equipment and people I need to ensure profitable operations. I seem to be trapped either way. Cutting back to maintain the informal atmosphere that we have grown up with is certainly consistent with my personal objectives.

"But I'm convinced that it would just be a matter of time until the technology and the competition would pass us by, perhaps forcing Flyte Craft to get out of boat production. I have to trade that off against the enjoyment I get out of designing and building boats—going back to just retailing someone else's boats doesn't hold much interest either.

"A couple of months ago I spoke briefly to a government consultant who visited us as part of a loan request we submitted to one of the government agencies. After spending some time here he was convinced that either we broaden our product line so we could get a larger share of our local market or get involved with a distribution system that would open much broader markets to our limited product line. Either way there are major implications for almost everything we do. I know we lack the management skills, financing, control and marketing. Vaguely, I know what has to be done but I'm sure the bank manager will want a detailed plan that looks at the various ways Flyte Craft might develop and frankly, I'm not really sure how to go about this task. We build a good boat; for the price and class, it's among the best available but the more I talk to various people about what happens next to Flyte Craft, the more I feel I will have to move away from my primary interests as a boat designer and builder and concentrate on management. On the other hand, I don't exactly relish the role of standing behind the counter taking orders for somebody else's boat."

Exhibit 1
Flyte Craft
Boat Shipments by Category

	1961	1963	1965	1967	1969
Unit Shipments					
Canoes	5 163	4 959	8 260	9 540	12 389
Rowboats	2 463	3 951	2 810	8 845	8 778
Sailboats	438	1 810	6 631	2 561	2 748
Outboards					
Aluminum	7 591	10 781	12 540	15 775	22 772
Plastic	7 057	7 856	10 141	11 840	17 422
Wood	4 857	4 832	2 789	1 099	599
Commercial	505	615	754	399	488
Cruisers & Yachts	—	—	183	652	818
$000's Shipments					
Canoes	$ 597	$ 671	$1 042	$1 229	$1 565
Rowboats	241	482	320	1 305	1 514
Sailboats	451	2 218	3 885	5 251	8 642
Outboards					
Aluminum	1 675	2 456	2 626	3 332	4 593
Plastic	3 910	5 055	6 289	7 550	12 027
Wood	2 085	2 324	1 708	908	250
Commercial	3 030	4 501	2 815	3 355	4 258
Cruisers & Yachts	—	—	2 321	4 548	6 726

Exhibit 2
Flyte Craft
Boats in Use by Material

Material	1963	1968	1973	1978 (projected)
Aluminum	22.3%	28.6%	33.0%	36.0%
Reinforced plastic	19.4	31.3	40.0	46.0
Steel	2.7	2.6	2.0	2.0
Wood	50.7	34.7	22.0	12.0
Other	4.9	2.8	3.0	4.0

Exhibit 3
Flyte Craft
Age Distribution of Boating Participants

Age	North American Population	North American Boating Participants
Under 25	46.4%	10.5%
25-34	12.1	21.2
35-44	11.5	25.7
45-54	11.4	23.7
55-64	9.0	13.9
Over 65	9.6	5.0
	100.0%	100.0%

Exhibit 4
Flyte Craft
Income Distribution of Boating Participants (U.S.)

Household Income	Total	Boating Participants
Under $2 000	12.6%	2.0%
$2 000-$3 999	13.9	7.9
$4 000-$5 999	14.2	12.1
$6 000-$7 999	15.9	14.1
$8 000-$9 000	13.5	17.5
$10 000-$14 999	19.4	19.5
Over $15 000	10.5	26.9

Exhibit 5
Flyte Craft
Canadian Exports—Pleasure Craft U.S.

Year	$000's
1966	$ 3 400
1967	4 400
1968	7 300
1969	10 700
1970	11 000

Exhibit 6[1]
Flyte Craft
Flyte Craft Sales

Year	Sales Units	Boat Dollars	Other Equipment[2]	Total Sales	Profit (Loss)
1967	13	37 570	31 240	68 610	$ 2 120
1968	8	24 960	47 920	72 880	(4 680)
1969	21	68 040	81 600	149 640	4 489
1970	31	112 220	96 470	208 690	6 678
1971	35	138 985	105 980	244 965	8 328
1972	43	179 310	121 240	300 550	(2 322)
1973	41	178 824	146 312	325 136	13 005
1974	29	129 630	128 610	258 240	(11 247)

[1] Flyte Craft's books were audited in 1973. The auditors at that time also reviewed (and changed) the statements for the years 1967 on.

[2] Includes outboard motors, parts, boating equipment, snowmobiles, etc.

Exhibit 7
Flyte Craft Organization

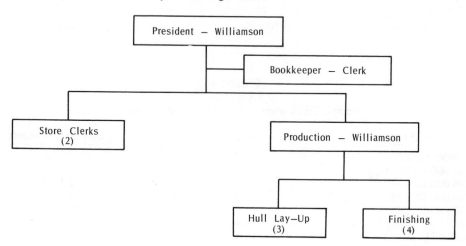

Exhibit 8
Layout — Flyte Craft Plant

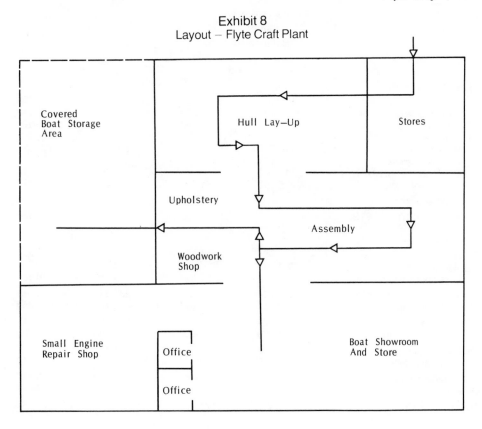

Exhibit 9
Flyte Craft
Profit and Loss Statements

	1973		1974	
Sales retail[1]	$146 312		$128 610	
Cost of goods	98 029		90 035	
Gross profit	48 283		38 575	
Direct expenses	31 279		32 590	
Contribution		$17 004		$5 985
Boat sales	178 824		129 630	
Cost of goods sold	141 343		112 778	
Gross profit	37 481	37 481	16 852	16 852
		$54 485		$22 837
Operating expenses		24 970		21 464
Selling and administrative expenses		16 510		12 620
Net profit (loss)		13 005		$(11 247)

[1] Excludes sale of boats manufactured by Flyte Craft.

Exhibit 10
Flyte Craft
Balance Sheet

	1973		1974	
ASSETS—CURRENT				
Cash		$ 720		$ 659
Accounts receivable (net)		7 210		6 140
Due-Finance Co.		590		620
Inventories				
Materials	$14 710		$16 420	
Work-in-process	9 974		10 274	
Finish goods—boats	11 460		13 260	
parts and motors	15 590	51 734	14 420	54 374
Prepaid and other		1 978		2 095
TOTAL CURRENT ASSETS		$ 62 232		$ 63 888
ASSETS—FIXED				
Land		14 290		14 290
Buildings	$54 790		$54 790	
Less depreciation	21 916	32 874	24 655	30 135
Machinery and equipment	$31 724		$37 620	
Less depreciation	18 710	13 014	21 165	16 455
Furniture and fixtures	$ 2 174		$ 2 490	
Less depreciation	1 570	604	1 760	730
Other equipment	$ 7 129		$ 7 129	
Less depreciation	3 610	3 519	4 410	2 719
Jigs, patterns and moulds		35 460		35 460
Other assets		9 710		7 071
TOTAL ASSETS		$171 703		$170 748
LIABILITIES—CURRENT				
Accounts payable		$ 10 390		$ 13 970
Accrued expenses		5 610		6 170
Employees' tax and pension		705		812
Federal and provincial taxes		7 470		8 271
Notes—short term		19 110		20 270
Customer deposits		4 082		5 724
		$ 47 367		$ 55 217
LIABILITIES—LONG TERM				
Notes payable		$ 18 320		$ 21 700
Bank loan		14 910		16 316
Mortgages		31 844		29 500
		65 074		67 516
CAPITAL				
Preferred stock		12 000		12 000
Common stock		5 000		5 000
Retained earnings		42 262		31 015
		$171 703		$170 748

47

Rebel Fire Apparatus Ltd.

THE FIRE EQUIPMENT INDUSTRY

The products of the fire equipment industry included fire trucks, hoses, fire extinguishers, sprinkler systems, and component parts such as nozzles, valves, siamese[1] and couplings. Firms in this industry usually specialized in a particular line of products (such as trucks) and no firm produced a complete line in any product.

Certain minimum standards must be met by all fire equipment products before they can be placed in public buildings. These requirements ensure that the public will be protected from faulty emergency equipment that could result in unnecessary property damage and personal harm. Recommended standards used in drawing up provisions for the regional fire prevention codes were prepared by several government agencies, national technical societies and trade associations.

Fire prevention codes varied throughout the different regions of Canada. Presently, there were over twelve regional screw thread patterns in existence in Canada and although some attempts had been made to standardize threads, a conversion to a single national thread was nearly impossible due to the expense of such a conversion. Companies required a thorough knowledge of regional standards if national distribution of their products was to be achieved.

Because of the large number of different nozzle sizes and the many different regional threads used on them, mass production of fire prevention equipment was nearly impossible. Consequently, each order had to be produced separately. This characteristic of the fire equipment industry explained why several small firms had been able to carve out a niche for themselves in a very competitive situation.

The markets in the fire equipment industry were broken into four major areas—construction, fire equipment, industrial fire protection and special equipment.

The construction segment required basic equipment for installation in new buildings. This equipment must conform to building and fire prevention codes. The major proportion of products was used in hose cabinets which were installed in public buildings at the time of construction. Products included hose racks, valves, hoses, nozzles and extinguishers. Products for this market segment were produced and sold in large quantity compared to products for other market segments. Product design did not vary significantly with the producer. The major problem in the construction segment was to ensure that the right threads were being used on orders that went to various regions of the country. Price was the major consideration when selling these products. Rapid delivery was much less important.

Although fire equipment must be installed when a factory is constructed, additional equipment may be required because of the nature of the business conducted in the factory. The additional equipment falls under the segment termed industrial fire protection. The equipment was more sophisticated than the equipment installed by the contractor. For example, if the company had a computer, carbon dioxide equipment was required at the site. Larger nozzles of more complex design were required in the industrial segment. Due to the limited market and product complexity, prices were higher than in the construction segment.

The fire department market segment required highly sophisticated equipment. Fire departments must have equipment designed for use in fighting many different classes of fires. Also, each piece of equipment must have technical qualities that enable it to perform

---

[1] Y-shaped outlets used on apartment and commercial buildings for water supply.

its function in the best possible manner. The producer of this equipment must be competent in technical product design, have research for new products, and have facilities for testing each piece of equipment sold. Because a fire department cannot afford to be without a piece of equipment for any length of time, delivery was the prime consideration in this market segment. Price was not as important because a fire department expected to pay a premium for the quality set down on its specifications.

Products in the special equipment segment were generally unique ones requiring a large amount of work. They were produced in small numbers and were very expensive. These products came about as a result of the user's needs and designer/producer's skill in meeting those needs. In many cases, the manufacturer worked on the cost-plus basis. (The producer accumulated all costs associated with the job and added a profit margin to this cost figure when the job was completed.)

MANUFACTURING COMPANIES

Most of the firms in the Canadian fire equipment industry were subsidiaries of large American firms. Among the more prominent companies were Elkart, Wilson and Cousins, Fyr-Fyter and Akron. Most of these companies imported partially completed products from parent firms in the United States and finished them in their Canadian plants. Nearly every firm produced products for the construction segment and each specialized in another line in a different segment of the market. The product range in this industry was so broad that even the bigger firms did not produce a complete line.

Product distribution in this industry took place in two ways. Some of the large manufacturers had their own sales force and distribution system although most manufacturers also supplied a separate distributor-warehousing network.

Most distributors handled competing products from many companies. Independent distributors did not like to handle products of companies who sold directly, and went to great lengths to obtain products from the smaller companies who used independent distributors exclusively. In addition, most distributors handled products for the safety equipment industry such as plastic coats, goggles and safety clothing. Prominent national distributors included such companies as Dyer and Miller, Safety Supply, Canadian Electric Box and Stamping Ltd., Wilson and Cousins, and National Fire Hose.

FOREIGN COMPETITION

Foreign competition in Canada was limited in most market segments where delivery was important. Canadian buyers purchased few foreign products because of the difficulty in getting repair parts from the foreign manufacturers. However, Canadian distributors did buy some items from American manufacturers. These items consisted of certain replacement parts which Canadian manufacturers had stopped making and certain specialty items which were either not produced in Canada or cost three or four times as much to purchase in Canada.

FUTURE OF THE FIRE EQUIPMENT INDUSTRY

The fire department, special equipment and industrial protection segments had grown in proportion to the overall population increase. Equipment in these segments had become more sophisticated as demands became more complex.

Growth in the construction segment depended on economic conditions. It followed the cyclical patterns of the construction industry and in the long run increased as the demand for housing increased.

As far as new products were concerned, a trend toward the use of plastics was growing. Many of the initial problems confronted by plastic manufacturers had been remedied and major companies such as Wilson and Cousins and Akron had begun to sell plastic nozzles. As the cost of brass continued to increase, plastic probably would occupy an even greater portion of the market.

THE COMPANY—REBEL FIRE APPARATUS LTD.

Rebel Fire Apparatus was a Hamilton-based manufacturer of brass components employed in fire fighting equipment. Its product line, which was continually expanding, included nozzles, valves, siamese and adapters. The company machined and assembled a limited line of fire equipment apparatus and sold it through distributors nationwide as well as in regions of the United States.

Don Steen, the owner of the company, had worked for eighteen years with Wilson and Cousins, producers of a wide line of fire fighting apparatus. In 1966, at the age of thirty-eight, Mr. Steen decided to resign from his job as plant manager and establish his own company. With virtually no general management experience but with an excellent knowledge of the products and the industry, Mr. Steen personally began to machine and sell fog nozzles to a number of fire equipment dealers.

Mr. Steen had an aptitude for improving old products and designing new ones. Because his products were of high quality, advanced design and competitively priced, Mr. Steen's reputation as a manufacturer grew. Sales rose steadily (Exhibit 1) from $50 000 in 1967, the first full year of operation, to a projected $300 000 in 1970. Mr. Steen predicted that the present sales level would double within three years. (The company's balance sheets for 1967-69 are presented in Exhibit 2.)

With orders constantly increasing, few problems existed in obtaining higher sales but Mr. Steen became alarmed with the backlog of orders. Fewer deadlines were being met each week. Mr. Steen felt the company was getting too large for him personally to continue supervising each area. The problem of preparing Rebel Fire Apparatus for future growth needed attention but Mr. Steen had less and less time to think about it.

MARKETING

Rebel competed mostly in the construction segment of the fire apparatus market. By promising fast delivery and underselling the competition by 10 per cent Rebel had been able to gain a large portion of the market. In addition, Mr. Steen felt his personal contact with distributors had been a big reason for repeat business.

Rebel used independent distributors exclusively to market its products. It did not sell directly to jobbers or employ any salesmen of its own. As a result, Rebel's distributors had been very loyal. Rebel had a limited number of customers and in 1969 five major purchasers accounted for almost 75 per cent of Rebel sales (Exhibit 3).

PRODUCTS

The three main products produced by Rebel were fog nozzles, siamese and adapters. A comparative analysis of sales by product for the months of December 1968 and November 1969 is given in Exhibit 4.

Nozzles used in fire fighting are similar to the common garden hose nozzle except that they can be subjected to very high water pressures. Prices range from ten dollars per unit for a small basic nozzle to five hundred dollars per unit for more sophisticated nozzles. The company's major line was the one-inch nozzle. Mr. Steen estimated that he held a 50 per cent share of an 18 000-unit total market for this size nozzle.

Siamese are Y-shaped fire hydrants attached to the outside of buildings. The annual total market for siamese was approximately 65 000 a year, of which Rebel held approximately 80 per cent.

Adapters are brass couplings which enable two pieces of equipment with different thread sizes to be joined. Mr. Steen estimated the market to be 40 000 annually and noted that Rebel sold almost 60 per cent of Canadian needs.

FOUNDRY

Initially, Rebel purchased all its castings from an outside foundry, but due to slow delivery and poor service the arrangement was not successful. In September 1968, Mr. Steen acquired the bankrupt Jeffery Foundry with a loss to carry forward of $29 000[2] which could be applied to the profits of the company over the next five years. Mr. Steen retained 100 per cent ownership of the foundry himself and it remained a separate legal entity from Rebel Fire Apparatus.

Rebel purchased the materials needed for the foundry; Jeffery Foundry then formed castings from the material owned by Rebel and charged $.55 per pound for the service. This transfer price (somewhat above the market price for casting services) allowed the foundry to generate a profit to be used against the $29 000 loss carry forward and still left Rebel competitive in its product pricing. The capacity of the foundry was approximately 18 000 lbs of castings per month although it was presently producing only 12 000 lbs per month. Mr. Steen felt the capacity of the foundry could be doubled if an additional man was hired and equipment costing approximately $4000 was purchased.

The foundry cast only for Rebel and did not accept outside orders. Mr. Steen felt he had enough to do without having to handle potential foundry sales to outside companies. The former owners continued to manage the foundry. Mr. Steen had very little contact with the foundry except for the few minutes each morning when he picked up the day's castings for the machine shop. These were no time clocks, expense reports or budgets used in the foundry. As long as it produced the castings needed for the machine shop, Mr. Steen raised few questions.

PERSONNEL

When Mr. Steen started his company, he persuaded six experienced employees to join him at Rebel. As an incentive, Mr. Steen gave each of these six men a financial interest in the company. As a result, the workers were a very task-oriented group whose goal was building a new company. It was not uncommon for the men to work overtime at regular rates if there was a large backlog of orders to be completed. Payments for overtime were figured into the Christmas bonus that each man received.

There was no formal organization chart in the company but Bill Turner, who looked after expediting and shipping, assumed responsibility for the shop when Mr. Steen was absent. At one time, Mr. Steen had been ill for two weeks and Bill managed the company in an excellent manner. Remal Biggs was considered the head machinist, and he had little trouble supervising the other machinists and training new help. Remal had a thorough knowledge of all the company products and knew exactly how much time was required to machine each item.

---

[2] Under the tax laws, a loss suffered by a company in any year could be used to offset an equal amount of profit generated by that company within a five-year period following the loss. By taking advantage of this loss carry forward, a company paid lower taxes than it otherwise would.

COMPETITION

Rebel's two largest competitors were Wilson and Cousins, a subsidiary of Purex, and Coulter Brass. Wilson and Cousins was a very large company with substantial financial resources. It offered a very wide range of products and had its own distributors which sold only Wilson and Cousins's products. It accounted for about $200 000 of sales in the fire apparatus market and this represented only 12 per cent of Wilson and Cousins's total yearly sales. The remaining products sold were purchased from outside suppliers. As this company placed more emphasis on becoming a distributor, Mr. Steen felt that his company had a good chance of becoming a supplier of the brass components needed by Wilson and Cousins.

Coulter Brass was the other major competitor for Rebel. Coulter Brass's sales were smaller than Rebel's and since they were having problems meeting the prices offered by other companies their sales were expected to decrease in the future.

Akron Manufacturing, an American firm, had a subsidiary operation in Aylmer, Ontario. They produced mostly for the fire department segment of the market and as such were only limited competitors of Rebel. This market segment required high quality and technical expertise on the part of competing firms. Akron had a highly regarded research and development department as well as a staff of trained engineers. Mr. Steen felt, however, that the fire department segment offered some opportunities that could be serviced profitably by Rebel.

ORDER PROCESS

The majority of orders were received by phone from the distributor, who preferred to speak to Mr. Steen personally. Usually Mr. Steen quoted a price when the order was phoned in but if it was a custom job he called the customer back within a few hours once he had determined a price. For most orders, a customer was promised delivery in a week or ten days although Mr. Steen realized he might not be able to meet it.

A phone order was first recorded on any scrap piece of paper that happened to be lying near the phone and then placed in a file folder. Customers usually followed up a phone order with a letter or purchase order and upon receipt of the confirmation, the piece of paper was removed from the file and replaced by the order itself. These orders were batched together and constituted a file of back orders.

When the castings were available from the foundry, Bill Turner checked the back order file and made a list of all the parts that had to be machined before the order could be completed. This information was verbally relayed to the head machinist, who added it to the products that had to be machined during the rest of the week.

There were no written schedules used by the machinists and output was dependent upon what castings were available and the number of rush orders that popped up. Often Mr. Steen took a rush order without considering what work was already in the plant at the time. Shuffling jobs to accommodate rush orders had resulted in missed delivery dates for the remaining backlog of orders. On one occasion, the assembly of 150 fog nozzles was held up because one part had been forgotten although all the other parts were completed.

At all times, there was a considerable amount of work in process. Components and castings waiting for further work were stacked on the floor in the vicinity of the machines.

COSTING

Very little costing was done by Mr. Steen but he sometimes referred to costing data salvaged from his previous employer. Although these data were outdated, Mr. Steen adjusted for increases due to higher wages and slightly better machine efficiency. He considered casting a time-consuming and expensive undertaking since every machinist worked at a different rate, and each "performed according to how he felt on any particular day."

As a rule of thumb, he established the cost of a finished product at twice the material cost. If his competitors sold below this estimate cost, he often chose not to manufacture the product. Normally his price was slightly below his competitors'.

When asked by the casewriter whether this method would yield a profit for all product lines, Mr. Steen replied, "Some people have told me ways of determining costs and profits. They all involve too much paperwork and time. I have yet to hear a method which is easier than mine. All I have to do is figure the cost I pay for materials and anything above that is profit because all my overhead and wages are fixed. If I pay $10 for a casting from the foundry, I can sell it for $11 and make a dollar profit." After a moment's pause, he added, "Although since I hired the last couple of employees, I don't think my profits have been as high as they were."

FINANCE

The majority of funds for Rebel Fire Apparatus Ltd. came from a bank loan and a loan from the Industrial Development Bank (I.D.B.). The bank loan was callable and was secured by assignment of accounts receivable. The I.D.B. had imposed restrictions on further capital expansion and required, among other things, that quarterly statements be submitted to them.

The growth increase had placed continual pressure on the company's working capital position (Exhibit 2). Mr. Steen had tried to combat this problem by offering a discount for prompt payment and selling only to relatively quick-paying distributors. Fortunately, the company had been operating at capacity, which permitted Rebel to be somewhat selective in the orders it accepted. (Exhibit 5 presents some selected ratios.)

CONCLUSION

As Mr. Steen reviewed his operation, he knew that there were problems needing immediate attention if the company were to develop its full potential. He was unsure about which problems should receive priority and what could be done to alleviate them. He felt any changes should leave the organization in a flexible position to meet changing demands and greater future growth. Mr. Steen stated, "I want to be the only manufacturer of fire equipment in Canada," and he was aware that some of the decisions he was going to make shortly would play an important role in deciding whether he would meet this objective.

Exhibit 1
Rebel Fire Apparatus Ltd.
Income Statements 1967-1969

	Seven Months May 31, 1967	Year Ended May 31, 1968	Year Ended May 31, 1969
Sales	$37 230	$101 608	$151 278
Cost of goods sold	25 979	79 084	119 185
Gross Profit	$11 251	$ 22 524	$ 32 093
General and adminis- tration expenses	8 775	17 032	24 165
Profit	$ 2 476	$ 5 492	$ 7 928
Other income		584	765
Profit on sale of fixed assets		234	
Income before tax	2 476	6 310	8 693
Income tax	NA	1 380	2 011
Net income	$ NA	$ 4 930	$ 6 682

Exhibit 2
Rebel Fire Apparatus Ltd.
Summary of Balance Sheets 1967-1969

	Year Ending May 31, 1967	Year Ending May 31, 1968	Year Ending May 31, 1969
ASSETS			
Current assets:			
Cash	$ 673	$ 687	$ 1 437
Accounts receivable	4 191	12 650	14 617
Inventory	6 395	5 530	9 305
Pre-paid insurance	204	426	567
Total current assets	11 463	19 293	25 926
Fixed Assets:			
Machinery and equipment	12 756	32 185	43 169
Less: depreciation	2 143	8 211	15 645
Net	10 613	23 974	27 524
Incorporation expense		535	535
Goodwill	10 336	10 336	10 336
TOTAL ASSETS	$32 412	$54 138	$64 321
LIABILITIES			
Current liabilities:			
Bank loan	$ 1 900	$ 7 000	$ 6 000
Accounts payable	5 747	7 225	12 671
Tax payable	223	697	1 863
Current portion L.T.D.		7 179	6 885
Total Current liabilities	7 870	22 101	27 419
I.D.B.		7 600	6 400
Note—truck		2 064	885
Note—non-interest	4 542	3 242	2 042
Long-term liabilities	4 542	12 906	9 327
Less: current portion		7 179	6 885
Total long-term liabilities	4 542	5 727	2 442
Deferred income tax		1 380	2 848
TOTAL LIABILITIES	12 412	29 208	32 709
CAPITAL STOCK			
Issued:			
1 900 preference shares	19 000	19 000	19 000
103 common shares	1 000	1 000	1 000
Earned surplus		4 930	11 612
	20 000	24 930	31 612
TOTAL LIABILITIES AND EQUITY	$32 412	$54 138	$64 321

Exhibit 3
Rebel Fire Apparatus Ltd.
Rebel Customer Purchases

Rebel Customers Purchasing	*Number of Customers*
More than $25 000 annually	3
Between $15 000-$25 000	2
Between $5 000-$15 000	3
Under $5 000	20

Exhibit 4
Rebel Fire Apparatus Ltd.
Sales by Product

	December 1968	November 1969
Fog nozzles (all sizes)	$ 6 840.00	$ 8 756.00
Siamese	3 115.00	4 740.00
Brass couplings	2 122.00	4 506.80
Miscellaneous products[1]	863.00	1 273.20
Total monthly sales	$12 940.00	$19 276.00

[1] Includes some special products and custom orders.

Exhibit 5
Rebel Fire Apparatus Ltd.
Ratio Calculations

	1967[1]	1968	1969
PROFITABILITY			
Return on investment (R.O.I.)	12.3%	22%	23.6%
Net profit %	—	5%	4.4%
Gross profit %	30 %	22%	21 %
LIQUIDITY			
Current ratio	1.4	.87	.9
Working capital	$3 593	($2 808)	($1 493)
Age of receivables	24 days	45 days	35 days
Age of payables	46 days	33 days	38 days
Age of inventory	52 days	25 days	28 days
STABILITY			
Net worth to total assets	62%	46%	49%
Debt to equity	17%	28%	16%
GROWTH			
Sales growth		+172%	+49%
Profit growth		—	+35%
Asset growth		+67%	+18%
Equity growth		+25%	+27%

[1] 7 months; used 210 days

48

Recycling Workshop Inc. (A)

Within the near future, Donald Riggin, executive director of Recycling Workshop Inc.(RW), knew he would have to come to grips with a number of serious problems which threatened the continuing viability of his business.

Riggin founded RW early in 1972 for the purpose of recycling industrial wood scraps into saleable products using technically "unemployable" people in the production process. The company's initial funding was a grant from the federal government's Local Initiatives Program (LIP) and Riggin summed up the operation's original objective this way: "The original intent was to prove recycling as a support system for poor people."

At the end of February 1974, as Riggin was pondering the status of his request for further government subsidization, he mentally reviewed his company's performance to date. It was not promising: sales revenues for the last fiscal year represented just over 10 per cent of total direct labour, materials and expenses (see Exhibit 1); the company's present facilities were totally inadequate; and Riggin was all too aware that he could not count on government subsidization for RW indefinitely.

THE LIP PERIOD: NOVEMBER 1971-MAY 1973

Riggin, who originally came from Vancouver, had always taken a keen interest in the problems of the disadvantaged and of minority groups. He had devoted much of his spare time to organizing these groups. In the late 1960s he left his job in the wood crafts industry and came to Toronto. He immediately became active in community projects and was a principal organizer in the struggle between City Hall and Yorkville residents in the early 1970s over that area's future development. In 1971 Riggin was twenty-nine years old.

Late in 1971 Riggin conceived the idea of combining the recycling of industrial wood scraps with that of providing meaningful employment for disadvantaged people. Both parts of his idea reflected what were then popular contemporary issues and, financed by a small grant from LIP, he researched the concept for four months. At the end of this period, he had provided employment for twenty people and had demonstrated that there was sufficient quantity of industrial scraps to manufacture a line of day-care centre products. Based upon these positive results, LIP provided a $56 000 grant in February 1972 to fund the establishment of what Riggin called the Recycling Workshop.

In June the grant was renewed for $47 000. This subsidy was to last until September. Riggin viewed it as an important step for RW. Existing LIP projects were always given second priority for funding and, the renewal indicated a positive government interest in the company.

In view of the renewal of the LIP grant and the degree of continuity the project now boasted, RW was incorporated in June as a non-profit organization. The corporation's officers were designated as Riggin, executive director; Mary Omelesh (who had worked on the recycling concept with Riggin since 1971), chief financial officer; and Gerry King, the lawyer, who handled the incorporation but did not take an active part in the business. Among the usual advantages of incorporating a business, RW's non-profit status exempted the company from paying corporate tax.

With the expiration of the second LIP grant in September, a two-month renewal amounting to $24 000 was granted. The rationale for the two-month renewal period was simple: the LIP program still had funds allocated to it and, as of October, found that it was in a position to subsidize RW further.

Considering that at that time sales revenues were paying less than 10 per cent of the expenses of the company, the reasoning behind the renewal served to point out the tenuous nature of RW. Without subsidization the business could not survive.

However, in January a further grant renewal for $70 000 through LIP assured the future of RW at least until May 1973.

During this initial period, Riggin developed what he termed the skill of "grantsmanship." Essentially this meant learning the peculiarities of the various federal grant-awarding programs, what it was they valued in a project and, possibly more significant, what the area directors for these programs liked and did not like.

LIP GRANT CONSTRAINTS

To a large extent, much of RW's predicament was rooted in constraints inherent in the using of government grants to subsidize operations. Notwithstanding the usually close-fisted control representatives of the various programs exercised over grant-funded projects, a number of specific guidelines hindered the improvement of the project's efficiency.

Because the major objective of LIP and its related programs was the creation of jobs, the bulk of grant monies had to be used for direct wages and materials. The use of grant monies for the acquisition of capital assets was monitored closely and the purchase of anything much more sophisticated than a saw had to be paid for from other sources of revenue. This constraint resulted in RW's production process being essentially a labour intensive operation. There were no other revenues available to purchase machinery. Toward the end of the LIP period, Riggin was able to divert some grant monies into capital assets, but they were largely confined to used equipment such as the old truck purchased in May 1973 for $1250.

Grant monies were received in a lump sum payment at the beginning of a grant period. LIP guidelines forbade the placing of grant monies in anything other than a current account. As a result, no interest was ever collected on LIP monies. Riggin pointed out that although he brought this inefficiency to the attention of the LIP personnel, they would not allow him to deviate from the guideline. Their reasoning was that grant monies could never be used to "make money," only to pay people.

Another guideline concerned the competitive position of LIP projects relative to private firms. Riggin was constantly warned that should RW ever pose a serious market threat to a commercial competitor, all financial assistance would cease upon receipt of a complaint.

THE CORPORATE FOCUS

By the very nature of its funding, the corporate focus of RW was to provide jobs for technically "unemployable" people as designated by the Department of Manpower and Immigration. This generally meant people whose mental and physical capabilities were such that they could not find or hold a regular job. A cross-section would include marginally retarded persons, immigrants with a negligible command of English, chronic alcoholics and some young people who had "dropped out" and had drug problems.

The number of people employed by RW fluctuated constantly. At its peak, when the recycling and manufacturing operations were running, the company had a workforce in excess of thirty-five. At other times, when the recycling operation was closed because of lack of materials, space or people, the workforce might total fifteen. On the average, RW provided between twenty and twenty-five jobs.

Every week, reports were submitted to LIP detailing the exact number of man working weeks that had been created and paid for. It was important that Riggin employ as many persons as possible with the funds he had available because future funding decisions were based on RW's job-creating performance.

Employees were paid minimum wages to start and could increase their rates by acquiring further skills. These skills were learned by spending a period of time on different operations in the manufacturing process. However, since the measurement of RW's performance was based on the number of jobs created and not on the improvement of a worker's ability, wages were never competitive with those of commercial wood-manufacturing operations.

This created a problem for RW because as employees acquired skills they would move to better paying jobs with other firms. Riggin personally viewed this as a measure of RW's success at rehabilitating people and his records showed that the majority of persons who left RW went on to better jobs. Unfortunately, it also meant RW had a high turnover of unskilled workers and this was reflected in low productivity.

SIGNS OF IMPROVEMENT

Throughout the first half of 1973, some signs of improvement were evident in RW's operation. Labour turnover was reduced as a few employees who had developed necessary skills combined to form the nucleus of a permanent workforce. A sense of responsibility toward RW became apparent and Riggin felt that the operation's productivity was increasing. By May 1973 RW employed over thirty-two persons, many of them for longer than four months. One man had been trained to manage the workshop and his performance was satisfactory.

Originally the company had manufactured small gift items such as spice racks and bookends and some day-care centre furniture. By 1973 a complete day-care centre line had been developed and was selling reasonably well. The line consisted of approximately thirty products, a number of which were designed by Riggin and the balance of which were designed by RW's management groups. (Drawings of one of the more popular designs are shown as Exhibits 2 and 3.)

The production operation was basically a job shop process. The initial operation was the preparation of the wood. Recycling was proving to be prohibitively expensive because of the handling and preparation required to bring the scraps to a workable condition. The pieces had to be collected by truck, sorted by size and type of wood, denailed, sanded and finished. Finishing included the filling of knots and nailholes. By the spring of 1973, most of the wood used in RW's products was purchased new, but each product contained some recycled wood if any was available.

The decision as to which products to manufacture each week was determined first by outstanding customer orders and second by inventory levels. Production runs were generally small lots. For example, a typical product such as the 022 Mini Chair was seldom manufactured in lots greater than twelve.

The production process was straightforward. With the Mini Chair, the total process required seven operations from the raw material stage to the finished product. The first operation was the sawing of larger sheets of wood to the 4 ft by 8 ft size required for each set of components. From each sheet a certain number of components could be fabricated (see Exhibit 2) and, using special jigs, the sheets were cut into the component shapes. The required angles and grooves were obtained by routing and dadoing the pieces. The pieces were then assembled (see Exhibit 3), sanded and finished. Usually one man was employed in each operation.

RW's customers were subsidized, non-profit day-care centres situated in large apartment complexes and local neighbourhoods. Cost was an important consideration in their choice of furniture and RW was forced to compete with its more efficient competitors on a price basis. Exhibit 4 shows the 1973 price list.

Riggin's marketing strategy was to provide better quality products at a competitive price. In addition, he was able to manufacture some special designs to customer specifications. His major competitors, Educational Supplies and Educare Pre-School Services, were less flexible and RW was able to carve a niche in the local market. Apparently for this reason, these companies never complained that RW was in direct competition.

Because of the price sensitivity of the market and the relative inefficiency of his operation, Riggin was aware that all his products were sold at a substantial loss. For example, twelve Mini Chairs which sold for $180, cost between $300 to $325 in labour, materials and overhead to manufacture.

The company had always had trouble finding adequate facilities. During its first two weeks of operation in 1971, the project had been located in an abandoned warehouse at 11 River Street near the Toronto harbour. With temperatures below freezing, this facility proved to be wholly inadequate. Riggin found another warehouse at 896 Queen Street West, which proved to be only marginally better than the River Street location. RW stayed here for five months. In the summer of 1972, new facilities were rented at 86 Parliament Street. This was the present location of RW.

The present facility had some advantages. It was closer to the homes of most of RW's employees. This was important as most of them had to rely on public transportation. Also, it had a showroom of sorts in which to display some pieces of giftware and furniture. Walk-in business, however, proved to be minimal.

Its disadvantages far outweighed its advantages. The production operation was situated in the basement while the finishing operation, offices and showroom were located on the first floor. This layout caused many material-handling problems. The heating and electrical systems were inadequate and with only 8 500 sq ft of space at RW's disposal, the whole operation suffered from over-crowding. Worst of all, the building itself was about to be condemned and Riggin was desperately searching for new quarters.

NEAR DISASTER

In May 1973 an incident occurred which nearly resulted in the permanent closing of RW. As a condition of the last LIP grant in December, Riggin had signed an agreement stating he would not seek further help from the program. He received assurances, however, that monies would be made available to RW through the Entrepreneurial Local Initiative Program (ELIP), a new program which was being instituted through the LIP bureaucracy. Even though another federal program, the Local Employment Assistance Program (LEAP), had expressed interest in funding RW, the LIP agency maintained its priority over the company until May. With two days left in May and no sign of ELIP funds, Riggin went to Ottawa. He was informed that ELIP was not yet operational and could not make any grants at that time.

Without funds, RW was forced to lay off all its production staff on May 31, 1973. Seven workers returned the following day and continued working on speculation along with the four management people. By the following week, LEAP provided an $87 000 grant to cover the balance of 1973. The company had been saved but Riggin knew that the morale he had built over the last two years had been seriously weakened.

THE LEAP PERIOD: JUNE 1973-FEBRUARY 1974

Following the problem encountered in May, Riggin set about securing a more permanent funding arrangement for RW. He made an immediate request for a further LEAP grant but by December his request was still under consideration. An interim three-month grant for $53 000 was approved pending a decision on his application.

During the latter half of 1973, Riggin and his team had worked at restoring RW to its former condition. Although some of the former nucleus of workers were unable or unwilling to return, by December 1973 the morale of the workforce was restored. LEAP regulations proved to be less stringent with regard to capital expenditures and RW had been able to secure a used belt sander, two planers and numerous other power tools. All these developments combined to make the production process more efficient. The power tools speeded up certain operations but the loss of some skilled workers negated any significant cost improvement.

Because of the $10 000 salary ceiling imposed by LEAP, RW had difficulty in attracting management personnel. However, late in 1973 the company was able to secure the service of an experienced manager. Bob Slee was sixty-three years of age and had held senior management positions with a number of major corporations. A heart condition had forced him to retire early but his health had improved and he joined RW because of a personal desire to help disadvantaged people. At the same time RW's production manager quit the firm when his salary reached the LEAP ceiling.

A gradual change in RW's product line became evident throughout 1973. The day-care line had never been very successful and, because of their interest in antiques, Riggin and Omelesh had started producing experimental reproductions of early Canadian furniture designs. As positive customer reaction increased with the new products in the showroom, RW began to concentrate more and more on this product line. By February 1974 a number of designs were being produced in the shop. Omelesh, who also acted as sales manager, felt that certain pieces sold better than others but that it was too soon to tell which designs would prove feasible from a marketing point of view. Neither she nor Riggin were knowledgeable about the competitors in this field and had done little promotion save a few advertisements in a weekly magazine, *Toronto Life*.

THE FUTURE?

As Riggin anticipated the outcome of LEAP's deliberations on his renewal, he was troubled by a request on the part of Ottawa that he furnish proof of his and his firm's "management capabilities." He had been given to understand that the deputy minister in charge of all grant-awarding programs was concerned about management inefficiency at RW. Riggin felt sure RW was not being singled out but that, rather, all projects receiving large grants were being carefully reviewed. Still, he was troubled as to how he could "prove" his competence.

Exhibit 1
Recycling Workshop Inc. (A)
Income Statements
for 12-Month Period Ending
February 28

	1973		1974	
Sales		$ 13 354		$ 22 430
Cost of goods sold				
Direct labour	$104 338		$110 354	
Materials	4 688		6 546	
Total		109 026		116 900
Gross profit		$ (95 672)		$ (94 470)
Selling and administrative[1] expenses		68 688		85 720
Net profit		$(164 360)		$(180 190)
Grant income		—		—
LIP		162 260		34 983
LEAP		—		140 457
Total		$162 260		$175 440
Deficit[2]		(2 100)		(4 750)

[1] Managerial salaries in 1973 amounted to approximately $30 000 and in 1974 to approximately $38 000.

[2] Deficit was covered by short-term demand note with local bank.

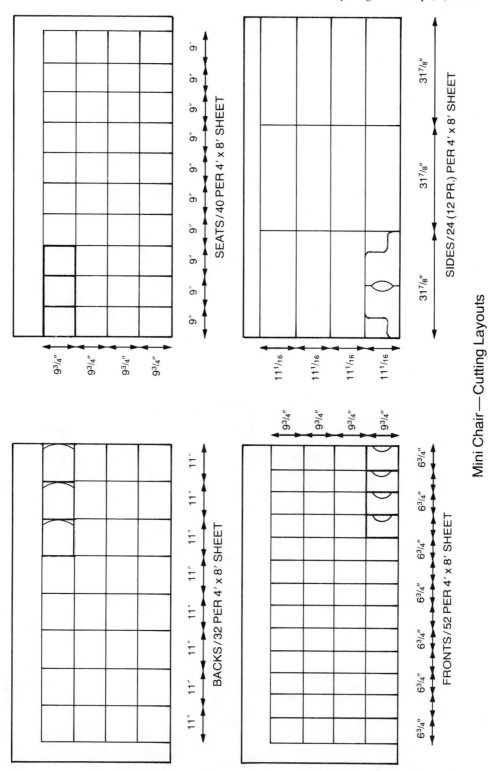

Exhibit 2
Recycling Workshop Inc. (A)

SEATS / 40 PER 4' x 8' SHEET

SIDES / 24 (12 PR.) PER 4' x 8' SHEET

BACKS / 32 PER 4' x 8' SHEET

FRONTS / 52 PER 4' x 8' SHEET

Mini Chair—Cutting Layouts

Exhibit 3
Recycling Workshop Inc. (A)
Minichair Assembly

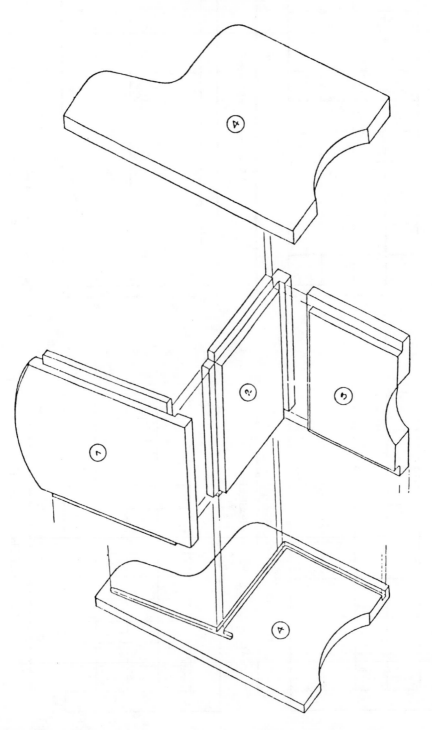

Exhibit 4
Recycling Workshop Inc. (A)
Canadian Recycled Wood Products

Recycling Workshop is unique in its field, that of recycling industrial wood waste into useful and attractive furniture, day-care and gift items. Recycling Workshop is also the only manufacturer of recycled day-care items in Canada.

A few of our day-care products are made from plywood which is not recycled; however, we will continue to manufacture these items as long as the demand for them exists.

Showrooms at:

Recycling Workshop Inc.,
86 Parliament St.,
Toronto, Ontario.
M5A 2Y6

Hours:
Monday to Thursday & Saturday
10 a.m. to 6 p.m.
Telephone: (416) 364-6103

DAY-CARE PRICE LIST

Design Number	Item	Price
001	Infant chair	$12.50
022	Mini chair	15.00
003	Small stool	12.50
007	Puzzle box (round peg, square hole)	40.00
006	Stacking box for jigsaw puzzle	10.00
010	Child's shaker table	65.00
012	Hobby horse (unpainted)	8.50
014	Wall easel (masonite board)	30.00
014a	Wall easel (black board)	30.00
015	Doll house	35.00
016	Climbing frame with slide	125.00
019	Pine cradle	40.00
023	Large folding cupboard	105.00
024	Large table (arborite top)	35.00
025	Picket fence	35.00
026	Small coat tree	20.00
027	Small boot and coat rack	40.00
032	Work bench	50.00
034	Room divider (folding)	35.00
036	Teeter-totter	40.00
037	Hollow blocks (birch)	3.00
	Hollow blocks (chipboard)	2.00
038	Cut-out table	85.00
008	Mahogany block box (while supply lasts)	15.00
028	Block chair	15.00
064	Single rockers	80.00
070	Small pine table	20.00
072	Ironing board	7.00

Prices subject to change without notice; please confirm before ordering.
Note: Furniture and giftware price list available upon request.

Recycling Workshop Inc. (B)

Donald Riggin, executive director of Recycling Workshop Inc. (RW), could look back over his company's performance in 1974 with some satisfaction. Financially, RW had become more stable than at any time since its inception in late 1971. The company was now manufacturing a line of early Canadian furniture which promised to be more successful than the day-care centre furniture manufactured since the company was founded. A more satisfactory building had been leased and because of its improved working conditions, the morale of the work force was greatly improved. In addition, the new facility provided badly needed showroom space. In all, RW had undergone some major changes during its fiscal year March 1974 through February 1975.

Early in 1974, in conjunction with officials of the Local Employment Assistance Program (LEAP), Riggin had formulated a three-phase strategy designed to bring RW to a self-sufficient state by 1977. However, by January 1975, LEAP had developed reservations about RW's ability to attain this objective. Before approving the company's 1975-1976 grant, LEAP's executive committee hired John Donaldson, a Toronto business consultant, to evaluate RW's operation and the probability of its becoming self-sufficient within two more years.

In early February 1975, Mr. Donaldson started collecting data on the company as a first step towards providing LEAP with his evaluation.

NOVEMBER 1971 TO MAY 1973

Donald Riggin conceived the idea of combining the recycling of industrial wood scraps and providing meaningful employment for disadvantaged people in late 1971. Funded by a grant from the Local Initiatives Program (LIP), Riggin researched the concept for four months. At the end of this period, he had provided employment for twenty people and demonstrated that there was a sufficient supply of industrial wood waste to manufacture a line of day-care centre furniture.

From February 1972 to May 1973, the company was subsidized by four successive LIP grants totalling $197 000 and revenues from the sale of furniture and giftware amounting to approximately $20 000. Exhibit 1 is a detailed grant history and employment record. During this period, RW hired 177 new employees of which thirty-two were still employed in May 1973. Further details of the company's early development can be found in Recycling Workshop Inc. (A).

JUNE 1973 TO FEBRUARY 1974

With the discontinuation of LIP funding in May 1973, RW was thrown into a crisis. As a condition of the final LIP grant made in December 1972, Riggin had signed an agreement stating he would not seek further help from the program. He received assurances, however, that funding would be made available through the Entrepreneurial Local Initiatives Program (ELIP), a new program which was being instituted through the LIP bureaucracy. At the end of May, ELIP informed RW that funding would not be made available and Riggin was forced to fire his work force and shut down his operation.

One week later, another federal subsidy program, LEAP, granted RW $87 000 with which to operate until November. LEAP was established under the auspices of the Job Creation Branch of the Department of Manpower and Immigration. The program's objective was to assist groups of individuals who were classified as unemployable and help them obtain new employment opportunities. This was to be achieved through funding projects which demonstrated potential for producing long-term employment. Because of this objective, many projects which LEAP subsidized had as their eventual goal a self-sufficient state. LEAP was prepared to fund such projects for up to three years, excluding a six-month research and development stage. Funds could be used for wages, overhead and special costs such as evaluation and counselling reports and consulting fees. The ratio for distribution was as follows: wages 80 per cent of total funding, overhead $35 per person working week created or 25 per cent of wages paid, and special costs not to exceed 20 per cent of wages and overhead paid.

In the period through to November, Riggin engaged in negotiations with LEAP to establish a more permanent funding arrangement. Riggin argued that the short-term funding arrangements RW had operated with to date had resulted in the company's inability to formulate a strategy which would lead to self-sufficiency.

Negotiations did not produce any agreement by November and LEAP made an interim grant of $53 000 in December to fund operations pending more permanent arrangements. A major issue-stalling settlement was the question of Riggin's and his administrative team's ability to successfully manage the operation. In January 1974, the team was asked to prove their competence.

By February RW had convinced LEAP of its competence by demonstrating the improvements made in the company's productivity through to January (see Recycling Workshop Inc. (A)) and by presenting a three-phase strategy leading to self-sufficiency. As Riggin understood the arrangement which followed from this exercise, RW was to receive three consecutive $200 000 grants running from March 1974 through to February 1977. The grants would be renewable each year conditional upon RW providing the agreed-upon man weeks of employment. Again, as Riggin understood the arrangement, the renewal process was really a formality provided that the funds were used to produce jobs.

THE THREE-PHASE STRATEGY

Riggin formulated the three-phase, three-year strategy as a compromise. He originally believed that RW could not attain self-sufficiency in less than five years. However, it was clear from the beginning of his negotiations with LEAP that funding for this time period would be impossible. Table 1 gives the basic strategy as it appeared in the company's proposal to LEAP.

Table 1

Phase I   To produce a product, either knowing or not knowing its cost, but disposing of it at a competitive price. Sustained by means of a subsidy.

Phase II   To produce a product knowing its cost, while at the same time maintaining a training program that involves some disadvantaged persons, and disposing of the product competitively, whether below or at cost. Sustained by means of a subsidy.

Phase III   All of Phase II with the emphasis on more selective training, with a view to completing this phase with a fairly well-trained crew capable of producing an item for sale at a profit. Sustained by means of a full subsidy because of the continuing training inefficiency, which must of necessity continue throughout the phase.

Appended to this plan was a Phase IV which stated that if all conditions and objectives throughout Phase I through III were achieved, RW would be an on-going, profitable business venture. Of course, LEAP assumed no responsibility for funding RW in Phase IV.

To back up this strategy, RW's management provided budgets and sales projections for the period March 1974 through February 1975. This information was based primarily on the company's intention to actively manufacture and market early Canadian reproductions and to seek newer, more appropriate facilities. Riggin was confident that RW could achieve sales of $50 000 if the new product line caught on as expected.

THE NEW PLANT

With the assurance that subsidization would be available for three years, Riggin began looking for a new plant with the capacity necessary to produce large furniture pieces. A plant was found at 276 Main Street in the east end, some ten miles from downtown Toronto.

The new plant had many advantages over the facility on Parliament Street. The production area was approximately 10 000 sq ft and the showroom 3000 sq ft. In addition to representing a significant increase in usable space over the former location's total 8500 sq ft, the new plant had convenient toilet facilities, good lighting and ventilation and a pleasant lounge area for employees at coffee breaks and lunch hours. Exhibit 2 shows the main production area, finished goods inventory and lounge area.

The showroom facility fronted on Main Street with sidewalk to ceiling window (Exhibit 3). Shortly after moving in the showroom was redecorated and carpeting was laid at a cost of $2500. The showroom was large enough to accommodate samples of the entire RW line of furniture and giftware. These samples were generally arranged in pleasant room groupings. During the summer, a number of local artists arranged to hang samples of their work in the showroom and arrangements were made with another LEAP project which produced pottery and batiks to display their merchandise. As a result of these efforts, the showroom took on an attractive, professional look which Riggin felt helped boost sales. Exhibit 4 shows various views of the showroom.

MARKETING DEVELOPMENTS

With the additional space which the new facility offered, RW concentrated more and more on the production and sales of early Canadian furniture. Although considerable experimenting with new designs and finishes still continued, the product line stabilized around fifteen basic pieces. Exhibit 5 lists the standard product line and their retail prices as at January 1975. Exhibit 6 is a drawing of the bureau desk design.

In conjunction with the new product line, RW upgraded its selling approach. Credit was made available through Chargex and Master Charge. Showroom hours were extended to include Saturdays and Thursday and Friday evenings. The showroom staff began to meet regularly to discuss new designs, finishes and processes and to explore the feasibility of any new design suggestions obtained from customers, competitors or magazines.

To complement this increased emphasis on marketing, RW undertook, by comparison with prior years, a major promotional campaign. In April, a booth was set up at the National Home Show on the Canadian National Exhibition grounds. The booth contained much of RW's established product line plus a number of new early Canadian pieces under consideration at that time. The booth staff felt that response to the products had been quite favourable. During the week-long show, over 7000 brochures depicting the new line were handed out.

In August, another booth was opened during the Canadian National Exhibition. This time the booth contained the full furniture line. Riggin and his staff used this opportunity to gather customer feedback on the new products. The consensus was favourable. At this point RW became fully committed to the development of this product line.

In September, $15 000 was committed for one year for one-third page ads in *Toronto Life* and *Toronto Calendar* magazines. These ads featured a different early Canadian design every week. Exhibit 7 is a sample ad from *Toronto Calendar* showing the bureau desk design.

Although unable to afford television advertising, RW received considerable free coverage on a number of Toronto stations. This coverage was usually on public service programs and local talk shows during which the training of disadvantaged people and the recycling of wood were the main topics. On one program, Riggin was challenged by a Toronto alderman for using federal monies. The alderman made insinuations about "welfare rip-offs," and the program ended on a hostile note. Notwithstanding that unfortunate incident, Riggin felt that RW benefited from the exposure these programs provided.

A number of newspaper and magazine articles on the company's concept also appeared throughout 1974. In addition to the *Globe and Mail* and *Financial Post,* articles appeared in local newspapers. Exhibit 8 is an article which was featured in *The News in East York*.

THE COMPETITION

RW's major competitors in the early Canadian furniture market were Pinecraft Canada Ltd., Early Canadian Furniture Ltd., Pack-Rat Ltd. and Pre-Confederation Furniture Ltd.

Riggin had little information on his competitor's volume but he believed the biggest company in the market was Pinecraft Canada Ltd., which manufactured a standardized line of early Canadian furniture in a plant at Almonte, just outside Ottawa. The company retailed its products through outlets in Toronto, Ottawa and Edmonton. The Toronto outlet was located in Yorkville, a highly fashionable area close to downtown and populated primarily by expensive boutiques and restaurants. The store was large, featured a number of room settings and was staffed by several attractive young saleswomen. Pinecraft's product line was extensive, offering over seventy pieces, including a full line of bedroom furniture.

Early Canadian Furniture and Pack-Rat were small businesses operating from old stores just outside Toronto's core area. Their product lines were considered to be spotty and there was little evidence of product standardization. Pre-Confederation Furniture, a manufacturer located in London, Ontario, had recently opened a retail outlet in Oakville but Riggin knew little about the company's product line or its operation.

None of RW's competitors used television or radio advertising and those that advertised at all employed the same print media as RW. Riggin had no data on how much any of his competitors spent on advertising but he guessed that their budgets equalled RW's new level of spending.

Because of the profusion of different designs in early Canadian furniture, it was difficult to compare prices. Late in 1974, Mary Omelesh undertook a small survey of prices on comparable competitive designs. Although she found only a few pieces with which any comparison could be made, it appeared that RW's prices were generally 10 to 20 per cent lower than any of the competition. Mary did not consider this overly important: she believed customers purchased early Canadian furniture on the basis of design, quality and finish. Delivery did not appear to be important since none of the competitors in this market could promise delivery any sooner than eight weeks.

The bulk of the new product line was retailed through the Main Street showroom. Riggin, however, had made three wholesale contacts in late 1974: two in Toronto and one in Ottawa. Although these accounts to date had purchased only a few items, all had placed repeat orders and it was hoped that these accounts could be expanded.

1974 PERFORMANCE

With the growth of the company, LEAP had strongly recommended that RW hire an accounting firm to prepare its annual statements. Arthur Anderson and Company were retained in January 1975 and had by February produced the unaudited statements shown in Exhibits 9 and 10. Revenues from sales for the 1974 fiscal year represented 28 per cent of total direct labour, materials and overhead costs. Riggin pointed out that this was a significant improvement over RW's 1973 performance when sales revenues had represented just over 10 per cent of total costs.

In spite of the improvement, it was clear that RW was still a long way from achieving a self-sufficient state. Riggin felt two factors were primarily responsible for the company's continuing poor performance: the problems associated with the production process, and the constant experimentation with product design and finish. An example which illustrates the first problem occurred in late 1974. A run of corner cupboards had been scheduled. This product had never been produced in any large quantity and it was hoped that the scheduled run of six would significantly reduce costs because of learning curve efficiencies. However, the shop foreman took ill for most of the week and at the same time, two new employees were hired. As as result, the direct costs for the six cupboards were far greater than their selling price.

Product experimentation, necessary because of management's relative unfamiliarity with the market, was costly. During the summer of 1974, three large desks were produced at an approximate direct cost of $2700. The desks were not successful and in order to clear them from inventory, two were sold for $400 each. The remaining desk was kept for use in the office.

It was in the area of manpower training and turnover that Riggin felt the most valuable contribution had been made. By February 1975, eighteen full-time positions had been created and turnover had dropped from approximately 200 per cent of this figure in the period December 1972 through May 1973 (Exhibit 1) to approximately 130 per cent during the 1974 fiscal year. Of the twenty-three persons who left RW in this period, fifteen went on to better positions, eight were let go because it was felt they were beyond hope of improvement, one left for health reasons and one returned to school.

Although Mr. Donaldson would have liked more information, he was aware that his evaluation would have to be made right away. On the basis of what he knew so far, he set about to evaluate RW's chances of attaining self-sufficiency by 1977.

Exhibit 1
Recycling Workshop Inc. (B)
Summarized Grant History

Period Covered	Government Grant	Sales Revenues	No. New Employees
February 1, 1972—May 31, 1972	$ 55 763	—	71
[1]June 1, 1972—September 30, 1972	47 295	4 166	39
[1]October 1, 1972—December 1, 1972	24 219	2 540	21
[1]December 2, 1972—May 31, 1973	69 966	13 297	46
Total	$197 243	$20 003	177

[1] These are extensions of the original grant.

No. Employees Leaving	No. Person Weeks Budget	Actual
42	528	487
47	401	403
19	207	212
37	598	610
145	1 734	1 712

Exhibit 2
Recycling Workshop Inc. (B)
The New Production Facilities
276 Main Street

Exhibit 2 (Continued)

Exhibit 3
Recycling Workshop Inc. (B)
The New Plant
276 Main Street

Exhibit 4
Recycling Workshop Inc. (B)
The New Showroom Facility
276 Main Street

Exhibit 5
Recycling Workshop Inc. (B)
Retail Price List—January 1975

Product

Blanket box	
Large	$170
Small	130
Bookcase	340
Chairs	
Ladderback	75
Straightback	75
Pantry tables	110
Corner cupboard	340
Dry sink	300
End table	70
Flatback	425
Shaker table	310
Trestle table	260
Trestle bench	75
Hutch	600
Bureau desk	650

Exhibit 6
Recycling Workshop Inc. (B)
Bureau Desk

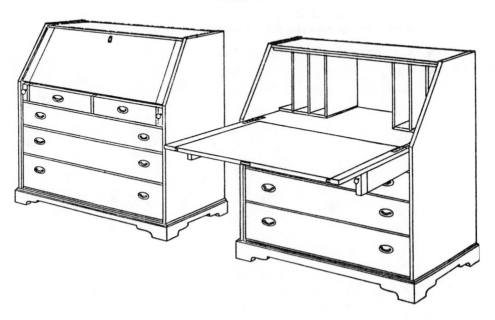

Exhibit 7
Recycling Workshop Inc. (B)
Ad in *Toronto Calendar* magazine, October 1975

RECYCLING WORKSHOP
HAND CRAFTED FURNITURE

Beautiful
Strong
Solid Pine

278 MAIN ST TORONTO 890-7797

44 TORONTO CALENDAR MAGAZINE

Exhibit 8
Recycling Workshop Inc.
Article from *The News in East York,* August 21, 1974

by John Cotter

NEW LIFE FOR OLD BOARDS AND CRATES

Wooden nickels are getting to be a good buy.

Real wood has become a premium commodity. Particularly in the home.

Once upon a time, say, when your grandmother was a girl, all the furniture in her home was built of wood. Good, solid wood.

Oak and cherry, mahogany and pine, maple, birch and fir. And sometimes even plywood. But it was real.

But today, as we all know, wood is a vanishing resource—vanishing from the marketplace at least—and of course the price is soaring.

Today's homemakers have the choice of hunting high and low for bargains, paying the price, building what they need themselves, or settling for the arborite, pressboard, near-woods or veneer.

Unless they buy second-hand. And that's exactly what the Recycling Workshop at 276 Main Street has in mind. The store is new, the furniture is all new, but the wood itself isn't.

What would you say to, for example, an all-mahogany coffee table? Or a solid maple desk, or a custom-made pine bookcase? All at reasonable prices (not cheap, not even really bargain prices, but not arm-and-leg prices either).

The Recycling Workshop, you see, is not a conventional furniture manufacturer or retailer. For one thing, they're a non-profit-making organization. So far, at least.

Newly located on Main Street, just below Danforth Avenue, the workshop is largely supported by government funds. Workshop spokeswoman Mary Omelesh hopes to see the operation in the black for 1976. Currently, sales are covering less than 30% of their costs.

And this is despite the fact that the raw materials, from which they craft some unusual furniture, are free.

"A lot of people are under the impression we refinish furniture," says Mary Omelesh. "But we start from scratch—with old wood."

The workshop's raw materials often began life as packing crates, industrial skids or dunnage—the material packed in the holds of ships to keep cargo from slipping around in high seas. This wood comes to the workshop free—or at a token cost for haulage.

"The harbour commission alone throws out 100 tons of good wood a year." says Omelesh. Other frequent suppliers are Pilkington Glass and the Douglas Aircraft Co.

The wood arrives at the Recycling Workshop as broken up crates and skids,—full of nails and looking for all the world like the garbage it used to be. There is a lot of hard labour, and satisfaction, in turning this cast-off material into fine furniture. They have been doing it for two and one-half years.

Beginning in February 1972, under a local initiatives grant of $60,000 the workshop set about to study the problem by doing the job.

"We were all pretty well amateurs," says Omelesh of the 30-odd people who set to work on the garbage wood. "We started off with one 14" planer, hand planers, hammers and saws."

Their first product was a small child's chair—still a popular item today—and work was carried on in a west-end warehouse basement. Without so much as lavatory facilities. But the furniture began to appear where once there was only refuse.

"We gave everything away to daycare centres at first," says Mary Omelash, "then we began to ask for token amounts to help meet expenses."

Under a government local assistance program last year, the workshop began to experiment with adult furniture. A full-time draftsman has been added to the staff to work on design and eighteen workers contribute ideas, based on the kinds and quality of wood available at any given time.

Mary Omelesh, whose background included clothing design, has been behind some of the workshop's more popular products.

"At first we spent time going through old antique books for designs," says she. "We favour nice straight clean lines."

All of the workshop's products have a distinctive—almost Scandinavian—look about them. The stain is usually clear and the finish is often plastic Urethane for durability and beauty.

Functional and beautiful

All designs are basic and functional. The workshoppers may not see it this way, but it is a great place to go for do-it-yourself ideas.

Prices, particularly for the children's items, begin around $15 dollars for the solid wooden chairs (that should last several lifetimes) running to $125 for the large climbing frames and slides.

Shaker-tables—a new idea to this reporter at least—incorporate a full-size dining table, a deacon's bench type seat and a linen or blanket chest. It all depends on how you open, swing and turn it. Believe me, you'd have to see it.

This item—the most popular—runs from $185 to $250 in price.

The workshop came to the present Main Street location after a three-stop odyssey around Toronto.

"Here we are fairly accessible to people from all over the city," says Mary Omelesh, "and we're fairly pleased with the reception, although there hasn't been a lot of off-the-street traffic. East Yorkers are gradually discovering we're here."

At the moment, the group is incorporating both new and used wood in their products, although it's almost impossible to tell the difference. The new workshop has no room for the expanding recycling operation and an additional location will have to be found, preferably close by. Storage and working outside is almost impossible.

This is despite the fact that the Main Street location was originally a wood-working shop. A great deal of the space has been used up with the beautifully appointed showroom and the new equipment.

The new wood is just carrying them over the summer, however. They don't intend to abandon the recycling operation now that they've proved its feasibility.

"Recycling was very expensive in terms of labour, but the costs went down and productivity rose as we got the proper equipment," says Mary.

"It's a long, time-consuming, physical job. First all the nails have to be pulled out and then the wood must be cut to size."

Today production averages from 50 to 200 pieces of furniture a month, but it has taken the workshop a long time to develop this kind of pace. There's really no way to automate the operation.

The Recycling Workshop will do work to order for customers who come in with an idea, but they charge a minimum of $10 for making up an estimate complete with a detailed drawing.

"We do it for people because we know how difficult it is to find just what you want in solid wood."

The store's hours run from 10:00 a.m. to 6:00 p.m. daily, including Saturdays, and from 10:00 a.m. to 9:00 p.m. on Thursdays and Fridays. But if you're on your way to the CNE, despite the strike, you can also see some of the finer handiwork on display at the Better Living exhibition.

"I think we've proved the feasibility of recycling," says Mary Omelesh. And it looks like they have.

Exhibit 9
Recycling Workshop Inc. (B)
Income Statement
For 12-Month Period Ending
February 28

		1973		1974		1975
Sales		$ 13 354		$ 22 430		$ 36 548
Cost of goods sold						
Direct labour	104 338		110 354		119 521	
Materials	4 688		6 546		11 500	
Total		109 026		116 900		131 021
Gross profit		$ (95 672)		$ (94 470)		$ (94 473)
Operating expenses[1]						
Management salaries		30 000		38 000		44 000
Selling		—		—		27 000
Administration		38 688		47 720		26 179
Net profit		$(164 360)		$(180 190)		$(191 652)
Grant income						
LIP		162 260		34 983		—
LEAP		—		140 457		199 230
Excess or deficit		$ (2 100)		$ (4 750)		$ 7 578

[1] 1973 and 1974 breakdowns are approximations.

Exhibit 10
Recycling Workshop Inc. (B)
Balance Sheet
as at February 28, 1975

ASSETS

Current:	
Cash	$ 6 919
Accounts receivable	4 118
Inventory	24 257
Ppd expenses	2 104
Total	$37 398

Fixed assets:	
Production equipment	14 440
Office equipment	6 852
Truck	1 250
Less: accumulated dep.	6 258
Total	$16 284

Rental deposit	1 750

TOTAL ASSETS	$55 432

LIABILITIES

Current:	
Accounts payable	$10 709
Total	$10 709

EXCESS OF REVENUE OVER EXPENSES
AND CONTRIBUTED SURPLUS
(See Note)

Balance, February 28, 1974	$37 145
Excess of revenue over expense	7 587
	$44 723

TOTAL	$55 432

Note: Excess of revenue over expense and contributed surplus.
    Residual net assets upon completion of a particular grant are contributed to the succeeding grant period. For accounting purposes, as of February 28, 1975, $37 145 in residual net assets had been acquired under various government grants from inception.
    It is the director's opinion that the residual net assets could be sold, should the company cease to operate as currently incorporated.

49

Stillwell Ice Cream Ltd.

Early in 1971, Mr. Jack Thompson and Mr. Neil Dudley decided to pool their resources and buy a business with apparent growth potential. Neil Dudley was fifty-two years old. He had spent most of his life developing and expanding a small restaurant which he sold for considerable gain in 1966. He had been semi-retired since that time. Mr. Dudley found that retirement did not fit his "get-up-and-go" personality and consequently he was eager to get back into business. Jack Thompson, thirty-six years old and a close neighbour of Mr. Dudley, had started as a salesman for a large ice cream producer following his graduation from university and in 1971 became sales manager. Among the several businesses Mr. Dudley and Mr. Thompson had looked at was a local ice cream plant that seemed particularly inviting.

Stillwell Ice Cream Ltd. was the largest ice cream producer in Simcoe Country. It was owned by two elderly partners, John Cole and Earl Stillwell, who had spent their entire lives building up the company. Since both men were approaching seventy years of age and neither of their families showed any interest in running the business, they were receptive to the idea of selling and retiring. Mr. Thompson and Mr. Dudley decided to spend the next four weeks looking into the ice cream industry in general before making any firm purchase plans. In particular, they were concerned with the current operating problems facing Stillwell Ice Cream Ltd., as well as the problems that they might face in expanding the business. Finally, there was a price question. Messrs. Thompson and Dudley realized that they had to come up with an offer that would be acceptable to the present owners as well as one which would provide an adequate return on their investment.

THE ICE CREAM INDUSTRY

Ice cream was first produced in the United States and soon after gained world-wide popularity. This popularity was evident in Ontario where, in 1970, ice cream production reached a new peak of 19 557 000 gallons. Market forecasts predicted that this figure would be exceeded in 1971 and 1972.

Before 1940, there were hundreds of locally owned ice cream producers. These plants served their own city or town and the surrounding rural area. The townspeople were loyal to their local producer and appeared more concerned with supporting a member of the community than buying ice cream at the lowest price. After 1940, larger ice cream manufacturers began to take over the market by producing and advertising a good quality ice cream at prices lower than the local plants were offering. As the price of ingredients, labour and overhead began to climb, the small local producers found their operations becoming unprofitable. Consolidation in the ice cream industry began with the big companies purchasing many of the smaller plants.

Ice cream production in Ontario was divided among four large firms with several plant operations and eighty-five regional one-plant operations. The four major producers were: Silverwood, Sealtest (Dominion Dairies Ltd.), Borden and Neilsen. Ice cream plant concentration could be broken into the following regions:

Toronto	18 plants
Central (Belleville-Orillia)	16 plants (Stillwell)
Eastern (Ottawa-Kingston)	17 plants
Northern	18 plants
Southwest	36 plants

There was downward pressure on the selling price of ice cream. Ice cream which sold at $.89 per half-gallon in 1960-65 was regularly featured at $.69 and $.79 in 1970. Costs of production were climbing for small ice cream producers and mass production seemed necessary to stay competitive. The larger companies were still purchasing the smaller operations and using them as distribution rather than production centres. (During the next ten years, it was expected that consolidation and merger would play an even greater role as the two major concerns who shared 80 per cent of the market worked to improve their positions.)

In the past, ice cream companies had placed refrigerated dispensers in outlets that handled their products as an incentive for dealers to sell their brand of ice cream. Almost any small store that handled a producer's ice cream would receive an ice cream case. In more recent years, companies who handled large numbers of small store accounts had been forced to take a critical look at this practice, although little action resulted.

With the cost of refrigerated cases as high as $1000 and repair costs up, many companies no longer supplied freezers to dealers who sold under 400 gallons per year. The average cost of stopping a truck to service an account was estimated at approximately $8 and many of the larger companies had been forced to place the minimum sale level per stop at $25.

A drastic shift in the sales of package products like ice cream from the corner store to the chain store had taken place in the past several years. The introduction of the $.69 half-gallon packages by the supermarkets had disastrous results for the corner store since it often could not meet the chain store price on ice cream. In many instances there were drastic reductions in sales. Furthermore, the major share of ice cream sales by corner stores was now in the less profitable novelty items such as popsicles and drumsticks.

To ensure a minimum quality of ice cream, the Food and Drug Regulations prescribed the ingredients for marketable ice cream. Specified minimum amounts of solids, milk fat, stabilizer and bacteria were required in any sample. The quality of ice cream was determined by the amount of butterfat in the product as well as the over run.[1] Butterfat gave ice cream the cream texture. Lower quality ice cream (low butterfat concentration) tended to taste and feel more "icy."

Winter temperatures were not conducive to ice cream sales. As a result, production in July was three times that of January. Because the shelf life of ice cream was, at most, five months (three months for a high quality product) and because refrigerated space was extremely expensive to build and maintain, ice cream was not stockpiled. Consequently, heavy production demands had to be met in the summer, while the winter months afforded a more leisurely production pace.

Studies by the Ice Cream Institute indicated that the average shopper was generally unaware of the ingredients of ice cream and therefore unable to render a sound judgement on its quality. This inability to discriminate quality forced the buyer to rely on the appearance of the package and the price of the ice cream to determine the quality of the product. Most people assumed that high quality and high price were synonymous.

There had been a great growth in substitutes for ice cream such as mousse, mellorine, ice milk and sherbet. The cost of equipment to produce these products was high and often one producer would buy a machine and then supply all the companies in the industry with the new substitute. The appearance of these products had sensitized the price of ice cream to the price of substitutes. The use of substitutes was expected to grow in the future and price competition from other desserts and snack goods would likely become more intense.

---

[1] When a quantity of mix was placed in an ice cream machine, the machine forced air into the mix while freezing it. The increase in volume of the mix due to air was called over run.

STILLWELL ICE CREAM LTD.

Stillwell Ice Cream Ltd. grew out of a small family-owned dairy operation near Barrie, Ontario, which began in 1876. In 1902, the operation was moved to its existing location two miles from the city. The business was expanded to include the manufacture and sale of butter. Although the company produced ice cream as early as 1920, it was not until 1946, after the purchase of a semi-automatic ice cream maker, that the ice cream sales began to flourish.

During the previous five years sales growth had levelled off while material, operation and selling costs continued to climb (Exhibit 1).

Stillwell Ice Cream Ltd. had produced its own line of top quality ice cream for over half a century. In central Simcoe County the name Stillwell was almost a family word. Many customers demanded Stillwell ice cream by name. It was not uncommon for people who lived outside of Stillwell's distribution area to make special trips to purchase Stillwell ice cream. Many retailers who handled other brands also stocked Stillwell ice cream for those who demanded it. One dealer suggested that many customers would seek out Stillwell ice cream rather than buying the store brand.

Stillwell ice cream had a 12 per cent butterfat content, which made it one of the highest quality ice creams on the market. A comparable ice cream, qualitywise, was Silverwood "Deluxe" which had an 11 per cent butterfat rating. Stillwell felt that the high quality of the product resulted in customer acceptance and loyalty. Stillwell ice cream sold generally for $1.05 per half gallon but it varied from $.99 to $1.10. Silverwood "Deluxe" sold for $1.15 to $1.19 per half gallon. Silverwood had a lower quality second line of ice cream, Medigold, which sold at approximately the same price as Stillwell ice cream. Stillwell sold its ice cream to dealers for $.85 plus a $.05 per half gallon freezer charge, while Silverwood sold "Deluxe" to the dealer for $.99 and Medigold for $.95 per half gallon.

In 1970 ingredients for a gallon of ice cream cost Stillwell $.76 and the package cost $.03. The direct labour and overhead amounted to $.15 and $.08 respectively while the fixed overhead was $.06 per gallon. The administrative and selling expenses were $.27 and $.54 per gallon respectively.

THE ICE CREAM PLANT

Earl Stillwell, a hard worker who knew the production of ice cream well, was in charge of the ice cream plant. As plant manager, he was responsible for general management, production and sales. Although John Cole knew the operation within the plant, he had assumed the role of a silent partner. He had put a large amount of capital into Stillwell Ice Cream and was always consulted before any major decisions concerning the business were made. Mr. Cole had many other activities aside from the ice cream business which demanded his time and attention. One of his major interests was photography and he was in constant demand for weddings and special occasions.

In addition to Mr. Stillwell the plant employed a bookkeeper, four production men and two driver-salesmen. The four production employees, with the exception of the youngest man (fifty-one), had an average age of sixty-eight and an average length of service with the company of forty-three years. Relations within the plant were excellent and everyone was on a first-name basis. After many years on the job together, the men had developed strong friendships and it was not uncommon for them and their wives to get together socially.

Stillwell paid its production men relatively low wages and had no pension or insurance plans. It considered the low wages one of the big factors in its ability to stay competitive and profitable. Although one of the eldest workers had given notice that he intended to retire in the fall, Earl Stillwell felt that the remaining workers would not retire in the near future because they did not have sufficient savings. As Mr. Stillwell stated, "They need the income from the plant to supplement their government pensions."

The two driver-salesmen were young and had been with the company for only two years. They were paid a small salary plus commission which made their total wages comparable to other driver-salesmen doing a similar job.

PRODUCTION

The production of ice cream at Stillwell was mainly a manual operation. There was very little automatic equipment and a man was needed at each step of the process. The making of the ice cream mix was the first step in the production of a final product. A man measured out specific quantities of milk, milk solids, glucose, emulsifier and stabilizer and placed them in a pasteurizer where the mixture was steam heated to remove all bacteria. Once the temperature reached 150°F the fluid was piped to a homogenizer where the solids were broken down to create a smooth uniform product. The batch, consisting of 208 gallons, was then poured into eight-gallon milk cans which were manually transported to a cool storage room where the mixture sat for a minimum of sixteen hours but no longer than two weeks. Stillwell used two pasteurizers for this process. The pasteurizing equipment, old and inefficient, required a man in constant attendance to see that the mixture did not overheat.

The pasteurized formula, along with required flavouring, nuts, fruits, etc., was poured into the ice cream machine by an operator. The operator then poured the ice cream manually into half-gallon cardboard containers. (The machine required approximately thirty minutes before production could begin. Thereafter, the operation was continuous until a change in flavour took place.) He placed the filled container on a table near the machine where a second worker sealed the open end and placed the containers on hardening racks in a cold storage room (at −10°F) for a minimum of four hours. The ice cream machine produced at a rate of ninety gallons per hour but the production was limited by the capacity of the hardening room. It held 278 gallons of ice cream. At peak production during the summer some ice cream was taken from the racks before four hours. The quality of the product was lowered as a result.

The only way to increase the capacity of the hardening facilities was to increase the size of the freezers. It was estimated that the cost of increasing Stillwell's hardening capacity to 550 gallons every four hours was between $5000 and $6000.

In the winter, ice cream was produced four days a week for six hours a day. During the summer when demand exceeded production capabilities, the plant atmosphere was hectic. Scheduled production increased to ten hours a day for a six-day week.

Vanilla and butterscotch ripple flavours made up 50 per cent of the sales. This proportion was quite stable throughout the year. The demand for other flavours was also fairly constant. The production employees simply checked the cooler to see what ice cream the salesmen had taken. They then replenished the stock.

MARKETING

The Stillwell distributors were generally small stores in small towns. In 1969 30 per cent of Stillwell's ice cream sales came from within Barrie, while the other 70 per cent came from a variety of 145 accounts spread in a thirty-mile radius around Barrie. The majority of Stillwell sales were made to general food stores and dairy bars but other accounts consisted of restaurants, service stations, golf clubs, resorts, hotels and chain stores. These accounts ranged in size from 16 gallons to 6575 gallons per year.

Stillwell employed two driver-salesmen to distribute ice cream. It was the driver-salesman's responsibility to stock his own refrigerated truck and to see that his customers did not run out of flavours. Each salesman followed a weekly route; one man covered Barrie and local accounts while the other man covered the remaining accounts. In Collingwood, Ontario, about forty miles away, Northern Dairy distributed Stillwell ice cream to local merchants.

It was Stillwell's policy to supply refrigerated cabinets to accounts if they did not have their own and if they were able to attain a volume of 100 gallons per year. If the cabinets were supplied, the wholesale price per half-gallon was increased by $.05 to make the final wholesale price $.90 per half-gallon. An analysis of the accounts showed that this policy was not tightly enforced because at least fifty accounts with cabinets did not meet the required minimum. Management explained the exceptions as long-time accounts. "The cabinets are very old and thus do not really mean a loss to Stillwell."

The seasonal nature of the ice cream market had been a constant concern to Stillwell. The amount of ice cream sold in the summer months of May to August almost equalled the amount sold in the remaining eight months. The problem was slightly more peaked for Stillwell than for the rest of the industry, which sold approximately 45 per cent of the total year's production during the four summer months. The maximum shelf life for high quality ice cream was three months. If it sat for a longer period it began to change, losing its smooth and creamy texture and becoming granular.

Stillwell supplied many outlets in the summer resort areas surrounding Barrie, including the area of Wasaga Beach. Many of these accounts were strictly four-month summer operations. An analysis of Stillwell's accounts showed that only 4.15 per cent of their total annual sales were to these four-month summer accounts. This analysis further showed that the major factor causing the fluctuating sales for Stillwell was consumption habits.

Earl Stillwell quickly admitted that the company was not market oriented. He credited its success to their high quality reputation and the company's long history in Simcoe County. "If anything, our problem has been producing enough ice cream to meet the demand rather than trying to find a buyer once the ice cream is produced," Mr. Stillwell stated. On another occasion Mr. Stillwell said, "Hell, John and I know we could be making lots more money if we wanted to invest the capital needed to increase our volume and to spend the time necessary to take advantage of the growth in our market area. But why should we bother when the company is making us a comfortable living now and when we are going to retire shortly?"

This philosophy of letting the customer come to Stillwell was evident in the amount of advertising done by the company. In the past, Stillwell spent very little money to advertise its products. The small advertising budget was held at one per cent of sales. The advertising mix consisted mostly of radio spots over a local radio station and a full page ad in a Barrie newspaper during June. In addition, Stillwell bought a half-page advertisement in a local monthly advertising booklet. Stillwell seldom made an effort to push any type of specials or to concentrate on any one product for a period of time. The advertisements were geared more toward the name Stillwell than toward a particular product.

Unlike the competition who ran specials and discounted their prices to the dealers, Stillwell seldom cut its price. If the dealer wanted to use a Stillwell product as a drawing card the dealer had to take a drop in margin him or herself. Competition in this respect was very tough with some ice cream companies often featuring their products below cost.

FUTURE PROSPECTS

As Mr. Dudley and Mr. Thompson became more acquainted with Stillwell and the ice cream industry, they began to discuss several alternatives which might aid the expansion of ice cream sales.

They considered the possibility of adding a second line of lower quality ice cream that could be marketed under a different brand name. The line would be aimed at the market where price, not quality, was the major purchase factor. Mr. Thompson felt there could be a market of approximately 15 000 gallons for this second line of ice cream. It was his feeling that the production cost of a gallon of this ice cream would be approximately the same in all aspects as the high quality line, with the ingredient cost the only exception. Mr. Thompson felt that the ingredient cost could be trimmed to approximately $.70 per gallon. With Stillwell "Supreme" holding approximately 50 per cent of the present market in central Simcoe County the men wondered how much the lower quality line would cannibalize on their present line. They also wondered what effect the lower quality line might have on the quality reputation Stillwell had built over the years.

The second alternative was to build the sales of Stillwell ice cream outside the existing market area and concentrate on the more populated areas around Toronto, sixty miles away. To do this Stillwell would have to buy more trucks to deliver ice cream to these areas or establish a relationship with a distributor who would receive a commission on sales. Messrs. Thompson and Dudley realized that the name "Stillwell" was not known outside their current market area and that great amounts of money would have to be spent to advertise their product.

As the men discussed these proposals they were concerned with the effects of such changes on present customers as well as on the plant itself. They would not want to hurt the present relationship that the company held with its old customers but, at the same time, they were not sure that it was good business to stand still. They also were concerned about the changes that would have to be made in the plant to meet the increased production and wondered if it could be undertaken without too many complications.

Exhibit 1
Stillwell Ice Cream Ltd.
Summary of Earnings

		1970		1969		1968
Sales[1]						
Bulk ice cream		$159 037		$140 106		$131 297
Ice cream specialities		16 940		15 597		12 169
Butter		156 780		151 657		156 964
Total sales		$332 757		$307 360		$300 430
Cost of goods						
Ingredients	$233 996		$218 945		$215 833	
Other costs	28 160		23 400		20 440	
Total cost of goods		$262 156		$242 345		$236 273
Gross profit		$ 70 601		$ 65 015		$ 64 157
Admin. expense	$ 23 760		$ 20 280		$ 18 250	
Selling expense	47 520		40 560		36 500	
Total expenses		$ 71 280		$ 60 840		$ 54 750
Net profit (loss)		(679)		$ 4 175		$ 9 407
Tax		—		840		1 880
Net profit after tax		$ (679)		$ 3 335		$ 7 527

[1] Both butter and ice cream specialities were purchased from other manufacturers. Butter was purchased at dealer list less $.02 per pound (dealer list $.62 per pound). Ice cream specialities were purchased at dealer list less 10 per cent.

Exhibit 2
Stillwell Ice Cream Ltd.
Summary of Balance Sheets

	1970	1969	1968
Current assets	$ 59 653	$ 54 926	$ 53 271
Mortgage receivable	3 100	3 500	3 800
Fixed assets (net)	71 010	75 200	65 737
Total assets	$134 763	$133 626	$122 806
Current liabilities	$ 36 500	$ 34 684	$ 27 199
Capital stock	80 000	80 000	80 000
Retained earnings	18 263	18 942	15 607
	$134 763	$133 626	$122 806

Exhibit 3
Stillwell Ice Cream Ltd.
Size of Accounts

	Under 100	100-700	700-1500	Over 1500
		(Annual Gallonage)		
Barrie	5	12	4	3
Outside Barrie	43	78	16	8

Exhibit 4
Stillwell Ice Cream Ltd.
Percentage Breakdown of Sales

	1965	1966	1967	1968
May-August	48%	49%	49%	47%
September-April	52	51	51	53
Total	100	100	100	100

50

Wayfarer Products Ltd.

"From the first time I saw Graplin tent stakes, I was certain that they had potential," said Mr. Tom Kendall in the fall of 1971. "And although our last year has not been a very successful one financially, nothing has occurred to change my belief in the future of the product."

Mr. Tom Kendall was president of Wayfarer Products Ltd., a firm which he had incorporated in 1970 to manufacture and market a patented tent peg called Graplin. The patent for the product was held by the South African designer. Wayfarer had an agreement with him for the manufacture and sale of Graplin tent stakes in North America.

During Wayfarer's first year of operations, the company lost over $13 000 on sales of $4800. While sales for the current year were up substantially, Mr. Kendall predicted that even greater losses would result in 1972.

THE CAMPING EQUIPMENT INDUSTRY—THE TENT STAKE MARKET

During the previous twenty years, the camping equipment industry had undergone dramatic expansion. Although the available statistics of camping growth were general, substantial evidence existed to document the market's growth. Exhibit 1 shows the number of overnight stays by campers in the U.S. National Park System for 1950 through 1968, while Exhibit 2 presents similar information for the State Park System. Exhibit 3 presents data on tent sales in Canada.

Although the figures in these exhibits do not show either primary or secondary tent stake sales, general industry growth was apparent. Best estimates in 1967 placed tent stake sales in North America at thirty-three million units (twenty-two million original equipment and eleven million replacement stakes). While increasing trailer and pick-up camper sales during the latter half of the 1960s slowed the growth of tent stake sales, the more recent emphasis on hiking equipment and the use of auxiliary shelters gave new impetus to tent stake prospects. Standard and Poor's Industry Survey, *Amusement,* described the U.S. camping market as follows: "The camping market is currently one of the most dynamic in American business." The survey projected 1969 consumer purchases of tents at $83 400 000 in the U.S., up from $60 500 000 in 1964.

The major tent manufacturers in North America were located in the U.S. with four companies reportedly supplying 35 per cent of the new tent market. Original equipment manufacturers looked for several features in the tent stakes they purchased: quality, appearance, safety, cost, and producer stability, with cost and stability of supply ranking as the key factors.

In the secondary market the individual camper was influenced by appearance and the word of other campers. They looked for durability and safety but seemed reluctant to pay an excessive premium for these features. The purchases were seasonal, often spur of the moment, and usually with little product loyalty. Wholesale purchases were made between January and June and retail purchases between February and August. Original equipment purchases remained relatively stable year round.

Small firms in the business of equipment rental purchased tent stakes in large quantities. Other uses included anchors for mobile and prefabricated homes, military uses and farm uses such as temporary grain storage under tarpaulins. Potential uses for Graplins included tension structures covering swimming pools, tennis courts and skating rinks, as well as portable garages. Many of these applications required larger stakes than used for ordinary tents.

Government influenced several factors key to tent stake sales, including the development of new camp grounds, grants for the development of new products, government and military purchases, currency exchange rates, tariffs and export and market development assistance. These were all factors influencing the operations of a small company competing in the North American market.

Three broad product types competed for the tent stake market—wood, metal and plastic—each with distinct price and performance characteristics. While some of the major tent manufacturers owned captive operations which produced their own pegs, most purchased their stake requirements from specialty producers. The specialty producers were material oriented and usually sold a number of products made from the same material and using the same basic process. For example, producers of wood stakes also made pallets, specialized shelving and cabinets, while those producing lightweight metal pegs used the same production equipment to fabricate automotive parts, components for the appliance industry, and miscellaneous metal products for households and industry. Few of Wayfarer's competitors were dependent on the production of tent stakes for a large portion of their business.

WAYFARER PRODUCTS LTD.—THE COMPANY

Wayfarer was incorporated early in 1970 to produce and market a revolutionary new tent stake known as the Graplin. The product was developed in the late 1950s in South Africa[1] and had attained a market share of over 70 per cent in that country. The inventor, a Mr. Calhoun, anxious to have the product introduced into the North American market, contacted the Department of Industry in Ottawa and listed it for Canadian licence in 1966.

At that time, Mr. Kendall was employed by Niagara Steel Products. Part of his job responsibility was the identification and development of new products for Niagara. He noticed the information on Graplin in a Department of Industry publication advertisement and followed up on this lead. In 1969, after two years of correspondence and a visit by Mr. Calhoun, Niagara obtained a licence to produce and market Graplins in North America. Niagara, in turn, had reached an agreement with Canadian Coleman whereby that firm would have exclusive rights to service the Canadian replacement market until mid-1972. In return, Coleman agreed to purchase a minimum of 300 000 Graplins prior to that date. Niagara produced the 300 000 Graplins immediately. Part of this production run was shipped to Coleman. The rest was inventoried for future delivery.

A short time later, Niagara encountered major operating problems and, in an effort to curtail increasing costs, product and market development of all new products, including Graplin, was discontinued. This change in plan by Niagara abrogated the company's agreement with Mr. Calhoun.

Mr. Kendall, who had great faith in the potential of Graplin, contacted Mr. Calhoun about obtaining the North American licence. Mr. Calhoun was enthusiastic and in a short time the two men reached an agreement that resulted in the formation of Wayfarer Products by Mr. Kendall. Mr. Calhoun provided major financing for the new firm. Mr. Kendall, however, retained control.

Canadian Coleman retained the exclusive rights to the Canadian replacement market until mid-1972. Wayfarer Products would supply any Graplins required beyond the 300 000 in Canadian Coleman's original agreement. Aside from this, the firm had the exclusive rights to the manufacture and sale of Graplins in North America.

[1] The product had been tested and used by the military and this market had been extremely important in the initial development of the product.

At its inception, Mr. Kendall had no well-defined objectives for the firm. It was his belief that he should be seeking to replace competitive products, although he was aware that this was likely to take considerable time. Both Mr. Kendall and Mr. Calhoun agreed that maintenance of their ownership position was important.

Several months after the new company was formed, Mr. Kendall resigned from his job at Niagara Steel Products. At the same time he purchased substantial production equipment including dies and fixtures for Graplin from Niagara Steel Products.

The Product

The patent protecting Graplin covered the design and the principle upon which it worked. The Graplin worked on a very simple principle whereby the tension at the hook was transferred through the resilient shoulder to the entire length of the shank in such a manner that the shank seeks a firmer hold when under strain rather than pulling over. This feature, coupled with its unique surface arm that "gives" to compensate for shrinking guy ropes or buffeting winds, insured that once erected the tent needed no further attention (Exhibit 4).

The Graplin was easy to insert and remove. Its ground level profile was safe against tripping and the "give" feature was effective under a variety of weather conditions. The product, which could be made in a variety of sizes, was currently offered only in the 9-in size.[2] Since this was by far the most popular tent peg, Wayfarer had not purchased tools to mass produce other sizes.

Production

Graplins were made from high-carbon, high-tensile steel. Stelco was the only Canadian supplier of the steel and because custom production of many sizes of steel rods was required, Stelco had a 10 000 lb minimum order size for each diameter of steel rod. For a 9-in Graplin, the minimum steel order was the equivalent of 65 000 stakes.

The steel rod was purchased in lengths adequate for producing two Graplins. The material was delivered to Brantford Stampers where it was cut in two. The cut, made at a 45° angle, provided a sharp point which permitted easy insertion into the ground. These blanks were then shipped to Wayfarer's facilities, located in rented space at the rear of Patrick's Iron Works in Hespeler, Ontario.

The Wayfarer process was centred around a 42-ton Toledo horn press with dies and fixtures for producing the Graplin. The process also included a heat-treating unit. The pre-cut blanks were fed into an air-activated feed chute, three at a time. From here the blanks were placed into a forming die that gave the Graplin its shape. As the press ram rose, the formed blanks were ejected onto a slanted rail which allowed the blanks to slide into a gas-fired furnace. This process added strength and resilience to the elbow of the Graplin, permitting it to regain its original shape after it had been under stress. The heat-treated pieces dropped off the end of the heat-treating unit into a work-in-process rack holding approximately 160 units.

The formed parts were rustproofed and painted before removal to the packing area. The parts were removed from the in-process racks six at a time, taped in bundles of six and placed in boxes, two bundles to each. The display boxes were placed in a carton and then palletized for storage.[3]

Since the equipment was not operating at capacity, Mr. Kendall did not schedule the plant operations nor did he feel it necessary to develop any complex system for inventory control.

---

[2] Mr. Kendall estimated that 65 to 70 per cent of the tent stake market could be served with the 9-in Graplin.

[3] Subsequently the rustproofing operation was eliminated by using galvanized stock.

Marketing

Due to some delay in the start of production, Mr. Kendall was unable to begin selling the Graplin stake until early 1971 and, as a result, missed the major sales of the 1971 camping season. Mr. Kendall's current attention was focussed on obtaining distribution throughout the United States in the replacement market. In Canada, Coleman had included the item in their catalogue and had advertised the product extensively although they did not require all Coleman dealers to carry it. By late 1971, Wayfarer had received only a few small orders from Coleman.

In the United States, Mr. Kendall was working to establish three types of distribution: (1) direct selling to tent manufacturers, (2) direct selling to distributors, and (3) the use of manufacturers' representatives. The latter two serviced the replacement market through dealers. Mr. Kendall felt that manufacturers' representatives would provide the best coverage since they had to live on commission. In addition, because the Graplin was a radically different product, selling it required direct and frequent contact with the dealers.

1. Pricing

Sales to the tent manufacturers in both Canada and the United States were difficult because of price. Prior to 1970, some of the largest producers had switched to plastic from wood and had paid a premium for the new product. However, since Mr. Kendall's original study of the market in 1970, prices in plastic stakes had dropped over 40 per cent. Tent manufacturers in the U.S. had looked at the Graplin but felt that the added cost of this product in the tent pack would make the total product noncompetitive. The addition of Graplin would not, in the opinion of most, influence many consumers to select their product.

Price was also an important factor in the replacement market. Exhibit 5 shows the pricing structure in this market. Many retailers believed that customers were unwilling to pay a premium price for tent stakes and planned their inventory accordingly. Retail margins for all stakes varied between 40 and 50 per cent. Wayfarer had recently quoted Coleman a price of 5½ cents per stake. Coleman, in turn, sold to dealers at $1.50 per dozen and the retail price varied between $2.66 and $2.99 per dozen.

Tariffs and shipping charges associated with selling into the United States market from Canada amounted to from 17 to 20 per cent of Wayfarer's selling price. Mr. Kendall felt that U.S. facilities might be required if a major market breakthrough was achieved. However, he was reluctant to invest further in facilities until the product gained a degree of market acceptance.

2. Advertising

Because the Graplin was radically different from competitive products, Mr. Kendall believed that the consumer had to be convinced that the product would work and that it was worth the premium price. At the same time, he was reluctant to spend his limited funds on consumer advertising. As an alternative, he was working on the development of word-of-mouth communication to develop consumer knowledge and interest in the product. In this respect, he visited campgrounds and handed out samples, provided samples to the Boy Scouts and other camping groups, and did some dealer oriented advertising in the trade sporting publications.

In an effort to demonstrate the Graplin, Mr. Kendall had promoted it at such events as the International Plowing Matches, National Hikers and Campers Association and at various camping and sporting goods shows. While such exposure had not yet resulted in significant sales, Mr. Kendall felt that it was important in the long-run development of the product.

Accounting and Finance

Mr. Kendall summed up the finance and accounting aspect of Wayfarer as "an area I know very little about." However, since pricing was important, Mr. Kendall had attempted to develop realistic costs, but the lack of good information made accurate costing difficult. The information in Exhibits 6 and 7 were used in his calculations.

Mr. Kendall had been approached by the stamping company with a subcontract that involved $1000 per year space rental plus $4.75 per hour for labour. Mr. Kendall currently paid $2.75 per hour for labour but unlike the subcontract arrangement, his current labour cost was not totally variable. Manufacture of some of the large size pegs used on various structures was currently subcontracted.

Wayfarer had no cost system and its accounting procedures were set up by the auditors. The most recent statements, as prepared by the auditors, appear as Exhibits 8, 9, and 10.

Wayfarer Management

After one year as an incorporated company, Wayfarer consisted basically of Mr. Kendall. And while he contemplated hiring a part-time bookkeeper-secretary to facilitate his absence from the office, no other additions seemed necessary. In the plant there were two part-time employees but even here substantial sales increases were required to justify permanent employment for the workers.

Mr. Kendall's major concern and interest lay in the area of marketing. He was aware that major improvements in production both in terms of capacity and cost reduction could be effected, but until sales were increased, any internal improvements would only add to his unutilized capacity. Financing the inception and growth of Wayfarer was also singled out as a potential problem, but thus far Mr. Kendall had not given it much attention. He personally felt that a 10 per cent return on his investment was more than adequate and both he and his principal in South Africa were more interested in penetrating the North American camping equipment market with a product they believed was a substantial improvement over anything else available. On the subject of ownership, Mr. Kendall felt that both he and Mr. Calhoun preferred to maintain control until the potential of Wayfarer could be more realistically appraised. Certainly any future outside investors would not get controlling interest in the company if Mr. Kendall could help it, although this stance would be reconsidered if the owners felt that such outside involvement was the only way to success. A number of vital issues faced Mr. Kendall. How could Wayfarer break into the original equipment and replacement markets? What overall strategy had the highest probability of success? Should the company consider contracting out production of the Graplin in both the U.S. and Canada to save on shipping costs and get around the tariffs involved in shipping into the U.S. market? Should he be volume pricing to get an order from one of the major original equipment producers or should his concentration be on the replacement market where prices seemed somewhat less important? Should he be concerned about the company's ability to finance the period of market development and did the various alternatives facing the company make any significant difference on the probability of Wayfarer's success?

The major concern was summed up when Mr. Kendall stated that he and Wayfarer could last for some time if the approach to the market was low key and evolutionary. In this situation, almost all of his costs could be kept variable. However, he was unsure about the ultimate impact of such an approach in a rapidly growing market. Even the product patent raised some questions. Neither he nor Mr. Calhoun were completely sure that it would stand up in a court of law and both were certain that they wanted no part of a long, high-cost court battle to protect the patent. This led Mr. Kendall to his second option, which involved quick penetration of the market at a reasonable price. This, he felt, would remove the possibility of other producers jumping on the bandwagon.

"I also am aware," said Mr. Kendall, "that Wayfarer, small as it is, has numerous options aside from Graplin. We could be developing other products for the camping market, for example, although I don't really see that I will have time for this kind of activity until Graplin is off the ground and running. At the same time, perhaps I should be exploring some of these choices in greater depth than I have to date, because some of them may have important implications for the company and my own future."

Exhibit 1
Wayfarer Products Ltd.
Overnight Stays by Campers in U.S. National Park System

Year Ending June 30	Camping Nights
1950	2 231 000
1955	3 275 000
1960	4 846 000
1965	8 085 000
1966	9 000 000
1967	9 314 000
1968	10 967 000

Source: Statistical Abstract of the United States, 1969.

Exhibit 2
Wayfarer Products Ltd.
Overnight Stays by Campers in U.S. State Park System (000's)

	1950	1955	1959	1960	1961	1962	1967
Total overnight visits	6 079	11 057	17 994	20 569	22 999	24 050	36 244
Organized camps overnight stays	1 480	1 697	2 096	2 235	2 206	2 249	2 055
Tent and trailer overnight stays	3 377	7 650	13 734	16 217	18 563	18 753	31 839

Source: Statistical Abstract of the United States, 1969.

Exhibit 3
Wayfarer Products Ltd.
Tents Manufactured and Shipped in Canada

	1962		1964		1966		1968		1970	
	Quantity	Value $000's	Quantity	Value $000's	Quantity	Value $000's	Quantity	Value $000 s	Quantity	Value $000's
Regular tourist	55 044	1 372	36 043	1 276	54 420	1 710	76 747	2 195	NA	1 233
Cottage or cabin style	21 129	1 067	32 300	1 750	21 426	991	25 330	1 025	NA	1 269
Standard wall	4 163	188	5 677	309	8 333	295	NA	NA	NA	NA
Trailer tents	NA	NA	NA	NA	NA	NA	NA	2 124	NA	2 419
Hiker or children's play tent	NA	NA	NA	NA	NA	NA	15 707	192	NA	237
Other domestic	13 970	601	25 665	934	22 666	1 101	18 914	640	NA	842

Source: Dominion Bureau of Statistics, *Canvas Products Industry*, Catalogue No. 34-202.

Exhibit 4
Wayfarer Products Ltd.

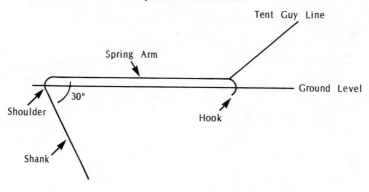

Exhibit 5
Wayfarer Products Ltd.
1971 Canadian Prices for Tent Stakes

Type of Stake[1]	Factory Selling Price 1000[2]	Wholesale Selling Price Dozen	Retail Selling Price Dozen
Wayfarer	60.00	1.49	2.98
Wood	34.00	.60	1.19
Metal—Light sheet	21.00	.36	.69
—Die cast	55.00	.85	1.99
Plastic—Lightweight	32.00	.56	1.09
—Heavyweight	50.00	.80	1.79

[1] These were approximate prices for stakes competitive with the 9-in Graplin.
[2] While the factory selling price could be reduced on extremely large orders, the prices shown are approximately what the original equipment producers were paying for tent stake supplies.

Exhibit 6
Wayfarer Products Ltd.
Labour Productivity Data

	Hours Per 1000 Pieces	Capacity
Forming	.670	1 500 units/hour
Heat treating	.670	1 500 units/hour
Packing	1.735	2 000 units/hour
Storage and material handling (no estimate)		

Exhibit 7
Wayfarer Products Ltd.
Material Cost Per 1 000 Pieces (Model 9190A—9-in Graplin)

Steel galvanized	$20.00	
Point of sale, display box	6.50	
Carton	.84	
Pallets	1.00	
Polyethylene	.06	
Strapping	.25	
TOTAL		$28.65
Indirect items:		
Cut and clean	2.50	
Propane gas	1.00	3.50
TOTAL		$32.15

Exhibit 8
Wayfarer Products Ltd.
Balance Sheet as of May 31, 1971

ASSETS—CURRENT		
Cash	$ 5 830	
Accounts receivable—Trade	2 253	
Sales tax refundable	193	
Inventory	2 050	
Prepaid expenses	50	$10 376
ASSETS—FIXED		
Plant and equipment	12 253	
Dies (at cost)	1 066	
Automobile (at cost)	3 325	
Office equipment	686	
	17 330	
Less: accumulated depreciation	4 262	13 068
OTHER ASSETS AT COST		
Incorporation	655	
Trademark	203	858
TOTAL		$24 302
LIABILITIES—CURRENT		
Accounts payable	2 902	
Royalties payable	104	
Advances from shareholders	4 350	7 356
EQUITY		
Preference stock (27 953) issued)	27 953	
Common stock (4000 shares)	1 998	
	29 951	
Operating deficit	(13 005)	16 946
TOTAL		$24 302

Exhibit 9
Wayfarer Products Ltd.
Statement of Earnings for the Year Ending May 31, 1971

Sales		$4 806
Cost of sales		
Inventory (beginning)	$ —	
Purchases	5 084	
Inventory	2 050	3 034
Gross profit		1 772
Expenses		
Salary[1]	2 000	
Bank charges	10	
Legal fees	1 241	
Automobile expenses	1 554	
Telephone	541	
Freight	555	
Office expenses	564	
Promotion and display	2 717	
Sales commission	40	
Travel	1 311	
Postage	200	
Repairs and maintenance	148	
Life insurance	359	
Royalties	104	
Depreciation	4 262	15 606
Operating loss	13 834	
Miscellaneous income	829	
Net loss for the period		$13 005

[1] Mr. Kendall's wife had a full-time job and this enabled him to draw a minimum salary from the firm.

Exhibit 10
Wayfarer Products Ltd.

ANCHOR YOUR TENT WITH

the Patented

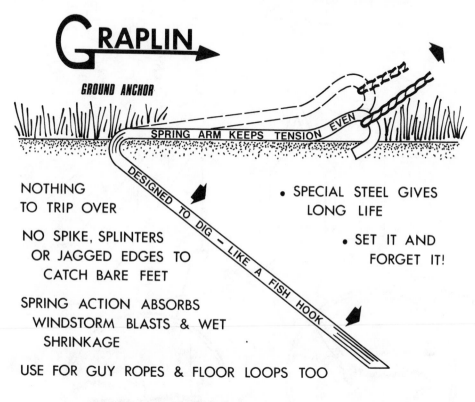

**NOTHING
TO TRIP OVER**

**NO SPIKE, SPLINTERS
OR JAGGED EDGES TO
CATCH BARE FEET**

**SPRING ACTION ABSORBS
WINDSTORM BLASTS & WET
SHRINKAGE**

USE FOR GUY ROPES & FLOOR LOOPS TOO

• **SPECIAL STEEL GIVES
LONG LIFE**

• **SET IT AND
FORGET IT!**

HOLDS AFTER STRAIGHT STAKES HAVE QUIT

CAMPING PRODUCTS LTD.

Exhibit 11
Wayfarer Products Ltd.

this is how it works

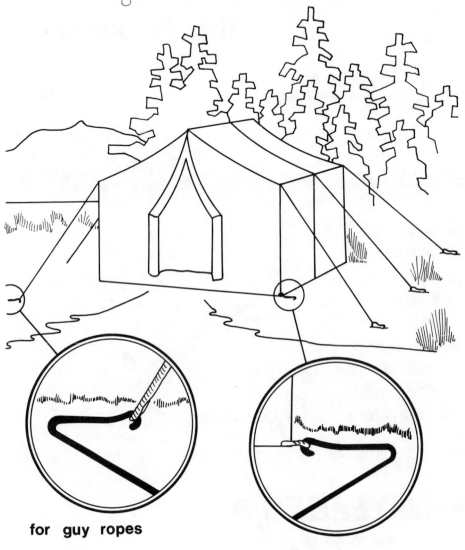

for guy ropes

for floor loops

51

W & W Enterprises

One day late in December 1974, Gary Webster was contemplating some major policy decisions which were facing his company. Gary was general manager and part owner of W & W Enterprises, the only producer of custom wool carpets in Canada. Company sales were expected to double over the next year and the building the company occupied would be cramped for space. With the possible necessity of a relocation, Gary realized that the time had come to consider the various directions in which the company could develop.

THE INDUSTRY

The Canadian carpet industry was predominantly domestic. Less than 10 per cent of 1970 carpet purchases consisted of imports, while only 2 per cent of Canadian production was exported. In 1972 there were thirty-three establishments listed by Statistics Canada that belonged to the carpet, mat and rug industry. No small group of companies dominated the industry and no one company dominated a segment of the market. The largest carpet manufacturer was Harding Carpets of Brantford, Ontario, with about 15 per cent of the market. The remaining producers each held 7 per cent of the market or less. Industry officials were optimistic about the future of the Canadian market for carpeting. During the 1960s industry sales had quadrupled in both unit and dollar terms. A further doubling of sales was expected to occur in the 1970-80 period (Exhibit 1).

The carpet market was made up of two main customer classes: the commercial (contract) market and the residential market. The contract market, which included builders, apartment house developers, mobile home producers, institutions, and commercial offices, made up 30 per cent of the total market in 1970. This segment of the market was expected to increase to 50 per cent by 1980. The home market for carpets was served at the retail level by a wide variety of stores ranging from hardware and building supply stores to decorator stores. There was no forward integration of carpet manufacturers into retailing, but several of the larger manufacturers owned their own wholesalers.

Over 400 styles of carpets were produced by Canadian manufacturers in 1970. A style was considered to be a particular combination of pile fibre, backing, construction, and pile types. The most frequently used fibres were nylon, acrylic, polypropylene, polyester, viscose and wool. Usually, only one fibre was used in the face of the carpet, but blends such as wool/nylon were not uncommon. Typical backings were jute or latex (foam rubber). The three main carpet manufacturing processes in use were weaving, tufting and needlepunch. Woven carpets were on the decline as this century-old process was slow and expensive. Construction of carpets by tufting (pushing the face yarn through a prefabricated backing and cutting it to the desired length) had been introduced in the 1940s. Tufted carpets accounted for about 70 per cent of 1970 production. Needlepunch, which produced indoor/outdoor carpeting, was the most recent innovation in carpet construction. As for pile types, the most popular were shag, plush, twist, and loop.

The majority of carpeting was produced in a standard width (12 ft) and sold to retailers in rolls. A home consumer would purchase whatever length he required, and it would be cut for him from the roll.

Recent studies conducted in Canada and the United States indicated that home carpet consumers tended to rely on colour, pattern, texture and price when purchasing a carpet. Shoppers typically lacked knowledge of brand names, technical product features, and appropriate price levels. The carpet salesman was found to be the major influence in the purchase decision.

COMPANY BACKGROUND

W & W Enterprises was located in Stratford, Ontario. The company had been established in 1971 as an equal partnership between Gary Webster and his friend Bob Wheelan. Previously Gary age 27, had been employed as a production scheduler by a large shoe manufacturer and had one year of business training at a local college. Bob age 26, still held his position as an executive employee of the large yarn manufacturer near Stratford which was W & W's major supplier. Bob was not actually working at W & W but, as a major shareholder, participated in all policy decisions.

With the limited capital available to them, the two partners bought one tufting machine and set up production in a rented building in St. Jacobs, Ontario. Because of Bob's unique relationship with a major supplier of yarns, the company was able to buy small amounts of yarn to fill customer carpet orders. W & W could buy as little as 150 lbs of yarn in a single order. By way of contrast, a yarn wholesaler normally required a 10 to 20 thousand lb minimum order.

In the early days of the company, Gary's idea was to manufacture area rugs which could be stockpiled in various predetermined sizes and colours. He visited sales agents in Toronto and London to get distribution for the company's products. At this time the company only went through the first stage of the manufacturing process. Carpets in semi-completed state were shipped to a Belleville carpet manufacturer to be backed. In the spring of 1972 another tufting machine was purchased and two product lines were established. This meant that in addition to the original ½-in plush carpet, the company also produced 2-in shag carpet. In September of that year a sales agent in Toronto suggested making custom carpets. This would mean ordering a style of carpet rather than having to cut a piece off a roll in whatever colour and style were available at that moment. The company entered a design show that year and had good response to this idea.

A third man, Ken Litwell, joined the company in December so that production of the new line could begin. He had no prior experience in the carpet industry. Ken and Gary split certain responsibilities between them. Basically, Ken took charge of production of the carpets while Gary took charge of sales.

In early 1973, W & W moved to Stratford and made custom carpet manufacture its sole business, dropping area carpets. With the move, it became possible for the company to complete all stages of the manufacturing process, including the backing of carpets. In August 1974 several more tufting machines were purchased and additional space rented.

THE MARKET

In 1974, W & W Enterprises' sole product was high quality all-wool custom carpets. Exhibit 2 is a sample price list for the company and shows the number of styles that were available. The company offered certain yarn colours as standard. The customer, however, could order a special colour to be custom produced. The price ranged from $15 to $35 per sq yd with an average selling price of $19. This compared very favourably with the prices charged by volume producers of rolls of broadloom (carpets wider than 54 in) who charged $15 to $30 per sq yd for wool, $7 to $20 for acrylic, and $5 to $20 for nylon.

W & W Enterprises was the only producer of custom wool carpet in Canada. Some imported wool carpet came from the U.S. but tariff duties made it unfeasible for competitive sale. There were also some imports from Britain, East Asia and India. As an indication of their cost, it was estimated that Indian carpets were sold at around $30 per sq yd.

W & W's main customers were interior designers, architects and discriminating people who had heard of the company's superior products and wanted something special for their floors. For example, lawyers frequently ordered carpets from W & W for their offices. Geographically, the company sold in all major Canadian urban centres, with

Toronto, Montreal and Vancouver of prime importance. The Maritimes had negligible volume.

In December 1974 the company had seven sales agents who received a 6 per cent commission. In addition, there were two wholesalers who received a 10 per cent discount from the list price. They used sample books to demonstrate styles and colours to potential customers. Gary had considered the possibility of either opening up wholly owned retail outlets or allowing independent retailers to hold exclusive franchise rights for his products. Gary estimated that a suitable sized store would rent for $500 per month. Staff wages would amount to an additional $1200 per month and miscellaneous expenses (insurance, advertising, heat, etc.) would cost $300 per month. Gary knew that retail carpet stores usually carried about $50 000 in inventory. However, he thought he might decrease this investment by selling from sample books. If the company opened up its own stores, he would use them to sell wool yarn and yarn-related hobby items in addition to carpets. Without some sort of retailing arrangement the only way a member of the general public could buy a W & W carpet was either by contacting them directly, or by dealing with an interior decorator or architect who had connections with W & W. Gary was not sure how efficient his present distribution system was in reaching new customers.

Promotion was carried on through wool journals, trade magazines and direct mailings to previous buyers and other potentially interested purchasers. W & W also entered annual interior design shows in the three major cities. There was no direct advertising to the general public.

PRODUCTION PROCESS

When an order for a carpet was received from a customer, Gary first calculated the amount of wool required. He then contacted the yarn manufacturing firm where Bob worked and ordered the wool. If it was to be custom coloured, the yarn manufacturer would dye it, and two or three days later it would be ready for pick up. The first step in the process was tufting. Wool yarn was tufted or threaded into a loose mesh woven plastic sheet by the tufting machine's 18-in row of needles. On average this process might take two hours for an ordinary size (9 by 12 ft) carpet. This process left the sheet of plastic with numerous short pieces of yarn sticking through it. W & W's tufting machine capacity, now that it had five machines in operation, was 1200 sq yds per week. Both shag and plush carpets could be produced on all machines, though considerable set-up time was required for each change in style or colour.

After this tufting was completed, the carpet was put in a metal rack and mended by an air gun that shot loops of yarn through the plastic in places missed by the tufting machine. These loops were then cut off to the level of the carpet. The whole mending process usually took no more than one hour.

The carpet was then stapled to the floor where a latex adhesive was applied and covered by a burlap backing. This backing was flattened by two men pulling a rubber scraper laboriously over the burlap. This was then gone over with a heavy steel roller, and the edges of the carpet were ironed by hand. The backing process took an average of one and a half hours and was considered the most back-breaking part of the process. The carpet was left on the floor for fourteen hours to dry, then was cut, rolled and wrapped.

Floor space for drying was very limited in the plant. There was enough room for carpets with a total combined length of no more than 65 ft (and any normal width) on the floor each day. This, however, was not a great problem because W & W had an arrangement with a local volume producer of carpet.

W & W Enterprises had to back all its own nonstandard (wider than 12 ft) carpets. However, if the carpets that had to be completed on any one day had a total combined length greater than 65 ft, then the excess carpets, as long as they were standard width, could be sent to be backed to the local carpet company, which had automatic backing equipment. A small automatic finishing machine (160 yards per hour capacity) would cost $100 000 and would save $.10 per yard over subcontracting the work or doing it themselves by hand.

All completed carpets were sent to the customers via private truck lines. Delivery time was four to six weeks after an order was placed. The only stockpiled carpets were ones that were returned or flawed. These were sold at reduced prices to the local general public.

THE PEOPLE

Every stage in the production process involved a great deal of manual labour with the exception of the actual tufting of the carpet on the tufting machines. All other steps required two people in order to be executed efficiently. In addition to Gary and Ken, a third man, Dave Slater, had also been hired to work on the production of the carpets. These three and an additional person in the office were the only employees of the company. Since Gary took charge of all sales and marketing functions and Ken was in charge of production, Dave was left with all the unassigned tasks. As a jack-of-all-trades Dave was indispensable.

At the current level of production all three men had to work very hard. Gary was forced to turn away orders because they could not be produced without hiring more employees. Gary had been considering the possibility of moving to a more mechanized mass-production system. One of his concerns though was how this would affect the personalized friendly relations of the three men who, under the present system, exercised considerable skill in the production of carpets.

THE FUTURE

For a number of reasons, sales were expected to increase dramatically in 1975, hitting an expected range of from $300 000 to $555 000. The first was the increase in production capacity over previous years. In addition, entry into the U.S. market and further penetration into Quebec were being planned. The product mix was also going to be improved through the addition of new wool lines and the introduction of synthetic carpets, largely nylon and acrylic. No new equipment was going to be necessary for the synthetic carpets but the selling price, at an expected maximum of $15 per sq yd, would be considerably lower than wool. Better sales coverage was planned by splitting up territories for sales agents and having them carry this increased product line.

Some of these planned changes were sure to change the character of the company. As Gary sat contemplating them, he realized that with a probable relocation of facilities necessary in the near future, now was the time to consider the directions for future growth. Although his personal satisfaction was derived from having a small company with high interpersonal interaction and making exclusive custom products, he recognized that future growth in profits might come from moves into new areas. He also realized that this might mean hiring new people, although he was not sure how many would be required. He wondered what alternatives existed and what implications they had for the company. (Exhibits 3 and 4 present the financial statements for W & W Enterprises.)

Exhibit 1
W & W Enterprises
Canadian Carpet, Mat and Rug Industry

	1960	1965	1970	1971	1972
Number of Establishments	15	25	33	33	33
Factory shipments of tufted carpets					
sq yds (000's)	3 769	11 225	23 341	29 840	44 786
$(000's)	12 373	39 998	98 560	121 301	174 626
Total ($000's)	31 513	76 766	159 568	187 755	241 001
Material ($000's)	15 443	47 661	101 467	115 680	148 733
Wool	5 607	5 248	2 363	2 391	3 108
Synthetics	1 597	19 800	49 498	60 885	75 997
Other yarn	4 723	3 568	6 440	3 721	7 823
Non-yarn	3 516	19 045	43 166	48 683	61 805

Source: Statistics Canada Catalogue 34-221.

Exhibit 2
W & W Enterprises
Canadiana Collection
Custom Wool Carpet

PRICE LIST   Effective June 1/74

Style	Description[1]	Stock Roll	Colours Cut	Custom Roll	Colours Cut	Special Sizes or Widths
Villager	Loop	$15.40	16.94	17.40	18.94	$2.00 per sq yd
Colonial	Loop	19.80	21.78	21.80	23.78	
Acadian	Cut Plush	17.43	19.17	19.43	21.17	
La Maison	Cut Plush	21.45	23.60	23.45	25.60	
Heirloom	Cut Plush	26.95	29.65	28.95	31.65	
Habitant	Cut Plush	23.65	26.02	25.65	28.02	
Squire	Hardtwist	18.98	20.88	20.98	22.88	
Voyageur	Hardtwist	21.89	24.08	23.89	26.08	
Provincial	Cut Pile	29.15	32.07	31.15	34.07	
Folklore	Plush	21.78	23.96	23.78	25.96	
Homestead	Plush	19.69	21.66	21.69	23.66	
Estate	Plush	24.20	26.62	26.20	28.62	
Heritage	Plush	28.49	31.34	30.49	33.34	
Pioneer	Shag	20.85	22.94	22.85	24.94	
Courier	Shag	26.95	29.65	28.95	31.65	
Frontier	Shag	23.54	25.89	25.54	27.89	
Legacy	Shag	29.42	32.36	31.42	34.36	
Hearthside	Shag	25.59	32.55	31.59	34.55	

[1] Roll price is minimum of 75 sq yds. Less than 75 sq yds is cut price.

Above prices include 12 per cent federal sales tax.

Exhibit 3
W & W Enterprises
Profit and Loss Statement

	For the year Ended December 31, 1973		For the 10 months Ended October 31, 1974	
Sales less discounts		$125 279		$206 968
				1 255
Net sales		$125 279		$205 713
Cost of sales:				
Material	$91 558		$123 261	
Freight	2 282		2 517	
Labour	16 108	109 948	12 253	138 031
Gross profit		$ 15 331		$67 682
Expenses				
Bad debt expense	—		$ 5 263	
Office costs	$1 772		2 949	
Commissions	4 856		10 497	
Factory supplies	2 505		5 111	
Rent	3 400		3 078	
Travel	2 457		4 038	
Advertising	3 417		4 528	
Business tax	288		627	
Insurance	648		540	
Interest	1 636		1 357	
Utilities	157		1 217	
Depreciation	1 817	22 953	3 975	43 180
Net profit (Loss)		$ (7 622)		$ 24 502

Exhibit 4
W & W Enterprises
Balance Sheet as of

ASSETS	December 31, 1973		October 31, 1974	
Current Assets				
Inventory		$ 8 771		$25 573
Accounts receivable	33 498		65 820	
Less: allow. for doubtful accounts	—		2 630	
		33 498		63 190
Total current assets		$42 269		$86 763
Machinery & equipment	10 405		17 038	
Less: accumulated depreciation	3 137	7 268	7 112	9 926
TOTAL ASSETS		$49 537		$96 689
LIABILITIES				
Accounts payable		$30 206		$41 806
Bank overdraft		1 043		1 300
Bank loan		15 000		20 800
Miscell. accruals pay.		3 644		1 537
Note pay., Ken Litwell		—		2 300
Total Liabilities		49 893		67 743
CAPITAL				
Capital stock		16 800		23 600
Retained earnings opening balance	(9 534)		(17 156)	
Profit (Loss) to date	(7 622)		24 502	
Retained earnings closing balance		(17 156)		7 346
Total Capital		(356)		30 946
TOTAL LIABILITIES AND CAPITAL		$49 537		$98 689